STATISTICAL HANDBOOK ON THE WORLD'S CHILDREN

Recent Titles in Oryx Statistical Handbooks

Statistical Handbook on U.S. Hispanics
Frank L. Schick and Renee Schick, compilers and editors

Statistical Handbook on Aging Americans: 1994 Edition
Frank L. Shick and Renee Schick, editors

Statistical Handbook on Violence in America
Adam Dobrin, Brian Wiersema, Colin Loftin and David McDowall, editors

Statistical Handbook on Women in America: Second Edition
Cynthia M. Taeuber, compiler and editor

Statistical Handbook on Adolescents in America
Bruce A. Chadwick and Tim B. Heaton, editors

Statistical Handbook on the American Family: Second Edition
Bruce A. Chadwick and Tim B. Heaton, editors

Statistical Handbook on Poverty in the Developing World
Chandrika Kaul and Valerie Tomaselli-Moschovitis, editors

Statistical Handbook on Consumption and Wealth in the United States
Chandrika Kaul and Valerie Tomaselli-Moschovitis, editors

Statistical Handbook on Technology
Paula Berinstein, editor

Statistical Handbook on Racial Groups in the United States
Tim B. Heaton, Bruce A. Chadwick, and Cardell K. Jacobson, editors

STATISTICAL HANDBOOK ON THE WORLD'S CHILDREN

Chandrika Kaul

Oryx Press
Westport, Connecticut • London

The rare Arabian Oryx is believed to have inspired the myth of the unicorn. This desert antelope became virtually extinct in the early 1960s. At that time, several groups of international conservationists arranged to have nine animals sent to the Phoenix Zoo to be the nucleus of a captive breeding herd. Today, the Oryx population is over 1,000, and over 500 have been returned to the Middle East.

Library of Congress Cataloging Publication information is available.

British Library Cataloguing in Publication Data is available.

ISBN: 1–57356–390–0

First published in 2002

Oryx Press, 88 Post Road West, Westport, CT 06881
An imprint of Greenwood Publishing Group, Inc.
www.oryxpress.com

Printed in the United States of America

∞ ™

The paper used in this book complies with the Permanent Paper Standard issued by the National Information Standards Organization (Z39.48–1984).

10 9 8 7 6 5 4 3 2 1

Dedicated to the thousands of children
orphaned by the January 2001 earthquake
in Gujarat, India.

Contents

Introduction

OVERVIEW

Almost 40 percent of the world's population is children. Yet, until the last half of the twentieth century, the world's children were invisible, their experiences and problems not worthy of recording. It was only after the international community established child-oriented agencies, such as UNICEF, that a portrait of the children's world emerged. Most children lived in a world of poverty and disease with their future limited by a lack of even the most basic social services. Over the last 50 years, the international community has attempted to address these problems. As a result, more of today's children are born healthy and more are immunized, more can read and write, and more are free to play and simply live as children than would have been thought possible even a few decades ago. But despite the marked progress, a large portion of the world's children are still growing up in circumstances that limit the development of their potential, compromise their health, restrict their sense of self, and generally curtail their chances for successful lives.

At the beginning of the twenty-first century there is a growing global consciousness of the issues affecting children and a commitment to address them. Given this focus, there is a significant need for a collection of international statistical material on children. Statistical data are often limited and what does exist is frequently hard to access and difficult to comprehend, scattered across a huge array of resources. The purpose of this handbook, then, is to compile statistics from a wide variety of sources into a comprehensive portrait of the world's children and make that information accessible to the general researcher.

SCOPE AND DEFINITION

This handbook attempts to create a comprehensive picture of the state of the world's children, present-ing statistics on various aspects their health and education as well as their family, social, and economic lives. In some key areas international data are limited or nonexistent. There are few international statistics on juvenile crime, despite concerns that crime rates among the young are rising, and there are none on such serious issues as child abuse. In many cases data exist only for the general population, even for issues in which children have the greatest stake. For example, diseases such as measles and diphtheria affect children primarily, yet international agencies do not present data by age. In compiling this volume, the editor also looked for information on the lighter aspects of children's lives—how they spend their leisure time; how they play. The editor found almost nothing, perhaps because most children in the developing world grow up in poverty, since play must give way to efforts for survival. The preponderance of the available statistics reflects the priorities of the international community: providing children the basic services necessary for survival and for a stable future.

There is no universally accepted definition of "child." It varies considerably among countries in accordance with the socio-economic-cultural context. The Convention on the Rights of Children defines "child" as any person under age 18 living in a civilian or non-institutionalized setting. Some of the major international agencies that collect data on children employ slightly different definitions. The Joint United Nations Program on HIV/AIDS (UNAIDS), for example, defines children as those aged 0-14 years. The World Health Organization considers the period between 10 and 19 "adolescence," while the United Nations terms the age group of 15 to 24 as "youth." Thus, age ranges in this book vary depending on the data source.

ORGANIZATION AND CONTENT

Organized into eight sections covering such general subject areas as demography, education, health and disease, economics, social life and crime, this handbook offers data on some of the most important aspects of these broad-ranging topics. Section A covers demographics and vital statistics including population, infant mortality, and life expectancy. Section B investigates the education status of children, presenting data on enrollment ratios, compulsory education duration, and illiteracy, among others. Section C turns the discussion to health and nutrition with information on access to health care, immunization, and food aid. Next, Section D focuses on the major causes of child deaths and the enormous problem of malnutrition. Because of the staggering impact AIDS has and will continue to have on children, the volume devotes a separate section, Section E, to the deadly epidemic. Sections F and G explore the economic and social aspects of children's well-being, respectively. Section F covers such topics as poverty and child labor. Section G presents measures of family composition and leisure. Section H covers some of the most daunting obstacles to full human development such as crime and violence committed by and against children, drug use, armed conflict, land mines, and the problem of child soldiers.

Each section begins with a general introduction and explanations of indicators. The introduction offers a quick snapshot of what will be presented in the section while the explanations of indicators provides material to help the user make sense of the data. The statistical material follows. Most data are presented in short-term time frames—within the last 10 years. In some instances, when applicable and available, longer time frames are used to give a deeper historical context to indicators.

The volume concludes with appendixes containing the text of several of the most important international documents related to children, as well as a glossary of useful terms and a list of important organizations devoted to children.

DATA SOURCES METHODOLOGY AND PRESENTATION

Data were compiled from a wide range of internationally recognized sources including: the United Nations Children's Fund (UNICEF); the United Nations Educational, Scientific and Cultural Organization (UNESCO); the United Nations Population Division (UNPD); the Food and Agriculture Organization of the United Nations (FAO); the United Na-

tions High Commissioner for Refugees (UNHCR); the World Health Organization (WHO); the International Criminal Police Organization (ICPO-Interpol); the U.S. Census Bureau; and the World Bank. In using such well-respected international sources, consistency and a high level of standardization of data are ensured. The editor has also consulted a wide range of regional and government reports, studies from nongovernmental organizations, and private research papers.

In most cases, tables are reproduced in their original format, but in some instances the presentation has been modified to make the information more understandable and readable. Such modifications include breaking very large, complex tables into several different tables, re-labeling column headings to ensure clarity, and omitting columns and rows of information not applicable to the topic at hand. Occasionally numbers are rounded to make the presentation clearer. Most tables present data in simple alphabetical order by country. However, the volume also uses continental and regional breakdowns to present broad trends. Graphs frequently summarize data. When data are being presented only for specific age groups, and not for "children" (age 18 and under), this is indicated in the title text (e.g., children ages 0-4).

Where necessary, the tables and graphs contain footnotes needed to understand the indicators. These notes are based on those found in the source material. However, they are not necessarily taken verbatim and may include information not found in the original data notes if it was thought the original explanations needed further clarification. Frequently, table notes repeat what is highlighted in the explanation of indicators. This was done for ease of use, so researchers do not have to flip between pages of the volume. Citations of print and electronic sources follow each table or graph.

TIMELINESS OF DATA

Care has been taken to include the latest available data for all indicators. Nevertheless, some of the statistics in this book cover dates no later than the early or mid-nineties. The age of those numbers stems from several realities. First, taking and compiling international surveys requires time as data are filtered through various governmental systems and institutional structures. Second, international data are often presented in publications that go through an extensive review process, resulting in issuance of data long after the research was completed. Third, some international data are updated only once every five or ten years. Finally, some surveys were conducted for studies that have not been repeated. We have included aging data only when they are the only indicators available on important topics.

Agencies frequently post statistical updates on their Web sites; in those cases, readers can use the Web citation in the source notes to check for more recent data. Users need to keep in mind that governments and organizations constantly revise older figures, sometimes without indicating that such figures have changed. Also, agencies are continually adding and removing documents and data from their Web sites. What was there a month ago may be gone now, and even if something similar appears in its place, it may offer the data sliced a different way. Readers may also use the Web citations for access to the international reports from which the handbook drew its tables.

When dealing with massive amounts of statistical data, it is possible that mistakes and omissions may occur. While the editor has tried to prevent such occurrences, she will appreciate being informed of any errors that readers detect so that corrections can be made in future editions of this book.

List of Tables and Figures

C. HEALTH AND NUTRITION

A. Demographics and Vital Statistics

GENERAL OVERVIEW

The indicators in this chapter cover the most basic measures of the child population—numbers and vital statistics. Indicators include population projections and growth rate; gender breakdowns and sex ratio at birth; infant and under-five-year mortality rates; and life expectancy. The section also includes several measures dealing with mothers and maternal well-being. At first glance they may seem out of place in a volume on children. Nevertheless, experts see the welfare of the child so interconnected with that of the mother that they routinely include maternal indicators in vital statistics on children.

EXPLANATION OF INDICATORS

A1-1–A1-8. Child population: The eight tables in this cluster offer basic population data by age group and gender. The first two graphs give an overview of population by continent; the next six offer an in-depth view by country. The data include all residents regardless of legal status or citizenship, and represent population aged 0 to 19 within the physical boundaries of a country and under the jurisdiction of that country's political control. Refugees not permanently settled in the country of asylum are generally considered to be part of the population of their country of origin. Population numbers are either current census data or historical census data extrapolated through certain demographic models.

A2-1. Sex ratio at birth: Sex ratio is calculated as the number of male live births per one female live birth. Barring some endemic health problems, abortion decisions based on fetal sex, and medical intervention, this indicator will remain close to a value of 100 for all countries. Values over 100 indicate that more boys are born than girls, and values under 100 indicate more girls are born than boys. Female infanticide practiced in some developing countries will skew this ratio in favor of male children.

A3-1–A3-2. Population growth rates: The average annual percent change in the population results from a surplus (or deficit) of births over deaths and the balance of migrants entering and leaving a country. Also known as average annual rate of growth, it may be positive or negative. Table A3-1 is an overview of growth rates from 1995 to 2000 by region; A3-2 offers a historical look at growth from 1980 to 1997 by country.

A4-1–A4-2. Child population projections: A4-1 and A4-2 offer population projections for the year 2025 by gender and with sex ratio, the former by continent, the latter by country. The data and assumptions upon which population projections are based vary from country to country. Some nations use population censuses, whereas others use vital registration systems, or population sample surveys.

A5-1–A5-3. Youth dependency ratio: Youth dependency ratio is a measure of the proportion of children to working-age adults. It is calculated as youth population (under age 15) per 100 working-age population (ages 15 to 64, although official working and retirement ages may differ slightly among countries). The ratio varies with economic development. It is lowest in the industrialized regions of the world, and highest in Africa. As a result of the decrease in fertility and increase in life expectancy, the proportion of children aged less than 15 years is expected to get smaller. Nevertheless, experts estimate that children will account for three-fourths of the world's population in the year 2025. A5-1 and A5-2 offer an overview of current and projected ratios by region and area; A5-3 presents historical data for selected countries.

A6-1–A6-7. Infant mortality rate (IMR): The next set of tables and graphs focuses on one of the most dangerous times in a young child's life, the period between birth and age one. IMR is the probability of an infant dying between birth and exactly one year of age per 1,000 live births. Accurate statistics on infant mortality are not available for many developing countries because they lack adequate vital records systems. In these cases the U.S. Census Bureau has calculated its estimates through the use of sampling methods. A6-1–A6-4 contrast current infant mortality by continent and trace IMR from 1980 to 2000. The final three tables in the cluster offer projected infant mortality for the years 2025 and 2050.

A7-1–A7-4. Under-five mortality rate (U5MR): U5MR is the probability of dying between birth and exactly five years of age per 1,000 live births. Leading international agencies such as United Nations Children's Fund (UNICEF) consider it the single most important indicator of young children's health. A high U5MR reflects a lack of overall safety in the child's environment as well as problems such as malnutrition, poverty, inadequate health care facilities, lack of sanitation, safe water, and immunization.

A8-1–A8-3. Gender difference in mortality: Although there has been an overall decline in death rates among children, boys continue to die at a rate about 50 percent higher than girls. The disparity between male and female death rates is particularly striking in industrial countries. UNICEF attributes the higher male death rate in these areas to injuries due to social violence and excessive alcohol. A8-1 and A8-2 present the most recent figures for male and female deaths under age five, by region and country. A8-3 shows trends for children ages 0-19 over time for selected industrial nations.

A9-1–A9-6. Births to adolescents: In the absence of country-level statistics about the diverse forces that shape the lives of teenagers, reproduction patterns remains one of the only measures available to compare adolescent girls around the world. Teenage births (approximately 15 million each year) can limit a young woman's education and economic opportunities and pose serious health risks for both mother and child. For the infants born to teenage mothers, poverty, poor care, and instability may mark their childhood. A9-1 and A9-2 offer regional breakdowns of births per 1,000 women ages 15 to 19 and births to adolescents as a percentage of all births, respectively, as well as projections to the year 2020. A9-3 presents birth rates by country for 1995 and 2000. The final three tables show how urban and rural residence as well as educational attainment affect birth rates.

A10-1–A10-4. Maternal mortality: Every minute somewhere in the world a woman dies as a result of pregnancy-related complications. Ninety-nine percent of these deaths take place in the developing world. A mother's death has such a dramatic impact on the life of her child that international organizations such as Save the Children insist that saving children starts with saving their mothers. This cluster of tables looks at three facets of maternal mortality. A10-1 and A10-2 provide figures on total annual and daily deaths by region. A10-3 presents the maternal mortality ratio, the number of maternal deaths divided by the number of live births for a given year. The ratio is expressed per 100,000 live births. The final table lists the nations that World Health Organization (WHO) and UNICEF classify as having the highest and lowest risk of maternal death and indicates the country's risk ratio. These tables should be approached with caution. According to WHO, most maternal deaths go unregistered in areas where maternal mortality rates are the highest.

A11. The Mothers' Index: The Mothers' Index is a composite indicator that measures the overall status of mothers by looking at important data on both women and children. For women, indicators used to calculate the Index are: lifetime risk of maternal death; modern contraceptive use; percent of births attended by trained personnel; percent of pregnant women with anemia; adult female literacy rate; and participation as national government officeholders. For children, the measures are: infant mortality rate; access to safe water; primary school enrollment; and nutritional status.

A12-1–A12-7. Life Expectancy (LE): LE is considered the best general indicator of a country's health status and is often used as an overall measure of a population's quality of life. It indicates the number of years a newborn infant would live if prevailing patterns of mortality at the time of its birth were to stay the same throughout its life. Life expectancy is a result of several factors including economic resources; nutrition and food availability; and access to health care facilities, safe water, and sanitation. Among the factors responsible for the lower life expectancy in some developing countries are the presence of civil war and geographic calamities such as drought. For reasons not yet fully understood, female LE is higher than male. A12-1–A12-3 trace life expectancy from 1980 to 2000, while A12-4 contrasts current life expectancy by continent. The final three tables in the cluster offer projected life expectancy for the years 2025 and 2050.

A13. Healthy Life Expectancy (HLE): While life expectancy is based on overall length of life, healthy life expectancy (HLE) is based upon Disability Adjusted Life Expectancy (DALE). DALE summarizes the expected number of years to be lived in what might be termed the equivalent of "full health." To calculate DALE, years of ill health are weighted according to severity and subtracted from the expected overall life expectancy to give the equivalent years of healthy life.

A1. CHILD POPULATION

A1-1. Child Population by Continent, 2000

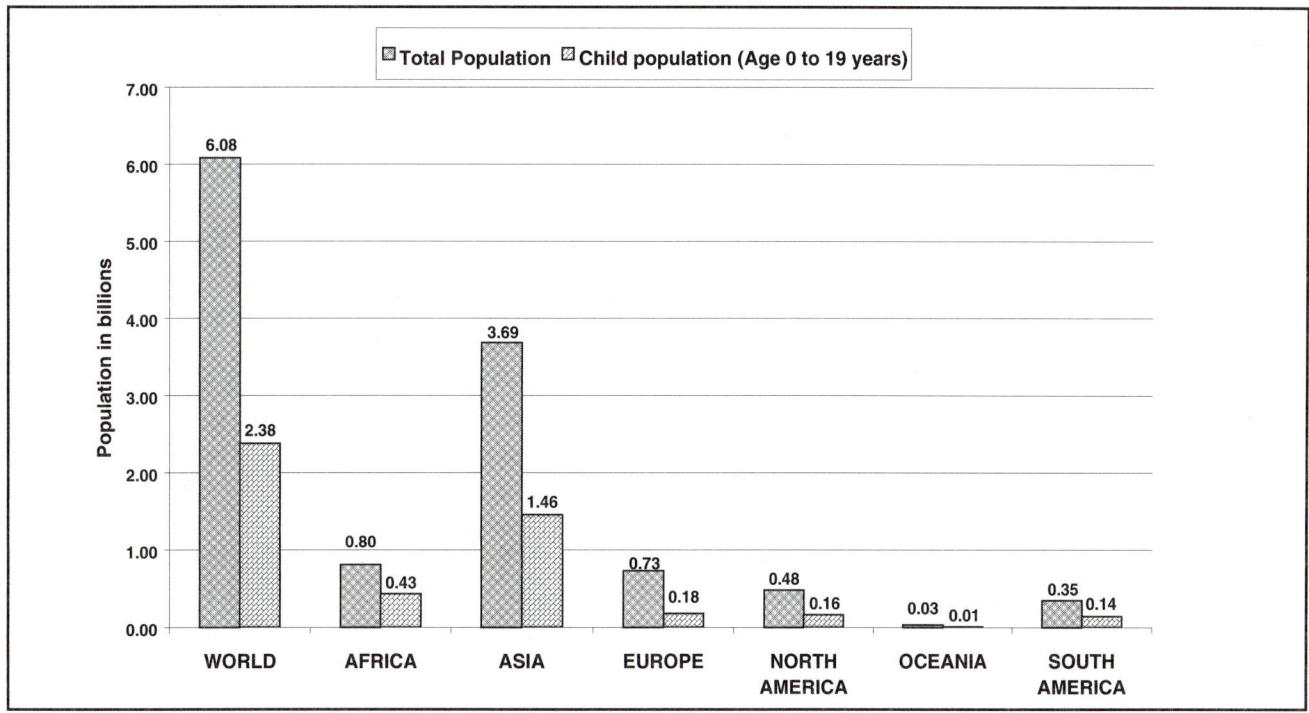

Source: U.S. Census International Database, 2000: Table 010. Infant Mortality Rates and Deaths, and Life Expectancy at Birth, by Sex; Table 028. Total Fertility Rate; Table 008. Vital Rates and Events; <http://www.census.gov/ipc/www/idbagg.html>. Underlying data from U.S. Bureau of the Census.

A1-2. Age Group (0 to 19 Years) as a Percentage of Total Population, 2000

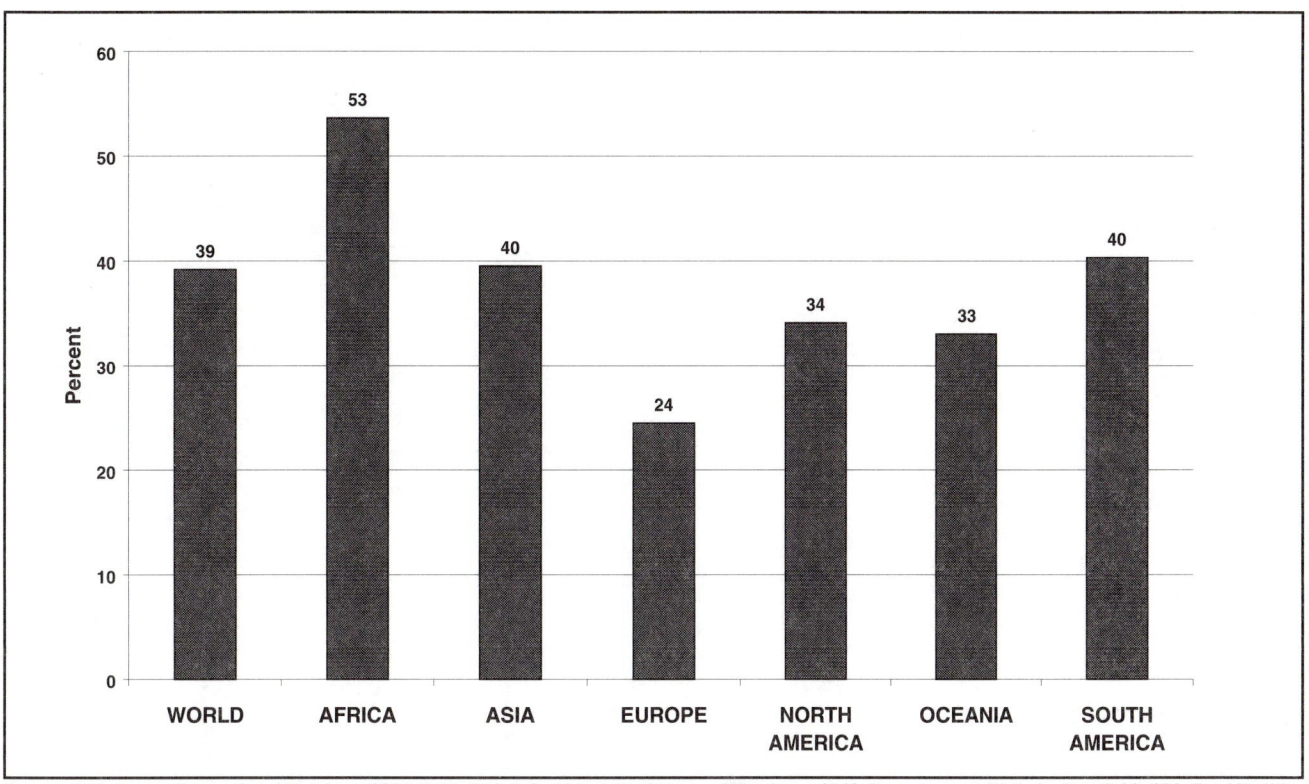

Source: U.S. Census International Database, 2000: Table 010. Infant Mortality Rates and Deaths, and Life Expectancy at Birth, by Sex; Table 028. Total Fertility Rate Table 008 Vital Rates and Events; <http://www.census.gov/ipc/www/idbagg.html>. Underlying data from U.S. Bureau of the Census.

A1-3. Population, Age 0 to 19 Years, Total, Male, and Female, and Percentages, 2000

	0-19 Age Group			Age Group 0-19 as % of population		
	Total	Male	Female	Total	% male	% female
Afghanistan	14,210,788	7,250,426	6,960,362	53.3	51.0	49.0
Albania	1,435,760	743,175	692,585	42.2	51.8	48.2
Algeria	15,459,046	7,869,850	7,589,196	48.6	50.9	49.1
American Samoa	31,625	16,219	15,406	48.3	51.3	48.7
Andorra	13,168	6,809	6,359	19.5	51.7	48.3
Angola	6,327,919	3,204,776	3,123,143	55.1	50.6	49.4
Anguilla	4,162	2,108	2,054	35.0	50.6	49.4
Antigua and Barbuda	21,709	11,025	10,684	33.7	50.8	49.2
Argentina	13,356,006	6,801,695	6,554,311	35.9	50.9	49.1
Armenia	1,159,125	590,272	568,853	34.1	50.9	49.1
Aruba	19,233	10,083	9,150	27.8	52.4	47.6
Australia	5,236,597	2,682,329	2,554,268	27.6	51.2	48.8
Austria	1,834,203	940,787	893,416	22.5	51.3	48.7
Azerbaijan	3,259,524	1,663,548	1,595,976	41.0	51.0	49.0
Bahamas, the	105,812	53,263	52,549	36.8	50.3	49.7
Bahrain	244,691	124,113	120,578	38.1	50.7	49.3
Bangladesh	63,914,671	32,773,223	31,141,448	49.5	51.3	48.7
Barbados	78,701	39,832	38,869	30.4	50.6	49.4
Belarus	2,773,514	1,413,853	1,359,661	26.7	51.0	49.0
Belgium	2,340,126	1,198,064	1,142,062	23.0	51.2	48.8
Belize	126,205	64,308	61,897	52.2	51.0	49.0
Benin	3,815,265	1,913,185	1,902,080	58.5	50.1	49.9
Bermuda	16,013	8,114	7,899	25.5	50.7	49.3
Bhutan	993,999	516,013	477,986	49.8	51.9	48.1
Bolivia	4,023,227	2,031,199	1,992,028	49.4	50.5	49.5
Bosnia and Herzegovina	896,376	458,552	437,824	25.0	51.2	48.8
Botswana	804,259	406,729	397,530	54.4	50.6	49.4
Brazil	68,706,322	34,973,344	33,732,978	39.5	50.9	49.1
Brunei	137,563	70,397	67,166	41.6	51.2	48.8
Bulgaria	1,835,876	941,257	894,619	22.5	51.3	48.7
Burkina Faso	7,020,353	3,529,933	3,490,420	59.0	50.3	49.7
Burundi	3,479,546	1,740,577	1,738,969	58.7	50.0	50.0
Cambodia	6,621,372	3,359,965	3,261,407	55.6	50.7	49.3
Cameroon	9,019,165	4,528,814	4,490,351	56.8	50.2	49.8
Canada	8,140,911	4,166,536	3,974,375	26.0	51.2	48.8
Cape Verde	230,055	116,133	113,922	55.9	50.5	49.5
Central African Republic	1,926,452	968,271	958,181	54.8	50.3	49.7
Chad	4,226,555	2,115,910	2,110,645	54.5	50.1	49.9
Chile	5,507,331	2,811,334	2,695,997	36.3	51.0	49.0
China	414,369,853	219,351,760	195,018,093	33.0	52.9	47.1
Colombia	16,821,800	8,504,329	8,317,471	42.0	50.6	49.4
Comoros	305,321	152,916	152,405	52.6	50.1	49.9
Congo, Dem. Rep. (Zaire)	30,673,691	15,373,623	15,300,068	59.0	50.1	49.9
Congo, Rep.	1,498,710	753,038	745,672	54.0	50.2	49.8
Costa Rica	1,592,621	816,462	776,159	42.5	51.3	48.7
Cote d'Ivoire	9,369,041	4,710,381	4,658,660	57.9	50.3	49.7
Croatia	1,092,579	560,755	531,824	23.3	51.3	48.7
Cuba	3,122,338	1,602,515	1,519,823	28.0	51.3	48.7
Cyprus	241,222	123,900	117,322	31.8	51.4	48.6
Czech Republic	2,395,474	1,226,911	1,168,563	23.3	51.2	48.8
Denmark	1,273,167	653,085	620,082	23.7	51.3	48.7
Djibouti	239,346	119,952	119,394	52.7	50.1	49.9
Dominica	22,373	11,244	11,129	35.0	50.3	49.7
Dominican Republic	3,691,425	1,880,417	1,811,008	44.7	50.9	49.1
Ecuador	5,771,050	2,934,460	2,836,590	45.1	50.8	49.2

A1-3. Population, Age 0 to 19 Years, Total, Male, and Female, and Percentages, 2000 *(continued)*

	0-19 Age Group			Age Group 0-19 as % of population		
	Total	**Male**	**Female**	**Total**	**% male**	**% female**
Egypt	31,286,367	15,978,894	15,307,473	45.7	51.1	48.9
El Salvador	2,787,488	1,421,214	1,366,274	47.0	51.0	49.0
Equatorial Guinea	254,731	127,626	127,105	53.3	50.1	49.9
Eritrea	2,212,826	1,111,694	1,101,132	53.4	50.2	49.8
Estonia	352,530	179,284	173,246	25.2	50.9	49.1
Ethiopia	34,956,818	17,522,842	17,433,976	57.3	50.1	49.9
Faroe Islands	11,932	6,117	5,815	29.7	51.3	48.7
Fiji	362,554	185,104	177,450	44.0	51.1	48.9
Finland	1,268,654	647,566	621,088	24.6	51.0	49.0
France	14,812,356	7,581,145	7,231,211	25.1	51.2	48.8
French Guiana	67,421	34,471	32,950	38.9	51.1	48.9
French Polynesia	103,105	52,482	50,623	41.9	50.9	49.1
Gabon	532,984	266,558	266,426	42.8	50.0	50.0
Gambia, the	771,325	385,978	385,347	55.8	50.0	50.0
Gaza Strip	719,307	368,731	350,576	61.9	51.3	48.7
Georgia	1,439,614	733,346	706,268	28.6	50.9	49.1
Germany	17,063,241	8,749,094	8,314,147	20.8	51.3	48.7
Ghana	10,083,406	5,062,298	5,021,108	52.3	50.2	49.8
Gibraltar	7,726	4,144	3,582	26.4	53.6	46.4
Greece	2,395,243	1,237,437	1,157,806	22.3	51.7	48.3
Greenland	20,125	10,152	9,973	33.4	50.4	49.6
Grenada	52,438	26,731	25,707	53.6	51.0	49.0
Guadeloupe	137,761	70,164	67,597	32.4	50.9	49.1
Guam	65,971	34,314	31,657	42.8	52.0	48.0
Guatemala	6,750,717	3,444,477	3,306,240	53.3	51.0	49.0
Guernsey	15,912	8,079	7,833	24.0	50.8	49.2
Guinea	4,117,281	2,052,168	2,065,113	54.1	49.8	50.2
Guinea-Bissau	666,085	333,581	332,504	52.7	50.1	49.9
Guyana	291,186	148,777	142,409	41.4	51.1	48.9
Haiti	3,728,372	1,890,269	1,838,103	53.3	50.7	49.3
Honduras	3,209,521	1,632,504	1,577,017	52.4	50.9	49.1
Hong Kong SAR, China	1,703,601	880,611	822,990	24.5	51.7	48.3
Hungary	2,408,049	1,232,474	1,175,575	23.7	51.2	48.8
Iceland	84,555	43,351	41,204	30.8	51.3	48.7
India	445,691,622	229,799,302	215,892,320	43.8	51.6	48.4
Indonesia	88,016,401	44,608,118	43,408,283	40.1	50.7	49.3
Iran	31,360,938	15,996,516	15,364,422	47.6	51.0	49.0
Iraq	12,717,583	6,456,558	6,261,025	54.9	50.8	49.2
Ireland	1,089,044	559,773	529,271	29.9	51.4	48.6
Israel	2,125,021	1,087,723	1,037,298	36.3	51.2	48.8
Italy	11,019,094	5,666,956	5,352,138	19.4	51.4	48.6
Jamaica	1,079,868	552,311	527,557	40.5	51.1	48.9
Japan	26,322,817	13,478,809	12,844,008	20.8	51.2	48.8
Jersey	20,649	10,670	9,979	22.9	51.7	48.3
Jordan	2,513,387	1,288,479	1,224,908	53.5	51.3	48.7
Kazakhstan	6,288,498	3,188,286	3,100,212	37.4	50.7	49.3
Kenya	16,119,624	8,147,959	7,971,665	55.1	50.5	49.5
Kuwait	838,643	459,613	379,030	40.6	54.8	45.2
Kyrgyzstan	2,060,958	1,040,110	1,020,848	45.0	50.5	49.5
Laos	3,088,285	1,564,317	1,523,968	55.6	50.7	49.3
Latvia	578,534	295,016	283,518	24.9	51.0	49.0
Lebanon	1,420,640	723,362	697,278	39.2	50.9	49.1
Lesotho	1,095,403	548,593	546,810	50.6	50.1	49.9
Liberia	1,690,913	849,748	841,165	54.7	50.3	49.7
Libya	2,441,686	1,246,920	1,194,766	47.7	51.1	48.9
Liechtenstein	8,065	4,128	3,937	24.9	51.2	48.8
Lithuania	963,226	491,272	471,954	27.0	51.0	49.0
Luxembourg	102,127	52,180	49,947	23.6	51.1	48.9

A1-3. Population, Age 0 to 19 Years, Total, Male, and Female, and Percentages, 2000 *(continued)*

	0-19 Age Group			Age Group 0-19 as % of population		
	Total	**Male**	**Female**	**Total**	**% male**	**% female**
Macau	137,753	70,871	66,882	30.9	51.4	48.6
Macedonia, FYRO	635,185	327,204	307,981	31.2	51.5	48.5
Madagascar	8,422,018	4,257,680	4,164,338	55.1	50.6	49.4
Malawi	5,790,329	2,909,857	2,880,472	57.0	50.3	49.7
Malaysia	9,808,455	5,031,456	4,776,999	45.0	51.3	48.7
Maldives	177,165	90,766	86,399	57.1	51.2	48.8
Mali	6,251,645	3,137,529	3,114,116	58.2	50.2	49.8
Malta	104,924	53,858	51,066	27.4	51.3	48.7
Man, Isle of	17,939	9,167	8,772	23.5	51.1	48.9
Marshall Islands	41,500	21,176	20,324	61.0	51.0	49.0
Martinique	124,122	62,797	61,325	29.9	50.6	49.4
Mauritania	1,519,028	758,559	760,469	57.1	49.9	50.1
Mauritius	419,204	211,616	207,588	35.0	50.5	49.5
Mayotte	87,584	43,822	43,762	55.8	50.0	50.0
Mexico	46,226,550	23,546,302	22,680,248	45.3	50.9	49.1
Moldova	1,470,640	747,520	723,120	32.9	50.8	49.2
Monaco	7,337	3,710	3,627	22.8	50.6	49.4
Mongolia	1,229,106	624,062	605,044	46.3	50.8	49.2
Morocco	13,959,791	7,106,459	6,853,332	46.2	50.9	49.1
Mozambique	10,887,501	5,384,772	5,502,729	55.5	49.5	50.5
Myanmar (Burma)	22,581,335	11,511,753	11,069,582	46.2	51.0	49.0
Namibia	938,777	474,684	464,093	56.1	50.6	49.4
Nepal	12,987,751	6,698,898	6,288,853	52.1	51.6	48.4
Netherlands	3,801,374	1,943,407	1,857,967	23.9	51.1	48.9
Netherlands Antilles	69,853	35,440	34,413	33.3	50.7	49.3
New Caledonia	76,424	38,879	37,545	38.1	50.9	49.1
New Zealand	1,091,931	559,327	532,604	29.5	51.2	48.8
Nicaragua	2,652,561	1,335,241	1,317,320	54.7	50.3	49.7
Niger	5,992,053	3,060,767	2,931,286	58.4	51.1	48.9
Nigeria	64,921,119	32,592,205	32,328,914	55.4	50.2	49.8
North Korea, Dem. Rep.	7,305,662	3,738,007	3,567,655	33.7	51.2	48.8
Northern Mariana Islands	21,692	10,739	10,953	30.1	49.5	50.5
Norway	1,139,811	585,152	554,659	25.6	51.3	48.7
Oman	1,287,589	656,602	630,987	50.8	51.0	49.0
Pakistan	72,902,155	37,538,647	35,363,508	51.7	51.5	48.5
Palau	6,487	3,349	3,138	34.5	51.6	48.4
Panama	1,147,634	585,098	562,536	40.7	51.0	49.0
Papua New Guinea	2,408,229	1,235,791	1,172,438	50.0	51.3	48.7
Paraguay	2,737,078	1,388,827	1,348,251	49.1	50.7	49.3
Peru	12,286,137	6,236,941	6,049,196	45.3	50.8	49.2
Philippines	38,455,536	19,539,700	18,915,836	47.5	50.8	49.2
Poland	10,764,828	5,506,995	5,257,833	27.9	51.2	48.8
Portugal	2,319,038	1,188,251	1,130,787	23.4	51.2	48.8
Puerto Rico	1,254,292	640,890	613,402	32.1	51.1	48.9
Qatar	259,283	133,570	125,713	34.6	51.5	48.5
Reunion	294,559	150,727	143,832	40.3	51.2	48.8
Romania	5,691,505	2,905,914	2,785,591	25.5	51.1	48.9
Russia	38,776,152	19,740,732	19,035,420	26.6	50.9	49.1
Rwanda	4,733,690	2,375,465	2,358,225	56.8	50.2	49.8
Saint Helena	1,923	970	953	26.7	50.4	49.6
Saint Kitts and Nevis	19,018	9,753	9,265	43.8	51.3	48.7
Saint Lucia	68,074	34,448	33,626	43.7	50.6	49.4
Saint Vincent and the Grenadines	49,066	24,994	24,072	40.5	50.9	49.1
Samoa	115,658	58,761	56,897	49.2	50.8	49.2
San Marino	5,390	2,701	2,689	21.4	50.1	49.9
Sao Tome and Principe	93,888	47,462	46,426	58.7	50.6	49.4

A1-3. Population, Age 0 to 19 Years, Total, Male, and Female, and Percentages, 2000 *(continued)*

	0-19 Age Group			Age Group 0-19 as % of population		
	Total	**Male**	**Female**	**Total**	**% male**	**% female**
Saudi Arabia	11,682,179	5,941,595	5,740,584	52.5	50.9	49.1
Senegal	6,075,419	3,027,324	3,048,095	58.5	49.8	50.2
Seychelles	30,971	15,540	15,431	38.9	50.2	49.8
Sierra Leone	3,048,950	1,497,501	1,551,449	55.3	49.1	50.9
Singapore	963,867	496,735	467,132	27.0	51.5	48.5
Slovakia	1,490,914	761,777	729,137	27.6	51.1	48.9
Slovenia	449,770	230,630	219,140	22.8	51.3	48.7
Solomon Islands	261,198	133,009	128,189	55.6	50.9	49.1
Somalia	4,069,110	2,029,573	2,039,537	54.7	49.9	50.1
South Africa	19,599,434	9,889,005	9,710,429	44.6	50.5	49.5
South Korea, Rep.	14,189,916	7,480,732	6,709,184	30.0	52.7	47.3
Spain	8,310,335	4,275,993	4,034,342	21.2	51.5	48.5
Sri Lanka	7,057,927	3,604,822	3,453,105	36.5	51.1	48.9
Sudan	19,829,463	10,118,972	9,710,491	55.8	51.0	49.0
Suriname	182,756	93,815	88,941	42.1	51.3	48.7
Swaziland	584,744	291,406	293,338	58.2	49.8	50.2
Sweden	2,185,093	1,121,241	1,063,852	24.4	51.3	48.7
Switzerland	1,654,347	846,125	808,222	22.7	51.1	48.9
Syria	10,054,510	5,150,639	4,903,871	56.6	51.2	48.8
Taiwan	6,723,749	3,478,024	3,245,725	30.1	51.7	48.3
Tajikistan	3,152,956	1,592,772	1,560,184	50.9	50.5	49.5
Tanzania	17,769,409	8,849,425	8,919,984	55.6	49.8	50.2
Thailand	19,950,951	10,152,316	9,798,635	32.6	50.9	49.1
Togo	3,098,280	1,555,427	1,542,853	58.9	50.2	49.8
Trinidad and Tobago	398,182	204,671	193,511	36.6	51.4	48.6
Tunisia	3,943,812	2,029,623	1,914,189	40.9	51.5	48.5
Turkey	26,587,689	13,530,004	13,057,685	39.9	50.9	49.1
Turkmenistan	2,129,719	1,084,107	1,045,612	48.0	50.9	49.1
Turks and Caicos Islands	6,985	3,544	3,441	40.0	50.7	49.3
Tuvalu	4,764	2,425	2,339	44.4	50.9	49.1
Uganda	14,566,017	7,305,799	7,260,218	62.1	50.2	49.8
Ukraine	12,646,821	6,446,655	6,200,166	25.5	51.0	49.0
United Arab Emirates	959,189	489,737	469,452	40.2	51.1	48.9
United Kingdom	15,010,858	7,707,624	7,303,234	25.3	51.3	48.7
United States	78,798,523	40,350,960	38,447,563	28.7	51.2	48.8
Uruguay	1,062,149	543,683	518,466	31.9	51.2	48.8
Uzbekistan	11,562,788	5,866,284	5,696,504	47.3	50.7	49.3
Vanuatu	94,684	48,163	46,521	49.1	50.9	49.1
Venezuela	10,124,674	5,219,637	4,905,037	42.9	51.6	48.4
Vietnam	34,336,103	17,645,088	16,691,015	43.8	51.4	48.6
Virgin Islands	43,451	22,046	21,405	35.8	50.7	49.3
Virgin Islands, British	5,768	2,928	2,840	29.4	50.8	49.2
West Bank	914,959	469,072	445,887	55.1	51.3	48.7
Yemen	10,386,869	5,326,288	5,060,581	59.3	51.3	48.7
Yugoslavia	3,070,521	1,589,404	1,481,117	27.3	51.7	48.2
Zambia	6,039,040	3,036,871	3,002,169	61.2	50.3	49.7
Zimbabwe	6,345,641	3,198,164	3,147,477	56.3	50.4	49.6

Source: U.S. Census International Database, 2000: Table 094. Midyear Population by Age and Sex; <http://www.census.gov/ipc/www/idbagg.html>. Underlying data from U.S. Bureau of the Census.

A1-4. Population, Age 0 to 14 Years, Total, Male, and Female, and Percentages, 2000

	0-14 Age Group			Age Group 0-14 as % of population		
	Total	Male	Female	Total	% male	% female
Afghanistan	11,396,242	5,811,021	5,585,221	42.7	42.4	43.1
Albania	1,089,538	563,870	525,668	32	34.6	29.6
Algeria	11,577,108	5,897,031	5,680,077	36.4	36.7	36.1
American Samoa	25,383	13,077	12,306	38.8	39.5	38
Andorra	9,576	4,964	4,612	14.2	13.9	14.4
Angola	5,156,733	2,613,884	2,542,849	44.9	45.2	44.5
Anguilla	3,141	1,596	1,545	26.5	26.5	26.4
Antigua and Barbuda	16,453	8,367	8,086	25.5	26.2	24.9
Argentina	10,154,533	5,174,753	4,979,780	27.3	28.2	26.4
Armenia	831,250	423,041	408,209	24.5	25.5	23.5
Aruba	14,766	7,665	7,101	21.4	23.0	19.8
Australia	3,942,335	2,019,336	1,922,999	20.8	21.4	20.2
Austria	1,352,211	693,808	658,403	16.6	17.4	15.8
Azerbaijan	2,508,178	1,278,714	1,229,464	31.5	33.0	30.2
Bahamas, the	78,420	39,478	38,942	27.3	28.1	26.5
Bahrain	194,402	98,512	95,890	30.3	27.2	34.3
Bangladesh	46,872,215	23,996,737	22,875,478	36.3	36.2	36.4
Barbados	58,640	29,663	28,977	22.6	23.6	21.7
Belarus	1,948,998	995,216	953,782	18.8	20.4	17.3
Belgium	1,733,189	887,636	845,553	17	17.8	16.3
Belize	98,958	50,450	48,508	41	41.2	40.8
Benin	3,105,069	1,557,197	1,547,872	47.6	48.8	46.5
Bermuda	12,124	6,143	5,981	19.3	20	18.6
Bhutan	799,364	414,452	384,912	40	40.3	39.8
Bolivia	3,138,376	1,586,324	1,552,052	38.6	39.5	37.6
Bosnia and Herzegovina	608,899	312,454	296,445	17	17.8	16.1
Botswana	614,195	310,528	303,667	41.5	43.2	40
Brazil	51,094,880	26,032,397	25,062,483	29.4	30.4	28.4
Brunei	107,480	54,995	52,485	32.5	31.9	33.2
Bulgaria	1,279,515	655,707	623,808	15.7	16.5	14.9
Burkina Faso	5,695,040	2,864,525	2,830,515	47.9	49.4	46.5
Burundi	2,766,679	1,386,292	1,380,387	46.6	47.7	45.7
Cambodia	5,361,363	2,721,708	2,639,655	45	47.1	43
Cameroon	7,280,278	3,657,964	3,622,314	45.8	46.2	45.4
Canada	6,055,006	3,100,639	2,954,367	19.3	20	18.7
Cape Verde	184,424	93,037	91,387	44.8	46.9	42.9
Central African Republic	1,530,040	769,517	760,523	43.5	44.4	42.7
Chad	3,429,164	1,718,332	1,710,832	44.2	44.9	43.5
Chile	4,186,397	2,140,042	2,046,355	27.6	28.5	26.8
China	315,502,305	168,091,842	147,410,463	25.1	25.9	24.3
Colombia	13,107,392	6,631,203	6,476,189	32.7	33.7	31.8
Comoros	248,676	124,560	124,116	42.8	43.3	42.4
Congo, Dem. Rep. (Zaire)	25,068,563	12,566,402	12,502,161	48.2	49	47.5
Congo, Rep.	1,174,936	590,465	584,471	42.3	43.2	41.4
Costa Rica	1,221,546	625,131	596,415	32.6	33	32.2
Côte d'Ivoire	7,511,879	3,774,080	3,737,799	46.4	46	46.8
Croatia	775,557	398,584	376,973	16.6	17.5	15.6
Cuba	2,379,160	1,221,437	1,157,723	21.4	21.9	20.8
Cyprus	178,099	91,175	86,924	23.5	24.1	22.9
Czech Republic	1,705,279	873,727	831,552	16.6	17.5	15.8
Denmark	991,065	508,577	482,488	18.4	19.1	17.7
Djibouti	194,546	97,334	97,212	42.8	41.5	44.2
Dominica	16,593	8,368	8,225	25.9	26.3	25.6
Dominican Republic	2,861,515	1,458,393	1,403,122	34.6	34.8	34.4
Ecuador	4,405,955	2,242,003	2,163,952	34.5	35.2	33.7
Egypt	24,120,558	12,339,803	11,780,755	35.2	35.7	34.7

A1-4. Population, Age 0 to 14 Years, Total, Male, and Female, and Percentages, 2000 *(continued)*

	0-14 Age Group			Age Group 0-14 as % of population		
	Total	**Male**	**Female**	**Total**	**% male**	**% female**
El Salvador	2,141,138	1,094,118	1,047,020	36.1	37.9	34.4
Equatorial Guinea	204,853	102,677	102,176	42.9	44.2	41.6
Eritrea	1,777,250	892,311	884,939	42.9	43.2	42.6
Estonia	247,079	125,970	121,109	17.7	19.5	16.1
Ethiopia	28,203,829	14,147,352	14,056,477	46.3	46.3	46.2
Faroe Islands	9,107	4,646	4,461	22.7	22.4	22.9
Fiji	270,757	138,013	132,744	32.9	33.4	32.4
Finland	937,742	478,387	459,355	18.2	19	17.4
France	10,915,010	5,588,263	5,326,747	18.5	19.4	17.6
French Guiana	53,478	27,353	26,125	30.9	29.8	32.1
French Polynesia	79,409	40,462	38,947	32.3	31.9	32.6
Gabon	416,079	207,865	208,214	33.4	33.3	33.5
Gambia, the	630,183	315,543	314,640	45.6	45.8	45.4
Gaza Strip	602,199	308,527	293,672	51.8	52.4	51.1
Georgia	1,029,497	525,221	504,276	20.5	21.9	19.1
Germany	12,511,667	6,414,373	6,097,294	15.2	16	14.6
Ghana	8,040,826	4,039,307	4,001,519	41.7	42.3	41.1
Gibraltar	5,884	3,120	2,764	20.1	19.7	20.5
Greece	1,678,430	869,575	808,855	15.6	16.3	14.9
Greenland	15,447	7,733	7,714	25.6	24.3	27
Grenada	41,254	20,967	20,287	42.1	41	43.4
Guadeloupe	104,845	53,537	51,308	24.7	25.6	23.8
Guam	53,572	27,962	25,610	34.7	34.7	34.9
Guatemala	5,380,588	2,745,858	2,634,730	42.5	43.1	41.9
Guernsey	12,206	6,178	6,028	18.4	19.4	17.5
Guinea	3,311,678	1,648,783	1,662,895	43.5	44.2	42.9
Guinea-Bissau	529,276	265,386	263,890	41.9	43.2	40.6
Guyana	208,410	106,221	102,189	29.6	30	29.2
Haiti	2,878,475	1,461,178	1,417,297	41.2	42.4	39.9
Honduras	2,504,539	1,274,847	1,229,692	40.9	41.5	40.2
Hong Kong SAR, China	1,254,742	651,285	603,457	18	19.1	17
Hungary	1,759,110	900,970	858,140	17.3	18.6	16.2
Iceland	63,643	32,627	31,016	23.2	23.8	22.6
Indonesia	66,013,343	33,487,193	32,526,150	30.1	30.6	29.6
Iran	22,806,963	11,659,377	11,147,586	34.6	34.9	34.3
Iraq	10,041,432	5,100,745	4,940,687	43.4	43.6	43.2
Ireland	764,836	393,289	371,547	21	21.7	20.3
Israel	1,620,516	829,573	790,943	27.7	28.5	26.9
Italy	8,044,101	4,140,877	3,903,224	14.2	15	13.4
Jamaica	814,614	416,481	398,133	30.5	31.3	29.7
Japan	18,802,894	9,627,899	9,174,995	14.9	15.6	14.2
Jersey	16,183	8,438	7,745	17.9	19.1	16.8
Jordan	2,002,846	1,027,090	975,756	42.6	42.6	42.6
Kazakhstan	4,675,933	2,374,503	2,301,430	27.8	29.3	26.4
Kenya	12,312,582	6,226,692	6,085,890	42.1	42.5	41.7
Kuwait	637,503	347,011	290,492	30.8	27.4	36.2
Kyrgyzstan	1,567,664	792,027	775,637	34.2	35.4	33
Laos	2,497,232	1,265,434	1,231,798	44.9	46	43.9
Latvia	402,423	205,683	196,740	17.3	19.3	15.6
Lebanon	1,059,458	539,714	519,744	29.3	30.8	27.8
Lesotho	853,740	427,610	426,130	39.4	40.4	38.4
Liberia	1,376,845	692,119	684,726	44.6	44.2	44.9
Libya	1,835,203	937,701	897,502	35.9	35.6	36.2
Liechtenstein	6,045	3,083	2,962	18.7	19.3	18
Lithuania	693,985	354,503	339,482	19.4	21.2	17.9
Luxembourg	77,668	39,626	38,042	18	18.5	17.4

A1-4. Population, Age 0 to 14 Years, Total, Male, and Female, and Percentages, 2000 *(continued)*

	0-14 Age Group			Age Group 0-14 as % of population		
	Total	**Male**	**Female**	**Total**	**% male**	**% female**
Macau	104,106	53,848	50,258	23.4	25.2	21.6
Macedonia, FYRO	467,173	241,114	226,059	23	23.7	22.2
Madagascar	6,802,969	3,440,488	3,362,481	44.5	45.0	43.9
Malawi	4,542,000	2,280,265	2,261,735	44.7	45.2	44.2
Malaysia	7,631,186	3,914,974	3,716,212	35	35.8	34.2
Maldives	145,252	74,534	70,718	46.8	46.9	46.7
Mali	5,097,183	2,558,961	2,538,222	47.4	48.8	46.1
Malta	76,486	39,356	37,130	20.0	20.7	19.2
Man, Isle of	13,667	6,984	6,683	17.9	18.9	17.0
Marshall Islands	33,705	17,198	16,507	49.5	49.5	49.5
Martinique	95,846	48,416	47,430	23.1	23.8	22.4
Mauritania	1,237,789	619,192	618,597	46.5	47.4	45.7
Mauritius	313,081	157,785	155,296	26.2	26.7	25.6
Mayotte	73,258	36,648	36,610	46.7	44.6	49.0
Mexico	35,456,116	18,080,325	17,375,791	34.8	35.9	33.6
Moldova	1,064,542	541,775	522,767	23.8	25.5	22.3
Monaco	5,346	2,715	2,631	16.6	18.0	15.4
Mongolia	932,908	474,421	458,487	35.1	35.7	34.6
Morocco	10,631,972	5,417,432	5,214,540	35.2	35.9	34.5
Mozambique	8,762,590	4,344,012	4,418,578	44.7	45.2	44.2
Myanmar (Burma)	17,576,499	8,961,005	8,615,494	36	36.5	35.4
Namibia	731,144	369,533	361,611	43.7	44.4	42.9
Nepal	10,242,409	5,279,874	4,962,535	41.1	41.4	40.8
Netherlands	2,884,292	1,475,002	1,409,290	18.2	18.7	17.6
Netherlands Antilles	53,361	27,225	26,136	25.4	27.1	23.9
New Caledonia	58,565	29,855	28,710	29.2	29.5	28.9
New Zealand	842,801	431,871	410,930	22.8	23.5	22.1
Nicaragua	2,092,440	1,056,152	1,036,288	43.1	44.1	42.2
Niger	4,933,767	2,517,193	2,416,574	48.1	49.0	47.2
Nigeria	52,526,002	26,375,522	26,150,480	44.8	44.5	45.1
North Korea, Dem. Rep.	5,548,456	2,843,250	2,705,206	25.6	27.0	24.2
Northern Mariana Islands	17,236	8,758	8,478	23.9	25.2	22.7
Norway	875,523	449,794	425,729	19.6	20.4	18.9
Oman	1,041,592	530,891	510,701	41.1	36.9	46.7
Pakistan	57,782,132	29,720,709	28,061,423	40.9	41.1	40.7
Palau	5,134	2,641	2,493	27.3	26.3	28.4
Panama	877,294	446,998	430,296	31.1	31.3	30.9
Papua New Guinea	1,884,285	966,966	917,319	39.2	39.0	39.4
Paraguay	2,182,554	1,110,056	1,072,498	39.1	39.6	38.7
Peru	9,516,224	4,833,798	4,682,426	35.1	35.4	34.7
Philippines	29,974,520	15,245,218	14,729,302	37	37.8	36.2
Poland	7,403,208	3,793,059	3,610,149	19.2	20.2	18.2
Portugal	1,660,659	852,708	807,951	16.8	17.9	15.7
Puerto Rico	938,984	480,777	458,207	24	25.5	22.6
Qatar	198,030	100,989	97,041	26.4	20.4	38
Reunion	233,890	119,733	114,157	32	33.2	30.9
Romania	4,039,965	2,063,685	1,976,280	18.1	19.0	17.3
Russia	26,873,430	13,710,360	13,163,070	18.4	20.1	16.9
Rwanda	3,644,367	1,829,769	1,814,598	43.7	44.2	43.3
Saint Helena	1,393	704	689	19.4	19.2	19.5
Saint Kitts and Nevis	13,957	7,150	6,807	32.1	32.9	31.4
Saint Lucia	50,690	25,798	24,892	32.6	33.8	31.4
Saint Vincent and the Grenadines	34,893	17,762	17,131	28.8	29.2	28.4
Samoa	90,926	46,239	44,687	38.6	38.3	39.0

A1-4. Population, Age 0 to 14 Years, Total, Male, and Female, and Percentages, 2000 *(continued)*

	0-14 Age Group			Age Group 0-14 as % of population		
	Total	**Male**	**Female**	**Total**	**% male**	**% female**
San Marino	4,088	2,034	2,054	16.2	16.5	16.0
Sao Tome and Principe	76,189	38,557	37,632	47.7	49.0	46.4
Saudi Arabia	9,552,151	4,863,293	4,688,858	42.9	39.5	47.1
Senegal	4,965,593	2,475,864	2,489,729	47.8	48.9	46.7
Seychelles	23,086	11,640	11,446	29	30.2	27.8
Sierra Leone	2,502,888	1,231,907	1,270,981	45.4	46.1	44.8
Singapore	754,368	389,522	364,846	21.1	21.9	20.4
Slovakia	1,046,116	534,554	511,562	19.4	20.3	18.5
Slovenia	311,345	159,799	151,546	15.8	16.7	14.9
Solomon Islands	208,593	106,292	102,301	44.4	44.6	44.2
Somalia	3,319,970	1,662,896	1,657,074	44.7	44.7	44.6
South Africa	15,009,939	7,575,222	7,434,717	34.1	34.8	33.5
South Korea, Rep.	10,383,042	5,514,168	4,868,874	21.9	23.1	20.8
Spain	5,786,296	2,982,066	2,804,230	14.8	15.6	14.0
Sri Lanka	5,145,310	2,629,549	2,515,761	26.6	27.5	25.7
Sudan	15,913,993	8,124,225	7,789,768	44.8	45.2	44.4
Suriname	141,016	72,231	68,785	32.5	32.8	32.2
Swaziland	464,293	231,669	232,624	46.2	47.2	45.3
Sweden	1,677,227	860,485	816,742	18.8	19.5	18.1
Switzerland	1,245,090	636,721	608,369	17.1	17.7	16.5
Syria	8,052,370	4,123,924	3,928,446	45.3	45.5	45.2
Taiwan	4,810,169	2,493,788	2,316,381	21.6	21.8	21.3
Tajikistan	2,452,365	1,238,357	1,214,008	39.6	40.2	39.0
Tanzania	14,152,339	7,055,129	7,097,210	44.3	44.9	43.7
Thailand	14,351,178	7,309,374	7,041,804	23.5	24.2	22.7
Togo	2,525,705	1,267,889	1,257,816	48	48.9	47.1
Trinidad and Tobago	278,038	142,096	135,942	25.6	25.4	25.8
Tunisia	2,898,682	1,497,574	1,401,108	30.1	30.8	29.3
Turkey	19,885,765	10,127,369	9,758,396	29.8	30.1	29.6
Turkmenistan	1,654,714	844,622	810,092	37.3	38.5	36.1
Turks and Caicos Islands	5,686	2,886	2,800	32.5	32.0	33.1
Tuvalu	3,655	1,862	1,793	34.1	35.6	32.6
Uganda	12,018,071	6,026,496	5,991,575	51.2	51.4	51.1
Ukraine	8,882,783	4,535,524	4,347,259	17.9	19.8	16.4
United Arab Emirate	714,926	365,377	349,549	30	25.4	36.8
United Kingdom	11,300,376	5,799,848	5,500,528	19.1	19.9	18.3
United States	58,963,139	30,182,352	28,780,787	21.4	22.4	20.5
Uruguay	803,412	411,742	391,670	24.1	25.3	22.9
Uzbekistan	8,860,969	4,503,709	4,357,260	36.3	37.2	35.3
Vanuatu	73,081	37,176	35,905	37.9	37.7	38.1
Venezuela	7,738,486	3,993,048	3,745,438	32.8	33.6	32.0
Vietnam	25,592,959	13,180,924	12,412,035	32.7	34.2	31.1
Virgin Islands	33,946	17,428	16,518	28	30.6	25.7
Virgin Islands, British	3,993	2,020	1,973	20.4	20.0	20.7
West Bank	742,022	380,105	361,917	44.7	45.2	44.1
Yemen	8,317,605	4,229,753	4,087,852	47.5	47.4	47.6
Yugoslavia	2,234,329	1,157,999	1,076,330	20.5	21.3	19.6
Zambia	4,816,864	2,421,789	2,395,075	48.8	49.4	48.2
Zimbabwe	4,797,188	2,421,116	2,376,072	42.6	43.2	42.0

Source: U.S. Census International Database, 2000, Table 094. Midyear Population by Age and Sex; <http://www.census.gov/ipc/www/idbagg.html>. Underlying data from U.S. Bureau of the Census.

A1-5. Population, Age 15 to 19 Years, Total, Male, and Female, and Percentages, 2000

	15-19 Age Group			Age Group 15-19 as % of population		
	Total	Male	Female	Total	% male	% female
Afghanistan	2,814,546	1,439,405	1,375,141	10.6	51.1	48.9
Albania	346,222	179,305	166,917	10.2	51.8	48.2
Algeria	3,881,938	1,972,819	1,909,119	12.2	50.8	49.2
American Samoa	6,250	3,148	3,102	9.5	50.4	49.6
Andorra	3,592	1,845	1,747	5.3	51.4	48.6
Angola	1,171,186	590,892	580,294	10.2	50.5	49.5
Anguilla	1,021	512	509	8.6	50.1	49.9
Antigua and Barbuda	5,256	2,658	2,598	8.2	50.6	49.4
Argentina	3,201,473	1,626,942	1,574,531	8.6	50.8	49.2
Armenia	327,875	167,231	160,644	9.7	51.0	49.0
Aruba	4,467	2,418	2,049	6.5	54.1	45.9
Australia	1,294,262	662,993	631,269	6.8	51.2	48.8
Austria	481,992	246,979	235,013	5.9	51.2	48.8
Azerbaijan	751,346	384,834	366,512	9.4	51.2	48.8
Bahamas, the	27,392	13,785	13,607	9.5	50.3	49.7
Bahrain	50,289	25,601	24,688	7.8	50.9	49.1
Bangladesh	17,042,456	8,776,486	8,265,970	13.2	51.5	48.5
Barbados	20,061	10,169	9,892	7.7	50.7	49.3
Belarus	824,516	418,637	405,879	7.9	50.8	49.2
Belgium	606,937	310,428	296,509	6.0	51.1	48.9
Belize	27,247	13,858	13,389	11.3	50.9	49.1
Benin	710,196	355,988	354,208	10.9	50.1	49.9
Bermuda	3,889	1,971	1,918	6.2	50.7	49.3
Bhutan	194,635	101,561	93,074	9.8	52.2	47.8
Bolivia	884,851	444,875	439,976	10.9	50.3	49.7
Bosnia and Herzegovina	287,477	146,098	141,379	8.0	50.8	49.2
Botswana	190,064	96,201	93,863	12.9	50.6	49.4
Brazil	17,611,442	8,940,947	8,670,495	10.1	50.8	49.2
Brunei	30,083	15,402	14,681	9.1	51.2	48.8
Bulgaria	556,361	285,550	270,811	6.8	51.3	48.7
Burkina Faso	1,325,313	665,408	659,905	11.1	50.2	49.8
Burundi	712,867	354,285	358,582	12.0	49.7	50.3
Cambodia	1,260,009	638,257	621,752	10.6	50.7	49.3
Cameroon	1,738,887	870,850	868,037	10.9	50.1	49.9
Canada	2,085,905	1,065,897	1,020,008	6.7	51.1	48.9
Cape Verde	45,631	23,096	22,535	11.1	50.6	49.4
Central African Republic	396,412	198,754	197,658	11.3	50.1	49.9
Chad	797,391	397,578	399,813	10.3	49.9	50.1
Chile	1,320,934	671,292	649,642	8.7	50.8	49.2
China	98,867,548	51,259,918	47,607,630	7.9	51.8	48.2
Colombia	3,714,408	1,873,126	1,841,282	9.3	50.4	49.6
Comoros	56,645	28,356	28,289	9.8	50.1	49.9
Congo, Dem. Rep. (Zaire)	5,605,128	2,807,221	2,797,907	10.8	50.1	49.9
Congo, Rep.	323,774	162,573	161,201	11.7	50.2	49.8
Costa Rica	371,075	191,331	179,744	9.9	51.6	48.4
Côte d'Ivoire	1,857,162	936,301	920,861	11.5	50.4	49.6
Croatia	317,022	162,171	154,851	6.8	51.2	48.8
Cuba	743,178	381,078	362,100	6.7	51.3	48.7
Cyprus	63,123	32,725	30,398	8.3	51.8	48.2
Czech Republic	690,195	353,184	337,011	6.7	51.2	48.8
Denmark	282,102	144,508	137,594	5.2	51.2	48.8
Djibouti	44,800	22,618	22,182	9.9	50.5	49.5
Dominica	5,780	2,876	2,904	9.0	49.8	50.2
Dominican Republic	829,910	422,024	407,886	10.0	50.9	49.1
Ecuador	1,365,095	692,457	672,638	10.7	50.7	49.3
Egypt	7,165,809	3,639,091	3,526,718	10.5	50.8	49.2

A1-5. Population, Age 15 to 19 Years, Total, Male, and Female, and Percentages, 2000 *(continued)*

	15-19 Age Group			Age Group 15-19 as % of population		
	Total	**Male**	**Female**	**Total**	**% male**	**% female**
El Salvador	646,350	327,096	319,254	10.9	50.6	49.4
Equatorial Guinea	49,878	24,949	24,929	10.4	50.0	50.0
Eritrea	435,576	219,383	216,193	10.5	50.4	49.6
Estonia	105,451	53,314	52,137	7.5	50.6	49.4
Ethiopia	6,752,989	3,375,490	3,377,499	11.1	50.0	50.0
Faroe Islands	2,825	1,471	1,354	7.0	52.1	47.9
Fiji	91,797	47,091	44,706	11.1	51.3	48.7
Finland	330,912	169,179	161,733	6.4	51.1	48.9
France	3,897,346	1,992,882	1,904,464	6.6	51.1	48.9
French Guiana	13,943	7,118	6,825	8.0	51.1	48.9
French Polynesia	23,696	12,020	11,676	9.6	50.7	49.3
Gabon	116,905	58,693	58,212	9.4	50.2	49.8
Gambia, the	141,142	70,435	70,707	10.2	49.9	50.1
Gaza Strip	117,108	60,204	56,904	10.1	51.4	48.6
Georgia	410,117	208,125	201,992	8.1	50.7	49.3
Germany	4,551,574	2,334,721	2,216,853	5.5	51.3	48.7
Ghana	2,042,580	1,022,991	1,019,589	10.6	50.1	49.9
Gibraltar	1,842	1,024	818	6.3	55.6	44.4
Greece	716,813	367,862	348,951	6.7	51.3	48.7
Greenland	4,678	2,419	2,259	7.8	51.7	48.3
Grenada	11,184	5,764	5,420	11.4	51.5	48.5
Guadeloupe	32,916	16,627	16,289	7.7	50.5	49.5
Guam	12,011	6,081	5,930	7.8	50.6	49.4
Guatemala	1,370,129	698,619	671,510	10.8	51.0	49.0
Guernsey	3,706	1,901	1,805	5.6	51.3	48.7
Guinea	805,603	403,385	402,218	10.6	50.1	49.9
Guinea-Bissau	136,809	68,195	68,614	10.8	49.8	50.2
Guyana	82,776	42,556	40,220	11.8	51.4	48.6
Haiti	849,897	429,091	420,806	12.2	50.5	49.5
Honduras	704,982	357,657	347,325	11.5	50.7	49.3
Hong Kong SAR, China	448,859	229,326	219,533	6.4	51.1	48.9
Hungary	648,939	331,504	317,435	6.4	51.1	48.9
Iceland	20,912	10,724	10,188	7.6	51.3	48.7
India	102,957,258	53,573,598	49,383,660	10.1	52.0	48.0
Indonesia	22,003,058	11,120,925	10,882,133	10.0	50.5	49.5
Iran	8,553,975	4,337,139	4,216,836	13.0	50.7	49.3
Iraq	2,676,151	1,355,813	1,320,338	11.6	50.7	49.3
Ireland	324,208	166,484	157,724	8.9	51.4	48.6
Israel	504,505	258,150	246,355	8.6	51.2	48.8
Italy	2,974,993	1,526,079	1,448,914	5.2	51.3	48.7
Jamaica	265,254	135,830	129,424	9.9	51.2	48.8
Japan	7,519,923	3,850,910	3,669,013	5.9	51.2	48.8
Jersey	4,466	2,232	2,234	4.9	50.0	50.0
Jordan	510,541	261,389	249,152	10.9	51.2	48.8
Kazakhstan	1,612,565	813,783	798,782	9.6	50.5	49.5
Kenya	3,807,042	1,921,267	1,885,775	13.0	50.5	49.5
Kuwait	201,140	112,602	88,538	9.7	56.0	44.0
Kyrgyzstan	493,294	248,083	245,211	10.8	50.3	49.7
Laos	591,053	298,883	292,170	10.6	50.6	49.4
Latvia	176,111	89,333	86,778	7.6	50.7	49.3
Lebanon	361,182	183,648	177,534	10.0	50.8	49.2
Lesotho	241,663	120,983	120,680	11.2	50.1	49.9
Liberia	314,068	157,629	156,439	10.2	50.2	49.8
Libya	606,483	309,219	297,264	11.9	51.0	49.0
Liechtenstein	2,020	1,045	975	6.2	51.7	48.3
Lithuania	269,241	136,769	132,472	7.5	50.8	49.2

A1-5. Population, Age 15 to 19 Years, Total, Male, and Female, and Percentages, 2000 *(continued)*

	15-19 Age Group			Age Group 15-19 as % of population		
	Total	Male	Female	Total	% male	% female
Luxembourg	24,459	12,554	11,905	5.7	51.3	48.7
Macau	33,647	17,023	16,624	7.6	50.6	49.4
Macedonia, FYRO	168,012	86,090	81,922	8.3	51.2	48.8
Madagascar	1,619,049	817,192	801,857	10.6	50.5	49.5
Malawi	1,248,329	629,592	618,737	12.3	50.4	49.6
Malaysia	2,177,269	1,116,482	1,060,787	10.0	51.3	48.7
Maldives	31,913	16,232	15,681	10.3	50.9	49.1
Mali	1,154,462	578,568	575,894	10.7	50.1	49.9
Malta	28,438	14,502	13,936	7.4	51.0	49.0
Man, Isle of	4,272	2,183	2,089	5.6	51.1	48.9
Marshall Islands	7,795	3,978	3,817	11.4	51.0	49.0
Martinique	28,276	14,381	13,895	6.8	50.9	49.1
Mauritania	281,239	139,367	141,872	10.6	49.6	50.4
Mauritius	106,123	53,831	52,292	8.9	50.7	49.3
Mayotte	14,326	7,174	7,152	9.1	50.1	49.9
Mexico	10,770,434	5,465,977	5,304,457	10.6	50.7	49.3
Moldova	406,098	205,745	200,353	9.1	50.7	49.3
Monaco	1,991	995	996	6.2	50.0	50.0
Mongolia	296,198	149,641	146,557	11.2	50.5	49.5
Morocco	3,327,819	1,689,027	1,638,792	11.0	50.8	49.2
Mozambique	2,124,911	1,040,760	1,084,151	10.8	49.0	51.0
Myanmar (Burma)	5,004,836	2,550,748	2,454,088	10.2	51.0	49.0
Namibia	207,633	105,151	102,482	12.4	50.6	49.4
Nepal	2,745,342	1,419,024	1,326,318	11.0	51.7	48.3
Netherlands	917,082	468,405	448,677	5.8	51.1	48.9
Netherlands Antilles	16,492	8,215	8,277	7.9	49.8	50.2
New Caledonia	17,859	9,024	8,835	8.9	50.5	49.5
New Zealand	249,130	127,456	121,674	6.7	51.2	48.8
Nicaragua	560,121	279,089	281,032	11.5	49.8	50.2
Niger	1,058,286	543,574	514,712	10.3	51.4	48.6
Nigeria	12,395,117	6,216,683	6,178,434	10.6	50.2	49.8
North Korea, Dem. Rep.	1,757,206	894,757	862,449	8.1	50.9	49.1
Northern Mariana Islands	4,663	2,087	2,576	6.5	44.8	55.2
Norway	264,288	135,358	128,930	5.9	51.2	48.8
Oman	245,997	125,711	120,286	9.7	51.1	48.9
Pakistan	15,120,023	7,817,938	7,302,085	10.7	51.7	48.3
Palau	1,353	708	645	7.2	52.3	47.7
Panama	270,340	138,100	132,240	9.6	51.1	48.9
Papua New Guinea	523,944	268,825	255,119	10.9	51.3	48.7
Paraguay	554,524	278,771	275,753	9.9	50.3	49.7
Peru	2,769,913	1,403,143	1,366,770	10.2	50.7	49.3
Philippines	8,481,016	4,294,482	4,186,534	10.5	50.6	49.4
Poland	3,361,620	1,713,936	1,647,684	8.7	51.0	49.0
Portugal	658,379	335,543	322,836	6.6	51.0	49.0
Puerto Rico	316,508	160,790	155,718	8.1	50.8	49.2
Qatar	61,253	32,581	28,672	8.2	53.2	46.8
Reunion	60,669	30,994	29,675	8.3	51.1	48.9
Romania	1,651,540	842,229	809,311	7.4	51.0	49.0
Russia	11,902,722	6,030,372	5,872,350	8.2	50.7	49.3
Rwanda	1,089,323	545,696	543,627	13.1	50.1	49.9
Saint Helena	530	266	264	7.4	50.2	49.8
Saint Kitts and Nevis	5,061	2,603	2,458	11.7	51.4	48.6
Saint Lucia	17,384	8,650	8,734	11.2	49.8	50.2
Saint Vincent and the Grenadines	14,173	7,232	6,941	11.7	51.0	49.0
Samoa	24,732	12,522	12,210	10.5	50.6	49.4

A1-5. Population, Age 15 to 19 Years, Total, Male, and Female, and Percentages, 2000 *(continued)*

	15-19 Age Group			Age Group 15-19 as % of population		
	Total	Male	Female	Total	% male	% female
San Marino	1,302	667	635	5.2	51.2	48.8
Sao Tome and Principe	17,699	8,905	8,794	11.1	50.3	49.7
Saudi Arabia	2,130,028	1,078,302	1,051,726	9.6	50.6	49.4
Senegal	1,109,826	551,460	558,366	10.7	49.7	50.3
Seychelles	7,885	3,900	3,985	9.9	49.5	50.5
Sierra Leone	546,062	265,594	280,468	9.9	48.6	51.4
Singapore	209,499	107,213	102,286	5.9	51.2	48.8
Slovakia	444,798	227,223	217,575	8.2	51.1	48.9
Slovenia	138,425	70,831	67,594	7.0	51.2	48.8
Solomon Islands	52,605	26,717	25,888	11.2	50.8	49.2
Somalia	749,140	366,677	382,463	10.1	48.9	51.1
South Africa	4,589,495	2,313,783	2,275,712	10.4	50.4	49.6
South Korea, Rep.	3,806,874	1,966,564	1,840,310	8.0	51.7	48.3
Spain	2,524,039	1,293,927	1,230,112	6.4	51.3	48.7
Sri Lanka	1,912,617	975,273	937,344	9.9	51.0	49.0
Sudan	3,915,470	1,994,747	1,920,723	11.0	50.9	49.1
Suriname	41,740	21,584	20,156	9.6	51.7	48.3
Swaziland	120,451	59,737	60,714	12.0	49.6	50.4
Sweden	507,866	260,756	247,110	5.7	51.3	48.7
Switzerland	409,257	209,404	199,853	5.6	51.2	48.8
Syria	2,002,140	1,026,715	975,425	11.3	51.3	48.7
Taiwan	1,913,580	984,236	929,344	8.6	51.4	48.6
Tajikistan	700,591	354,415	346,176	11.3	50.6	49.4
Tanzania	3,617,070	1,794,296	1,822,774	11.3	49.6	50.4
Thailand	5,599,773	2,842,942	2,756,831	9.2	50.8	49.2
Togo	572,575	287,538	285,037	10.9	50.2	49.8
Trinidad and Tobago	120,144	62,575	57,569	11.1	52.1	47.9
Tunisia	1,045,130	532,049	513,081	10.8	50.9	49.1
Turkey	6,701,924	3,402,635	3,299,289	10.1	50.8	49.2
Turkmenistan	475,005	239,485	235,520	10.7	50.4	49.6
Turks and Caicos Islands	1,299	658	641	7.4	50.7	49.3
Tuvalu	1,109	563	546	10.3	50.8	49.2
Uganda	2,547,946	1,279,303	1,268,643	10.9	50.2	49.8
Ukraine	3,764,038	1,911,131	1,852,907	7.6	50.8	49.2
United Arab Emirates	244,263	124,360	119,903	10.2	50.9	49.1
United Kingdom	3,710,482	1,907,776	1,802,706	6.3	51.4	48.6
United States	19,835,384	10,168,608	9,666,776	7.2	51.3	48.7
Uruguay	258,737	131,941	126,796	7.8	51.0	49.0
Uzbekistan	2,701,819	1,362,575	1,339,244	11.1	50.4	49.6
Vanuatu	21,603	10,987	10,616	11.2	50.9	49.1
Venezuela	2,386,188	1,226,589	1,159,599	10.1	51.4	48.6
Vietnam	8,743,144	4,464,164	4,278,980	11.2	51.1	48.9
Virgin Islands	9,834	4,788	5,046	8.1	48.7	51.3
Virgin Islands, British	1,775	908	867	9.1	51.2	48.8
West Bank	172,937	88,967	83,970	10.4	51.4	48.6
Yemen	2,069,264	1,096,535	972,729	11.8	53.0	47.0
Yugoslavia	836,192	431,405	404,787	7.5	51.5	48.5
Zambia	1,222,176	615,082	607,094	12.4	50.3	49.7
Zimbabwe	1,548,453	777,048	771,405	13.7	50.2	49.8

Source: U.S. Census International Database, 2000: Table 094. Midyear Population by Age and Sex; <http://www.census.gov/ipc/www/idbagg.html>. Underlying data from U.S. Bureau of the Census.

A1-6. Population, Age 10 to 14 Years, Total, Male, and Female, and Percentages, 2000

	10-14 Age Group			Age Group 10-14 as % of population		
	Total	**Male**	**Female**	**Total**	**% male**	**% female**
Afghanistan	3,265,573	1,667,081	1,598,492	12.2	12.1	12.3
Albania	377,730	195,612	182,118	11.1	12.0	10.3
Algeria	3,747,145	1,907,944	1,839,201	11.8	11.9	11.7
American Samoa	7,579	3,927	3,652	11.6	11.9	11.3
Andorra	3,203	1,679	1,524	4.7	4.7	4.8
Angola	1,441,723	731,853	709,870	12.6	12.7	12.4
Anguilla	1,130	575	555	9.5	9.6	9.5
Antigua and Barbuda	5,324	2,702	2,622	8.3	8.5	8.1
Argentina	3,265,076	1,662,055	1,603,021	8.8	9.0	8.5
Armenia	341,316	174,020	167,296	10.0	10.5	9.6
Aruba	4,919	2,623	2,296	7.1	7.9	6.4
Australia	1,336,373	684,182	652,191	7.1	7.2	6.9
Austria	471,728	242,112	229,616	5.8	6.1	5.5
Azerbaijan	835,978	428,430	407,548	10.5	11.0	10.0
Bahamas, the	22,823	11,484	11,339	7.9	8.2	7.7
Bahrain	60,615	30,893	29,722	9.4	8.5	10.6
Bangladesh	18,576,204	9,490,659	9,085,545	14.4	14.3	14.5
Barbados	19,135	9,712	9,423	7.4	7.7	7.0
Belarus	811,768	414,456	397,312	7.8	8.5	7.2
Belgium	606,768	311,177	295,591	6.0	6.2	5.7
Belize	31,187	15,890	15,297	12.9	13	12.9
Benin	857,595	429,759	427,836	13.2	13.5	12.9
Bermuda	4,039	2,016	2,023	6.4	6.5	6.3
Bhutan	228,889	119,180	109,709	11.5	11.6	11.4
Bolivia	974,990	490,470	484,520	12.0	12.2	11.7
Bosnia and Herzegovina	272,636	139,725	132,911	7.6	8.0	7.2
Botswana	198,027	100,009	98,018	13.4	13.9	12.9
Brazil	17,463,432	8,887,826	8,575,606	10.0	10.4	9.7
Brunei	33,783	17,260	16,523	10.2	10	10.4
Bulgaria	522,366	267,524	254,842	6.4	6.7	6.1
Burkina Faso	1,596,879	801,996	794,883	13.4	13.8	13
Burundi	813,598	407,456	406,142	13.7	14.0	13.4
Cambodia	1,535,788	779,273	756,515	12.9	13.5	12.3
Cameroon	2,053,984	1,028,973	1,025,011	12.9	13	12.9
Canada	2,075,826	1,062,457	1,013,369	6.6	6.9	6.4
Cape Verde	57,346	28,963	28,383	13.9	14.6	13.3
Central African Republic	459,658	230,499	229,159	13.1	13.3	12.9
Chad	945,452	472,507	472,945	12.2	12.3	12.0
Chile	1,402,829	716,441	686,388	9.3	9.5	9.0
China	119,854,295	62,766,592	57,087,703	9.5	9.7	9.4
Colombia	4,070,604	2,058,699	2,011,905	10.2	10.5	9.9
Comoros	67,575	33,820	33,755	11.6	11.7	11.5
Congo, Dem. Rep. (Zaire)	6,843,458	3,429,886	3,413,572	13.2	13.4	13.0
Congo, Rep.	344,570	173,124	171,446	12.4	12.7	12.2
Costa Rica	405,153	207,288	197,865	10.8	10.9	10.7
Côte d'Ivoire	2,199,382	1,106,470	1,092,912	13.6	13.5	13.7
Croatia	281,466	144,155	137,311	6.0	6.3	5.7
Cuba	876,130	449,388	426,742	7.9	8.1	7.7
Cyprus	64,307	33,044	31,263	8.5	8.7	8.2
Czech Republic	645,670	330,502	315,168	6.3	6.6	6.0
Denmark	307,616	158,008	149,608	5.7	5.9	5.5
Djibouti	53,587	26,761	26,826	11.8	11.4	12.2
Dominica	5,744	2,869	2,875	9.0	9.0	9.0
Dominican Republic	900,851	458,415	442,436	10.9	11	10.9
Ecuador	1,487,575	756,554	731,021	11.6	11.9	11.4
Egypt	7,822,379	3,998,194	3,824,185	11.4	11.6	11.3

A1-6. Population, Age 10 to 14 Years, Total, Male, and Female, and Percentages, 2000 *(continued)*

	10-14 Age Group			Age Group 10-14 as % of population		
	Total	**Male**	**Female**	**Total**	**% male**	**% female**
El Salvador	685,499	349,886	335,613	11.6	12.1	11
Equatorial Guinea	59,180	29,601	29,579	12.4	12.7	12.1
Eritrea	488,219	245,788	242,431	11.8	11.9	11.7
Estonia	107,839	54,899	52,940	7.7	8.5	7.1
Ethiopia	7,968,668	3,996,434	3,972,234	13.1	13.1	13.1
Faroe Islands	3,267	1,648	1,619	8.1	8.0	8.3
Fiji	92,374	47,036	45,338	11.2	11.4	11.1
Finland	316,113	161,557	154,556	6.1	6.4	5.8
France	3,813,264	1,949,541	1,863,723	6.4	6.8	6.2
French Guiana	16,364	8,365	7,999	9.4	9.1	9.8
French Polynesia	26,477	13,466	13,011	10.8	10.6	10.9
Gabon	126,701	63,369	63,332	10.2	10.2	10.2
Gambia, the	172,398	86,130	86,268	12.5	12.5	12.5
Gaza Strip	149,585	76,656	72,929	12.9	13	12.7
Georgia	409,399	209,287	200,112	8.1	8.7	7.6
Germany	4,682,427	2,400,423	2,282,004	5.7	6.0	5.5
Ghana	2,557,094	1,282,372	1,274,722	13.3	13.4	13.1
Gibraltar	1,705	938	767	5.8	5.9	5.7
Greece	602,203	310,899	291,304	5.6	5.8	5.4
Greenland	5,375	2,710	2,665	8.9	8.5	9.3
Grenada	14,005	7,169	6,836	14.3	14	14.6
Guadeloupe	34,437	17,539	16,898	8.1	8.4	7.8
Guam	14,109	7,255	6,854	9.2	9.0	9.3
Guatemala	1,586,513	809,682	776,831	12.5	12.7	12.3
Guernsey	3,833	1,924	1,909	5.8	6.1	5.5
Guinea	958,788	475,930	482,858	12.6	12.8	12.4
Guinea-Bissau	154,443	77,200	77,243	12.2	12.6	11.9
Guyana	77,406	39,519	37,887	11	11.2	10.8
Haiti	975,374	494,489	480,885	14	14.4	13.5
Honduras	769,924	391,011	378,913	12.6	12.7	12.4
Hong Kong SAR, China	425,126	218,676	206,450	6.1	6.4	5.8
Hungary	617,336	315,856	301,480	6.1	6.5	5.7
Iceland	21,021	10,835	10,186	7.7	7.9	7.4
Indonesia	21,287,881	10,782,044	10,505,837	9.7	9.9	9.6
Iran	8,840,376	4,516,403	4,323,973	13.4	13.5	13.3
Iraq	2,959,642	1,502,610	1,457,032	12.8	12.8	12.7
Ireland	276,336	141,574	134,762	7.6	7.8	7.3
Israel	522,336	267,401	254,935	8.9	9.2	8.7
Italy	2,753,489	1,415,744	1,337,745	4.9	5.1	4.6
Jamaica	267,039	136,683	130,356	10	10.3	9.7
Japan	6,539,163	3,350,103	3,189,060	5.2	5.4	4.9
Jersey	4,875	2,527	2,348	5.4	5.7	5.1
Jordan	578,989	296,794	282,195	12.3	12.3	12.3
Kazakhstan	1,763,072	892,848	870,224	10.5	11	10
Kenya	4,132,624	2,088,563	2,044,061	14.1	14.2	14
Kuwait	216,541	122,256	94,285	10.5	9.7	11.8
Kyrgyzstan	567,458	286,489	280,969	12.4	12.8	12
Laos	718,577	363,237	355,340	12.9	13.2	12.7
Latvia	181,116	92,480	88,636	7.8	8.7	7.0
Lebanon	334,209	170,091	164,118	9.2	9.7	8.8
Lesotho	268,908	134,469	134,439	12.4	12.7	12.1
Liberia	377,140	189,338	187,802	12.2	12.1	12.3
Libya	606,005	309,337	296,668	11.8	11.8	11.9
Liechtenstein	1,996	1,033	963	6.2	6.5	5.9
Lithuania	276,095	140,923	135,172	7.7	8.4	7.1
Luxembourg	25,463	12,970	12,493	5.9	6.1	5.7

A1-6. Population, Age 10 to 14 Years, Total, Male, and Female, and Percentages, 2000 *(continued)*

	10-14 Age Group			Age Group 10-14 as % of population		
	Total	Male	Female	Total	% male	% female
Macau	41,720	21,558	20,162	9.4	10.1	8.7
Macedonia, FYRO	158,228	81,451	76,777	7.8	7.0	7.6
Madagascar	1,907,693	965,330	942,363	12.5	12.6	12.3
Malawi	1,406,246	706,358	699,888	13.8	14.0	13.7
Malaysia	2,380,906	1,221,684	1,159,222	10.9	11.2	10.7
Maldives	41,168	21,156	20,012	13.3	13.3	13.2
Mali	1,360,947	681,953	678,994	12.7	13.0	12.3
Malta	27,248	14,040	13,208	7.1	7.4	6.8
Man, Isle of	4,314	2,185	2,129	5.7	5.9	5.4
Marshall Islands	9,358	4,764	4,594	13.7	13.7	13.8
Martinique	30,799	15,586	15,213	7.4	7.7	7.2
Mauritania	337,420	167,780	169,640	12.7	12.8	12.5
Mauritius	98,097	50,088	48,009	8.2	8.5	7.9
Mayotte	18,527	9,222	9,305	11.8	11.2	12.4
Mexico	11,402,118	5,808,925	5,593,193	11.2	11.5	10.8
Moldova	421,054	214,083	206,971	9.4	10.1	8.8
Monaco	1,860	935	925	5.8	6.2	5.4
Mongolia	343,001	173,356	169,645	12.9	13.1	12.8
Morocco	3,494,062	1,777,917	1,716,145	11.6	11.8	11.3
Mozambique	2,391,879	1,171,279	1,220,600	12.2	12.2	12.2
Myanmar (Burma)	5,485,356	2,793,555	2,691,801	11.2	11.4	11.1
Namibia	229,169	115,756	113,413	13.7	13.9	13.5
Nepal	3,050,234	1,577,185	1,473,049	12.2	12.4	12.1
Netherlands	967,391	494,182	473,209	6.1	6.3	5.9
Netherlands Antilles	17,062	8,634	8,428	8.1	8.6	7.7
New Caledonia	18,763	9,545	9,218	9.4	9.4	9.3
New Zealand	277,776	141,847	135,929	7.5	7.7	7.3
Nicaragua	618,453	310,817	307,636	12.7	13.0	12.5
Niger	1,286,399	657,619	628,780	12.5	12.8	12.3
Nigeria	14,476,261	7,249,341	7,226,920	12.4	12.2	12.5
North Korea, Dem. Rep.	1,899,356	970,737	928,619	8.8	9.2	8.3
Northern Mariana Islands	4,549	2,277	2,272	6.3	6.5	6.1
Norway	283,390	145,251	138,139	6.4	6.6	6.1
Oman	269,238	137,130	132,108	10.6	9.5	12.1
Pakistan	17,848,035	9,201,642	8,646,393	12.6	12.7	12.5
Palau	1,491	766	725	7.9	7.6	8.3
Panama	291,676	149,534	142,142	10.3	10.5	10.2
Papua New Guinea	569,615	292,183	277,432	11.8	11.8	11.9
Paraguay	644,048	326,419	317,629	11.5	11.6	11.4
Peru	2,973,572	1,508,813	1,464,759	11	11.1	10.9
Philippines	9,229,490	4,681,951	4,547,539	11.4	11.6	11.2
Poland	2,927,165	1,499,170	1,427,995	7.6	8.0	7.2
Portugal	567,104	290,499	276,605	5.7	6.1	5.4
Puerto Rico	308,189	157,033	151,156	7.9	8.3	7.5
Qatar	69,807	35,565	34,242	9.3	7.2	13.4
Reunion	73,277	37,510	35,767	10.0	10.4	9.7
Romania	1,712,083	872,652	839,431	7.7	8.0	7.4
Russia	11,861,187	6,040,175	5,821,012	8.1	8.9	7.5
Rwanda	1,182,613	592,986	589,627	14.2	14.3	14.1
Saint Helena	456	229	227	6.3	6.3	6.4
Saint Kitts and Nevis	4,590	2,350	2,240	10.6	10.8	10.3
Saint Lucia	16,925	8,414	8,511	10.9	11.0	10.7
Saint Vincent and the Grenadines	12,419	6,332	6,087	10.2	10.4	10.1
Samoa	27,966	14,187	13,779	11.9	11.7	12
San Marino	1,265	625	640	5.0	5.1	5.0
Sao Tome and Principe	20,971	10,595	10,376	13.1	13.5	12.8

A1-6. Population, Age 10 to 14 Years, Total, Male, and Female, and Percentages, 2000 *(continued)*

	10-14 Age Group			Age Group 10-14 as % of population		
	Total	**Male**	**Female**	**Total**	**% male**	**% female**
Saudi Arabia	2,670,508	1,346,193	1,324,315	12	10.9	13.3
Senegal	1,371,301	679,074	692,227	13.2	13.4	13
Seychelles	7,736	3,874	3,862	9.7	10	9.4
Sierra Leone	667,778	325,933	341,845	12.1	12.2	12.1
Singapore	266,665	136,955	129,710	7.5	7.7	7.2
Slovakia	405,571	206,969	198,602	7.5	7.9	7.2
Slovenia	122,141	62,721	59,420	6.2	6.6	5.9
Solomon Islands	60,824	30,948	29,876	12.9	13	12.9
Somalia	941,122	469,187	471,935	12.7	12.6	12.7
South Africa	4,692,631	2,362,787	2,329,844	10.7	10.8	10.5
South Korea, Rep.	3,251,286	1,716,850	1,534,436	6.9	7.2	6.5
Spain	2,061,757	1,060,043	1,001,714	5.3	5.5	5.0
Sri Lanka	1,725,278	881,462	843,816	8.9	9.2	8.6
Sudan	4,551,470	2,317,788	2,233,682	12.8	12.9	12.7
Suriname	46,440	23,853	22,587	10.7	10.8	10.6
Swaziland	137,263	68,224	69,039	13.7	13.9	13.5
Sweden	567,851	291,458	276,393	6.4	6.6	6.1
Switzerland	418,367	213,480	204,887	5.7	5.9	5.6
Syria	2,339,747	1,199,115	1,140,632	13.2	13.2	13.1
Taiwan	1,601,049	829,252	771,797	7.2	7.3	7.1
Tajikistan	882,126	446,167	435,959	14.2	14.5	14.0
Tanzania	4,086,531	2,031,050	2,055,481	12.8	12.9	12.6
Thailand	4,644,311	2,361,794	2,282,517	7.6	7.8	7.4
Togo	700,156	351,106	349,050	13.3	13.5	13.1
Trinidad and Tobago	111,375	57,259	54,116	10.2	10.2	10.3
Tunisia	1,019,458	525,137	494,321	10.6	10.8	10.3
Turkey	6,658,500	3,386,241	3,272,259	10	10.1	9.9
Turkmenistan	565,330	286,070	279,260	12.7	13.1	12.4
Turks and Caicos Islands	1,416	714	702	8.1	7.9	8.3
Tuvalu	1,264	643	621	11.8	12.3	11.3
Uganda	3,265,384	1,638,664	1,626,720	13.9	14	13.9
Ukraine	3,654,424	1,863,355	1,791,069	7.4	8.1	6.7
United Arab Emirate	281,528	143,576	137,952	11.8	10	14.5
United Kingdom	3,897,814	2,003,629	1,894,185	6.6	6.9	6.3
United States	20,056,779	10,272,582	9,784,197	7.3	7.6	7.0
Uruguay	262,987	134,690	128,297	7.9	8.3	7.5
Uzbekistan	3,211,827	1,627,581	1,584,246	13.2	13.5	12.9
Vanuatu	23,585	11,992	11,593	12.2	12.2	12.3
Venezuela	2,476,868	1,277,630	1,199,238	10.5	10.7	10.3
Vietnam	8,862,726	4,564,470	4,298,256	11.3	11.9	10.8
Virgin Islands	11,497	5,897	5,600	9.5	10.4	8.7
Virgin Islands, British	1,658	851	807	8.5	8.4	8.5
West Bank	204,347	104,840	99,507	12.3	12.5	12.1
Yemen	2,392,854	1,213,427	1,179,427	13.7	13.6	13.7
Yugoslavia	811,102	419,978	391,124	7.2	7.5	7.0
Zambia	1,427,328	716,379	710,949	14.5	14.6	14.3
Zimbabwe	1,640,366	826,321	814,045	14.6	14.7	14.4

Source: U.S. Census International Database, 2000: Table 094. Midyear Population by Age and Sex; <http://www.census.gov/ipc/www/idbagg.html>. Underlying data from U.S. Bureau of the Census.

A1-7. Population, Age 5 to 9 Years, Total, Male, and Female, and Percentages, 2000

	5-9 Age Group			Age Group 5-9 as % of population		
	Total	**Male**	**Female**	**Total**	**% male**	**% female**
Afghanistan	3,724,624	1,898,887	1,825,737	14	13.8	14.1
Albania	371,388	192,199	179,189	10.9	11.8	10.1
Algeria	3,850,751	1,961,718	1,889,033	12.1	12.2	12
American Samoa	9,412	4,843	4,569	14.4	14.6	14.1
Andorra	2,921	1,510	1,411	4.3	4.2	4.4
Angola	1,718,167	873,211	844,956	15	15.1	14.8
Anguilla	1,021	521	500	8.6	8.7	8.5
Antigua and Barbuda	5,847	2,973	2,874	9.1	9.3	8.8
Argentina	3,359,022	1,711,883	1,647,139	9.0	9.3	8.7
Armenia	272,715	138,549	134,166	8.0	8.4	7.7
Aruba	5,135	2,634	2,501	7.4	7.9	7
Australia	1,338,207	685,218	652,989	7.1	7.3	6.9
Austria	473,096	242,748	230,348	5.8	6.1	5.5
Azerbaijan	871,630	442,262	429,368	11	11.4	10.5
Bahamas, the	26,791	13,482	13,309	9.3	9.6	9.1
Bahrain	66,001	33,343	32,658	10.3	9.2	11.7
Bangladesh	13,743,158	7,017,143	6,726,015	10.6	10.6	10.7
Barbados	20,615	10,410	10,205	8.0	8.3	7.6
Belarus	629,877	321,498	308,379	6.1	6.6	5.6
Belgium	603,608	308,910	294,698	5.9	6.2	5.7
Belize	33,454	17,054	16,400	13.8	13.9	13.8
Benin	1,024,572	513,430	511,142	15.7	16.1	15.4
Bermuda	4,269	2,173	2,096	6.8	7.1	6.5
Bhutan	265,525	137,912	127,613	13.3	13.4	13.2
Bolivia	1,045,917	528,302	517,615	12.9	13.2	12.5
Bosnia and Herzegovina	171,624	88,152	83,472	4.8	5.0	4.5
Botswana	204,499	103,378	101,121	13.8	14.4	13.3
Brazil	16,581,348	8,447,814	8,133,534	9.5	9.9	9.2
Brunei	35,543	18,184	17,359	10.7	10.5	11
Bulgaria	418,052	214,264	203,788	5.1	5.4	4.9
Burkina Faso	1,873,695	942,002	931,693	15.8	16.2	15.3
Burundi	923,010	462,065	460,945	15.6	15.9	15.3
Cambodia	1,782,285	904,555	877,730	15	15.6	14.3
Cameroon	2,399,101	1,205,050	1,194,051	15.1	15.2	15.0
Canada	2,085,764	1,068,755	1,017,009	6.7	6.9	6.4
Cape Verde	62,957	31,721	31,236	15.3	16	14.7
Central African Republic	504,554	253,970	250,584	14.4	14.6	14.1
Chad	1,123,445	562,283	561,162	14.5	14.7	14.3
Chile	1,440,241	736,128	704,113	9.5	9.8	9.2
China	102,032,621	54,751,545	47,281,076	8.1	8.4	7.8
Colombia	4,368,900	2,210,201	2,158,699	10.9	11.2	10.6
Comoros	81,841	40,949	40,892	14.1	14.2	14
Congo, Dem. Rep. (Zaire)	8,242,508	4,128,236	4,114,272	15.9	16.1	15.6
Congo, Rep.	388,397	195,056	193,341	14	14.3	13.7
Costa Rica	409,085	209,348	199,737	10.9	11.1	10.8
Côte d'Ivoire	2,473,363	1,240,952	1,232,411	15.3	15.1	15.4
Croatia	247,671	127,445	120,226	5.3	5.6	5.0
Cuba	782,930	401,980	380,950	7.0	7.2	6.8
Cyprus	61,324	31,315	30,009	8.1	8.3	7.9
Czech Republic	585,931	300,412	285,519	5.7	6	5.4
Denmark	349,887	179,472	170,415	6.5	6.8	6.3
Djibouti	63,540	31,735	31,805	14.0	13.5	14.5
Dominica	5,465	2,758	2,707	8.5	8.7	8.4
Dominican Republic	959,664	489,179	470,485	11.6	11.7	11.5
Ecuador	1,531,975	778,894	753,081	12	12.2	11.7
Egypt	7,998,705	4,095,528	3,903,177	11.7	11.8	11.5

A1-7. Population, Age 5 to 9 Years, Total, Male, and Female, and Percentages, 2000 *(continued)*

	5-9 Age Group			Age Group 5-9 as % of population		
	Total	**Male**	**Female**	**Total**	**% male**	**% female**
El Salvador	722,567	369,426	353,141	12.2	12.8	11.6
Equatorial Guinea	67,952	34,031	33,921	14.2	14.6	13.8
Eritrea	558,797	279,292	279,505	13.5	13.5	13.5
Estonia	76,378	38,960	37,418	5.5	6.0	5.0
Ethiopia	9,297,526	4,660,055	4,637,471	15.2	15.2	15.3
Faroe Islands	3,263	1,669	1,594	8.1	8.1	8.2
Fiji	88,995	45,328	43,667	10.8	11.0	10.7
Finland	327,363	166,849	160,514	6.3	6.6	6.1
France	3,652,018	1,870,816	1,781,202	6.2	6.5	5.9
French Guiana	18,059	9,236	8,823	10.4	10.1	10.8
French Polynesia	26,433	13,469	12,964	10.7	10.6	10.9
Gabon	137,618	68,562	69,056	11.1	11.0	11.1
Gambia, the	208,437	104,236	104,201	15.1	15.1	15
Gaza Strip	204,241	104,647	99,594	17.6	17.8	17.3
Georgia	338,074	172,373	165,701	6.7	7.2	6.3
Germany	4,170,002	2,136,706	2,033,296	5.1	5.3	4.9
Ghana	2,723,008	1,367,145	1,355,863	14.1	14.3	13.9
Gibraltar	2,266	1,197	1,069	7.7	7.6	7.9
Greece	552,434	287,037	265,397	5.1	5.4	4.9
Greenland	5,422	2,704	2,718	9	8.5	9.5
Grenada	13,899	7,058	6,841	14.2	13.8	14.6
Guadeloupe	35,855	18,328	17,527	8.4	8.8	8.1
Guam	19,165	10,074	9,091	12.4	12.5	12.4
Guatemala	1,775,872	906,192	869,680	14	14.2	13.8
Guernsey	3,922	1,990	1,932	5.9	6.3	5.6
Guinea	1,093,105	543,246	549,859	14.4	14.6	14.2
Guinea-Bissau	174,400	87,400	87,000	13.8	14.2	13.4
Guyana	68,912	35,072	33,840	9.8	9.9	9.7
Haiti	929,881	472,290	457,591	13.3	13.7	12.9
Honduras	852,793	433,938	418,855	13.9	14.1	13.7
Hong Kong SAR, China	397,145	207,935	189,210	5.7	6.1	5.3
Hungary	596,380	305,584	290,796	5.9	6.3	5.5
Iceland	22,286	11,377	10,909	8.1	8.3	8
Indonesia	21,876,449	11,089,995	10,786,454	10.0	10.1	9.8
Iran	7,407,274	3,789,234	3,618,040	11.2	11.3	11.1
Iraq	3,228,024	1,638,273	1,589,751	13.9	14	13.9
Ireland	246,906	127,151	119,755	6.8	7	6.5
Israel	537,699	275,260	262,439	9.2	9.5	8.9
Italy	2,731,872	1,406,747	1,325,125	4.8	5.1	4.5
Jamaica	277,116	141,615	135,501	10.4	10.7	10.1
Japan	5,954,608	3,047,835	2,906,773	4.7	4.9	4.5
Jersey	5,757	2,991	2,766	6.4	6.8	6
Jordan	678,099	347,686	330,413	14.4	14.4	14.4
Kazakhstan	1,543,277	784,123	759,154	9.2	9.7	8.7
Kenya	4,043,422	2,044,719	1,998,703	13.8	13.9	13.7
Kuwait	213,908	117,922	95,986	10.3	9.3	12
Kyrgyzstan	540,280	273,142	267,138	11.8	12.2	11.4
Laos	833,785	422,433	411,352	15.0	15.4	14.7
Latvia	127,529	65,256	62,273	5.5	6.1	4.9
Lebanon	345,932	176,190	169,742	9.6	10	9.1
Lesotho	284,718	142,517	142,201	13.1	13.5	12.8
Liberia	462,799	232,624	230,175	15	14.9	15.1
Libya	596,547	304,770	291,777	11.7	11.6	11.8
Liechtenstein	2,008	1,009	999	6.2	6.3	6.1
Lithuania	230,495	117,793	112,702	6.5	7	5.9
Luxembourg	27,607	14,161	13,446	6.4	6.6	6.2

A1-7. Population, Age 5 to 9 Years, Total, Male, and Female, and Percentages, 2000 *(continued)*

	5-9 Age Group			Age Group 5-9 as % of population		
	Total	Male	Female	Total	% male	% female
Macau	34,539	17,960	16,579	7.8	8.4	7.1
Macedonia, FYRO	155,511	80,138	75,373	7.6	7.9	7.4
Madagascar	2,235,695	1,130,041	1,105,654	14.6	14.8	14.4
Malawi	1,511,250	757,616	753,634	14.9	15	14.7
Malaysia	2,555,417	1,310,950	1,244,467	11.7	12	11.4
Maldives	48,963	25,126	23,837	15.8	15.8	15.7
Mali	1,646,551	825,668	820,883	15.3	15.7	14.9
Malta	26,500	13,622	12,878	6.9	7.2	6.7
Man, Isle of	4,633	2,380	2,253	6.1	6.4	5.7
Marshall Islands	11,009	5,616	5,393	16.2	16.2	16.2
Martinique	31,799	16,021	15,778	7.6	7.9	7.4
Mauritania	405,914	202,648	203,266	15.3	15.5	15
Mauritius	108,163	54,469	53,694	9	9.2	8.9
Mayotte	24,367	12,184	12,183	15.5	14.8	16.3
Mexico	11,888,651	6,062,131	5,826,520	11.7	12	11.3
Moldova	338,277	172,170	166,107	7.6	8.1	7.1
Monaco	1,766	900	866	5.5	6	5.1
Mongolia	308,171	157,322	150,849	11.6	11.8	11.4
Morocco	3,529,087	1,797,819	1,731,268	11.7	11.9	11.4
Mozambique	2,903,052	1,429,834	1,473,218	14.8	14.9	14.7
Myanmar (Burma)	5,876,887	2,994,158	2,882,729	12	12.2	11.8
Namibia	239,656	121,131	118,525	14.3	14.6	14.1
Nepal	3,371,072	1,740,106	1,630,966	13.5	13.6	13.4
Netherlands	997,657	510,357	487,300	6.3	6.5	6.1
Netherlands Antilles	18,326	9,389	8,937	8.7	9.3	8.2
New Caledonia	19,676	10,031	9,645	9.8	9.9	9.7
New Zealand	294,115	151,172	142,943	8.0	8.2	7.7
Nicaragua	690,148	348,367	341,781	14.2	14.5	13.9
Niger	1,590,184	813,330	776,854	15.5	15.8	15.2
Nigeria	17,329,456	8,685,553	8,643,903	14.8	14.7	14.9
North Korea, Dem. Rep.	1,915,693	985,575	930,118	8.8	9.4	8.3
Northern Mariana Islands	6,150	3,129	3,021	8.5	9	8.1
Norway	303,524	156,080	147,444	6.8	7.1	6.6
Oman	345,006	175,645	169,361	13.6	12.2	15.5
Pakistan	19,414,914	9,994,680	9,420,234	13.8	13.8	13.7
Palau	1,769	912	857	9.4	9.1	9.8
Panama	294,226	149,454	144,772	10.4	10.5	10.4
Papua New Guinea	623,977	320,371	303,606	13	12.9	13
Paraguay	728,665	370,682	357,983	13.1	13.2	12.9
Peru	3,230,688	1,640,529	1,590,159	11.9	12	11.8
Philippines	10,162,423	5,168,039	4,994,384	12.6	12.8	12.3
Poland	2,478,253	1,269,800	1,208,453	6.4	6.8	6.1
Portugal	568,249	291,915	276,334	5.7	6.1	5.4
Puerto Rico	321,944	164,943	157,001	8.2	8.7	7.8
Qatar	65,743	33,544	32,199	8.8	6.8	12.6
Reunion	80,706	41,317	39,389	11.1	11.4	10.7
Romania	1,231,755	630,203	601,552	5.5	5.8	5.3
Russia	8,089,719	4,131,653	3,958,066	5.5	6.1	5.1
Rwanda	1,149,896	576,821	573,075	13.8	13.9	13.7
Saint Helena	455	231	224	6.3	6.3	6.3
Saint Kitts and Nevis	4,655	2,383	2,272	10.7	11	10.5
Saint Lucia	16,984	8,721	8,263	10.9	11.4	10.4
Saint Vincent and the Grena	11,621	5,918	5,703	9.6	9.7	9.4
Samoa	30,911	15,717	15,194	13.1	13	13.3
San Marino	1,469	734	735	5.8	5.9	5.7
Sao Tome and Principe	25,030	12,681	12,349	15.7	16.1	15.2

A1-7. Population, Age 5 to 9 Years, Total, Male, and Female, and Percentages, 2000 *(continued)*

	5-9 Age Group			Age Group 5-9 as % of population		
	Total	**Male**	**Female**	**Total**	**% male**	**% female**
Saudi Arabia	3,186,601	1,628,470	1,558,131	14.3	13.2	15.7
Senegal	1,643,262	818,213	825,049	15.8	16.2	15.5
Seychelles	7,812	3,950	3,862	9.8	10.2	9.4
Sierra Leone	827,355	405,927	421,428	15.0	15.2	14.9
Singapore	248,300	128,091	120,209	7.0	7.2	6.7
Slovakia	362,847	185,581	177,266	6.7	7.1	6.4
Slovenia	100,364	51,454	48,910	5.1	5.4	4.8
Solomon Islands	69,832	35,577	34,255	14.9	14.9	14.8
Somalia	1,029,851	515,837	514,014	13.9	13.9	13.8
South Africa	5,066,938	2,559,923	2,507,015	11.5	11.7	11.3
South Korea, Rep.	3,453,415	1,841,250	1,612,165	7.3	7.7	6.9
Spain	1,857,438	958,208	899,230	4.7	5	4.5
Sri Lanka	1,717,049	877,589	839,460	8.9	9.2	8.6
Sudan	5,318,214	2,715,266	2,602,948	15	15.1	14.8
Suriname	48,186	24,677	23,509	11.1	11.2	11
Swaziland	156,050	77,730	78,320	15.5	15.8	15.3
Sweden	593,310	304,346	288,964	6.6	6.9	6.4
Switzerland	432,894	221,377	211,517	5.9	6.1	5.7
Syria	2,709,783	1,387,875	1,321,908	15.3	15.3	15.2
Taiwan	1,597,526	828,457	769,069	7.2	7.3	7.1
Tajikistan	830,991	419,778	411,213	13.4	13.6	13.2
Tanzania	4,645,813	2,312,446	2,333,367	14.5	14.7	14.4
Thailand	4,844,663	2,467,069	2,377,594	7.9	8.2	7.7
Togo	833,702	418,104	415,598	15.8	16.1	15.6
Trinidad and Tobago	88,506	45,173	43,333	8.1	8.1	8.2
Tunisia	969,882	501,773	468,109	10.1	10.3	9.8
Turkey	6,609,122	3,365,208	3,243,914	9.9	10	9.9
Turkmenistan	565,329	289,650	275,679	12.7	13.2	12.3
Turks and Caicos Islands	2,087	1,059	1,028	11.9	11.7	12.2
Tuvalu	1,240	631	609	11.6	12.1	11.1
Uganda	3,990,665	1,997,930	1,992,735	17.0	17	17
Ukraine	2,870,402	1,466,607	1,403,795	5.8	6.4	5.3
United Arab Emirate	222,049	113,583	108,466	9.3	7.9	11.4
United Kingdom	3,846,997	1,972,203	1,874,794	6.5	6.8	6.2
United States	19,919,840	10,197,744	9,722,096	7.2	7.6	6.9
Uruguay	267,524	137,118	130,406	8..0	8.4	7.6
Uzbekistan	3,020,269	1,535,879	1,484,390	12.4	12.7	12
Vanuatu	24,445	12,428	12,017	12.7	12.6	12.8
Venezuela	2,710,818	1,399,022	1,311,796	11.5	11.8	11.2
Vietnam	8,814,040	4,542,157	4,271,883	11.2	11.8	10.7
Virgin Islands	12,222	6,276	5,946	10.1	11	9.2
Virgin Islands, British	1,143	564	579	5.8	5.6	6.1
West Bank	261,711	134,134	127,577	15.7	15.9	15.5
Yemen	2,704,509	1,376,718	1,327,791	15.4	15.4	15.5
Yugoslavia	731,595	379,079	352,516	6.8	7.1	6.6
Zambia	1,565,772	786,494	779,278	15.9	16	15.7
Zimbabwe	1,576,909	795,731	781,178	14.0	14.2	13.8

Source: U.S. Census International Database, 2000. Table 094. Midyear Population by Age and Sex; <http://www.census.gov/ipc/www/idbagg.html>. Underlying data from U.S. Bureau of the Census.

A1-8. Population, Age 0 to 4 Years, Total, Male, and Female, and Percentages, 2000

	0-4 Age Group			Age Group 0-4 as % of population		
	Total	**Male**	**Female**	**Total**	**% male**	**% female**
Afghanistan	4,406,045	2,245,053	2,160,992	16.5	16.4	16.7
Albania	340,420	176,059	164,361	10.0	10.8	9.3
Algeria	3,979,212	2,027,369	1,951,843	12.5	12.6	12.4
American Samoa	8,392	4,307	4,085	12.8	13	12.6
Andorra	3,452	1,775	1,677	5.1	5.0	5.2
Angola	1,996,843	1,008,820	988,023	17.4	17.5	17.3
Anguilla	990	500	490	8.3	8.3	8.4
Antigua and Barbuda	5,282	2,692	2,590	8.2	8.4	8.0
Argentina	3,530,435	1,800,815	1,729,620	9.5	9.8	9.2
Armenia	217,219	110,472	106,747	6.4	6.7	6.1
Aruba	4,712	2,408	2,304	6.8	7.2	6.4
Australia	1,267,755	649,936	617,819	6.7	6.9	6.5
Austria	407,387	208,948	198,439	5.0	5.2	4.8
Azerbaijan	800,570	408,022	392,548	10.1	10.5	9.6
Bahamas, the	28,806	14,512	14,294	10	10.3	9.7
Bahrain	67,786	34,276	33,510	10.6	9.5	12
Bangladesh	14,552,853	7,488,935	7,063,918	11.3	11.3	11.2
Barbados	18,890	9,541	9,349	7.3	7.6	7.0
Belarus	507,353	259,262	248,091	4.9	5.3	4.5
Belgium	522,813	267,549	255,264	5.1	5.4	4.9
Belize	34,317	17,506	16,811	14.2	14.3	14.1
Benin	1,222,902	614,008	608,894	18.8	19.2	18.3
Bermuda	3,816	1,954	1,862	6.1	6.3	5.8
Bhutan	304,950	157,360	147,590	15.3	15.3	15.3
Bolivia	1,117,469	567,552	549,917	13.7	14.1	13.3
Bosnia and Herzegovina	164,639	84,577	80,062	4.6	4.8	4.4
Botswana	211,669	107,141	104,528	14.3	14.9	13.8
Brazil	17,050,100	8,696,757	8,353,343	9.8	10.2	9.5
Brunei	38,154	19,551	18,603	11.5	11.3	11.8
Bulgaria	339,097	173,919	165,178	4.2	4.4	3.9
Burkina Faso	2,224,466	1,120,527	1,103,939	18.7	19.3	18.1
Burundi	1,030,071	516,771	513,300	17.4	17.8	17
Cambodia	2,043,290	1,037,880	1,005,410	17.1	17.9	16.4
Cameroon	2,827,193	1,423,941	1,403,252	17.8	18	17.6
Canada	1,893,416	969,427	923,989	6.0	6.3	5.8
Cape Verde	64,121	32,353	31,768	15.6	16.3	14.9
Central African Republic	565,828	285,048	280,780	16.1	16.4	15.8
Chad	1,360,267	683,542	676,725	17.5	17.9	17.2
Chile	1,343,327	687,473	655,854	8.9	9.1	8.6
China	93,615,389	50,573,705	43,041,684	7.5	7.8	7.1
Colombia	4,667,888	2,362,303	2,305,585	11.7	12	11.3
Comoros	99,260	49,791	49,469	17.1	17.3	16.9
Congo, Dem. Rep. (Zaire)	9,982,597	5,008,280	4,974,317	19.2	19.5	18.9
Congo, Rep.	441,969	222,285	219,684	15.9	16.3	15.6
Costa Rica	407,308	208,495	198,813	10.9	11	10.7
Côte d'Ivoire	2,839,134	1,426,658	1,412,476	17.5	17.4	17.7
Croatia	246,420	126,984	119,436	5.3	5.6	5.0
Cuba	720,100	370,069	350,031	6.5	6.6	6.3
Cyprus	52,468	26,816	25,652	6.9	7.1	6.7
Czech Republic	473,678	242,813	230,865	4.6	4.8	4.4
Denmark	333,562	171,097	162,465	6.2	6.4	6.0
Djibouti	77,419	38,838	38,581	17	16.6	17.5
Dominica	5,384	2,741	2,643	8.4	8.6	8.2
Dominican Republic	1,001,000	510,799	490,201	12.1	12.2	12
Ecuador	1,386,405	706,555	679,850	10.8	11.1	10.6
Egypt	8,299,474	4,246,081	4,053,393	12.1	12.3	11.9

A1-8. Population, Age 0 to 4 Years, Total, Male, and Female, and Percentages, 2000 *(continued)*

	0-4 Age Group			Age Group 0-4 as % of population		
	Total	Male	Female	Total	% male	% female
El Salvador	733,072	374,806	358,266	12.4	13	11.8
Equatorial Guinea	77,721	39,045	38,676	16.3	16.8	15.8
Eritrea	730,234	367,231	363,003	17.6	17.8	17.5
Estonia	62,862	32,111	30,751	4.5	5.0	4.1
Ethiopia	10,937,635	5,490,863	5,446,772	17.9	18	17.9
Faroe Islands	2,577	1,329	1,248	6.4	6.4	6.4
Fiji	89,388	45,649	43,739	10.9	11	10.7
Finland	294,266	149,981	144,285	5.7	5.9	5.5
France	3,449,728	1,767,906	1,681,822	5.8	6.1	5.6
French Guiana	19,055	9,752	9,303	11	10.6	11.4
French Polynesia	26,499	13,527	12,972	10.8	10.7	10.9
Gabon	151,760	75,934	75,826	12.2	12.2	12.2
Gambia, the	249,348	125,177	124,171	18	18.2	17.9
Gaza Strip	248,373	127,224	121,149	21.4	21.6	21.1
Georgia	282,024	143,561	138,463	5.6	6.0	5.2
Germany	3,659,238	1,877,244	1,781,994	4.5	4.7	4.3
Ghana	2,760,724	1,389,790	1,370,934	14.3	14.6	14.1
Gibraltar	1,913	985	928	6.5	6.2	6.9
Greece	523,793	271,639	252,154	4.9	5.1	4.6
Greenland	4,650	2,319	2,331	7.7	7.3	8.2
Grenada	13,350	6,740	6,610	13.6	13.2	14.1
Guadeloupe	34,553	17,670	16,883	8.1	8.4	7.8
Guam	20,298	10,633	9,665	13.2	13.2	13.2
Guatemala	2,018,203	1,029,984	988,219	15.9	16.2	15.7
Guernsey	4,451	2,264	2,187	6.7	7.1	6.4
Guinea	1,259,785	629,607	630,178	16.6	16.9	16.2
Guinea-Bissau	200,433	100,786	99,647	15.9	16.4	15.3
Guyana	62,092	31,630	30,462	8.8	8.9	8.7
Haiti	973,220	494,399	478,821	13.9	14.4	13.5
Honduras	881,822	449,898	431,924	14.4	14.6	14.1
Hong Kong SAR, China	432,471	224,674	207,797	6.2	6.6	5.8
Hungary	545,394	279,530	265,864	5.4	5.8	5.0
Iceland	20,336	10,415	9,921	7.4	7.6	7.2
Indonesia	22,849,013	11,615,154	11,233,859	10.4	10.6	10.2
Iran	6,559,313	3,353,740	3,205,573	10	10	9.9
Iraq	3,853,766	1,959,862	1,893,904	16.6	16.7	16.5
Ireland	241,594	124,564	117,030	6.6	6.9	6.4
Israel	560,481	286,912	273,569	9.6	9.9	9.3
Italy	2,558,740	1,318,386	1,240,354	4.5	4.8	4.3
Jamaica	270,459	138,183	132,276	10.1	10.4	9.9
Japan	6,309,123	3,229,961	3,079,162	5.0	5.2	4.8
Jersey	5,551	2,920	2,631	6.2	6.6	5.7
Jordan	745,758	382,610	363,148	15.9	15.9	15.8
Kazakhstan	1,369,584	697,532	672,052	8.1	8.6	7.7
Kenya	4,136,536	2,093,410	2,043,126	14.1	14.3	14
Kuwait	207,054	106,833	100,221	10	8.4	12.5
Kyrgyzstan	459,926	232,396	227,530	10	10.4	9.7
Laos	944,870	479,764	465,106	17	17.4	16.6
Latvia	93,778	47,947	45,831	4.0	4.5	3.6
Lebanon	379,317	193,433	185,884	10.5	11	10
Lesotho	300,114	150,624	149,490	13.9	14.2	13.5
Liberia	536,906	270,157	266,749	17.4	17.3	17.5
Libya	632,651	323,594	309,057	12.4	12.3	12.4
Liechtenstein	2,041	1,041	1,000	6.3	6.5	6.1
Lithuania	187,395	95,787	91,608	5.2	5.7	4.8
Luxembourg	24,598	12,495	12,103	5.7	5.8	5.5

A1-8. Population, Age 0 to 4 Years, Total, Male, and Female, and Percentages, 2000 *(continued)*

	0-4 Age Group			Age Group 0-4 as % of population		
	Total	**Male**	**Female**	**Total**	**% male**	**% female**
Macau	27,847	14,330	13,517	6.3	6.7	5.8
Macedonia, FYRO	153,434	79,525	73,909	7.5	7.8	7.3
Madagascar	2,659,581	1,345,117	1,314,464	17.4	17.6	17.2
Malawi	1,624,504	816,291	808,213	16	16.2	15.8
Malaysia	2,694,863	1,382,340	1,312,523	12.4	12.6	12.1
Maldives	55,121	28,252	26,869	17.8	17.8	17.7
Mali	2,089,685	1,051,340	1,038,345	19.4	20	18.9
Malta	22,738	11,694	11,044	5.9	6.1	5.7
Man, Isle of	4,720	2,419	2,301	6.2	6.5	5.9
Marshall Islands	13,338	6,818	6,520	19.6	19.6	19.5
Martinique	33,248	16,809	16,439	8.0	8.3	7.8
Mauritania	494,455	248,764	245,691	18.6	19.1	18.1
Mauritius	106,821	53,228	53,593	8.9	9.0	8.8
Mayotte	30,364	15,242	15,122	19.4	18.6	20.2
Mexico	12,165,347	6,209,269	5,956,078	11.9	12.3	11.5
Moldova	305,211	155,522	149,689	6.8	7.3	6.4
Monaco	1,720	880	840	5.3	5.8	4.9
Mongolia	281,736	143,743	137,993	10.6	10.8	10.4
Morocco	3,608,823	1,841,696	1,767,127	11.9	12.2	11.7
Mozambique	3,467,659	1,742,899	1,724,760	17.7	18.1	17.2
Myanmar (Burma)	6,214,256	3,173,292	3,040,964	12.7	12.9	12.5
Namibia	262,319	132,646	129,673	15.7	15.9	15.4
Nepal	3,821,103	1,962,583	1,858,520	15.3	15.4	15.3
Netherlands	919,244	470,463	448,781	5.8	6.0	5.6
Netherlands Antilles	17,973	9,202	8,771	8.6	9.2	8.0
New Caledonia	20,126	10,279	9,847	10	10.2	9.9
New Zealand	270,910	138,852	132,058	7.3	7.6	7.1
Nicaragua	783,839	396,968	386,871	16.2	16.6	15.8
Niger	2,057,184	1,046,244	1,010,940	20	20.3	19.7
Nigeria	20,720,285	10,440,628	10,279,657	17.7	17.6	17.7
North Korea, Dem. Rep.	1,733,407	886,938	846,469	8.0	8.4	7.6
Northern Mariana Islands	6,537	3,352	3,185	9.1	9.6	8.5
Norway	288,609	148,463	140,146	6.5	6.7	6.2
Oman	427,348	218,116	209,232	16.9	15.2	19.1
Pakistan	20,519,183	10,524,387	9,994,796	14.5	14.6	14.5
Palau	1,874	963	911	10	9.6	10.4
Panama	291,392	148,010	143,382	10.3	10.4	10.3
Papua New Guinea	690,693	354,412	336,281	14.4	14.3	14.4
Paraguay	809,841	412,955	396,886	14.5	14.7	14.3
Peru	3,311,964	1,684,456	1,627,508	12.2	12.3	12.1
Philippines	10,582,607	5,395,228	5,187,379	13.1	13.4	12.8
Poland	1,997,790	1,024,089	973,701	5.2	5.5	4.9
Portugal	525,306	270,294	255,012	5.3	5.7	5.0
Puerto Rico	308,851	158,801	150,050	7.9	8.4	7.4
Qatar	62,480	31,880	30,600	8.3	6.5	12
Reunion	79,907	40,906	39,001	10.9	11.3	10.6
Romania	1,096,127	560,830	535,297	4.9	5.2	4.7
Russia	6,922,524	3,538,532	3,383,992	4.7	5.2	4.3
Rwanda	1,311,858	659,962	651,896	15.7	15.9	15.5
Saint Helena	482	244	238	6.7	6.7	6.7
Saint Kitts and Nevis	4,712	2,417	2,295	10.8	11.1	10.6
Saint Lucia	16,781	8,663	8,118	10.8	11.4	10.2
Saint Vincent and the Grenadines	10,853	5,512	5,341	9.0	9.1	8.8
Samoa	32,049	16,335	15,714	13.6	13.5	13.7
San Marino	1,354	675	679	5.4	5.5	5.3
Sao Tome and Principe	30,188	15,281	14,907	18.9	19.4	18.4

A1-8. Population, Age 0 to 4 Years, Total, Male, and Female, and Percentages, 2000 *(continued)*

	0-4 Age Group			Age Group 0-4 as % of population		
	Total	**Male**	**Female**	**Total**	**% male**	**% female**
Saudi Arabia	3,695,042	1,888,630	1,806,412	16.6	15.4	18.2
Senegal	1,951,030	978,577	972,453	18.8	19.3	18.3
Seychelles	7,538	3,816	3,722	9.5	9.9	9.1
Sierra Leone	1,007,755	500,047	507,708	18.3	18.7	17.9
Singapore	239,403	124,476	114,927	6.7	7.0	6.4
Slovakia	277,698	142,004	135,694	5.1	5.4	4.9
Slovenia	88,840	45,624	43,216	4.5	4.8	4.3
Solomon Islands	77,937	39,767	38,170	16.6	16.7	16.5
Somalia	1,348,997	677,872	671,125	18.1	18.2	18.1
South Africa	5,250,370	2,652,512	2,597,858	11.9	12.2	11.7
South Korea, Rep.	3,678,341	1,956,068	1,722,273	7.8	8.2	7.3
Spain	1,867,101	963,815	903,286	4.8	5.0	4.5
Sri Lanka	1,702,983	870,498	832,485	8.8	9.1	8.5
Sudan	6,044,309	3,091,171	2,953,138	17	17.2	16.8
Suriname	46,390	23,701	22,689	10.7	10.8	10.6
Swaziland	170,980	85,715	85,265	17	17.5	16.6
Sweden	516,066	264,681	251,385	5.8	6.0	5.6
Switzerland	393,829	201,864	191,965	5.4	5.6	5.2
Syria	3,002,840	1,536,934	1,465,906	16.9	16.9	16.9
Taiwan	1,611,594	836,079	775,515	7.2	7.3	7.1
Tajikistan	739,248	372,412	366,836	11.9	12.1	11.8
Tanzania	5,419,995	2,711,633	2,708,362	17	17.3	16.7
Thailand	4,862,204	2,480,511	2,381,693	7.9	8.2	7.7
Togo	991,847	498,679	493,168	18.8	19.2	18.5
Trinidad and Tobago	78,157	39,664	38,493	7.2	7.1	7.3
Tunisia	909,342	470,664	438,678	9.4	9.7	9.2
Turkey	6,618,143	3,375,920	3,242,223	9.9	10	9.8
Turkmenistan	524,055	268,902	255,153	11.8	12.3	11.4
Turks and Caicos Islands	2,183	1,113	1,070	12.5	12.3	12.7
Tuvalu	1,151	588	563	10.7	11.2	10.2
Uganda	4,762,022	2,389,902	2,372,120	20.3	20.4	20.2
Ukraine	2,357,957	1,205,562	1,152,395	4.8	5.3	4.3
United Arab Emirate	211,349	108,218	103,131	8.9	7.5	10.9
United Kingdom	3,555,565	1,824,016	1,731,549	10.1	6.3	5.7
United States	18,986,520	9,712,026	9,274,494	6.9	7.2	6.6
Uruguay	272,901	139,934	132,967	8.2	8.6	7.8
Uzbekistan	2,628,873	1,340,249	1,288,624	10.8	11.1	10.5
Vanuatu	25,051	12,756	12,295	13	12.9	13.1
Venezuela	2,550,800	1,316,396	1,234,404	10.8	11.1	10.6
Vietnam	7,916,193	4,074,297	3,841,896	10.1	10.6	9.6
Virgin Islands	10,227	5,255	4,972	8.4	9.2	7.7
Virgin Islands, British	1,192	605	587	6.1	6.0	6.2
West Bank	275,964	141,131	134,833	16.6	16.8	16.4
Yemen	3,220,242	1,639,608	1,580,634	18.4	18.4	18.4
Yugoslavia	691,632	358,942	332,690	6.4	6.7	6.1
Zambia	1,823,764	918,916	904,848	18.5	18.7	18.2
Zimbabwe	1,579,913	799,064	780,849	14.0	14.2	13.8

Source: U.S. Census International Database, 2000: Table 094. Midyear Population by Age and Sex; <http://www.census.gov/ipc/www/idbagg.html>. Underlying data from U.S. Bureau of the Census.

A2. SEX RATIO AT BIRTH

A2-1. Sex Ratio at Birth, Males per Females, 2000

	Sex ratio at birth
Afghanistan	1.050
Albania	1.077
Algeria	1.043
American Samoa	1.060
Andorra	1.060
Angola	1.050
Anguilla	1.032
Antigua and Barbuda	1.051
Argentina	1.046
Armenia	1.050
Australia	1.055
Austria	1.054
Azerbaijan	1.050
Bahamas, the	1.020
Bahrain	1.029
Bangladesh	1.060
Barbados	1.025
Belarus	1.050
Belgium	1.050
Belize	1.050
Benin	1.030
Bermuda	1.051
Bhutan	1.050
Bolivia	1.050
Bosnia and Herzegovina	1.066
Botswana	1.030
Brazil	1.050
Brunei	1.055
Bulgaria	1.057
Burkina Faso	1.030
Burma	1.060
Burundi	1.030
Cambodia	1.050
Cameroon	1.030
Canada	1.050
Cape Verde	1.030
Central African Republic	1.030
Chad	1.040
Chile	1.050
China	1.150
Colombia	1.034
Comoros	1.030
Congo, Dem. Rep. (Zaire)	1.030
Congo, Rep.	1.030
Costa Rica	1.050
Côte d'Ivoire	1.030
Croatia	1.065
Cuba	1.060
Cyprus	1.050
Czech Republic	1.054
Denmark	1.055
Djibouti	1.030
Dominica	1.051
Dominican Republic	1.050
Ecuador	1.050
Egypt	1.050

A2-1. Sex Ratio at Birth, Males per Females, 2000 *(continued)*

	Sex ratio at birth
El Salvador	1.050
Equatorial Guinea	1.030
Eritrea	1.030
Estonia	1.050
Ethiopia	1.030
Fiji	1.050
Finland	1.040
France	1.053
French Guiana	1.050
Gabon	1.030
Gambia, The	1.030
Gaza Strip	1.050
Georgia	1.050
Germany	1.056
Ghana	1.030
Greece	1.073
Grenada	1.017
Guadeloupe	1.049
Guatemala	1.050
Guinea	1.030
Guinea-Bissau	1.030
Guyana	1.050
Haiti	1.050
Honduras	1.050
Hong Kong, China	1.070
Hungary	1.054
Iceland	1.057
India	1.050
Indonesia	1.050
Iran	1.050
Iraq	1.050
Ireland	1.065
Israel	1.050
Italy	1.064
Jamaica	1.050
Japan	1.050
Jordan	1.060
Kazakhstan	1.050
Kenya	1.030
Kuwait	1.049
Kyrgyzstan	1.050
Laos	1.050
Latvia	1.050
Lebanon	1.050
Lesotho	1.030
Liberia	1.030
Libya	1.050
Liechtenstein	1.042
Lithuania	1.050
Luxembourg	1.033
Macedonia, FYRO	1.077
Madagascar	1.030
Malawi	1.030
Malaysia	1.064
Maldives	1.050
Mali	1.030
Malta	1.063
Marshall Islands	1.050

A2-1. Sex Ratio at Birth, Males per Females, 2000 *(continued)*

	Sex ratio at birth
Martinique	1.024
Mauritania	1.030
Mauritius	0.998
Mexico	1.050
Moldova	1.050
Monaco	1.048
Mongolia	1.050
Morocco	1.050
Mozambique	1.030
Namibia	1.030
Nepal	1.050
Netherlands, the	1.050
New Zealand	1.054
Nicaragua	1.040
Niger	1.030
Nigeria	1.030
North Korea	1.050
Norway	1.061
Oman	1.050
Pakistan	1.050
Palau	1.060
Panama	1.037
Papua New Guinea	1.050
Paraguay	1.050
Peru	1.046
Philippines	1.050
Poland	1.055
Portugal	1.062
Puerto Rico	1.055
Qatar	1.051
Reunion	1.050
Romania	1.053
Russia	1.050
Rwanda	1.030
Saint Helena	1.064
Saint Kitts and Nevis	1.062
Saint Lucia	1.071
Saint Vincent and the Grenadines	1.030
Samoa	1.050
San Marino	1.000
Sao Tome and Principe	1.030
Saudi Arabia	1.050
Senegal	1.030
Seychelles	1.031
Sierra Leone	1.030
Singapore	1.084
Slovakia	1.049
Slovenia	1.057
Solomon Islands	1.050
Somalia	1.030
South Africa	1.030
South Korea, Rep.	1.128
Spain	1.069
Sri Lanka	1.050
Sudan	1.050
Suriname	1.050
Swaziland	1.030

A2-1. Sex Ratio at Birth, Males per Females, 2000 *(continued)*

	Sex ratio at birth
Sweden	1.054
Switzerland	1.053
Syria	1.050
Taiwan	1.080
Tajikistan	1.050
Tanzania	1.030
Thailand	1.050
Togo	1.030
Trinidad and Tobago	1.027
Tunisia	1.079
Turkey	1.050
Turkmenistan	1.050
Turks and Caicos Islands	1.050
Tuvalu	1.053
Uganda	1.030
Ukraine	1.050
United Arab Emirates	1.050
United Kingdom	1.054
United States	1.048
Uruguay	1.056
Uzbekistan	1.050
Vanuatu	1.050
Venezuela	1.075
Vietnam	1.060
West Bank	1.050
Yemen	1.050
Zambia	1.030
Zimbabwe	1.030

Source: U.S. Census International Database, 2000: Table 094. Midyear population by Age and Sex; <http://www.census.gov/ipc/www/idbagg.html>. Underlying data from U.S. Bureau of the Census.

A3. POPULATION GROWTH RATES

A3-1. Average Population Growth Rate (%), by Region, 1995–2000

	Sub Region	% Growth Rate
Africa		**2.4**
	Eastern Africa	2.6
	Middle Africa	2.7
	Northern Africa	2.0
	Southern Africa	1.6
	Western Africa	2.5
Asia		**1.4**
	Eastern Asia	0.9
	South Central Asia	1.8
	South Eastern Asia	N/A
	Western Asia	2.2
Europe		**0.0**
	Eastern Europe	-0.2
	Northern Europe	0.2
	Southern Europe	0.1
	Western Europe	0.3
Latin America and Caribbean		**1.6**
	Caribbean	1.1
	Central America	1.9
	South America	1.5
Northern America		**0.9**
Oceania		**1.3**
	Australia and New Zealand	1.0
	Melanesia	2.2
	Micronesia	N/A
	Polynesia	N/A
Countries with Economies in Transition of the Former USSR		**N/A**

N/A   Not Available

Source: The State of World Population, 1999; <http://www.unfpa.org/swp/1999/Swp99_action.cfm>. Underlying data from United Nations (UN).

A3-2. Average Annual Children's Population Growth Rates, Ages 0-14, 1980–1997

	Average Annual Growth Rate (%)
Albania	0.38
Algeria	1.46
Angola	3.35
Argentina	0.98
Armenia	0.41
Australia	0.30
Austria	-0.57
Azerbaijan	0.58
Bangladesh	1.42
Belarus	-0.36
Belgium	-0.61
Benin	3.26
Bolivia	1.84
Bosnia and Herzegovina	-4.62
Botswana	2.32
Brazil	0.47
Bulgaria	-1.88
Burkina Faso	2.35
Burundi	2.77
Cambodia	3.17
Cameroon	2.77
Canada	0.37
Central African Republic	2.45
Chad	3.85
Chile	0.74
China	-0.57
Colombia	0.91
Congo, Dem. Rep. (Zaire)	3.39
Congo, Rep.	2.97
Costa Rica	1.64
Côte d'Ivoire	2.89
Croatia	-0.66
Cuba	-1.46
Czech Republic	-1.59
Denmark	-0.74
Dominican Republic	0.87
Ecuador	1.24
Egypt	1.82
El Salvador	0.30
Eritrea	N/A
Estonia	-0.83
Ethiopia	2.89
Finland	-0.04
France	-0.42
Gabon	3.79
Gambia, the	3.47
Georgia	-0.40
Germany	-0.64
Ghana	2.92
Greece	-1.53
Guatemala	2.30
Guinea	2.56
Guinea-Bissau	2.61
Haiti	1.97
Honduras	2.47
Hong Kong SAR, China	-0.35
Hungary	-1.58
India	1.38

A3-2. Average Annual Children's Population Growth Rates, Ages 0-14, 1980–1997 *(continued)*

	Average Annual Growth Rate (%)
Indonesia	0.35
Iran	1.64
Iraq	2.42
Ireland	-1.28
Israel	1.54
Italy	-2.32
Jamaica	-0.24
Japan	-2.03
Jordan	3.05
Kazakhstan	N/A
Kenya	2.55
Kuwait	0.78
Kyrgyzstan	1.21
Laos	2.64
Latvia	-0.57
Lebanon	0.77
Lesotho	2.14
Libya	2.26
Lithuania	-0.31
Macedonia, FYRO	-0.79
Madagascar	2.87
Malawi	2.84
Malaysia	1.98
Mali	2.66
Mauritania	2.75
Mauritius	-0.80
Mexico	0.39
Moldova	0.02
Mongolia	1.58
Morocco	0.62
Mozambique	2.09
Myanmar (Burma)	-0.08
Namibia	2.48
Nepal	2.40
Netherlands, the	-0.58
New Zealand	0.02
Nicaragua	2.26
Niger	3.53
Nigeria	2.78
North Korea, Dem. Rep.	-0.70
Norway	-0.33
Oman	4.20
Pakistan	2.34
Panama	0.67
Papua New Guinea	1.67
Paraguay	2.64
Peru	0.99
Philippines	1.83
Poland	-0.25
Portugal	-2.18
Puerto Rico	-0.44
Romania	-1.73
Russia	-0.13
Rwanda	1.55
Saudi Arabia	4.12
Senegal	2.69
Sierra Leone	2.60
Singapore	0.68

A3-2. Average Annual Children's Population Growth Rates, Ages 0-14, 1980–1997 *(continued)*

	Average Annual Growth Rate (%)
Slovakia	-0.72
Slovenia	-1.51
South Africa	1.36
South Korea, Rep.	-1.33
Spain	-2.86
Sri Lanka	0.02
Sudan	1.68
Sweden	0.14
Switzerland	-0.12
Syria	2.45
Tajikistan	2.23
Tanzania	2.83
Thailand	-0.84
Togo	3.13
Trinidad and Tobago	-0.01
Tunisia	0.76
Turkey	0.53
Turkmenistan	2.41
Uganda	2.82
Ukraine	-0.60
United Arab Emirates	5.22
United Kingdom	-0.27
United States	0.80
Uruguay	0.21
Uzbekistan	2.02
Venezuela	1.58
Vietnam	1.00
Yemen	3.58
Yugoslavia	-0.29
Zambia	2.53
Zimbabwe	2.15

Source: World Bank, *World Development Indicators, 1999:* Table 2.2.

A4. CHILD POPULATION PROJECTIONS

A4-1. Population Projections, Children (0 to 19 Years), by Continent, 2025

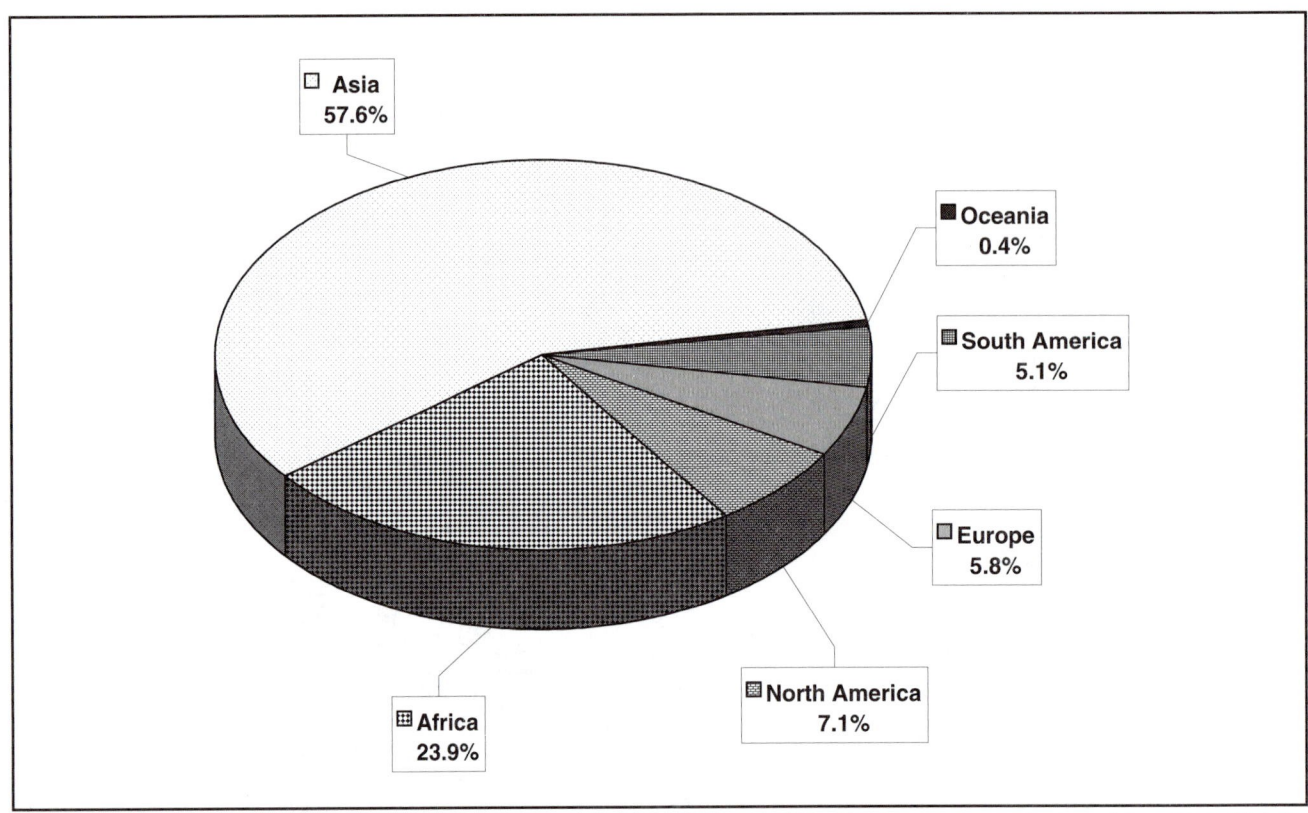

Asia
57.6%

Oceania
0.4%

South America
5.1%

Europe
5.8%

North America
7.1%

Africa
23.9%

Source: U.S. Census International Database, 2000: Table 094. Midyear Population by Age and Sex; <http://www.census.gov/ipc/www/idbagg.html>. Underlying data from U.S. Bureau of the Census.

A4-2. Population Projections, Children (0 to 19 Years), Total Population, Male, Female, Sex Ratio, by Country, 2025

		Child Population		
	Total	**Male**	**Female**	**Sex ratio**
Afghanistan	21,651,345	11,087,298	10,564,047	105.0
Albania	1,160,015	599,214	560,801	106.8
Algeria	13,978,441	7,121,444	6,856,997	103.9
American Samoa	35,211	18,069	17,142	105.4
Andorra	12,106	6,250	5,856	106.7
Angola	8,844,671	4,467,145	4,377,526	102.0
Anguilla	3,745	1,890	1,855	101.9
Antigua and Barbuda	21,652	11,046	10,606	104.1
Argentina	13,038,934	6,674,111	6,364,823	104.9
Armenia	939,302	478,817	460,485	104.0
Aruba	15,874	8,123	7,751	104.8
Australia	5,261,755	2,692,184	2,569,571	104.8
Austria	1,528,336	781,836	746,500	104.7
Azerbaijan	3,145,602	1,605,586	1,540,016	104.3
Bahamas, the	93,625	47,236	46,389	101.8
Bahrain	251,865	127,412	124,453	102.4
Bangladesh	58,290,880	29,942,163	28,348,717	105.6
Barbados	67,105	33,514	33,591	99.8
Belarus	2,263,806	1,156,534	1,107,272	104.4
Belgium	2,060,048	1,054,273	1,005,775	104.8

A4-2. Population Projections, Children (0 to 19 Years), Total Population, Male, Female, Sex Ratio, by Country, 2025 *(continued)*

		Child Population		
	Total	**Male**	**Female**	**Sex ratio**
Belize	172,147	87,883	84,264	104.3
Benin	6,012,751	3,039,580	2,973,171	102.2
Bermuda	14,580	7,066	7,514	94.0
Bhutan	1,447,362	747,566	699,796	106.8
Bolivia	3,818,349	1,946,783	1,871,566	104.0
Bosnia and Herzegovina	923,074	475,423	447,651	106.2
Botswana	538,412	272,360	266,052	102.4
Brazil	54,221,089	27,675,169	26,545,920	104.3
Brunei	148,178	75,843	72,335	104.8
Bulgaria	930,740	478,458	452,282	105.8
Burkina Faso	11,427,749	5,766,205	5,661,544	101.8
Burundi	5,581,344	2,819,942	2,761,402	102.1
Cambodia	8,675,019	4,410,542	4,264,477	103.4
Cameroon	11,263,369	5,687,866	5,575,503	102.0
Canada	8,095,355	4,146,515	3,948,840	105.0
Cape Verde	157,306	79,582	77,724	102.4
Cayman Islands	11,306	5,263	6,043	87.1
Central African Republic	2,294,067	1,156,124	1,137,943	101.6
Chad	9,948,154	5,001,682	4,946,472	101.1
Chile	4,758,511	2,434,843	2,323,668	104.8
China	355,026,243	183,289,122	171,737,121	106.7
Colombia	17,597,137	8,903,505	8,693,632	102.4
Comoros	534,998	268,937	266,061	101.1
Congo, Dem Rep. (Zaire)	57,449,364	28,887,961	28,561,403	101.1
Congo, Rep.	2,222,212	1,119,080	1,103,132	101.4
Costa Rica	1,454,442	744,649	709,793	104.9
Côte d'Ivoire	12,905,270	6,490,829	6,414,441	101.2
Croatia	1,049,462	539,044	510,418	105.6
Cuba	2,425,393	1,246,428	1,178,965	105.7
Cyprus	200,462	102,503	97,959	104.6
Czech Republic	1,597,017	820,204	776,813	105.6
Denmark	1,190,653	611,451	579,202	105.6
Djibouti	393,862	197,599	196,263	100.7
Dominica	19,894	10,147	9,747	104.1
Dominican Republic	4,241,901	2,166,933	2,074,968	104.4
Ecuador	6,541,364	3,332,678	3,208,686	103.9
Egypt	31,296,020	16,000,104	15,295,916	104.6
El Salvador	3,512,355	1,791,973	1,720,382	104.2
Equatorial Guinea	387,292	194,692	192,600	101.1
Eritrea	4,116,154	2,063,277	2,052,877	100.5
Estonia	273,106	139,460	133,646	104.4
Ethiopia	64,091,502	32,321,597	31,769,905	101.7
Faroe Islands	13,379	6,690	6,689	100.0
Fiji	402,077	205,430	196,647	104.5
Finland	1,082,372	549,722	532,650	103.2
France	13,242,096	6,793,688	6,448,408	105.4
French Guiana	85,397	43,685	41,712	104.7
French Polynesia	91,323	46,722	44,601	104.8
Gabon	598,750	300,635	298,115	100.8
Gambia, the	1,309,748	658,074	651,674	101.0
Gaza Strip	1,302,680	666,574	636,106	104.8
Georgia	1,165,770	595,275	570,495	104.3
Germany	15,829,998	8,125,787	7,704,211	105.5
Ghana	9,745,835	4,910,093	4,835,742	101.5
Gibraltar	5,795	2,971	2,824	105.2
Greece	1,861,419	960,532	900,887	106.6

A4-2. Population Projections, Children (0 to 19 Years), Total Population, Male, Female, Sex Ratio, by Country, 2025 *(continued)*

		Child Population		
	Total	Male	Female	Sex ratio
Greenland	16,186	8,262	7,924	104.3
Grenada	33,022	16,592	16,430	101.0
Guadeloupe	126,935	64,886	62,049	104.6
Guam	73,642	39,222	34,420	114.0
Guatemala	9,610,885	4,901,043	4,709,842	104.1
Guernsey	11,826	6,002	5,824	103.1
Guinea	5,963,677	2,968,062	2,995,615	99.1
Guinea-Bissau	1,026,987	512,518	514,469	99.6
Guyana	231,287	118,055	113,232	104.3
Haiti	3,910,617	1,981,967	1,928,650	102.8
Honduras	3,682,637	1,883,059	1,799,578	104.6
Hong Kong SAR (China)	1,666,392	874,623	791,769	110.5
Hungary	1,654,612	854,311	800,301	106.7
Iceland	70,713	36,683	34,030	107.8
India	449,451,873	230,542,261	218,909,612	105.3
Indonesia	91,044,813	46,408,972	44,635,841	104.0
Iran	27,279,697	13,949,417	13,330,280	104.6
Iraq	16,607,043	8,445,018	8,162,025	103.5
Ireland	1,088,418	561,385	527,033	106.5
Israel	2,196,292	1,123,959	1,072,333	104.8
Italy	8,212,189	4,231,657	3,980,532	106.3
Jamaica	860,328	440,132	420,196	104.7
Japan	20,920,044	10,714,663	10,205,381	105.0
Jersey	17,056	8,835	8,221	107.5
Jordan	2,695,630	1,375,619	1,320,011	104.2
Kazakhstan	6,168,515	3,133,162	3,035,353	103.2
Kenya	12,851,698	6,502,763	6,348,935	102.4
Kiribati	69,707	35,395	34,312	103.2
Kuwait	1,329,844	670,347	659,497	101.6
Kyrgyzstan	2,590,618	1,315,510	1,275,108	103.2
Laos	4,243,659	2,150,012	2,093,647	102.7
Latvia	421,731	215,429	206,302	104.4
Lebanon	1,221,295	623,555	597,740	104.3
Lesotho	1,067,579	538,529	529,050	101.8
Liberia	3,049,390	1,537,622	1,511,768	101.7
Libya	2,996,221	1,530,972	1,465,249	104.5
Liechtenstein	7,381	3,671	3,710	98.9
Lithuania	824,138	420,917	403,221	104.4
Luxembourg	127,813	65,850	61,963	106.3
Macau, SAR	154,062	79,659	74,403	107.1
Macedonia, FYRO	514,087	266,863	247,224	107.9
Madagascar	17,561,674	8,807,705	8,753,969	100.6
Malawi	5,670,891	2,847,756	2,823,135	100.9
Malaysia	11,863,979	6,113,907	5,750,072	106.3
Maldives	251,413	128,993	122,420	105.4
Mali	11,506,443	5,779,663	5,726,780	100.9
Malta	102,274	53,403	48,871	109.3
Man, Isle of	17,065	8,734	8,331	104.8
Marshall Islands	95,344	48,677	46,667	104.3
Martinique	109,332	55,436	53,896	102.9
Mauritania	2,722,763	1,365,734	1,357,029	100.6
Mauritius	364,951	183,359	181,592	101.0
Mayotte	182,805	92,130	90,675	101.6
Mexico	42,370,102	21,626,581	20,743,521	104.3
Moldova	1,344,683	684,724	659,959	103.8
Monaco	6,646	3,404	3,242	105.0

A4-2. Population Projections, Children (0 to 19 Years), Total Population, Male, Female, Sex Ratio, by Country, 2025 *(continued)*

		Child Population		
	Total	**Male**	**Female**	**Sex ratio**
Mongolia	1,171,385	598,283	573,102	104.4
Montserrat	2,954	1,508	1,446	104.3
Morocco	13,867,248	7,070,604	6,796,644	104.0
Mozambique	9,513,539	4,804,403	4,709,136	102.0
Myanmar (Burma)	12,754,792	6,521,104	6,233,688	104.6
Namibia	987,580	500,887	486,693	102.9
Nauru	6,713	3,424	3,289	104.1
Nepal	16,356,718	8,428,364	7,928,354	106.3
Netherlands, the	3,515,435	1,793,371	1,722,064	104.1
Netherlands Antilles	63,286	32,430	30,856	105.1
New Caledonia	75,635	38,660	36,975	104.6
New Zealand	1,118,701	570,668	548,033	104.1
Nicaragua	2,530,251	1,290,042	1,240,209	104.0
Niger	9,803,355	4,985,462	4,817,893	103.5
Nigeria	100,530,110	50,642,210	49,887,900	101.5
North Korea, Dem. Rep.	6,554,058	3,353,474	3,200,584	104.8
Northern Mariana Islands	33,962	17,223	16,739	102.9
Norway	1,110,651	572,750	537,901	106.5
Oman	2,549,252	1,302,038	1,247,214	104.4
Pakistan	77,242,917	39,620,419	37,622,498	105.3
Palau	7,013	3,600	3,413	105.5
Panama	954,553	484,963	469,590	103.3
Papua New Guinea	3,166,957	1,612,785	1,554,172	103.8
Paraguay	4,125,043	2,099,236	2,025,807	103.6
Peru	12,026,907	6,118,248	5,908,659	103.5
Philippines	44,401,414	22,643,619	21,757,795	104.1
Poland	7,706,837	3,953,857	3,752,980	105.4
Portugal	1,969,543	1,015,129	954,414	106.4
Puerto Rico	1,027,970	526,325	501,645	104.9
Qatar	316,328	161,497	154,831	104.3
Reunion	302,052	154,570	147,482	104.8
Romania	4,133,062	2,123,117	2,009,945	105.6
Russia	29,773,513	15,205,793	14,567,720	104.4
Rwanda	3,368,971	1,692,987	1,675,984	101.0
Saint Helena	1,563	795	768	103.5
Saint Kitts and Nevis	14,073	7,228	6,845	105.6
Saint Lucia	61,429	31,702	29,727	106.6
Saint Pierre and Miquelon	1,735	888	847	104.8
Saint Vincent and the Grenadines	29,274	15,000	14,274	105.1
Samoa	55,167	28,247	26,920	104.9
San Marino	7,036	3,632	3,404	106.7
Sao Tome and Principe	166,410	84,241	82,169	102.5
Saudi Arabia	24,991,737	12,768,772	12,222,965	104.5
Senegal	8,409,919	4,233,910	4,176,009	101.4
Seychelles	23,308	11,821	11,487	102.9
Sierra Leone	4,988,103	2,448,502	2,539,601	96.4
Singapore	1,715,462	884,593	830,869	106.5
Slovakia	1,010,188	517,400	492,788	105.0
Slovenia	327,057	167,812	159,245	105.4
Solomon Islands	321,289	164,047	157,242	104.3
Somalia	7,848,108	3,930,576	3,917,532	100.3
South Africa	12,140,285	6,134,714	6,005,571	102.2
South Korea, Rep.	11,747,922	6,084,626	5,663,296	107.4
Spain	6,260,806	3,230,534	3,030,272	106.6
Sri Lanka	5,801,199	2,964,715	2,836,484	104.5
Sudan	26,679,230	13,614,104	13,065,126	104.2

A4-2. Population Projections, Children (0 to 19 Years), Total Population, Male, Female, Sex Ratio, by Country, 2025 *(continued)*

	Child Population			Sex ratio
	Total	**Male**	**Female**	
Suriname	131,479	68,002	63,477	107.1
Swaziland	749,873	375,432	374,441	100.3
Sweden	1,771,425	909,863	861,562	105.6
Switzerland	1,327,451	680,666	646,785	105.2
Syria	9,823,335	5,053,372	4,769,963	105.9
Taiwan	5,738,917	2,961,594	2,777,323	106.6
Tajikistan	4,801,060	2,428,993	2,372,067	102.4
Tanzania	29,138,759	14,677,385	14,461,374	101.5
Thailand	17,258,704	8,809,371	8,449,333	104.3
Togo	3,224,147	1,619,243	1,604,904	100.9
Tonga	50,259	25,680	24,579	104.5
Trinidad and Tobago	224,280	115,732	108,548	106.6
Tunisia	3,122,328	1,615,438	1,506,890	107.2
Turkey	21,447,947	10,937,123	10,510,824	104.1
Turkmenistan	2,781,228	1,413,021	1,368,207	103.3
Turks and Caicos Islands	10,799	5,511	5,288	104.2
Tuvalu	5,835	2,977	2,858	104.2
Uganda	27,430,633	13,792,902	13,637,731	101.1
Ukraine	9,471,400	4,838,675	4,632,725	104.4
United Arab Emirates	1,039,618	531,114	508,504	104.4
United Kingdom	12,961,898	6,643,617	6,318,281	105.1
United States	89,253,092	45,692,246	43,560,846	104.9
Uruguay	1,152,806	590,981	561,825	105.2
Uzbekistan	13,828,424	7,022,041	6,806,383	103.2
Vanuatu	86,589	44,208	42,381	104.3
Venezuela	9,551,135	4,931,678	4,619,457	106.8
Vietnam	31,911,216	16,440,787	15,470,429	106.3
Virgin Islands	39,959	20,447	19,512	104.8
Virgin Islands, British	7,567	3,852	3,715	103.7
West Bank	1,656,057	850,010	806,047	105.5
Yemen	21,292,936	10,853,581	10,439,355	104.0
Yugoslavia	2,368,015	1,227,310	1,140,706	N/A
Zambia	7,474,283	3,764,656	3,709,627	101.5
Zimbabwe	3,928,659	1,991,048	1,937,611	102.8

N/A Not Available

Source: U.S. Census International Database, 2000: Table 094. Midyear population by Age and Sex; <http://www.census.gov/ipc/www/idbagg.html>. Underlying data from U.S. Bureau of the Census.

A5. YOUTH DEPENDENCY RATIO

A5-1. Youth Dependency Ratio (Ratio of Population under Age 15 to Population Age 15 to 64), by Region, 1998 and 2025

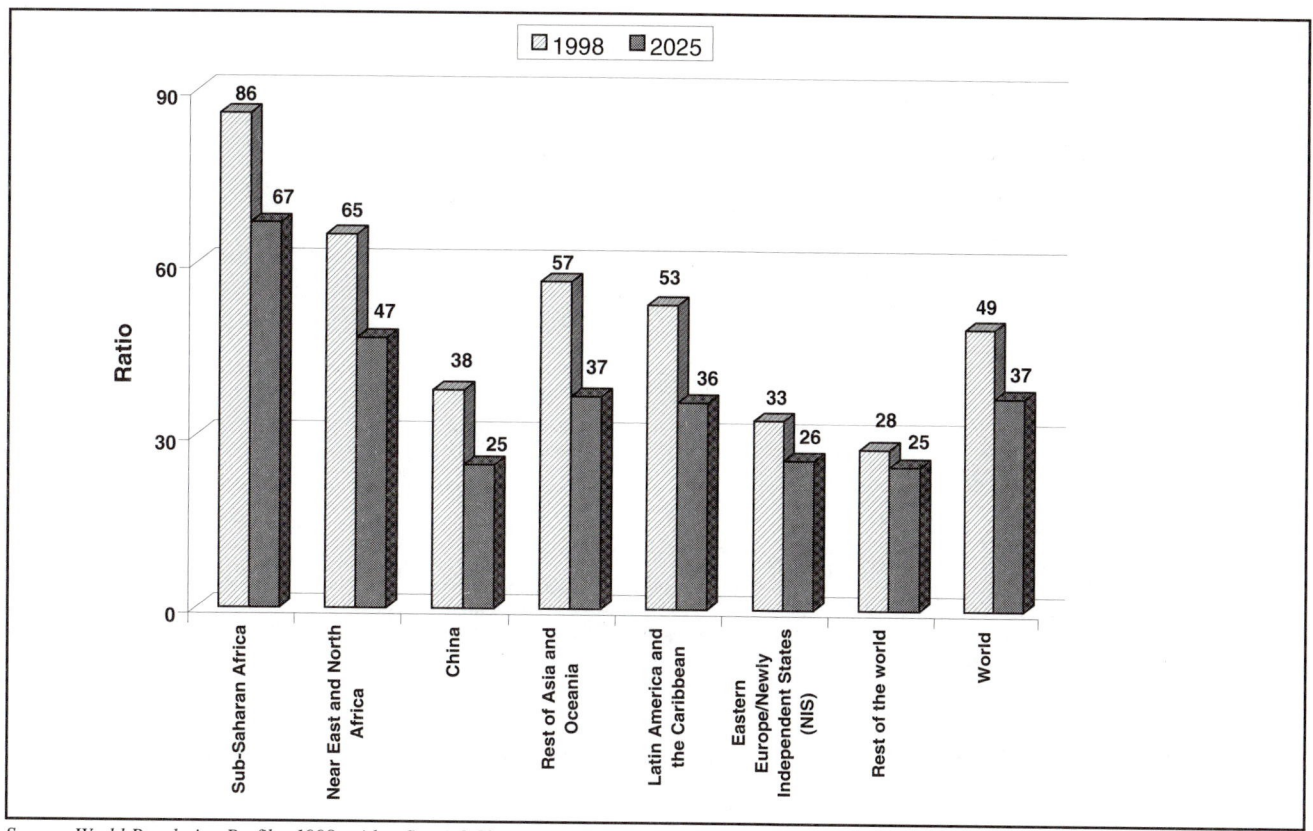

Source: World Population Profile: 1998, with a Special Chapter Focusing on HIV/AIDS in the Developing World, Population Composition and Distribution; <http://www.census.gov/ipc/www/wp98.html>. Underlying data from U.S. Department of Commerce, Economics and Statistics Administration, U.S. Bureau of the Census.

A5-2. Youth Dependency Ratio (Ratio of Population under Age 15 to Population Age 15 to 64), by Major Areas and Regions, 1950–2025

	1950–1955	1960–1965	1970–1975	1980–1985	1990–1995	2000–2005	2010–2015	2020–2025
Africa	78.3	81.1	85.8	85.9	84.4	78.2	70.3	61.1
Asia	61.7	70.0	72.5	64.9	53.6	46.6	38.2	34.1
Europe	39.9	41.4	39.5	33.9	30.6	25.8	22.2	22.7
South America	69.1	76.0	75.4	66.0	58.3	47.6	40.4	36.3
North America*	42.1	51.9	46.1	33.9	33.1	32.0	27.8	28.0
Oceania	47.3	55.3	53.3	46.7	40.8	38.7	35.3	34.0
Central America and Caribbean	71.1	78.5	79.4	70.8	60.0	50.0	42.2	37.2
World	56.9	63.8	65.7	59.8	52.6	46.9	40.2	36.9
*United States and Canada								

Source: World Population Prospects: The 1998 Revision, Volume 1, Comprehensive Tables, Table A.29, Dependency Ratios. Underlying data from United Nations Population Division, Department of Economic and Social Affairs of the United Nations Secretariat, United Nations New York, 1999.

A5-2. Youth Dependency Ratio (Ratio of Population under Age 15 to Population Age 15 to 64), by Major Areas and Regions, 1950–2025 (continued)

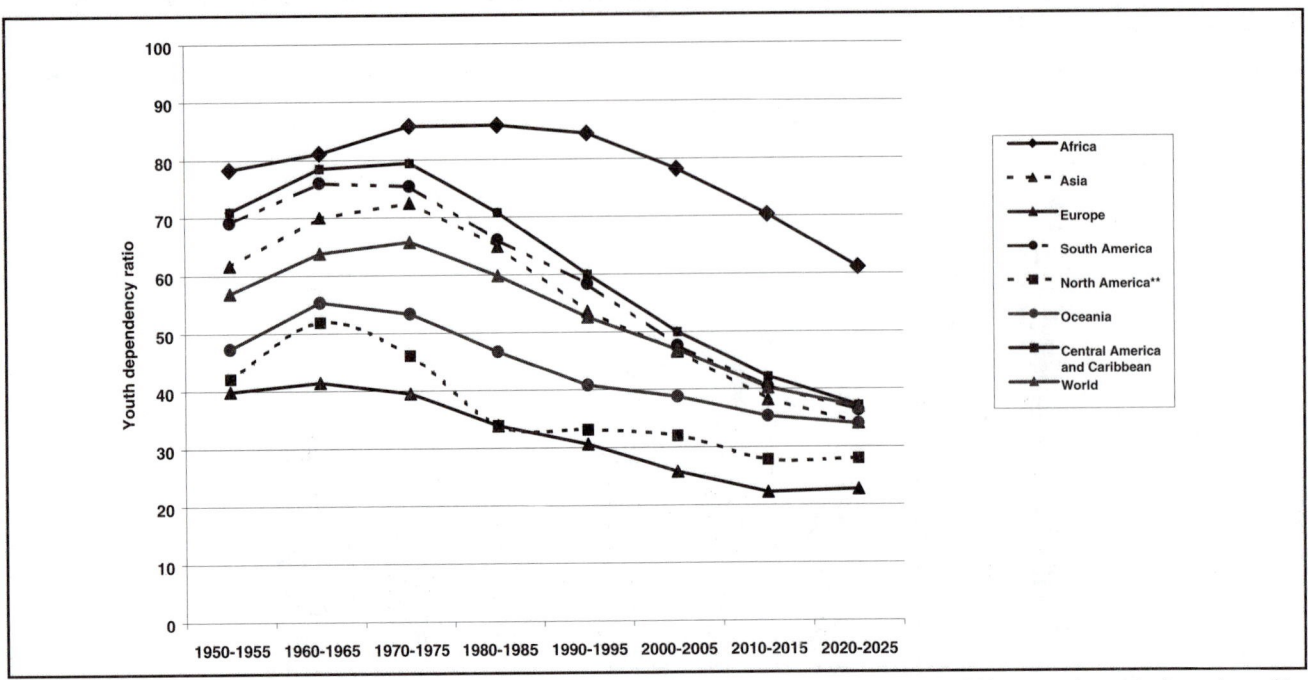

Source: TransMONEE 2000 database, United Nations Children's Fund (UNICEF); <http://www.eurochild.gla.ac.uk/documents/monee/welcome.htm>. Underlying data from UNICEF Innocenti Research Centre, Florence.

A5-3. Youth Dependency Ratio (Ratio of Population under Age 15 to Population Age 15 to 64), Selected Countries, 1990–1998

	1990	1991	1992	1993	1994	1995	1996	1997	1998	1999
Albania	55.1	55.8	57.9	60.4	61.3	60.9	60.0	59.1	58.1	56.9
Armenia	63.2	64.0	63.8	63.5	62.8	61.6	60.1	58.4	56.3	54.4
Azerbaijan	56.0	56.6	57.1	57.4	57.5	57.2	56.3	56.3	56.2	56.3
Belarus	38.1	38.3	38.1	37.9	37.3	36.5	35.5	34.5	33.4	32.0
Bosnia-Herzegovina	N/A	N/A	N/A	N/A	33.1	31.6	29.9	28.7	27.9	27.1
Bulgaria	34.1	33.3	32.4	31.4	30.7	29.8	29.0	28.1	27.2	26.2
Croatia	N/A	N/A	30.5	30.0	30.0	29.4	28.8	28.3	27.8	27.4
Czech Republic	35.9	34.6	33.4	32.2	31.1	29.9	28.8	27.9	27.0	26.2
Estonia	36.8	36.8	36.4	35.7	34.9	34.1	33.2	32.3	31.4	30.3
Georgia	40.7	40.7	40.5	40.0	39.2	38.3	37.3	36.2	35.0	33.6
Hungary	33.9	32.7	31.7	30.7	29.9	29.3	28.7	28.2	27.7	27.4
Kazakhstan	54.1	53.7	53.1	52.5	51.6	50.9	50.2	49.3	48.3	47.4
Kyrgyzstan	69.2	69.6	69.5	70.1	70.5	69.9	69.4	68.2	66.5	64.8
Latvia	35.2	35.4	35.5	35.3	34.9	34.3	33.6	32.7	31.6	30.3
Lithuania	36.8	37.0	36.8	36.7	36.4	35.9	35.3	34.7	34.0	33.1
Macedonia	N/A	N/A	38.0	37.6	38.8	39.9	39.3	38.7	38.1	37.5
Moldova	47.2	47.0	46.7	46.3	45.6	44.7	43.6	42.3	42.0	40.0
Poland	42.1	41.5	40.8	39.9	38.9	37.8	36.5	35.2	33.7	32.1
Romania	39.0	38.2	37.3	36.1	34.9	33.7	32.5	31.4	30.8	30.2
Russia	37.7	37.5	37.2	36.6	35.6	34.7	33.7	32.7	31.6	30.2
Slovakia	42.6	41.6	40.6	39.5	38.3	36.9	35.6	34.3	33.0	31.8
Slovenia	33.0	32.4	31.5	30.8	29.9	29.0	28.3	27.3	26.4	25.7
Tajikistan	84.8	85.8	85.8	87.2	87.9	87.4	86.6	84.6	82.3	79.4
Turkmenistan	76.0	75.8	75.5	75.4	74.8	75.7	74.5	73.6	72.0	70.6
Ukraine	35.7	35.6	35.2	34.9	34.2	33.5	32.7	32.0	31.3	30.2
Uzbekistan	77.5	78.0	78.0	78.3	77.9	77.2	76.5	75.3	73.7	71.6
Yugoslavia	37.6	37.3	37.2	36.8	36.3	35.8	35.3	34.9	34.3	33.7

Source: TransMONEE 2000 database, United Nations Children's Fund (UNICEF); <http://www.eurochild.gla.ac.uk/documents/monee/welcome.htm>. Underlying data from UNICEF Innocenti Research Centre, Florence.

A6. INFANT MORTALITY RATE

A6-1. Infant Mortality Rate (Infant Deaths per 1,000 Live Births), by Continent, 2000

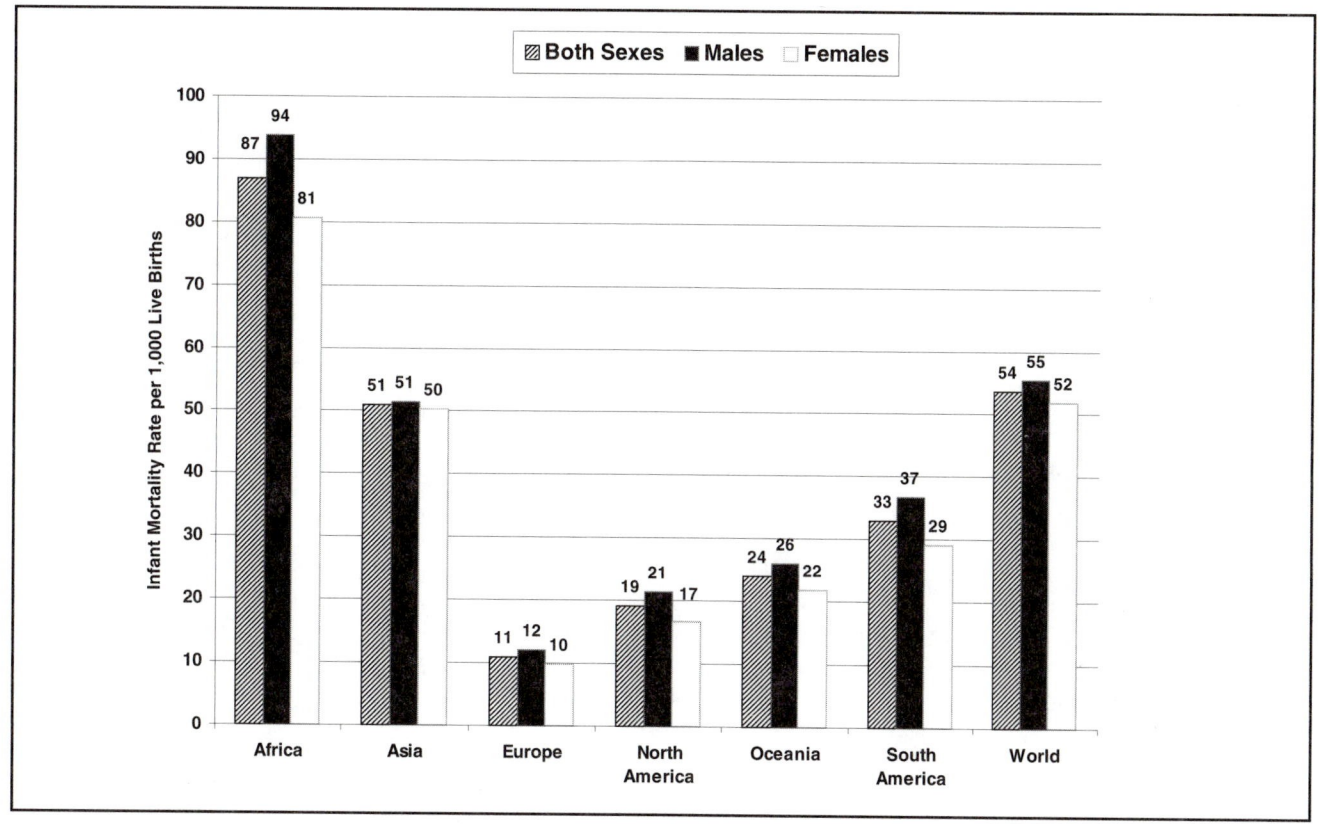

Source: U.S. Census International Database, 2000: Table 010. Infant Mortality Rates and Deaths, and Life Expectancy at Birth, by Sex; Table 028. Total Fertility Rate; Table 008. Vital Rates and Events; <http://www.census.gov/ipc/www/idbagg.html>. Underlying data from U.S. Bureau of the Census.

A6-2. Infant Mortality Rate (Infant Deaths per 1,000 Live Births), 1980

	Both sexes	Male	Female
Afghanistan	182.9	189.2	176.2
Albania	N/A	N/A	N/A
Algeria	102.8	107.0	98.5
American Samoa	16.6	N/A	N/A
Andorra	N/A	N/A	N/A
Angola	189.2	201.6	176.1
Anguilla	N/A	N/A	N/A
Antigua and Barbuda	N/A	N/A	N/A
Argentina	32.4	35.8	28.9
Armenia	N/A	N/A	N/A
Aruba	N/A	N/A	N/A
Australia	10.7	11.9	9.4
Austria	N/A	N/A	N/A
Azerbaijan	N/A	N/A	N/A
Bahamas, the	29.3	30.5	28.0
Bahrain	N/A	N/A	N/A
Bangladesh	N/A	N/A	N/A
Barbados	26.2	26.9	25.6
Belarus	N/A	N/A	N/A
Belgium	N/A	N/A	N/A
Belize	49.2	55.0	43.2

A6-2. Infant Mortality Rate (Infant Deaths per 1,000 Live Births), 1980 *(continued)*

	Both sexes	Male	Female
Benin	146.5	156.2	136.5
Bermuda	14.0	18.1	9.9
Bhutan	153.9	153.3	154.6
Bolivia	95.4	103.2	87.3
Bosnia and Herzegovina	N/A	N/A	N/A
Botswana	N/A	N/A	N/A
Brazil	73.7	80.2	66.9
Brunei	N/A	N/A	N/A
Bulgaria	20.2	23.0	17.0
Burkina Faso	N/A	N/A	N/A
Burundi	126.2	137.3	114.8
Cambodia	185.1	200.4	169.1
Cameroon	107.9	114.1	101.4
Canada	10.0	12.0	9.0
Cape Verde	85.6	93.5	77.4
Cayman Islands	N/A	N/A	N/A
Central African Republic	N/A	N/A	N/A
Chad	147.1	159.7	134.1
Chile	35.0	N/A	N/A
China	N/A	N/A	N/A
Colombia	56.7	60.8	52.5
Comoros	112.4	121.6	103.0
Congo, Dem. Rep. of (Zaire)	N/A	N/A	N/A
Congo, Rep.	N/A	N/A	N/A
Cook Islands	22.4	N/A	N/A
Costa Rica	N/A	N/A	N/A
Côte d'Ivoire	N/A	N/A	N/A
Croatia	N/A	N/A	N/A
Cuba	N/A	N/A	N/A
Cyprus	N/A	N/A	N/A
Czech Republic	N/A	N/A	N/A
Denmark	N/A	N/A	N/A
Djibouti	N/A	N/A	N/A
Dominica	N/A	N/A	N/A
Dominican Republic	80.2	86.7	73.5
Ecuador	N/A	N/A	N/A
Egypt	N/A	N/A	N/A
El Salvador	81.9	89.6	73.9
Equatorial Guinea	N/A	N/A	N/A
Eritrea	N/A	N/A	N/A
Estonia	N/A	N/A	N/A
Ethiopia	N/A	N/A	N/A
Faroe Islands	10.1	11.0	9.1
Fiji	N/A	N/A	N/A
Finland	7.6	8.4	6.8
France	10.0	N/A	N/A
French Guiana	N/A	N/A	N/A
French Polynesia	N/A	N/A	N/A
Gabon	130.4	143.0	117.4
Gambia, the	N/A	N/A	N/A
Gaza Strip	N/A	N/A	N/A
Georgia	N/A	N/A	N/A
Germany	N/A	N/A	N/A
Ghana	96.0	103.1	88.7
Gibraltar	N/A	N/A	N/A
Greece	17.9	19.9	15.9
Greenland	32.1	N/A	N/A
Grenada	N/A	N/A	N/A

A6-2. Infant Mortality Rate (Infant Deaths per 1,000 Live Births), 1980 *(continued)*

	Both sexes	Male	Female
Guadeloupe	17.5	N/A	N/A
Guam	16.3	N/A	N/A
Guatemala	77.6	83.4	71.4
Guernsey	12.4	N/A	N/A
Guinea	173.9	186.5	160.9
Guinea-Bissau	148.8	160.3	136.9
Guyana	60.4	65.8	54.8
Haiti	N/A	N/A	N/A
Honduras	N/A	N/A	N/A
Hong Kong SAR (China)	11.2	N/A	N/A
Hungary	23.2	25.9	20.3
Iceland	N/A	N/A	N/A
India	116.4	113.9	119.0
Indonesia	99.7	106.8	92.2
Iran	N/A	N/A	N/A
Iraq	N/A	N/A	N/A
Ireland	N/A	N/A	N/A
Israel	N/A	N/A	N/A
Italy	14.0	N/A	N/A
Jamaica	N/A	N/A	N/A
Japan	7.5	N/A	N/A
Jersey	10.6	N/A	N/A
Jordan	59.3	61.6	56.8
Kazakhstan	N/A	N/A	N/A
Kenya	81.4	85.2	77.5
Kiribati	N/A	N/A	N/A
Kuwait	27.7	29.5	25.8
Kyrgyzstan	N/A	N/A	N/A
Laos	N/A	N/A	N/A
Latvia	N/A	N/A	N/A
Lebanon	49.0	52.6	45.1
Lesotho	104.5	113.6	95.1
Liberia	146.8	154.8	138.7
Libya	69.0	72.8	65.1
Liechtenstein	7.6	N/A	N/A
Lithuania	N/A	N/A	N/A
Luxembourg	11.5	10.1	12.9
Macau	N/A	N/A	N/A
Macedonia, FYRO	N/A	N/A	N/A
Madagascar	115.4	120.5	110.2
Malawi	162.0	169.4	154.4
Malaysia	40.9	46.6	34.9
Maldives	N/A	N/A	N/A
Mali	N/A	N/A	N/A
Malta	14.6	18.4	11.6
Man, Isle of	8.1	N/A	N/A
Marshall Islands	N/A	N/A	N/A
Martinique	14.7	N/A	N/A
Mauritania	109.6	110.3	109.0
Mauritius	33.0	35.0	31.0
Mayotte	N/A	N/A	N/A
Mexico	52.6	57.9	46.9
Micronesia	N/A	N/A	N/A
Moldova	N/A	N/A	N/A
Monaco	10.6	11.4	9.7
Mongolia	N/A	N/A	N/A
Montenegro	N/A	N/A	N/A

A6-2. Infant Mortality Rate (Infant Deaths per 1,000 Live Births), 1980 *(continued)*

	Both sexes	Male	Female
Montserrat	40.2	N/A	N/A
Morocco	N/A	N/A	N/A
Mozambique	156.1	168.5	143.3
Myanmar (Burma)	102.0	110.7	92.7
Namibia	N/A	N/A	N/A
Nauru	N/A	N/A	N/A
Nepal	113.5	113.9	113.1
Netherlands Antilles	N/A	N/A	N/A
Netherlands, the	8.6	N/A	N/A
New Caledonia	N/A	N/A	N/A
New Zealand	12.9	N/A	N/A
Nicaragua	86.8	97.7	75.4
Niger	N/A	N/A	N/A
Nigeria	106.1	108.3	103.8
North Korea, Dem. Rep.	39.5	43.7	35.1
Northern Mariana Islands	26.1	N/A	N/A
Norway	8.1	9.0	7.1
Oman	N/A	N/A	N/A
Pakistan	N/A	N/A	N/A
Palau	N/A	N/A	N/A
Panama	34.6	37.1	32.1
Papua New Guinea	85.4	84.6	86.2
Paraguay	56.9	63.1	50.4
Peru	N/A	N/A	N/A
Philippines	56.9	64.6	48.8
Poland	21.3	24.3	18.0
Portugal	23.9	27.2	21.2
Puerto Rico	19.0	N/A	N/A
Qatar	N/A	N/A	N/A
Reunion	N/A	N/A	N/A
Romania	29.3	32.3	26.1
Russia	N/A	N/A	N/A
Rwanda	138.5	148.5	128.2
Saint Helena	N/A	N/A	N/A
Saint Kitts and Nevis	52.5	57.3	47.2
Saint Lucia	25.7	27.9	23.5
Saint Pierre and Miquelon	N/A	N/A	N/A
Saint Vincent and the Grenadines	50.2	54.5	45.8
Samoa	N/A	N/A	N/A
San Marino	12.1	10.4	14.1
Sao Tome and Principe	N/A	N/A	N/A
Saudi Arabia	106.7	108.8	104.5
Senegal	N/A	N/A	N/A
Serbia	N/A	N/A	N/A
Seychelles	17.7	18.9	16.6
Sierra Leone	184.2	200.1	167.7
Singapore	12.8	12.8	12.8
Slovakia	N/A	N/A	N/A
Slovenia	N/A	N/A	N/A
Solomon Islands	47.1	52.6	41.4
Somalia	161.2	177.1	144.9
South Africa	79.0	81.0	77.0
South Korea, Rep.	N/A	N/A	N/A
Spain	12.3	13.9	10.7
Sri Lanka	N/A	N/A	N/A
Sudan	99.0	99.3	98.6
Suriname	48.9	56.4	41.0
Swaziland	129.3	139.2	119.0

A6-2. Infant Mortality Rate (Infant Deaths per 1,000 Live Births), 1980 *(continued)*

	Both sexes	Male	Female
Sweden	6.9	8.1	5.7
Switzerland	9.8	11.2	8.3
Syria	N/A	N/A	N/A
Taiwan	N/A	N/A	N/A
Tajikistan	N/A	N/A	N/A
Tanzania	128.8	141.4	115.9
Thailand	N/A	N/A	N/A
Togo	N/A	N/A	N/A
Tonga	N/A	N/A	N/A
Trinidad and Tobago	37.7	42.1	33.1
Tunisia	N/A	N/A	N/A
Turkey	95.3	100.1	90.3
Turkmenistan	N/A	N/A	N/A
Turks and Caicos Islands	28.9	N/A	N/A
Tuvalu	40.4	45.2	35.5
Uganda	130.0	140.1	119.5
Ukraine	N/A	N/A	N/A
United Arab Emirates	N/A	N/A	N/A
United Kingdom	N/A	N/A	N/A
United States	12.6	13.9	11.2
Uruguay	37.1	N/A	N/A
Uzbekistan	N/A	N/A	N/A
Vanuatu	95.8	100.0	91.4
Venezuela	N/A	N/A	N/A
Vietnam	N/A	N/A	N/A
Virgin Islands	24.4	N/A	N/A
Virgin Islands, British	44.1	67.2	26.1
Wallis and Futuna	N/A	N/A	N/A
West Bank	N/A	N/A	N/A
Yemen	125.7	139.9	110.7
Zambia	93.1	97.6	88.5
Zimbabwe	N/A	N/A	N/A

N/A Not Available

Source: U.S. Census International Database, 2000: Table 010. Infant Mortality Rates and Deaths, and Life Expectancy at Birth, by Sex; <http://www.census.gov/ipc/www.idbagg.html>. Underlying data from U.S. Bureau of the Census.

A6-3. Infant Mortality Rate (Infant Deaths per 1,000 Live Births), 1990

	Both sexes	Male	Female
Afghanistan	167.9	173.4	162.2
Albania	41.7	44.7	38.5
Algeria	59.5	62.7	56.3
American Samoa	14.0	16.4	11.6
Andorra	9.0	9.5	8.4
Angola	158.2	170.5	145.4
Anguilla	17.3	22.6	11.9
Antigua and Barbuda	27.2	32.7	21.5
Argentina	26.0	28.8	23.1
Armenia	35.7	38.2	33.0
Aruba	8.9	10.3	7.5
Australia	8.3	9.2	7.3
Austria	7.8	8.9	6.7
Azerbaijan	58.6	65.0	52.0
Bahamas, the	23.2	26.6	19.7
Bahrain	23.4	27.1	19.5

A6-3. Infant Mortality Rate (Infant Deaths per 1,000 Live Births), 1990 *(continued)*

	Both sexes	Male	Female
Bangladesh	N/A	N/A	N/A
Barbados	25.6	28.6	22.4
Belarus	11.7	13.7	9.6
Belgium	8.0	9.3	6.7
Belize	39.1	44.0	34.1
Benin	120.3	129.6	110.8
Bermuda	13.2	15.3	10.6
Bhutan	130.4	128.4	132.5
Bolivia	78.7	85.0	72.0
Bosnia and Herzegovina	N/A	N/A	N/A
Botswana	60.7	63.4	58.0
Brazil	50.1	54.5	45.5
Brunei	27.3	30.2	24.3
Bulgaria	N/A	N/A	N/A
Burkina Faso	125.4	132.4	118.2
Burundi	116.3	127.0	105.2
Cambodia	115.6	124.0	106.9
Cameroon	86.5	94.1	78.8
Canada	7.1	7.9	6.4
Cape Verde	65.1	71.1	58.9
Cayman Islands	8.4	10.1	6.7
Central African Republic	124.4	133.0	115.6
Chad	130.5	142.3	118.2
Chile	16.9	18.6	15.3
China	52.2	39.7	65.9
Colombia	35.7	39.4	31.9
Comoros	104.4	114.9	93.7
Congo, Dem. Rep. of (Zaire)	119.2	129.9	108.3
Congo, Rep.	119.7	126.5	112.6
Cook Islands	24.7	28.4	20.8
Costa Rica	16.3	17.9	14.6
Côte d'Ivoire	111.0	120.7	101.0
Croatia	N/A	N/A	N/A
Cuba	10.8	12.3	9.2
Cyprus	10.2	13.0	7.2
Czech Republic	N/A	N/A	N/A
Denmark	7.7	8.7	6.6
Djibouti	119.7	128.7	110.5
Dominica	11.9	15.4	8.1
Dominican Republic	59.7	64.6	54.5
Ecuador	44.5	50.6	38.0
Egypt	84.0	85.9	82.1
El Salvador	43.5	47.8	39.0
Equatorial Guinea	111.9	119.1	104.4
Eritrea	92.0	99.7	84.1
Estonia	12.1	14.0	10.1
Ethiopia	134.7	145.9	123.1
Faroe Islands	9.0	10.3	7.6
Fiji	19.5	21.2	17.7
Finland	5.7	5.6	5.8
France	7.4	8.5	6.3
French Guiana	18.8	19.7	17.9
French Polynesia	11.6	13.3	9.8
Gabon	104.7	116.7	92.3
Gambia, the	91.2	99.6	82.5
Gaza Strip	36.0	36.8	35.2
Georgia	20.6	22.1	19.0
Germany	7.2	8.2	6.2

A6-3. Infant Mortality Rate (Infant Deaths per 1,000 Live Births), 1990 *(continued)*

	Both sexes	Male	Female
Ghana	88.8	95.6	81.7
Gibraltar	9.1	10.4	7.9
Greece	9.7	10.0	9.5
Greenland	33.3	40.5	26.1
Grenada	13.5	14.9	12.1
Guadeloupe	9.9	11.0	8.6
Guam	9.1	11.7	6.2
Guatemala	60.7	64.9	56.3
Guernsey	7.1	9.2	5.0
Guinea	149.3	161.0	137.3
Guinea-Bissau	128.3	137.7	118.7
Guyana	51.7	56.6	46.6
Haiti	110.0	116.8	102.8
Honduras	53.2	57.3	49.0
Hong Kong SAR (China)	N/A	N/A	N/A
Hungary	15.0	16.6	13.3
Iceland	4.1	4.2	3.9
India	79.9	79.5	80.4
Indonesia	76.4	82.3	70.2
Iran	N/A	N/A	N/A
Iraq	67.4	72.3	62.2
Ireland	8.3	9.0	7.5
Israel	9.6	10.4	8.7
Italy	N/A	N/A	N/A
Jamaica	19.6	21.7	17.4
Japan	4.6	5.0	4.2
Jersey	N/A	N/A	N/A
Jordan	38.5	40.8	36.0
Kazakhstan	49.2	53.8	44.4
Kenya	62.6	65.9	59.2
Kiribati	65.2	N/A	N/A
Kuwait	14.3	15.8	12.8
Kyrgyzstan	59.5	66.0	52.7
Laos	112.1	123.5	100.2
Latvia	17.9	19.4	16.4
Lebanon	41.5	45.3	37.5
Lesotho	86.0	95.6	76.1
Liberia	123.8	131.9	115.5
Libya	45.2	47.8	42.5
Liechtenstein	5.4	5.2	5.1
Lithuania	11.8	12.3	11.2
Luxembourg	7.5	8.5	6.3
Macau	N/A	N/A	N/A
Macedonia, FYRO	N/A	N/A	N/A
Madagascar	102.5	103.2	101.8
Malawi	147.2	154.7	139.4
Malaysia	29.3	34.3	23.9
Maldives	68.9	68.1	69.8
Mali	139.8	147.3	132.0
Malta	9.0	10.0	7.8
Man, Isle of	9.3	10.4	8.1
Marshall Islands	54.3	55.8	52.7
Martinique	8.9	9.8	8.0
Mauritania	92.3	94.5	90.0
Mauritius	20.9	23.8	17.8
Mayotte	88.5	97.0	79.6
Mexico	37.0	40.9	33.0
Micronesia	41.0	46.3	35.6

A6-3. Infant Mortality Rate (Infant Deaths per 1,000 Live Births), 1990 *(continued)*

	Both sexes	Male	Female
Moldova	34.1	38.6	29.4
Monaco	7.8	8.8	6.8
Mongolia	71.4	75.4	67.2
Montenegro	N/A	N/A	N/A
Montserrat	11.2	13.3	9.1
Morocco	69.8	73.9	65.3
Mozambique	141.0	152.4	129.2
Myanmar (Burma)	97.3	105.8	88.4
Namibia	73.3	78.0	68.6
Nauru	40.6	N/A	N/A
Nepal	93.7	94.0	93.5
Netherlands Antilles	13.1	14.0	12.2
Netherlands, the	6.6	7.4	5.8
New Caledonia	18.2	21.2	15.0
New Zealand	8.5	9.8	7.1
Nicaragua	58.0	65.7	50.1
Niger	126.7	127.9	125.5
Nigeria	84.7	87.3	82.0
North Korea, Dem. Rep.	31.3	34.7	27.8
Northern Mariana Islands	10.5	13.0	7.8
Norway	6.8	7.6	6.0
Oman	33.4	37.7	28.8
Pakistan	108.6	109.9	107.2
Palau	19.8	21.7	17.8
Panama	29.7	32.1	27.2
Papua New Guinea	69.8	69.6	70.0
Paraguay	45.8	50.4	41.0
Peru	57.8	64.2	51.0
Philippines	41.0	46.6	35.2
Poland	15.8	17.6	13.8
Portugal	N/A	N/A	N/A
Puerto Rico	14.2	15.9	12.4
Qatar	26.2	30.6	21.5
Reunion	8.9	9.4	8.3
Romania	N/A	N/A	N/A
Russia	23.8	25.9	21.5
Rwanda	116.8	125.1	108.2
Saint Helena	36.1	42.0	29.9
Saint Kitts and Nevis	22.2	24.3	19.9
Saint Lucia	19.8	21.1	18.5
Saint Pierre and Miquelon	18.1	20.9	14.8
Saint Vincent and the Grenadines	21.4	23.2	19.5
Samoa	43.0	49.2	36.5
San Marino	5.8	7.0	4.7
Sao Tome and Principe	65.8	68.4	63.2
Saudi Arabia	64.8	66.8	62.6
Senegal	72.5	79.8	65.1
Serbia	N/A	N/A	N/A
Seychelles	13.1	15.6	10.4
Sierra Leone	154.4	170.5	137.8
Singapore	6.7	7.2	6.2
Slovakia	N/A	N/A	N/A
Slovenia	N/A	N/A	N/A
Solomon Islands	32.4	36.6	27.9
Somalia	125.8	135.5	115.8
South Africa	53.7	59.0	48.3
South Korea, Rep.	10.4	10.4	10.3
Spain	N/A	N/A	N/A

A6-3. Infant Mortality Rate (Infant Deaths per 1,000 Live Births), 1990 *(continued)*

	Both sexes	Male	Female
Sri Lanka	18.9	20.1	17.5
Sudan	86.5	86.6	86.4
Suriname	35.6	41.5	29.5
Swaziland	115.6	125.0	105.9
Sweden	6.1	6.8	5.4
Switzerland	7.0	7.8	6.1
Syria	47.9	48.7	47.1
Taiwan	18.5	20.2	16.7
Tajikistan	75.1	81.8	68.2
Tanzania	110.8	122.9	98.2
Thailand	42.5	44.6	40.4
Togo	98.5	105.4	91.3
Tonga	46.2	N/A	N/A
Trinidad and Tobago	22.4	25.4	19.3
Tunisia	43.8	46.6	40.8
Turkey	61.6	65.5	57.5
Turkmenistan	69.5	76.9	61.6
Turks and Caicos Islands	26.8	30.8	22.7
Tuvalu	32.1	35.6	28.4
Uganda	105.7	114.9	96.3
Ukraine	18.7	20.1	17.2
United Arab Emirates	21.5	23.4	19.6
United Kingdom	N/A	N/A	N/A
United States	N/A	N/A	N/A
Uruguay	20.6	22.8	18.3
Uzbekistan	62.8	69.3	56.0
Vanuatu	75.3	80.0	70.3
Venezuela	34.0	38.2	29.6
Vietnam	46.1	46.6	45.7
Virgin Islands	14.8	16.3	13.3
Virgin Islands, British	20.2	23.4	16.8
Wallis and Futuna	31.8	32.4	31.1
West Bank	34.4	34.8	33.9
Yemen	94.1	98.8	89.2
Zambia	97.7	104.2	91.0
Zimbabwe	66.3	70.3	62.2

N/A Not Available

Source: U.S. Census International Database, 2000: Table 010. Infant Mortality Rates and Deaths, and Life Expectancy at Birth, by Sex; <http://www.census.gov/ipc/www/idbagg.html>. Underlying data from U.S. Bureau of the Census.

A6-4. Infant Mortality Rate (Infant Deaths per 1,000 Live Births), 2000

	Both sexes	Male	Female
Afghanistan	137.5	141.8	132.9
Albania	40.8	43.3	38.1
Algeria	42.2	44.3	40.0
American Samoa	10.6	12.5	8.6
Andorra	4.1	4.4	3.7
Angola	125.9	137.7	113.6
Anguilla	17.3	22.8	11.6
Antigua and Barbuda	20.0	24.2	15.6
Argentina	17.8	19.8	15.7
Armenia	41.5	46.2	36.5
Aruba	7.7	9.1	6.3
Australia	5.0	5.5	4.4
Austria	5.0	5.5	4.5
Azerbaijan	83.4	85.6	81.1
Bahamas, the	17.8	19.9	15.6
Bahrain	13.9	16.4	11.4
Bangladesh	67.1	68.6	65.5
Barbados	16.2	17.9	14.5
Belarus	14.6	16.4	12.8
Belgium	6.1	6.7	5.4
Belize	30.8	34.4	27.0
Benin	95.3	104.2	86.2
Bermuda	9.0	10.2	7.7
Bhutan	107.0	104.2	110.0
Bolivia	60.2	65.5	54.6
Bosnia and Herzegovina	18.2	19.6	16.7
Botswana	58.9	61.4	56.3
Brazil	33.8	37.4	29.9
Brunei	22.4	23.7	20.9
Bulgaria	12.0	13.5	10.4
Burkina Faso	105.2	111.8	98.4
Burundi	97.5	107.3	87.5
Cambodia	103.4	110.6	95.8
Cameroon	74.5	80.9	67.9
Canada	5.4	5.8	4.9
Cape Verde	43.5	48.2	38.6
Cayman Islands	8.4	10.1	6.7
Central African Republic	101.1	108.6	93.4
Chad	113.6	124.4	102.2
Chile	9.6	10.2	9.0
China	41.1	34.3	49.0
Colombia	23.2	27.5	18.7
Comoros	78.7	88.8	68.3
Congo, Dem. Rep. of (Zaire)	97.3	107.1	87.2
Congo, Rep.	98.5	105.5	91.2
Cook Islands	24.7	28.4	20.8
Costa Rica	12.7	13.4	11.9
Côte d'Ivoire	92.4	101.2	83.4
Croatia	7.7	8.3	7.0
Cuba	7.7	8.8	6.7
Cyprus	7.4	9.1	5.6
Czech Republic	6.6	7.5	5.5
Denmark	5.0	5.7	4.4
Djibouti	98.1	106.8	89.1
Dominica	8.4	10.7	6.1
Dominican Republic	40.8	44.5	36.9
Ecuador	29.3	33.4	25.0
Egypt	65.7	67.5	63.7

A6-4. Infant Mortality Rate (Infant Deaths per 1,000 Live Births), 2000 *(continued)*

	Both sexes	Male	Female
El Salvador	27.2	29.3	24.9
Equatorial Guinea	88.9	96.3	81.2
Eritrea	75.2	81.3	68.8
Estonia	13.7	15.5	11.8
Ethiopia	123.5	132.9	113.7
Faroe Islands	10.0	12.5	7.5
Fiji	15.9	17.6	14.2
Finland	3.8	4.1	3.4
France	5.6	6.3	4.8
French Guiana	12.4	13.1	11.6
French Polynesia	13.5	15.7	11.2
Gabon	80.8	91.9	69.3
Gambia, the	73.6	81.5	65.5
Gaza Strip	21.4	21.5	21.2
Georgia	52.9	59.6	45.9
Germany	5.1	5.6	4.5
Ghana	74.8	81.0	68.3
Gibraltar	6.3	7.4	5.2
Greece	7.0	7.4	6.6
Greenland	18.8	22.7	14.8
Grenada	10.9	12.4	9.3
Guadeloupe	8.3	9.3	7.2
Guam	6.8	7.0	6.7
Guatemala	44.6	48.3	40.7
Guernsey	8.2	9.1	7.2
Guinea	123.7	135.1	112.0
Guinea-Bissau	107.4	114.5	100.0
Guyana	48.6	52.9	44.1
Haiti	96.3	104.2	88.0
Honduras	39.8	43.8	35.6
Hong Kong SAR (China)	5.2	5.8	4.4
Hungary	9.2	10.4	8.0
Iceland	5.2	6.3	4.0
India	58.5	59.8	57.1
Indonesia	55.4	61.2	49.3
Iran	28.1	29.7	26.4
Iraq	62.4	68.4	56.1
Ireland	5.8	6.3	5.4
Israel	7.5	8.1	7.0
Italy	6.2	6.7	5.7
Jamaica	13.4	15.3	11.4
Japan	4.0	4.5	3.6
Jersey	2.8	2.0	3.6
Jordan	32.1	34.7	29.3
Kazakhstan	59.4	64.2	54.3
Kenya	58.8	61.5	56.0
Kiribati	46.8	N/A	N/A
Kuwait	9.8	10.7	8.9
Kyrgyzstan	77.1	87.5	66.2
Laos	86.8	94.8	78.5
Latvia	16.9	19.2	14.6
Lebanon	29.4	33.3	25.4
Lesotho	76.9	86.7	66.7
Liberia	98.1	106.4	89.6
Libya	26.4	27.5	25.4
Liechtenstein	5.2	7.0	3.3
Lithuania	14.7	16.8	12.4
Luxembourg	4.9	5.3	4.5

A6-4. Infant Mortality Rate (Infant Deaths per 1,000 Live Births), 2000 *(continued)*

	Both sexes	Male	Female
Macau	4.1	4.0	4.1
Macedonia, FYRO	17.9	18.4	17.4
Madagascar	87.6	89.4	85.8
Malawi	130.5	138.1	122.8
Malaysia	20.9	25.2	16.4
Maldives	35.1	34.9	35.4
Mali	117.2	124.8	109.3
Malta	7.3	8.9	5.5
Man, Isle of	2.5	2.5	2.5
Marshall Islands	42.2	43.4	40.9
Martinique	6.6	7.3	5.9
Mauritania	74.7	78.3	71.0
Mauritius	15.9	18.1	13.7
Mayotte	67.0	74.9	58.8
Mexico	23.4	26.5	20.2
Micronesia	33.5	38.1	28.7
Moldova	43.3	47.3	39.1
Monaco	6.3	7.0	5.6
Mongolia	62.9	67.3	58.4
Montenegro	10.7	12.0	9.4
Montserrat	12.1	14.3	9.8
Morocco	48.9	51.8	45.9
Mozambique	114.9	122.9	106.5
Myanmar (Burma)	74.2	81.3	66.6
Namibia	65.1	68.8	61.4
Nauru	N/A	N/A	N/A
Nepal	71.2	71.3	71.0
Netherlands Antilles	12.2	13.0	11.4
Netherlands, the	5.0	5.7	4.3
New Caledonia	11.6	13.6	9.5
New Zealand	6.1	7.1	4.9
Nicaragua	38.7	44.1	33.0
Niger	111.2	112.6	109.7
Nigeria	68.2	72.1	64.1
North Korea, Dem. Rep.	24.3	25.1	23.5
Northern Mariana Islands	5.8	6.9	4.6
Norway	4.9	5.4	4.3
Oman	23.9	26.9	20.7
Pakistan	90.3	91.9	88.5
Palau	18.2	20.0	16.2
Panama	22.7	25.0	20.3
Papua New Guinea	54.1	52.9	55.3
Paraguay	35.3	38.7	31.8
Peru	37.1	41.7	32.4
Philippines	33.2	37.2	29.1
Poland	12.4	13.7	11.0
Portugal	6.6	7.3	5.8
Puerto Rico	9.7	10.8	8.5
Qatar	16.4	19.3	13.3
Reunion	6.7	7.2	6.2
Romania	17.4	19.7	15.1
Russia	22.7	24.4	20.9
Rwanda	112.4	119.7	104.9
Saint Helena	27.2	33.3	20.7
Saint Kitts and Nevis	16.9	19.1	14.6
Saint Lucia	16.2	17.5	14.7
Saint Pierre and Miquelon	7.7	9.1	6.0
Saint Vincent and the Grenadines	14.6	15.2	14.0

A6-4. Infant Mortality Rate (Infant Deaths per 1,000 Live Births), 2000 *(continued)*

	Both sexes	Male	Female
Samoa	29.2	33.2	25.1
San Marino	5.3	6.2	4.5
Sao Tome and Principe	51.3	54.2	48.3
Saudi Arabia	36.3	38.2	34.2
Senegal	58.4	65.6	51.0
Serbia	15.9	16.9	14.8
Seychelles	16.3	18.6	13.9
Sierra Leone	123.1	138.5	107.1
Singapore	3.8	4.1	3.4
Slovakia	9.2	10.3	8.1
Slovenia	5.2	5.7	4.8
Solomon Islands	22.1	25.3	18.7
Somalia	125.8	135.5	115.8
South Africa	52.0	56.3	47.5
South Korea, Rep.	7.3	7.7	7.0
Spain	6.3	7.1	5.5
Sri Lanka	15.9	17.8	14.0
Sudan	69.2	69.5	68.9
Suriname	25.6	30.0	21.0
Swaziland	100.4	108.8	91.7
Sweden	3.9	4.4	3.4
Switzerland	4.8	5.4	4.3
Syria	35.2	36.4	34.1
Taiwan	5.7	6.5	4.8
Tajikistan	117.4	132.9	101.2
Tanzania	93.6	104.8	82.0
Thailand	28.2	31.5	24.8
Togo	75.3	82.4	68.0
Tonga	37.3	N/A	N/A
Trinidad and Tobago	18.3	20.9	15.6
Tunisia	30.1	32.5	27.5
Turkey	33.3	36.6	29.9
Turkmenistan	73.3	76.9	69.5
Turks and Caicos Islands	20.5	23.3	17.6
Tuvalu	24.8	27.4	22.1
Uganda	88.5	97.2	79.5
Ukraine	21.7	23.2	20.1
United Arab Emirates	13.4	13.5	13.3
United Kingdom	5.7	6.3	5.0
United States	6.7	7.2	5.2
Uruguay	12.9	14.2	11.4
Uzbekistan	72.1	76.0	68.0
Vanuatu	57.9	62.9	52.6
Venezuela	25.5	28.9	21.9
Vietnam	33.7	34.1	33.2
Virgin Islands	9.6	10.8	8.4
Virgin Islands, British	21.4	24.4	18.2
Wallis and Futuna	N/A	N/A	N/A
West Bank	24.1	26.1	21.9
Yemen	67.4	72.8	61.8
Zambia	91.1	96.9	85.2
Zimbabwe	60.7	63.6	57.6

N/A Not Available

Source: U.S. Census International Database, 2000: Table 010. Infant Mortality Rates and Deaths, and Life Expectancy at Birth, by Sex; <http://www.census.gov/ipc/www/idbagg.html>. Underlying data from U.S. Bureau of the Census.

A6-5. Projected Infant Mortality Rate (Infant Deaths per 1,000 Live Births), by Continent, 2025 and 2050

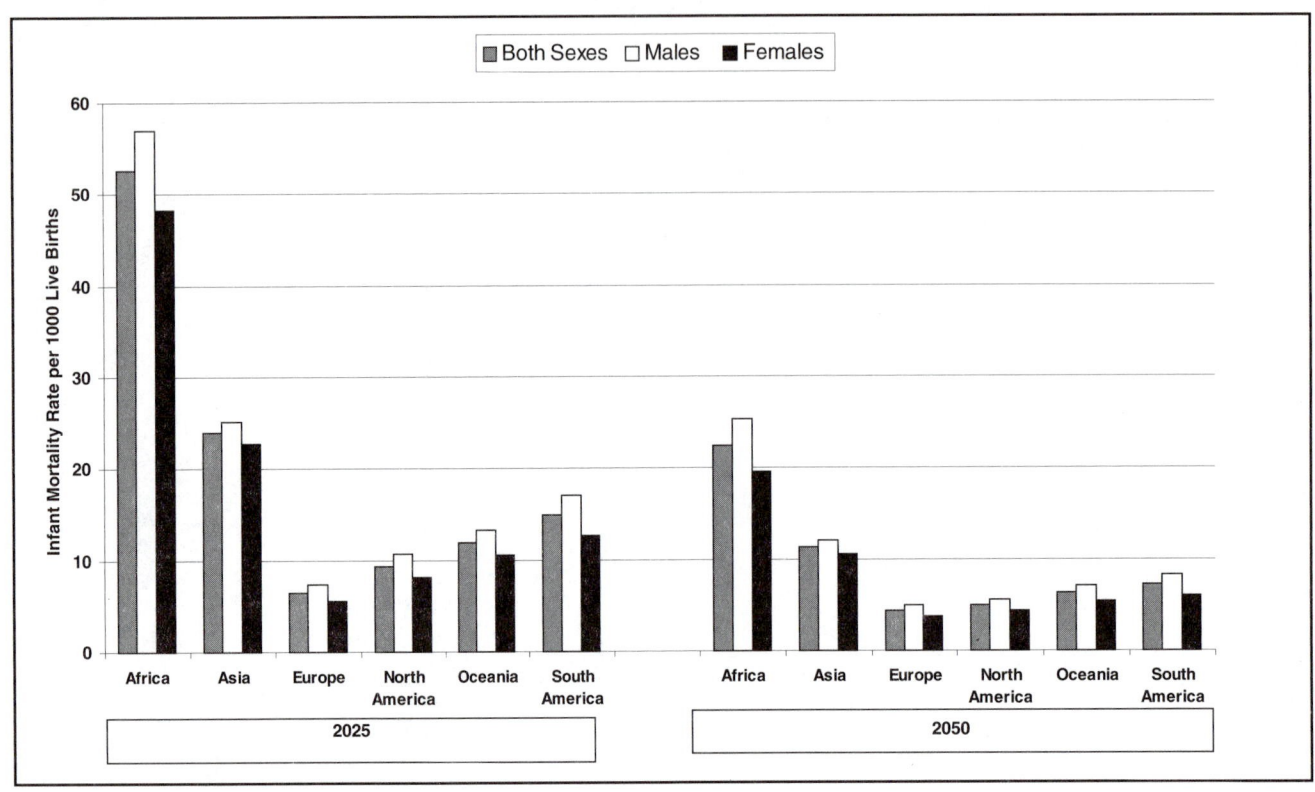

Projected Infant Mortality Rate (IMR), Infant Deaths per 1,000 Live Births			
	2025		
	Both sexes	Male	Female
Africa	52.6	57.0	48.2
Asia	24.0	25.2	22.7
Europe	6.5	7.4	5.6
North America	9.4	10.7	8.2
Oceania	11.9	13.2	10.5
South America	14.9	17.0	12.6
	2050		
	Both sexes	Male	Female
Africa	22.5	25.4	19.6
Asia	11.3	12.1	10.5
Europe	4.3	4.9	3.7
North America	4.9	5.6	4.3
Oceania	6.3	7.1	5.5
South America	7.2	8.3	6.0

Source: U.S. Census International Database, 2000; <http://www.census.gov/ipc/www/idbagg.html>. Underlying data from U.S. Bureau of the Census.

A6-6. Projected Infant Mortality Rate (Infant Deaths per 1,000 Live Births), 2025

	Both sexes	**Male**	**Female**
Afghanistan	93.5	94.9	92.2
Albania	16.6	18.2	14.8
Algeria	16.6	18.2	14.9
American Samoa	5.9	7.0	4.8
Andorra	3.9	4.3	3.6
Angola	141.0	152.5	128.9
Anguilla	10.6	13.7	7.4
Antigua and Barbuda	10.4	12.4	8.2
Argentina	8.7	9.6	7.7
Armenia	18.9	21.6	16.1
Aruba	4.3	4.9	3.7
Australia	3.8	4.1	3.4
Austria	3.5	3.7	3.3
Azerbaijan	38.1	40.5	35.5
Bahamas, the	13.2	14.1	12.2
Bahrain	9.3	10.8	7.7
Bangladesh	33.8	34.6	33.0
Barbados	6.6	7.6	5.6
Belarus	8.2	9.2	7.1
Belgium	3.6	4.0	3.2
Belize	11.3	13.0	9.4
Benin	55.8	59.0	52.4
Bermuda	5.4	6.3	4.5
Bhutan	62.3	60.2	64.4
Bolivia	30.2	32.8	27.5
Bosnia and Herzegovina	11.1	12.6	9.3
Botswana	53.8	56.0	51.4
Brazil	17.4	19.6	15.1
Brunei	7.3	8.9	5.5
Bulgaria	7.4	8.7	6.1
Burkina Faso	62.6	66.1	59.1
Burundi	44.3	48.3	40.3
Cambodia	34.9	38.8	30.7
Cameroon	40.7	44.0	37.4
Canada	3.8	4.2	3.5
Cape Verde	26.4	30.2	22.6
Cayman Islands	5.7	6.6	4.9
Central African Republic	64.2	68.7	59.6
Chad	58.4	65.4	51.0
Chile	5.5	6.0	4.9
China	10.6	11.8	9.5
Colombia	11.3	14.0	8.5
Comoros	39.4	45.3	33.3
Congo, Dem. Rep. (Zaire)	56.4	62.3	50.3
Congo, Rep.	55.6	60.2	50.9
Costa Rica	6.2	6.8	5.5
Côte d'Ivoire	53.8	59.0	48.4
Croatia	4.8	5.4	4.1
Cuba	5.1	5.7	4.5
Cyprus	5.0	5.9	4.0
Czech Republic	4.0	4.5	3.6
Denmark	3.8	4.1	3.5
Djibouti	60.6	66.9	54.1
Dominica	7.7	9.9	5.5
Dominican Republic	13.9	15.8	11.9
Ecuador	15.6	18.5	12.5
Egypt	26.2	27.6	24.7

A6-6. Projected Infant Mortality Rate (Infant Deaths per 1,000 Live Births), 2025 *(continued)*

	Both sexes	Male	Female
El Salvador	13.8	16.3	11.2
Equatorial Guinea	51.2	56.2	46.0
Eritrea	42.3	47.9	36.5
Estonia	7.4	8.9	5.8
Ethiopia	59.9	64.2	55.4
Faroe Islands	4.5	5.3	3.7
Fiji	7.6	8.5	6.6
Finland	3.2	3.6	2.8
France	3.6	4.0	3.1
French Guiana	7.2	7.9	6.6
French Polynesia	5.9	6.8	5.0
Gabon	56.3	63.1	49.3
Gambia, the	45.7	50.7	40.5
Gaza Strip	14.3	14.9	13.8
Georgia	15.5	18.0	13.0
Germany	3.6	4.0	3.2
Ghana	33.3	37.8	28.7
Gibraltar	4.0	4.4	3.5
Greece	4.3	4.7	3.8
Greenland	9.2	10.4	8.0
Grenada	8.8	9.0	8.6
Guadeloupe	5.7	6.4	4.8
Guam	4.6	4.9	4.2
Guatemala	22.1	24.9	19.2
Guernsey	3.8	4.2	3.3
Guinea	82.9	93.4	72.0
Guinea-Bissau	67.8	76.5	58.7
Guyana	24.1	26.3	21.7
Haiti	53.7	59.4	47.7
Honduras	18.4	19.9	16.9
Hong Kong, SAR (China)	4.2	4.2	4.1
Hungary	5.6	6.5	4.7
Iceland	3.1	3.4	2.8
India	29.8	30.3	29.3
Indonesia	17.9	20.7	15.0
Iran	12.7	13.7	11.7
Iraq	24.5	28.7	20.1
Ireland	4.0	4.4	3.5
Israel	5.0	5.5	4.4
Italy	4.1	4.6	3.7
Jamaica	7.1	7.7	6.4
Japan	3.3	3.5	3.0
Jersey	4.0	4.3	3.7
Jordan	8.8	10.4	7.1
Kazakhstan	31.4	37.1	25.4
Kenya	41.1	43.3	38.8
Kiribati	27.0	30.9	22.9
Kuwait	6.1	6.8	5.4
Kyrgyzstan	35.1	40.6	29.4
Laos	51.6	58.3	44.6
Latvia	8.6	10.3	6.9
Lebanon	12.4	14.0	10.6
Lesotho	54.9	58.6	51.1
Liberia	82.6	87.8	77.2
Libya	11.6	13.1	10.1
Liechtenstein	3.7	4.7	2.8
Lithuania	8.5	10.2	6.8
Luxembourg	3.7	3.9	3.5

A6-6. Projected Infant Mortality Rate (Infant Deaths per 1,000 Live Births), 2025 *(continued)*

	Both sexes	Male	Female
Macau SAR (China)	4.0	3.7	4.4
Macedonia, FYRO	6.6	7.3	5.9
Madagascar	47.1	53.4	40.7
Malawi	78.7	84.0	73.3
Malaysia	9.6	11.1	7.9
Maldives	29.0	28.6	29.5
Mali	78.5	84.2	72.5
Malta	4.0	4.3	3.8
Man, Isle of	4.4	5.0	3.7
Marshall Islands	18.6	20.2	17.0
Martinique	4.9	3.9	5.8
Mauritania	44.4	47.8	40.9
Mauritius	8.4	9.9	6.8
Mayotte	34.1	38.2	29.9
Mexico	11.4	13.3	9.5
Moldova	18.2	21.8	14.5
Monaco	4.1	4.7	3.5
Mongolia	25.4	27.1	23.6
Montserrat	4.9	5.6	4.2
Morocco	19.8	22.4	17.1
Mozambique	95.9	100.0	91.8
Myanmar (Burma)	39.2	42.8	35.3
Namibia	55.2	56.8	53.6
Nauru	7.0	8.7	5.2
Nepal	37.8	36.1	39.6
Netherlands, the	3.5	3.8	3.1
Netherlands Antilles	6.0	6.6	5.5
New Caledonia	5.4	5.9	4.7
New Zealand	4.4	5.0	3.8
Nicaragua	14.7	16.6	12.6
Niger	89.8	92.3	87.2
Nigeria	45.7	48.9	42.4
North Korea, Dem. Rep.	11.9	12.1	11.7
Northern Mariana Islands	4.1	4.8	3.4
Norway	3.3	3.6	2.9
Oman	10.2	11.8	8.6
Pakistan	40.1	40.6	39.5
Palau	8.8	10.1	7.4
Panama	9.8	11.1	8.5
Papua New Guinea	26.6	29.6	23.6
Paraguay	12.6	15.3	9.8
Peru	17.7	20.5	14.8
Philippines	13.8	16.1	11.3
Poland	5.7	6.5	4.8
Portugal	4.1	4.6	3.7
Puerto Rico	5.9	6.8	5.0
Qatar	9.9	11.7	8.0
Reunion	5.4	6.0	4.7
Romania	9.7	11.1	8.1
Russia	11.7	13.6	9.7
Rwanda	76.0	82.1	69.7
Saint Helena	9.4	11.3	7.4
Saint Kitts and Nevis	8.5	9.7	7.2
Saint Lucia	8.0	8.9	7.0
Saint Pierre and Miquelon	5.0	5.7	4.3
Saint Vincent and the Grenadines	8.7	9.5	7.8
Samoa	14.3	17.1	11.4
San Marino	4.2	4.6	3.8

A6-6. Projected Infant Mortality Rate (Infant Deaths per 1,000 Live Births), 2025 *(continued)*

	Both sexes	Male	Female
Sao Tome and Principe	22.2	23.6	20.7
Saudi Arabia	21.6	23.4	19.7
Senegal	29.1	33.0	25.2
Seychelles	9.2	11.6	6.7
Sierra Leone	95.8	112.1	79.0
Singapore	3.2	3.5	2.9
Slovakia	5.4	6.1	4.7
Slovenia	3.7	4.4	2.9
Solomon Islands	11.2	12.9	9.4
Somalia	81.0	88.8	73.0
South Africa	44.5	45.7	43.2
South Korea, Rep.	5.5	5.8	5.2
Spain	3.7	4.1	3.4
Sri Lanka	8.4	9.4	7.4
Sudan	36.5	37.8	35.1
Suriname	11.0	13.1	8.8
Swaziland	76.9	85.0	68.6
Sweden	3.1	3.4	2.7
Switzerland	3.5	3.7	3.3
Syria	15.2	15.6	14.7
Taiwan	4.7	5.0	4.4
Tajikistan	49.3	56.6	41.6
Tanzania	42.6	46.7	38.3
Thailand	13.6	15.1	12.0
Togo	40.5	46.1	34.7
Tonga	7.6	8.5	6.6
Trinidad and Tobago	11.7	13.2	10.2
Tunisia	11.9	13.8	9.9
Turkey	19.8	22.2	17.3
Turkmenistan	44.7	51.0	38.0
Turks and Caicos Islands	8.5	9.8	7.1
Tuvalu	11.0	12.8	9.2
Uganda	51.8	57.0	46.5
Ukraine	11.5	13.2	9.8
United Arab Emirates	8.1	9.5	6.7
United Kingdom	4.0	4.4	3.5
United States	5.0	5.5	4.5
Uruguay	7.5	8.5	6.4
Uzbekistan	41.7	48.1	35.0
Vanuatu	31.4	33.3	29.3
Venezuela	12.0	13.9	9.9
Vietnam	14.2	14.8	13.5
Virgin Islands	5.8	6.5	4.9
Virgin Islands, British	8.8	10.3	7.3
West Bank	12.1	13.5	10.7
Yemen	33.7	36.8	30.4
Zambia	54.6	59.0	50.1
Zimbabwe	49.1	50.9	47.2

Source: U.S. Census International Database, 2000; <http://www.census.gov/ipc/www/idbsprd.html>. Underlying data from U.S. Bureau of the Census.

A6-7. Projected Infant Mortality Rate (Infant Deaths per 1,000 Live Births), 2050

	Both sexes	Male	Female
Afghanistan	48.6	49.2	48.0
Albania	7.7	8.6	6.7
Algeria	7.7	8.6	6.8
American Samoa	4.1	4.7	3.5
Andorra	3.7	4.1	3.4
Angola	85.9	95.3	76.0
Anguilla	5.7	7.0	4.4
Antigua and Barbuda	5.8	6.7	4.7
Argentina	5.2	5.8	4.6
Armenia	8.7	10.3	7.1
Aruba	3.4	3.8	3.0
Australia	3.2	3.5	2.9
Austria	3.1	3.3	2.8
Azerbaijan	16.2	17.9	14.4
Bahamas, The	5.2	5.8	4.6
Bahrain	5.4	6.2	4.6
Bangladesh	14.6	15.3	13.9
Barbados	4.4	5.0	3.8
Belarus	5.2	6.0	4.4
Belgium	3.1	3.4	2.8
Belize	6.1	6.9	5.1
Benin	24.3	26.4	22.2
Bermuda	3.8	4.4	3.4
Bhutan	28.9	28.2	29.6
Bolivia	14.4	16.1	12.8
Bosnia and Herzegovina	6.1	7.0	5.2
Botswana	11.8	13.1	10.4
Brazil	7.5	8.7	6.4
Brunei	4.6	5.4	3.8
Bulgaria	4.7	5.4	3.9
Burkina Faso	24.1	26.1	22.2
Burundi	17.4	19.6	15.3
Cambodia	14.9	17.2	12.5
Cameroon	15.8	17.8	13.7
Canada	3.2	3.5	2.9
Cape Verde	12.2	14.3	10.1
Cayman Islands	4.0	4.6	3.5
Central African Republic	26.4	28.8	23.8
Chad	29.6	34.5	24.6
Chile	3.9	4.3	3.5
China	5.8	6.3	5.3
Colombia	6.2	7.6	4.7
Comoros	16.4	19.4	13.3
Congo, Dem. Rep. (Zaire)	24.0	27.4	20.5
Congo, Rep.	21.6	24.5	18.6
Costa Rica	4.2	4.6	3.7
Côte d'Ivoire	19.5	22.4	16.5
Croatia	3.6	4.1	3.2
Cuba	3.9	4.3	3.5
Cyprus	3.7	4.3	3.1
Czech Republic	3.3	3.7	3.0
Denmark	3.2	3.5	3.0
Djibouti	29.7	34.0	25.3
Dominica	4.7	5.7	3.7
Dominican Republic	6.7	7.6	5.7
Ecuador	7.8	9.2	6.3
Egypt	11.2	12.2	10.2
El Salvador	7.3	8.8	5.8

A6-7. Projected Infant Mortality Rate (Infant Deaths per 1,000 Live Births), 2050 *(continued)*

	Both sexes	Male	Female
Equatorial Guinea	23.6	26.9	20.2
Eritrea	20.3	23.8	16.6
Estonia	4.9	5.8	3.9
Ethiopia	22.3	24.8	19.6
Faroe Islands	3.5	4.0	3.0
Fiji	4.8	5.4	4.2
Finland	3.0	3.3	2.6
France	3.1	3.4	2.8
French Guiana	4.7	5.1	4.2
French Polynesia	4.2	4.7	3.6
Gabon	22.1	26.0	18.1
Gambia, The	22.6	25.8	19.2
Gaza Strip	8.9	9.3	8.5
Georgia	7.8	9.1	6.4
Germany	3.1	3.4	2.8
Ghana	13.9	16.2	11.4
Gibraltar	3.3	3.6	3.0
Greece	3.4	3.7	3.1
Greenland	5.5	6.2	4.7
Grenada	5.3	5.7	4.9
Guadeloupe	4.0	4.5	3.5
Guam	3.6	3.9	3.3
Guatemala	10.5	12.1	8.8
Guernsey	3.2	3.5	2.9
Guinea	43.6	51.3	35.7
Guinea-Bissau	34.1	40.2	27.9
Guyana	8.8	10.0	7.7
Haiti	23.0	26.4	19.5
Honduras	7.3	8.1	6.4
Hong Kong, SAR (China)	3.4	3.6	3.2
Hungary	4.1	4.6	3.5
Iceland	2.9	3.1	2.6
India	13.0	13.6	12.4
Indonesia	8.5	9.8	7.2
Iran	6.5	7.2	5.9
Iraq	10.5	12.6	8.3
Ireland	3.3	3.6	2.9
Israel	3.7	4.1	3.3
Italy	3.4	3.7	3.0
Jamaica	4.5	5.0	4.1
Japan	3.0	3.2	2.7
Jersey	3.3	3.6	3.0
Jordan	5.0	5.8	4.2
Kazakhstan	13.6	16.5	10.4
Kenya	13.3	14.6	11.9
Kiribati	12.5	14.7	10.2
Kuwait	4.1	4.6	3.7
Kyrgyzstan	14.7	17.5	11.8
Laos	24.2	27.9	20.3
Latvia	5.4	6.5	4.3
Lebanon	6.4	7.3	5.5
Lesotho	17.4	19.6	15.2
Liberia	44.1	47.7	40.5
Libya	6.0	6.7	5.2
Liechtenstein	3.2	3.8	2.6
Lithuania	5.4	6.4	4.2
Luxembourg	3.2	3.4	2.9
Macau SAR (China)	3.8	3.6	4.1

A6-7. Projected Infant Mortality Rate (Infant Deaths per 1,000 Live Births), 2050 *(continued)*

	Both sexes	Male	Female
Macedonia, FYRO	4.3	4.8	3.9
Madagascar	22.4	26.2	18.5
Malawi	29.6	33.6	25.6
Malaysia	5.5	6.3	4.6
Maldives	12.3	12.5	12.1
Mali	41.5	45.8	37.1
Malta	3.3	3.6	3.1
Man, Isle of	3.5	3.9	3.0
Marshall Islands	8.8	9.8	7.8
Martinique	3.6	3.4	3.9
Mauritania	21.2	24.0	18.3
Mauritius	5.0	5.8	4.2
Mayotte	15.0	17.3	12.7
Mexico	6.2	7.1	5.2
Moldova	8.7	10.5	6.8
Monaco	3.4	3.8	2.9
Mongolia	13.0	13.5	12.5
Montserrat	3.7	4.1	3.2
Morocco	8.8	10.1	7.4
Mozambique	36.5	39.4	33.5
Myanmar (Burma)	16.8	18.9	14.6
Namibia	13.9	14.9	12.8
Nauru	4.8	5.8	3.8
Nepal	16.9	16.4	17.5
Netherlands	3.0	3.3	2.8
Netherlands Antilles	4.1	4.5	3.7
New Caledonia	3.9	4.4	3.5
New Zealand	3.5	3.9	3.1
Nicaragua	7.3	8.3	6.2
Niger	54.9	56.3	53.4
Nigeria	17.6	19.9	15.3
North Korea, Dem. Rep.	7.7	7.6	7.8
Northern Mariana Islands	3.4	3.8	2.9
Norway	3.0	3.3	2.7
Oman	5.7	6.5	4.9
Pakistan	17.1	18.0	16.2
Palau	5.4	6.1	4.5
Panama	5.7	6.4	4.9
Papua New Guinea	11.8	13.4	10.1
Paraguay	6.4	7.6	5.1
Peru	8.5	9.8	7.1
Philippines	7.2	8.4	5.9
Poland	4.1	4.6	3.5
Portugal	3.4	3.7	3.0
Puerto Rico	4.2	4.8	3.6
Qatar	5.6	6.5	4.7
Reunion	3.9	4.4	3.5
Romania	5.6	6.4	4.7
Russia	6.6	7.9	5.3
Rwanda	28.8	32.6	24.8
Saint Helena	5.3	6.2	4.3
Saint Kitts and Nevis	5.2	5.9	4.4
Saint Lucia	5.0	5.5	4.4
Saint Pierre and Miquelon	3.7	4.1	3.3
Saint Vincent and the Grenadines	5.2	5.7	4.7
Samoa	7.2	8.5	5.9
San Marino	3.4	3.7	3.1
Sao Tome and Principe	10.1	11.1	9.2

A6-7. Projected Infant Mortality Rate (Infant Deaths per 1,000 Live Births), 2050 *(continued)*

	Both sexes	Male	Female
Saudi Arabia	9.4	10.5	8.3
Senegal	13.2	15.7	10.5
Seychelles	5.5	6.6	4.3
Sierra Leone	51.6	64.0	38.8
Singapore	2.9	3.2	2.7
Slovakia	3.9	4.4	3.4
Slovenia	3.2	3.7	2.7
Solomon Islands	6.1	6.9	5.2
Somalia	43.8	49.4	38.0
South Africa	9.2	9.5	8.8
South Korea, Rep.	4.5	4.6	4.4
Spain	3.2	3.5	2.9
Sri Lanka	5.1	5.8	4.4
Sudan	16.9	18.2	15.5
Suriname	6.0	7.0	4.9
Swaziland	23.2	27.9	18.2
Sweden	2.9	3.1	2.6
Switzerland	3.1	3.3	2.8
Syria	7.5	8.0	7.0
Taiwan	3.6	3.9	3.3
Tajikistan	21.2	25.1	17.1
Tanzania	15.1	17.4	12.6
Thailand	6.7	7.5	5.8
Togo	14.8	17.7	11.8
Tonga	4.8	5.4	4.2
Trinidad and Tobago	6.4	7.2	5.5
Tunisia	6.1	7.0	5.1
Turkey	8.9	10.1	7.7
Turkmenistan	18.8	22.3	15.2
Turks and Caicos Islands	5.0	5.7	4.3
Tuvalu	6.0	6.9	5.0
Uganda	20.5	23.7	17.3
Ukraine	6.5	7.6	5.3
United Arab Emirates	4.9	5.6	4.2
United Kingdom	3.3	3.6	3.0
United States	3.3	3.6	3.0
Uruguay	4.7	5.3	4.1
Uzbekistan	17.6	20.9	14.1
Vanuatu	14.4	15.8	13.0
Venezuela	6.5	7.5	5.5
Vietnam	7.2	7.8	6.7
Virgin Islands	4.1	4.6	3.5
Virgin Islands, British	5.1	5.8	4.3
West Bank	7.6	8.6	6.5
Yemen	15.0	16.8	13.1
Zambia	18.5	21.1	15.8
Zimbabwe	11.4	12.4	10.3

Source: U.S. Census International Database, 2000; <http://www.census.gov/ipc/www/idbsprd.html>. Underlying data from U.S. Bureau of the Census.

A7. UNDER-5 MORTALITY RATE

A7-1. Under-5 Mortality Values (Probability of Dying under Age 5 per 1,000 Live Births) and Rankings, 1960

Rank		Rate per 1,000
1	Mali	400
2	Sierra Leone	385
3	Gambia	375
4	Malawi	365
5	Madagascar	364
6	Afghanistan	360
7	Angola	345
8	Yemen	340
9	Guinea	337
10	Guinea-Bissau	336
11	Mozambique	331
12	Chad	325
13	Bhutan	324
14	Mauritania	321
15	Niger	320
16	Burkina Faso	318
17	Benin	310
18	Senegal	303
19	Côte d'Ivoire	300
19	Oman	300
20	Somalia	294
20	Eritrea	294
20	Ethiopia	294
20	Central African Republic	294
21	Sudan	292
21	Saudi Arabia	292
22	Nepal	290
23	Liberia	288
24	Gabon	287
25	Congo, Dem. Rep. (Zaire)	286
26	Libya	269
27	Togo	264
27	Cameroon	264
28	Haiti	260
29	Egypt	258
30	Burundi	255
31	Bolivia	252
32	Tanzania	249
33	Papua New Guinea	248
34	Bangladesh	247
35	Tunisia	244
36	Algeria	243
37	United Arab Emirates	240
38	Myanmar (Burma)	237
39	India	236
39	Peru	236
40	Laos	233
40	Iran	233
42	Pakistan	221
41	Zambia	220
41	Congo, Rep.	220
42	Vietnam	219
43	Uganda	218
44	Cambodia	217
44	Turkey	217
45	Indonesia	216

A7-1. Under-5 Mortality Values (Probability of Dying under Age 5 per 1,000 Live Births) and Rankings, 1960 *(continued)*

Rank		Rate per 1,000
46	Morocco	215
47	Ghana	213
48	El Salvador	210
49	Nicaragua	209
49	China	209
50	Namibia	206
51	Guatemala	205
52	Nigeria	204
52	Lesotho	204
53	Honduras	203
54	Kenya	202
55	Syria	201
56	Rwanda	191
57	Mongolia	185
58	Zimbabwe	181
58	Brazil	181
59	Ecuador	180
60	Macedonia, FYRO	177
61	Iraq	171
62	Botswana	170
63	Bosnia and Herzegovina	155
64	Dominican Republic	152
65	Albania	151
66	Jordan	149
67	Mexico	148
68	Thailand	146
69	Chile	138
70	Colombia	132
71	Sri Lanka	130
72	Kuwait	128
73	South Africa	126
74	South Korea, Rep. of	124
75	North Korea, Dem. Rep.	120
75	Yugoslavia	120
76	Costa Rica	112
76	Portugal	112
77	Malaysia	105
78	Panama	104
79	Philippines	102
80	Croatia	98
81	Paraguay	90
82	Lebanon	85
83	Mauritius	84
84	Romania	82
85	Jamaica	76
86	Trinidad and Tobago	73
87	Venezuela	70
87	Bulgaria	70
87	Poland	70
88	Argentina	68
89	Greece	64
90	Hungary	57
90	Spain	57
91	Hong Kong, SAR (China)	52
92	Cuba	50
92	Italy	50
93	Uruguay	47
94	Slovenia	45
95	Austria	43

A7-1. Under-5 Mortality Values (Probability of Dying under Age 5 per 1,000 Live Births) and Rankings, 1960 *(continued)*

Rank		Rate per 1,000
96	Germany	40
96	Japan	40
96	Singapore	40
97	Israel	39
98	Ireland	36
99	Belgium	35
100	France	34
101	Canada	33
102	United States	30
103	Finland	28
104	United Kingdom	27
104	Switzerland	27
105	New Zealand	26
106	Denmark	25
107	Australia	24
108	Norway	23
109	Netherlands, the	22
110	Sweden	20

Source: State of the World's Children 1997 < http://www.unicef.org/sowc97/>. Underlying data from United Nations Children's Fund (UNICEF) .

A7-2. Under-5 Mortality Values (Probability of Dying under Age 5 per 1,000 Live Births) and Rankings, 1980

Rank		Rate per 1,000
1	Cambodia	330
2	Niger	320
3	Mali	310
4	Sierra Leone	301
5	Guinea-Bissau	290
5	Malawi	290
6	Afghanistan	280
7	Gambia, the	278
8	Guinea	276
9	Mozambique	269
10	Angola	261
11	Eritrea	260
11	Ethiopia	260
12	Chad	254
13	Mauritania	249
13	Bhutan	249
14	Somalia	246
14	Burkina Faso	246
15	Liberia	235
16	Rwanda	222
17	Senegal	221
18	Madagascar	216
19	Bangladesh	211
20	Yemen	210
21	Congo, Dem. Rep. (Zaire)	204
22	Central African Republic	202
22	Tanzania	202
23	Sudan	200

A7-2. Under-5 Mortality Values (Probability of Dying under Age 5 per 1,000 Live Births) and Rankings, 1980 *(continued)*

Rank		Rate per 1,000
24	Nigeria	196
25	Haiti	195
26	Gabon	194
27	Burundi	193
28	Laos	190
29	Uganda	181
30	Nepal	180
30	Egypt	180
31	India	177
32	Benin	176
33	Togo	175
34	Lesotho	173
34	Cameroon	173
35	Côte d'Ivoire	170
35	Bolivia	170
36	Zambia	160
37	Ghana	155
38	Pakistan	151
39	Libya	150
40	Myanmar	146
41	Algeria	145
41	Morocco	145
42	Nicaragua	143
43	Turkey	141
44	Guatemala	136
45	Peru	130
46	Indonesia	128
47	Iran	126
48	Congo, Rep.	125
48	Zimbabwe	125
49	El Salvador	120
50	Namibia	114
51	Kenya	112
51	Mongolia	112
52	Vietnam	105
53	Tunisia	102
54	Ecuador	101
55	Honduras	100
56	Papua New Guinea	95
56	Oman	95
57	Botswana	94
57	Dominican Republic	94
58	Brazil	93
59	South Africa	91
60	Saudi Arabia	90
61	Mexico	87
62	Iraq	83
63	Syria	73
64	Philippines	70
65	Macedonia, FYRO	69
66	Jordan	66
67	China	65
68	United Arab Emirates	64
69	Paraguay	61
69	Thailand	61
70	Colombia	59
71	Albania	57

A7-2. Under-5 Mortality Values (Probability of Dying under Age 5 per 1,000 Live Births) and Rankings, 1980 *(continued)*

Rank		Rate per 1,000
72	Sri Lanka	52
73	Yugoslavia	44
74	North Korea, Dem. Rep.	43
75	Venezuela	42
75	Mauritius	42
75	Uruguay	42
75	Malaysia	42
76	Argentina	41
77	Lebanon	40
77	Trinidad and Tobago	40
78	Jamaica	39
79	Bosnia and Herzegovina	38
80	Romania	36
81	Chile	35
81	Kuwait	35
82	Panama	31
82	Portugal	31
83	Costa Rica	29
84	Hungary	26
84	Cuba	26
85	Bulgaria	25
86	Poland	24
87	Croatia	23
87	Greece	23
88	Israel	19
89	South Korea, Rep.	18
89	Slovenia	18
90	Italy	17
90	Austria	17
91	Spain	16
91	New Zealand	16
91	Germany	16
92	United States	15
92	Belgium	15
93	United Kingdom	14
93	Ireland	14
94	France	13
94	Australia	13
94	Canada	13
94	Hong Kong, SAR (China)	13
94	Singapore	13
95	Netherlands, the	11
95	Norway	11
95	Switzerland	11
95	Japan	11
96	Denmark	10
97	Finland	9
97	Sweden	9

Source: State of the World's Children 1996 <http://www.unicef.org/sowc96/swc96t9x.htm>. Underlying data from United Nations Children's Fund (UNICEF).

A7-3. Under-5 Mortality Values (Probability of Dying under Age 5 per 1,000 Live Births) and Rankings, 1990

Rank		Rate per 1,000
1	Sierra Leone	323
2	Niger	320
3	Angola	297
4	Afghanistan	260
5	Mali	254
6	Guinea-Bissau	246
7	Guinea	237
8	Liberia	235
9	Mozambique	235
10	Malawi	230
11	Somalia	215
12	Congo, Dem. Rep. (Zaire)	207
13	Equatorial Guinea	206
14	Chad	198
15	Burkina Faso	196
16	Cambodia	193
17	Zambia	192
18	Nigeria	190
18	Ethiopia	190
20	Benin	185
21	Mauritania	183
22	Burundi	180
22	Central African Republic	177
24	Madagascar	168
25	Bhutan	166
26	Uganda	165
27	Djibouti	164
28	Gabon	164
28	Laos	163
30	Rwanda	161
30	Eritrea	160
32	Togo	152
33	Côte d'Ivoire	150
33	Mongolia	150
35	Tanzania	150
36	Lesotho	148
37	Haiti	148
38	Senegal	147
38	Yemen	142
40	Bangladesh	140
41	Cameroon	139
41	Pakistan	138
43	Nepal	138
44	India	131
45	Myanmar (Burma)	130
45	Ghana	127
47	Gambia	127
48	Sudan	125
49	Bolivia	122
49	Comoros	120
51	Swaziland	115
52	Maldives	115
53	Papua New Guinea	112
53	Congo, Rep.	110
55	Egypt	106
56	Kenya	97
57	Marshall Islands	92

A7-3. Under-5 Mortality Values (Probability of Dying under Age 5 per 1,000 Live Births) and Rankings, 1990 *(continued)*

Rank		Rate per 1,000
58	Indonesia	91
59	Guyana	90
60	Sao Tome and Principe	90
61	Kiribati	88
62	Namibia	84
62	Morocco	83
62	Kyrgyzstan	83
65	South Africa	81
66	Guatemala	81
67	Zimbabwe	80
68	Tajikistan	78
69	Turkmenistan	76
70	Peru	75
71	Cape Verde	73
71	Vanuatu	70
73	Turkey	70
74	Nicaragua	66
75	Philippines	66
76	Dominican Republic	65
77	Botswana	62
77	Honduras	61
79	Brazil	60
80	Iran	59
81	Uzbekistan	58
81	Tuvalu	56
83	Vietnam	55
83	El Salvador	54
85	Tunisia	52
85	Iraq	50
85	Ecuador	50
88	Belize	49
89	Kazakhstan	48
90	Algeria	48
90	China	47
90	Mexico	46
93	Saudi Arabia	45
94	Azerbaijan	44
94	Saint Kitts and Nevis	44
94	Suriname	44
97	Syria	44
97	Samoa	42
97	Libya	42
100	Albania	41
100	Thailand	41
102	Macedonia, FYRO	41
102	Lebanon	40
104	Colombia	40
104	Jordan	38
104	Moldova	37
104	Paraguay	37
104	Grenada	37
109	Solomon Islands	36
110	Qatar	36
110	North Korea, Dem. Rep.	35
110	Palau	34
113	Cook Islands	32
113	Romania	32

A7-3. Under-5 Mortality Values (Probability of Dying under Age 5 per 1,000 Live Births) and Rankings, 1990 *(continued)*

Rank		Rate per 1,000
115	Armenia	31
115	Micronesia	31
117	Fiji	31
117	Yugoslavia	30
117	Oman	30
120	Georgia	29
120	Bahamas, the	29
120	Argentina	28
120	Venezuela	27
120	Tonga	27
120	Russia	26
126	Saint Vincent and Grenadines	26
126	Mauritius	25
126	Saint Lucia	24
126	Uruguay	24
130	Trinidad and Tobago	24
130	Bahrain	23
130	Dominica	23
133	Sri Lanka	23
133	Estonia	22
133	Ukraine	22
133	Bosnia and Herzegovina	22
137	Lithuania	21
137	Panama	21
137	Seychelles	21
140	Malaysia	21
140	Latvia	20
140	Chile	20
140	Belarus	19
144	Poland	19
145	Bulgaria	18
146	Costa Rica	16
147	Kuwait	16
148	Hungary	16
149	Jamaica	16
149	Barbados	15
149	Slovakia	15
149	Portugal	15
153	United Arab Emirates	14
153	Malta	14
153	Croatia	13
156	Cuba	13
156	Cyprus	12
156	Israel	12
156	Brunei	11
160	Greece	11
160	Czech Republic	11
162	New Zealand	11
162	United States	10
162	Italy	10
165	San Marino	10
165	Australia	10
165	Ireland	9
165	Belgium	9
165	Canada	9
165	Spain	9
165	United Kingdom	9

A7-3. Under-5 Mortality Values (Probability of Dying under Age 5 per 1,000 Live Births) and Rankings, 1990 *(continued)*

Rank		Rate per 1,000
165	Austria	9
165	Denmark	9
165	France	9
175	Germany	9
175	South Korea, Rep.	9
175	Luxembourg	9
175	Slovenia	9
175	Norway	9
175	Netherlands, the	8
175	Singapore	8
175	Switzerland	8
175	Finland	7
175	Japan	6
175	Sweden	6
175	Iceland	5
175	Nauru	N/A
175	Antigua and Barbuda	N/A
189	Liechtenstein	N/A
189	Andorra	N/A
189	Monaco	N/A

N/A Not Available

Source: State of the World's Children 2000, Table 8 <http://www.unicef.org/sowc00/>. Underlying data from United Nations Children's Fund (UNICEF).

A7-4. Under-5 Mortality Values (Probability of Dying under Age 5 per 1,000 Live Births) and Rankings, 1998

Rank		Rate per 1,000
1	Sierra Leone	316
2	Angola	292
3	Niger	280
4	Afghanistan	257
5	Mali	237
6	Liberia	235
7	Malawi	213
8	Somalia	211
9	Congo, Dem. Rep. (Zaire)	207
10	Mozambique	206
11	Guinea-Bissau	205
12	Zambia	202
13	Chad	198
14	Guinea	197
15	Nigeria	187
16	Mauritania	183
17	Burundi	176
18	Central African Republic	173
18	Ethiopia	173
20	Equatorial Guinea	171
21	Rwanda	170
22	Benin	165
22	Burkina Faso	165
24	Cambodia	163
25	Madagascar	157

A7-4. Under-5 Mortality Values (Probability of Dying under Age 5 per 1,000 Live Births) and Rankings, 1998 *(continued)*

Rank		Rate per 1,000
26	Djibouti	156
27	Cameroon	153
28	Côte d'Ivoire	150
28	Mongolia	150
30	Gabon	144
30	Togo	144
32	Tanzania	142
33	Lesotho	136
33	Pakistan	136
35	Uganda	134
36	Haiti	130
37	Iraq	125
38	Senegal	121
38	Yemen	121
40	Kenya	117
41	Bhutan	116
41	Laos	116
43	Sudan	115
44	Myanmar	113
45	Eritrea	112
45	Papua New Guinea	112
47	Congo	108
48	Bangladesh	106
49	Ghana	105
49	India	105
51	Nepal	100
52	Marshall Islands	92
53	Comoros	90
53	Swaziland	90
55	Zimbabwe	89
56	Maldives	87
57	Bolivia	85
58	South Africa	83
59	Gambia	82
60	Guyana	79
61	Sao Tome and Principe	77
62	Kiribati	74
62	Namibia	74
62	Tajikistan	74
65	Cape Verde	73
66	Turkmenistan	72
67	Morocco	70
68	Egypt	69
69	Kyrgyzstan	66
70	Uzbekistan	58
71	Indonesia	56
71	Tuvalu	56
73	Peru	54
74	Guatemala	52
75	Dominican Republic	51
76	Vanuatu	49
77	Botswana	48
77	Nicaragua	48
79	China	47
80	Azerbaijan	46
81	Honduras	44
81	Philippines	44

A7-4. Under-5 Mortality Values (Probability of Dying under Age 5 per 1,000 Live Births) and Rankings, 1998 *(continued)*

Rank		Rate per 1,000
83	Belize	43
83	Kazakhstan	43
85	Brazil	42
85	Turkey	42
85	Viet Nam	42
88	Algeria	40
89	Ecuador	39
90	Albania	37
90	Saint Kitts and Nevis	37
90	Thailand	37
93	Jordan	36
94	Lebanon	35
94	Moldova	35
94	Suriname	35
97	El Salvador	34
97	Mexico	34
97	Palau	34
100	Iran	33
100	Paraguay	33
102	Syria	32
102	Tunisia	32
104	Armenia	30
104	Colombia	30
104	Cook Islands	30
107	North Korea, Dem. Rep.	104
104	Nauru	30
109	Grenada	28
110	Belarus	27
110	Samoa	27
110	Macedonia, FYRO	27
113	Saudi Arabia	26
113	Solomon Islands	26
115	Russia	25
115	Venezuela	25
117	Libya	24
117	Micronesia	24
117	Romania	24
120	Fiji	23
120	Georgia	23
120	Lithuania	23
120	Mauritius	23
120	Saint Vincent and the Grenadines	23
120	Tonga	23
126	Argentina	22
126	Estonia	22
126	Latvia	22
126	Ukraine	22
130	Bahamas, the	21
130	Saint Lucia	21
130	Yugoslavia	21
133	Antigua and Barbuda	20
133	Bahrain	20
133	Dominica	20
133	Panama	20
137	Bosnia and Herzegovina	19
137	Sri Lanka	19
137	Uruguay	19

A7-4. Under-5 Mortality Values (Probability of Dying under Age 5 per 1,000 Live Births) and Rankings, 1998 *(continued)*

Rank		Rate per 1,000
140	Oman	18
140	Qatar	18
140	Seychelles	18
140	Trinidad and Tobago	18
144	Bulgaria	17
145	Costa Rica	16
146	Barbados	15
147	Kuwait	13
148	Chile	12
149	Hungary	11
149	Jamaica	11
149	Liechtenstein	11
149	Poland	11
153	Malaysia	10
153	Slovakia	10
153	United Arab Emirates	10
156	Brunei	9
156	Crotia	9
156	Cyprus	9
156	Portugal	9
160	Cuba	8
160	United States	8
162	Greece	7
162	Ireland	7
162	Malta	7
165	Andorra	6
165	Belgium	6
165	Canada	6
165	Czech Republic	6
165	Israel	6
165	Italy	6
165	New Zealand	6
165	San Marino	6
165	Spain	6
165	United Kingdom	6
175	Australia	5
175	Austria	5
175	Denmark	5
175	Finland	5
175	France	5
175	Germany	5
175	Iceland	5
175	South Korea, Rep. of	5
175	Luxembourg	5
175	Monaco	5
175	Netherlands, the	5
175	Singapore	5
175	Slovenia	5
175	Switzerland	5
189	Japan	4
189	Norway	4
189	Sweden	4

Source: State of the World's Children 2000 <http://www.unicef.org/sowc00/>. Underlying data from United Nations Children's Fund (UNICEF) .

A8. GENDER DIFFERENCE IN MORTALITY

A8-1. Under-5 Mortality (per 1,000 Live Births), Male and Female, by Regions and Sub-regions, 1998

Sub-region	Under-5 mortality (per 1,000 live births) Male	Under-5 mortality (per 1,000 live births) Female
Africa	**146**	**133**
Eastern Africa	169	154
Middle Africa	158	139
Northern Africa	73	67
Southern Africa	102	82
Western Africa	162	149
Asia	**71**	**77**
Eastern Asia	39	50
South Central Asia	91	101
South Eastern Asia	N/A	N/A
Western Asia	69	61
Europe	**16**	**12**
Eastern Europe	25	18
Northern Europe	10	8
Southern Europe	13	11
Western Europe	8	6
Latin America and Caribbean	**49**	**39**
Caribbean	57	48
Central America	45	38
South America	50	39
Northern America	**9**	**7**
Oceania	**31**	**32**
Australia and New Zealand	8	6
Melanesia	68	73
Micronesia	47	40
Polynesia	20	21
Countries with Economies in Transition of the Former USSR	**N/A**	**N/A**

N/A   Not Available

Source: The State of World Population 1999; <http://www.unfpa.org/swp/1999/Swp99_action.cfm>. Underlying data from: United Nations (UN).

A8-2. Under-5 Mortality Values (Probability of Dying under Age 5 per 1,000 Persons), by Gender, 1999

	Males	Females
Afghanistan	279	249
Albania	61	49
Algeria	50	48
Andorra	5	5
Angola	209	192
Antigua and Barbuda	22	20
Argentina	23	20
Armenia	19	16
Australia	7	5
Austria	6	6
Azerbaijan	32	25
Bahamas, the	24	21
Bahrain	23	20
Bangladesh	113	116
Barbados	11	10
Belarus	16	11
Belgium	9	6
Belize	30	25
Benin	157	148
Bhutan	113	114
Bolivia	91	81
Bosnia and Herzegovina	22	17
Botswana	99	97
Brazil	47	42
Brunei	12	9
Bulgaria	21	16
Burkina Faso	182	171
Burundi	170	166
Cambodia	138	129
Cameroon	123	120
Canada	6	5
Cape Verde	55	50
Central African Republic	153	143
Chad	184	165
Chile	11	8
China	35	40
Colombia	31	26
Comoros	113	92
Congo, Dem. Rep. (Zaire)	170	153
Congo, Rep.	112	102
Cook Islands	29	24
Costa Rica	13	14
Côte d'Ivoire	145	124
Croatia	9	7
Cuba	10	8
Cyprus	9	8
Czech Republic	6	5
Denmark	7	6
Djibouti	169	162
Dominica	9	7
Dominican Republic	52	46
Ecuador	40	33
Egypt	74	72
El Salvador	42	35
Equatorial Guinea	146	131
Eritrea	144	134
Estonia	12	11

A8-2. Under-5 Mortality Values (Probability of Dying under Age 5 per 1,000 Persons), by Gender, 1999 *(continued)*

	Males	Females
Ethiopia	188	177
Fiji	25	19
Finland	5	4
France	7	5
Gabon	94	85
Gambia	103	93
Georgia	20	16
Germany	6	5
Ghana	118	109
Greece	8	7
Grenada	27	22
Guatemala	58	44
Guinea	217	193
Guinea-Bissau	207	196
Guyana	75	58
Haiti	120	111
Honduras	42	37
Hungary	12	10
Iceland	5	3
India	97	104
Indonesia	63	53
Iran	48	42
Iraq	67	54
Ireland	7	6
Israel	8	7
Italy	6	5
Jamaica	29	25
Japan	5	5
Jordan	29	25
Kazakhstan	48	36
Kenya	100	99
Kiribati	62	58
Kuwait	19	17
Kyrgyzstan	73	68
Laos	143	126
Latvia	21	16
Lebanon	31	25
Lesotho	147	134
Liberia	214	196
Libya	39	35
Lithuania	16	9
Luxembourg	6	6
Macedonia, FYRO	27	23
Madagascar	179	157
Malawi	222	215
Malaysia	15	13
Maldives	90	86
Mali	240	229
Malta	9	6
Marshall Islands	60	51
Mauritania	189	168
Mauritius	26	15
Mexico	26	23
Micronesia	44	31
Moldova	20	17
Monaco	9	7

A8-2. Under-5 Mortality Values (Probability of Dying under Age 5 per 1,000 Persons), by Gender, 1999 *(continued)*

	Males	Females
Mongolia	123	104
Morocco	69	61
Mozambique	196	189
Myanmar (Burma)	142	126
Namibia	113	112
Nauru	19	15
Nepal	119	107
Netherlands, the	7	6
New Zealand	9	7
Nicaragua	50	44
Niger	331	339
Nigeria	173	170
Niue	33	30
North Korea, Dem. Rep.	100	99
Norway	6	5
Oman	18	18
Pakistan	100	98
Palau	23	16
Panama	35	32
Papua New Guinea	129	106
Paraguay	37	33
Peru	52	45
Philippines	48	41
Poland	13	11
Portugal	9	7
Qatar	19	19
Romania	29	22
Russian Federation	24	19
Rwanda	189	163
Saint Kitts and Nevis	34	28
Saint Lucia	27	19
Saint Vincent and the Grenadines	28	26
Samoa	28	25
San Marino	7	6
Sao Tome and Principe	82	51
Saudi Arabia	21	20
Senegal	134	126
Seychelles	21	12
Sierra Leone	326	298
Singapore	4	3
Slovakia	12	10
Slovenia	6	4
Solomon Islands	49	47
Somalia	206	196
South Africa	85	67
South Korea, Rep.	12	10
Spain	6	6
Sri Lanka	25	19
Sudan	117	103
Suriname	34	27
Swaziland	107	97
Sweden	5	4
Switzerland	6	6
Syria	44	40
Tajikistan	69	59
Tanzania	157	148
Thailand	40	27

A8-2. Under-5 Mortality Values (Probability of Dying under Age 5 per 1,000 Persons), by Gender, 1999 *(continued)*

	Males	**Females**
Togo	142	122
Tonga	29	23
Trinidad and Tobago	10	7
Tunisia	36	31
Turkey	45	42
Turkmenistan	83	77
Tuvalu	45	32
Uganda	165	153
Ukraine	16	12
United Arab Emirates	19	16
United Kingdom	7	6
United States	8	8
Uruguay	20	16
Uzbekistan	48	38
Vanuatu	64	57
Venezuela	22	23
Vietnam	39	31
Yemen	113	108
Yugoslavia	29	22
Zambia	174	163
Zimbabwe	122	113

Source: World Health Report 2000—Health Systems: Improving Performance, Table 2. <http://filestore.who.int/~who/whr/2000/en/excel/AnnexTable02.xls>. Underlying data from World Health Organization (WHO).

A8-3. Gender Differences in Death Rates, Selected Countries, 1993

	Percent decline in mortaility rates, 1970–93		**Percent by which male rate exceeds female rate, 1993**
	Male	**Female**	
Australia	61	62	49
Austria	65	66	55
Bulgaria	45	46	41
Canada	57	57	49
Czech Republic	N/A	N/A	58
Denmark	51	47	45
Finland	56	54	53
France	56	58	53
Germany	N/A	N/A	44
Greece	69	72	39
Hungary	61	62	41
Israel	N/A	N/A	25
Japan	67	68	54
Netherlands, the	53	50	40
New Zealand	45	46	52
Norway	53	51	56
Poland	52	54	45
Portugal	N/A	N/A	72
Romania	60	65	41
Russia	N/A	N/A	65
Spain	N/A	N/A	54
Sweden	52	48	39
Switzerland	58	56	44
United Kingdom	60	60	42
United States	45	45	51

N/A Not Available

Source: Progress of Nations 1998; United Nations Children's Fund (UNICEF); <http://www.unicef.org/pon98/>. Underlying data from: World Health Organization (WHO).

A9. BIRTHS TO ADOLESCENTS

A9-1. Annual Births per 1,000 Women Ages 15 to 19, by Region, 1995, 2000, 2005, 2010, 2020

	1995	2000	2005	2010	2020
World	60	56	53	52	48
Sub-Saharan Africa	143	132	121	110	87
Asia/Near East/North Africa	66	58	54	50	45
North Africa	54	49	46	44	41
Asia, excluding Near East, China, and Japan	66	57	53	49	44
Near East	79	72	70	67	60
Latin America/Caribbean	60	52	46	43	38
Remaining world	25	25	24	25	25
Asia: China and Japan	14	13	13	14	13
Europe	34	34	33	31	31
North America	55	56	56	58	59
Oceania	39	37	34	32	30

Source: Trends in Adolescent Fertility and Contraceptive Use in the Developing World, by Thomas M. McDevitt with Arjun Adlakha, Timothy B. Fowler and Vera Harris-Bourne; IPC/95-1. Table 2, 1995. < http://www.census.gov/ipc/prod/ipc95-1/ipc95_1j.pdf>. Underlying data from U.S. Bureau of the Census.

A9-2. Births to Adolescents as a Percentage of All Births, by Region, 1995, 2000, 2005, 2010, 2020

	1995	2000	2005	2010	2020
World	11	11	11	11	10
Sub-Saharan Africa	17	17	17	17	14
Asia/Near East/North Africa	11	11	10	10	10
North Africa	10	11	10	9	9
Asia, excluding Near East, China, and Japan	11	11	10	10	9
Near East	12	11	12	12	11
Latin America/Caribbean	13	12	11	10	9
Remaining world	6	6	7	7	6
Asia: China and Japan	3	3	4	4	3
Europe	9	9	9	8	8
North America	12	14	15	15	14
Oceania	8	8	8	8	7

Source: Trends in Adolescent Fertility and Contraceptive Use in the Developing World, by Thomas M. McDevitt with Arjun Adlakha, Timothy B. Fowler and Vera Harris-Bourne; IPC/95-1. Table 2, 1995. < http://www.census.gov/ipc/prod/ipc95-1/ipc95_1j.pdf>. Underlying data from U.S. Bureau of the Census.

A9-3. Annual Births per 1,000 Women Ages 15 to 19, 1995 and 2000

	Number of 15 to 19 year old women (in thousands), 1995	Annual births per 1,000 women aged 15 to 19 years, 1995	Number of 15 to 19 year old women (in thousands), 2000	Annual births per 1,000 women aged 15 to 19 years, 2000
World	253,809	60	315,393	48
Afghanistan	971	101	2,146	67
Albania	153	14	154	10
Algeria	1,599	46	1,964	35
Andorra	2	19	2	18
Angola	501	119	1,037	75
Anguilla	-	14	-	23
Antigua and Barbuda	3	65	2	66
Argentina	1584	56	1,658	39
Armenia	141	86	142	57
Aruba	2	41	2	40
Australia	631	20	679	20
Austria	221	22	204	24
Azerbaijan	334	26	344	19
Bahamas, the	15	48	13	46
Bahrain	24	53	42	51
Bangladesh	7,112	113	10,128	49
Barbados	10	60	9	59
Belarus	361	43	319	40
Belgium	299	12	249	12
Belize	11	106	17	43
Benin	300	143	663	92
Bhutan	81	87	146	62
Bolivia	419	75	583	43
Bosnia and Hercegovina	179	36	139	37
Botswana	80	90	97	36
Brazil	8,337	45	7,361	31
Brunei	14	42	20	40
Bulgaria	318	69	242	69
Burkina	561	145	1,090	84
Burma	2,242	46	2,898	31
Burundi	327	57	602	76
Cambodia	398	71	1,032	55
Cameroon	733	132	1,486	98
Canada	924	26	965	25
Cape Verde	23	62	45	44
Central African Republic	163	146	267	86
Chad	293	196	500	114
Chile	608	58	702	45
China	46,979	15	41,126	14
China, Taiwan	966	17	790	16
Colombia	1,722	53	1,765	32
Comoros	29	136	69	82
Congo	134	116	214	64
Costa Rica	156	84	209	64
Côte d'Ivoire	777	223	1,727	107
Croatia	159	30	122	30
Cuba	373	90	363	87
Cyprus	26	35	28	32
Czech Republic	427	44	335	42
Denmark	156	10	145	10
Djibouti	22	202	40	112
Dominica	4	50	4	46
Dominican Republic	401	75	423	35
Ecuador	584	62	635	36
Egypt	3,280	59	4,071	39

A9-3. Annual Births per 1,000 Women Ages15 to 19, 1995 and 2000 *(continued)*

	Number of 15 to 19 year old women (in thousands), 1995	Annual births per 1,000 women aged 15 to 19 years, 1995	Number of 15 to 19 year old women (in thousands), 2000	Annual births per 1,000 women aged 15 to 19 years, 2000
El Salvador	377	112	430	50
Equatorial Guinea	21	161	41	95
Estonia	56	50	57	44
Ethiopia	3,115	112	6,732	72
Europe	27,824	34	25,506	31
Faroe Islands	2	24	2	18
Fiji	41	60	44	49
Finland	160	12	142	12
France	1,779	9	1,737	9
French Guiana	5	100	10	77
French Polynesia	11	77	15	50
Gabon	54	155	79	87
Gambia, the	53	192	113	113
Gaza Strip	40	80	87	52
Georgia	206	59	197	51
Germany	2,036	17	1,970	16
Ghana	859	116	1,883	74
Gibraltar	1	13	1	10
Greece	368	24	275	26
Greenland	2	63	2	51
Grenada	5	105	6	53
Guadeloupe	17	32	15	27
Guatemala	602	102	879	46
Guernsey	2	21	2	21
Guinea	337	169	611	66
Guinea-Bissau	61	96	99	56
Guyana	42	41	29	30
Haiti	326	81	498	45
Honduras	306	95	434	41
Hong Kong SAR, China	183	7	143	7
Hungary	402	42	313	41
Iceland	10	27	9	23
India	43,939	71	54,701	41
Indonesia	11,068	58	11,240	38
Iran	3,363	111	7,435	63
Iraq	1,124	100	2,475	68
Ireland	162	14	121	13
Isle of Man	2	32	3	31
Israel	229	19	265	17
Italy	1,780	11	1,509	12
Jamaica	124	62	124	31
Japan	4,190	3	3,473	4
Jersey	2	12	2	13
Jordan	208	51	376	37
Kazakhstan	756	46	689	38
Kenya	1,667	128	2,596	52
Kuwait	85	60	172	70
Kyrgyzstan	222	42	269	30
Laos	254	105	476	54
Latvia	91	49	99	44
Lebanon	231	44	266	36
Lesotho	106	65	159	42
Liberia	152	173	338	102
Libya	261	142	655	94
Liechtenstein	1	4	1	4
Lithuania	132	41	134	37
Luxembourg	11	12	11	12

A9-3. Annual Births per 1,000 Women Ages 15 to 19, 1995 and 2000 *(continued)*

	Number of 15 to 19 year old women (in thousands), 1995	Annual births per 1,000 women aged 15 to 19 years, 1995	Number of 15 to 19 year old women (in thousands), 2000	Annual births per 1,000 women aged 15 to 19 years, 2000
Macau	17	7	15	8
Macedonia, FYRO	92	42	76	38
Madagascar	710	137	1,593	84
Malawi	523	159	989	97
Malaysia	881	31	1,365	35
Maldives	12	121	29	56
Mali	504	244	1,128	152
Malta	14	11	12	10
Marshall Islands	3	153	8	109
Martinique	16	25	16	23
Mauritania	121	165	273	96
Mauritius	55	47	51	41
Mayotte	5	260	13	139
Mexico	5170	69	5,848	40
Moldova	177	54	159	45
Monaco	1	9	1	9
Mongolia	130	71	206	46
Morocco	1,566	42	1,898	35
Mozambique	953	124	1,903	77
Namibia	84	81	197	57
Near East	7,609	79	13,418	60
Nepal	1,155	100	1,934	58
Netherlands, the	445	6	409	6
Netherlands Antilles	5	42	6	38
New Caledonia	9	43	10	35
New Zealand	122	31	103	27
Nicaragua	243	116	331	42
Niger	491	259	1,175	157
Nigeria	5,199	176	11,631	100
North Korea, Dem. Rep.	956	9	1,124	7
Norway	130	17	109	15
Oceania	1,102	39	1,274	30
Oman	92	124	218	83
Pakistan	6,482	67	12,792	72
Panama	133	84	154	43
Papua New Guinea	244	79	348	43
Paraguay	266	82	437	45
Peru	1,290	55	1,380	36
Philippines	3,874	42	4,342	35
Poland	1,574	29	1,285	26
Portugal	403	25	304	27
Puerto Rico	165	42	132	30
Qatar	18	52	24	35
Reunion	28	51	37	41
Romania	945	50	736	48
Russia	5,381	54	4,840	51
Rwanda	477	76	906	56
Saint Kitts and Nevis	2	72	2	40
Saint Lucia	9	55	7	34
Saint Vincent and the Grenadines	7	46	5	30
San Marino	1	10	1	10
Sao Tome and Principe	8	87	11	45
Saudi Arabia	758	107	2,067	87
Senegal	488	141	1,014	91
Seychelles	4	46	3	40
Sierra Leone	244	219	493	119

A9-3. Annual Births per 1,000 Women Ages 15 to 19, 1995 and 2000 *(continued)*

	Number of 15 to 19 year old women (in thousands), 1995	Annual births per 1,000 women aged 15 to 19 years, 1995	Number of 15 to 19 year old women (in thousands), 2000	Annual births per 1,000 women aged 15 to 19 years, 2000
Singapore	92	8	91	7
Slovakia	234	43	190	39
Slovenia	72	28	54	28
Solomon Islands	23	95	40	43
Somalia	367	57	900	74
South Africa	2,228	81	4,072	54
South Korea, Rep.	1,919	6	1,683	6
Spain	1,504	15	1,102	17
Sri Lanka	873	31	779	30
Sudan	1,561	103	3,060	57
Suriname	20	47	23	34
Swaziland	55	68	114	63
Sweden	246	13	257	12
Switzerland	191	7	196	7
Syria	801	108	1,841	63
Tajikistan	299	36	484	23
Tanzania	1,630	157	2,898	99
Thailand	2,892	42	2,327	29
Togo	231	151	551	94
Trinidad and Tobago	65	49	62	31
Tunisia	468	33	458	34
Turkey	3,164	54	3,754	36
Turkmenistan	203	22	269	15
Tuvalu	-	28	1	24
Uganda	1,040	170	1,816	92
Ukraine	1,774	58	1,516	56
United Arab Emirates	95	81	247	49
United Kingdom	1,665	32	1,643	31
United States	8,790	58	10,325	62
Uruguay	136	53	136	37
Uzbekistan	1,141	40	1,560	27
Vanuatu	9	65	12	37
Venezuela	1,105	61	1,273	38
Vietnam	3,690	21	4,082	14
West Bank	78	63	102	34
Western Samoa	10	56	16	39
Yemen	635	140	1,454	83
Yugoslavia	402	69	363	62
Zaire	2,394	173	5,269	108
Zambia	533	160	954	98
Zimbabwe	685	93	809	40

- Represents less than 500

Source: Trends in Adolescent Fertility and Contraceptive Use in the Developing World, by Thomas M. McDevitt with Arjun Adlakha, Timothy B. Fowler and Vera Harris-Bourne; IPC/95-1. Table 3, 1995. < http://www.census.gov/ipc/prod/ipc95-1/ipc95_1j.pdf>. Underlying data from U.S. Bureau of the Census.

A9-4. Percentage of Women Ages 15 to 19 Who Have Begun Childbearing by Residence—Urban and Rural, Selected Countries, various years

Country	Urban	Rural
Egypt, 1992	5	14
Philippines, 1993	5	9
Indonesia, 1991	6	16
Jordan, 1990	7	8
Peru, 1991/1992	8	25
Pakistan, 1990/1991	10	19
Rwanda, 1992	10	11
Turkey, 1993	10	7
Yemen, 1991/1992	11	15
Colombia, 1990	12	16
Dominican Republic, 1991	13	27
Paraguay, 1990	13	21
Senegal, 1992/1993	13	33
Brazil*, 1991	14	16
Bolivia, 1994	15	22
Madagascar, 1992	15	33
Zimbabwe,1988	15	24
Ghana, 1993	16	26
Kenya, 1993	17	21
Nigeria, 1990	17	33
Burkina Faso, 1993	19	35
Namibia, 1992	24	20
Botswana, 1988	26	29
Tanzania, 1991/1992	28	29
Cameroon, 1991	29	40
Malawi, 1992	29	36
Niger, 1992	29	38
Zambia, 1992	29	40

* Data are only for some parts of the country.

Note: Data refer to all women ages 15 to 19. Women who have begun childbearing includes those who are mothers or are pregnant with their first child.

Source: Trends in Adolescent Fertility and Contraceptive Use in the Developing World, by Thomas M. McDevitt with Arjun Adlakha, Timothy B. Fowler and Vera Harris-Bourne; IPC/95-1. Table 7, 1995. < http://www.census.gov/ipc/prod/ipc95-1/ipc95_1j.pdf>. Underlying data from U.S. Bureau of the Census.

A9-5. Percentage of Women Ages 15 to 19 Who Have Begun Childbearing by Level of Education, Selected Countries, various years

Country	Year	No education	Primary	Secondary or higher
Bolivia	1994	37.6	24.0	9.4
Burkina Faso	1993	36.3	23.5	9.0
Cameroon	1991	53.4	37.8	21.3
Colombia	1990	62.4	20.3	7.5
Ghana	1993	33.3	30.2	16.3
Kenya	1993	29.9	22.4	12.1
Malawi	1992	42.8	32.2	19.6
Morocco	1992	10.5	7.0	2.1
Niger*	1992	38.9	24.8	N/A
Peru	1991/1992	38.6	27.6	6.9
Philippines	1993	15.2	13.5	4.8
Rwanda	1992	22.1	8.1	3.1
Senegal	1992/1993	32.1	13.6	5.4
Turkey	1993	19.7	10.7	3.0
Zambia	1992	45.4	36.5	21.2
Zimbabwe	1988	42.3	22.8	17.5

N/A Not Available

*Primary education data refer to primary education or higher.

Source: Trends in Adolescent Fertility and Contraceptive Use in the Developing World, by Thomas M. McDevitt with Arjun Adlakha, Timothy B. Fowler and Vera Harris-Bourne; IPC/95-1. Table 10, 1995. < http://www.census.gov/ipc/prod/ipc95-1/ipc95_1j.pdf>. Underlying data from U.S. Bureau of the Census.

A9-6. Adolescent Fertility (Children per 1,000 Women Ages 15 to 19) and Educational Attainment, Selected Countries, mid-1980s to early 1990s

	Year of survey	Children per 1,000 women ages 15–19	Percentage of women	
			Primary or higher education	Secondary or higher education
Bolivia	1994	96.0	97.4	46.5
Botswana	1988	125.0	94.5	37.8
Brazil	1986	81.0	97.4	66.2
Burkina	1993	154.0	26.2	11.1
Burundi	1987	52.0	26.6	1.2
Cameroon	1991	174.0	74.3	36.7
Colombia	1990	73.0	97.7	64.0
Dominican Republic	1991	91.0	97.0	39.8
Ecuador	1987	88.0	96.9	56.1
Egypt	1992	69.0	76.3	65.3
El Salvador	1985	124.0	91.0	17.6
Ghana	1993	119.0	80.9	11.6
Guatemala	1987	139.0	77.5	21.2
Indonesia	1991	70.0	96.9	48.1
Jordan	1990	52.0	97.0	87.7
Kenya	1993	118.0	95.7	18.9
Liberia	1986	184.0	63.3	22.2
Madagascar	1992	156.0	85.4	27.4
Malawi	1992	159.0	69.7	4.1
Mexico	1987	84.0	96.1	62.2
Morocco	1992	43.0	54.0	31.0
Namibia	1992	101.0	93.2	21.4
Niger	1992	219.0	18.9	5.4
Nigeria	1990	144.0	64.2	30.5
Pakistan	1990/1991	84.0	45.0	18.9
Peru	1991/1992	68.0	98.8	77.9
Philippines	1993	52.0	98.9	80.3
Rwanda	1992	56.0	79.0	9.7
Senegal	1992/1993	132.0	38.9	11.7
Sudan*	1989/1990	69.0	76.5	16.6
Tanzania	1991/1992	139.0	88.8	5.7
Togo	1988	127.0	62.4	15.6
Trinidad and Tobago	1987	84.0	100.0	86.7
Turkey	1993	57.0	92.6	36.7
Uganda	1988/1989	187.0	79.4	12.3
Zambia	1992	152.0	89.9	24.1
Zimbabwe	1988	109.0	97.5	49.8

* Data is only for some parts of the country.
Note: Percentages are for persons attending, rather than completing, primary and secondary schooling, or better. Intermediate and middle levels are classed with primary levels throughout.

Source: Trends in Adolescent Fertility and Contraceptive Use in the Developing World, by Thomas M. McDevitt with Arjun Adlakha, Timothy B. Fowler and Vera Harris-Bourne; IPC/95-1. Table 9, 1995. < http://www.census.gov/ipc/prod/ipc95-1/ipc95_1j.pdf>. Underlying data from U.S. Bureau of the Census.

A10. MATERNAL MORTALITY

A10-1. Estimated Worldwide Total Maternal Deaths per Year, by World Regions, mid-1990s

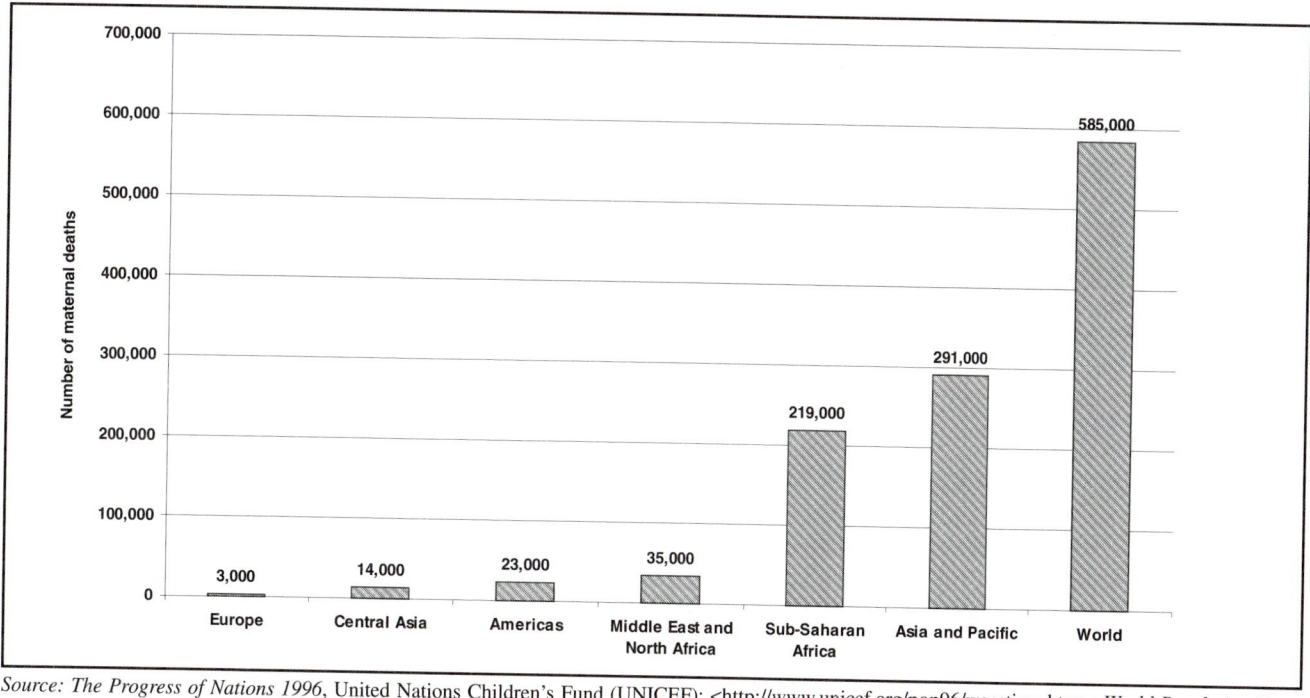

Source: The Progress of Nations 1996, United Nations Children's Fund (UNICEF); <http://www.unicef.org/pon96/woestima.htm>; *World Population Prospects: The 1994 Revision.* Underlying data from United Nations Population Division.

A10-2. Maternal Deaths per Day in Pregnancy and Childbirth, by World Regions, mid-1990s

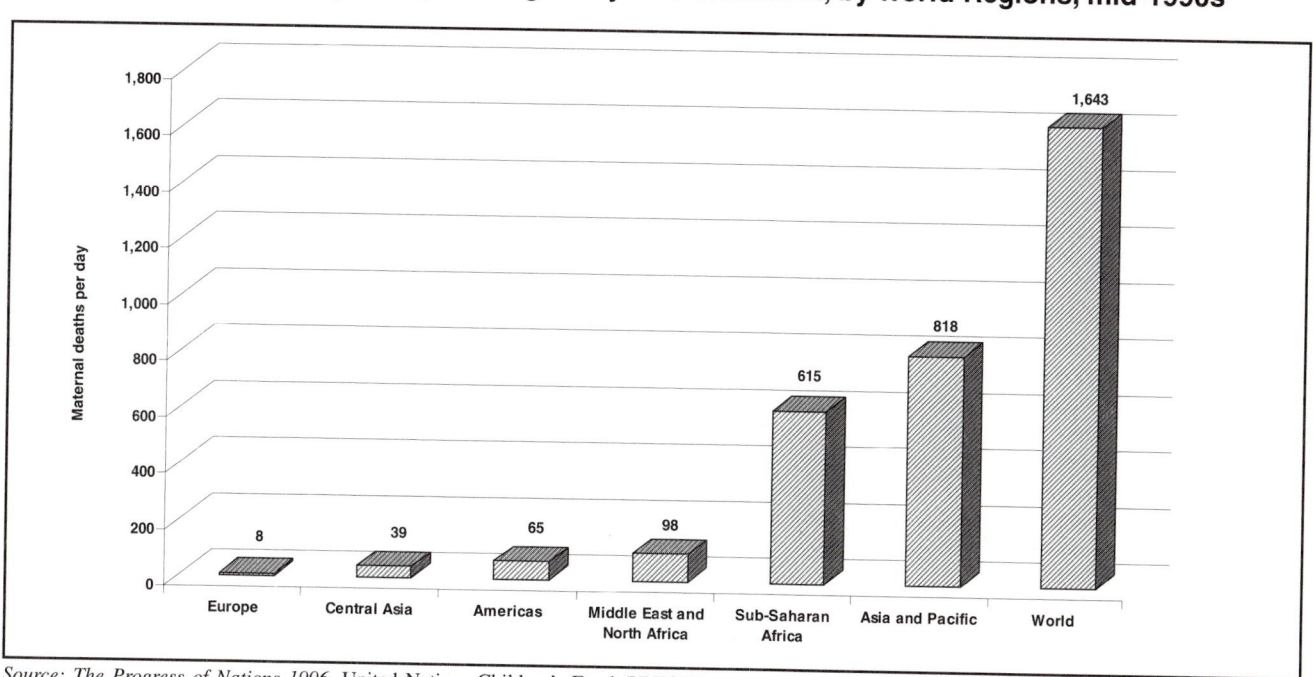

Source: The Progress of Nations 1996, United Nations Children's Fund (UNICEF); <http://www.unicef.org/pon96/woestima.htm>; *World Population Prospects: The 1994 Revision,* Underlying data from United Nations Population Division.

A10-3. Maternal Mortality Ratio* per 100,000 Live Births, 1990–1996

Country	Maternal mortality rate per 100,000 live births 1990–96
Albania	28
Algeria	140
Angola	1,500
Argentina	100
Armenia	21
Australia	9
Austria	10
Azerbaijan	44
Bangladesh	850
Belarus	22
Belgium	10
Benin	500
Bolivia	370
Botswana	250
Brazil	160
Bulgaria	20
Burkina Faso	930
Burundi	1,300
Cambodia	900
Cameroon	550
Canada	6
Central African Republic	700
Chad	900
Chile	180
China	115
Colombia	100
Congo, Rep.	890
Costa Rica	55
Côte d'Ivoire	600
Croatia	12
Cuba	36
Czech Republic	7
Denmark	9
Dominican Republic	110
Ecuador	150
Egypt	170
El Salvador	300
Eritrea	1,400
Estonia	52
Ethiopia	1,400
Finland	11
France	15
Gabon	500
Gambia	1,100
Georgia	19
Germany	22
Ghana	740
Greece	10
Guatemala	190
Guinea	880
Guinea-Bissau	910
Haiti	600
Honduras	220
Hong Kong	7
Hungary	14
India	437
Indonesia	390

A10-3. Maternal Mortality Ratio* per 100,000 Live Births, 1990–1996 *(continued)*

Country	Maternal mortality rate per 100,000 live births 1990–96
Iran	120
Iraq	310
Ireland	10
Israel	7
Italy	12
Jamaica	120
Japan	8
Jordan	150
Kazakhstan	53
Kenya	650
Kuwait	18
Kyrgyzstan	32
Laos	650
Latvia	15
Lebanon	300
Lesotho	610
Libya	220
Lithuania	13
Macedonia, FYRO	22
Madagascar	660
Malawi	620
Malaysia	43
Mali	580
Mauritania	800
Mauritius	112
Mexico	110
Moldova	33
Mongolia	65
Morocco	372
Mozambique	1,500
Myanmar (Burma)	580
Namibia	220
Nepal	1,500
Netherlands	12
New Zealand	25
Nicaragua	160
Niger	593
Nigeria	1,000
Norway	6
Pakistan	340
Panama	55
Papua New Guinea	930
Paraguay	190
Peru	280
Philippines	208
Poland	10
Portugal	15
Romania	41
Russia	53
Rwanda	1,300
Saudi Arabia	18
Senegal	510
Sierra Leone	1,800
Singapore	10
Slovakia	8
Slovenia	5
South Africa	230

A10-3. Maternal Mortality Ratio* per 100,000 Live Births, 1990–1996 *(continued)*

Country	Maternal mortality rate per 100,000 live births 1990–96
South Korea, Rep.	30
Spain	7
Sri Lanka	30
Sudan	370
Sweden	7
Switzerland	6
Syria	179
Tajikistan	74
Tanzania	530
Thailand	200
Togo	640
Trinidad and Tobago	90
Turkey	180
Turkmenistan	44
Uganda	550
Ukraine	30
United Kingdom	9
United States	12
Uruguay	85
Uzbekistan	24
Venezuela	200
Vietnam	105
Yemen	1,400
Yugoslavia	12
Zambia	230
Zimbabwe	280

* Maternal mortality ratio is the number of maternal deaths divided by the number of live births for a given year and expressed per 100,000 live births.

Source: World Bank, *World Development Indicators 1998*, Table 2.15. Underlying data from World Bank, United Nations Children's Fund (UNICEF); and United nations (UN).

A10-4. Lifetime Risk of Maternal Death: Risk Ratios and Risk Categories, 1997

Country	Risk ratio (1996)	Risk category
Afghanistan	1 in 7	Highest risk
Angola	1 in 8	Highest risk
Bhutan	1 in 9	Highest risk
Burundi	1 in 9	Highest risk
Chad	1 in 9	Highest risk
Eritrea	1 in 10	Highest risk
Ethiopia	1 in 9	Highest risk
Guinea	1 in 7	Highest risk
Mali	1 in 10	Highest risk
Mozambique	1 in 9	Highest risk
Nepal	1 in 10	Highest risk
Niger	1 in 9	Highest risk
Rwanda	1 in 9	Highest risk
Sierra Leone	1 in 7	Highest risk
Somalia	1 in 7	Highest risk
Uganda	1 in 10	Highest risk
Yemen	1 in 8	Highest risk
Australia	1 in 4,900	Lowest risk
Austria	1 in 5,600	Lowest risk

A10-4. Lifetime Risk of Maternal Death: Risk Ratios and Risk Categories, 1997

Country	Risk ratio (1996)	Risk category
Belgium	1 in 5,200	Lowest risk
Canada	1 in 7,700	Lowest risk
Denmark	1 in 5,800	Lowest risk
Finland	1 in 4,200	Lowest risk
Greece	1 in 5,600	Lowest risk
Italy	1 in 5,300	Lowest risk
Netherlands, the	1 in 4,300	Lowest risk
Norway	1 in 7,300	Lowest risk
Singapore	1 in 4,900	Lowest risk
Slovenia	1 in 4,000	Lowest risk
Spain	1 in 9,200	Lowest risk
Sweden	1 in 6,000	Lowest risk
Switzerland	1 in 8,700	Lowest risk
United Kingdom	1 in 5,100	Lowest risk

Source: *Progress of Nations 1997, Revised 1990 Estimates of Maternal Mortality, A New Approach by WHO and UNICEF*, April 1996. <http://www.unicef.org/pon97/>. Underlying data from United Nations Children's Fund (UNICEF) and World Health Organization (WHO).

A11. THE MOTHERS' INDEX

A11-1. Mothers' Index Ranking, 2000

Mothers' Index Ranking, 2000	Mothers' Index Rank	Women's Index* Rank	Children's Index** Rank
Norway	1	1	10
Canada	2	2	9
Australia	3	3	3
Switzerland	4	5	3
United States	4	4	15
Netherlands, the	6	6	5
United Kingdom	7	8	1
Finland	8	7	12
France	9	11	5
Cyprus	10	10	12
New Zealand	11	9	22
Costa Rica	12	12	8
Singapore	13	13	7
Colombia	14	14	18
Japan	15	14	18
Chile	16	16	12
Portugal	16	18	2
Hungary	18	17	29
Cuba	19	19	18
Uruguay	20	21	10
Jamaica	21	24	26
South Korea, Rep.	21	21	33
Panama	21	29	24
Kazakhstan	24	20	37
Trinidad and Tobago	24	23	31
Mexico	26	26	30
Russia	27	26	32
Brazil	28	26	35
Philippines	29	30	37
Argentina	30	30	42
Ecuador	31	33	40
Dominican Republic	32	32	35
Honduras	33	38	28

A11-1. Mothers' Index Ranking, 2000 *(continued)*

Mothers' Index Ranking, 2000	Mothers' Index Rank	Women's Index* Rank	Children's Index** Rank
Romania	34	35	35
Czech Republic	35	43	21
South Africa	36	44	22
El Salvador	37	34	50
Venezuela	38	40	41
Paraguay	39	44	39
Lebanon	40	49	25
Mauritius	41	38	55
Thailand	42	41	51
Jordan	43	54	26
China	44	48	42
Peru	44	51	34
Zimbabwe	44	47	46
Moldova	47	37	63
Sri Lanka	47	35	66
Uzbekistan	47	24	81
Kuwait	50	49	54
Malaysia	51	54	44
Tajikistan	52	42	72
Tunisia	52	64	16
Namibia	54	51	59
Nicaragua	54	58	47
United Arab Emirates	56	56	58
Vietnam	56	46	74
Mongolia	58	53	61
Botswana	59	60	49
Libya	60	70	16
Iran	61	67	44
Turkey	62	59	65
Lesotho	63	57	70
Guatemala	64	65	57
Bolivia	65	61	63
Indonesia	66	63	68
Syria	67	72	51
Algeria	68	71	56
Kenya	69	65	76
Egypt	70	74	53
Myanmar (Burma)	71	69	73
Zambia	72	61	90
Papua New Guinea	73	68	89
Oman	74	77	67
Cameroon	75	76	69
Uganda	76	73	86
Iraq	77	79	75
Ghana	78	77	83
Togo	79	88	59
Morocco	80	86	61
Tanzania	81	75	93
Malawi	82	81	77
Haiti	83	80	96
Nigeria	84	84	88
India	85	92	79
Senegal	86	94	80
Yemen	86	91	83
Central African Republic	88	82	99
Côte d'Ivoire	89	96	78
Madagascar	90	87	95
Sudan	91	83	97

A11-1. Mothers' Index Ranking, 2000 *(continued)*

Mothers' Index Ranking, 2000	Mothers' Index Rank	Women's Index* Rank	Children's Index** Rank
Benin	**92**	85	98
Mozambique	**93**	93	92
Bangladesh	**94**	97	87
Mauritania	**94**	100	82
Pakistan	**96**	99	85
Angola	**97**	89	100
Gambia, the	**98**	102	90
Nepal	**99**	106	71
Burkina Faso	**100**	97	101
Chad	**101**	90	104
Burundi	**102**	104	94
Ethiopia	**102**	95	103
Guinea	**104**	103	102
Mali	**105**	101	105
Niger	**106**	104	106

*Indicators include: Lifetime Risk of Maternal Death; Percent of Women Using Modern Contraception; Percent of Births Attended by Trained Personnel; Percent of Pregnant Women with Anemia; Female (Adult) Literacy Rate; Percent of National Government Positions Held by Women.
**Indicators include: Infant Mortality Rate; Gross Primary Enrollment Ratio; Percent of Population with Access to Safe Water.

Source: State of the World's Mothers 2000, release date May 9, 2000; <http://www.savethechildren.org/worldsmothers00/maintable.html>. Underlying data from Save the Children Organization.

A12. LIFE EXPECTANCY

A12-1. Life Expectancy at Birth in Years, by Gender, and Difference Between Male and Female Life Expectancy, 1980

	Both sexes	Male	Female	Difference between male and female life expectancy (in years)
Afghanistan	40.8	41.6	39.9	-1.7
Albania	69.5	67.0	72.0	5.0
Algeria	57.4	55.9	58.8	2.9
Angola	39.2	37.9	40.6	2.7
Argentina	69.6	66.4	73.0	6.6
Australia	74.5	71.0	78.1	7.1
Bahamas, the	66.8	62.7	71.1	8.4
Barbados	72.0	70.2	73.9	3.7
Belize	64.7	62.8	66.7	3.9
Benin	45.5	44.4	46.7	2.3
Bhutan	44.9	45.6	44.1	-1.5
Bolivia	50.8	48.4	53.4	5.0
Brazil	62.5	59.1	66.2	7.1
Burundi	49.1	47.5	50.8	3.3
Cambodia	35.8	34.1	37.5	3.4
Cameroon	51.5	49.7	53.2	3.5
Cape Verde	60.8	57.8	63.8	6.0
Chad	42.5	40.5	44.5	4.0
Colombia	64.5	62.4	66.6	4.2
Comoros	51.5	50.0	53.0	3.0
Dominican Republic	63.1	61.2	65.1	3.9
El Salvador	55.8	49.9	62.0	12.1
Faroe Islands	76.3	73.4	79.5	6.1

A12-1. Life Expectancy at Birth in Years, by Gender, and Difference Between Male and Female Life Expectancy, 1980 *(continued)*

	Both sexes	Male	Female	Difference between male and female life expectancy (in years)
Finland	73.3	69.2	77.6	8.4
France	74.2	70.2	78.4	8.2
Gabon	48.2	46.2	50.4	4.2
Ghana	52.6	50.9	54.4	3.5
Gibraltar	73.0	71.0	75.0	4.0
Greece	74.2	72.2	76.3	4.1
Guatemala	57.3	55.1	59.6	4.5
Guinea	38.2	36.5	40.0	3.5
Guinea-Bissau	42.0	40.4	43.6	3.2
Guyana	62.0	58.8	65.4	6.6
Hungary	69.5	66.0	73.2	7.2
India	52.5	52.9	52.1	-0.8
Indonesia	53.4	52.0	55.0	3.0
Jordan	67.7	66.3	69.2	2.9
Kenya	57.4	55.9	58.9	3.0
Lebanon	66.5	64.4	68.7	4.3
Lesotho	55.6	53.2	58.0	4.8
Liberia	51.5	49.7	53.2	3.5
Libya	66.2	64.3	68.2	3.9
Madagascar	47.7	46.5	49.0	2.5
Malawi	43.1	42.3	44.0	1.7
Malaysia	64.2	62.0	66.7	4.7
Malta	70.5	68.5	72.7	4.2
Mauritania	41.9	39.7	44.1	4.4
Mexico	66.9	63.6	70.3	6.7
Monaco	73.9	70.0	78.0	8.0
Mozambique	43.2	41.9	44.7	2.8
Myanmar (Burma)	51.8	50.5	53.1	2.6
Nepal	46.4	47.1	45.6	-1.5
New Zealand	72.7	70.0	75.6	5.6
Nicaragua	56.0	53.3	58.7	5.4
Nigeria	46.8	46.4	47.2	0.8
North Korea, Dem. Rep.	65.7	62.7	69.0	6.3
Panama	70.5	68.1	73.1	5.0
Papua New Guinea	51.1	50.9	51.5	0.6
Paraguay	67.6	65.4	69.9	4.5
Philippines	62.3	60.0	64.7	4.7
Puerto Rico	74.1	70.5	77.6	7.1
Rwanda	47.3	45.9	48.7	2.8
Saint Kitts and Nevis	64.2	61.4	67.3	5.9
Saint Lucia	68.8	67.2	70.5	3.3
Saint Vincent and the Grenadine	68.1	66.4	69.8	3.4
San Marino	76.1	73.8	78.7	4.9
Saudi Arabia	56.2	55.5	56.9	1.4
Seychelles	70.5	66.3	74.6	8.3
Sierra Leone	39.6	37.5	41.8	4.3
Singapore	71.6	69.0	74.4	5.4
Solomon Islands	65.2	63.2	67.4	4.2
Somalia	49.5	49.2	49.9	0.7
South Africa	57.9	54.4	61.5	7.1
Spain	75.6	72.5	78.6	6.1
Sudan	49.2	49.6	49.8	0.2
Suriname	64.9	62.6	67.3	4.7
Swaziland	50.2	46.6	54.0	7.4

A12-1. Life Expectancy at Birth in Years, by Gender, and Difference Between Male and Female Life Expectancy, 1980 *(continued)*

	Both sexes	Male	Female	Difference between male and female life expectancy (in years)
Sweden	75.7	72.8	78.8	6.0
Switzerland	75.7	72.4	79.1	6.7
Tanzania	47.0	45.1	49.0	3.9
Trinidad and Tobago	67.4	65.2	69.7	4.5
Turkey	62.6	60.9	64.5	3.6
Tuvalu	58.8	57.2	60.4	3.2
Uganda	43.9	43.2	44.7	1.5
United States	73.7	70.0	77.4	7.4
Vanuatu	52.6	51.7	53.5	1.8
Yemen	49.3	47.1	51.6	4.5
Zambia	51.7	50.4	53.0	2.6

Source: U.S. Census International Database, 2000: Table 010. Infant Mortality Rates and Deaths, and Life Expectancy at Birth, by Sex; <http://www.census.gov/cgi-bin/ipc/agggen>. Underlying data from U.S. Bureau of the Census.

A12-2. Life Expectancy at Birth in Years, by Gender, and Difference Between Male and Female Life Expectancy, 1990

	Both sexes	Male	Female	Difference between male and female life expectancy (in years)
Afghanistan	43.0	43.8	42.2	-1.6
Albania	69.2	66.0	72.6	6.6
Algeria	66.4	65.4	67.4	2.0
American Samoa	70.8	65.7	76.2	10.5
Andorra	77.5	74.8	80.8	6.0
Angola	43.8	41.9	45.7	3.8
Anguilla	75.2	72.5	78.0	5.5
Antigua and Barbuda	69.0	66.8	71.3	4.5
Argentina	72.5	69.1	76.0	6.9
Armenia	70.6	67.2	74.0	6.8
Aruba	75.9	72.3	79.7	7.4
Australia	77.4	74.2	80.8	6.6
Austria	75.7	72.4	79.1	6.7
Azerbaijan	68.4	64.3	72.8	8.5
Bahamas, the	72.2	68.6	76.0	7.4
Bahrain	71.9	69.6	74.3	4.7
Barbados	72.3	69.6	75.2	5.6
Belarus	70.9	66.2	75.8	9.6
Belgium	76.0	72.7	79.6	6.9
Belize	67.2	65.2	69.2	4.0
Benin	50.0	48.3	51.6	3.3
Bhutan	48.9	49.5	48.3	-1.2
Bolivia	56.5	53.8	59.4	5.6
Botswana	42.5	40.5	44.5	4.0
Brazil	67.0	63.0	71.1	8.1
Brunei	70.4	68.7	72.3	3.6
Burkina Faso	47.8	47.9	47.6	-0.3
Burundi	46.9	45.7	48.0	2.3
Cambodia	47.4	45.9	49.0	3.1

A12-2. Life Expectancy at Birth in Years, by Gender, and Difference Between Male and Female Life Expectancy, 1990 *(continued)*

	Both sexes	Male	Female	Difference between male and female life expectancy (in years)
Cameroon	52.9	51.1	54.7	3.6
Canada	77.6	74.1	81.3	7.2
Cape Verde	66.6	63.4	69.9	6.5
Cayman Islands	77.1	75.4	78.8	3.4
Central African Republic	44.7	43.3	46.0	2.7
Chad	45.6	43.4	47.9	4.5
Chile	72.4	69.1	76.0	6.9
China	67.7	66.9	68.5	1.6
Colombia	68.1	64.7	71.5	6.8
Comoros	56.5	54.5	58.5	4.0
Congo, Dem. Rep. of (Zaire)	48.3	46.8	49.8	3.0
Congo, Rep.	46.9	45.6	48.2	2.6
Cook Islands	71.1	69.2	73.1	3.9
Costa Rica	75.7	73.3	78.2	4.9
Côte d'Ivoire	47.3	46.2	48.4	2.2
Cuba	75.1	72.8	77.6	4.8
Cyprus	74.5	72.4	76.7	4.3
Denmark	74.7	71.8	77.7	5.9
Djibouti	47.4	45.8	49.1	3.3
Dominica	76.0	73.2	79.0	5.8
Dominican Republic	66.9	64.8	69.1	4.3
Ecuador	68.8	66.2	71.5	5.3
Egypt	59.5	57.7	61.4	3.7
El Salvador	65.7	62.5	69.1	6.6
Equatorial Guinea	50.3	48.4	52.2	3.8
Eritrea	51.9	49.9	54.0	4.1
Estonia	69.7	64.7	74.9	10.2
Ethiopia	44.2	43.6	44.8	1.2
Faroe Islands	77.4	73.9	81.0	7.1
Fiji	64.0	61.9	66.3	4.4
Finland	74.8	70.9	78.9	8.0
France	77.0	72.9	81.2	8.3
French Guiana	73.9	70.6	77.4	6.8
French Polynesia	70.8	68.6	73.2	4.6
Gabon	52.8	50.2	55.5	5.3
Gambia, the	50.1	48.2	52.1	3.9
Gaza Strip	69.6	68.5	70.8	2.3
Georgia	72.2	68.6	76.0	7.4
Germany	75.2	72.0	78.5	6.5
Ghana	54.2	52.4	56.1	3.7
Gibraltar	75.3	72.4	78.1	5.7
Greece	76.9	74.5	79.5	5.0
Greenland	64.1	59.6	68.7	9.1
Grenada	69.4	67.2	71.7	4.5
Guadeloupe	74.8	71.6	78.0	6.4
Guam	74.3	71.0	77.9	6.9
Guatemala	62.7	60.3	65.3	5.0
Guernsey	77.4	74.8	80.1	5.3
Guinea	42.3	40.3	44.4	4.1
Guinea-Bissau	45.8	44.2	47.5	3.3
Guyana	63.8	60.4	67.3	6.9
Haiti	49.7	47.8	51.6	3.8
Honduras	65.3	62.9	67.9	5.0
Hungary	69.3	65.1	73.8	8.7

A12-2. Life Expectancy at Birth in Years, by Gender, and Difference Between Male and Female Life Expectancy, 1990 *(continued)*

	Both sexes	Male	Female	Difference between male and female life expectancy (in years)
Iceland	78.3	76.1	80.5	4.4
India	57.2	56.9	57.5	0.6
Indonesia	58.9	57.0	60.8	3.8
Iraq	66.5	65.5	67.6	2.1
Ireland	74.5	71.7	77.5	5.8
Israel	77.2	75.4	79.1	3.7
Jamaica	73.3	71.2	75.4	4.2
Japan	78.9	76.0	82.0	6.0
Jordan	71.1	69.4	72.9	3.5
Kazakhstan	66.9	62.2	71.7	9.5
Kenya	52.6	52.1	53.2	1.1
Kiribati	60.0	58.3	61.9	3.6
Kuwait	74.3	72.1	76.5	4.4
Kyrgyzstan	66.5	62.2	70.9	8.7
Laos	49.7	48.2	51.2	3.0
Latvia	69.0	64.0	74.2	10.2
Lebanon	68.2	65.9	70.6	4.7
Lesotho	58.3	55.2	61.4	6.2
Liberia	56.0	53.7	58.3	4.6
Libya	72.5	70.6	74.5	3.9
Liechtenstein	77.0	73.3	80.5	7.2
Lithuania	71.1	66.4	76.2	9.8
Luxembourg	75.7	71.9	79.7	7.8
Madagascar	50.1	49.3	50.9	1.6
Malawi	39.5	39.4	39.6	0.2
Malaysia	67.8	65.1	70.7	5.6
Maldives	61.5	60.4	62.7	2.3
Mali	43.4	42.4	44.4	2.0
Malta	75.8	73.7	78.1	4.4
Man, Isle of	75.2	72.5	78.1	5.6
Marshall Islands	61.8	60.3	63.3	3.0
Martinique	77.2	74.4	80.0	5.6
Mauritania	46.2	43.6	49.0	5.4
Mauritius	69.4	65.5	73.5	8.0
Mayotte	56.0	54.0	58.1	4.1
Mexico	68.5	65.5	71.5	6.0
Micronesia	66.7	64.8	68.7	3.9
Moldova	67.3	63.9	71.0	7.1
Monaco	76.9	73.0	81.0	8.0
Mongolia	60.4	58.5	62.4	3.9
Montserrat	75.9	74.1	77.7	3.6
Morocco	65.7	63.8	67.8	4.0
Mozambique	41.9	40.8	43.1	2.3
Myanmar (Burma)	52.0	50.6	53.6	3.0
Namibia	44.3	43.5	45.2	1.7
Nauru	66.7	64.3	69.2	4.9
Nepal	53.8	54.3	53.2	-1.1
Netherlands Antilles	74.0	72.0	76.2	4.2
Netherlands, the	77.0	73.9	80.2	6.3
New Caledonia	72.1	68.8	75.6	6.8
New Zealand	75.5	72.5	78.6	6.1
Nicaragua	62.9	60.7	65.1	4.4
Niger	38.2	38.9	37.6	-1.3
Nigeria	52.5	51.5	53.6	2.1

A12-2. Life Expectancy at Birth in Years, by Gender, and Difference Between Male and Female Life Expectancy, 1990 *(continued)*

	Both sexes	Male	Female	Difference between male and female life expectancy (in years)
North Korea, Dem. Rep.	68.7	65.6	72.0	6.4
Northern Mariana Islands	71.9	68.6	75.5	6.9
Norway	76.5	73.1	80.1	7.0
Oman	68.8	66.9	70.8	3.9
Pakistan	56.2	55.8	56.7	0.9
Palau	66.9	63.9	70.2	6.3
Panama	72.9	70.2	75.6	5.4
Papua New Guinea	54.8	54.0	55.6	1.6
Paraguay	70.4	68.4	72.5	4.1
Peru	65.7	63.6	68.0	4.4
Philippines	64.3	61.3	67.5	6.2
Poland	70.9	66.5	75.5	9.0
Puerto Rico	74.3	70.0	78.9	8.9
Qatar	71.0	68.7	73.5	4.8
Reunion	72.6	69.5	75.8	6.3
Russia	68.5	63.4	73.9	10.5
Rwanda	48.1	47.1	49.2	2.1
Saint Helena	74.5	71.6	77.5	5.9
Saint Kitts and Nevis	64.6	61.7	67.6	5.9
Saint Lucia	70.2	66.5	74.0	7.5
Saint Pierre and Miquelon	73.1	71.3	75.2	3.9
Saint Vincent and the Grenadines	70.7	69.1	72.3	3.2
Samoa	66.4	64.0	68.9	4.9
San Marino	81.0	76.8	85.2	8.4
Sao Tome and Principe	61.9	60.8	63.0	2.2
Saudi Arabia	65.6	64.1	67.2	3.1
Senegal	53.8	51.4	56.3	4.9
Seychelles	69.2	64.0	74.8	10.8
Sierra Leone	44.3	41.7	47.0	5.3
Singapore	76.1	73.5	78.8	5.3
Solomon Islands	69.1	66.8	71.5	4.7
Somalia	46.2	44.7	47.9	3.2
South Africa	61.4	58.1	64.7	6.6
South Korea, Rep.	70.8	67.1	75.2	8.1
Sri Lanka	71.0	68.6	73.5	4.9
Sudan	52.6	51.8	53.4	1.6
Suriname	68.2	65.8	70.8	5.0
Swaziland	41.5	39.2	43.9	4.7
Sweden	77.6	74.8	80.5	5.7
Switzerland	77.5	74.0	81.0	7.0
Syria	65.1	64.2	66.0	1.8
Taiwan	73.2	70.6	76.0	5.4
Tajikistan	67.2	64.5	70.1	5.6
Tanzania	47.7	46.3	49.3	3.0
Thailand	68.1	65.2	71.1	5.9
Togo	55.1	53.2	57.0	3.8
Tonga	67.3	65.4	69.5	4.1
Trinidad and Tobago	69.6	67.3	71.9	4.6
Tunisia	71.0	69.8	72.3	2.5
Turkey	68.9	66.7	71.2	4.5
Turkmenistan	64.7	61.2	68.4	7.2
Turks and Caicos Islands	70.5	68.6	72.5	3.9
Tuvalu	61.7	60.4	63.0	2.6
Uganda	44.4	44.5	44.4	-0.1

A12-2. Life Expectancy at Birth in Years, by Gender, and Difference Between Male and Female Life Expectancy, 1990 *(continued)*

	Both sexes	Male	Female	Difference between male and female life expectancy (in years)
Ukraine	69.7	65.2	74.4	9.2
United Arab Emirates	72.3	70.6	74.0	3.4
Uruguay	72.6	69.4	76.1	6.7
Uzbekistan	67.4	64.1	70.8	6.7
Vanuatu	57.5	56.0	59.1	3.1
Venezuela	70.9	67.9	74.0	6.1
Vietnam	64.7	62.6	67.0	4.4
Virgin Islands	75.7	71.7	80.0	8.3
Virgin Islands, British	72.5	70.6	74.4	3.8
Wallis and Futuna	69.7	69.1	70.4	1.3
West Bank	70.0	69.0	71.0	2.0
Yemen	55.0	54.0	56.1	2.1
Zambia	38.5	38.1	38.8	0.7
Zimbabwe	41.4	41.1	41.7	0.6

Source: U.S. Census International Database, 2000: Table 010. Infant Mortality Rates and Deaths, and Life Expectancy at Birth, by Sex; <http://www.census.gov/cgi-bin/ipc/agggen>. Underlying data from U.S. Bureau of the Census.

A12-3. Life Expectancy at Birth in Years, by Gender, and Difference Between Male and Female Life Expectancy, 2000

	Both sexes	Male	Female	Difference between male and female life expectancy (in years)
Afghanistan	47.8	48.3	47.4	0.9
Albania	69.4	66.3	72.7	6.4
Algeria	69.5	68.4	70.8	2.4
American Samoa	75.1	70.7	79.8	9.1
Andorra	83.5	80.6	86.6	6.0
Angola	48.9	46.6	51.4	4.8
Anguilla	78.0	75.0	81.1	6.1
Antigua and Barbuda	71.7	69.3	74.3	5.0
Argentina	75.0	71.4	78.8	7.4
Armenia	66.4	62.0	71.0	9.0
Aruba	77.2	73.4	81.1	7.7
Australia	80.4	77.5	83.5	6.0
Austria	77.6	74.5	81.0	6.5
Azerbaijan	62.9	58.5	67.5	9.0
Bahamas, the	74.5	71.2	77.9	6.7
Bahrain	75.7	73.1	78.3	5.2
Bangladesh	61.1	61.2	61.1	-0.1
Barbados	75.2	72.4	78.0	5.6
Belarus	68.0	61.8	74.5	12.7
Belgium	77.7	74.5	81.0	6.5
Belize	69.4	67.5	71.5	4.0
Benin	54.5	52.4	56.8	4.4
Bermuda	77.2	75.4	79.0	3.6
Bhutan	53.2	53.6	52.8	-0.8
Bolivia	62.0	59.0	65.1	6.1
Bosnia and Herzegovina	71.3	67.2	75.7	8.5
Botswana	39.7	39.4	40.0	0.6

A12-3. Life Expectancy at Birth in Years, by Gender, and Difference Between Male and Female Life Expectancy, 2000 *(continued)*

	Both sexes	Male	Female	Difference between male and female life expectancy (in years)
Brazil	63.8	59.3	68.4	9.1
Brunei	72.0	70.5	73.5	3.0
Bulgaria	72.6	69.0	76.3	7.3
Burkina Faso	45.7	44.6	46.8	2.2
Burundi	45.3	43.3	47.4	4.1
Cambodia	48.5	47.0	50.1	3.1
Cameroon	51.2	49.6	52.8	3.2
Canada	79.6	76.4	82.9	6.5
Cape Verde	71.4	68.1	74.8	6.7
Cayman Islands	77.1	75.4	78.8	3.4
Central African Republic	47.6	45.7	49.5	3.8
Chad	48.9	46.5	51.5	5.0
Chile	75.8	72.7	79.0	6.3
China	70.2	68.8	71.9	3.1
Colombia	70.9	66.9	75.0	8.1
Comoros	61.3	58.8	63.9	5.1
Congo, Dem. Rep. of (Zaire)	49.6	47.3	51.9	4.6
Congo, Rep.	47.2	45.5	48.9	3.4
Cook Islands	71.1	69.2	73.1	3.9
Costa Rica	76.2	73.7	78.7	5.0
Côte d'Ivoire	45.9	44.2	47.5	3.3
Croatia	74.2	71.0	77.8	6.8
Cuba	75.9	73.5	78.5	5.0
Cyprus	77.4	75.2	79.7	4.5
Czech Republic	74.6	71.3	78.1	6.8
Denmark	76.7	74.0	79.5	5.5
Djibouti	52.0	49.9	54.2	4.3
Dominica	78.2	75.3	81.2	5.9
Dominican Republic	70.4	68.2	72.8	4.6
Ecuador	72.5	69.9	75.3	5.4
Egypt	62.7	60.7	64.8	4.1
El Salvador	70.4	67.1	73.9	6.8
Equatorial Guinea	54.9	52.5	57.4	4.9
Eritrea	56.2	54.0	58.4	4.4
Estonia	68.8	62.7	75.2	12.5
Ethiopia	40.1	38.7	41.5	2.8
Faroe Islands	78.7	75.8	81.7	5.9
Fiji	66.9	64.5	69.4	4.9
Finland	77.5	74.0	81.1	7.1
France	78.8	74.9	82.8	7.9
French Guiana	76.9	73.7	80.2	6.5
French Polynesia	72.4	70.0	75.0	5.0
Gabon	57.5	54.4	60.6	6.2
Gambia, the	54.9	52.5	57.4	4.9
Gaza Strip	73.9	72.5	75.5	3.0
Georgia	64.5	60.9	68.2	7.3
Germany	77.3	74.2	80.7	6.5
Ghana	57.5	55.4	59.6	4.2
Gibraltar	78.6	75.3	82.0	6.7
Greece	78.6	76.0	81.3	5.3
Greenland	70.8	66.7	74.8	8.1
Grenada	71.8	69.2	74.6	5.4
Guadeloupe	78.2	75.2	81.4	6.2
Guam	77.8	75.5	80.4	4.9

A12-3. Life Expectancy at Birth in Years, by Gender, and Difference Between Male and Female Life Expectancy, 2000 *(continued)*

	Both sexes	Male	Female	Difference between male and female life expectancy (in years)
Guatemala	66.8	64.2	69.7	5.5
Guernsey	78.9	76.0	81.9	5.9
Guinea	47.0	44.5	49.6	5.1
Guinea-Bissau	50.0	48.3	51.7	3.4
Guyana	61.3	58.8	63.9	5.1
Haiti	51.9	49.7	54.2	4.5
Honduras	64.3	63.0	65.7	2.7
Hong Kong SAR (China)	79.0	76.2	82.0	5.8
Hungary	71.5	67.2	76.0	8.8
Iceland	79.1	76.9	81.3	4.4
India	63.9	63.0	64.9	1.9
Indonesia	63.4	61.1	65.8	4.7
Iran	70.2	68.8	71.7	2.9
Iraq	66.5	65.5	67.6	2.1
Ireland	76.6	73.8	79.5	5.7
Israel	78.8	76.9	80.8	3.9
Italy	78.6	75.5	81.9	6.4
Jamaica	75.9	73.4	78.4	5.0
Japan	80.2	77.1	83.5	6.4
Jersey	79.0	76.2	82.0	5.8
Jordan	73.3	71.3	75.3	4.0
Kazakhstan	63.2	57.7	68.9	11.2
Kenya	46.5	46.1	46.9	0.8
Kiribati	63.1	61.3	65.3	4.0
Kuwait	77.5	75.5	79.7	4.2
Kyrgyzstan	63.4	59.1	67.9	8.8
Laos	54.7	53.1	56.4	3.3
Latvia	67.5	61.5	73.8	12.3
Lebanon	71.2	68.6	74.0	5.4
Lesotho	52.0	50.6	53.5	2.9
Liberia	60.3	57.6	63.1	5.5
Libya	76.0	74.1	78.0	3.9
Liechtenstein	78.2	75.8	80.8	5.0
Lithuania	69.1	63.1	75.4	12.3
Luxembourg	77.8	74.7	81.0	6.3
Macau	82.2	78.9	85.6	6.7
Macedonia, FYRO	73.3	71.2	75.7	4.5
Madagascar	53.6	52.3	54.9	2.6
Malawi	36.0	36.3	35.7	-0.6
Malaysia	71.0	67.9	74.2	6.3
Maldives	69.0	67.2	71.0	3.8
Mali	48.0	46.5	49.5	3.0
Malta	77.9	75.6	80.4	4.8
Man, Isle of	78.0	74.5	81.7	7.2
Marshall Islands	65.2	63.5	66.8	3.3
Martinique	79.4	76.6	82.3	5.7
Mauritania	51.0	47.8	54.2	6.4
Mauritius	71.3	67.4	75.2	7.8
Mayotte	60.5	58.0	63.0	5.0
Mexico	72.4	69.3	75.6	6.3
Micronesia	68.6	66.7	70.6	3.9
Moldova	64.5	59.9	69.2	9.3
Monaco	78.8	75.2	82.5	7.3
Mongolia	62.2	60.0	64.4	4.4

A12-3. Life Expectancy at Birth in Years, by Gender, and Difference Between Male and Female Life Expectancy, 2000 *(continued)*

	Both sexes	Male	Female	Difference between male and female life expectancy (in years)
Montenegro	76.5	73.1	80.2	7.1
Montserrat	75.5	73.8	77.3	3.5
Morocco	69.2	67.2	71.3	4.1
Mozambique	46.4	45.2	47.6	2.4
Myanmar (Burma)	55.0	53.5	56.5	3.0
Namibia	41.0	41.6	40.5	-1.1
Nepal	59.0	58.9	59.0	0.1
Netherlands Antilles	74.5	72.4	76.6	4.2
Netherlands, the	78.3	75.4	81.3	5.9
New Caledonia	75.7	72.5	79.1	6.6
New Zealand	78.1	74.8	81.6	6.8
Nicaragua	67.5	65.1	70.0	4.9
Niger	42.4	42.6	42.2	-0.4
Nigeria	53.0	52.4	53.7	1.3
North Korea, Dem. Rep.	70.7	67.8	73.9	6.1
Northern Mariana Islands	75.5	72.5	78.8	6.3
Norway	78.5	75.7	81.5	5.8
Oman	71.6	69.6	73.7	4.1
Pakistan	59.7	58.8	60.6	1.8
Palau	68.0	64.9	71.2	6.3
Panama	74.8	72.1	77.7	5.6
Papua New Guinea	58.9	58.0	59.8	1.8
Paraguay	72.6	70.7	74.7	4.0
Peru	70.8	68.5	73.2	4.7
Philippines	66.8	64.0	69.7	5.7
Poland	73.3	69.2	77.7	8.5
Portugal	76.1	72.8	79.7	6.9
Puerto Rico	75.5	71.0	80.3	9.3
Qatar	74.6	72.0	77.3	5.3
Reunion	76.1	73.0	79.3	6.3
Romania	71.2	67.4	75.1	7.7
Russia	65.3	59.1	71.8	12.7
Rwanda	40.7	40.2	41.2	1.0
Saint Helena	76.0	72.9	79.3	6.4
Saint Kitts and Nevis	68.3	65.2	71.6	6.4
Saint Lucia	72.0	68.3	76.0	7.7
Saint Pierre and Miquelon	77.3	75.8	79.2	3.4
Saint Vincent and the Grenadines	74.1	72.6	75.7	3.1
Samoa	70.2	67.8	72.7	4.9
San Marino	81.5	77.7	85.4	7.7
Sao Tome and Principe	65.1	63.5	66.7	3.2
Saudi Arabia	71.1	69.2	73.1	3.9
Senegal	58.3	55.4	61.3	5.9
Serbia	73.7	71.3	76.3	5.0
Seychelles	71.2	67.1	75.3	8.2
Sierra Leone	49.7	46.6	52.9	6.3
Singapore	79.2	76.1	82.5	6.4
Slovakia	73.7	70.0	77.6	7.6
Slovenia	75.6	71.9	79.4	7.5
Solomon Islands	72.4	69.8	75.1	5.3
Somalia	46.2	44.7	47.9	3.2
South Africa	53.9	51.8	56.0	4.2
South Korea, Rep.	74.7	71.1	78.7	7.6
Spain	77.9	74.2	81.8	7.6

A12-3. Life Expectancy at Birth in Years, by Gender, and Difference Between Male and Female Life Expectancy, 2000 *(continued)*

	Both sexes	Male	Female	Difference between male and female life expectancy (in years)
Sri Lanka	72.8	70.0	75.8	5.8
Sudan	56.8	55.8	57.9	2.1
Suriname	71.2	68.6	73.9	5.3
Swaziland	37.7	36.4	39.0	2.6
Sweden	79.4	76.7	82.2	5.5
Switzerland	79.1	76.0	82.4	6.4
Syria	68.4	67.0	69.9	2.9
Taiwan	78.2	75.0	81.7	6.7
Tajikistan	64.1	61.0	67.4	6.4
Tanzania	46.0	43.5	48.5	5.0
Thailand	69.4	65.8	73.2	7.4
Togo	59.7	57.4	62.2	4.8
Tonga	70.0	68.0	72.5	4.5
Trinidad and Tobago	70.8	68.3	73.3	5.0
Tunisia	73.6	72.2	75.1	2.9
Turkey	73.8	71.2	76.4	5.2
Turkmenistan	60.9	57.3	64.7	7.4
Turks and Caicos Islands	72.6	70.6	74.6	4.0
Tuvalu	64.4	63.3	65.6	2.3
Uganda	43.5	42.6	44.5	1.9
Ukraine	66.0	60.4	71.8	11.4
United Arab Emirates	75.6	74.2	77.0	2.8
United Kingdom	77.5	74.9	80.3	5.4
United States	76.3	73.0	79.8	6.8
Uruguay	76.1	73.0	79.5	6.5
Uzbekistan	63.7	60.1	67.5	7.4
Vanuatu	61.9	59.8	64.1	4.3
Venezuela	73.2	70.3	76.5	6.2
Vietnam	68.5	66.1	71.0	4.9
Virgin Islands	78.1	74.2	82.2	8.0
Virgin Islands, British	75.3	74.5	76.1	1.6
West Bank	73.2	71.2	75.2	4.0
Yemen	60.5	58.6	62.5	3.9
Zambia	36.9	36.6	37.1	0.5
Zimbabwe	38.6	38.4	38.7	0.3

Source: U.S. Census International Database, 2000: Table 010. Infant Mortality Rates and Deaths, and Life Expectancy at Birth, by Sex; <http://www.census.gov/cgi-bin/ipc/agggen>. Underlying data from U.S. Bureau of the Census.

A12-4. Life Expectancy at Birth, Total, Male, and Female, by Continent, 2000

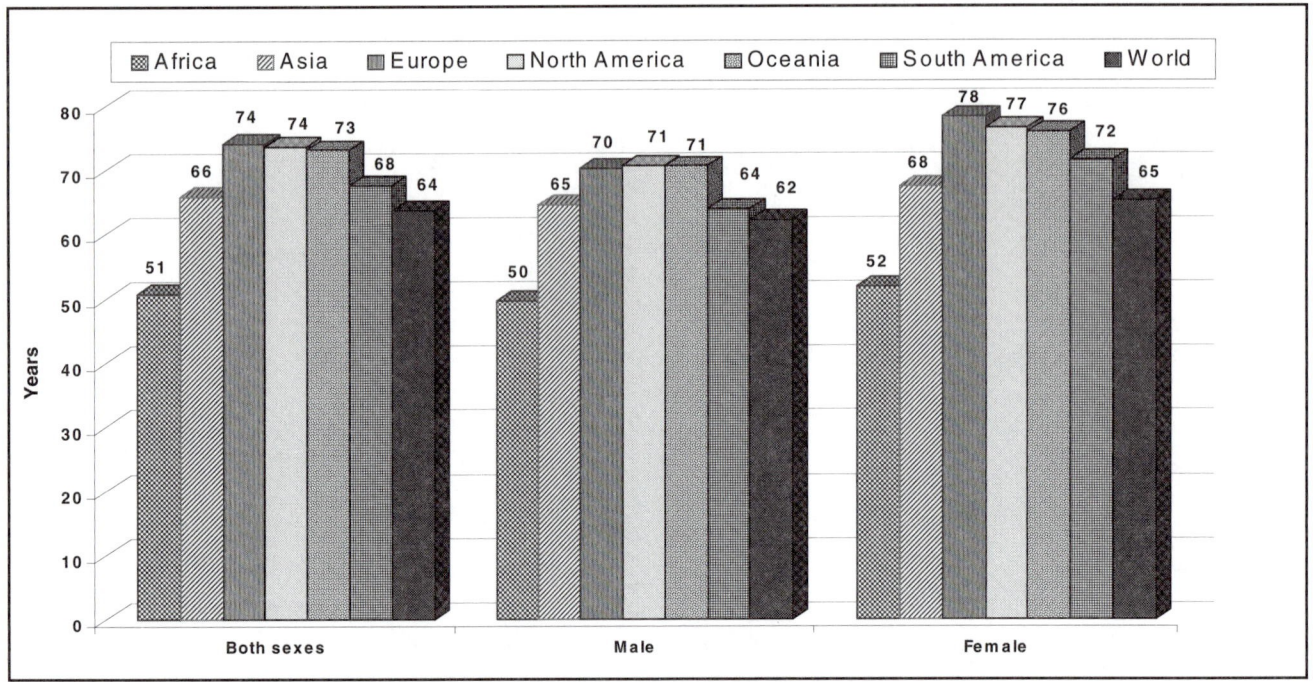

Source: U.S. Census International Database, 2000: Table 010. Infant Mortality Rates and Deaths, and Life Expectancy at Birth, by Sex; Table 028. Total Fertility Rate; Table 008. Vital Rates and Events; <http://www.census.gov/ipc/www/agggen.html>. Underlying data from U.S. Bureau of the Census.

A12-5. Projected Life Expectancy (Expectation of Life at Birth in Years), by Continent, 2025 and 2050

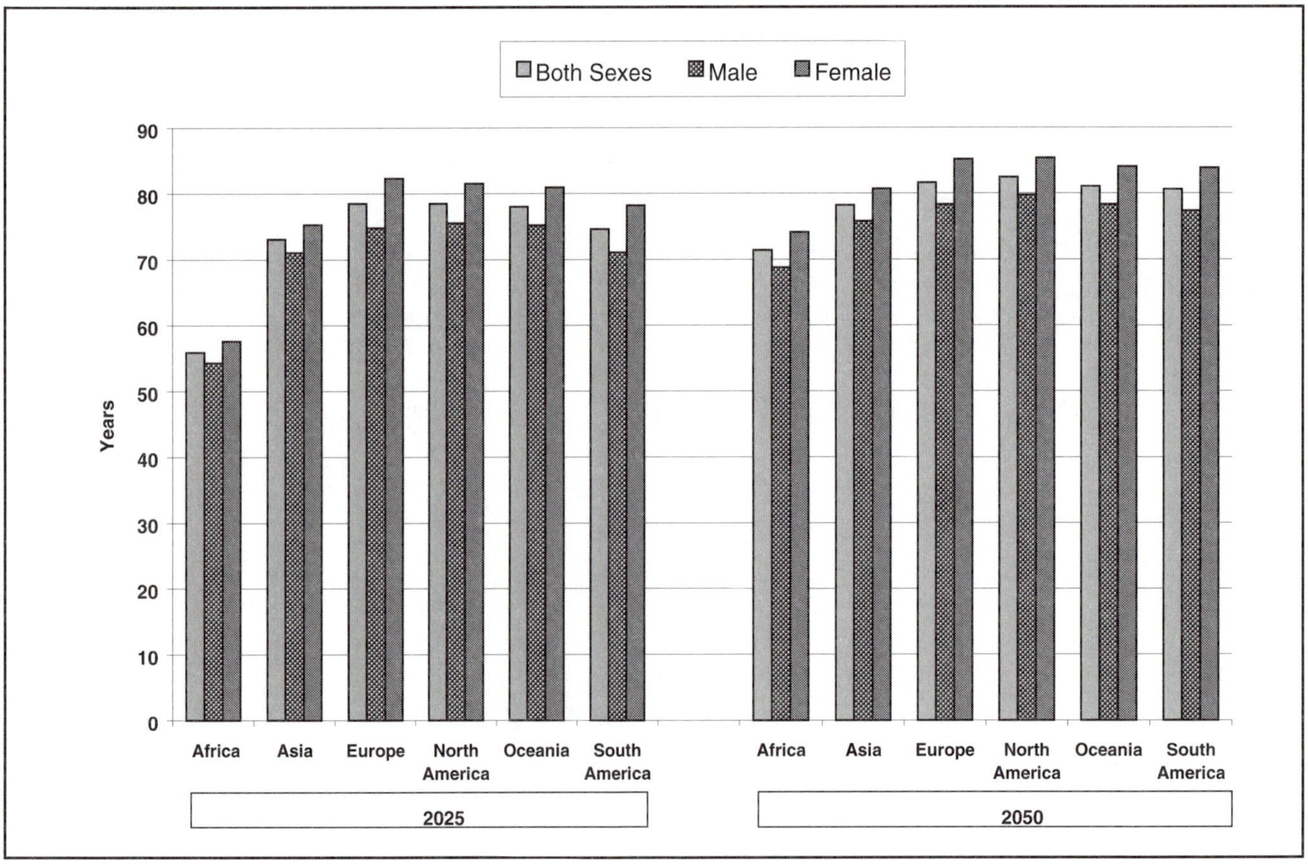

A12-5. Projected Life Expectancy (Expectation of Life at Birth in Years), by Continent, 2025 and 2050 *(continued)*

2025			
Country	Both Sexes	Male	Female
Africa	55.9	54.3	57.6
Asia	73.1	71.1	75.3
Europe	78.5	74.8	82.3
North America	78.5	75.5	81.5
Oceania	78.0	75.2	80.9
South America	74.6	71.1	78.2

2050			
Country	Both Sexes	Male	Female
Africa	71.4	68.8	74.1
Asia	78.2	75.8	80.7
Europe	81.6	78.3	85.2
North America	82.5	79.7	85.4
Oceania	81.1	78.3	84.1
South America	80.6	77.3	83.9

Source: U.S. Census International Database, 2000; <http://www.census.gov/ipc/www/idbagg.html>. Underlying data from U.S. Bureau of the Census.

A12-6. Projected Life Expectancy (Expectation of Life at Birth in Years), 2025

	Both sexes	Male	Female
Afghanistan	55.5	55.7	55.3
Albania	77.4	74.4	80.5
Algeria	76.1	74.1	78.2
American Samoa	79.6	75.6	83.8
Andorra	83.7	80.8	86.8
Angola	46.4	44.4	48.5
Anguilla	80.2	77.3	83.3
Antigua and Barbuda	76.6	74.0	79.4
Argentina	79.6	76.3	83.0
Armenia	73.7	69.9	77.7
Aruba	81.5	78.3	84.9
Australia	82.3	79.4	85.4
Austria	81.1	78.0	84.4
Azerbaijan	71.5	67.6	75.5
Bahamas, The	70.0	63.6	76.5
Bahrain	78.3	75.6	81.1
Bangladesh	69.0	68.3	69.8
Barbados	78.3	75.5	81.2
Belarus	74.5	69.6	79.7
Belgium	81.2	78.0	84.6
Belize	76.9	74.3	79.7
Benin	54.6	53.3	55.9
Bermuda	80.8	78.3	83.2
Bhutan	62.2	61.9	62.6
Bolivia	71.8	68.9	74.9
Bosnia and Herzegovina	77.3	74.4	80.4
Botswana	33.2	33.7	32.7
Brazil	70.5	66.7	74.6
Brunei	78.7	76.0	81.5
Bulgaria	77.0	73.5	80.7
Burkina Faso	51.8	50.9	52.7
Burundi	51.6	50.1	53.1

A12-6. Projected Life Expectancy (Expectation of Life at Birth in Years), 2025 *(continued)*

	Both sexes	Male	Female
Cambodia	65.3	62.4	68.4
Cameroon	58.7	57.4	60.1
Canada	82.2	78.9	85.5
Cape Verde	75.6	72.2	79.0
Cayman Islands	82.0	79.0	84.6
Central African Republic	49.2	47.8	50.7
Chad	60.4	57.7	63.2
Chile	80.0	76.8	83.4
China	77.4	74.9	80.1
Colombia	76.5	72.8	80.3
Comoros	69.0	66.3	71.8
Congo, Dem. Rep. (Zaire)	56.9	54.7	59.2
Congo, Rep.	54.7	51.0	58.5
Costa Rica	80.0	77.3	82.9
Côte d'Ivoire	49.7	48.1	51.4
Croatia	78.7	75.2	82.4
Cuba	80.3	77.6	83.1
Cyprus	80.6	78.0	83.3
Czech Republic	79.2	75.9	82.8
Denmark	80.5	77.7	83.4
Djibouti	60.7	58.2	63.3
Dominica	78.6	75.6	81.7
Dominican Republic	78.4	75.9	81.0
Ecuador	77.0	74.0	80.2
Egypt	71.6	69.0	74.2
El Salvador	76.1	72.6	79.9
Equatorial Guinea	63.3	60.7	66.1
Eritrea	65.4	62.4	68.4
Estonia	75.8	70.6	81.3
Ethiopia	48.4	47.4	49.5
Faroe Islands	81.6	78.3	84.9
Fiji	74.9	72.2	77.8
Finland	81.0	77.6	84.5
France	81.8	78.2	85.5
French Guiana	80.2	77.0	83.6
French Polynesia	79.4	76.8	82.2
Gabon	52.1	49.8	54.4
Gambia, the	63.0	60.5	65.7
Gaza Strip	75.2	73.6	76.8
Georgia	73.6	70.4	76.9
Germany	81.0	77.9	84.3
Ghana	61.3	58.7	64.0
Gibraltar	81.9	79.0	85.0
Greece	81.6	78.9	84.5
Greenland	75.0	71.4	78.7
Grenada	71.1	68.8	73.4
Guadeloupe	80.7	77.6	84.0
Guam	81.2	78.6	84.0
Guatemala	73.7	70.7	76.8
Guernsey	82.3	79.3	85.4
Guinea	55.2	51.9	58.5
Guinea-Bissau	58.9	55.9	62.0
Guyana	62.3	60.2	64.5
Haiti	57.8	55.8	59.8
Honduras	68.1	66.2	70.0
Hong Kong, SAR (China)	82.2	79.4	85.2
Hungary	77.2	73.2	81.5

A12-6. Projected Life Expectancy (Expectation of Life at Birth in Years), 2025 *(continued)*

	Both sexes	Male	Female
Iceland	82.1	79.6	84.9
India	70.9	69.5	72.4
Indonesia	74.9	72.2	77.8
Iran	76.1	74.1	78.2
Iraq	74.3	72.5	76.2
Ireland	80.6	77.8	83.7
Israel	81.6	79.2	84.2
Italy	81.8	78.7	85.1
Jamaica	79.7	77.3	82.2
Japan	82.9	79.8	86.1
Jersey	81.6	79.0	84.5
Jordan	81.0	78.3	83.8
Kazakhstan	70.8	65.9	75.9
Kenya	50.3	49.5	51.1
Kiribati	68.8	65.5	72.2
Kuwait	79.9	78.2	81.7
Kyrgyzstan	70.9	66.9	75.2
Laos	62.9	60.4	65.5
Latvia	75.1	69.9	80.6
Lebanon	77.2	74.5	80.0
Lesotho	43.7	42.1	45.4
Liberia	60.9	58.8	63.1
Libya	79.8	77.3	82.5
Liechtenstein	81.8	78.4	85.3
Lithuania	75.1	70.0	80.5
Luxembourg	80.8	77.6	84.2
Macau SAR (China)	83.4	80.5	86.4
Macedonia, FYRO	78.8	76.2	81.5
Madagascar	64.6	61.8	67.5
Malawi	42.0	41.4	42.6
Malaysia	76.9	74.0	79.9
Maldives	70.7	68.8	72.7
Mali	56.4	54.5	58.4
Malta	81.3	78.6	84.2
Man, Isle of	81.0	77.8	84.4
Marshall Islands	73.2	70.9	75.6
Martinique	81.5	80.7	82.3
Mauritania	60.6	57.9	63.5
Mauritius	77.0	73.2	80.8
Mayotte	68.5	65.9	71.2
Mexico	77.3	74.2	80.6
Moldova	72.1	68.2	76.2
Monaco	81.8	78.3	85.5
Mongolia	72.0	69.4	74.7
Montserrat	81.3	78.8	83.9
Morocco	75.8	73.1	78.5
Mozambique	37.1	37.6	36.5
Myanmar (Burma)	63.4	60.7	66.3
Namibia	37.7	38.6	36.8
Nauru	69.6	65.9	73.5
Nepal	67.1	66.7	67.6
Netherlands	81.5	78.6	84.6
Netherlands Antilles	79.4	76.8	82.0
New Caledonia	78.2	75.1	81.3
New Zealand	81.2	78.2	84.4
Nicaragua	75.5	73.1	78.1
Niger	50.2	49.9	50.5

A12-6. Projected Life Expectancy (Expectation of Life at Birth in Years), 2025 *(continued)*

	Both sexes	Male	Female
Nigeria	53.4	51.8	55.0
North Korea, Dem. Rep.	76.8	73.7	80.1
Northern Mariana Islands	79.9	76.8	83.1
Norway	81.7	78.8	84.9
Oman	77.5	75.0	80.2
Pakistan	69.8	68.2	71.5
Palau	75.4	72.1	78.8
Panama	79.8	77.0	82.8
Papua New Guinea	71.4	68.8	74.1
Paraguay	78.7	76.0	81.6
Peru	76.4	73.6	79.2
Philippines	74.6	71.5	77.8
Poland	78.4	74.5	82.4
Portugal	80.0	76.6	83.5
Puerto Rico	79.9	75.9	84.0
Qatar	77.9	75.2	80.8
Reunion	78.1	74.7	81.6
Romania	76.0	72.4	79.9
Russia	73.0	68.2	78.1
Rwanda	42.6	41.9	43.3
Saint Helena	80.7	77.7	83.8
Saint Kitts and Nevis	76.8	73.8	80.0
Saint Lucia	77.8	74.4	81.5
Saint Pierre and Miquelon	81.1	78.5	83.8
Saint Vincent and the Grenadine	77.9	75.6	80.2
Samoa	75.8	72.8	78.9
San Marino	83.1	79.8	86.6
Sao Tome and Principe	73.0	70.9	75.2
Saudi Arabia	74.8	72.6	77.2
Senegal	70.7	68.5	73.0
Seychelles	76.5	71.7	81.5
Sierra Leone	54.8	51.0	58.7
Singapore	82.5	79.6	85.7
Slovakia	78.7	75.0	82.6
Slovenia	79.4	75.8	83.2
Solomon Islands	77.2	74.5	80.0
Somalia	56.0	53.6	58.4
South Africa	42.7	42.9	42.5
South Korea, Rep.	79.2	75.7	83.0
Spain	81.8	78.5	85.3
Sri Lanka	77.5	74.8	80.5
Sudan	66.0	64.3	67.9
Suriname	77.2	74.4	80.3
Swaziland	34.9	34.9	34.9
Sweden	82.2	79.5	85.2
Switzerland	82.3	79.4	85.3
Syria	75.3	73.4	77.3
Taiwan	80.4	77.5	83.4
Tajikistan	71.5	68.2	74.9
Tanzania	56.5	55.4	57.6
Thailand	75.3	72.3	78.5
Togo	57.0	54.6	59.5
Tonga	74.9	72.2	77.8
Trinidad and Tobago	74.9	72.1	77.9
Tunisia	78.7	76.6	81.0
Turkey	77.0	74.3	79.8
Turkmenistan	69.3	65.6	73.1
Turks and Caicos Islands	78.5	76.0	81.1

A12-6. Projected Life Expectancy (Expectation of Life at Birth in Years), 2025 *(continued)*

	Both sexes	Male	Female
Tuvalu	73.8	71.2	76.5
Uganda	53.0	51.5	54.6
Ukraine	72.8	67.9	78.0
United Arab Emirates	79.0	76.3	81.8
United Kingdom	81.1	78.3	84.1
United States	80.6	77.6	83.6
Uruguay	79.7	76.4	83.1
Uzbekistan	71.2	67.6	75.0
Vanuatu	69.4	67.4	71.5
Venezuela	78.3	75.2	81.6
Vietnam	75.8	73.1	78.8
Virgin Islands	81.4	77.9	85.1
Virgin Islands, British	79.8	78.1	81.7
West Bank	76.4	74.4	78.6
Yemen	68.8	66.5	71.3
Zambia	45.0	44.2	45.8
Zimbabwe	37.3	38.5	36.1

Source: U.S. Census International Database, 2000; <http://www.census.gov/ipc/www/idbsprd.html>. Underlying data from U.S. Bureau of the Census.

A12-7. Projected Life Expectancy (Expectation of Life at Birth in Years), 2050

	Both sexes	Male	Female
Afghanistan	65.1	64.5	65.8
Albania	80.9	78.0	84.2
Algeria	80.2	77.8	82.8
American Samoa	82.2	78.7	86.0
Andorra	83.9	81.0	87.0
Angola	56.1	53.3	59.0
Anguilla	82.6	79.7	85.7
Antigua and Barbuda	80.5	77.7	83.5
Argentina	82.2	79.1	85.5
Armenia	78.7	75.2	82.5
Aruba	83.4	80.3	86.6
Australia	83.8	80.9	86.8
Austria	83.1	80.1	86.3
Azerbaijan	77.3	73.6	81.2
Bahamas, the	82.0	78.4	85.7
Bahrain	81.5	78.7	84.5
Bangladesh	75.7	74.1	77.4
Barbados	81.5	78.6	84.5
Belarus	79.2	75.0	83.7
Belgium	83.2	80.1	86.4
Belize	80.7	77.9	83.7
Benin	69.8	67.5	72.3
Bermuda	83.0	80.2	85.6
Bhutan	70.7	69.5	72.0
Bolivia	77.5	74.5	80.7
Bosnia and Herzegovina	80.9	78.0	84.1
Botswana	69.2	66.5	72.0
Brazil	79.9	76.5	83.4
Brunei	81.7	78.9	84.7
Bulgaria	80.7	77.4	84.3
Burkina Faso	70.6	68.5	72.8
Burundi	71.2	68.7	73.8

A12-7. Projected Life Expectancy (Expectation of Life at Birth in Years), 2050 *(continued)*

	Both sexes	Male	Female
Cambodia	75.2	72.3	78.2
Cameroon	75.1	72.6	77.7
Canada	83.7	80.6	86.9
Cape Verde	79.9	76.6	83.3
Cayman Islands	83.7	80.6	86.4
Central African Republic	71.4	68.6	74.3
Chad	69.2	66.1	72.5
Chile	82.5	79.4	85.8
China	80.9	78.3	83.7
Colombia	80.5	77.0	84.0
Comoros	75.7	72.7	78.7
Congo, Dem. Rep. (Zaire)	71.0	68.1	74.1
Congo, Rep.	72.0	68.9	75.3
Costa Rica	82.5	79.7	85.5
Côte d'Ivoire	71.4	68.5	74.4
Croatia	81.7	78.5	85.2
Cuba	82.6	79.9	85.6
Cyprus	82.8	80.1	85.7
Czech Republic	82.0	78.8	85.4
Denmark	82.8	79.9	85.8
Djibouti	69.5	66.6	72.6
Dominica	81.7	78.7	84.8
Dominican Republic	81.6	78.9	84.4
Ecuador	80.8	77.8	83.9
Egypt	77.4	74.6	80.3
El Salvador	80.2	76.9	83.8
Equatorial Guinea	71.6	68.5	74.7
Eritrea	73.1	69.9	76.4
Estonia	80.0	75.6	84.6
Ethiopia	70.2	67.6	72.8
Faroe Islands	83.4	80.3	86.6
Fiji	79.5	76.6	82.5
Finland	83.0	79.8	86.4
France	83.5	80.2	86.9
French Guiana	82.6	79.5	85.9
French Polynesia	82.2	79.4	85.1
Gabon	70.6	67.4	73.9
Gambia, the	71.3	68.4	74.4
Gaza Strip	78.2	76.4	80.2
Georgia	78.7	75.5	82.0
Germany	83.0	80.0	86.2
Ghana	75.0	72.1	78.0
Gibraltar	83.5	80.6	86.6
Greece	83.4	80.5	86.4
Greenland	79.5	76.1	83.0
Grenada	77.1	74.4	79.8
Guadeloupe	82.9	79.9	86.1
Guam	83.1	80.4	86.1
Guatemala	78.7	75.7	81.9
Guernsey	83.8	80.8	86.8
Guinea	64.8	61.0	68.7
Guinea-Bissau	68.0	64.6	71.5
Guyana	77.7	74.5	81.0
Haiti	72.2	69.5	75.1
Honduras	80.2	77.5	82.9
Hong Kong, SAR (China)	83.7	80.9	86.7
Hungary	80.8	77.2	84.7
Iceland	83.7	81.0	86.5

A12-7. Projected Life Expectancy (Expectation of Life at Birth in Years), 2050 *(continued)*

	Both sexes	Male	Female
India	77.0	74.9	79.1
Indonesia	79.5	76.6	82.5
Iran	80.2	77.8	82.8
Iraq	79.1	76.8	81.5
Ireland	82.8	79.9	85.9
Israel	83.4	80.7	86.2
Italy	83.5	80.5	86.7
Jamaica	82.3	79.7	85.1
Japan	84.1	81.1	87.2
Jersey	83.4	80.6	86.3
Jordan	83.0	80.2	86.0
Kazakhstan	76.8	72.4	81.4
Kenya	74.2	71.8	76.5
Kiribati	75.5	72.1	79.0
Kuwait	82.4	80.2	84.6
Kyrgyzstan	76.9	73.1	80.9
Laos	71.2	68.3	74.3
Latvia	79.5	75.2	84.2
Lebanon	80.9	78.0	83.8
Lesotho	71.4	68.5	74.4
Liberia	69.7	67.0	72.4
Libya	82.4	79.7	85.2
Liechtenstein	83.5	80.3	86.8
Lithuania	79.6	75.2	84.1
Luxembourg	82.9	79.9	86.2
Macau SAR (China)	84.3	81.5	87.4
Macedonia, FYRO	81.8	79.0	84.7
Madagascar	72.5	69.4	75.8
Malawi	67.1	64.4	69.9
Malaysia	80.7	77.7	83.8
Maldives	76.8	74.4	79.3
Mali	65.9	63.4	68.5
Malta	83.2	80.4	86.2
Man, Isle of	83.0	80.0	86.3
Marshall Islands	78.4	75.8	81.2
Martinique	83.3	81.5	85.2
Mauritania	69.5	66.3	72.7
Mauritius	80.7	77.2	84.3
Mayotte	75.3	72.4	78.3
Mexico	80.9	77.9	84.2
Moldova	77.7	74.0	81.6
Monaco	83.5	80.2	86.9
Mongolia	77.7	74.8	80.6
Montserrat	83.2	80.5	86.0
Morocco	80.0	77.2	82.9
Mozambique	64.0	62.1	66.0
Myanmar (Burma)	73.8	71.0	76.7
Namibia	70.2	68.5	71.9
Nauru	76.0	72.4	79.8
Nepal	74.4	73.0	75.8
Netherlands, the	83.3	80.4	86.4
Netherlands Antilles	82.1	79.4	85.0
New Caledonia	81.4	78.4	84.6
New Zealand	83.2	80.2	86.3
Nicaragua	79.9	77.2	82.7
Niger	60.1	59.1	61.1
Nigeria	71.7	69.3	74.1
North Korea, Dem. Rep.	80.7	77.6	83.9

A12-7. Projected Life Expectancy (Expectation of Life at Birth in Years), 2050 *(continued)*

	Both sexes	Male	Female
Northern Mariana Islands	82.4	79.4	85.6
Norway	83.4	80.5	86.5
Oman	81.1	78.3	83.9
Pakistan	76.2	74.0	78.5
Palau	79.8	76.6	83.1
Panama	82.4	79.5	85.5
Papua New Guinea	77.3	74.4	80.2
Paraguay	81.8	78.9	84.8
Peru	80.4	77.5	83.4
Philippines	79.3	76.2	82.5
Poland	81.5	78.1	85.2
Portugal	82.5	79.3	85.8
Puerto Rico	82.4	78.9	86.1
Qatar	81.3	78.4	84.3
Reunion	81.4	78.2	84.7
Romania	80.2	76.8	83.8
Russia	78.3	74.0	82.7
Rwanda	67.2	64.6	69.8
Saint Helena	82.9	79.9	86.0
Saint Kitts and Nevis	80.6	77.6	83.8
Saint Lucia	81.2	78.0	84.7
Saint Pierre and Miquelon	83.1	80.4	86.0
Saint Vincent and the Grenadines	81.3	78.7	84.0
Samoa	80.0	77.0	83.2
San Marino	84.2	81.1	87.5
Sao Tome and Principe	78.3	75.8	80.9
Saudi Arabia	79.4	76.9	82.1
Senegal	76.8	74.2	79.5
Seychelles	80.4	76.3	84.7
Sierra Leone	64.4	60.2	68.8
Singapore	83.9	81.0	87.0
Slovakia	81.8	78.3	85.3
Slovenia	82.2	78.8	85.7
Solomon Islands	80.9	78.0	83.9
Somalia	65.5	62.6	68.5
South Africa	72.3	70.2	74.6
South Korea, Rep.	82.0	78.7	85.5
Spain	83.5	80.4	86.8
Sri Lanka	81.1	78.2	84.1
Sudan	73.6	71.3	76.0
Suriname	80.9	77.9	84.0
Swaziland	66.5	63.3	69.8
Sweden	83.7	80.9	86.7
Switzerland	83.7	80.8	86.8
Syria	79.7	77.4	82.2
Taiwan	82.7	79.8	85.8
Tajikistan	77.3	74.0	80.7
Tanzania	75.2	72.6	77.9
Thailand	80.6	77.5	83.8
Togo	74.7	71.5	77.9
Tonga	79.5	76.6	82.5
Trinidad and Tobago	79.5	76.6	82.6
Tunisia	81.8	79.3	84.4
Turkey	80.7	77.9	83.7
Turkmenistan	75.8	72.2	79.6
Turks and Caicos Islands	81.6	78.9	84.5
Tuvalu	78.8	76.0	81.7
Uganda	70.2	67.8	72.6

A12-7. Projected Life Expectancy (Expectation of Life at Birth in Years), 2050 *(continued)*

	Both sexes	Male	Female
Ukraine	78.1	73.8	82.6
United Arab Emirates	81.9	79.1	84.9
United Kingdom	83.1	80.3	86.2
United States	83.9	81.2	86.6
Uruguay	82.3	79.2	85.6
Uzbekistan	77.1	73.6	80.8
Vanuatu	75.9	73.5	78.5
Venezuela	81.5	78.5	84.8
Vietnam	80.0	77.2	83.1
Virgin Islands	83.2	80.0	86.7
Virgin Islands, British	82.4	80.1	84.8
West Bank	79.3	77.0	81.8
Yemen	75.5	72.8	78.4
Zambia	70.5	67.9	73.2
Zimbabwe	71.4	69.7	73.2

Source: U.S. Census International Database, 2000; <http://www.census.gov/ipc/www/idbsprd.html>. Underlying data from U.S. Bureau of the Census.

A13. HEALTHY LIFE EXPECTANCY

A13-1. Healthy Life Expectancy (Disability-Adjusted Life Expectancy) at Birth, 1999

	Males	Females
Afghanistan	36.7	38.7
Albania	56.5	63.4
Algeria	62.5	60.7
Andorra	69.3	75.2
Angola	37.0	38.9
Antigua and Barbuda	63.4	68.3
Argentina	63.8	69.6
Armenia	65.0	68.3
Australia	70.8	75.5
Austria	68.8	74.4
Azerbaijan	60.6	66.7
Bahamas, the	56.7	61.6
Bahrain	63.9	64.9
Bangladesh	50.1	49.8
Barbados	62.4	67.6
Belarus	56.2	67.2
Belgium	68.7	74.6
Belize	58.5	63.3
Benin	41.9	42.6
Bhutan	51.4	52.2
Bolivia	52.5	54.1
Bosnia and Herzegovina	63.4	66.4
Botswana	32.3	32.2
Brazil	55.2	62.9
Brunei	63.4	65.4
Bulgaria	61.2	67.7
Burkina Faso	35.3	35.7
Burundi	34.6	34.6
Cambodia	43.9	47.5
Cameroon	41.5	43.0
Canada	70.0	74.0
Cape Verde	54.6	60.6
Central African Republic	35.6	36.5

A13-1. Healthy Life Expectancy (Disability-Adjusted Life Expectancy) at Birth, 1999 *(continued)*

	Males	Females
Chad	38.6	40.2
Chile	66.0	71.3
China	61.2	63.3
Colombia	60.3	65.5
Comoros	46.1	47.5
Congo	44.3	45.9
Congo, Dem. Rep. (Zaire)	36.4	36.2
Cook Islands	62.2	64.5
Costa Rica	65.2	68.1
Côte d'Ivoire	42.2	43.3
Croatia	63.3	70.6
Cuba	67.4	69.4
Cyprus	68.7	70.9
Czech Republic	65.2	70.8
Denmark	67.2	71.5
Djibouti	37.7	38.1
Dominica	67.2	72.3
Dominican Republic	62.1	62.9
Ecuador	59.9	62.1
Egypt	58.6	58.3
El Salvador	58.6	64.5
Equatorial Guinea	42.8	45.4
Eritrea	38.5	36.9
Estonia	58.1	68.1
Ethiopia	33.5	33.5
Fiji	57.7	61.1
Finland	67.2	73.7
France	69.3	76.9
Gabon	46.6	49.0
Gambia, the	47.2	49.4
Georgia	63.1	69.4
Germany	67.4	73.5
Ghana	45.0	46.0
Greece	70.5	74.6
Grenada	62.4	68.5
Guatemala	52.1	56.4
Guinea	37.0	38.5
Guinea-Bissau	36.8	37.5
Guyana	57.1	63.3
Haiti	42.4	45.2
Honduras	60.0	62.3
Hungary	60.4	67.9
Iceland	69.2	72.3
India	52.8	53.5
Indonesia	58.8	60.6
Iran	61.3	59.8
Iraq	55.4	55.1
Ireland	67.5	71.7
Israel	69.2	71.6
Italy	70.0	75.4
Jamaica	66.8	67.9
Japan	71.9	77.2
Jordan	60.7	59.3
Kazakhstan	51.5	61.2
Kenya	39.0	39.6
Kiribati	53.9	56.6
Kuwait	63.0	63.4
Kyrgyzstan	53.4	59.1

A13-1. Healthy Life Expectancy (Disability-Adjusted Life Expectancy) at Birth, 1999 *(continued)*

	Males	Females
Laos	45.0	47.1
Latvia	57.1	67.2
Lebanon	61.2	60.1
Lesotho	36.6	37.2
Liberia	33.8	34.2
Libya	59.7	58.9
Lithuania	60.6	67.5
Luxembourg	68.0	74.2
Macedonia, FYRO	61.8	65.6
Madagascar	36.5	36.8
Malawi	29.3	29.4
Malaysia	61.3	61.6
Maldives	54.4	53.3
Mali	32.6	33.5
Malta	68.4	72.5
Marshall Islands	56.0	57.6
Mauritania	40.2	42.5
Mauritius	59.0	66.3
Mexico	62.4	67.6
Micronesia, Federated States of	58.7	60.6
Moldova	58.5	64.5
Monaco	68.5	76.3
Mongolia	51.3	56.3
Morocco	58.7	59.4
Mozambique	33.7	35.1
Myanmar	51.4	51.9
Namibia	35.8	35.4
Nauru	49.8	55.1
Nepal	49.4	49.5
Netherlands, the	69.6	74.4
New Zealand	67.1	71.2
Nicaragua	56.4	59.9
Niger	28.1	30.1
Nigeria	38.1	38.4
Niue	61.0	62.2
North Korea, Dem. Rep.	51.4	53.1
Norway	68.8	74.6
Oman	61.8	64.1
Pakistan	55.0	56.8
Palau	57.4	60.7
Panama	64.9	67.2
Papua New Guinea	45.5	48.5
Paraguay	60.7	65.3
Peru	58.0	60.8
Philippines	57.1	60.7
Poland	62.3	70.1
Portugal	65.9	72.7
Qatar	64.2	62.8
Romania	58.8	65.8
Russia	56.1	66.4
Rwanda	32.9	32.7
Saint Kitts and Nevis	58.7	64.4
Saint Lucia	62.4	67.6
Saint Vincent and the Grenadines	65.0	67.8
Samoa	58.7	62.3
San Marino	69.5	75.0
Sao Tome and Principe	52.1	54.8
Saudi Arabia	65.1	64.0

A13-1. Healthy Life Expectancy (Disability-Adjusted Life Expectancy) at Birth, 1999 *(continued)*

	Males	Females
Senegal	43.5	45.6
Seychelles	56.4	62.1
Sierra Leone	25.8	26.0
Singapore	67.4	71.2
Slovakia	63.5	69.7
Slovenia	64.9	71.9
Solomon Islands	54.5	55.3
Somalia	35.9	36.9
South Africa	38.6	41.0
South Korea. Rep.	59.9	64.7
Spain	69.8	75.7
Sri Lanka	59.3	66.3
Sudan	42.6	43.5
Suriname	60.2	65.2
Swaziland	37.8	38.4
Sweden	71.2	74.9
Switzerland	69.5	75.5
Syria	58.8	58.9
Tajikistan	55.1	59.4
Tanzania	35.9	36.1
Thailand	58.4	62.1
Togo	40.0	41.4
Tonga	61.4	64.3
Trinidad and Tobago	62.8	66.4
Tunisia	62.0	60.7
Turkey	64.0	61.8
Turkmenistan	51.9	56.7
Tuvalu	57.1	57.6
Uganda	32.9	32.5
Ukraine	58.5	67.5
United Arab Emirates	65.0	65.8
United Kingdom	69.7	73.7
United States of America	67.5	72.6
Uruguay	64.1	69.9
Uzbekistan	58.0	62.3
Vanuatu	51.3	54.4
Venezuela	62.9	67.1
Vietnam	56.7	59.6
Yemen	49.7	49.7
Yugoslavia	64.2	68.1
Zambia	30.0	30.7
Zimbabwe	33.4	32.4

Source: World Health Report 2000—Health Systems: Improving Performance, Table 5. <http://filestore.who.int/~who/whr/2000/en/excel/AnnexTable05.xls>. Underlying data from World Health Organization (WHO).

B. Education

GENERAL OVERVIEW

Education is one of the most important elements in a child's world, affecting quality of life and determining the future. The indicators in this section compile statistics on a broad range of topics that are needed to understand the environment in which children learn and the educational challenges they face. Subjects include enrollment, gender issues, funding, educational resources, student performances, and literacy.

Over the past decades the overall percentage and number of children attending schools has risen. According to UNESCO primary school attendance increased by 10 million annually during the 1990s—nearly double the rate of the 1980s. Yet, there are still dramatic differences in educational opportunities for the world's children. Ninety-seven percent of children not attending primary school live in the developing countries. One in three children in developing countries does not complete five years of education—the minimum required for achieving basic literacy. Throughout the world, ethnic minorities as well as children in geographically remote or rural areas and urban slums also lag behind in enrollment. In some nations girls are at particular risk. More than 60 percent of the 110 million out-of-school children in the developing world are girls—a result of religious, cultural, and economic factors.

Providing basic education remains a challenge for developing nations struggling to offer social services with limited resources. Government funding is essential for universal schooling, yet almost half of the developing countries reported public spending on primary education of less than 1.7 percent of their GNPs in 1998. One-tenth of the countries reported spending of less than 0.7 percent. Many children in the developing world go to schools with few educational resources. Basic elements such as running water and sanitation are lacking. Books, and even chalk, may be scarce. UNESCO estimates that millions of children are taught by untrained and underpaid teachers in overcrowded and poorly equipped classrooms.

While providing basic education consumes the developing world, the industrialized world focuses on the type and quality of education. These countries struggle with issues such as math and science achievement, reading proficiency, and geographic literacy to prepare their children for their future in a global economy.

EXPLANATION OF INDICATORS

B1-1–B1-2. Number of schools: This set of tables presents numbers of schools for pre-primary and primary institutions. UNESCO defines a school as an educational institute where a group of students of one or more grades is organized to receive instruction of a given type and level under one or more than one teacher. Under the International Standard Classification of Education guidelines, pre-primary schools are institutions for children who are not old enough to enter school at the primary level. These include nursery schools, kindergartens, and infant schools. Nurseries as well as childcare and play centers are generally excluded. Elementary school, middle school, intermediate school, and junior high school through the eighth grade are classified as primary schools. Primary schools provide the basic tools of learning such as reading, writing, and math. Secondary and high schools provide educational emphasis on skills beyond basic reading, writing, and math.

B2. Compulsory education: This indicator shows the age at which a child is first required by the prevailing law of the country to attend school, as well as the age at which he or she may legally leave the education system. It also gives compulsory education duration, the number of years of school attendance that are required by law, providing there is a suitable school within reasonable distance of a child's home.

Compulsory education is meant to provide every child with a fundamental education in math, reading, and writing. A greater number of years of compulsory education generally corresponds to higher education levels in a society. Nevertheless, in spite of compulsory education laws, school attendance is not always possible in many developing countries because economic conditions force children to seek work to help families. Other factors limiting the effectiveness of education laws are a shortage of trained teachers, inadequate school buildings and classrooms, and long distances from homes to schools.

B3-1–B3-3. Entrance age and duration of schooling by level: These three indicators give the age at which children are accepted for pre-primary, primary, and secondary education, as well as the number of years of schooling at each level. Entrance age at different levels and duration of years varies significantly among countries, a result of diverse educational philosophies and traditions. Comparisons among nations, therefore, must be made with caution.

B4. Net Apparent Intake Rate (NAIR): The net intake rate (also known as net admission rate) is the number of new entrants (of official admission age) into the first grade of primary education. It is expressed as a percentage of the population of the same age. The NAIR is a significant indicator of the level of access to primary education. Countries with a policy goal of universal primary education aim for a NAIR of 100 percent.

B5-1–B5-5. Enrollment ratios: The five tables in this cluster present gross enrollment ratios for primary and secondary schools. UNESCO defines gross enrollment ratio (GER) as the actual school enrollment in a particular sector (pre-primary, primary, secondary) as a percentage of the official school age population of that sector. Gross enrollment ratio is used to analyze the development and accessibility of all levels of education in a country. The higher the GER, the closer a nation comes to educating all the children of a given age range. The GER can exceed 100 percent in countries where students outside the normal age group attend schools.

B6-1–B6-2. Age-specific enrollment ratio (ASER): These tables offer the ASER for primary and secondary schools by age: from age 5 to 14 for primary school and from age 10 to 20 for secondary school. Age specific enrollment ratio is the percentage of the population of a specified age enrolled, irrespective of the level of education. The indicator shows the extent of the participation of a specified age cohort in educational activities. A high ASER denotes a high degree of educational participation of the population of the particular age.

B7-1–B7-6. Gender and wealth: The first two tables in this cluster present enrollment by gender, permitting comparisons of the relative educational opportunities for the sexes. B7-3 and B7-4 focus the disparity between the sexes and percent of girls out of school. Worldwide, more than 60 percent of the out-of-school children are girls—a result of many factors such as inadequate number of schools for girls in societies where segregation of sexes exists and social and religious beliefs. The World Health Organization (WHO) considers raising the education levels of girls critical for any society, because educated mothers can improve the quality of life of their children. According to WHO, improved education facilities for women and girls is also closely related to improvements in health and to falling fertility rates. Table B7-5 shows the relationship of education to wealth in selected developing countries. There are often enormous gaps between the educational attainment of the rich and of the poor children within countries. In India, for example, 15–19-year-olds from the richest 20 percent of households have completed on average 10 years of schooling; children from the poorest 40 percent of households have on average no schooling. The final table shows how the death of a parent can affect a child's education. Studies have shown that children who have lost a parent or parents are less likely to attend school than those whose parents are alive. These children frequently leave school because they must contribute to the family income or because they are needed to help in the home.

B8-1–B8-2. Types of education: B8-1 and B8-2 present enrollment figures for two major types of secondary education: vocational and general. General education provides general or specialized education which does not aim at preparing the pupils directly for a given trade or occupation, and offers the programs necessary for college admission. These schools may be known by a variety of names, and duration of training may vary greatly. Vocational education prepares pupils directly for a trade or occupation other than teaching. Many countries have composite schools that offer both general and vocational education. Numbers for these schools are included in general education.

B9-1–B9-5. Class size and pupil-teacher ratio: This cluster of tables offers limited figures on class size (B9-1 and B9-2) as well as tables on pupil-teacher ratio for pre-primary, primary, and secondary schools (B9-3–B9-5). Pupil-teacher ratio is calculated by dividing the number of students at a particular school level by the total number of teachers at that level. It measures the human resources input in educating the student population. Education experts use pupil-teacher ratios as an indicator of the quality of a nation's education system because they associate individual care with academic performance. Thus lower pupil-teacher ratios are thought to reflect a better education system.

B10-1. Coefficient of efficiency: The coefficient of efficiency is the ideal number of pupil-years required to produce a number of graduates from a given school-cohort. It is expressed as a percentage of the actual number of pupil-years spent to produce the same number of graduates. One school year spent in a grade by a pupil is counted as one pupil-year. This indicator summarizes the consequences of repetition and dropout and measures the internal efficiency of an educational system.

B11-1. Students repeating grades: This indicator measures the extent and patterns of repetition of grades as part of the internal efficiency of education system. The total number of pupils who are enrolled in the same grade as they were in the previous year is expressed as a percentage of the total enrollment. Ideally, the percentage of repeaters should be zero, indicating absence of grade repetition. A high percent of repeaters means there are serious problems with the effectiveness of the education system. UNESCO reports that grade repetition coincides strongly with poverty and low maternal education levels.

B12-1. Survival ratios: The survival ratio is the percentage of a cohort of students enrolled in the first grade of a given level or cycle of education in a given school year who are expected to reach successive grades. Survival ratios measure the holding power and internal efficiency of an education system and conversely the magnitude of dropout by grade. A survival ratio approaching 100 percent indicates a high level of retention and low incidence of dropout. Education experts look particularly at the survival rate to grade 5 of primary education because they view five years of schooling as the prerequisite for sustainable literacy.

B13-1. Transition rate: Transition rate is the number of students admitted to the first grade of a higher level of education in a given year expressed as a percentage of the number of students enrolled in the final grade of the lower level of education in the previous year. This indicator conveys information on the degree of access from one level of education to a higher one. It can also help in assessing the relative selectivity of an education system. High transition rates indicate a high level of access and intake capacity at the next level of education.

B14-1. School life expectancy (SLE): School life expectancy is an indicator of the overall level of development of an educational system in terms of the number of years of education that a child can expect to achieve. SLE is defined as the total number of years of schooling that a child of a certain age can expect to receive in the future, assuming that the probability of his or her being enrolled in school at any particular age is equal to the current enrollment ratio for that age. The expected number of years does not necessarily coincide with the expected number of grades of education completed because grade repetition is included in the calculation. Education systems vary greatly from country to country, so a grade completed in one country is not necessarily the same as a grade completed in another country in terms of educational content or quality. Comparing the SLE figures for males and females may reveal a gender disparity because cultural and economic factors may prompt a country to emphasize educational opportunities for males.

B15-1–B15-5. Facilities: The first three tables in this grouping offer a glimpse of the physical conditions and resources children encounter in some of the poorest countries of the developing world. B15-1 furnishes information on one of the most basic elements of the physical plant—running water and adequate sanitation. B15-2 presents figures on the availability of chalkboards in the classroom. B15-3 surveys library facilities in schools below the tertiary level for selected nations. In contrast, the last two tables (B15-4 and B15-5) present figures on use of modern technology—computers and calculators—in schools in the industrialized world. The data are dated, but this is the only material available. School and library facilities are a measure of the quality of a nation's education system. According to the UNESCO, better facilities generally provide students extra incentive to learn and contribute to the economic-socio-cultural development of a society.

B16-1–B16-8. Public spending on education: This cluster of indicators present an overview of public spending on education. The first two tables provide figures on total public expenditure on education expressed as a percentage of the GNP. (GNP is the sum of value added by all resident producers plus net receipts of income from nonresident sources.) B16-3 shows the proportion of a government's total expenditure devoted to education. Expenditures include all types of funding by all levels of government for public and private education. Experts consider these indicators a significant gauge of public policy towards education. In principle, a high percentage of the GNP or of public expenditure on education denotes a high level of attention, but the percentage is also affected by the age of the population. Ideally countries with a larger share of young people would devote larger proportions of their budgets to education than those nations with older populations. B16-4 offers data on primary school spending as a percentage of total education expenditures, and B16-5 and B16-6 on spending per pupil. Again, in principle a high rate of spending per pupil indicates interest in education, but some experts question the relationship between per pupil spending and educational achievement. The final two tables focus on funds devoted to teaching materials: textbooks, books, and other scholastic supplies. These figures are one measure of the educational expenditures that directly affect the student. UNESCO defines spending on teaching materials as the ratio of public expenditure on teaching materials to total public expenditure on education for a particular level of education.

B17-1. Time spent in overall instruction: This table presents time spent in formal instruction for 13-year-olds in selected industrial countries. The data are for overall instruction as well as math and science education. Some experts consider length of hours in the classroom an indicator of a nation's commitment to education and a measure of the quality of its education system. The inclusion of specific figures for math and science reflect the importance contemporary educators place on these subjects.

B18-1. Homework: There are only very limited data available on homework patterns. B18 presents figures for 9- and 13-year-olds in 14 industrial nations. UNESCO views homework as a form of practice, and most educators believe that it improves student achievement. This indicator must be viewed with caution. It does not address the quality of the homework assigned, the degrees to which students actually complete homework, or the effort and care students take in completing it.

B19-1–B19-11. Student performance and achievement: The following 11 indicators present figures on achievement in core curriculum subjects: math, science, geography and reading. The measures for math, science and geography are based on standardized tests given by the International Assessment of Educational Progress. Those for reading come from a test administered by International Association for the Evaluation of Educational Achievement.

B20-1. Literacy rates: Literacy rate is defined as the percentage of population that can both read and write with understanding a short simple statement on his or her everyday life. A person who can only write figures, his or her name, or a memorized ritual phrase is not considered literate. Generally calculated for people 15 years and over, basic literacy rate is a crucial indicator of a population's education attainment. Raising levels of literacy, especially in developing countries, is crucial for expanding economic opportunity and ensuring a prosperous future for children.

B21-1–B21-2. Illiteracy: Two indicators illustrate the problem of illiteracy. B21-1 lists the population aged 15 to 19 years who cannot both read and write, with understanding, a short simple statement on everyday life. It also compares this portion of the illiterate population to that of the illiterate population as a whole. B21-2 surveys women ages 15 to 19 with no education. It illustrates the fact that there are still many countries, mostly developing nations in Africa and Asia, where much more emphasis is given to educating boys than girls.

B1. NUMBER OF SCHOOLS

B1-1. Number of Pre-Primary Schools, various years

	Year	Number of schools
Argentina	1997	15,219
Australia	1997	N/A
Austria	1996	4,467
Belarus	1996	4,494
Benin	1997	N/A
Brazil	1997	N/A
Bulgaria	1996	3,713
Burkina Faso	1997	147
Cambodia	1997	843
Chad	1997	31
China	1997	182,485
Costa Rica	1997	1,128
Croatia	1996	960
Czech Republic	1996	6,935
Dominican Republic	1997	3,462
Ecuador	1997	4,009
Ethiopia	1997	761
Finland	1996	2,505
Germany	1996	41,594
Gibraltar	1996	N/A
Greece	1996	5,542
Guinea	1997	N/A
Iceland	1996	257
India	1997	41,788
Japan	1997	14,690
Jordan	1997	932
Kiribati	1997	N/A
Kuwait	1997	215
Laos	1997	735
Latvia	1996	611
Lithuania	1996	729
Macedonia , FYRO	1996	417
Maldives	1997	N/A
Mali	1997	197
Malta	1996	49
Mauritius	1997	1,145
Monaco	1996	9
Netherlands, the	1996	7,287
New Zealand	1997	3,789
Nicaragua	1997	3,443
Niger	1997	123
Norway	1996	6,409
Oman	1997	5
Pakistan	1997	N/A
Peru	1997	N/A
Philippines	1997	7,317
Romania	1996	12,951
San Marino	1996	15
Senegal	1997	270
Slovakia	1996	3,396
Slovenia	1996	800
Swaziland	1997	N/A
Sweden	1996	8,356
Tanzania	1997	N/A
Tunisia	1997	N/A

B1-1. Number of Pre-Primary Schools, various years *(continued)*

	Year	Number of schools
United Kingdom	1996	1,538
Yugoslavia	1996	1,748
Zimbabwe	1997	N/A

N/A Not Available

Source: UNESCO Statistical Yearbook 1999; <http://unescostat.unesco.org/uisen/stats/stats0.htm>. Underlying data from United Nations Educational, Scientific and Cultural Organization (UNESCO).

B1-2. Number of Primary Schools, 1997

	Number of schools
Algeria	15,426
Anguilla	7
Argentina	22,437
Armenia	1,402
Australia	8,123
Austria	3,703
Azerbaijan	4,454
Bahamas, the	113
Benin	3,072
Bermuda	26
Brazil	196,479
Brunei	72
Bulgaria	3,170
Cambodia	4,899
Cameroon	8,514
Chad	N/A
China	645,983
Costa Rica	3,671
Côte d'Ivoire	7,599
Croatia	1,094
Cuba	9,926
Cyprus	376
Ecuador	17,367
Egypt	18,522
Eritrea	549
Ethiopia	10,256
Finland	3,766
France	N/A
Georgia	3,201
Germany	17,892
Gibraltar	11
Greece	6,651
Guinea	3,534
Guyana	420
Iceland	193
India	598,354
Indonesia	173,893
Iran	63,101
Ireland	N/A
Jamaica	N/A
Japan	24,482
Jordan	2,575
Kiribati	86
Kuwait	275
Latvia	1,074

B1-2. Number of Primary Schools, 1997 *(continued)*

	Number of schools
Lebanon	2,160
Lithuania	N/A
Luxembourg	N/A
Macedonia, FYRO	1,086
Malaysia	N/A
Maldives	230
Mali	2,133
Mauritania	2,392
Mauritius	283
Mexico	95,855
Moldova	N/A
Monaco	7
Mongolia	N/A
Morocco	5,806
Netherlands, the	7,287
New Zealand	2,296
Nicaragua	7,098
Niger	3,063
Oman	429
Palestine	1,118
Peru	33,017
Philippines	37,645
Romania	6,188
San Marino	14
Saudi Arabia	11,506
Senegal	3,530
Slovakia	N/A
Slovenia	824
South Korea, Rep.	5,733
St. Lucia	89
Sudan	11,158
Swaziland	529
Sweden	N/A
Syria	10,783
Tajikistan	3,432
Tanzania	11,290
Togo	N/A
Trinidad and Tobago	476
Tunisia	4,428
Turkey	47,313
Turks and Caicos Islands	21
United Arab Emirates	N/A
United Kingdom	23,306
Venezuela	N/A
Vietnam	N/A
Yemen	N/A
Zimbabwe	4,670

N/A   Not Available

Source: UNESCO Statistical Yearbook 1999; <http://unescostat.unesco.org/uisen/stats/stats0.htm>. Underlying data from United Nations Educational, Scientific and Cultural Organization (UNESCO).

B2. COMPULSORY EDUCATION

B2-1. Compulsory Education—Beginning and Ending Ages and Duration in Years, 1999

	Beginning age	End age	Duration (years) 1999
Afghanistan	7	13	6
Albania	6	14	8
Algeria	6	15	9
American Samoa	6	18	12
Andorra	N/A	N/A	N/A
Angola	7	15	8
Anguilla	5	16	12
Antigua and Barbuda	5	16	11
Argentina	5	14	10
Armenia	6	17	11
Australia	6	15	10
Austria	6	15	9
Azerbaijan	6	17	11
Bahamas, the	5	14	9
Bahrain	6	15	9
Bangladesh	5	10	5
Barbados	5	16	11
Belarus	6	15	9
Belgium	6	18	12
Belize	5	14	10
Benin	6	11	6
Bermuda	5	16	11
Bolivia	6	14	8
Brazil	7	14	8
British Virgin Islands	5	16	11
Brunei	5	16	12
Bulgaria	7	16	8
Burkina Faso	7	14	7
Burundi	7	13	6
Cameroon	6	12	6
Canada	6	16	10
Cape Verde	7	13	6
Cayman Islands	5	15	10
Central African Republic	6	14	6
Chad	6	12	6
Chile	6	13	8
China	7	15	9
Colombia	6	12	5
Comoros	7	16	9
Congo	6	16	10
Cook Islands	6	15	9
Costa Rica	6	18	10
Côte d'Ivoire	7	13	6
Croatia	7	15	8
Cuba	6	16	9
Cyprus	5	15	9
Czech Republic	6	15	9
Denmark	7	16	9
Djibouti	6	12	6
Dominica	5	16	11
Dominican Republic	5	14	10
Ecuador	5	15	10
Egypt	6	14	8
El Salvador	7	15	9
Equatorial Guinea	6	11	5

B2-1. Compulsory Education—Beginning and Ending Ages and Duration in Years, 1999 *(continued)*

	Beginning age	End age	Duration (years) 1999
Eritrea	7	13	7
Estonia	7	16	9
Ethiopia	7	13	6
Falkland Islands (Malvinas)	5	16	11
Fiji	6	15	8
Finland	7	16	9
France	6	16	10
French Guiana	6	16	10
French Polynesia	6	16	10
Gabon	6	16	10
Georgia	6	14	9
Germany	6	18	12
Ghana	6	14	8
Gibraltar	4	15	12
Greece	6	15	9
Grenada	5	16	11
Guadeloupe	6	16	10
Guam	5	16	11
Guatemala	7	14	6
Guinea	7	13	6
Guinea-Bissau	7	13	6
Guyana	6	14	8
Haiti	6	12	6
Honduras	7	12	6
Hong Kong, SAR (China)	7	15	9
Hungary	6	16	10
Iceland	6	16	10
India	6	14	8
Indonesia	7	15	9
Iran	6	11	5
Iraq	6	12	6
Ireland	6	15	9
Israel	5	15	11
Italy	6	14	8
Jamaica	6	12	6
Japan	6	15	9
Jordan	6	15	9
Kazakhstan	6	17	11
Kenya	6	14	8
Kiribati	6	15	9
Kuwait	6	14	8
Kyrgyzstan	7	16	10
Laos	6	15	5
Lebanon	7	15	9
Lesotho	6	13	7
Liberia	6	16	10
Libya	6	15	9
Liechtenstein	7	16	8
Lithuania	7	15	9
Luxembourg	6	15	9
Macau	6	12	5
Macedonia, FYRO	6	15	9
Madagascar	6	13	6
Malawi	6	14	8
Malaysia	N/A	N/A	N/A
Mali	7	16	9
Malta	5	16	11
Martinique	6	16	10

B2-1. Compulsory Education—Beginning and Ending Ages and Duration in Years, 1999 _(continued)_

	Beginning age	End age	Duration (years) 1999
Mauritania	6	12	6
Mauritius	5	12	7
Mexico	6	14	6
Moldova	6	17	11
Monaco	6	16	10
Mongolia	8	16	8
Montserrat	5	14	9
Morocco	7	16	6
Mozambique	7	14	7
Myanmar (Burma)	5	10	5
Namibia	6	16	10
Nauru	6	16	10
Nepal	6	11	5
Netherlands, the	5	18	13
New Caledonia	6	16	10
New Zealand	6	16	10
Nicaragua	6	12	6
Niger	7	15	8
Nigeria	6	12	6
Niue	5	14	8
North Korea, Dem. Rep.	5	15	10
Norway	7	15	9
Pakistan	N/A	N/A	N/A
Palau	6	14	8
Panama	6	15	6
Paraguay	6	12	6
Peru	6	12	6
Philippines	6	12	6
Poland	7	15	8
Portugal	6	15	9
Puerto Rico	6	16	10
Reunion	6	16	10
Romania	7	14	8
Russia	6	15	9
Rwanda	7	13	6
Samoa	5	14	8
San Marino	6	14	8
Sao Tome and Principe	6	14	4
Senegal	7	13	6
Seychelles	6	16	10
Slovakia	6	15	9
Slovenia	7	15	8
Somalia	6	14	8
South Africa	6	14	9
South Korea, Rep.	6	15	9
Spain	6	16	10
Sri Lanka	5	14	9
St. Helena	5	15	10
St. Kitts and Nevis	5	17	12
St. Lucia	5	15	10
St. Pierre and Miquelon	6	16	10
St. Vincent and the Grenadines	5	15	10
Sudan	6	13	8
Suriname	7	12	6
Swaziland	6	13	7
Sweden	7	15	9
Switzerland	6	16	9
Syria	6	12	6

B2-1. Compulsory Education—Beginning and Ending Ages and Duration in Years, 1999 *(continued)*

	Beginning age	End age	Duration (years) 1999
Tajikistan	7	17	9
Tanzania	7	14	7
Thailand	7	15	6
Togo	6	12	6
Tokelau	5	16	12
Tonga	6	14	8
Trinidad and Tobago	5	12	7
Tunisia	6	16	9
Turkey	6	14	8
Turks and Caicos Islands	7	14	7
Tuvalu	7	14	7
Ukraine	6	15	9
United Arab Emirates	6	12	6
United Kingdom	5	16	11
United States	6	16	10
Uruguay	6	14	6
Vanuatu	6	12	6
Venezuela	6	15	10
Vietnam	6	11	5
Virgin Islands	6	16	10
Yemen	6	15	9
Yugoslavia	7	15	8
Zambia	7	14	7
Zimbabwe	7	15	8
N/A Not Available			

Source: UNESCO Statistical Yearbook 1999; <http://unescostat.unesco.org/uisen/stats/stats0.htm>. Underlying data from United Nations Educational, Scientific and Cultural Organization (UNESCO).

B3. ENTRANCE AGE AND DURATION OF SCHOOLING BY LEVEL

B3-1. Entrance Age and Duration in Years, Pre-Primary Education, 1999

	Entrance age	Duration (years)
Afghanistan	3	4
Albania	3	3
Algeria	4	2
American Samoa	3	3
Andorra	3	3
Angola	5	1
Anguilla	3	2
Antigua and Barbuda	3	2
Argentina	3	3
Armenia	3	4
Australia	4	1
Austria	3	3
Azerbaijan	3	3
Bahamas, the	3	2
Bahrain	3	3
Bangladesh	5	1
Barbados	3	2
Belarus	3	3
Belgium	3	3
Belize	3	2
Benin	3	3
Bermuda	4	1

B3-1. Entrance Age and Duration in Years, Pre-Primary Education, 1999 *(continued)*

	Entrance age	Duration (years)
Bhutan	5	1
Bolivia	4	2
Botswana	N/A	N/A
Brazil	4	3
Brunei	3	3
Bulgaria	3	4
Burkina Faso	4	3
Burundi	4	3
Cambodia	3	3
Cameroon	4	2
Canada	4	2
Cape Verde	5	2
Cayman Islands	N/A	N/A
Central African Republic	3	3
Chad	3	3
Chile	5	1
China	3	4
Colombia	3	3
Comoros	4	3
Congo, Dem. Rep. (Zaire)	3	3
Congo, Rep.	3	3
Cook Islands	4	1
Costa Rica	5	1
Côte d'Ivoire	3	3
Croatia	3	4
Cuba	5	1
Cyprus	2	4
Czech Republic	3	3
Denmark	3	4
Djibouti	4	2
Dominica	3	2
Dominican Republic	3	3
Ecuador	5	1
Egypt	4	2
El Salvador	4	3
Equatorial Guinea	3	3
Eritrea	5	2
Estonia	3	4
Ethiopia	4	3
Falkland Islands (Malvinas)	4	1
Fiji	3	3
Finland	3	4
France	2	4
French Guiana	2	4
French Polynesia	3	3
Gabon	3	3
Gambia, the	5	2
Georgia	3	3
Germany	3	3
Ghana	4	2
Gibraltar	3	1
Greece	4	2
Grenada	3	2
Guadeloupe	2	4
Guam	5	1
Guatemala	5	2
Guinea	4	3
Guinea-Bissau	4	3

B3-1. Entrance Age and Duration in Years, Pre-Primary Education, 1999 *(continued)*

	Entrance age	Duration (years)
Guyana	4	2
Haiti	3	3
Honduras	4	3
Hong Kong SAR , China	3	3
Hungary	3	3
Iceland	2	4
India	4	2
Indonesia	5	2
Iran	5	1
Iraq	4	2
Ireland	4	2
Israel	2	4
Italy	3	3
Jamaica	3	3
Japan	3	3
Jordan	4	2
Kazakhstan	3	4
Kenya	3	3
Kiribati	4	2
Kuwait	4	2
Kyrgyzstan	3	4
Laos	3	3
Latvia	3	4
Lebanon	3	3
Lesotho	N/A	N/A
Liberia	4	3
Libya	4	2
Liechtenstein	4	2
Lithuania	3	...
Luxembourg	4	2
Macau	3	3
Macedonia, FYRO	3	4
Madagascar	3	3
Malawi	N/A	N/A
Malaysia	4	2
Maldives	4	2
Mali	3	4
Malta	3	2
Martinique	2	4
Mauritania	3	3
Mauritius	3	2
Mexico	4	2
Moldova	3	4
Monaco	3	3
Mongolia	4	5
Montserrat	3	2
Morocco	5	N/A
Mozambique	N/A	N/A
Myanmar (Burma)	4	1
Namibia	6	1
Nauru	5	1
Nepal	3	3
Netherlands, the	4	2
New Caledonia	3	3
New Zealand	2	3
Nicaragua	3	4
Niger	4	3
Nigeria	3	3

B3-1. Entrance Age and Duration in Years, Pre-Primary Education, 1999 *(continued)*

	Entrance age	Duration (years)
Niue	4	1
North Korea, Dem. Rep.	4	2
Norway	4	3
Oman	4	2
Pakistan	3	2
Palestine	4	2
Panama	5	1
Papua New Guinea	5	2
Paraguay	5	1
Peru	3	3
Philippines	5	2
Poland	3	4
Portugal	3	3
Puerto Rico	3	2
Qatar	4	2
Reunion	2	4
Romania	3	4
Russia	3	4
Rwanda	4	3
Samoa	3	2
San Marino	3	3
Sao Tome and Principe	3	4
Saudi Arabia	4	2
Senegal	4	3
Seychelles	4	2
Sierra Leone	3	2
Singapore	4	2
Slovakia	3	3
Slovenia	3	4
Solomon Islands	3	3
Somalia	4	2
South Africa	5	1
South Korea, Rep.	5	1
Spain	2	4
Sri Lanka	4	1
St. Helena	3	2
St. Kitts and Nevis	3	2
St. Lucia	2	3
St. Pierre and Miquelon	2	4
St. Vincent and the Grenadines	3	2
Sudan	4	2
Suriname	4	2
Swaziland	3	3
Sweden	3	4
Switzerland	5	2
Syria	3	3
Tajikistan	3	4
Tanzania	4	2
Thailand	3	3
Togo	3	3
Tokelau	3	2
Tonga	3	3
Trinidad and Tobago	3	2
Tunisia	3	3
Turkey	4	2
Turkmenistan	3	4
Turks and Caicos Islands	4	2
Tuvalu	3	3

B3-1. Entrance Age and Duration in Years, Pre-Primary Education, 1999 *(continued)*

	Entrance age	Duration (years)
Uganda	N/A	N/A
Ukraine	3	4
United Arab Emirates	4	2
United Kingdom	3	2
United States	3	3
Uruguay	3	3
Uzbekistan	3	3
Vanuatu	3	3
Venezuela	3	3
Vietnam	3	3
Virgin Islands	5	1
Virgin Islands, British	3	2
Yemen	3	3
Yugoslavia	3	4
Zambia	3	4
Zimbabwe	5	1

N/A Not Available

Source: UNESCO Statistical Yearbook 1999; <http://unescostat.unesco.org/uisen/stats/stats0.htm>. Underlying data from United Nations Educational, Scientific and Cultural Organization (UNESCO).

B3-2. Entrance Age and Duration in Years, Primary Education, 1997

	Entrance age	Duration (years)
Afghanistan	7	6
Albania	6	8
Algeria	6	6
American Samoa	6	8
Andorra	6	5
Angola	6	4
Anguilla	5	7
Antigua and Barbuda	5	7
Argentina	6	7
Armenia	7	4
Australia	5	7
Austria	6	4
Azerbaijan	6	4
Bahamas	5	6
Bahrain	6	6
Bangladesh	6	5
Barbados	5	7
Belarus	6	4
Belgium	6	6
Belize	5	8
Benin	6	6
Bermuda	5	7
Bhutan	6	7
Bolivia	6	8
Bosnia and Herzegovina	7	4
Botswana	6	7
Brazil	7	8
British Virgin Islands	5	7
Brunei	6	6
Bulgaria	7	4
Burkina Faso	7	6

B3-2. Entrance Age and Duration in Years, Primary Education, 1997 *(continued)*

	Entrance age	Duration (years)
Burundi	7	6
Cambodia	6	6
Cameroon	6	6
Canada	6	6
Cape Verde	7	6
Cayman Islands	5	6
Central African Republic	6	6
Chad	6	6
Chile	6	8
China	7	5
Colombia	6	5
Comoros	7	6
Congo	6	6
Congo, Dem. Rep. (Zaire)	6	6
Cook Islands	5	6
Costa Rica	6	6
Côte d'Ivoire	6	6
Croatia	7	4
Cuba	6	6
Cyprus	6	6
Czech Republic	6	4
Denmark	7	6
Djibouti	6	6
Dominica	5	7
Dominican Republic	6	8
East Timor	6	4
Ecuador	6	6
Egypt	6	5
El Salvador	7	9
Equatorial Guinea	6	5
Eritrea	7	5
Estonia	7	6
Ethiopia	7	6
Falkland Islands (Malvinas)	5	7
Fiji	6	6
Finland	7	6
France	6	5
French Guiana	6	5
French Polynesia	6	5
Gabon	6	6
Gambia	7	6
Georgia	6	4
Germany	6	4
Ghana	6	6
Gibraltar	4	8
Greece	6	6
Grenada	5	7
Guadeloupe	6	5
Guam	6	8
Guatemala	7	6
Guinea	7	6
Guinea-Bissau	7	6
Guyana	6	6
Haiti	6	6
Honduras	7	6
Hong Kong SAR, China	6	6
Hungary	6	4
Iceland	6	7

B3-2. Entrance Age and Duration in Years, Primary Education, 1997 *(continued)*

	Entrance age	Duration (years)
India	6	5
Indonesia	7	6
Iran	6	5
Iraq	6	6
Ireland	6	6
Israel	6	6
Italy	6	5
Jamaica	6	6
Japan	6	6
Jordan	6	10
Kazakstan	7	4
Kenya	6	8
Kiribati	6	7
Kuwait	6	4
Kyrgyzstan	7	4
Laos	6	5
Latvia	7	4
Lebanon	6	5
Lesotho	6	7
Liberia	7	6
Libya	6	9
Liechtenstein	6	5
Luxembourg	6	6
Macau	6	6
Macedonia, FYRO	7	8
Madagascar	6	5
Malawi	6	8
Malaysia	6	6
Maldives	6	5
Mali	7	6
Malta	5	6
Martinique	6	5
Mauritania	6	6
Mauritius	5	6
Mexico	6	6
Moldova	7	4
Monaco	6	5
Mongolia	8	4
Montserrat	5	7
Mozambique	7	5
Myanmar (Burma)	5	5
Namibia	7	7
Nauru	6	7
Nepal	6	5
Netherlands Antilles	6	6
Netherlands, the	6	6
New Caledonia	6	5
New Zealand	5	6
Nicaragua	7	6
Niger	7	6
Nigeria	6	6
Niue	5	6
Norfolk Island	5	7
North Korea, Dem. Rep.	6	4
Norway	7	6
Oman	6	6
Pacific Islands (Palau)	6	8
Pakistan	5	5

B3-2. Entrance Age and Duration in Years, Primary Education, 1997 *(continued)*

	Entrance age	Duration (years)
Palestine	6	10
Panama	6	6
Papua New Guinea	7	6
Paraguay	6	6
Peru	6	6
Philippines	7	6
Poland	7	8
Portugal	6	6
Puerto Rico	5	8
Qatar	6	6
Reunion	6	5
Romania	7	4
Russia	7	3
Rwanda	7	7
Samoa	5	8
San Marino	6	5
Sao Tome and Principe	7	4
Saudi Arabia	6	6
Senegal	7	6
Seychelles	6	6
Sierra Leone	5	7
Singapore	6	6
Slovakia	6	4
Slovenia	7	4
Solomon Islands	6	6
Somalia	6	8
South Africa	6	7
South Korea, Rep.	6	6
Spain	6	6
Sri Lanka	5	5
St. Helena	5	6
St. Kitts and Nevis	5	7
St. Lucia	5	7
St. Pierre and Miquelon	6	5
St. Vincent and the Grenadines	5	7
Sudan	6	8
Suriname	6	6
Swaziland	6	7
Sweden	7	6
Switzerland	7	6
Syria	6	6
Tajikistan	7	4
Tanzania	7	7
Thailand	6	6
Togo	6	6
Tokelau	5	9
Tonga	6	6
Trinidad and Tobago	5	7
Tunisia	6	6
Turkey	6	5
Turkmenistan	7	4
Turks and Caicos Islands	6	6
Tuvalu	6	8
U.S. Virgin Islands	6	6
Uganda	6	7
Ukraine	7	4
United Arab Emirates	6	6
United Kingdom	5	6

B3-2. Entrance Age and Duration in Years, Primary Education, 1997 *(continued)*

	Entrance age	Duration (years)
United States	6	6
Uruguay	6	6
Uzbekistan	6	4
Vanuatu	6	6
Venezuela	6	9
Vietnam	6	5
Yemen	6	9
Yugoslavia	7	4
Zambia	7	7
Zimbabwe	6	7

Source: UNESCO Statistical Yearbook 1999; <http://unescostat.unesco.org/uisen/stats/stats0.htm>. Underlying data from United Nations Educational, Scientific and Cultural Organization (UNESCO).

B3-3. Entrance Age and Duration in Years, Secondary Education, 1997

	Entrance age	Duration (years)
Afghanistan	13	6
Albania	14	4
Algeria	12	6
American Samoa	14	4
Andorra	11	7
Angola	10	7
Anguilla	12	5
Antigua and Barbuda	12	5
Argentina	13	5
Armenia	11	6
Australia	12	6
Austria	10	8
Azerbaijan	10	7
Bahamas	11	6
Bahrain	12	6
Bangladesh	11	7
Barbados	12	6
Belarus	10	7
Belgium	12	6
Belize	13	4
Benin	12	7
Bermuda	12	5
Bhutan	13	4
Bolivia	14	4
Bosnia and Herzegovina	11	8
Botswana	13	5
Brazil	15	3
Brune	12	7
Bulgaria	11	8
Burkina Faso	13	7
Burundi	13	7
Cambodia	12	6
Cameroon	12	7
Canada	12	6
Cape Verde	13	6
Cayman Islands	11	7
Central African Republic	12	7
Chad	12	7
Chile	14	4

B3-3. Entrance Age and Duration in Years, Secondary Education, 1997 *(continued)*

	Entrance age	Duration (years)
China	12	5
Colombia	11	6
Comoros	13	7
Congo, Dem. Rep. (Zaire)	12	6
Congo, Rep.	12	7
Cook Islands	11	6
Costa Rica	12	5
Côte d'Ivoire	12	7
Croatia	11	8
Cuba	12	6
Cyprus	12	6
Czech Republic	10	8
Denmark	13	6
Djibouti	12	7
Dominica	12	5
Dominican Republic	14	4
East Timor	10	7
Ecuador	12	6
Egypt	11	6
El Salvador	16	3
Equatorial Guinea	11	7
Eritrea	12	6
Estonia	13	5
Ethiopia	13	6
Falkland Islands (Malvinas)	12	5
Fiji	12	6
Finland	13	6
France	11	7
French Guiana	11	7
French Polynesia	11	7
Gabon	12	7
Gambia, the	13	6
Georgia	10	7
Germany	10	9
Ghana	12	7
Gibraltar	12	6
Greece	12	6
Grenada	12	5
Guadeloupe	11	7
Guam	14	4
Guatemala	13	6
Guinea	13	7
Guinea-Bissau	13	5
Guyana	12	5
Haiti	12	6
Honduras	13	5
Hong Kong, SAR (China)	12	7
Hungary	10	8
Iceland	13	7
India	11	7
Indonesia	13	6
Iran	11	7
Iraq	12	6
Ireland	12	5
Israel	12	6
Italy	11	8
Jamaica	12	7
Japan	12	6

B3-3. Entrance Age and Duration in Years, Secondary Education, 1997 *(continued)*

	Entrance age	Duration (years)
Jordan	16	2
Kazakhstan	11	7
Kenya	14	4
Kiribati	13	5
Kuwait	10	8
Kyrgyzstan	11	7
Laos	11	6
Latvia	11	8
Lebanon	11	7
Lesotho	13	5
Liberia	13	6
Libya	15	3
Liechtenstein	11	6
Lithuania	11	8
Luxembourg	12	7
Macau	12	6
Macedonia, FYRO	15	4
Madagascar	11	7
Malawi	14	4
Malaysia	12	7
Maldives	11	7
Mali	13	6
Malta	11	7
Martinique	11	7
Mauritania	12	6
Mauritius	11	7
Mexico	12	6
Moldova	11	7
Monaco	11	7
Mongolia	12	6
Montserrat	12	5
Mozambique	12	7
Myanmar (Burma)	10	6
Namibia	14	5
Nauru	13	4
Nepal	11	5
Netherlands Antilles	12	5
Netherlands, the	12	6
New Caledonia	11	7
New Zealand	11	7
Nicaragua	13	5
Niger	13	7
Nigeria	12	6
Niue	11	6
Norfolk Island	12	4
North Korea, Dem. Rep.	10	6
Norway	13	6
Oman	12	6
Pakistan	10	7
Palestine	16	2
Panama	12	6
Papua New Guinea	13	6
Paraguay	12	6
Peru	12	5
Philippines	13	4
Poland	15	4
Portugal	12	6
Puerto Rico	13	4

B3-3. Entrance Age and Duration in Years, Secondary Education, 1997 *(continued)*

	Entrance age	Duration (years)
Qatar	12	6
Reunion	11	7
Romania	11	8
Russia	10	7
Rwanda	14	6
Samoa	13	5
San Marino	11	8
Sao Tome and Principe	11	7
Saudi Arabia	12	6
Senegal	13	7
Seychelles	12	5
Sierra Leone	12	7
Singapore	12	7
Slovakia	10	8
Slovenia	11	8
Solomon Islands	12	5
Somalia	14	4
South Africa	13	5
South Korea, Rep.	12	6
Spain	12	6
Sri Lanka	10	8
St. Helena	11	6
St. Kitts and Nevis	12	6
St. Lucia	12	5
St. Pierre and Miquelon	11	7
St. Vincent and the Grenadines	12	7
Sudan	14	3
Suriname	12	7
Swaziland	13	5
Sweden	13	6
Switzerland	13	7
Syria	12	6
Tajikistan	11	7
Tanzania	14	6
Thailand	12	6
Togo	12	7
Tokelau	14	2
Tonga	12	7
Trinidad and Tobago	12	5
Tunisia	12	7
Turkey	11	6
Turkmenistan	11	7
Turks and Caicos Islands	12	5
Tuvalu	14	4
Uganda	13	6
Ukraine	11	7
United Arab Emirates	12	6
United Kingdom	11	7
United States	12	6
Uruguay	12	6
Uzbekistan	10	7
Vanuatu	12	7
Venezuela	15	2
Vietnam	11	7
Virgin Islands, British	12	5
Virgin Islands, US	12	6
Yemen	15	3
Yugoslavia	11	8
Zambia	14	5
Zimbabwe	13	6

Source: UNESCO Statistical Yearbook 1999; <http://unescostat.unesco.org/uisen/stats/stats0.htm>. Underlying data from United Nations Educational, Scientific and Cultural Organization (UNESCO).

B4. NET APPARENT INTAKE RATE

B4-1. Net Apparent Intake Rate or Net Admission Rate (New Entrants in First Grade), by Sex, 1995

	Intake rate		
	Both sexes	**Male**	**Female**
Albania	99.8	99.1	100.5
Algeria	103.3	105.9	100.6
Azerbaijan	105.0	104.4	105.6
Bahrain	103.9	102.8	105.0
Belarus	98.2	100.5	95.7
Benin	80.0	95.1	64.9
Botswana	113.8	115.0	112.6
Brunei	100.4	N/A	N/A
Bulgaria	101.6	102.7	100.5
Burkina Faso	43.3	52.8	33.7
Chad	65.5	82.3	48.7
Chile	99.7	100.5	98.9
China	107.6	106.7	108.7
Colombia	136.2	139.9	132.4
Costa Rica	100.6	101.0	100.1
Côte d'Ivoire	67.4	75.8	59.0
Croatia	85.9	86.4	85.4
Cuba	103.0	N/A	N/A
Cyprus	82.2	83.3	81.2
Czech Republic	101.4	101.5	101.4
Denmark	102.1	102.3	101.9
Djibouti	37.6	N/A	N/A
Ecuador	130.0	130.9	129.1
El Salvador	126.9	128.8	125.0
Eritrea	49.6	55.7	43.6
Estonia	97.2	97.5	97.0
Ethiopia	72.5	94.9	50.2
Finland	101.6	101.7	101.5
Gabon	138.8	139.6	138.1
Gambia	95.0	104.5	85.5
Georgia	83.6	N/A	N/A
Germany	102.8	103.3	102.2
Guinea	47.8	N/A	N/A
Guyana	94.4	97.9	90.8
Hong Kong, SAR (China)	97.7	N/A	N/A
Iceland	103.1	101.9	104.4
Indonesia	108.2	110.9	105.3
Italy	98.3	98.9	97.7
Jordan	68.4	67.6	69.3
Kuwait	71.8	73.4	70.2
Kyrgyzstan	103.2	N/A	N/A
Laos	113.6	121.1	105.7
Latvia	93.4	N/A	N/A
Lithuania	94.0	94.4	93.5
Macedonia, FYRO	104.1	105.5	102.6
Madagascar	102.3	102.5	102.1
Malawi	223.2	225.7	220.7
Mali	41.7	48.7	34.6
Malta	106.3	105.6	107.0
Mauritania	91.5	96.8	86.2
Mauritius	109.2	109.9	108.5
Mexico	114.2	114.4	113.9
Moldova	98.7	99.3	98.1
Mongolia	95.1	94.9	95.2

B4-1. Net Apparent Intake Rate or Net Admission Rate (New Entrants in First Grade), by Sex, 1995 *(continued)*

	Intake rate		
	Both sexes	**Male**	**Female**
Mozambique	68.8	77.1	60.6
Namibia	110.4	N/A	N/A
New Zealand	104.1	103.4	104.8
Nicaragua	131.8	133.2	130.3
Niger	31.5	38.7	24.4
Norway	102.3	102.2	102.4
Oman	67.5	68.4	66.6
Papua New Guinea	104.0	110.3	97.4
Paraguay	125.0	126.8	123.1
Peru	123.6	123.7	123.5
Poland	95.0	N/A	N/A
Qatar	53.6	50.5	56.9
Romania	99.9	N/A	N/A
Samoa	106.4	N/A	N/A
Saudi Arabia	75.0	74.5	75.6
Senegal	75.7	80.3	71.0
Slovakia	99.1	99.3	98.9
Slovenia	100.2	N/A	N/A
South Korea, Rep.	98.9	98.2	99.7
Sudan	69.0	74.8	63.0
Swaziland	117.5	119.0	115.9
Sweden	110.5	110.1	111.0
Switzerland	101.0	101.1	100.8
Syria	97.0	100.6	93.3
Togo	128.1	141.3	114.9
Trinidad and Tobago	87.3	88.1	86.5
Tunisia	95.7	96.6	94.7
United Arab Emirates	89.7	89.9	89.4
Uruguay	100.0	99.2	100.8
Venezuela	100.8	101.5	100.0
Yugoslavia	69.5	N/A	N/A
Zimbabwe	127.5	129.5	125.5

N/A Not Available

Source: UNESCO Statistical Yearbook 1999; <http://unescostat.unesco.org/uisen/stats/stats0.htm>. Underlying data from United Nations Educational, Scientific and Cultural Organization (UNESCO).

B5. ENROLLMENT RATIOS

B5-1. Gross Enrollment Ratios, Pre-Primary Schools, various years

	Year	Ratio
Albania	1995	40
Algeria	1996	2
Angola	1990	54
Argentina	1996	54
Armenia	1996	26
Australia	1997	80
Austria	1996	80
Azerbaijan	1996	19
Bahamas, the	1994	7
Bahrain	1996	33
Belarus	1996	82
Belgium	1995	118
Belize	1994	27
Bolivia	1990	32
Brazil	1997	58
Bulgaria	1996	63
Burkina Faso	1996	2
Cambodia	1997	5
Cameroon	1994	11
Canada	1995	64
Chile	1996	98
China	1997	28
Colombia	1996	33
Costa Rica	1998	79
Croatia	1996	40
Cuba	1996	88
Czech Republic	1995	91
Denmark	1995	83
Djibouti	1996	0.7
Dominican Republic	1997	33
Ecuador	1996	56
El Salvador	1997	40
Eritrea	1996	4
Estonia	1996	68
Ethiopia	1996	1
Fiji	1992	15
Finland	1996	45
France	1996	83
French Polynesia	1995	99
Georgia	1996	30
Germany	1996	89
Greece	1996	64
Guatemala	1996	35
Guinea	1997	4
Guyana	1996	89
Haiti	1990	34
Honduras	1994	14
Hong Kong, SAR (China)	1995	83
Hungary	1995	109
Iceland	1996	80
India	1996	5
Indonesia	1996	19
Iran	1996	11
Iraq	1995	7
Ireland	1996	114
Israel	1995	71

B5-1. Gross Enrollment Ratios, Pre-Primary Schools, various years *(continued)*

	Year	Ratio
Italy	1996	95
Japan	1995	49
Jordan	1992	25
Kuwait	1997	63
Kyrgyzstan	1995	7
Laos	1996	8
Latvia	1996	47
Lebanon	1996	75
Liberia	1980	67
Lithuania	1996	40
Luxembourg	1996	98
Macau	1992	87
Macedonia, FYRO	1996	26
Maldives	1997	66
Mali	1997	2
Malta	1996	107
Mauritius	1997	104
Mexico	1996	73
Moldova	1996	45
Mongolia	1996	25
Morocco	1996	68
Netherlands, the	1996	100
New Zealand	1997	76
Nicaragua	1998	24
Niger	1996	1
Norway	1996	103
Panama	1996	76
Papua New Guinea	1995	1
Paraguay	1997	61
Peru	1995	36
Philippines	1995	12
Poland	1995	46
Portugal	1995	61
Qatar	1995	32
Romania	1996	53
Samoa	1996	33
Saudi Arabia	1996	8
Senegal	1997	2
Slovakia	1996	76
Slovenia	1996	61
Solomon Islands	1994	36
Somalia	1985	0.3
South Africa	1995	33
South Korea, Rep.	1997	88
Spain	1996	74
Sudan	1996	23
Sweden	1996	73
Switzerland	1995	95
Syria	1996	7
Tajikistan	1996	10
Thailand	1996	62
Togo	1996	2
Turkey	1996	8
Ukraine	1993	54
United Arab Emirates	1996	57
United Kingdom	1996	30
United States	1995	70
Uruguay	1995	42

B5-1. Gross Enrollment Ratios, Pre-Primary Schools, various years *(continued)*

	Year	Ratio
Uzbekistan	1994	55
Vanuatu	1992	35
Venezuela	1996	44
Vietnam	1997	40
Yugoslavia	1996	31

Source: UNESCO Statistical Yearbook 1999; <http://unescostat.unesco.org/uisen/stats/stats0.htm>. Underlying data from United Nations Educational, Scientific and Cultural Organization (UNESCO).

B5-2. Gross Enrollment Ratios, Primary Schools, various years

	Year	Ratio
Afghanistan	1995	49
Albania	1995	107
Algeria	1996	107
Angola	1990	92
Argentina	1996	113
Armenia	1996	87
Australia	1997	101
Austria	1996	100
Azerbaijan	1996	106
Bahrain	1996	106
Bangladesh	1990	72
Barbados	1991	90
Belarus	1996	98
Belgium	1995	103
Belize	1994	121
Bolivia	1990	95
Botswana	1996	108
Brazil	1997	125
Brunei	1996	106
Bulgaria	1996	99
Burundi	1995	51
Cambodia	1997	113
Cameroon	1994	88
Canada	1995	102
Cape Verde	1997	148
Central African Republic	1991	57
Chad	1996	57
Chile	1996	101
China	1997	123
Colombia	1996	113
Comoros	1995	75
Congo, Dem. Rep. (Zaire)	1994	72
Congo, Rep.	1995	114
Costa Rica	1998	104
Croatia	1996	87
Cuba	1996	106
Cyprus	1996	100
Czech Republic	1995	104
Denmark	1995	101
Djibouti	1996	39
Ecuador	1996	127
Egypt	1997	101

B5-2. Gross Enrollment Ratios, Primary Schools, various years *(continued)*

	Year	Ratio
El Salvador	1997	97
Eritrea	1996	53
Estonia	1996	94
Ethiopia	1996	43
Fiji	1992	128
Finland	1996	99
France	1996	105
French Polynesia	1995	116
Gambia, the	1995	77
Georgia	1996	88
Germany	1996	104
Ghana	1994	79
Greece	1996	93
Guatemala	1996	88
Guinea	1997	54
Guinea-Bissau	1994	62
Guyana	1996	96
Haiti	1990	48
Honduras	1994	111
Hong Kong, SAR (China)	1995	94
Hungary	1995	103
Iceland	1996	98
India	1996	100
Indonesia	1996	113
Iran	1996	98
Iraq	1995	85
Ireland	1996	104
Israel	1995	98
Italy	1996	101
Jamaica	1996	100
Japan	1995	103
Jordan	1992	94
Kazakhstan	1996	98
Kenya	1995	85
Kuwait	1997	77
Kyrgyzstan	1995	104
Laos	1996	112
Latvia	1996	96
Lebanon	1996	111
Lesotho	1996	108
Liberia	1980	48
Libya	1993	111
Lithuania	1996	98
Luxembourg	1996	99
Macau	1992	99
Macedonia, FYRO	1996	99
Madagascar	1995	92
Malawi	1995	134
Malaysia	1997	101
Maldives	1997	128
Mali	1997	49
Malta	1996	107
Mauritania	1995	75
Mauritius	1997	106
Mexico	1996	114
Moldova	1996	97
Mongolia	1996	88
Morocco	1996	86

B5-2. Gross Enrollment Ratios, Primary Schools, various years *(continued)*

	Year	Ratio
Mozambique	1995	60
Myanmar (Burma)	1994	120
Namibia	1997	131
Nepal	1996	113
Netherlands, the	1996	108
New Zealand	1997	101
Nicaragua	1998	101
Niger	1996	29
Nigeria	1994	98
Norway	1996	100
Oman	1997	76
Pakistan	1991	65
Panama	1996	105
Papua New Guinea	1995	80
Paraguay	1997	111
Peru	1995	123
Philippines	1995	114
Poland	1995	96
Portugal	1995	128
Qatar	1995	86
Romania	1996	103
Russian	1994	107
Rwanda	1991	81
Samoa	1996	100
Saudi Arabia	1996	76
Senegal	1997	71
Sierra Leone	1990	50
Singapore	1996	94
Slovakia	1996	102
Slovenia	1996	98
Solomon Islands	1994	97
Somalia	1985	14
South Africa	1995	133
South Korea, Rep.	1997	94
Spain	1996	109
Sri Lanka	1995	113
Sudan	1996	51
Swaziland	1996	118
Sweden	1996	107
Syria	1996	101
Tajikistan	1996	95
Tanzania	1997	66
Thailand	1996	87
Togo	1996	120
Trinidad and Tobago	1995	98
Tunisia	1997	118
Turkey	1996	107
Uganda	1995	74
Ukraine	1993	87
United Arab Emirates	1996	89
United Kingdom	1996	116
United States	1995	102
Uruguay	1995	108
Uzbekistan	1994	78
Vanuatu	1992	98
Venezuela	1996	91
Vietnam	1997	113

B5-2. Gross Enrollment Ratios, Primary Schools, various years *(continued)*

	Year	Ratio
Yemen	1996	70
Yugoslavia	1996	69
Zambia	1994	91
Zimbabwe	1996	113

Source: UNESCO Statistical Yearbook 1999; <http://unescostat.unesco.org/uisen/stats/stats0.htm>. Underlying data from United Nations Educational, Scientific and Cultural Organization (UNESCO).

B5-3. Countries with Primary Gross Enrollment Ratios of Less than 50 Percent, various years

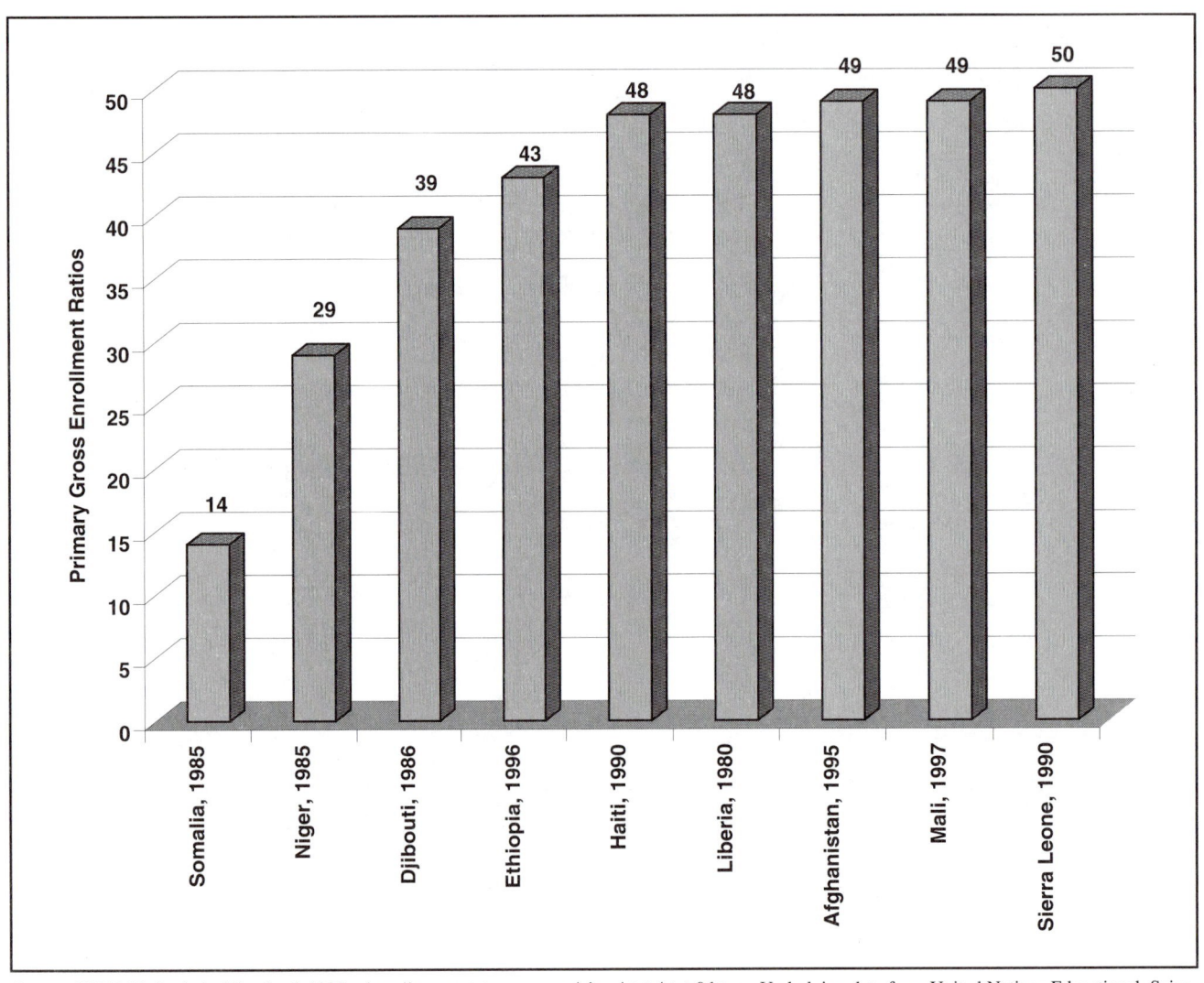

Source: UNESCO Statistical Yearbook 1999; <http://unescostat.unesco.org/uisen/stats/stats0.htm>. Underlying data from United Nations Educational, Scientific and Cultural Organization (UNESCO).

B5-4. Gross Enrollment Ratios, Secondary Schools, various years

	Year	Ratio
Afghanistan	1995	22
Albania	1995	38
Algeria	1996	63
Angola	1990	12
Argentina	1996	77
Armenia	1996	90
Australia	1997	153
Austria	1996	103
Azerbaijan	1996	77
Bahamas, the	1994	90
Bahrain	1996	94
Bangladesh	1990	19
Belarus	1996	93
Belgium	1995	146
Belize	1994	49
Benin	1997	18
Bolivia	1990	37
Botswana	1996	65
Brazil	1997	62
Brunei	1996	77
Brunei	1996	49
Bulgaria	1996	77
Cambodia	1997	24
Cameroon	1994	27
Canada	1995	105
Cape Verde	1997	55
Central African Republic	1991	10
Chad	1996	9
Chile	1996	75
China	1997	70
Colombia	1996	67
Comoros	1995	21
Congo, Dem Rep. (Zaire)	1994	26
Congo, Rep.	1995	53
Côte d'Ivoire	1997	25
Croatia	1996	82
Cuba	1996	81
Cyprus	1996	97
Czech Republic	1995	99
Denmark	1995	121
Djibouti	1996	14
Dominican Republic	1997	54
Egypt	1997	78
El Salvador	1997	37
Eritrea	1996	20
Estonia	1996	104
Ethiopia	1996	12
Fiji	1992	64
Finland	1996	118
France	1996	111
Gambia, the	1995	25
Georgia	1996	77
Germany	1996	104
Greece	1996	95
Guatemala	1996	26
Guinea	1997	14
Guyana	1996	73
Haiti	1990	21

B5-4. Gross Enrollment Ratios, Secondary Schools, various years *(continued)*

	Year	Ratio
Hong Kong, SAR (China)	1995	73
Hungary	1995	98
Iceland	1996	109
India	1996	49
Indonesia	1996	56
Iran	1996	77
Iraq	1995	42
Ireland	1996	118
Israel	1995	88
Italy	1996	95
Japan	1995	103
Kazakhstan	1996	87
Kenya	1995	24
Kuwait	1997	65
Kyrgyzstan	1995	79
Laos	1996	28
Latvia	1996	84
Lebanon	1996	81
Lesotho	1996	31
Liberia	1980	22
Lithuania	1996	86
Luxembourg	1996	88
Macau	1992	71
Macedonia, FYRO	1996	63
Madagascar	1995	16
Malawi	1995	17
Malaysia	1997	64
Maldives	1997	69
Mali	1997	13
Malta	1996	84
Mauritania	1995	16
Mexico	1996	64
Moldova	1996	80
Mongolia	1996	56
Morocco	1996	39
Mozambique	1995	7
Myanmar (Zaire)	1994	30
Namibia	1997	62
Nepal	1996	42
Netherlands, the	1996	132
New Caledonia	1997	100
New Zealand	1997	113
Nicaragua	1998	57
Niger	1996	7
Nigeria	1994	33
Norway	1996	118
Oman	1997	67
Pakistan	1991	26
Panama	1996	69
Papua New Guinea	1995	14
Paraguay	1997	47
Peru	1995	70
Philippines	1995	77
Poland	1995	98
Portugal	1995	111
Qatar	1995	80
Romania	1996	78
Rwanda	1991	11

B5-4. Gross Enrollment Ratios, Secondary Schools, various years *(continued)*

	Year	Ratio
Samoa	1996	62
Saudi Arabia	1996	61
Senegal	1997	16
Sierra Leone	1990	17
Singapore	1996	74
Slovakia	1996	94
Slovenia	1996	92
Solomon Islands	1994	17
Somalia	1985	8
South Africa	1995	95
Spain	1996	120
Sri Lanka	1995	75
Sudan	1996	21
Swaziland	1996	54
Sweden	1996	140
Syria	1996	42
Tajikistan	1996	78
Tanzania	1997	6
Thailand	1996	56
Togo	1996	27
Trinidad and Tobago	1995	74
Tunisia	1997	64
Turkey	1996	58
Uganda	1995	12
Ukraine	1993	91
United Arab Emirates	1996	80
United Kingdom	1996	129
United States	1995	97
Uruguay	1995	82
Uzbekistan	1994	94
Vanuatu	1992	20
Venezuela	1996	40
Vietnam	1997	57
Yemen	1996	34
Yugoslavia	1996	62
Zambia	1994	27
Zimbabwe	1996	49

Source: UNESCO Statistical Yearbook 1999; <http://unescostat.unesco.org/uisen/stats/stats0.htm>. Underlying data from United Nations Educational, Scientific and Cultural Organization (UNESCO).

B5-5. Gross Enrollment Ratios (Total Primary plus Secondary), various years

	Year	Ratio
Afghanistan	1995	36
Albania	1995	85
Algeria	1996	86
Angola	1990	45
Argentina	1996	98
Armenia	1996	89
Australia	1997	125
Austria	1996	102
Azerbaijan	1996	88
Bahamas, the	1994	93
Bahrain	1996	100
Bangladesh	1990	44

B5-5. Gross Enrollment Ratios (Total Primary plus Secondary), various years *(continued)*

	Year	Ratio
Belarus	1996	95
Belgium	1995	125
Belize	1994	98
Bolivia	1990	77
Botswana	1996	91
Brazil	1997	107
Brunei	1996	92
Bulgaria	1996	84
Cambodia	1997	76
Cameroon	1994	58
Canada	1995	103
Cape Verde	1997	103
Central African Republic	1991	35
Chad	1996	35
Chile	1996	93
China	1997	98
Colombia	1996	88
Comoros	1995	48
Congo, Dem. Rep. (Zaire)	1994	52
Congo, Rep.	1995	85
Costa Rica	1998	80
Croatia	1996	83
Cuba	1996	94
Cyprus	1996	99
Czech Republic	1995	100
Denmark	1995	112
Djibouti	1996	26
Egypt	1997	89
Eritrea	1996	37
Estonia	1996	98
Ethiopia	1996	29
Fiji	1992	97
Finland	1996	108
France	1996	109
Gambia, the	1995	54
Georgia	1996	81
Germany	1996	104
Greece	1996	94
Guatemala	1996	59
Guinea	1997	35
Guyana	1996	86
Haiti	1990	36
Hong Kong, SAR (China)	1995	82
Hungary	1995	99
Iceland	1996	103
India	1996	72
Indonesia	1996	84
Iran	1996	86
Ireland	1996	111
Israel	1995	93
Italy	1996	97
Japan	1995	103
Kazakhstan	1996	91
Kenya	1995	67
Kuwait	1997	69
Kyrgyzstan	1995	89
Laos	1996	72
Latvia	1996	88

B5-5. Gross Enrollment Ratios (Total Primary plus Secondary), various years *(continued)*

	Year	Ratio
Lebanon	1996	94
Lesotho	1996	78
Liberia	1980	36
Lithuania	1996	90
Luxembourg	1996	93
Macau	1992	87
Macedonia, FYRO	1997	82
Madagascar	1995	51
Malawi	1995	100
Malaysia	1997	82
Maldives	1997	96
Mali	1997	32
Malta	1996	95
Mauritania	1995	48
Mexico	1996	90
Moldova	1996	87
Mongolia	1996	70
Morocco	1996	62
Mozambique	1995	32
Myanmar (Burma)	1994	69
Namibia	1997	105
Nepal	1996	80
Netherlands, the	1996	119
New Zealand	1997	107
Nicaragua	1998	82
Niger	1996	19
Nigeria	1994	69
Norway	1996	109
Pakistan	1991	44
Panama	1996	88
Papua New Guinea	1995	49
Paraguay	1997	81
Peru	1995	99
Philippines	1995	100
Poland	1995	97
Portugal	1995	118
Romania	1996	87
Rwanda	1991	53
Samoa	1996	86
Saudi Arabia	1996	69
Senegal	1997	44
Sierra Leone	1990	36
Singapore	1996	84
Slovakia	1996	96
Slovenia	1996	94
Solomon Islands	1994	64
Somalia	1985	12
South Africa	1995	118
South Korea, Rep.	1997	72
Spain	1996	115
Sri Lanka	1995	89
Sudan	1996	44
Swaziland	1996	94
Sweden	1996	123
Switzerland	1995	99
Syria	1996	74
Tajikistan	1996	85
Tanzania	1997	42

B5-5. Gross Enrollment Ratios (Total Primary plus Secondary), various years *(continued)*

	Year	Ratio
Thailand	1996	71
Togo	1996	76
Trinidad and Tobago	1995	88
Tunisia	1997	89
Turkey	1996	79
Uganda	1995	49
Ukraine	1993	90
United Arab Emirates	1996	85
United Kingdom	1996	123
United States	1995	100
Uruguay	1995	95
Uzbekistan	1994	87
Vanuatu	1992	61
Venezuela	1996	83
Vietnam	1997	81
Yemen	1996	63
Yugoslavia	1996	64
Zambia	1994	68
Zimbabwe	1996	86

Source: UNESCO Statistical Yearbook 1999; <http://unescostat.unesco.org/uisen/stats/stats0.htm>. Underlying data from United Nations Educational, Scientific and Cultural Organization (UNESCO).

B6. AGE-SPECIFIC ENROLLMENT RATIO

B6-1. Age-Specific Enrollment Ratios, Primary Schools (Age 5–14), 1995

	AGE 5	AGE 6	AGE 7	AGE 8	AGE 9	AGE 10	AGE 11	AGE 12	AGE 13	AGE 14
Albania	N/A	85.2	100.0	100.0	100.0	100.0	100.0	100.0	99.7	35.4
Algeria	14.0	91.1	96.3	97.0	94.9	100.0	89.7	36.2	13.9	4.5
Australia	74.0	98.8	98.2	98.4	98.5	99.1	97.2	39.5	2.5	0.1
Austria	N/A	61.7	97.5	96.4	96.6	43.8	5.5	0.8	0.8	N/A
Bahrain	12.0	99.9	100.0	100.0	100.0	97.6	90.5	20.1	8.7	3.8
Belgium	1.0	97.1	100.0	99.0	99.3	97.3	97.5	22.1	3.7	0.3
Benin	9.0	55.1	70.7	64.5	60.4	60.3	46.0	36.6	22.9	13.3
Botswana	2.0	21.4	68.5	89.6	95.0	99.1	100.0	100.0	90.7	62.7
Bulgaria	0.0	9.9	92.5	93.6	95.9	77.9	8.9	4.0	2.2	1.1
Canada	27.0	91.0	99.2	100.0	100.0	89.4	87.1	13.3	1.6	0.1
Chad	5.0	26.5	41.7	47.3	45.8	44.1	33.8	29.0	21.7	15.7
Chile	0.0	39.2	92.8	93.6	91.9	90.9	91.8	92.2	98.7	67.9
China	1.0	19.5	98.7	100.0	99.6	94.7	90.1	61.7	18.0	5.3
Colombia	14.0	58.3	83.9	89.9	89.9	82.0	54.7	37.3	22.3	12.2
Costa Rica	N/A	52.8	88.3	98.6	100.0	100.0	89.5	58.6	22.0	8.0
Côte d'Ivoire	21.0	49.2	56.7	59.2	57.5	50.1	45.3	38.7	27.7	15.2
Cuba	7.0	100.0	100.0	99.8	96.0	100.0	84.4	21.7	6.6	1.7
Cyprus	15.0	80.3	80.3	81.8	84.7	83.6	73.5	3.8	N/A	N/A
Czech Republic	N/A	54.8	95.2	97.9	99.1	60.4	6.4	0.2	0.2	0.2
Denmark	N/A	4.6	91.8	100.0	100.0	100.0	100.0	95.8	9.7	0.6
Djibouti	1.0	28.6	35.5	35.5	34.4	31.2	28.0	24.4	13.6	2.2
Ecuador	16.0	91.6	97.0	97.8	97.3	95.8	82.0	44.7	20.9	10.3
El Salvador	3.0	33.6	81.3	86.2	82.9	87.8	80.6	84.5	80.9	71.3
Eritrea	N/A	0.9	19.3	28.3	32.3	38.8	37.2	39.1	37.3	28.7
Estonia	0.0	13.8	93.6	95.1	91.8	92.7	95.0	50.2	9.4	3.4
Ethiopia	N/A	2.5	18.3	26.5	26.4	36.4	29.3	32.9	31.5	28.4
Finland	N/A	0.8	100.0	95.3	95.8	97.7	100.0	100.0	3.1	0.1
France	2.0	100.0	100.0	100.0	100.0	97.2	21.9	2.8	1.3	1.1

B6-1. Age-Specific Enrollment Ratios, Primary Schools (Age 5–14), 1995 *(continued)*

	AGE 5	AGE 6	AGE 7	AGE 8	AGE 9	AGE 10	AGE 11	AGE 12	AGE 13	AGE 14
French Polynesia	N/A	98.2	100.0	100.0	100.0	100.0	46.0	20.4	6.1	1.0
Gambia	N/A	17.7	70.7	73.6	68.6	64.0	58.0	50.5	37.4	17.4
Georgia	0.0	82.8	86.1	85.9	84.8	0.3	N/A	N/A	N/A	N/A
Germany	N/A	44.7	98.4	99.1	97.4	59.9	8.0	0.8	N/A	N/A
Greece	23.0	90.9	90.9	88.8	92.1	98.1	80.1	1.7	0.4	0.1
Guyana	N/A	75.0	93.7	99.2	96.9	88.8	70.4	41.7	N/A	N/A
Hong Kong, SAR (China)	12.0	95.3	98.1	90.1	88.6	88.8	78.2	11.2	2.2	0.7
Hungary	3.0	86.4	100.0	100.0	98.5	17.2	4.1	1.4	0.5	0.2
Iceland	0.0	100.0	100.0	96.8	90.3	90.9	95.9	100.0	0.2	N/A
Indonesia	N/A	55.1	100.0	100.0	100.0	93.5	83.9	68.0	33.3	18.0
Iraq	8.0	71.7	76.6	77.6	78.3	79.7	72.6	30.2	14.5	5.9
Ireland	0.0	44.3	97.3	100.0	100.0	99.0	98.0	62.5	6.1	0.5
Italy	1.0	100.0	100.0	99.7	99.3	97.1	3.6	0.5	N/A	N/A
Jordan	20.0	65.0	68.5	67.4	68.7	69.6	71.0	71.0	71.0	67.5
Kuwait	23.0	66.4	66.6	66.8	47.1	13.7	4.9	2.2	0.8	0.3
Kyrgyzstan	N/A	36.3	92.8	100.0	99.8	84.5	N/A	N/A	N/A	N/A
Laos	N/A	47.0	70.6	76.3	75.4	84.1	73.9	71.6	57.0	34.2
Latvia	N/A	4.2	81.4	94.4	95.0	63.1	12.4	3.1	1.0	0.4
Lesotho	2.0	30.5	63.6	71.4	77.6	83.5	86.1	87.4	89.1	73.2
Macedonia, FYRO	N/A	23.8	100.0	100.0	99.7	100.0	98.2	96.3	95.8	68.2
Madagascar	14.0	56.3	61.6	63.7	60.1	61.6	51.7	43.1	31.0	17.8
Mali	N/A	14.8	30.6	35.9	36.1	33.1	27.7	23.4	18.4	11.6
Malta	80.0	100.0	100.0	100.0	100.0	99.0	36.7	3.0	0.1	N/A
Martinique	3.0	100.0	100.0	100.0	100.0	100.0	27.4	2.8	0.3	N/A
Mauritania	N/A	27.7	63.8	73.0	65.4	62.6	52.4	41.8	31.8	21.9
Mauritius	79.0	100.0	100.0	97.9	92.8	95.4	51.9	7.4	N/A	N/A
Mexico	6.0	100.0	100.0	100.0	100.0	100.0	88.6	42.3	19.9	8.4
Mongolia	N/A	0.6	8.8	83.3	86.1	68.8	13.9	2.8	0.5	0.1
Mozambique	N/A	10.5	34.2	40.3	39.6	46.5	39.0	41.5	31.2	18.8
Namibia	1.0	43.4	80.4	87.5	91.7	98.0	96.3	98.5	91.5	75.3
Netherlands, the	1.0	98.2	99.0	100.0	100.0	99.7	97.3	42.2	4.9	0.5
New Zealand	100.0	96.6	98.1	93.3	94.0	93.3	18.8	0.0	N/A	N/A
Nicaragua	3.0	43.3	75.6	81.8	83.5	84.4	72.4	68.1	50.0	34.5
Norway	N/A	0.8	100.0	98.3	98.4	97.8	98.5	98.5	1.0	N/A
Oman	7.0	65.0	68.8	70.9	73.9	75.0	68.5	31.8	14.4	6.0
Paraguay	1.0	58.9	93.1	95.5	96.1	95.6	92.8	77.0	40.3	24.0
Peru	9.0	84.7	92.0	93.5	94.3	93.7	86.5	54.5	38.9	24.2
Philippines	N/A	5.8	90.8	100.0	100.0	100.0	100.0	87.9	41.7	19.7
Poland	N/A	0.7	92.1	92.3	91.0	92.4	95.2	96.4	99.4	96.7
Portugal	N/A	100.0	100.0	100.0	100.0	100.0	100.0	39.8	19.4	9.8
Romania	N/A	17.7	92.1	99.2	98.8	77.3	11.5	3.5	N/A	N/A
Samoa	95.0	98.4	100.0	100.0	98.9	97.8	95.2	82.3	36.0	10.3
Saudi Arabia	5.0	47.6	61.5	66.4	68.9	69.4	67.8	47.9	23.2	11.7
Senegal	1.0	12.5	55.7	57.8	55.6	55.4	51.2	46.7	35.1	17.2
Singapore	1.0	100.0	100.0	83.0	93.0	92.1	90.3	6.6	3.3	0.4
Slovenia	N/A	7.3	99.2	99.3	92.9	87.5	4.5	0.5	0.1	0.0
South Africa	N/A	95.9	100.0	100.0	100.0	100.0	100.0	100.0	74.2	49.0
South Korea, Rep	N/A	91.5	95.5	93.4	93.5	90.3	95.7	9.5	0.4	0.1
Spain	N/A	100.0	100.0	100.0	100.0	100.0	100.0	17.7	3.4	0.8
Swaziland	14.0	67.6	87.6	100.0	100.0	100.0	96.9	100.0	75.1	56.6
Sweden	N/A	7.7	99.8	100.0	100.0	100.0	100.0	100.0	N/A	N/A
Switzerland	0.0	29.4	98.3	97.9	99.0	94.9	85.6	62.8	10.3	0.8
Syria	29.0	88.6	95.1	95.6	93.4	100.0	74.0	21.8	7.2	N/A
Tanzania	0.0	0.2	11.8	29.0	45.4	58.3	65.0	66.7	66.6	60.9
Togo	19.0	71.1	86.2	90.6	91.2	93.8	78.0	73.5	60.5	40.0
Trinidad and Tobago	84.0	90.6	91.2	94.1	96.8	95.5	74.8	28.7	13.1	5.1
Tunisia	10.0	92.0	98.1	100.0	100.0	100.0	93.5	57.4	35.9	11.6

B6-1. Age-Specific Enrollment Ratios, Primary Schools (Age 5–14), 1995 *(continued)*

	AGE 5	AGE 6	AGE 7	AGE 8	AGE 9	AGE 10	AGE 11	AGE 12	AGE 13	AGE 14
United Arab Emirates	36.0	79.0	82.9	83.4	83.0	83.4	64.6	19.2	9.0	4.5
United Kingdom	100.0	99.4	100.0	99.4	93.6	93.6	11.9	0.1	N/A	N/A
United States	7.0	85.4	97.5	92.3	99.1	100.0	92.9	32.6	4.6	0.7
Uruguay	N/A	53.8	99.8	100.0	100.0	100.0	99.6	65.1	22.4	8.6
Venezuela	8.0	70.9	85.9	91.3	91.2	90.4	87.1	83.0	75.3	61.9
Zambia	N/A	5.6	43.0	71.1	83.8	84.8	84.7	81.3	78.0	55.5

N/A Not Available

Source: UNESCO Statistical Yearbook 1999; <http://unescostat.unesco.org/uisen/stats/stats0.htm>. Underlying data from United Nations Educational, Scientific and Cultural Organization (UNESCO).

B6-2. Age-Specific Enrollment Ratios, Higher Secondary Schools (Age 10–20), 1995

	AGE 10	AGE 11	AGE 12	AGE 13	AGE 14	AGE 15	AGE 16	AGE 17	AGE 18	AGE 19	AGE 20
Algeria	0.1	5.9	50.3	66.4	69.0	65.9	51.4	32.8	22.0	11.3	1.2
Australia	0.1	1.2	59.2	95.9	97.6	91.0	78.8	58.8	12.3	2.1	2.5
Austria	51.9	91.6	96.7	100.0	74.2	36.0	20.1	17.5	7.9	1.9	0.6
Bahrain	4.5	13.9	79.4	86.1	93.1	89.4	84.4	73.1	34.9	18.6	7.2
Belgium	1.5	77.8	98.9	78.9	84.1	95.7	99.3	71.1	47.3	29.5	17.5
Botswana	N/A	0.1	0.7	8.3	36.0	63.1	66.5	52.5	38.7	27.9	15.9
Bulgaria	16.3	87.3	90.7	89.8	86.6	81.2	78.0	62.6	29.1	2.6	0.8
Canada	11.0	13.3	86.9	99.6	99.7	98.0	92.8	69.4	34.3	10.5	13.4
Chad	0.0	0.2	0.9	2.3	3.3	6.4	9.0	10.4	9.2	8.9	7.5
Colombia	9.3	30.5	45.2	52.2	53.5	49.5	43.2	33.5	23.6	17.1	12.2
Costa Rica	N/A	0.3	19.9	42.1	42.6	34.5	26.5	14.5	4.0	1.0	0.4
Cyprus	N/A	14.6	85.5	88.8	81.9	82.7	75.3	61.1	8.3	1.5	9.9
Czech Republic	40.6	95.3	99.8	97.2	59.0	19.0	15.0	14.1	8.9	1.5	0.1
Eritrea	N/A	0.8	4.2	9.7	14.8	18.9	21.0	19.3	17.2	7.4	5.5
Estonia	0.0	2.0	48.1	85.0	91.3	87.7	81.9	70.6	28.1	10.3	4.6
France	3.4	74.8	93.4	100.0	100.0	100.0	97.4	88.8	56.7	30.8	14.0
Georgia	64.4	83.5	86.5	85.1	77.0	60.9	55.6	8.4	7.9	N/A	4.0
Germany	35.8	87.4	97.2	100.0	100.0	97.2	68.1	38.4	27.0	13.4	3.0
Greece	N/A	19.1	100.0	94.2	86.0	96.1	80.5	62.7	17.1	8.0	4.3
Guyana	N/A	27.2	66.6	79.6	76.9	62.5	39.2	21.3	N/A	N/A	4.0
Hong Kong SAR, (China)	N/A	7.8	80.0	85.3	85.5	80.2	75.0	43.1	33.0	13.9	4.4
Hungary	88.9	97.2	100.0	92.6	79.8	89.7	82.2	65.3	32.9	18.2	8.2
Ireland	N/A	0.1	36.9	96.2	100.0	100.0	91.7	67.6	24.2	2.3	0.3
Kuwait	68.3	61.4	75.6	86.4	65.9	57.6	46.2	25.8	11.9	5.6	3.6
Latvia	31.1	82.7	95.2	92.7	90.2	83.0	73.2	64.8	30.6	12.9	5.7
Malta	0.1	61.7	98.6	100.0	99.8	95.8	60.0	34.8	18.5	8.9	11.1
Martinique	4.1	77.6	100.0	100.0	100.0	100.0	96.2	79.4	57.8	38.6	25.5
Mexico	N/A	13.2	53.9	67.0	62.4	50.6	40.1	33.2	17.9	8.3	5.1
Mongolia	10.7	62.9	64.4	64.4	59.7	65.0	45.6	32.5	4.7	0.7	0.2
Mozambique	0.1	0.9	3.2	6.1	8.1	9.2	7.6	5.0	4.0	2.9	1.8
Netherlands, the	0.0	0.5	54.8	92.6	100.0	100.0	100.0	91.2	66.8	43.9	29.5
New Zealand	1.6	75.5	96.4	96.6	97.9	95.4	80.7	56.6	15.4	3.2	1.3
Peru	0.1	6.9	36.3	50.5	62.0	63.3	53.9	39.6	21.0	10.6	3.9
Philippines	N/A	1.5	15.8	55.7	65.9	62.7	50.9	26.6	13.8	20.0	8.0
Reunion	3.0	77.9	100.0	100.0	100.0	100.0	92.4	74.6	46.3	24.4	9.6
Romania	22.0	86.5	87.6	93.2	92.3	80.5	70.9	57.5	26.9	8.3	4.0
Samoa	N/A	0.6	7.2	39.3	73.7	71.5	55.8	41.7	25.0	10.4	1.8
Saudi Arabia	N/A	3.9	20.3	42.3	48.7	67.2	62.0	47.6	30.4	17.4	9.3
South Korea, Rep	N/A	1.7	83.4	100.0	100.0	97.4	94.2	89.8	23.1	2.8	0.4
Spain	N/A	0.0	86.9	100.0	92.0	77.8	61.8	54.8	24.7	12.3	7.9
Swaziland	0.1	0.4	4.9	18.3	32.6	47.2	48.1	43.2	32.6	22.3	12.3

B6-2. Age-Specific Enrollment Ratios, Higher Secondary Schools (Age 10–20), 1995 *(continued)*

	AGE 10	AGE 11	AGE 12	AGE 13	AGE 14	AGE 15	AGE 16	AGE 17	AGE 18	AGE 19	AGE 20
Switzerland	3.4	13.5	35.5	90.5	99.5	95.1	54.9	29.9	23.1	15.8	6.4
Syria	N/A	15.8	52.5	54.3	44.2	34.7	24.3	17.0	8.5	1.7	0.3
United Kingdom	10.6	85.2	98.4	98.8	100.0	100.0	84.9	68.2	29.4	14.8	9.9
United States	1.1	4.3	71.2	97.3	100.0	98.7	89.1	81.4	24.4	5.0	1.5

N/A Not Available

Source: UNESCO Statistical Yearbook 1999; <http://unescostat.unesco.org/uisen/stats/stats0.htm>. Underlying data from United Nations Educational, Scientific and Cultural Organization (UNESCO).

B7. GENDER AND WEALTH

B7-1. Enrollment by Gender, Primary Schools, 1997

	Enrollment	Percent female	Percent male
Algeria	4,674,947	46	54
Anguilla	1,557	49	51
Argentina	5,153,256	49	51
Armenia	256,475	N/A	N/A
Australia	1,855,789	49	51
Austria	381,927	49	51
Azerbaijan	719,013	48	52
Bahamas, the	34,199	N/A	N/A
Bahrain	72,876	49	51
Belarus	625,000	48	52
Benin	779,329	37	63
Bermuda	5,883	49	51
Brazil	34,229,388	N/A	N/A
Bulgaria	431,790	48	52
Cambodia	1,918,985	45	55
Cameroon	1,921,186	N/A	N/A
Chad	680,909	34	66
China	136,150,042	47	53
Costa Rica	525,273	49	51
Côte d'Ivoire	1,735,814	42	58
Croatia	203,933	49	51
Cuba	1,094,868	48	52
Cyprus	64,761	48	52
Djibouti	36,896	42	58
Dominican Republic	1,360,044	49	51
Ecuador	1,888,172	49	51
Egypt	8,243,137	45	55
El Salvador	1,191,052	49	51
Eritrea	240,737	45	55
Estonia	126,800	48	52
Ethiopia	4,007,694	36	64
Finland	380,932	49	51
France	4,004,704	49	51
Georgia	293,325	48	52
Germany	3,859,490	49	51
Gibraltar	2,729	47	53
Greece	652,040	48	52
Guatemala	1,544,709	46	54
Guinea	649,835	36	64
Guyana	102,000	49	51
Iceland	29,342	49	51
India	110,390,406	43	57
Indonesia	29,236,283	48	52

B7-1. Enrollment by Gender, Primary Schools, 1997 *(continued)*

	Enrollment	Percent female	Percent male
Iran	9,238,393	47	53
Ireland	358,830	49	51
Italy	2,810,158	48	52
Jamaica	293,863	49	51
Japan	8,105,629	49	51
Jordan	1,086,641	49	51
Kazakhstan	1,342,035	49	51
Kiribati	17,594	49	51
Kuwait	143,286	49	51
Latvia	146,653	48	52
Lebanon	382,309	48	52
Lithuania	225,701	48	52
Luxembourg	28,437	N/A	N/A
Macedonia, FYRO	260,917	48	52
Malaysia	2,840,667	49	51
Maldives	50,230	48	52
Mali	778,450	39	61
Malta	35,374	48	52
Mauritania	312,671	47	53
Mauritius	127,109	49	51
Mexico	14,650,521	48	52
Moldova	320,725	49	51
Monaco	1,919	47	53
Mongolia	234,193	51	49
Morocco	3,160,907	42	58
Namibia	380,945	50	50
Netherlands, the	1,230,987	48	52
New Zealand	357,569	49	51
Nicaragua	777,917	50	50
Niger	464,267	38	62
Norway	330,619	49	51
Oman	311,955	48	52
Palestine	656,353	49	51
Paraguay	905,813	48	52
Peru	4,163,180	N/A	N/A
Philippines	11,902,501	N/A	N/A
Romania	1,405,308	49	51
Samoa	35,649	48	52
San Marino	1,170	48	52
Saudi Arabia	2,256,185	48	52
Senegal	954,758	45	55
Slovakia	329,880	N/A	N/A
Slovenia	98,866	49	51
South Korea, Rep.	3,810,932	48	52
Spain	2,702,553	48	52
St. Lucia	31,615	49	51
Sudan	3,000,048	45	55
Swaziland	205,829	49	51
Sweden	690,630	49	51
Syria	2,690,205	47	53
Tajikistan	638,674	49	51
Tanzania	4,057,965	50	50
Thailand	5,909,618	N/A	N/A
Togo	859,574	41	59
Trinidad and Tobago	181,030	49	51
Tunisia	1,450,916	47	53
Turkey	6,389,060	47	53
Turks and Caicos Islands	1,573	49	51

B7-1. Enrollment by Gender, Primary Schools, 1997 *(continued)*

	Enrollment	Percent female	Percent male
United Arab Emirates	259,509	48	52
United Kingdom	5,328,219	49	51
Venezuela	4,262,221	50	50
Vietnam	10,431,300	N/A	N/A
Yemen	2,699,788	28	72
Yugoslavia	437,780	49	51
Zimbabwe	2,510,605	N/A	N/A
N/A Not Available			

Source: UNESCO Statistical Yearbook 1999; <http://unescostat.unesco.org/uisen/stats/stats0.htm>. Underlying data from United Nations Educational, Scientific and Cultural Organization (UNESCO).

B7-2. Enrollment by Gender, Secondary Schools, various years

	Year	Total pupils enrolled	Female pupils enrolled	Percent pupils enrolled, female	Percent pupils enrolled, male
Afghanistan	1995	512,851	130,136	25	75
Albania	1996	89,895	43,745	49	51
Algeria	1997	2,618,242	1,253,576	48	52
American Samoa	1992	3,643	1,680	46	54
Andorra	1976	1,753	1,092	62	38
Angola	1992	218,987	N/A	N/A	N/A
Anguilla	1997	1,062	581	55	45
Antigua and Barbuda	1992	5,845	2,937	50	50
Argentina	1996	2,594,329	1,347,990	52	48
Armenia	1997	372,187	N/A	N/A	N/A
Australia	1997	2,367,692	1,173,470	50	50
Austria	1997	793,485	377,559	48	52
Azerbaijan	1997	819,625	420,304	51	49
Bahamas, the	1997	27,970	N/A	N/A	N/A
Bahrain	1997	57,184	29,014	51	49
Bangladesh	1990	3,592,995	1,180,440	33	N/A
Barbados	1991	N/A	N/A	N/A	N/A
Belarus	1997	1,064,700	N/A	N/A	N/A
Belgium	1996	1,058,998	535,324	51	49
Belize	1995	10,272	5,335	52	48
Benin	1997	N/A	N/A	N/A	N/A
Bermuda	1997	N/A	N/A	N/A	N/A
Bhutan	1994	N/A	N/A	N/A	N/A
Bolivia	1990	219,232	100,748	46	54
Botswana	1996	N/A	N/A	N/A	N/A
Brazil	1998	6,967,905	N/A	N/A	N/A
British Virgin Islands	1994	1,309	668	51	49
Brunei	1996	30,470	15,868	52	48
Bulgaria	1997	733,362	356,083	49	51
Burkina Faso	1994	N/A	N/A	N/A	N/A
Burundi	1995	N/A	N/A	N/A	N/A
Cambodia	1998	312,934	108,917	35	65
Cameroon	1995	N/A	N/A	N/A	N/A
Canada	1996	2,505,389	1,218,403	49	51
Cape Verde	1998	31,602	16,125	51	49
Central African Republic	1992	43,740	12,851	29	71
Chad	1997	99,789	20,301	20	80
Chile	1996	739,316	377,256	51	49
China	1998	71,883,000	32,530,000	45	N/A
Colombia	1996	3,317,782	1,687,248	51	49

B7-2. Enrollment by Gender, Secondary Schools, various years *(continued)*

	Year	Total pupils enrolled	Female pupils enrolled	Percent pupils enrolled, female	Percent pupils enrolled, male
Comoros	1996	N/A	N/A	N/A	N/A
Congo, Dem. Rep. (Zaire)	1995	1,514,323	571,264	38	62
Congo, Rep.	1996	214,650	91,500	43	57
Costa Rica	1998	202,415	104,081	51	49
Côte d'Ivoire	1997	N/A	N/A	N/A	N/A
Croatia	1997	416,829	205,490	49	51
Cuba	1997	712,897	367,943	52	48
Cyprus	1997	61,266	30,303	49	51
Czech Republic	1996	1,190,725	591,073	50	50
Denmark	1996	438,809	217,156	49	51
Djibouti	1997	13,311	5,477	41	59
Dominica	1995	N/A	N/A	N/A	N/A
Dominican Republic	1998	N/A	N/A	N/A	N/A
Ecuador	1993	814,359	405,655	50	50
Egypt	1998	N/A	N/A	N/A	N/A
Equatorial Guinea	1994	16,616	5,741	35	65
Eritrea	1997	89,087	37,196	42	58
Estonia	1997	N/A	N/A	N/A	N/A
Ethiopia	1997	N/A	N/A	N/A	N/A
Falkland Islands (Malvinas)	1995	147	72	49	51
Fiji	1992	66,890	32,673	49	51
Finland	1997	469,933	244,760	52	48
France	1997	5,979,690	2,910,884	49	51
French Guiana	1996	15,989	8,036	50	N/A
French Polynesia	1993	22,366	12,241	55	45
Gabon	1996	80,552	38,076	47	53
Gambia, the	1996	32,097	12,354	38	62
Georgia	1997	444,058	215,969	49	51
Germany	1997	8,382,335	4,037,044	48	52
Ghana	1992	N/A	N/A	N/A	N/A
Gibraltar	1997	N/A	N/A	N/A	N/A
Greece	1997	817,566	400,097	49	51
Grenada	1993	10,213	5,489	54	46
Guadeloupe	1995	50,899	26,281	52	48
Guam	1986	14,557	N/A	N/A	N/A
Guatemala	1997	384,729	N/A	N/A	N/A
Guinea	1998	N/A	N/A	N/A	N/A
Guinea-Bissau	1981	4,757	939	20	80
Guyana	1997	62,043	31,845	51	49
Haiti	1991	N/A	N/A	N/A	N/A
Honduras	1993	203,192	N/A	N/A	N/A
Hong Kong, SAR (China)	1996	473,817	232,505	49	51
Hungary	1996	1,112,149	552,511	50	50
Iceland	1997	N/A	N/A	N/A	N/A
India	1997	68,872,393	26,269,449	38	62
Indonesia	1997	14,209,974	N/A	N/A	N/A
Iran	1997	8,776,792	4,065,233	46	54
Iraq	1996	1,160,421	437,633	38	62
Ireland	1997	389,353	197,386	51	49
Israel	1996	541,737	N/A	N/A	N/A
Italy	1997	4,602,243	2,244,975	49	51
Jamaica	1993	235,071	120,640	51	49
Japan	1995	9,878,568	4,852,217	49	51
Jordan	1998	155,008	77,240	50	50
Kazakhstan	1997	1,921,302	1,000,406	52	48
Kenya	1995	N/A	N/A	N/A	N/A
Kiribati	1997	N/A	N/A	N/A	N/A
Kuwait	1998	224,293	111,744	50	50

B7-2. Enrollment by Gender, Secondary Schools, various years *(continued)*

	Year	Total pupils enrolled	Female pupils enrolled	Percent pupils enrolled, female	Percent pupils enrolled, male
Kyrgyzstan	1996	530,854	N/A	N/A	N/A
Laos	1997	187,600	73,944	39	N/A
Latvia	1997	239,318	122,000	51	49
Lebanon	1997	347,850	179,629	52	48
Lesotho	1996	68,132	40,149	59	41
Liberia	1980	54,623	15,343	28	72
Libya	1994	N/A	N/A	N/A	N/A
Lithuania	1997	378,754	189,096	50	50
Luxembourg	1997	28,796	14,509	50	50
Macau	1993	20,383	10,721	53	47
Macedonia, FYRO	1997	83,746	40,447	48	52
Madagascar	1996	N/A	N/A	N/A	N/A
Malawi	1996	141,911	N/A	N/A	N/A
Malaysia	1998	1,889,592	957,790	51	49
Maldives	1998	36,905	18,885	51	49
Mali	1998	188,109	62,460	33	67
Malta	1997	34,211	16,237	47	53
Martinique	1996	47,706	24,093	51	49
Mauritania	1996	51,765	17,355	34	66
Mauritius	1997	N/A	N/A	N/A	N/A
Mexico	1997	7,914,165	3,906,783	49	51
Moldova	1997	445,501	223,162	50	N/A
Monaco	1997	2,886	1,458	51	49
Mongolia	1997	195,408	112,056	57	43
Montserrat	1994	N/A	N/A	N/A	N/A
Morocco	1997	1,442,049	610,727	42	58
Mozambique	1995	185,181	72,369	39	61
Myanmar (Burma)	1996	N/A	N/A	N/A	N/A
Namibia	1998	115,237	60,630	53	47
Nauru	1985	482	242	50	50
Nepal	1996	1,121,335	419,909	37	63
Netherlands, the	1997	1,415,712	677,314	48	52
Netherlands Antilles	1992	14,987	N/A	N/A	N/A
New Caledonia	1997	25,560	13,230	52	48
New Zealand	1997	433,347	216,630	50	50
Nicaragua	1998	N/A	N/A	N/A	N/A
Niger	1997	97,675	34,493	35	65
Nigeria	1994	4,451,329	2,031,547	46	54
Niue	1991	302	159	53	47
Norway	1997	368,074	176,073	48	52
Oman	1998	217,246	105,540	49	51
Pakistan	1994	N/A	N/A	N/A	N/A
Palestine	1997	56,467	26,833	48	52
Panama	1996	221,022	N/A	N/A	N/A
Papua New Guinea	1995	78,759	30,858	39	61
Paraguay	1997	327,775	165,780	51	49
Peru	1997	1,969,501	N/A	N/A	N/A
Philippines	1998	4,979,795	N/A	N/A	N/A
Poland	1996	2,539,138	1,239,331	49	51
Portugal	1996	947,478	484,773	51	49
Qatar	1996	38,594	18,804	49	51
Reunion	1996	91,548	46,016	50	50
Romania	1997	2,212,090	1,081,450	49	51
Russia	1994	13,732,000	N/A	N/A	N/A
Rwanda	1992	94,586	41,704	44	56
Samoa	1996	12,672	6,316	50	50
San Marino	1997	1,192	578	48	52

B7-2. Enrollment by Gender, Secondary Schools, various years *(continued)*

	Year	Total pupils enrolled	Female pupils enrolled	Percent pupils enrolled, female	Percent pupils enrolled, male
Sao Tome and Principe	1981	3,815	N/A	N/A	N/A
Saudi Arabia	1997	1,542,989	707,073	46	54
Senegal	1998	215,988	81,661	38	62
Seychelles	1996	9,099	4,497	49	51
Sierra Leone	1991	102,474	37,660	37	63
Singapore	1996	N/A	N/A	N/A	N/A
Slovakia	1997	677,377	329,135	N/A	N/A
Slovenia	1997	212,458	105,077	49	51
Solomon Islands	1994	7,811	2,940	38	N/A
Somalia	1986	45,686	16,036	35	65
South Africa	1995	N/A	N/A	N/A	N/A
South Korea, Rep.	1997	4,662,492	2,257,709	48	52
Spain	1997	3,852,102	1,934,449	50	50
Sri Lanka	1995	2,314,054	1,181,371	51	49
St. Helena	1986	513	252	49	51
St. Kitts and Nevis	1993	4,402	2,242	51	49
St. Lucia	1997	11,753	6,605	56	44
St. Pierre and Miquelon	1986	821	432	53	47
St. Vincent and the Grenadines	1994	N/A	N/A	N/A	N/A
Sudan	1997	405,583	189,958	47	53
Suriname	1994	N/A	N/A	N/A	N/A
Swaziland	1996	57,330	28,893	50	50
Sweden	1997	829,295	440,553	53	47
Switzerland	1996	559,924	264,398	47	53
Syria	1997	957,664	443,737	46	54
Tajikistan	1997	N/A	N/A	N/A	N/A
Tanzania	1997	234,743	104,782	45	55
Thailand	1998	4,097,331	N/A	N/A	N/A
Togo	1997	178,254	47,595	27	73
Tokelau	1991	N/A	N/A	N/A	N/A
Tonga	1993	16,570	7,908	48	52
Trinidad and Tobago	1997	N/A	N/A	N/A	N/A
Tunisia	1998	N/A	N/A	N/A	N/A
Turkey	1997	4,760,892	1,900,870	40	60
Turks and Caicos Islands	1997	N/A	N/A	N/A	N/A
Tuvalu	1990	345	178	52	48
Uganda	1995	N/A	N/A	N/A	N/A
Ukraine	1994	4,731,200	N/A	N/A	N/A
United Arab Emirates	1997	180,764	90,195	50	50
United Kingdom	1997	6,548,786	3,405,483	52	48
United States	1996	21,473,692	10,471,227	49	51
Uruguay	1996	269,826	N/A	N/A	N/A
Uzbekistan	1995	3,318,900	N/A	N/A	N/A
Vanuatu	1992	N/A	N/A	N/A	N/A
Venezuela	1997	377,984	217,894	58	42
Vietnam	1998	N/A	N/A	N/A	N/A
Virgin Islands, US	1993	12,502	6,191	50	50
Yemen	1997	354,288	71,309	20	80
Yugoslavia	1997	815,029	404,613	50	50
Zambia	1994	N/A	N/A	N/A	N/A
Zimbabwe	1998	847,296	N/A	N/A	N/A

N/A Not Available

Source: UNESCO Statistical Yearbook 1999; <http://unescostat.unesco.org/uisen/stats/stats0.htm>. Underlying data from United Nations Educational, Scientific and Cultural Organization (UNESCO).

B7-3. Percentage of 6–14-Year-Old Girls in School, Selected Countries, various years

	Survey Year	% 6–14-year-old girls in school	% 6–14-year-old boys in school	Male-female gap
High female disadvantage* countries				
Nepal	1996	55.5	76.1	20.6
Benin	1993	32.6	53.1	20.5
Pakistan	1990-91	44.3	64.7	20.4
Morocco	1992	45.8	63.9	18.1
Central Afr. Rep.	1994-95	48.9	65.9	17.0
India	1992-93	59.1	75.7	16.6
Cote d'Ivoire	1994	41.7	55.8	14.1
Turkey	1993	63.7	74.5	10.8
Egypt	1995-96	75.7	85.6	9.9
Burkina Faso	1992-93	22.1	31.9	9.8
Mozambique	1997	51.7	61.0	9.3
Comoros	1996	48.3	57.2	8.9
Senegal	1992-93	27.4	35.8	8.4
Mali	1995-96	22.3	30.4	8.1
Niger	1997	18.9	26.7	7.8
Low/no female disadvantage* countries				
Kenya	1998	87.0	87.9	0.9
Haiti	1994-95	73.4	73.7	0.3
Zambia	1996-97	60.4	60.1	-0.3
Brazil	1996	93.8	93.4	-0.4
Indonesia	1997	86.6	86.0	-0.6
Madagascar	1997	58.6	58.0	-0.6
Kazakhstan	1995	85.3	84.6	-0.7
Malawi	1996	89.7	88.9	-0.8
Bangladesh	1996-97	73.8	72.6	-1.2
Dominican Rep.	1996	94.2	92.8	-1.4
Colombia	1995	89.7	87.9	-1.8
Tanzania	1996	48.6	45.8	-2.8
Uzbekistan	1996	82.9	80.0	-2.9
Namibia	1992	87.1	83.6	-3.5
Philippines	1998	88.4	83.5	-4.9

* Refers to high and low percentage of girls enrolled in schools.

Source: Poverty Trends and Voices of the Poor, World Bank, December 2000. <http://www.worldbank.org/poverty/data/trends/girls.htm>. Underlying data from Deon Filmer (1999), *"The Structure of Social Disadvantage in Education: Gender and Wealth."* Table 19.

B7-4. Percentage of Primary School-Age Girls Out of School, Selected Countries, mid-1990s

	Percent out of school
Somalia	94
Afghanistan	86
Mali	86
Niger	86
Ethiopia	84
Eritrea	76
Burkina Faso	75
Haiti	74
Chad	73
Senegal	70
Guinea-Bissau	68
Benin	65
Mozambique	65
Yemen	65
Bhutan	64

B7-4. Percentage of Primary School-Age Girls Out of School, Selected Countries, mid-1990s (continued)

	Percent out of school
Morocco	55
Pakistan	55
Central African Republic	54
Gambia, the	54
Burundi	53
Zaire	53
Nigeria	51
Liberia	47
Nepal	47
Tanzania	47
Malawi	46
Madagascar	44
Saudi Arabia	43
Togo	42
Cameroon	40
India	39
Laos	39
Rwanda	39
Guatemala	34
Papua New Guinea	33
Yugoslavia	30
El Salvador	29
Lesotho	29
Myanmar (Burma)	29
Turkey	29
Oman	28
Bangladesh	27
Ghana	26
Iraq	26
Romania	24
Zambia	23
Colombia	21
Namibia	21
Croatia	20
Bulgaria	19
Nicaragua	19
Egypt	18
Kenya	17
Dominican Republic	16
Chile	13
Trinidad and Tobago	12
Algeria	11
Bolivia	11
Peru	11
Germany	10
Ireland	10
Venezuela	10
Zimbabwe	10
Austria	9
Honduras	9
Philippines	9
Syria	9
Hungary	8
Indonesia	8
Panama	8
Iran	7
Paraguay	7

B7-4. Percentage of Primary School-Age Girls Out of School, Selected Countries, mid-1990s *(continued)*

	Percent out of school
South Africa	7
Greece	6
Mauritius	6
Russia	6
Argentina	5
China	5
Switzerland	5
Tunisia	5
Uruguay	5
Uzbekistan	5
Libya	4
Netherlands, the	4
Poland	4
United Kingdom	4
Belgium	3
Canada	3
Jordan	3
South Korea, Rep.	3
Denmark	2
Mexico	2
Australia	1
France	1
Norway	1
Sweden	1
United Arab Emirates	1
Botswana	0
Cuba	0
Jamaica	0
Japan	0
Portugal	0
Singapore	0
United States	0

Source: The Progress of Nations 1996, <http://www.unicef.org/pon96/leag1edu.htm>. Underlying data from United Nations Educational, Scientific and Cultural Organization (UNESCO)and United Nations Children's Fund (UNICEF).

B7-5. Percentage of Poor 6–14-Year-Old Children in School, Selected Countries and Regions, various years

Country	Year	Poor 6–14-year-old children in school (%)	Rich 6–14-year-old children in school (%)	Rich-poor gap
Western Africa				
Senegal	1992-93	14.1	65.6	51.5
Ghana	1993	69.3	90.8	21.5
Eastern Africa				
Madagascar	1997	46.8	90.0	43.2
Malawi	1996	87.0	93.3	6.3
North Africa				
Morocco	1992	26.7	89.5	62.8
Egypt	1995-96	67.6	95.5	27.9
South Asia				
Pakistan	1990-91	36.6	85.6	49.0
Bangladesh	1996-97	66.8	83.4	16.6
East Asia				
Philippines	1993	70.0	86.3	16.3
Indonesia	1997	80.5	95.0	14.5
South America				
Colombia	1995	80.9	97.6	16.7
Peru	1996	85.8	94.6	8.8
Central America and the Caribbean				
Guatemala	1995	46.4	90.8	44.4
Dominican Republic	1996	88.7	97.8	9.1
Eastern Europe and Central Asia				
Turkey	1993	61.0	80.1	19.1
Uzbekistan	1996	80.2	81.1	0.9

Note: Poverty is defined with respect to ownership of assets.

Source: Poverty Trends and Voices of the Poor, World Bank, December 2000. <http://www.worldbank.org/poverty/data/trends/girls.htm#worse>. Underlying data from Deon Filmer (1999), *"The Structure of Social Disadvantage in Education: Gender and Wealth."* Table 20.

B7-6. Percentage of Orphaned Children (0–14 years) in School, Selected Countries, 1990s

	Unorphaned children* (0–14 years) in school, %	Orphaned children** (0–14 years) in school, %
Benin	50	17
Bolivia	94	77
Brazil	90	72
Cameroon	78	68
Central African Republic	65	33
Chad	40	32
Côte d'Ivoire	57	37
Guatemala	70	43
Haiti	82	56
Kenya	93	72
Madagascar	61	34
Mali	29	21
Mozambique	68	24
Niger	28	10
Peru	94	77
Tanzania	72	53
Togo	77	54
Uganda	80	70
Zambia	78	65
Zimbabwe	77	65

* Both parents alive; children living with at least one parent
** Both parents deceased

Source: The Progress of Nations, 2000; <http://www.unicef.org/pon00/>. Underlying data from United Nations Children's Fund (UNICEF).

B8. TYPES OF EDUCATION

B8-1. High School Pupil Enrollment in Vocational Education, by Gender, various years

	Year	Total enrollment, secondary school	Total female enrollment, secondary school	Percent pupils enrolled, female, secondary school	Percent pupils enrolled, male, secondary school	Total enrollment, vocational school	Female enrollment, vocational school	Percent female enrollment, vocational education	Percent male enrollment, vocational education
Afghanistan	1995	512,851	130,136	25	75	N/A	N/A	N/A	N/A
Albania	1996	89,895	43,745	49	51	18,504	5,746	31	69
Algeria	1997	2,618,242	1,253,576	48	52	138,074	49,726	36	64
American Samoa	1992	3,643	1,680	46	54	160	7	4	96
Andorra	1976	1,753	1,092	62	38	N/A	N/A	N/A	N/A
Angola	1992	218,987	N/A	N/A	N/A	12,116	N/A	N/A	N/A
Anguilla	1997	1,062	581	55	45	N/A	N/A	N/A	N/A
Antigua and Barbuda	1992	5,845	2,937	50	50	N/A	N/A	N/A	N/A
Argentina	1996	2,594,329	1,347,990	52	48	N/A	N/A	N/A	N/A
Armenia	1997	372,187	N/A	N/A	N/A	7,162	N/A	N/A	N/A
Australia	1997	2,367,692	1,173,470	50	50	1,051,857	519,288	49	51
Austria	1997	793,485	377,559	48	52	300,612	131,175	44	56
Azerbaijan	1997	819,625	420,304	51	49	17,287	5,653	33	67
Bahamas, the	1997	27,970	N/A	N/A	N/A	N/A	N/A	N/A	N/A
Bahrain	1997	57,184	29,014	51	49	7,287	2,270	31	69
Bangladesh	1990	3,592,995	1,180,440	33	N/A	25,791	1,970	8	92
Barbados	1991	N/A	N/A	N/A	N/A	161	40	25	75
Belarus	1997	1,064,700	N/A	N/A	N/A	112,200	N/A	N/A	N/A
Belgium	1996	1,058,998	535,324	51	49	569,041	288,549	51	49
Belize	1995	10,272	5,335	52	48	125	28	22	78
Benin	1997	N/A	N/A	N/A	N/A	N/A	N/A	N/A	N/A
Bermuda	1997	N/A	N/A	N/A	N/A	N/A	N/A	N/A	N/A
Bhutan	1994	N/A	N/A	N/A	N/A	N/A	N/A	N/A	N/A
Bolivia	1990	219,232	100,748	46	54	N/A	N/A	N/A	N/A
Botswana	1996	N/A	N/A	N/A	N/A	N/A	N/A	N/A	N/A
Brazil	1998	6,967,905	N/A	N/A	N/A	N/A	N/A	N/A	N/A
British Virgin Islands	1994	1,309	668	51	49	N/A	N/A	N/A	N/A
Brunei	1996	30,470	15,868	52	48	2,196	919	42	58
Bulgaria	1997	733,362	356,083	49	51	206,570	78,143	38	62
Burkina Faso	1994	N/A	N/A	N/A	N/A	8,808	4,335	49	51
Burundi	1995	N/A	N/A	N/A	N/A	N/A	N/A	N/A	N/A
Cambodia	1998	312,934	108,917	35	65	5,065	1,493	29	71
Cameroon	1995	N/A	N/A	N/A	N/A	91,779	37,674	41	59
Canada	1996	2,505,389	1,218,403	49	51	N/A	N/A	N/A	N/A
Cape Verde	1998	31,602	16,125	51	49	N/A	N/A	N/A	N/A
Central African Republic	1992	43,740	12,851	29	71	1,477	578	39	61
Chad	1997	99,789	20,301	20	80	2,153	647	30	70
Chile	1996	739,316	377,256	51	49	323,397	152,289	47	53
China	1998	71,883,000	32,530,000	45	N/A	10,793,000	N/A	N/A	N/A
Colombia	1996	3,317,782	1,687,248	51	49	849,010	460,489	54	46
Comoros	1996	N/A	N/A	N/A	N/A	N/A	N/A	N/A	N/A
Congo, Dem. Rep. (Zaire)	1995	1,514,323	571,264	38	62	N/A	N/A	N/A	N/A
Congo, Rep.	1996	214,650	91,500	43	57	25,191	11,133	44	56

B8-1. High School Pupil Enrollment in Vocational Education, by Gender, various years (continued)

	Year	Total enrollment, secondary school	Total female enrollment, secondary school	Percent pupils enrolled, female, secondary school	Percent pupils enrolled, male, secondary school	Total enrollment, vocational school	Female enrollment, vocational school	Percent female enrollment, vocational education	Percent male enrollment, vocational education
Costa Rica	1998	202,415	104,081	51	49	44,323	22,010	50	50
Côte d'Ivoire	1997	N/A	N/A	N/A	N/A	N/A	N/A	N/A	N/A
Croatia	1997	416,829	205,490	49	51	154,798	71,090	46	54
Cuba	1997	712,897	367,943	52	48	212,052	100,678	47	53
Cyprus	1997	61,266	30,303	49	51	4,614	945	20	80
Czech Republic	1996	1,190,725	591,073	50	50	544,457	262,904	48	52
Denmark	1996	438,809	217,156	49	51	122,059	54,123	44	56
Djibouti	1997	13,311	5,477	41	59	1,841	1,077	59	41
Dominica	1995	N/A	N/A	N/A	N/A	N/A	N/A	N/A	N/A
Dominican Republic	1998	N/A	N/A	N/A	N/A	N/A	N/A	N/A	N/A
Ecuador	1993	814,359	405,655	50	50	279,189	152,352	55	45
Egypt	1998	N/A	N/A	N/A	N/A	N/A	N/A	N/A	N/A
Equatorial Guinea	1994	16,616	5,741	35	65	1,496	472	32	68
Eritrea	1997	89,087	37,196	42	58	674	91	14	86
Estonia	1997	N/A	N/A	N/A	N/A	N/A	N/A	N/A	N/A
Ethiopia	1997	N/A	N/A	N/A	N/A	2,924	415	14	86
Falkland Islands (Malvinas)	1995	147	72	49	51	N/A	N/A	N/A	N/A
Fiji	1992	66,890	32,673	49	51	6,653	1,723	26	74
Finland	1997	469,933	244,760	52	48	140,632	72,035	51	49
France	1997	5,979,690	2,910,884	49	51	1,646,377	695,004	42	58
French Guiana	1996	15,989	8,036	50	50	2,404	1,187	49	51
French Polynesia	1993	22,366	12,241	55	45	3,730	1,749	47	53
Gabon	1996	80,552	38,076	47	53	7,588	2,638	35	65
Gambia, the	1996	32,097	12,354	38	62	N/A	N/A	N/A	N/A
Georgia	1997	444,058	215,969	49	51	19,593	9,358	48	52
Germany	1997	8,382,335	4,037,044	48	52	2,320,465	1,024,301	44	56
Ghana	1992	N/A	N/A	N/A	N/A	22,578	6,914	31	69
Gibraltar	1997	N/A	N/A	N/A	N/A	N/A	N/A	N/A	N/A
Greece	1997	817,566	400,097	49	51	135,365	53,708	40	60
Grenada	1993	10,213	5,489	54	46	N/A	N/A	N/A	N/A
Guadeloupe	1995	50,899	26,281	52	48	9,243	4,443	48	52
Guam	1986	14,557	N/A	N/A	N/A	N/A	N/A	N/A	N/A
Guatemala	1997	384,729	N/A	N/A	N/A	N/A	N/A	N/A	N/A
Guinea	1998	N/A	N/A	N/A	N/A	N/A	N/A	N/A	N/A
Guinea-Bissau	1981	4,757	939	20	80	277	38	14	86
Guyana	1997	62,043	31,845	51	49	N/A	N/A	N/A	N/A
Haiti	1991	N/A	N/A	N/A	N/A	N/A	N/A	N/A	N/A
Honduras	1993	203,192	N/A	N/A	N/A	N/A	N/A	N/A	N/A
Hong Kong, SAR (China)	1996	473,817	232,505	49	51	13,972	4,475	32	68
Hungary	1996	1,112,149	552,511	50	50	406,129	186,835	46	54
Iceland	1997	N/A	N/A	N/A	N/A	N/A	N/A	N/A	N/A
India	1997	68,872,393	26,269,449	38	62	770,688	119,113	15	85

B8-1. High School Pupil Enrollment in Vocational Education, by Gender, various years (continued)

	Year	Total enrollment, secondary school	Total female enrollment, secondary school	Percent pupils enrolled, female, secondary school	Percent pupils enrolled, male, secondary school	Total enrollment, vocational school	Female enrollment, vocational school	Percent female enrollment, vocational education	Percent male enrollment, vocational education
Indonesia	1997	14,209,974	N/A	N/A	N/A	1,767,161	N/A	N/A	N/A
Iraq	1996	1,160,421	437,633	38	62	99,405	17,488	18	82
Ireland	1997	389,353	197,386	51	49	36,083	19,917	55	45
Italy	1997	4,602,243	2,244,975	49	51	1,959,787	920,574	47	53
Jamaica	1993	235,071	120,640	51	49	N/A	N/A	N/A	N/A
Japan	1995	9,878,568	4,852,217	49	51	1,435,724	648,904	45	55
Jordan	1998	155,008	77,240	50	50	39,701	14,310	36	64
Kazakhstan	1997	1,921,302	1,000,406	52	48	154,670	84,180	54	46
Kenya	1995	N/A	N/A	N/A	N/A	N/A	N/A	N/A	N/A
Kiribati	1997	N/A	N/A	N/A	N/A	N/A	N/A	N/A	N/A
Kuwait	1998	224,293	111,744	50	50	2,214	792	36	64
Kyrgyzstan	1996	530,854	N/A	N/A	N/A	32,005	N/A	N/A	N/A
Laos	1997	187,600	73,944	39	N/A	N/A	N/A	N/A	54
Latvia	1997	239,318	122,000	51	49	43,170	19,680	46	54
Lebanon	1997	347,850	179,629	52	48	55,848	25,385	45	N/A
Lesotho	1996	68,132	40,149	59	41	678	437	64	36
Liberia	1980	54,623	15,343	28	72	2,322	627	27	73
Libya	1994	N/A	N/A	N/A	N/A	118,564	N/A	N/A	N/A
Lithuania	1997	378,754	189,096	50	50	53,274	20,882	39	61
Luxembourg	1997	28,796	14,509	50	50	19,333	9,325	48	52
Macau	1993	20,383	10,721	53	47	857	86	10	90
Macedonia, FYRO	1997	83,746	40,447	48	52	58,387	25,417	44	56
Madagascar	1996	N/A	N/A	N/A	N/A	8,138	2,430	30	70
Malawi	1996	141,911	N/A	N/A	N/A	1,054	N/A	N/A	N/A
Malaysia	1998	1,889,592	957,790	51	49	N/A	N/A	N/A	N/A
Maldives	1998	36,905	18,885	51	49	N/A	N/A	N/A	N/A
Mali	1998	188,109	62,460	33	67	20,191	6,706	33	67
Malta	1997	34,211	16,237	47	53	4,275	573	13	87
Martinique	1996	47,706	24,093	51	49	11,101	5,701	51	49
Mauritania	1996	51,765	17,355	34	66	1,414	415	29	71
Mauritius	1997	N/A	N/A	N/A	N/A	N/A	N/A	N/A	N/A
Mexico	1997	7,914,165	3,906,783	49	51	882,560	499,027	57	43
Moldova	1997	445,501	223,162	50	N/A	24,105	9,240	38	N/A
Monaco	1997	2,886	1,458	51	49	528	241	46	54
Mongolia	1997	195,408	112,056	57	43	11,308	5,946	53	47
Montserrat	1994	N/A	N/A	N/A	N/A	N/A	N/A	N/A	N/A
Morocco	1997	1,442,049	610,727	42	58	96,460	44,079	46	54
Mozambique	1995	185,181	72,369	39	61	14,582	3,769	26	74
Myanmar (Burma)	1996	N/A	N/A	N/A	N/A	N/A	N/A	N/A	N/A
Namibia	1998	115,237	60,630	53	47	90	70	78	22
Nauru	1985	482	242	50	50	17	8	47	53
Nepal	1996	1,121,335	419,909	37	63	N/A	N/A	N/A	N/A

B8-1. High School Pupil Enrollment in Vocational Education, by Gender, various years (continued)

	Year	Total enrollment, secondary school	Total female enrollment, secondary school	Percent pupils enrolled, female, secondary school	Percent pupils enrolled, male, secondary school	Total enrollment, vocational school	Female enrollment, vocational school	Percent female enrollment, vocational education	Percent male enrollment, vocational education
Netherlands, the	1997	1,415,712	677,314	48	52	583,901	256,290	44	56
Netherlands Antilles	1992	14,987	N/A	N/A	N/A	6,247	N/A	N/A	N/A
New Caledonia	1997	25,560	13,230	52	48	7,860	3,540	45	55
New Zealand	1997	433,347	216,630	50	50	78,640	40,458	51	49
Nicaragua	1998	N/A	N/A	N/A	N/A	N/A	N/A	N/A	N/A
Niger	1997	97,675	34,493	35	65	805	144	18	82
Nigeria	1994	4,451,329	2,031,547	46	54	N/A	N/A	N/A	N/A
Niue	1991	302	159	53	47	N/A	N/A	N/A	N/A
Norway	1997	368,074	176,073	48	52	124,682	51,128	41	59
Oman	1998	217,246	105,540	49	51	1,573	N/A	N/A	N/A
Pakistan	1994	N/A	N/A	N/A	N/A	92,000	30,000	33	81
Palestine	1997	56,467	26,833	48	52	1,775	332	19	81
Panama	1996	221,022	N/A	N/A	N/A	N/A	N/A	N/A	N/A
Papua New Guinea	1995	78,759	30,858	39	61	7,981	2,250	28	72
Paraguay	1997	327,775	165,780	51	49	N/A	N/A	N/A	N/A
Peru	1997	1,969,501	N/A	N/A	N/A	N/A	N/A	N/A	N/A
Philippines	1998	4,979,795	N/A	N/A	N/A	N/A	N/A	N/A	N/A
Poland	1996	2,539,138	1,239,331	49	51	1,745,884	719,247	41	59
Portugal	1996	947,478	484,773	51	49	126,004	57,994	46	54
Qatar	1996	38,594	18,804	49	51	670	N/A	N/A	N/A
Reunion	1996	91,548	46,016	50	50	13,547	6,020	44	56
Romania	1997	2,212,090	1,081,450	49	51	736,554	299,529	41	59
Russia	1994	13,732,000	N/A	N/A	N/A	1,007,000	N/A	N/A	N/A
Rwanda	1992	94,586	41,704	44	56	51,376	22,639	44	56
Samoa	1996	12,672	6,316	50	50	N/A	N/A	N/A	N/A
San Marino	1997	1,192	578	48	52	129	37	29	71
Sao Tome and Principe	1981	3,815	N/A	N/A	N/A	130	N/A	N/A	N/A
Saudi Arabia	1997	1,542,989	707,073	46	54	21,551	1,269	6	94
Senegal	1998	215,988	81,661	38	62	4,615	1,705	37	63
Seychelles	1996	9,099	4,497	49	51	711	288	41	59
Sierra Leone	1991	102,474	37,660	37	63	5,425	2,801	52	48
Singapore	1996	N/A	N/A	N/A	N/A	8,233	N/A	N/A	N/A
Slovakia	1997	677,377	329,135	N/A	N/A	256,361	122,576	N/A	N/A
Slovenia	1997	212,458	105,077	49	51	80,140	37,095	46	54
Solomon Islands	1994	7,811	2,940	38	65	N/A	N/A	N/A	N/A
Somalia	1986	45,686	16,036	35	65	5,933	1,361	23	77
South Africa	1995	N/A	N/A	N/A	N/A	N/A	N/A	N/A	N/A
South Korea, Rep.	1997	4,662,492	2,257,709	48	52	949,750	493,915	52	48
Spain	1997	3,852,102	1,934,449	50	50	905,911	452,202	50	50
Sri Lanka	1995	2,314,054	1,181,371	51	49	N/A	N/A	N/A	N/A
St. Helena	1986	513	252	49	51	32	N/A	N/A	N/A
St. Kitts and Nevis	1993	4,402	2,242	51	49	N/A	N/A	N/A	N/A

B8-1. High School Pupil Enrollment in Vocational Education, by Gender, various years *(continued)*

	Year	Total enrollment, secondary school	Total female enrollment, secondary school	Percent pupils enrolled, female, secondary school	Percent pupils enrolled, male, secondary school	Total enrollment, vocational school	Female enrollment, vocational school	Percent female enrollment, vocational education	Percent male enrollment, vocational education
St. Lucia	1997	11,753	6,605	56	44	N/A	N/A	N/A	N/A
St. Pierre and Miquelon	1986	821	432	53	47	265	135	51	49
Sudan	1997	405,583	189,958	47	53	26,421	9,977	38	62
Suriname	1994	N/A	N/A	N/A	N/A	N/A	N/A	N/A	N/A
Swaziland	1996	57,330	28,893	50	50	N/A	N/A	N/A	N/A
Sweden	1997	829,295	440,553	53	47	257,339	127,917	50	50
Switzerland	1996	559,924	264,398	47	53	172,266	64,742	38	62
Syria	1997	957,664	443,737	46	54	92,622	47,727	52	48
Tajikistan	1997	N/A	N/A	N/A	N/A	N/A	N/A	N/A	N/A
Tanzania	1997	234,743	104,782	45	55	N/A	N/A	N/A	N/A
Thailand	1998	4,097,331	N/A	N/A	N/A	738,861	N/A	N/A	N/A
Togo	1997	178,254	47,595	27	73	9,076	2,565	28	72
Tokelau	1991	N/A	N/A	N/A	N/A	N/A	N/A	N/A	N/A
Tonga	1993	16,570	7,908	48	52	787	330	42	58
Trinidad and Tobago	1997	N/A	N/A	N/A	N/A	N/A	N/A	N/A	N/A
Tunisia	1998	N/A	N/A	N/A	N/A	15,186	5,968	39	61
Turkey	1997	4,760,892	1,900,870	40	60	1,333,177	522,829	39	61
Turks and Caicos Islands	1997	N/A	N/A	N/A	N/A	N/A	N/A	N/A	N/A
Tuvalu	1990	345	178	52	48	31	N/A	N/A	N/A
Uganda	1995	N/A	N/A	N/A	N/A	13,360	N/A	N/A	N/A
Ukraine	1994	4,731,200	N/A	N/A	N/A	507,700	N/A	N/A	N/A
United Arab Emirates	1997	180,764	90,195	50	50	1,925	N/A	N/A	N/A
United Kingdom	1997	6,548,786	3,405,483	52	48	2,435,321	1,383,337	57	43
United States	1996	21,473,692	10,471,227	49	51	N/A	N/A	N/A	N/A
Uruguay	1996	269,826	N/A	N/A	N/A	43,284	19,348	45	55
Uzbekistan	1995	3,318,900	N/A	N/A	N/A	214,500	N/A	N/A	N/A
Vanuatu	1992	N/A	N/A	N/A	N/A	444	140	32	68
Venezuela	1997	377,984	217,894	58	42	N/A	N/A	N/A	N/A
Vietnam	1998	N/A	N/A	N/A	N/A	179,907	N/A	N/A	N/A
Virgin Islands, US	1993	12,502	6,191	50	50	N/A	N/A	N/A	N/A
Yemen	1997	354,288	71,309	20	80	52,349	7,725	15	85
Yugoslavia	1997	815,029	404,613	50	50	265,749	125,427	47	53
Zambia	1994	N/A	N/A	N/A	N/A	4,888	N/A	N/A	N/A
Zimbabwe	1998	847,296	N/A	N/A	N/A	N/A	N/A	N/A	N/A

N/A Not Available

Source: UNESCO Statistical Yearbook 1999, <http://unescostat.unesco.org/uisen/stats/stats0.htm>. Underlying data from United Nations Educational, Scientific and Cultural Organization (UNESCO).

B8-2. High School Pupil Enrollment in General Education, by Gender, various years

	Year	Total enrollment, secondary school	Total female enrollment, secondary school	Percent pupils enrolled, female, secondary school	Percent pupils enrolled, male, secondary school	Total enrollment, general education	Female enrollment, general education	Percent female enrollment, general education	Percent male enrollment, general education
Afghanistan	1995	512,851	130,136	25	75	512,851	130,136	25	75
Albania	1996	89,895	43,745	49	51	71,391	37,999	53	47
Algeria	1997	2,618,242	1,253,576	48	52	2,480,168	1,203,850	49	51
American Samoa	1992	3,643	1,680	46	54	3,483	1,673	48	52
Andorra	1976	1,753	1,092	62	38	1,753	1,092	62	38
Angola	1992	218,987	N/A	N/A	N/A	196,099	N/A	N/A	N/A
Anguilla	1997	1,062	581	55	45	1,062	581	55	45
Antigua and Barbuda	1992	5,845	2,937	50	50	5,845	2,937	50	50
Argentina	1996	2,594,329	1,347,990	52	48	N/A	N/A	N/A	N/A
Armenia	1997	372,187	N/A	N/A	N/A	365,025	N/A	N/A	N/A
Australia	1997	2,367,692	1,173,470	50	50	1,315,835	654,182	50	50
Austria	1997	793,485	377,559	48	52	480,966	237,446	49	51
Azerbaijan	1997	819,625	420,304	51	49	802,338	414,651	52	48
Bahamas, the	1997	27,970	N/A	N/A	N/A	27,970	N/A	N/A	N/A
Bahrain	1997	57,184	29,014	51	49	49,897	26,744	54	46
Bangladesh	1990	3,592,995	1,180,440	33	N/A	3,562,194	1,176,122	33	67
Barbados	1991	N/A	N/A	N/A	N/A	N/A	N/A	N/A	N/A
Belarus	1997	1,064,700	N/A	N/A	N/A	946,100	472,600	50	50
Belgium	1996	1,058,998	535,324	51	49	489,957	246,775	50	50
Belize	1995	10,272	5,335	52	48	10,147	5,307	52	48
Benin	1997	N/A	N/A	N/A	N/A	146,135	44,124	30	70
Bermuda	1997	N/A	N/A	N/A	N/A	3,726	1,890	51	49
Bhutan	1994	N/A	N/A	N/A	N/A	7,299	2,805	38	62
Bolivia	1990	219,232	100,748	46	54	N/A	N/A	N/A	N/A
Botswana	1996	N/A	N/A	N/A	N/A	109,843	58,468	53	47
Brazil	1998	6,967,905	N/A	N/A	N/A	N/A	N/A	N/A	N/A
British Virgin Islands	1994	1,309	668	51	49	1,309	668	51	49
Brunei	1996	30,470	15,868	52	48	28,274	14,949	53	47
Bulgaria	1997	733,362	356,083	49	51	526,792	277,940	53	47
Burkina Faso	1994	N/A	N/A	N/A	N/A	116,033	39,551	34	66
Burundi	1995	N/A	N/A	N/A	N/A	47,636	N/A	N/A	N/A
Cambodia	1998	312,934	108,917	35	65	302,951	105,440	35	65
Cameroon	1995	N/A	N/A	N/A	N/A	459,068	185,248	40	60
Canada	1996	2,505,389	1,218,403	49	51	2,505,389	1,218,403	49	51
Cape Verde	1998	31,602	16,125	51	49	N/A	N/A	N/A	N/A
Central African Republic	1992	43,740	12,851	29	71	42,263	12,273	29	71
Chad	1997	99,789	20,301	20	80	97,011	19,389	20	80
Chile	1996	739,316	377,256	51	49	415,919	224,967	54	46
China	1998	71,883,000	32,530,000	45	N/A	60,179,000	27,356,000	45	55
Colombia	1996	3,317,782	1,687,248	51	49	2,403,118	1,179,407	49	51
Comoros	1996	N/A	N/A	N/A	N/A	21,192	N/A	N/A	N/A
Congo, Dem. Rep. (Zaire)	1995	1,514,323	571,264	38	62	1,155,517	415,126	36	64
Congo, Rep.	1996	214,650	91,500	43	57	189,381	80,308	42	58

B8-2. High School Pupil Enrollment in General Education, by Gender, various years (continued)

	Year	Total enrollment, secondary school	Total female enrollment, secondary school	Percent pupils enrolled, female, secondary school	Percent pupils enrolled, male, secondary school	Total enrollment, general education	Female enrollment, general education	Percent female enrollment, general education	Percent male enrollment, general education
Costa Rica	1998	202,415	104,081	51	49	158,092	82,071	52	48
Côte d'Ivoire	1997	N/A	N/A	N/A	N/A	534,214	169,013	32	68
Croatia	1997	416,829	205,490	49	51	262,031	134,400	51	49
Cuba	1997	712,897	367,943	52	48	500,339	266,874	53	47
Cyprus	1997	61,266	30,303	49	51	56,652	29,358	52	48
Czech Republic	1996	1,190,725	591,073	50	50	643,191	325,382	51	49
Djibouti	1997	13,311	5,477	41	59	11,367	4,380	39	61
Dominica	1995	N/A	N/A	N/A	N/A	6,493	3,334	51	49
Dominican Republic	1998	N/A	N/A	N/A	N/A	329,944	184,384	56	44
Ecuador	1993	814,359	405,655	50	50	534,368	252,876	47	53
Egypt	1998	N/A	N/A	N/A	N/A	4,835,938	2,261,514	47	53
Equatorial Guinea	1994	16,616	5,741	35	65	14,511	5,119	35	65
Eritrea	1997	89,087	37,196	42	58	88,054	37,053	42	58
Estonia	1997	N/A	N/A	N/A	N/A	95,877	50,412	53	47
Ethiopia	1997	N/A	N/A	N/A	N/A	889,650	374,122	42	N/A
Falkland Islands (Malvinas)	1995	147	72	49	51	N/A	N/A	N/A	N/A
Fiji	1992	66,890	32,673	49	51	60,237	30,950	51	49
Finland	1997	469,933	244,760	52	48	329,301	172,725	52	48
France	1997	5,979,690	2,910,884	49	51	4,333,313	2,215,880	51	49
French Guiana	1996	15,989	8,036	50	N/A	13,585	6,849	50	50
French Polynesia	1993	22,366	12,241	55	45	18,636	10,492	56	44
Gabon	1996	80,552	38,076	47	53	72,888	35,402	49	51
Gambia, the	1996	32,097	12,354	38	62	N/A	N/A	N/A	N/A
Georgia	1997	444,058	215,969	49	51	424,465	206,611	49	51
Germany	1997	8,382,335	4,037,044	48	52	6,061,870	3,012,743	50	50
Ghana	1992	N/A	N/A	N/A	N/A	841,722	328,718	39	61
Gibraltar	1997	N/A	N/A	N/A	N/A	1,781	862	48	52
Greece	1997	817,566	400,097	49	51	682,201	346,389	51	49
Grenada	1993	10,213	5,489	54	46	10,213	5,489	54	46
Guam	1986	14,557	N/A	N/A	N/A	N/A	N/A	N/A	N/A
Guatemala	1997	384,729	N/A	N/A	N/A	N/A	N/A	N/A	N/A
Guinea	1998	N/A	N/A	N/A	N/A	153,661	39,449	26	74
Guinea-Bissau	1981	4,757	939	20	80	4,068	876	22	78
Guyana	1997	62,043	31,845	51	49	62,043	31,845	51	49
Haiti	1991	N/A	N/A	N/A	N/A	184,968	90,534	49	51
Honduras	1993	203,192	N/A	N/A	N/A	N/A	N/A	N/A	N/A
Hong Kong, SAR (China)	1996	473,817	232,505	49	51	459,845	228,030	50	50
Hungary	1996	1,112,149	552,511	50	50	702,641	362,515	52	48
Iceland	1997	N/A	N/A	N/A	N/A	25,477	13,341	52	48
India	1997	68,872,393	26,269,449	38	62	68,101,705	26,150,336	38	62
Indonesia	1997	14,209,974	N/A	N/A	N/A	12,442,813	N/A	N/A	N/A
Iran	1997	8,776,792	4,065,233	46	54	N/A	N/A	N/A	N/A
Iraq	1996	1,160,421	437,633	38	62	1,037,482	406,025	39	61
Ireland	1997	389,353	197,386	51	49	353,270	177,469	50	50

B8-2. High School Pupil Enrollment in General Education, by Gender, various years (continued)

	Year	Total enrollment, secondary school	Total female enrollment, secondary school	Percent pupils enrolled, female, secondary school	Percent pupils enrolled, male, secondary school	Total enrollment, general education	Female enrollment, general education	Percent female enrollment, general education	Percent male enrollment, general education
Israel	1996	541,737	N/A	N/A	N/A	419,122	N/A	N/A	N/A
Italy	1997	4,602,243	2,244,975	49	51	2,642,456	1,324,401	50	50
Jamaica	1993	235,071	120,640	51	49	N/A	N/A	N/A	N/A
Japan	1995	9,878,568	4,852,217	49	51	8,442,844	4,203,313	50	50
Jordan	1998	155,008	77,240	50	50	115,307	62,930	55	45
Kazakhstan	1997	1,921,302	1,000,406	52	48	1,743,623	894,457	51	49
Kenya	1995	N/A	N/A	N/A	N/A	632,388	290,581	46	N/A
Kiribati	1997	N/A	N/A	N/A	N/A	4,403	2,335	53	47
Kuwait	1998	224,293	111,744	50	50	222,079	110,952	50	50
Kyrgyzstan	1996	530,854	N/A	N/A	N/A	498,849	261,482	52	48
Laos	1997	187,600	73,944	39	N/A	180,160	71,164	40	60
Latvia	1997	239,318	122,000	51	49	196,148	102,320	52	48
Lebanon	1997	347,850	179,629	52	48	292,002	154,244	53	N/A
Lesotho	1996	68,132	40,149	59	41	67,454	39,712	59	41
Liberia	1980	54,623	15,343	28	72	51,666	14,632	28	72
Libya	1994	N/A	N/A	N/A	N/A	N/A	N/A	N/A	N/A
Lithuania	1997	378,754	189,096	50	50	325,480	168,214	52	48
Luxembourg	1997	28,796	14,509	50	50	9,463	5,184	55	45
Macau	1993	20,383	10,721	53	47	19,526	10,635	54	46
Macedonia, FYRO	1997	83,746	40,447	48	52	25,359	15,030	59	41
Madagascar	1996	N/A	N/A	N/A	N/A	302,035	151,493	50	50
Malawi	1996	141,911	N/A	N/A	N/A	139,386	49,383	35	65
Malaysia	1998	1,889,592	957,790	51	49	N/A	N/A	N/A	N/A
Maldives	1998	36,905	18,885	51	49	N/A	N/A	N/A	N/A
Mali	1998	188,109	62,460	33	67	166,372	55,260	33	67
Malta	1997	34,211	16,237	47	53	29,936	15,664	52	48
Martinique	1996	47,706	24,093	51	49	36,605	18,392	50	50
Mauritania	1996	51,765	17,355	34	66	49,221	16,613	34	66
Mauritius	1997	N/A	N/A	N/A	N/A	93,839	48,133	51	49
Mexico	1997	7,914,165	3,906,783	49	51	7,031,605	3,407,756	48	52
Moldova	1997	445,501	223,162	50	N/A	419,256	211,931	51	N/A
Monaco	1997	2,886	1,458	51	49	2,358	1,217	52	48
Mongolia	1997	195,408	112,056	57	43	184,100	106,110	58	42
Montserrat	1994	N/A	N/A	N/A	N/A	905	447	49	51
Morocco	1997	1,442,049	610,727	42	58	1,345,589	566,648	42	58
Mozambique	1995	185,181	72,369	39	61	165,868	66,549	40	60
Myanmar (Burma)	1996	N/A	N/A	N/A	N/A	1,923,323	N/A	N/A	N/A
Namibia	1998	115,237	60,630	53	47	115,147	60,560	53	47
Nauru	1985	482	242	50	50	465	234	50	50
Nepal	1996	1,121,335	419,909	37	63	N/A	N/A	N/A	N/A
Netherlands, the	1997	1,415,712	677,314	48	52	831,811	421,024	51	49
Netherlands Antilles	1992	14,987	N/A	N/A	N/A	8,740	N/A	N/A	N/A
New Caledonia	1997	25,560	13,230	52	48	17,700	9,690	55	45
New Zealand	1997	433,347	216,630	50	50	354,707	176,172	50	50

B8-2. High School Pupil Enrollment in General Education, by Gender, various years (continued)

	Year	Total enrollment, secondary school	Total female enrollment, secondary school	Percent pupils enrolled, female, secondary school	Percent pupils enrolled, male, secondary school	Total enrollment, general education	Female enrollment, general education	Percent female enrollment, general education	Percent male enrollment, general education
Nicaragua	1998	N/A	N/A	N/A	N/A	287,476	154,263	54	46
Niger	1997	97,675	34,493	35	65	95,530	34,016	36	64
Nigeria	1994	4,451,329	2,031,547	46	54	N/A	N/A	N/A	N/A
Niue	1991	302	159	53	47	302	159	53	47
Norway	1997	368,074	176,073	48	52	243,392	124,945	51	49
Oman	1998	217,246	105,540	49	51	215,673	105,540	49	51
Pakistan	1994	N/A	N/A	N/A	N/A	N/A	N/A	N/A	N/A
Palestine	1997	56,467	26,833	48	52	54,692	26,501	48	52
Panama	1996	221,022	N/A	N/A	N/A	N/A	N/A	N/A	N/A
Papua New Guinea	1995	78,759	30,858	39	61	68,818	27,693	40	60
Paraguay	1997	327,775	165,780	51	49	N/A	N/A	N/A	N/A
Peru	1997	1,969,501	N/A	N/A	N/A	1,969,501	N/A	N/A	N/A
Philippines	1998	4,979,795	N/A	N/A	N/A	4,979,795	N/A	N/A	N/A
Poland	1996	2,539,138	1,239,331	49	51	793,216	520,054	66	34
Portugal	1996	947,478	484,773	51	49	821,474	426,779	52	48
Qatar	1996	38,594	18,804	49	51	37,924	18,804	50	50
Reunion	1996	91,548	46,016	50	50	78,001	39,996	51	49
Romania	1997	2,212,090	1,081,450	49	51	1,457,608	764,985	52	48
Russia	1994	13,732,000	N/A	N/A	N/A	12,424,000	6,399,000	52	48
Rwanda	1992	94,586	41,704	44	56	23,039	8,734	38	62
Samoa	1996	12,672	6,316	50	50	12,672	6,316	50	50
San Marino	1997	1,192	578	48	52	1,063	541	51	49
Sao Tome and Principe	1981	3,815	N/A	N/A	N/A	3,685	N/A	N/A	N/A
Saudi Arabia	1997	1,542,989	707,073	46	54	1,500,072	684,438	46	54
Senegal	1998	215,988	81,661	38	62	210,798	79,862	38	62
Seychelles	1996	9,099	4,497	49	51	8,151	4,046	50	50
Sierra Leone	1991	102,474	37,660	37	63	97,049	34,859	36	64
Singapore	1996	N/A	N/A	N/A	N/A	207,719	N/A	N/A	N/A
Slovakia	1997	677,377	329,135	49	51	418,199	203,932	49	51
Slovenia	1997	212,458	105,077	49	51	131,573	67,257	51	49
Solomon Islands	1994	7,811	2,940	38	62	7,811	2,940	38	62
Somalia	1986	45,686	16,036	35	65	39,753	14,675	37	63
South Africa	1995	N/A	N/A	N/A	N/A	3,749,449	2,039,551	54	46
South Korea, Rep.	1997	4,662,492	2,257,709	48	52	3,712,742	1,763,794	48	52
Spain	1997	3,852,102	1,934,449	50	50	2,946,191	1,482,247	50	50
Sri Lanka	1995	2,314,054	1,181,371	51	49	2,314,054	1,181,371	51	49
St. Helena	1986	513	252	49	51	470	245	52	48
St. Kitts and Nevis	1993	4,402	2,242	51	49	4,402	2,242	51	49
St. Lucia	1997	11,753	6,605	56	44	556	297	53	47
St. Pierre and Miquelon	1994	821	432	53	47	N/A	N/A	N/A	N/A
St. Vincent and the Grenadines	1994	N/A	N/A	N/A	N/A	9,870	5,497	56	44
Sudan	1997	405,583	189,958	47	53	379,162	179,981	53	47
Suriname	1994	N/A	N/A	N/A	N/A	16,511	9,454	57	43
Swaziland	1996	57,330	28,893	50	50	57,330	28,893	50	50

B8-2. High School Pupil Enrollment in General Education, by Gender, various years (continued)

	Year	Total enrollment, secondary school	Total female enrollment, secondary school	Percent pupils enrolled, female, secondary school	Percent pupils enrolled, male, secondary school	Total enrollment, general education	Female enrollment, general education	Percent female enrollment, general education	Percent male enrollment, general education
Sweden	1997	829,295	440,553	53	47	571,956	312,636	55	45
Switzerland	1996	559,924	264,398	47	53	378,328	192,165	51	49
Syria	1997	957,664	443,737	46	54	865,042	396,010	46	54
Tajikistan	1997	N/A	N/A	N/A	N/A	688,150	322,468	47	53
Tanzania	1997	234,743	104,782	45	55	225,607	100,450	45	55
Thailand	1998	4,097,331	N/A	N/A	N/A	3,358,470	N/A	N/A	N/A
Togo	1997	178,254	47,595	27	73	169,178	45,030	27	73
Tokelau	1991	N/A	N/A	N/A	N/A	113	53	47	53
Tonga	1993	16,570	7,908	48	52	15,573	7,450	48	52
Trinidad and Tobago	1997	N/A	N/A	N/A	N/A	104,349	53,253	51	49
Tunisia	1998	N/A	N/A	N/A	N/A	833,372	418,409	50	50
Turkey	1997	4,760,892	1,900,870	40	60	3,427,715	1,378,041	40	60
Turks and Caicos Islands	1997	N/A	N/A	N/A	N/A	1,028	519	50	50
Tuvalu	1990	345	178	52	48	314	178	57	43
Uganda	1995	N/A	N/A	N/A	N/A	256,258	98,205	38	62
Ukraine	1994	4,731,200	N/A	N/A	N/A	4,202,200	2,139,400	51	49
United Arab Emirates	1997	180,764	90,195	50	50	178,839	90,195	50	50
United Kingdom	1997	6,548,786	3,405,483	52	48	4,113,465	2,022,146	49	51
United States	1996	21,473,692	10,471,227	49	51	21,473,692	10,471,227	49	51
Uzbekistan	1995	3,318,900	N/A	N/A	N/A	3,104,400	1,492,300	48	52
Vanuatu	1992	N/A	N/A	N/A	N/A	4,269	1,894	44	56
Venezuela	1997	377,984	217,894	58	42	6,642,350	3,118,775	N/A	N/A
Vietnam	1998	N/A	N/A	N/A	N/A	12,502	6,191	47	53
Virgin Islands, US	1993	12,502	6,191	50	50	286,405	60,939	50	50
Yemen	1997	354,288	71,309	20	80	548,953	278,947	21	79
Yugoslavia	1997	815,029	404,613	50	50	199,154	76,397	51	49
Zambia	1994	N/A	N/A	N/A	N/A	847,296	N/A	38	62
Zimbabwe	1998	847,296	N/A	N/A	N/A			N/A	N/A

N/A   Not Available

Source: UNESCO Statistical Yearbook 1999, <http://unescostat.unesco.org/uisen/stats/stats0.htm>. Underlying data from United Nations Educational, Scientific and Cultural Organization (UNESCO).

B9. CLASS SIZE AND PUPIL-TEACHER RATIO

B9-1. Average Class Size (Grade 1), Selected Countries, 1995

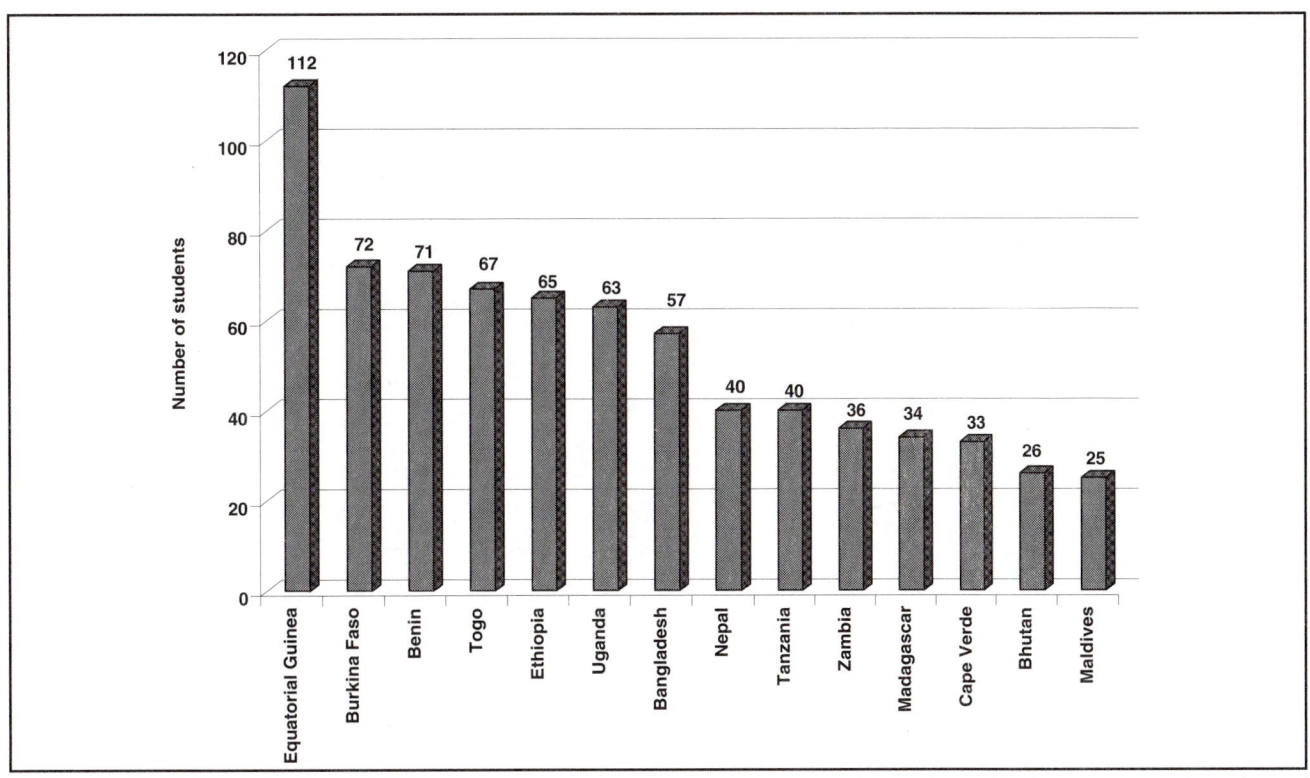

Source: The Progress of Nations 1996, <http://www.unicef.org/pon96/edstnds.htm>. Underlying data from *Andreas Schleicher, Maria Teresa Siniscalco, and Neville Postlethwaite, The Conditions of Primary Schools: A Pilot Study in the Least Developed Countries,* September 1995. Report to United Nations Educational, Scientific and Cultural Organization (UNESCO) and United Nations Children's Fund (UNICEF).

B9-2. Average Class Size for 13-Year-Olds, Selected Countries, 1991

	Number of students per class
South Korea, Rep.	49
Taiwan	44
Japan	36
Spain	29
Hungary	27
Ireland	27
Canada	25
France	25
Scotland (UK)	24
United States	23

Source: Educational Indicators: An International Perspective, Figure 21; <http://www.nces.ed.gov/pubs/eiip/eiipid21.html>. Underlying data from Educational Testing Service, International Assessment of Educational Progress, Learning Mathematics, 1992, National Center For Education Statistics.

B9-3. Pupil-Teacher Ratio, Pre-Primary Schools, 1995

	Pupils per teacher
Albania	19
Algeria	26
Argentina	15
Armenia	7
Austria	17
Azerbaijan	7
Bahrain	27
Belarus	6
Benin	27
Bulgaria	11
Burkina Faso	36
Cambodia	24
Canada	40
Chile	30
China	31
Colombia	21
Costa Rica	23
Croatia	12
Cuba	24
Cyprus	20
Czech Republic	12
Ecuador	16
Egypt	24
El Salvador	26
Eritrea	35
Estonia	8
Finland	12
France	24
French Polynesia	25
Georgia	8
Germany	20
Greece	15
Guatemala	32
Guinea	53
Guyana	16
Hong Kong, SAR (China)	21
Iceland	7
Iran	28
Iraq	18
Ireland	24
Italy	14
Japan	16
Jordan	22
Kuwait	16
Kyrgyzstan	9
Latvia	8
Lithuania	8
Macedonia, FYRO	11
Malta	14
Martinique	32
Mexico	24
Moldova	7
Monaco	22
Mongolia	12
New Zealand	15
Niger	22
Oman	20
Palestine	31

B9-3. Pupil-Teacher Ratio, Pre-Primary Schools, 1995 *(continued)*

	Pupils per teacher
Panama	22
Papua New Guinea	32
Paraguay	22
Peru	23
Poland	13
Qatar	22
Romania	18
San Marino	9
Saudi Arabia	11
Senegal	21
Seychelles	18
Slovakia	11
Slovenia	11
South Africa	26
South Korea, Rep.	25
Spain	19
Syria	22
Tajikistan	9
Togo	23
United Arab Emirates	20
United Kingdom	30
United States	28
Uruguay	26
Venezuela	23
Vietnam	26
Yugoslavia	11

Source: UNESCO Statistical Yearbook 1999; <http://unescostat.unesco.org/uisen/stats/stats0.htm>. Underlying data from United Nations Educational, Scientific and Cultural Organization (UNESCO).

B9-4. Pupil-Teacher Ratio, Primary Schools, 1995

	Pupils per teacher
Albania	18
Algeria	27
Argentina	18
Armenia	22
Australia	17
Austria	12
Azerbaijan	20
Bahamas, the	22
Benin	52
Bermuda	13
Botswana	25
Brazil	24
Bulgaria	17
Burkina Faso	50
Burundi	50
Cambodia	45
Canada	16
Chad	63
Chile	27
China	23
Colombia	25
Comoros	42
Congo, Rep.	70
Costa Rica	31

B9-4. Pupil-Teacher Ratio, Primary Schools, 1995 *(continued)*

	Pupils per teacher
Côte d'Ivoire	41
Croatia	20
Cuba	12
Cyprus	19
Czech Republic	19
Djibouti	36
Ecuador	29
Egypt	24
El Salvador	28
Eritrea	41
Estonia	17
Ethiopia	38
France	19
French Guiana	21
French Polynesia	14
Gabon	51
Gambia	30
Georgia	16
Germany	17
Greece	15
Guatemala	34
Guinea	49
Guyana	30
Hong Kong SAR, (China)	24
India	47
Iraq	20
Ireland	23
Italy	11
Jamaica	33
Japan	18
Jordan	21
Kenya	30
Kiribati	27
Kuwait	15
Kyrgyzstan	20
Latvia	14
Lesotho	48
Lithuania	17
Macedonia, FYRO	20
Madagascar	37
Malawi	59
Malaysia	19
Mali	70
Malta	19
Martinique	13
Mauritania	51
Mauritius	24
Mexico	28
Moldova	23
Monaco	19
Mongolia	25
Mozambique	58
New Zealand	18
Nicaragua	38
Niger	39
Oman	26
Palestine	42
Papua New Guinea	37

B9-4. Pupil-Teacher Ratio, Primary Schools, 1995 *(continued)*

	Pupils per teacher
Paraguay	21
Peru	28
Philippines	35
Poland	15
Qatar	9
Romania	20
Samoa	24
San Marino	5
Saudi Arabia	13
Senegal	58
Seychelles	17
Singapore	25
Slovakia	21
Slovenia	14
South Africa	37
South Korea, Rep.	32
Spain	17
Sri Lanka	28
St. Lucia	27
Sudan	31
Swaziland	34
Syria	24
Tajikistan	23
Tanzania	37
Togo	51
Trinidad and Tobago	25
Tunisia	25
Uganda	35
United Arab Emirates	17
United Kingdom	19
United States	16
Uruguay	20
Vietnam	34
Zambia	39
Zimbabwe	39

Source: UNESCO Statistical Yearbook 1999, <http://unescostat.unesco.org/uisen/stats/stats0.htm>. Underlying data from United Nations Educational, Scientific and Cultural Organization (UNESCO).

B9-5. Pupil-Teacher Ratio, Secondary Schools, 1995

	Pupils per teacher
Afghanistan	28
Albania	14
Algeria	17
Argentina	10
Armenia	10
Australia	13
Austria	10
Azerbaijan	9
Bahamas, the	16
Bahrain	13
Benin	29
Bermuda	9
Botswana	17
Brunei	12

B9-5. Pupil-Teacher Ratio, Secondary Schools, 1995 *(continued)*

	Pupils per teacher
Bulgaria	11
Cambodia	18
Canada	19
Chad	35
Chile	13
China	16
Colombia	21
Comoros	25
Congo, Rep.	30
Costa Rica	19
Côte d'Ivoire	27
Croatia	14
Cuba	10
Cyprus	11
Czech Republic	10
Djibouti	19
Egypt	17
El Salvador	20
Eritrea	37
Estonia	10
Ethiopia	32
Falkland Islands (Malvinas)	7
France	12
French Guiana	15
Gabon	26
Gambia, the	21
Georgia	6
Germany	15
Greece	10
Guatemala	16
Guinea	25
Guyana	29
Hong Kong SAR, (China)	20
India	32
Iran	32
Iraq	19
Ireland	15
Italy	10
Jordan	17
Kenya	15
Kiribati	14
Kuwait	11
Kyrgyzstan	13
Latvia	8
Lesotho	24
Lithuania	10
Macedonia, FYRO	17
Madagascar	17
Malawi	22
Malaysia	19
Mali	23
Malta	11
Martinique	13
Mauritania	25
Mauritius	20
Mexico	16
Moldova	13
Monaco	10

B9-5. Pupil-Teacher Ratio, Secondary Schools, 1995 *(continued)*

	Pupils per teacher
Mongolia	18
Mozambique	33
New Zealand	15
Nicaragua	34
Niger	26
Norway	7
Oman	17
Palestine	7
Panama	18
Peru	19
Philippines	35
Poland	21
Reunion	15
Romania	13
Samoa	19
Saudi Arabia	13
Senegal	24
Seychelles	13
Singapore	19
Slovakia	13
Slovenia	14
South Korea, Rep.	25
Spain	15
Sri Lanka	22
St. Lucia	19
Sudan	33
Swaziland	19
Syria	15
Tajikistan	8
Tanzania	17
Togo	31
Trinidad and Tobago	21
Tunisia	18
Uganda	18
United Arab Emirates	13
United Kingdom	14
United States	15
Vietnam	27
Zimbabwe	26

Source: UNESCO Statistical Yearbook 1999; <http://unescostat.unesco.org/uisen/stats/stats0.htm>. Underlying data from United Nations Educational, Scientific and Cultural Organization (UNESCO).

B10. COEFFICIENT OF EFFICIENCY

B10-1. Coefficient of Efficiency, Primary Education, Selected Countries, 1995

	Percent both sexes	Percent male	Percent female
Algeria	83.9	81.1	87.3
Armenia	99.8	N/A	N/A
Azerbaijan	96.8	98.7	88.5
Bahrain	84.6	83.7	85.7
Belarus	98.4	98.3	98.4
Botswana	90.7	86.9	94.3
Bulgaria	92.5	92.0	93.0
Chad	43.2	45.8	37.1
Chile	91.7	88.6	94.6
China	94.2	93.8	94.5
Colombia	84.6	83.1	86.1
Costa Rica	80.0	77.7	82.5
Côte d'Ivoire	65.6	67.2	60.5
Croatia	99.5	99.4	99.4
Cyprus	99.6	99.0	99.7
Djibouti	72.8	N/A	N/A
Ecuador	91.8	91.1	92.6
El Salvador	63.5	63.4	63.6
Eritrea	66.5	69.1	63.1
Georgia	98.6	N/A	N/A
Guatemala	57.1	57.9	56.3
Kazakhstan	94.9	N/A	N/A
Kiribati	96.3	94.7	95.7
Kuwait	93.8	93.1	94.6
Latvia	96.1	N/A	N/A
Lithuania	98.1	97.5	98.6
Macedonia, FYRO	92.2	91.0	93.5
Mali	66.4	N/A	N/A
Malta	97.9	96.8	98.4
Mauritania	61.0	61.1	60.7
Mauritius	94.9	94.4	95.1
Moldova	97.3	96.4	98.1
Mongolia	94.5	93.4	95.6
Namibia	69.2	N/A	N/A
New Zealand	93.0	92.6	93.3
Niger	68.6	68.3	69.2
Oman	87.1	85.8	88.5
Palestine	78.3	74.7	82.2
Romania	95.0	N/A	N/A
Samoa	89.1	N/A	N/A
San Marino	99.9	99.8	100.0
Saudi Arabia	87.5	84.8	90.4
Senegal	76.2	79.6	71.8
Seychelles	99.9	99.4	99.4
Slovakia	96.6	96.2	96.9
Slovenia	98.9	98.6	99.2
Sri Lanka	86.8	86.3	87.3
Sudan	77.4	74.4	81.0
Swaziland	61.3	58.7	63.9
Syria	86.4	86.2	86.7
Tunisia	76.1	74.1	78.3
United Arab Emirates	86.2	84.9	87.7
Uruguay	88.0	85.8	90.4
Venezuela	59.9	52.8	66.8
Yugoslavia	98.2	N/A	N/A
Zimbabwe	91.1	91.0	91.1

N/A Not Available

Source: UNESCO Statistical Yearbook 1999; <http://unescostat.unesco.org/uisen/stats/stats0.htm>. Underlying data from United Nations Educational, Scientific and Cultural Organization (UNESCO).

B11. STUDENTS REPEATING GRADES

B11-1. Percentage of Pupils Who Repeat a Grade, Primary Schools, various years

	Year	Percent
Afghanistan	1993	9
Albania	1995	5
Algeria	1996	10
Argentina	1996	6
Austria	1970	6
Azerbaijan	1993	N/A
Bahrain	1996	5
Belarus	1996	1
Belgium	1985	17
Benin	1995	25
Bhutan	1994	19
Bolivia	1990	3
Botswana	1996	3
Brazil	1993	18
Brunei	1994	9
Bulgaria	1996	3
Burkina Faso	1995	16
Burundi	1992	24
Cambodia	1997	26
Cameroon	1990	29
Cape Verde	1993	17
Central African Republic	1991	37
Chad	1996	32
Chile	1996	5
China	1996	2
Colombia	1996	7
Comoros	1992	41
Comoros	1993	36
Congo, Dem. Rep. (Zaire)	1993	21
Congo, Rep.	1995	33
Costa Rica	1998	10
Côte d'Ivoire	1996	24
Croatia	1996	N/A
Cuba	1995	3
Cuba	1994	3
Cyprus	1995	N/A
Czech Republic	1995	1
Djibouti	1996	16
Ecuador	1996	3
Egypt	1996	6
El Salvador	1995	6
Eritrea	1996	20
Estonia	1995	3
Ethiopia	1996	8
Fiji	1985	3
Finland	1996	N/A
Gabon	1994	39
Gambia, the	1995	13
Georgia	1996	N/A
Ghana	1991	3
Greece	1991	N/A
Guadeloupe	1990	8
Guatemala	1996	15
Guinea	1997	28
Guinea-Bissau	1980	29

B11-1. Percentage of Pupils Who Repeat a Grade, Primary Schools, various years *(continued)*

	Year	Percent
Guyana	1996	4
Haiti	1990	13
Honduras	1993	12
India	1994	4
Indonesia	1996	6
Iran	1996	6
Iraq	1992	16
Italy	1996	N/A
Jamaica	1992	3
Jordan	1992	4
Kazakhstan	1993	1
Kenya	1980	13
Kiribati	1996	N/A
Kuwait	1995	3
Kyrgyzstan	1995	N/A
Laos	1996	23
Latvia	1996	2
Lebanon	1996	13
Lesotho	1996	20
Lesotho	1992	21
Libya	1980	9
Lithuania	1996	1
Macau	1992	7
Macedonia, FYRO	1995	1
Madagascar	1995	34
Malawi	1990	19
Mali	1995	18
Malta	1996	2
Martinique	1991	5
Mauritania	1996	16
Mauritius	1996	4
Mexico	1996	7
Moldova	1996	1
Mongolia	1996	1
Morocco	1996	12
Mozambique	1995	26
Namibia	1996	13
Nepal	1992	27
New Caledonia	1990	13
Nicaragua	1995	15
Niger	1996	13
Oman	1996	9
Palestine	1995	4
Panama	1985	13
Paraguay	1996	9
Peru	1995	15
Philippines	1985	2
Poland	1994	1
Portugal	1990	14
Qatar	1995	5
Reunion	1985	16
Romania	1996	3
Russia	1994	2
Rwanda	1991	14
San Marino	1995	N/A
Saudi Arabia	1996	8
Senegal	1996	13
Singapore	1980	7

B11-1. Percentage of Pupils Who Repeat a Grade, Primary Schools, various years *(continued)*

	Year	Percent
Slovakia	1995	2
Slovenia	1995	1
Solomon Islands	1994	9
Spain	1993	3
Sri Lanka	1991	8
St. Pierre and Miquelon	1985	3
Suriname	1975	24
Swaziland	1996	15
Switzerland	1995	2
Syria	1995	7
Tajikistan	1996	N/A
Tanzania	1985	1
Thailand	1980	8
Togo	1995	24
Trinidad and Tobago	1995	6
Tunisia	1995	17
Turkey	1993	5
Ukraine	1993	1
United Arab Emirates	1996	4
Uruguay	1995	10
Vanuatu	1992	13
Venezuela	1996	10
Yugoslavia	1995	1
Zambia	1994	2

N/A Not Available

Source: UNESCO Statistical Yearbook 1999; <http://unescostat.unesco.org/uisen/stats/stats0.htm>. Underlying data from United Nations Educational, Scientific and Cultural Organization (UNESCO).

B12. SURVIVAL RATIOS

B12-1. Survival Ratios, Primary Education (Grade 1 to Grade 6), 1995

	Grade 1	Grade 2	Grade 3	Grade 4	Grade 5	Grade 6
Algeria	100	99	97	96	94	90
Armenia	100	100	100	100	N/A	N/A
Azerbaijan	100	96	95	93	N/A	N/A
Bahrain	100	99	98	96	95	85
Belarus	100	99	98	98	N/A	N/A
Botswana	100	93	92	92	90	89
Bulgaria	100	93	91	89	N/A	N/A
Chad	100	84	79	69	59	50
Chile	100	100	100	100	100	100
China	100	100	99	97	94	N/A
Colombia	100	76	76	76	73	N/A
Costa Rica	100	96	93	91	88	83
Côte d'Ivoire	100	90	85	78	75	74
Croatia	100	100	100	100	N/A	N/A
Cyprus	100	100	100	100	100	100
Djibouti	100	94	89	86	79	77
Ecuador	100	89	88	87	85	85
El Salvador	100	89	87	82	77	67
Eritrea	100	89	84	79	70	N/A
Ethiopia	100	66	N/A	N/A	51	47
Finland	100	100	N/A	N/A	100	100
Georgia	100	100	99	98	N/A	N/A

B12-1. Survival Ratios, Primary Education (Grade 1 to Grade 6), 1995 *(continued)*

	Grade 1	Grade 2	Grade 3	Grade 4	Grade 5	Grade 6
Guatemala	100	78	67	57	50	45
Guyana	100	100	N/A	N/A	91	88
Indonesia	100	98	N/A	N/A	88	83
Italy	100	100	N/A	N/A	99	N/A
Kazakhstan	100	98	96	92	N/A	N/A
Kiribati	100	93	93	92	89	89
Kuwait	100	97	96	94	N/A	N/A
Laos	100	78	N/A	N/A	55	N/A
Latvia	100	99	99	97	N/A	N/A
Lesotho	100	84	N/A	N/A	63	56
Lithuania	100	99	99	99	N/A	N/A
Macedonia, FYRO	100	99	98	97	95	93
Mali	100	99	94	89	84	75
Malta	100	100	100	100	100	100
Mauritania	100	90	84	74	64	58
Mauritius	100	100	100	99	99	99
Mexico	100	94	N/A	N/A	86	83
Moldova	100	96	96	95	N/A	N/A
Mongolia	100	94	90	87	N/A	N/A
Namibia	100	92	88	85	79	72
New Zealand	100	98	85	85	85	83
Niger	100	92	86	79	73	67
Oman	100	99	99	99	96	94
Palestine	100	100	100	100	100	99
Paraguay	100	92	N/A	N/A	78	72
Romania	100	97	96	95	N/A	N/A
Samoa	100	90	90	89	86	82
San Marino	100	100	100	100	100	N/A
Saudi Arabia	100	96	95	92	89	88
Senegal	100	94	92	87	85	81
Seychelles	100	100	100	100	100	100
Slovakia	100	97	97	96	N/A	N/A
Slovenia	100	100	100	100	N/A	N/A
South Korea, Rep.	100	100	N/A	N/A	98	98
Sri Lanka	100	100	95	91	83	N/A
Sudan	100	93	88	82	74	67
Swaziland	100	92	87	82	74	66
Sweden	100	97	N/A	N/A	97	97
Syria	100	99	97	96	94	89
Trinidad and Tobago	100	100	N/A	N/A	97	97
Tunisia	100	98	97	95	91	85
United Arab Emirates	100	93	89	87	83	80
Uruguay	100	99	99	99	98	96
Venezuela	100	96	95	92	89	85
Yugoslavia	100	99	99	98	N/A	N/A
Zimbabwe	100	88	84	81	79	79

N/A Not Available

Source: *UNESCO Statistical Yearbook 1999;* <http://unescostat.unesco.org/uisen/stats/stats0.htm>. Underlying data from United Nations Educational, Scientific and Cultural Organization (UNESCO).

B13. TRANSITION RATE

B13-1. Transition Rates of Students—Primary School to Secondary School, 1995

	Transition Rate		
	Both sexes	**Male**	**Female**
Algeria	77.5	73.8	82.0
Azerbaijan	98.2	102.0	94.5
Belarus	99.3	99.3	99.2
Bulgaria	94.5	94.2	94.8
Chile	53.1	49.7	56.5
China	87.9	89.4	86.3
Costa Rica	68.0	66.8	69.2
Côte d'Ivoire	38.8	41.7	34.0
Croatia	100.0	99.9	100.2
Cuba	93.8	N/A	N/A
Cyprus	100.5	101.3	99.7
Djibouti	39.2	N/A	N/A
Eritrea	76.5	79.2	72.7
Ethiopia	88.1	88.2	87.8
Georgia	97.9	N/A	N/A
Germany	99.5	99.3	99.6
Guyana	95.5	97.8	93.2
Ireland	97.7	97.5	97.9
Italy	99.7	99.9	99.4
Kazakhstan	99.4	N/A	N/A
Kiribati	46.9	45.9	47.9
Kuwait	104.4	107.3	101.3
Laos	63.5	64.9	61.7
Latvia	97.2	N/A	N/A
Lithuania	99.1	98.9	99.3
Macedonia, FYRO	23.0	N/A	N/A
Mauritius	60.8	57.3	64.6
Mexico	84.4	86.7	81.9
Moldova	98.4	97.9	98.9
Mongolia	82.2	80.0	84.3
Namibia	77.4	77.7	77.2
New Zealand	111.5	112.3	110.7
Niger	28.6	28.4	28.9
Oman	90.7	87.7	94.0
Palestine	85.4	83.1	87.7
Paraguay	80.0	82.1	77.9
Romania	98.5	N/A	N/A
Saudi Arabia	98.7	102.3	94.7
Senegal	30.2	31.1	28.9
Slovakia	98.2	98.0	98.4
South Korea, Rep.	99.6	99.6	99.7
Swaziland	76.8	N/A	N/A
Trinidad and Tobago	67.9	68.7	67.2
Tunisia	65.1	64.2	66.2
United Arab Emirates	94.9	93.3	96.8
Venezuela	82.5	80.6	83.9

N/A Not Available

Source: UNESCO Statistical Yearbook 1999; <http://unescostat.unesco.org/uisen/stats/stats0.htm>. Underlying data from United Nations Educational, Scientific and Cultural Organization (UNESCO).

B14. SCHOOL LIFE EXPECTANCY

B14-1. School Life Expectancy (Total Number of Years of Schooling Which a Child Can Expect to Receive in the Future), 1995

	School Life Expectancy		
	Both sexes	Male	Female
Algeria	10.8	11.4	10.1
Australia	16.8	16.8	16.7
Austria	14.4	14.5	14.3
Belgium	16.8	16.7	16.9
Botswana	11.3	11.1	11.4
Bulgaria	12.1	N/A	N/A
Canada	16.8	16.5	17.1
Chad	3.9	N/A	N/A
Chile	12.1	12.2	12.1
Colombia	10.0	N/A	N/A
Czech Republic	12.8	12.8	12.9
Denmark	14.8	14.6	15.0
El Salvador	9.8	9.7	9.9
Eritrea	4.3	4.9	3.7
Estonia	12.6	12.3	12.9
Finland	15.6	15.1	16.2
France	15.5	15.3	15.7
Georgia	10.7	10.5	10.8
Germany	15.3	15.6	15.1
Greece	13.5	13.5	13.5
Guyana	9.9	9.8	9.9
Hungary	12.9	12.7	13.1
Iceland	15.2	14.7	15.5
Ireland	13.7	13.5	13.9
Jordan	9.0	9.0	9.1
Kuwait	9.0	8.8	9.0
Latvia	11.6	11.3	11.9
Macedonia, FYRO	11.3	11.2	11.3
Malta	13.4	13.6	13.1
Mexico	11.1	N/A	N/A
Mongolia	7.5	6.6	8.5
Mozambique	3.7	4.3	3.0
Namibia	12.9	N/A	N/A
Netherlands, the	16.6	16.8	16.3
New Zealand	16.0	15.7	16.4
Norway	15.2	14.9	15.5
Paraguay	9.8	N/A	N/A
Peru	12.4	N/A	N/A
Philippines	11.2	N/A	N/A
Romania	11.3	N/A	N/A
Saudi Arabia	9.2	9.5	8.8
South Korea, Rep.	14.2	14.9	13.6
Swaziland	11.6	12.0	11.3
Sweden	14.7	14.4	15.1
Switzerland	14.1	14.7	13.5
United Kingdom	16.5	16.2	16.7
United States	15.9	15.5	16.4

N/A Not Available

Source: UNESCO Statistical Yearbook 1999; <http://unescostat.unesco.org/uisen/stats/stats0.htm>. Underlying data from United Nations Educational, Scientific and Cultural Organization (UNESCO).

B15. FACILITIES

B15-1. School Facilities, Selected Countries, 1995

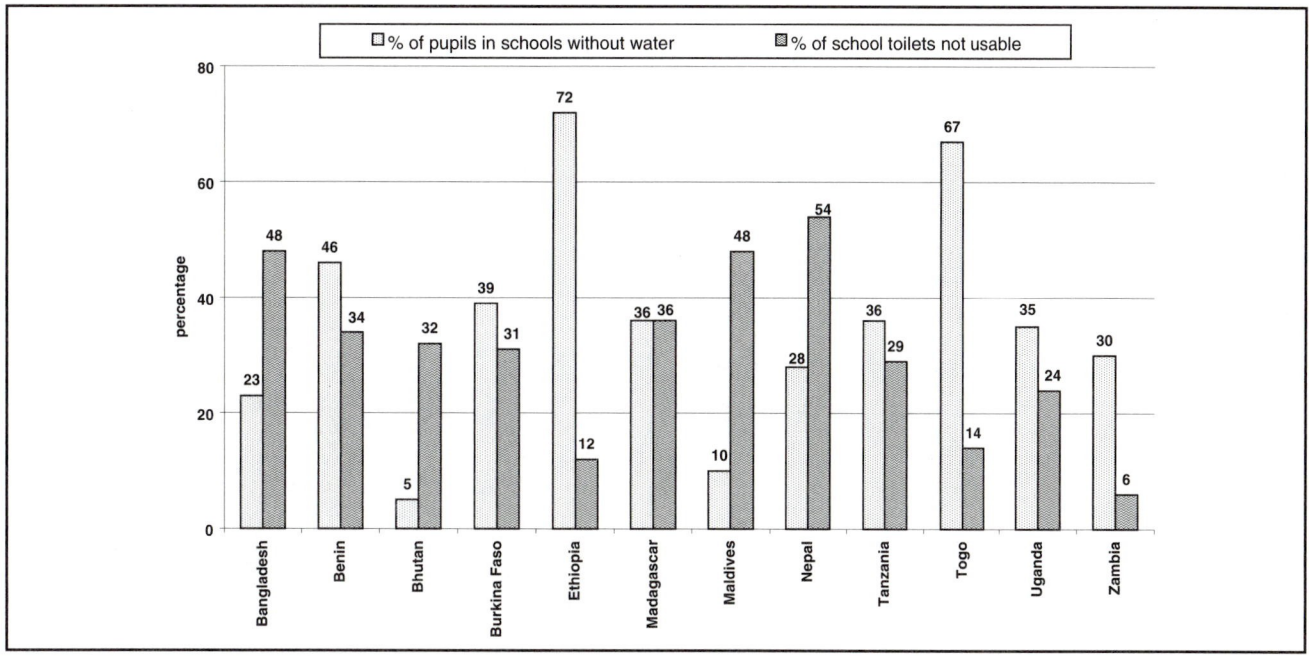

Source: The Progress of Nations 1996; <http://www.unicef.org/pon96/edstnds.htm>. Underlying data from *Andreas Schleicher, Maria Teresa Siniscalco, and Neville Postlethwaite, The Conditions of Primary Schools: A Pilot Study in the Least Developed Countries,* September 1995. Report to United Nations Educational, Scientific and Cultural Organization (UNESCO) and United Nations Children's Fund (UNICEF).

B15-2. Percent of Classrooms with No Usable Chalkboard, Selected Countries, 1995

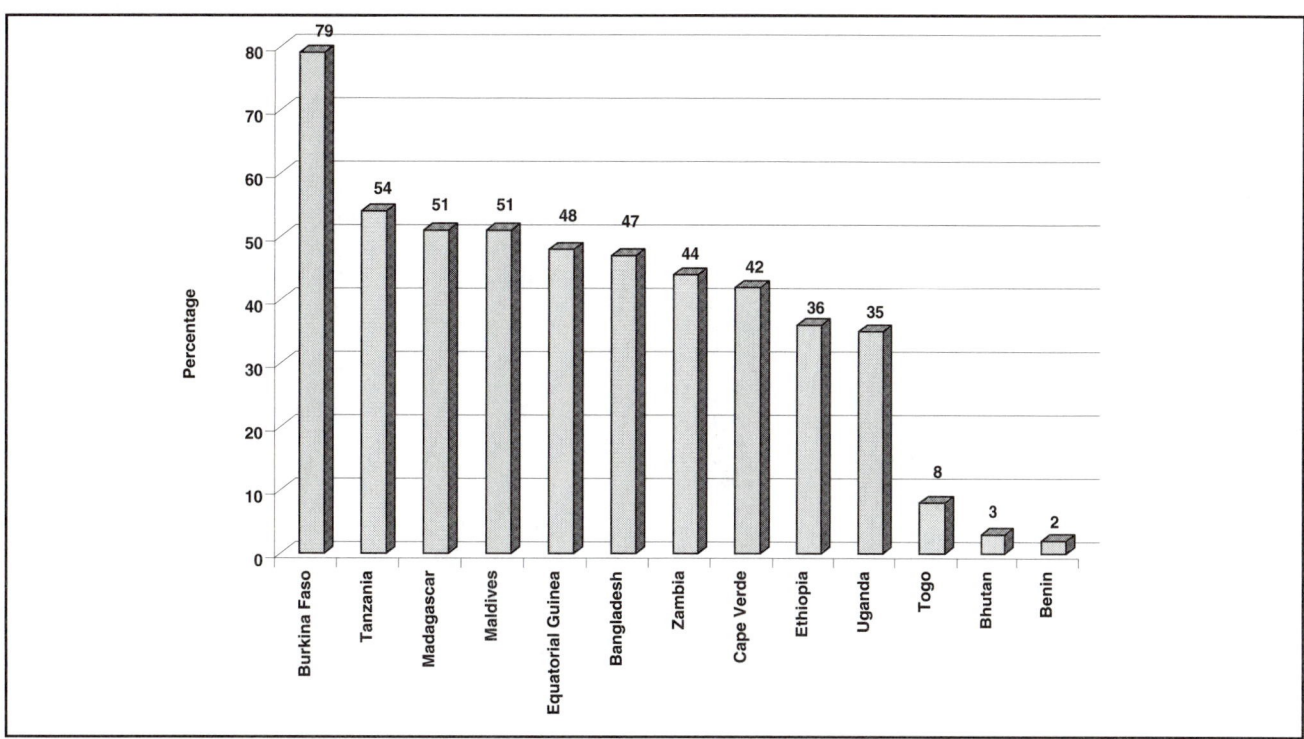

Source: The Progress of Nations 1996; <http://www.unicef.org/pon96/edstnds.htm>. Underlying data from *Andreas Schleicher, Maria Teresa Siniscalco, and Neville Postlethwaite, The Conditions of Primary Schools: A Pilot Study in the Least Developed Countries,* September 1995 Report to United Nations Educational, Scientific and Cultural Organization (UNESCO) and United Nations Children's Fund (UNICEF).

B15-3. School Libraries, Collection of Volumes, Audio-Visual Documents, and Other Library Materials, various years

	Year	Service points	Collections		
			Volumes of books	Audio-visual documents	Other library materials
Austria	1997	434	2,342	N/A	N/A
Bahrain	1990	184	166	10,000	N/A
Belarus	1993	4,867	95,957	N/A	N/A
Belgium	1997	927	8,969	N/A	N/A
Brunei	1991	23	287	2,205	8,200
Bulgaria	1997	2,876	15,787	70,247	N/A
Congo, Rep.	1990	1	10	N/A	N/A
Croatia	1992	1,127	5,530	N/A	134,210
Cuba	1993	3,800	N/A	N/A	N/A
Czech Republic	1997	4,108	30,858	N/A	N/A
Denmark	1997	1,784	22,197	410,057	1,328
Dominica	1993	7	15	N/A	N/A
Estonia	1997	571	6,107	28,976	N/A
Finland	1997	5,461	7,767	N/A	N/A
France	1997	5,556	53,734	N/A	N/A
Germany	1997	6,487	21,011	N/A	N/A
Greece	1997	978	9,461	N/A	N/A
Greenland	1990	24	177	N/A	N/A
Hong Kong SAR, China	1990	374	3,266	N/A	N/A
Hungary	1997	621	10,149	N/A	N/A
Iceland	1997	151	677	32,099	402
Iran	1993	4,001	16,068	N/A	N/A
Ireland	1997	455	4,404	N/A	N/A
Italy	1997	8,957	16,333	N/A	N/A
Kuwait	1990	587	3,117	2,000	N/A
Latvia	1997	569	8,404	N/A	N/A
Lebanon	1993	227	815	N/A	N/A
Liechtenstein	1997	2	10	N/A	N/A
Lithuania	1997	1,971	16,324	N/A	N/A
Luxembourg	1997	32	310	N/A	N/A
Macedonia, FYRO	1992	641	2,837	N/A	N/A
Mauritius	1990	26	161	N/A	N/A
Mexico	1993	4,017	14,260	939,062	752,214
Monaco	1995	8	57	5,665	N/A
Mongolia	1990	530	3,220	N/A	N/A
Netherlands, the	1997	1,499	14,501	N/A	N/A
Nicaragua	1990	174	N/A	150	N/A
Niue	1990	2	4	45	N/A
Norway	1997	3,075	7,725	N/A	N/A
Oman	1994	249	284	99	N/A
Poland	1997	21,538	157,901	N/A	N/A
Portugal	1997	900	5,234	N/A	N/A
Qatar	1994	162	465	1,220	N/A
Romania	1997	9,641	58,696	N/A	N/A
Russia	1993	64,318	1,180,774	N/A	N/A
San Marino	1983	17	22	2,056	635
Saudi Arabia	1993	5,206	8,698	N/A	N/A
Seychelles	1990	24	150	N/A	N/A
Singapore	1990	366	4,640	N/A	N/A
Slovakia	1997	6,537	10,953	19,569	N/A
Slovenia	1997	1,057	5,905	N/A	N/A
South Korea, Rep.	1994	9,117	29,725	N/A	N/A
Spain	1997	629	7,447	N/A	N/A
Sweden	1997	5,495	30,230	N/A	N/A

B15-3. School Libraries, Collection of Volumes, Audio-Visual Documents, and Other Library Materials, various years *(continued)*

	Year	Service points	Collections		
			Volumes of books	Audio-visual documents	Other library materials
Switzerland	1990	361	1,873	55,655	2,903
United Arab Emirates	1993	330	750	16,500	N/A
United Kingdom	1997	5,107	53,740	N/A	N/A
Uzbekistan	1993	8,863	39,276	N/A	N/A
Yugoslavia	1992	2,837	13,222	N/A	N/A
N/A Not Available					

Source: UNESCO Statistical Yearbook 1999; <http://unescostat.unesco.org/uisen/stats/stats0.htm>. Underlying data from United Nations Educational, Scientific and Cultural Organization (UNESCO).

B15-4. Percent of Schools Using Computers for Instructional Purposes and Median Student/Computer Ratio, by Level of Education, Selected Countries, 1989

	Percentage of schools using computers			Student/computer ratio		
	Primary	Lower secondary	Upper secondary	Primary	Lower secondary	Upper secondary
Austria	N/A	50	100	N/A	29	46
Belgium (Flemish)	78	98	N/A	N/A	28	35
Belgium (French)	54	93	93	28	34	38
British Columbia (Canada)	99	100	100	N/A	N/A	N/A
China	N/A	N/A	64	N/A	N/A	43
France	92	99	99	23	31	26
Greece	N/A	5	4	N/A	52	44
Hungary	N/A	N/A	100	N/A	N/A	27
India	N/A	N/A	8	N/A	N/A	95
Israel	62	N/A	81	25	N/A	29
Italy	43	58	80	116	90	36
Japan	12	35	94	14	143	32
Luxembourg	100	N/A	N/A	N/A	45	N/A
Netherlands, the	53	87	68	63	26	34
New Zealand	78	99	100	62	34	38
Poland	N/A	N/A	75	N/A	N/A	53
Portugal	29	53	72	301	287	289
Slovenia	N/A	N/A	94	N/A	N/A	50
Switzerland	N/A	64	98	N/A	21	21
United States	100	100	100	23	18	15
West Germany (former)	N/A	94	100	N/A	47	48
N/A Not Available						

Source: Educational Indicators: An International Perspective, Table 29; <http://www.nces.ed.gov/pubs/eiip/eiipid29.html>. Underlying data from Educational Testing Service, International Assessment of Educational Progress, Learning About the World, 1992, National Center For Education Statistics.

B15-5. Percent of 13-Year-Old Students Who Have a Calculator and Who Ever Use Calculators in School, Selected Countries, 1991

	Percent of students who have calculators	Percent of students who have used calculators in schools
South Korea, Rep.	0.3	3.7
Jordan	52.7	5.4
Soviet Union (former)	46.6	19.2
Ireland	57.5	25.3
Spain	85.9	45.0
Slovenia	85.6	46.1
Israel	93.6	48.5
Switzerland	84.9	51.3
United States	88.5	53.6
Taiwan	57.7	62.2
Hungary	86.7	71.0
Canada	91.1	74.7
France	97.9	94.2

Source: Educational Indicators: An International Perspective, Table 28; <http://www.nces.ed.gov/pubs/eiip/eiipid28.html>. Underlying data from Educational Testing Service, International Assessment of Educational Progress, Learning About the World, 1992, National Center For Education Statistics.

B16. PUBLIC SPENDING ON EDUCATION

B16-1. Estimated Percent of GNP per Capita Spent on Education, by Level of Education, for Regions and Sub-regions, 1990 and 1997

			% of GNP per capita		
	Number of countries	Year	Pre-primary and primary	Secondary	Pre-primary, primary, and secondary
WORLD TOTAL	109	1990	N/A	N/A	17.7
		1997	N/A	N/A	17.9
More developed regions* of which:	23	1990	N/A	N/A	18.4
Northern America	2	1990	N/A	N/A	19.1
		1997	N/A	N/A	20.3
Asia/Oceania	4	1990	N/A	N/A	17.0
		1997	N/A	N/A	17.0
Europe	17	1990	N/A	N/A	18.9
		1997	N/A	N/A	20.9
Countries in transition**	17	1990	N/A	N/A	15.8
		1997	N/A	N/A	19.0
Less developed regions*** of which:	69	1990	N/A	N/A	12.6
Sub-Saharan Africa	24	1990	8.7	22.8	11.5
		1997	6.1	16.0	8.1
Arab States	10	1990	N/A	N/A	16.4
		1997	N/A	N/A	18.7
Latin America/Caribbean	20	1990	9.5	14.5	10.9
		1997	9.8	16.2	11.7

B16-1. Estimated Percent of GNP per Capita Spent on Education, by Level of Education, for Regions and Sub-regions, 1990 and 1997 *(continued)*

	Number of countries	Year	% of GNP per capita		
			Pre-primary and primary	Secondary	Pre-primary, primary, and secondary
Eastern Asia/Oceania	9	1990	7.6	17.5	10.3
		1997	8.5	15.6	10.6
Southern Asia	5	1990	11	17.5	13.1
		1997	9.4	12.7	10.6
Least developed countries****	19	1990	7.8	22.6	10.5
		1997	7.6	22.5	10.4

N/A = Not Available.

*More Developed Regions:

Northern America: Canada and the United States.

Asia and Oceania: Australia, Israel, Japan and New Zealand.

Europe: Austria, Belgium, Denmark, Finland, France, Germany, Greece, Iceland, Ireland, Italy, Luxembourg, Monaco, Netherlands, Norway, Portugal, San Marino, Spain, Sweden, Switzerland and the United Kingdom.

**Countries in Transition: Albania, Armenia, Azerbaijan, Belarus, Bosnia and Herzegovina, Bulgaria, Croatia, Czech Republic, Estonia, Georgia, Hungary, Kazakhstan, Kyrgyzstan, Latvia, Lithuania, Poland, Republic of Moldova, Romania, Russian Federation, Slovakia, Slovenia, Tajikistan, The Former Yugoslav Republic of Macedonia, Turkmenistan, Ukraine, Uzbekistan and Yugoslavia.

***Less Developed Regions:

Sub-Saharan Africa: Angola, Benin, Botswana, Burkina Faso, Burundi, Cameroon, Cape Verde, Central African Republic, Chad, Comoros, Congo, Côte d'Ivoire, Democratic Republic of the Congo, Djibouti, Equatorial Guinea, Eritrea, Ethiopia, Gabon, Gambia, Ghana, Guinea, Guinea-Bissau, Kenya, Lesotho, Liberia, Madagascar, Malawi, Mali, Mauritania, Mauritius, Mozambique, Namibia, Niger, Nigeria, Rwanda, Sao Tome and Principe, Senegal, Seychelles, Sierra Leone, Somalia, South Africa, Sudan, Swaziland, Togo, Uganda, United Republic of Tanzania, Zambia and Zimbabwe.

Arab States: Algeria, Bahrain, Djibouti, Egypt, Iraq, Jordan, Kuwait, Lebanon, Libyan Arab Jamahiriya, Mauritania, Morocco, Oman, Palestinian Autonomous Territories, Qatar, Saudi Arabia, Somalia, Sudan, Syrian Arab Republic, Tunisia, United Arab Emirates and Yemen.

Latin America and the Caribbean: Antigua and Barbuda, Argentina, Bahamas, Barbados, Belize, Bolivia, Brazil, British Virgin Islands, Chile, Colombia, Costa Rica, Cuba, Dominica, Dominican Republic, Ecuador, El Salvador, Grenada, Guatemala, Guyana, Haiti, Honduras, Jamaica, Mexico, Netherlands Antilles, Nicaragua, Panama, Paraguay, Peru, Saint Kitts and Nevis, Saint Lucia, Saint Vincent and the Grenadines, Suriname, Trinidad and Tobago, Uruguay and Venezuela.

Eastern Asia and Oceania: Brunei Darussalam, Cambodia, China, Cook Islands, Democratic People's Republic of Korea, Fiji, Hong Kong Special Administrative Region of China, Indonesia, Kiribati, Lao People's Democratic Republic, Macau, Malaysia, Mongolia, Myanmar, Papua New Guinea, Philippines, Republic of Korea, Samoa, Singapore, Solomon Islands, Thailand, Tonga, Tuvalu, Vanuatu and Viet Nam.

Southern Asia: Afghanistan, Bangladesh, Bhutan, India, Islamic Republic of Iran, Maldives, Nepal, Pakistan and Sri Lanka.

****Least Developed Countries: Afghanistan, Angola, Bangladesh, Benin, Bhutan, Burkina Faso, Burundi, Cambodia, Cape Verde, Central African Republic, Chad, Comoros, Democratic Republic of the Congo, Djibouti, Equatorial Guinea, Eritrea, Ethiopia, Gambia, Guinea, Guinea-Bissau, Haiti, Kiribati, Lao People's Democratic Republic, Lesotho, Liberia, Madagascar, Malawi, Maldives, Mali, Mauritania, Mozambique, Myanmar, Nepal, Niger, Rwanda, Samoa, Sao Tome and Principe, Sierra Leone, Solomon Islands, Somalia, Sudan, Togo, Tuvalu, Uganda, United Republic of Tanzania, Vanuatu, Yemen and Zambia.

Source: UNESCO's World Education Indicators, World education report 2000, Table 13 - Estimated public current expenditure per pupil, by level of education, 1990 and 1997; <http://www.unesco.org/education/information/wer/WEBtables/regtabweb.xls> and <http://unescostat.unesco.org/uisen/pub/pub0.htm>. Underlying data from UNESCO.

B16-2. Public Expenditure on Education as Percentage of Gross National Product (GNP), various years

	Year	Public expenditure on education, as % of GNP
Algeria	1996	5.1
Argentina	1996	3.5
Armenia	1996	2.0
Aruba	1997	N/A
Australia	1995	5.5
Austria	1996	5.4
Azerbaijan	1997	3.0
Bahamas, the	1996	N/A
Bahrain	1997	4.4
Bangladesh	1996	2.2
Belarus	1996	5.9
Belgium	1996	3.1
Belize	1996	5.0
Benin	1995	3.2
Bhutan	1997	4.1
Bolivia	1996	4.9
Botswana	1997	8.6
Brazil	1995	5.1
Brunei	1995	0.7
Bulgaria	1996	3.2
Burkina Faso	1997	N/A
Burundi	1996	4.0
Cambodia	1996	2.9
Cameroon	1996	N/A
Central African Republic	1995	N/A
Chad	1996	N/A
Chile	1997	3.6
China	1996	2.3
Colombia	1996	4.4
Comoros	1995	N/A
Congo, Rep.	1995	6.1
Costa Rica	1996	5.4
Côte d'Ivoire	1997	5.0
Croatia	1995	5.3
Cuba	1996	6.7
Cyprus	1995	4.5
Czech Republic	1996	5.1
Denmark	1996	8.1
Dominican Republic	1997	2.3
Ecuador	1996	3.5
Egypt	1996	N/A
El Salvador	1997	2.5
Eritrea	1996	1.8
Estonia	1997	7.2
Ethiopia	1996	4.0
Falkland Islands	1996	N/A
Finland	1996	7.5
France	1996	6.0
Gabon	1995	2.9
Gambia, the	1996	4.9
Germany	1996	4.8
Ghana	1996	4.2
Greece	1996	3.1
Grenada	1996	4.7
Guatemala	1996	1.7
Guinea	1997	1.9

B16-2. Public Expenditure on Education as Percentage of Gross National Product (GNP), various years *(continued)*

	Year	Public expenditure on education, as % of GNP
Guyana	1996	5.0
Honduras	1995	3.6
Hong Kong, SAR (China)	1995	2.9
Hungary	1996	4.6
Iceland	1996	5.4
India	1996	3.2
Indonesia	1996	1.4
Iran	1995	4.0
Ireland	1996	6.0
Italy	1996	4.9
Jamaica	1996	7.5
Jordan	1996	7.9
Kazakhstan	1997	4.4
Kenya	1996	6.5
Kiribati	1996	N/A
Kuwait	1997	5.0
Kyrgyzstan	1996	5.3
Laos	1997	2.1
Latvia	1996	6.3
Lebanon	1996	2.5
Lesotho	1996	8.4
Lithuania	1996	5.5
Luxembourg	1996	4.0
Macedonia, FYRO	1996	5.1
Madagascar	1997	1.9
Malawi	1995	5.4
Malaysia	1997	4.9
Maldives	1995	6.4
Mali	1996	2.2
Malta	1996	5.1
Mauritania	1996	N/A
Mauritius	1996	4.6
Mexico	1995	4.9
Moldova	1996	10.6
Monaco	1997	N/A
Mongolia	1997	5.7
Morocco	1996	5.3
Namibia	1997	9.1
Nepal	1997	3.2
Netherlands, the	1996	5.1
New Zealand	1996	7.3
Nicaragua	1997	3.9
Niger	1997	2.3
Norway	1996	7.4
Oman	1997	N/A
Pakistan	1997	2.7
Panama	1997	5.1
Paraguay	1997	4.0
Peru	1996	2.9
Philippines	1997	3.4
Poland	1996	7.5
Portugal	1996	5.8
Romania	1996	3.6
Russia	1995	3.5
Saudi Arabia	1997	7.5
Senegal	1997	N/A

B16-2. Public Expenditure on Education as Percentage of Gross National Product (GNP), various years *(continued)*

	Year	Public expenditure on education, as % of GNP
Seychelles	1996	7.9
Singapore	1995	3.0
Slovakia	1996	5.0
Slovenia	1995	5.7
South Africa	1996	8.0
South Korea, Rep.	1995	3.7
Spain	1996	5.0
Sri Lanka	1996	3.4
St. Kitts and Nevis	1996	3.8
Sudan	1995	1.4
Swaziland	1996	5.7
Sweden	1996	8.3
Switzerland	1996	5.4
Syria	1997	3.1
Tajikistan	1996	2.2
Thailand	1996	4.8
Togo	1996	4.5
Tunisia	1997	7.7
Turkey	1995	2.2
Uganda	1995	2.6
Ukraine	1995	7.3
United Arab Emirates	1996	N/A
United Kingdom	1995	5.3
Uruguay	1996	3.3
Uzbekistan	1996	7.7
Vanuatu	1995	4.8
Venezuela	1995	N/A
Vietnam	1997	3.0
Yemen	1997	7.0
Zambia	1995	2.2

N/A Not Available

Source: UNESCO Statistical Yearbook 1999; <http://unescostat.unesco.org/uisen/stats/stats0.htm>. Underlying data from United Nations Educational, Scientific and Cultural Organization (UNESCO).

B16-3. Government Expenditure on Education as Percentage of Total Government Expenditure, various years

	Year	Percent
Algeria	1996	16.4
Argentina	1996	12.6
Armenia	1996	10.3
Aruba	1997	12.8
Australia	1995	13.5
Austria	1996	10.4
Azerbaijan	1997	18.8
Bahamas, the	1996	13.2
Bahrain	1997	12.0
Bangladesh	1996	N/A
Belarus	1996	17.8
Belgium	1996	6.0
Belize	1996	19.5
Benin	1995	15.2
Bhutan	1997	7.0
Bolivia	1996	11.1
Botswana	1997	20.6
Brazil	1995	N/A
Brunei	1995	11.5
Bulgaria	1996	7.0
Burkina Faso	1997	N/A
Burundi	1996	18.3
Cambodia	1996	N/A
Cameroon	1996	N/A
Central African Republic	1995	N/A
Chad	1996	N/A
Chile	1997	15.5
China	1996	N/A
Colombia	1996	19.0
Comoros	1995	N/A
Congo, Rep.	1995	14.7
Costa Rica	1996	22.8
Côte d'Ivoire	1997	24.9
Croatia	1995	N/A
Cuba	1996	12.6
Cyprus	1995	13.2
Czech Republic	1996	N/A
Denmark	1996	N/A
Dominican Republic	1997	13.8
Ecuador	1996	13.0
Egypt	1996	N/A
El Salvador	1997	16.0
Eritrea	1996	N/A
Estonia	1997	25.5
Ethiopia	1996	13.7
Falkland Islands	1996	5.4
Finland	1996	12.2
France	1996	10.9
Gabon	1995	N/A
Gambia, the	1996	21.2
Germany	1996	9.6
Ghana	1996	19.9
Greece	1996	N/A
Grenada	1996	10.6
Guatemala	1996	15.8
Guinea	1997	26.8
Guyana	1996	10.0

B16-3. Government Expenditure on Education as Percentage of Total Government Expenditure, various years *(continued)*

	Year	Percent
Honduras	1995	16.5
Hong Kong, SAR (China)	1995	N/A
Hungary	1996	N/A
Iceland	1996	13.6
India	1996	N/A
Indonesia	1996	7.9
Iran	1995	17.8
Ireland	1996	N/A
Italy	1996	9.1
Jamaica	1996	12.9
Jordan	1996	19.8
Kazakhstan	1997	N/A
Kenya	1996	16.7
Kiribati	1996	N/A
Kuwait	1997	14.0
Kyrgyzstan	1996	23.5
Laos	1997	8.7
Latvia	1996	14.1
Lebanon	1996	8.2
Lesotho	1996	N/A
Lithuania	1996	22.8
Luxembourg	1996	N/A
Macedonia, FYRO	1996	20.0
Madagascar	1997	N/A
Malawi	1995	N/A
Malaysia	1997	N/A
Maldives	1995	10.5
Mali	1996	N/A
Malta	1996	10.8
Mauritania	1996	N/A
Mauritius	1996	17.4
Mexico	1995	23.0
Moldova	1996	28.1
Monaco	1997	5.3
Mongolia	1997	15.1
Morocco	1996	24.9
Namibia	1997	N/A
Nepal	1997	N/A
Netherlands, the	1996	9.8
New Zealand	1996	N/A
Nicaragua	1997	8.8
Niger	1997	12.8
Norway	1996	15.8
Oman	1997	16.4
Pakistan	1997	7.1
Panama	1997	16.3
Paraguay	1997	19.8
Peru	1996	19.2
Philippines	1997	15.7
Poland	1996	24.8
Portugal	1996	N/A
Romania	1996	10.5
Russia	1995	N/A
Saudi Arabia	1997	22.8
Senegal	1997	N/A
Seychelles	1996	24.1
Singapore	1995	23.4

B16-3. Government Expenditure on Education as Percentage of Total Government Expenditure, various years *(continued)*

	Year	Percent
Slovakia	1996	N/A
Slovenia	1995	12.6
South Africa	1996	23.9
South Korea, Rep.	1995	17.5
Spain	1996	11.0
Sri Lanka	1996	8.9
St. Kitts and Nevis	1996	8.8
Sudan	1995	N/A
Swaziland	1996	18.1
Sweden	1996	12.2
Switzerland	1996	15.4
Syria	1997	N/A
Tajikistan	1996	11.5
Thailand	1996	N/A
Togo	1996	24.7
Tunisia	1997	19.9
Turkey	1995	N/A
Uganda	1995	21.4
Ukraine	1995	N/A
United Arab Emirates	1996	16.7
United Kingdom	1995	11.6
Uruguay	1996	15.5
Uzbekistan	1996	21.1
Vanuatu	1995	N/A
Venezuela	1995	N/A
Vietnam	1997	N/A
Yemen	1997	N/A
Zambia	1995	7.1

N/A Not Available

Source: UNESCO Statistical Yearbook 1999; <http://unescostat.unesco.org/uisen/stats/stats0.htm>. Underlying data from United Nations Educational, Scientific and Cultural Organization (UNESCO).

B16-4. Primary School Spending as a Percentage of Total Public Education Expenditures, 1990–1997

	Percent
Bangladesh	45
Brazil	50
Egypt	67
Guatemala	56
India	40
Kenya	59
Mexico	41
Nepal	49
Nicaragua	66
Pakistan	48
Peru	18
Philippines	48
South Africa	42
Tanzania	42
Thailand	50
Turkey	43

Source: By the Sweat & Toil of Children (Volume VI), An Economic Consideration of Child Labor, 2000. Page 64, Table IV-1; <http://www.dol.gov/dol/ilab/public/media/reports/iclp/sweat6/sweat6.pdf>. Underlying data from U.S. Department of Labor, Bureau of International Labor Affairs, 2000.

B16-5. Estimated Public Expenditure per Pupil, by Level of Education, for Regions and Sub-regions, 1990 and 1997

	Number of countries	Year	Pre-primary and primary US$	Secondary US$	Pre-primary, primary, and secondary US$
WORLD TOTAL	109	1990	N/A	N/A	839
		1997	N/A	N/A	999
More developed regions* of which:	23	1990	N/A	N/A	3,939
Northern America	2	1990	N/A	N/A	4,155
		1997	N/A	N/A	5,014
Asia/Oceania	4	1990	N/A	N/A	4,702
		1997	N/A	N/A	5,833
Europe	17	1990	N/A	N/A	3,370
		1997	N/A	N/A	4,583
Countries in transition*	17	1990	N/A	N/A	296
		1997	N/A	N/A	397
Less developed regions* of which:	69	1990	N/A	N/A	113
Sub-Saharan Africa	24	1990	134	351	177
		1997	143	378	190
Arab States	10	1990	N/A	N/A	332
		1997	N/A	N/A	494
Latin America/Caribbean	20	1990	266	407	305
		1997	331	546	392
Eastern Asia/Oceania	9	1990	57	129	77
		1997	108	199	136
Southern Asia	5	1990	47	75	56
		1997	40	53	44
Least developed countries*	19	1990	20	59	27
		1997	20	60	28

N/A = not available.

***More Developed Regions:**
Northern America: Canada and the United States.
Asia and Oceania: Australia, Israel, Japan and New Zealand.
Europe: Austria, Belgium, Denmark, Finland, France, Germany, Greece, Iceland, Ireland, Italy, Luxembourg, Monaco, Netherlands, Norway, Portugal, San Marino, Spain, Sweden, Switzerland and the United Kingdom.
****Countries in Transition:** Albania, Armenia, Azerbaijan, Belarus, Bosnia and Herzegovina, Bulgaria, Croatia, Czech Republic, Estonia, Georgia, Hungary, Kazakhstan, Kyrgyzstan, Latvia, Lithuania, Poland, Republic of Moldova, Romania, Russian Federation, Slovakia, Slovenia, Tajikistan, The Former Yugoslav Republic of Macedonia, Turkmenistan, Ukraine, Uzbekistan and Yugoslavia.
*****Less Developed Regions:**
Sub-Saharan Africa: Angola, Benin, Botswana, Burkina Faso, Burundi, Cameroon, Cape Verde, Central African Republic, Chad, Comoros, Congo, Côte d'Ivoire, Democratic Republic of the Congo, Djibouti, Equatorial Guinea, Eritrea, Ethiopia, Gabon, Gambia, Ghana, Guinea, Guinea-Bissau, Kenya, Lesotho, Liberia, Madagascar, Malawi, Mali, Mauritania, Mauritius, Mozambique, Namibia, Niger, Nigeria, Rwanda, Sao Tome and Principe, Senegal, Seychelles, Sierra Leone, Somalia, South Africa, Sudan, Swaziland, Togo, Uganda, United Republic of Tanzania, Zambia and Zimbabwe.
Arab States: Algeria, Bahrain, Djibouti, Egypt, Iraq, Jordan, Kuwait, Lebanon, Libyan Arab Jamahiriya, Mauritania, Morocco, Oman, Palestinian Autonomous Territories, Qatar, Saudi Arabia, Somalia, Sudan, Syrian Arab Republic, Tunisia, United Arab Emirates and Yemen.
Latin America and the Caribbean: Antigua and Barbuda, Argentina, Bahamas, Barbados, Belize, Bolivia, Brazil, British Virgin Islands, Chile, Colombia, Costa Rica, Cuba, Dominica, Dominican Republic, Ecuador, El Salvador, Grenada, Guatemala, Guyana, Haiti, Honduras, Jamaica, Mexico, Netherlands Antilles, Nicaragua, Panama, Paraguay, Peru, Saint Kitts and Nevis, Saint Lucia, Saint Vincent and the Grenadines, Suriname, Trinidad and Tobago, Uruguay and Venezuela.
Eastern Asia and Oceania: Brunei Darussalam, Cambodia, China, Cook Islands, Democratic People's Republic of Korea, Fiji, Hong Kong Special Administrative Region of China, Indonesia, Kiribati, Lao People's Democratic Republic, Macau, Malaysia, Mongolia, Myanmar, Papua New Guinea, Philippines, Republic of Korea, Samoa, Singapore, Solomon Islands, Thailand, Tonga, Tuvalu, Vanuatu and Viet Nam.
Southern Asia: Afghanistan, Bangladesh, Bhutan, India, Islamic Republic of Iran, Maldives, Nepal, Pakistan and Sri Lanka.
******Least Developed Countries:** Afghanistan, Angola, Bangladesh, Benin, Bhutan, Burkina Faso, Burundi, Cambodia, Cape Verde, Central African Republic, Chad, Comoros, Democratic Republic of the Congo, Djibouti, Equatorial Guinea, Eritrea, Ethiopia, Gambia, Guinea, Guinea-Bissau, Haiti, Kiribati, Lao People's Democratic Republic, Lesotho, Liberia, Madagascar, Malawi, Maldives, Mali, Mauritania, Mozambique, Myanmar, Nepal, Niger, Rwanda, Samoa, Sao Tome and Principe, Sierra Leone, Solomon Islands, Somalia, Sudan, Togo, Tuvalu, Uganda, United Republic of Tanzania, Vanuatu, Yemen and Zambia.

Source: UNESCO's World Education Indicators, World Education Report 2000: Table 13. Estimated public current expenditure per pupil, by level of education, 1990 and 1997; <http://www.unesco.org/education/information/wer/WEBtables/regtabweb.xls> and <http://unescostat.unesco.org/uisen/pub/pub0.htm>. Underlying data from UNESCO.

B16-6. Public Education Expenditures per Student, by Level of Education, Selected Countries, 1985, 1990, and 1992

Country	Primary			Secondary			Higher education		
	1985	1990	1992	1985	1990	1992	1985	1990	1992
Austria	3,451	3,526	4,010	3,943	4,632	6,420	6,557	6,369	5,820
Belgium	2,232	2,131	2,390	5,279	4,805	5,150	7,098	6,178	6,590
Denmark	3,570	4,446	4,220	5,045	5,301	4,940	8,570	8,332	6,710
France	N/A	N/A	2,900	N/A	N/A	5,430	N/A	N/A	6,020
Germany	N/A	N/A	2,980	N/A	N/A	4,260	N/A	N/A	N/A
Japan	N/A	N/A	3,530	N/A	N/A	3,900	N/A	N/A	11,850
Ireland	1,323	1,429	1,770	2,277	2,403	2,770	5,173	5,527	7,270
Norway	3,404	3,878	4,480	4,817	5,153	6,200	3,732	N/A	N/A
Portugal	1,330	1,931	N/A	1,759	N/A	N/A	3,732	3,156	3,770
Spain	1,439	1,800	2,030	1,998	2,706	3,140	1,907	3,156	3,770
Sweden	N/A	5,271	4,840	N/A	6,292	6,050	N/A	8,669	7,120
Switzerland	N/A	N/A	3,560	N/A	N/A	N/A	N/A	N/A	12,900
Turkey	N/A	N/A	N/A	N/A	N/A	N/A	N/A	N/A	N/A
United Kingdom	2,336	2,897	3,120	3,864	5,499	4,390	N/A	N/A	10,370
United States	4,364	5,223	5,600	5,282	6,546	6,470	10,221	12,013	11,880

N/A Not Available
NOTE—Data adjusted to 1992 US dollars using the purchasing power pariety (PPP) index.

Source: The Digest of Education Statistics 1996, International Comparisons, Table 406; <http://nces.ed.gov/pubs/D96/D96T406.html>. Underlying data from Organization for Economic Cooperation and Development, Education at a Glance, and unpublished data (table prepared May 1995).

B16-7. Spending on Teaching Materials as Percentage of Total Expenditure on Primary School Material, 1980, 1990, 1995

	1980	1990	1995
Afghanistan	4.97	N/A	N/A
Angola	N/A	0.67	N/A
Belgium	0.18	N/A	N/A
Brunei	5.86	N/A	N/A
Burkina Faso	0.84	N/A	N/A
Central African Republic	N/A	1.67	N/A
Chile	0.01	N/A	N/A
Congo, Rep.	0.09	N/A	N/A
Costa Rica	0.36	N/A	N/A
Cuba	N/A	2.53	1.42
Cyprus	3.00	1.53	2.18
Denmark	4.29	N/A	N/A
Djibouti	N/A	8.03	N/A
Ethiopia	N/A	0.75	N/A
Finland	6.21	4.99	N/A
France	N/A	1.29	N/A
Gambia, the	N/A	6.52	5.73
Guadeloupe	N/A	0.20	N/A
Guatemala	N/A	N/A	0.34
Haiti	1.49	0.01	N/A
Honduras	3.56	N/A	0.35
Hong Kong, SAR, (China)	0.32	N/A	N/A
Iceland	N/A	2.51	N/A
Ireland	0.33	0.34	N/A
Israel	9.92	14.35	N/A
Italy	N/A	0.52	N/A
Jamaica	1.70	N/A	0.66

B16-7. Spending on Teaching Materials as Percentage of Total Expenditure on Primary School Material, 1980, 1990, 1995 *(continued)*

	1980	1990	1995
Japan	4.86	N/A	N/A
Kuwait	6.28	N/A	N/A
Macedonia, FYRO	N/A	N/A	0.06
Madagascar	1.13	N/A	N/A
Malaysia	6.03	N/A	15.09
Mali	N/A	N/A	N/A
Malta	0.20	N/A	N/A
Martinique	N/A	0.21	N/A
Mauritius	0.01	N/A	N/A
Monaco	N/A	N/A	1.46
Nepal	7.23	N/A	N/A
Netherlands, the	3.11	1.59	N/A
New Zealand	7.89	N/A	N/A
Norway	2.04	1.61	N/A
Oman	N/A	2.42	1.27
Panama	1.82	N/A	N/A
Peru	0.73	N/A	N/A
Reunion	N/A	0.12	N/A
Rwanda	3.53	N/A	N/A
Senegal	4.00	N/A	N/A
Seychelles	N/A	3.83	1.68
Singapore	0.02	N/A	N/A
Slovenia	N/A	N/A	4.21
South Africa	N/A	N/A	3.89
South Korea	N/A	1.81	N/A
St. Vincent and the Grenadines	N/A	1.38	N/A
Suriname	N/A	4.02	N/A
Sweden	3.88	N/A	N/A
Switzerland	N/A	3.49	N/A
Syria	N/A	N/A	0.79
Thailand	1.03	3.36	3.18
Togo	0.19	N/A	N/A
Tunisia	2.01	N/A	N/A
Turkey	0.08	0.07	N/A
United Kingdom	2.92	3.91	N/A
Uruguay	5.80	N/A	N/A
Venezuela	0.71	N/A	N/A
Yugoslavia	N/A	N/A	12.72
Zambia	2.80	N/A	N/A
Zimbabwe	N/A	1.01	1.25

N/A Not Available

Source: World Bank, *World Development Indicators 1999:* Table 2.9. Series: Spending on Teaching Materials, Primary (% of primary total); <http://www.worldbank.org/data/>. Underlying data from World Bank.

B16-8. Spending on Teaching Materials as Percentage of Total Expenditure on Secondary School Material, 1980, 1990, 1995

	1980	1990	1995
Afghanistan	17.33	N/A	N/A
Bangladesh	0.15	N/A	N/A
Belgium	0.09	N/A	N/A
Brunei	7.01	N/A	N/A
Burkina Faso	0.62	N/A	N/A
Burundi	N/A	2.54	N/A
Canada	5.34	4.20	N/A
Central African Republic	N/A	3.23	N/A
Chile	0.20	N/A	N/A
Congo, Rep.	1.77	N/A	N/A
Cuba	N/A	1.73	1.23
Cyprus	2.25	0.39	0.34
Denmark	9.93	N/A	N/A
Djibouti	N/A	10.95	N/A
Egypt	0.66	N/A	0.71
El Salvador	N/A	N/A	N/A
Estonia	N/A	N/A	4.10
Ethiopia	N/A	1.37	N/A
Finland	6.28	5.71	N/A
France	0.29	0.25	N/A
French Guiana	N/A	0.78	N/A
French Polynesia	N/A	0.18	N/A
Gambia, the	N/A	2.60	2.80
Guadeloupe	N/A	0.94	N/A
Haiti	4.66	N/A	N/A
Honduras	1.86	N/A	0.30
Ireland	0.60	0.35	N/A
Israel	4.18	15.46	N/A
Italy	N/A	1.55	N/A
Jamaica	4.02	1.18	N/A
Japan	9.08	N/A	N/A
Lithuania	N/A	N/A	0.52
Madagascar	8.05	N/A	N/A
Malaysia	10.73	N/A	N/A
Malta	0.13	0.02	N/A
Martinique	N/A	0.81	N/A
Mauritius	0.05	4.29	N/A
Monaco	N/A	N/A	3.19
Netherlands, the	0.50	0.35	N/A
New Caledonia	N/A	1.98	N/A
New Zealand	5.35	N/A	N/A
Norway	5.43	5.53	N/A
Oman	N/A	2.54	1.38
Panama	4.28	N/A	N/A
Peru	0.72	N/A	N/A
Reunion	N/A	1.01	N/A
Rwanda	6.32	N/A	N/A
Senegal	13.57	N/A	N/A
Seychelles	N/A	5.44	N/A
Singapore	0.02	N/A	N/A
Slovenia	N/A	N/A	6.12
St. Lucia	3.27	N/A	N/A
St. Vincent and the Grenadines	N/A	3.43	N/A
Suriname	N/A	9.43	N/A
Sweden	5.22	N/A	N/A
Switzerland	3.08	1.91	N/A

B16-8. Spending on Teaching Materials as Percentage of Total Expenditure on Secondary School Material, 1980, 1990, 1995 *(continued)*

	1980	1990	1995
Syria	4.71	N/A	8.20
Tajikistan	N/A	N/A	0.51
Thailand	3.55	5.44	4.33
Togo	4.63	N/A	N/A
Trinidad and Tobago	12.97	N/A	N/A
Tunisia	8.58	N/A	N/A
Turkey	0.23	0.22	N/A
United Kingdom	4.69	7.68	N/A
Uruguay	6.30	N/A	N/A
Zambia	3.27	N/A	N/A
Zimbabwe	N/A	4.45	N/A

N/A Not Available

Source: World Bank, *World Development Indicators 1999*: Table 2.9. Series: Spending on Teaching Materials, Primary (% of primary total); <http://www.worldbank.org/data/>. Underlying data from World Bank.

B17. TIME SPENT IN OVERALL INSTRUCTION

B17-1. Time in Formal Instruction for 13-Year-Olds, Selected Countries, 1991

	Overall Instruction			Mathematics	Science
	Average hours	Average days	Average hours	Average hours	Average hours
Canada	5.1	188	959	3.8	2.6
France	6.2	174	1079	3.8	2.9
West Germany (former)	4.0	N/A	N/A	N/A	N/A
Japan	4.0	220	875	N/A	N/A
United States	5.6	178	997	3.8	3.7
Hungary	3.7	177	655	3.1	3.5
Ireland	5.4	173	934	3.2	2.7
Israel	4.6	215	989	3.4	3.0
South Korea, Rep.	4.4	222	977	3.0	2.4
Soviet Union (former)	4.1	198	812	4.3	6.5
Taiwan	5.3	222	1177	3.4	4.1

N/A Not Available

Note: All countries from Educational Testing Service, International Assessment of Educational Progress, Learning Mathematics, 1992; Learning Science, 1992; except the former West Germany: unpublihsed tabulations, International Association for the Evaluation of Educational Achievement (IEA) Study of Reading Literacy, 1992; and Japan: National Institute of Educational Research, Ministry of Education, Science, and Culture, Government of Japan, Monbusho, 1992.

Source: Educational Indicators: An International Perspective, November 1996, (NCES96-003), Table 24; <http://nces.ed.gov/pubs/eiip/eiipid24.html#table24>. Underlying data from National Center For Education Statistics.

B18. HOMEWORK

B18-1. Percentage of Students Reporting Number of Hours Spent on Homework Daily, by Age, Selected Countries, 1991

	Age 9			Age 13		
	None	**1 hour or less**	**2 hours or more**	**None**	**1 hour or less**	**2 hours or more**
Canada	29	58	13	8	65	27
France	N/A	N/A	N/A	0	44	55
Hungary	2	72	25	0	42	58
Ireland	2	80	18	1	35	63
Israel	4	60	35	1	49	50
Jordan	N/A	N/A	N/A	3	40	56
Scotland (UK)	18	78	4	16	70	14
Slovenia	4	81	15	1	70	28
South Korea, Rep.	2	77	22	3	56	41
Soviet Union	2	68	31	0	47	52
Spain	15	55	29	1	33	64
Switzerland	N/A	N/A	1	1	79	20
Taiwan	2	67	31	4	55	41
United States	20	59	20	10	61	29

N/A Not Available

Source: Educational Indicators: An International Perspective, Table 25a; <http://www.nces.ed.gov/pubs/eiip/eiipid25.html>. Underlying data from Educational Testing Service, International Assessment of Educational Progress, Learning Mathematics, 1992, National Center For Education Statistics.

B19. STUDENT PERFORMANCE AND ACHIEVEMENT

B19-1. Average Fourth-Grade Mathematics Scores, by Content Areas, and Average Time Spent Studying Mathematics out of School, Selected Countries: 1994–1995

	Overall mathematics scores	Whole numbers	Fractions and proportionality	Measurement, estimation, and number sense	Data representation, analysis, and probability	Geometry	Patterns, relations, and functions	Time spent studying math out of school			
								No time (%)	Less than 1 hour (%)	1 hour or more	Average hours
Australia	63	67	51	60	67	74	64	15	61	24	0.8
Austria	65	74	51	69	66	67	64	4	58	38	1.0
Canada	60	68	48	54	68	72	62	14	60	26	0.8
Cyprus	54	65	48	48	52	53	55	9	51	40	1.1
Czech Republic	66	75	53	68	67	71	67	9	69	22	0.7
England (UK)	57	58	45	52	64	74	55	N/A	N/A	N/A	N/A
Greece	51	62	42	48	50	53	47	6	38	56	1.6
Hong Kong, SAR (China)	73	79	66	69	76	74	73	6	44	50	1.3
Hungary	64	76	49	64	60	66	69	5	58	37	1.0
Iceland	50	56	36	44	58	63	48	10	63	27	0.8
Iran	38	51	32	36	23	42	40	5	17	78	2.3
Ireland	63	70	58	56	69	66	64	7	70	23	0.8
Israel	59	71	48	54	64	62	60	14	46	40	1.1
Japan	74	82	65	72	79	72	76	10	60	31	0.9
Kuwait	32	36	25	35	26	36	33	5	34	60	1.9
Latvia (Latvian speaking schools)	59	68	44	60	54	67	65	7	61	33	1.0
Netherlands, the	69	75	60	70	75	71	52	47	39	14	0.5
New Zealand	53	57	41	49	61	66	50	21	54	25	0.8
Norway	53	61	38	56	59	58	47	23	58	19	0.6
Portugal	48	57	38	49	43	52	57	3	55	42	1.3
Scotland	58	61	46	53	66	72	76	26	63	11	0.5
Singapore	76	83	74	67	81	72	68	N/A	N/A	N/A	N/A
Slovenia	64	74	50	64	64	72	83	3	57	40	1.0
South Korea, Rep.	76	88	65	72	80	72	50	14	44	42	1.0
Thailand	50	58	44	44	56	53	66	17	44	39	1.0
United States	63	71	51	53	73	71	66	8	60	32	1.0

N/A Not Available

Source: Digest of Education Statistics, 1999; Chapter 6, Table 409; <http://ncesedgov/pubs2000/digest99/tables/XLS/Tab409xls>. Underlying data from International Association for the Evaluation of Educational Achievement, Mathematics Achievement in the Primary School Years, IEA's Third International Mathematics and Science Study, 1997.

B19-2. Average Eighth-Grade Achievement in Mathematics Content Areas, Selected Countries, 1999

	Fractions and number sense	Measurement	Data representation, analysis, and probability	Geometry	Algebra
International average of 38 nations	*487*	*487*	*487*	*487*	*487*
Australia	519	529	522	497	520
Belgium (Flemish area only)	557	549	544	535	540
Bulgaria	503	497	493	524	512
Canada	533	521	521	507	525
Chile	403	412	429	412	399
Chinese (Taipei only)	576	566	559	557	586
Cyprus	481	471	472	484	479
Czech Republic	507	535	513	513	514
England	497	507	506	471	498
Finland	531	521	525	494	498
Hong Kong SAR, China	579	567	547	556	569
Hungary	526	538	520	489	536
Indonesia	406	395	423	441	424
Iran	437	401	430	447	434
(Israel)	472	457	468	462	479
Italy	471	501	484	482	481
Japan	570	558	555	575	569
Jordan	432	438	436	449	439
Latvia-	496	505	495	522	499
Lithuania	479	467	493	496	487
Macedonia, FYRO	437	451	442	460	465
Malaysia	532	514	491	497	505
Moldova	465	479	450	481	477
Morocco	335	348	383	407	353
Netherlands, the	545	538	538	515	522
New Zealand	493	496	497	478	497
Philippines	378	355	406	383	345
Romania	458	491	453	487	481
Russia	513	527	501	522	529
Singapore	608	599	562	560	576
Slovakia	525	537	521	527	525
Slovenia	527	523	530	506	525
South Africa	300	329	356	335	293
South Korea, Rep.	570	571	576	573	585
Thailand	471	463	476	484	456
Tunisia	443	442	446	484	455
Turkey	430	436	446	428	432
United States	509	482	506	473	506

Source: Pursuing Excellence: Comparisons of International Eighth-Grade Mathematics and Science Achievement from a U.S. Perspective, 1995 and 1999, NCES 2001–028; Initial Findings from the Third International Mathematics and Science Study—Repeat, National Center for Education Statistics, (NCES) December 2000, (TIMSS-R); Appendix 3, Table A 3.4; <http://nces.ed.gov/pubs2001/2001028.pdf>. Underlying data from Martin et al. (2000). TIMSS 1999 International Science Report: Findings from IEA's Repeat of the International Mathematics and Science Study at the Eighth Grade. Exhibit 3.1. Chestnut Hill, MA: Boston College.

B19-3. Average Mathematics Scores at the End of Secondary School, by Sex, and Average Time Spent Studying Mathematics out of School, Selected Countries, 1994–1995

| | Math Scores | | | Time Spent Studying | | | |
| | | | | Less than 1 hour (Percent) | One to two hours (Percent) | Three or more hours (Percent) | Average hours |
	Overall	Males	Females				
Australia	522	540	510	59	36	5	1.0
Austria	518	545	503	77	19	4	0.6
Canada	519	537	504	56	38	7	1.1
Cyprus	446	454	439	63	29	8	1.0
Czech Republic	466	488	443	92	8	0	0.4
Denmark	547	575	523	68	28	4	0.9
France	523	544	506	59	35	5	1.0
Germany	495	509	480	N/A	N/A	N/A	N/A
Hungary	483	485	481	74	24	2	0.7
Iceland	534	558	514	79	19	2	0.7
Italy	476	490	464	55	40	5	1.0
Lithuania	469	485	461	67	29	4	0.8
Netherlands, the	560	585	533	82	16	1	0.7
New Zealand	522	536	507	75	23	2	0.7
Norway	528	555	501	85	14	1	0.5
Russia	471	488	460	56	33	11	1.2
Slovenia	512	535	490	72	25	2	0.7
South Africa	356	365	348	33	51	17	1.7
Sweden	552	573	531	90	9	1	0.4
Switzerland	540	555	522	67	28	5	0.9
United States	461	466	456	76	22	2	0.7

N/A Not Available

Source: Digest of Education Statistics, 1999; Chapter 6, Table 411; <http://ncesedgov/pubs2000/digest99/d99t411html>. Underlying data from International Association for the Evaluation of Educational Achievement, Mathematics and Science Achievement in the Final Year of Secondary School: IEA's Third International Mathematics and Science Study, 1998.

B19-4. Average Mathematics and Science Achievement of Eighth-Grade Students, Selected Countries, 1999

Country	Mathematics Average	Science
International average of 38 nations	**487**	**488**
Australia	525	540
Belgium-Flemish	558	535
Bulgaria	511	518
Canada	531	533
Chile	392	420
Cyprus	476	460
Czech Republic	520	539
England (UK)	496	538
Finland	520	535
Hong Kong, SAR (China)	582	530
Hungary	532	552
Indonesia	403	435
Iran	422	448
(Israel)	466	468
Italy	479	493
Japan	579	550
Jordan	428	450
Latvia	505	503
Lithuania	482	488
Macedonia, FYRO	447	458
Malaysia	519	492
Moldova	469	459
Morocco	337	323
Netherlands, the	540	545
New Zealand	491	510
Philippines	345	345
Romania	472	472
Russia	526	529
Singapore	604	568
Slovakia	534	535
Slovenia	530	533
South Africa	275	243
South Korea, Republic	587	549
Taiwan	585	569
Thailand	467	482
Tunisia	448	430
Turkey	429	433
United States	502	515

Source: Pursuing Excellence: Comparisons of International Eighth-Grade Mathematics and Science Achievement from a U.S. Perspective, 1995 and 1999, NCES 2001–028; Initial Findings from the Third International Mathematics and Science Study—Repeat, National Center for Education Statistics, (NCES) December 2000, (TIMSS-R); Appendix 3, Table A3.1; <http://nces.ed.gov/pubs2001/2001028.pdf>. Underlying data from Martin et al. (2000). TIMSS 1999 International Science Report: Findings from IEA' s Repeat of the International Mathematics and Science Study at the Eighth Grade. Exhibit 3.1. Chestnut Hill, MA: Boston College.

B19-5. Average Fourth-Grade Science Scores, by Content Areas, and Average Time Spent Teaching Science in School, Selected Countries, 1994–1995

	Science content areas				Average number of hours science is taught			
	Overall science scores	Earth science	Life science	Physical science	Environmental issues and the nature of science	Less than 1 hour (Percent)	1 to 2 hours (Percent)	2 to 3 hours (Percent)	More than 3 hours (Percent)
Australia	66	61	72	63	63	35	55	5	5
Austria	66	62	72	64	54	0	0	97	3
Canada	64	62	68	61	56	8	42	27	23
Cyprus	51	48	55	50	42	N/A	N/A	N/A	N/A
Czech Republic	65	64	71	62	56	2	79	3	16
England	63	61	68	60	56	6	27	44	23
Greece	54	52	61	49	43	N/A	N/A	N/A	N/A
Hong Kong, SAR (China)	62	61	68	60	50	13	84	2	1
Hungary	62	62	66	59	50	6	72	8	14
Iceland	55	55	60	52	47	17	41	30	12
Iran	40	38	44	40	26	N/A	N/A	N/A	N/A
Ireland	61	60	66	57	55	47	40	11	2
Israel	57	51	61	55	51	0	53	32	15
Japan	70	66	73	70	62	2	1	95	2
Kuwait	39	36	45	37	25	0	1	96	4
Latvia (Latvian speaking schools)	56	57	60	54	46	89	5	5	1
Netherlands, the	67	61	73	65	61	38	44	9	9
New Zealand	60	57	66	57	54	29	48	14	9
Norway	60	60	67	55	53	73	27	0	0
Portugal	50	50	54	49	39	2	3	12	84
Scotland	60	58	65	57	53	35	44	14	7
Singapore	64	58	70	64	53	0	4	96	0
Slovenia	64	64	68	61	54	3	60	18	19
South Korea, Rep.	74	72	76	75	70	0	1	95	5
Thailand	49	48	52	46	48	2	9	17	73
United States	66	64	71	60	65	9	16	33	42

N/A Not Available

Source: Digest of Education Statistics, 1999; Chapter 6, Table 410; <http://ncesedgov/pubs2000/digest99/d99t410html>. Underlying data from International Association for the Evaluation of Educational Achievement, Science Achievement in the Primary School Years: IEA's Third International Mathematics and Science Study, 1997.

B19-6. Average Eighth-Grade Achievement in Science Content Areas, Selected Countries, 1999

	Earth science	Life science	Physics	Chemistry	Environmental and resource issues	Scientific inquiry and the nature of science
International average of 38 nations	*488*	*488*	*488*	*488*	*488*	*488*
Australia	519	530	531	520	530	535
Belgium (Flemish area only)	533	535	530	508	513	526
Bulgaria	520	514	505	527	483	479
Canada	519	523	521	521	521	532
Chile	435	431	428	435	449	441
Chinese (Taipei only)	538	550	552	563	567	540
Cyprus	459	468	459	470	475	467
Czech Republic	533	544	526	512	516	522
England	525	533	528	524	518	538
Finland	520	520	520	535	514	528
Hong Kong SAR, China	506	516	523	515	518	531
Hungary	560	535	543	548	501	526
Indonesia	431	448	452	425	489	446
Iran	459	437	445	487	470	446
(Israel)	472	463	484	479	458	476
Italy	502	488	480	493	491	489
Japan	533	534	544	530	506	543
Jordan	446	448	459	483	476	440
Latvia-	495	509	495	490	493	495
Lithuania	476	494	510	485	458	483
Macedonia, FYRO	464	468	463	481	432	464
Malaysia	491	479	494	485	502	488
Moldova	466	477	457	451	444	471
Morocco	363	347	352	372	396	391
Netherlands, the	534	536	537	515	526	534
New Zealand	504	501	499	503	503	521
Philippines	390	378	393	394	391	403
Romania	475	475	465	481	473	456
Russia	529	517	529	523	495	491
Singapore	521	541	570	545	577	550
Slovakia	537	535	518	525	512	507
Slovenia	541	521	525	509	519	513
South Africa	348	289	308	350	350	329
South Korea, Rep.	532	528	544	523	523	545
Thailand	470	508	475	439	507	462
Tunisia	442	441	425	439	462	451
Turkey	435	444	441	437	461	445
United States	504	520	498	508	509	522

Source: Pursuing Excellence: Comparisons of International Eighth-Grade Mathematics and Science Achievement from a U.S. Perspective, 1995 and 1999, NCES 2001–028; Initial Findings from the Third International Mathematics and Science Study—Repeat, National Center for Education Statistics, (NCES) December 2000, (TIMSS-R); Appendix 3, Table A 3.5; <http://nces.ed.gov/pubs2001/2001028.pdf>. Underlying data from Martin et al. (2000). TIMSS 1999 International Science Report: Findings from IEA' s Repeat of the International Mathematics and Science Study at the Eighth Grade. Exhibit 3.1. Chestnut Hill, MA: Boston College.

B19-7. Average Science Scores at the End of Secondary School, by Sex, and Average Time Spent Studying Mathematics out of School, Selected Countries, 1994–1995

	Science scores			Time spent studying			
	Overall	Males	Females	Less than 1 hour (Percent)	One to two hours (Percent)	Three or more hours (Percent)	Average hours
Australia	527	547	513	58	35	7	1.0
Austria	520	554	501	87	11	1	0.4
Canada	532	550	518	57	35	8	1.1
Cyprus	448	459	439	80	16	4	0.5
Czech Republic	487	512	460	84	14	3	0.5
Denmark	509	532	490	73	25	3	0.7
France	487	508	468	59	35	6	1.0
Germany	497	514	478	N/A	N/A	N/A	N/A
Hungary	471	484	455	67	27	6	0.9
Iceland	549	572	530	87	12	1	0.4
Italy	475	495	458	70	25	5	0.8
Lithuania	461	481	450	69	26	5	0.8
Netherlands, the	558	582	532	78	20	1	0.7
New Zealand	529	543	515	80	18	3	0.6
Norway	544	574	513	74	23	3	0.7
Russia	481	510	463	61	30	10	1.1
Slovenia	517	541	494	85	13	2	0.5
South Africa	349	367	333	47	35	18	1.5
Sweden	559	585	534	81	17	2	0.6
Switzerland	523	540	500	76	21	3	0.7
United States	480	492	469	76	21	2	0.7

N/A   Not Available

NOTE—End of secondary school is equivalent to 12th-grade in the U.S. and a few other countries, but ranges from 9th- to 14th-grade among the survey countries.

Source: Digest of Education Statistics, 1999; Chapter 6, Table 41; <http://nces.ed.gov/pubs2000/digest99/d99t412html>. Underlying data from International Association for the Evaluation of Educational Achievement, Mathematics and Science Achievement in the Final Year of Secondary School: IEA's Third International Mathematics and Science Study, 1998.

B19-8. Percentage of 13-Year-Old Students Who Took a Test or Quiz at Least Once a Week, by Subject, Selected Countries, 1991

	Mathematics	Science
Canada	53	26
France	64	47
Hungary	17	27
Ireland	19	18
Israel	36	28
Jordan	68	73
Slovenia	28	18
South Korea, Rep.	28	21
Soviet Union (former)	52	88
Spain	31	42
Switzerland	40	18
Taiwan	87	67
United States	68	69

Source: Educational Indicators: An International Perspective, Table 26; <http://www.nces.ed.gov/pubs/eiip/eiipid26.html>. Underlying data from Educational Testing Service, International Assessment of Educational Progress, Learning Mathematics; Learning Science, 1992, National Center For Education Statistics.

B19-9. Average Percent Correct for 13-Year-Olds on Geography Items, by Sex, Content Area, and Country, 1991

Country	Total	Male	Female	Skills	Content area: Physical geography	Content area: Cultural geography
Canada	63.0	65.5	60.5	69.5	61.0	58.2
Hungary	69.8	72.7	67.0	76.3	67.8	65.0
Ireland	58.5	61.4	55.7	62.7	59.5	52.3
Scotland (UK)	58.3	61.0	55.6	66.2	57.1	50.6
Slovenia	65.3	67.8	62.6	67.9	63.6	64.3
South Korea, Rep.	59.7	63.0	55.7	67.8	52.1	60.3
Soviet Union (former)	62.6	64.1	61.1	72.2	61.2	53.4
Spain	60.1	63.0	57.3	62.4	58.9	58.9
United States	61.9	64.6	59.4	69.4	58.3	58.1

Source: Educational Indicators: An International Perspective, Table 9; <http://www.nces.ed.gov/pubs/eiip/eiipid9.html>. Underlying data from Educational Testing Service, International Assessment of Educational Progress, Learning About the World, 1992, National Center For Education Statistics.

B19-10. Reading Literacy Test Scores for 9-Year-Olds, Selected Countries, 1992

	Grade tested	Mean age (years)	Overall mean score	Narrative* 1st quartile	Narrative* mean score	Narrative* 3rd quartile	Expository** mean score	Documents*** mean score
Belgium	4	9.8	507	439	510	558	505	506
Canada	3	8.9	500	437	502	566	499	500
Cyprus	4	9.8	481	421	492	548	475	476
Denmark	3	9.8	475	386	463	539	467	496
Finland	3	9.7	569	508	568	602	569	569
France	4	10.1	531	467	532	580	533	527
Germany (former East)	3	9.5	499	414	482	531	493	522
Germany (former West)	3	9.4	503	421	491	543	497	520
Greece	4	9.3	504	447	514	567	511	488
Hong Kong, SAR (China)	4	10.0	517	431	494	548	503	554
Hungary	3	9.3	499	437	496	541	493	509
Iceland	3	9.8	518	448	518	571	517	519
Indonesia	4	10.8	394	351	402	436	411	369
Ireland	4	9.3	509	445	518	571	514	495
Italy	4	9.9	529	468	533	576	538	517
Netherlands, the	3	9.2	485	425	494	539	480	481
New Zealand	5	10.0	528	452	534	594	531	521
Norway	3	9.8	524	455	525	576	528	519
Portugal	4	10.4	478	419	483	531	480	471
Singapore	3	9.3	515	450	521	567	519	504
Slovenia	3	9.7	498	435	502	570	489	503
Spain	4	10.0	504	429	497	543	505	509
Sweden	3	9.8	539	467	536	592	542	539
Switzerland	3	9.7	511	438	506	566	507	522
Trinidad and Tobago	4	9.6	451	383	455	502	458	440
United States	4	10.0	547	476	553	619	538	550
Venezuela	4	10.1	383	322	378	426	396	374

* Narrative prose is continuous text in which the writer's aim is to tell a story.
** Expository prose is continuous text designed to describe, explain, or otherwise convey factual information or opinion to the reader.
*** Documents are structured information presented in the form of charts, tables, maps, graphs, lists, or sets of instructions.

Source: Digest of Education Statistics, 1999; Chapter 6, Table 413; <http://nces.ed.gov/pubs2000/digest99/tables/XLS/Tab413xls>. Underlying data from International Association for the Evaluation of Educational Achievement, How in the World Do Students Read? 1992.

B19-11. Reading Literacy Test Scores for 14-Year-Olds, Selected Countries, 1992

	Grade tested	Mean age (years)	Overall mean score	Narrative* 1st quartile	Narrative* mean score	Narrative* 3rd quartile	Expository** mean score	Documents*** mean score
Belgium	8	14.3	481	484	415	477	522	483
Botswana	9	14.7	330	340	294	339	371	312
Canada	8	13.9	522	526	449	516	569	522
Cyprus	9	14.8	497	516	427	492	536	482
Denmark	8	14.8	525	517	458	524	573	532
Finland	8	14.7	560	559	493	541	575	580
France	9	15.4	549	556	484	546	580	544
Germany (former East)	8	14.4	526	512	464	523	566	543
Germany (former West)	8	14.6	522	514	453	521	573	532
Greece	9	14.4	509	526	450	508	548	493
Hong Kong, SAR (China)	9	15.2	535	509	480	540	576	557
Hungary	8	14.1	536	530	469	536	577	542
Iceland	8	14.8	536	550	472	548	617	509
Ireland	9	14.5	511	510	439	505	555	518
Italy	8	14.1	515	520	459	524	565	501
Netherlands, the	8	14.3	514	506	442	503	546	533
New Zealand	10	15.0	545	547	457	535	597	552
Nigeria	9	15.3	401	402	351	406	441	394
Norway	8	14.8	516	515	464	520	569	512
Philippines	8	14.5	430	421	378	439	472	430
Portugal	9	15.6	523	523	469	523	556	523
Singapore	8	14.4	534	530	476	539	574	533
Slovenia	8	14.7	532	534	471	525	576	537
Spain	8	14.2	490	500	435	495	536	475
Sweden	8	14.8	546	556	469	533	576	550
Switzerland	8	14.9	536	534	466	525	572	549
Thailand	9	15.2	477	468	429	486	533	478
Trinidad and Tobago	9	14.4	479	482	408	485	537	472
United States	9	15.0	535	539	456	539	599	528
Venezuela	9	15.5	417	407	381	433	482	412
Zimbabwe	9	15.5	372	367	326	374	411	373

* Narrative prose is continuous text in which the writer's aim is to tell a story.

** Expository prose is continuous text designed to describe, explain, or otherwise convey factual information or opinion to the reader.

*** Documents are structured information presented in the form of charts, tables, maps, graphs, lists, or sets of instructions.

Source: Digest of Education Statistics, 1999; Chapter 6, Table 414; <http://nces.ed.gov/pubs2000/digest99/d99t414html>. Underlying data from International Association for the Evaluation of Educational Achievement, How in the World Do Students Read? 1992.

B20. LITERACY RATES

B20-1. Percentage of Population Aged 15 Years and Over Who Can Both Read and Write, 1985–2000

	1985			1990			1995			2000		
	Total (%)	Male (%)	Female (%)	Total (%)	Male (%)	Female (%)	Total (%)	Male (%)	Female (%)	Total (%)	Male (%)	Female (%)
Afghanistan	22.1	35.3	8.1	26.5	40.4	11.6	31.5	46.2	16.1	36.3	51.0	20.8
Algeria	46.8	60.8	32.8	52.8	66.4	39.1	58.4	71.1	45.4	63.3	75.1	51.3
Argentina	95.1	95.3	94.8	95.8	95.9	95.6	96.4	96.5	96.3	96.9	96.9	96.9
Bahamas	94.2	93.5	94.9	95.0	94.3	95.7	95.6	95.0	96.3	96.1	95.4	96.8
Bahrain	76.9	83.3	66.5	82.3	86.9	74.8	85.3	89.2	79.5	87.6	91.0	82.7
Bangladesh	32.0	43.4	19.9	34.8	46.0	23.0	37.8	48.9	26.2	40.8	51.7	29.5
Belarus	96.5	99.1	94.3	97.9	99.4	96.7	98.8	99.6	98.2	99.4	99.7	99.2
Benin	22.0	31.9	12.6	26.5	38.1	15.5	31.6	44.9	19.1	37.5	52.2	23.6
Bhutan	32.5	46.2	18.8	37.3	51.3	23.2	42.2	56.3	28.2	47.3	61.1	33.6
Bolivia	73.9	83.8	64.5	78.4	87.1	70.1	82.3	89.9	75.1	85.6	92.1	79.4
Botswana	63.4	61.4	65.2	68.2	65.8	70.4	72.7	70.0	75.1	77.2	74.4	79.8
Brazil	78.3	79.6	77.1	81.7	82.1	81.2	83.2	83.4	83.0	85.3	85.1	85.4
Brunei	80.8	87.9	72.9	85.6	91.1	79.5	89.1	93.2	84.6	91.6	94.7	88.2
Bulgaria	96.5	97.9	95.0	97.4	98.4	96.4	98.0	98.8	97.4	98.5	99.1	98.0
Burkina Faso	13.2	21.0	5.7	16.0	24.7	7.6	19.2	28.7	10.0	23.0	33.2	13.1
Burundi	32.2	44.6	21.2	37.8	48.5	28.0	42.3	52.2	33.2	48.1	56.3	40.5
Cameroon	54.7	65.8	44.1	62.3	71.8	53.1	69.3	77.2	61.6	75.4	81.8	69.2
Cape Verde	57.5	71.6	47.5	62.4	74.7	52.9	69.4	80.7	60.7	73.5	84.3	65.3
Central African Republic	28.1	41.8	15.7	33.5	47.4	20.9	39.7	53.6	27.2	46.5	59.6	34.5
Chad	37.7	52.1	24.0	42.8	57.2	29.1	48.2	62.2	34.8	53.6	66.9	40.8
Chile	92.8	93.3	92.4	94.0	94.4	93.6	94.9	95.2	94.6	95.7	95.9	95.5
China	72.5	83.4	61.0	77.9	87.0	68.1	81.5	89.9	72.7	85.0	92.3	77.4
Colombia	86.8	87.5	86.3	88.7	89.1	88.4	90.4	90.6	90.3	91.8	91.8	91.8
Comoros	52.5	60.5	44.9	53.8	61.4	46.4	55.0	62.5	47.6	56.2	63.5	49.1
Congo, Rep.	59.1	70.8	48.3	67.2	77.3	57.9	74.4	82.7	66.8	80.7	87.5	74.4
Costa Rica	92.9	93.0	92.8	93.9	93.9	93.9	94.8	94.8	94.8	95.6	95.5	95.7
Côte d'Ivoire	27.9	37.4	17.6	33.4	42.8	23.4	40.0	48.7	30.6	46.8	54.6	38.5
Croatia	94.7	98.1	91.5	96.3	98.7	94.2	97.4	99.1	96.0	98.3	99.4	97.3
Cuba	93.6	93.4	93.7	94.8	94.8	94.8	95.6	95.6	95.6	96.4	96.5	96.4
Cyprus	91.9	96.9	87.0	93.8	97.6	90.0	95.3	98.2	92.6	96.9	98.7	95.0
Djibouti	36.2	50.4	22.5	41.2	55.5	27.4	46.3	60.4	32.8	51.4	65.0	38.4
Dominican Republic	76.9	77.6	76.1	79.5	80.0	79.0	81.8	82.1	81.5	83.8	84.0	83.7
Ecuador	85.2	88.2	82.1	88.4	90.5	86.2	90.1	92.2	88.0	91.9	93.6	90.2
Egypt	43.2	57.1	29.1	47.1	60.3	33.6	51.1	63.5	38.5	55.3	66.6	43.7
El Salvador	69.3	73.5	65.4	72.6	76.3	69.3	76.0	79.3	73.0	78.7	81.6	76.1
Equatorial Guinea	66.5	81.1	52.6	73.1	85.4	61.2	77.8	89.3	67.2	83.2	92.5	74.5
Ethiopia	23.8	32.1	15.6	28.3	36.0	20.6	33.2	39.9	26.5	38.7	43.9	33.4
Fiji	86.2	89.5	82.8	88.7	91.6	85.7	91.1	93.5	88.6	92.9	95.0	90.9
Gabon	48.5	61.4	36.4	56.0	67.7	44.9	63.3	73.7	53.4	70.8	79.8	62.2
Gambia, the	20.5	26.1	15.2	25.6	31.7	19.7	30.9	37.8	24.4	36.5	43.8	29.6
Ghana	50.3	63.5	37.5	57.3	69.4	45.6	63.9	74.7	53.4	70.2	79.5	61.2
Greece	92.9	96.9	89.1	94.8	97.6	92.2	96.2	98.2	94.3	97.2	98.6	96.0
Guatemala	57.7	65.6	49.6	61.5	69.3	53.7	65.3	73.0	57.6	68.7	76.2	61.1
Guinea	26.6	39.5	13.8	31.1	44.7	17.6	35.9	50.0	22.0	41.1	55.1	27.0
Guinea-Bissau	22.6	36.7	9.2	26.7	42.0	12.2	31.5	47.5	16.3	36.8	53.0	21.4
Guyana	96.1	97.4	94.8	97.2	98.0	96.3	97.9	98.6	97.2	98.5	99.0	98.1

B20-1. Percentage of Population Aged 15 Years and Over Who Can Both Read and Write, 1985–2000 (continued)

	1985			1990			1995			2000		
	Total (%)	Male (%)	Female (%)	Total (%)	Male (%)	Female (%)	Total (%)	Male (%)	Female (%)	Total (%)	Male (%)	Female (%)
Haiti	35.2	38.5	32.1	39.3	42.4	36.5	43.9	46.6	41.5	48.6	51.0	46.5
Honduras	64.1	65.5	62.7	67.0	68.0	66.0	69.7	70.3	69.1	72.2	72.5	72.0
Hungary	98.9	99.2	98.6	99.1	99.3	98.9	99.3	99.5	99.1	99.4	99.5	99.3
India	44.7	59.0	29.4	48.5	62.4	33.5	52.1	65.5	37.7	55.8	68.6	42.1
Indonesia	74.8	83.4	66.5	81.6	88.0	75.2	83.7	89.7	77.9	87.0	91.9	82.1
Iran	50.8	62.3	39.0	64.3	73.2	55.3	71.0	78.9	63.1	76.9	83.7	70.0
Israel	92.7	95.9	89.6	94.1	96.7	91.5	95.1	97.4	93.0	96.1	97.9	94.3
Italy	97.0	97.9	96.3	97.7	98.4	97.1	98.2	98.7	97.8	98.5	98.9	98.1
Jamaica	80.5	76.2	84.6	82.7	78.3	86.9	84.8	80.5	88.9	86.7	82.5	90.7
Jordan	75.0	85.6	63.4	81.2	89.9	71.7	85.6	90.5	80.1	89.8	94.9	84.4
Kenya	64.2	76.4	52.3	71.1	81.4	61.0	77.3	85.6	69.1	82.5	89.0	76.0
Kuwait	74.5	78.2	68.8	76.9	79.5	72.9	79.3	82.3	76.0	82.3	84.3	79.9
Laos	46.8	60.5	33.0	51.6	65.1	38.6	56.7	69.5	44.4	61.8	73.6	50.5
Latvia	99.2	99.7	98.7	99.4	99.8	99.1	99.6	99.8	99.4	99.7	99.8	99.6
Lebanon	76.4	85.6	68.3	80.4	88.5	73.2	83.4	90.5	77.0	86.1	92.3	80.4
Lesotho	75.1	62.3	86.6	78.4	66.3	89.5	81.4	70.1	91.9	83.9	73.6	93.6
Liberia	33.5	48.7	18.0	39.2	55.3	22.9	45.2	61.6	28.4	53.4	69.9	36.8
Libya	60.9	77.7	41.0	68.0	83.0	50.9	74.3	87.4	59.8	79.8	90.9	67.6
Lithuania	97.7	98.9	96.7	98.7	99.3	98.1	99.2	99.6	99.0	99.5	99.7	99.4
Malawi	48.2	66.3	31.8	51.9	68.8	36.3	56.0	71.7	41.3	60.3	74.5	46.7
Malaysia	76.5	84.1	69.1	80.9	87.0	74.6	84.5	89.5	79.4	87.5	91.5	83.6
Maldives	92.3	92.2	92.4	94.2	94.2	94.1	95.3	95.4	95.2	96.3	96.3	96.4
Mali	18.9	25.5	12.8	25.0	32.3	18.2	32.3	40.0	25.1	40.3	47.9	33.2
Malta	86.2	86.0	86.4	88.5	88.0	89.1	90.5	89.9	91.1	92.1	91.4	92.8
Martinique	94.1	93.4	94.6	95.5	94.8	96.1	96.5	96.0	97.1	97.4	97.0	97.9
Mauritania	32.0	43.8	20.9	34.9	46.4	23.9	37.5	48.7	26.7	39.9	50.6	29.5
Mauritius	77.2	83.1	71.5	80.0	85.2	74.7	82.2	86.4	78.2	84.3	87.7	81.0
Mexico	85.1	88.3	82.0	87.7	90.4	85.0	89.5	91.8	87.2	91.0	93.1	89.1
Moldova	94.5	97.8	91.7	96.5	98.7	94.7	98.0	99.2	96.9	98.9	99.6	98.3
Mongolia	98.5	98.9	98.2	98.8	99.0	98.7	99.1	99.1	99.0	99.3	99.2	99.3
Morocco	33.5	47.4	20.0	38.7	52.7	25.0	44.0	57.7	30.5	48.9	61.9	36.0
Mozambique	28.9	44.1	14.5	33.5	49.4	18.3	38.3	54.6	22.9	43.8	59.9	28.4
Myanmar (Burma)	78.3	86.5	70.5	80.8	87.4	74.4	82.9	88.2	77.7	84.7	89.0	80.6
Namibia	70.6	74.3	67.0	74.7	77.3	72.2	78.4	80.1	76.8	82.1	82.9	81.2
Nepal	27.1	43.4	10.2	30.8	47.8	14.2	35.9	53.6	18.6	41.4	59.1	23.8
Netherlands Antilles	94.5	94.6	94.5	95.4	95.4	95.4	96.1	96.1	96.0	96.6	96.6	96.6
Nicaragua	59.8	60.0	59.6	61.3	61.4	61.2	62.8	62.8	62.8	64.3	64.2	64.4
Niger	9.7	15.7	3.9	11.4	18.0	5.1	13.4	20.6	6.6	15.7	23.5	8.3
Nigeria	40.9	52.4	29.9	48.8	59.5	38.5	56.5	66.1	47.3	64.1	72.3	56.2
Oman	46.0	60.6	26.8	55.0	67.9	38.4	64.0	74.6	50.7	71.9	80.4	61.7
Pakistan	31.5	44.8	16.8	35.5	49.4	20.2	39.4	53.7	23.8	43.3	57.6	27.8
Panama	87.2	87.9	86.5	88.8	89.3	88.2	90.6	91.3	90.0	91.9	92.6	91.3
Papua New Guinea	63.5	74.4	51.7	68.1	77.9	57.5	72.2	81.0	62.7	76.0	83.7	67.7

B20-1. Percentage of Population Aged 15 Years and Over Who Can Both Read and Write, 1985–2000 (continued)

	1985			1990			1995			2000		
	Total (%)	Male (%)	Female (%)	Total (%)	Male (%)	Female (%)	Total (%)	Male (%)	Female (%)	Total (%)	Male (%)	Female (%)
Paraguay	88.4	91.1	85.7	90.3	92.3	88.3	91.9	93.4	90.4	93.3	94.4	92.2
Peru	83.0	90.4	75.6	85.7	92.1	79.4	88.0	93.5	82.7	89.9	94.7	85.4
Philippines	91.0	91.7	90.3	92.5	93.1	92.0	94.1	94.4	93.8	95.4	95.5	95.2
Poland	99.4	99.6	99.2	99.6	99.7	99.5	99.7	99.8	99.7	99.8	99.8	99.8
Portugal	84.3	88.8	80.4	87.3	91.0	83.9	90.0	93.1	87.2	92.2	94.8	90.0
Puerto Rico	90.0	90.2	89.8	91.4	91.5	91.4	92.8	92.7	92.8	93.8	93.7	94.0
Qatar	74.4	75.5	71.5	77.1	77.4	76.1	79.3	79.0	80.0	81.3	80.5	83.2
Reunion	78.6	76.4	80.6	82.0	79.5	84.3	84.8	82.5	87.0	87.1	84.8	89.2
Romania	95.6	98.1	93.3	96.8	98.6	95.2	97.6	98.9	96.4	98.2	99.1	97.3
Russia	97.2	99.3	95.5	98.3	99.5	97.3	99.1	99.7	98.6	99.4	99.8	99.2
Rwanda	46.7	57.5	36.3	53.4	63.0	44.2	60.4	68.7	52.4	67.0	73.7	60.6
Saudi Arabia	60.5	73.0	41.7	67.2	77.6	50.6	72.2	80.8	59.7	77.0	84.1	67.2
Senegal	24.7	34.4	15.0	28.5	38.4	18.7	32.8	42.8	23.0	37.3	47.2	27.6
Sierra Leone	22.7	35.0	11.2	26.9	40.2	14.4	31.5	45.4	18.2	36.3	50.7	22.6
Singapore	85.8	93.1	78.3	89.1	95.1	83.0	90.8	95.6	86.1	92.4	96.4	88.5
Slovenia	99.5	99.6	99.4	99.6	99.6	99.5	99.6	99.7	99.6	99.7	99.7	99.6
South Africa	79.1	80.2	77.9	81.3	82.3	80.3	83.3	84.1	82.5	85.1	85.8	84.5
South Korea, Rep.	94.5	97.8	91.2	95.9	98.4	93.4	96.9	98.8	95.0	97.8	99.2	96.4
Spain	95.1	97.2	93.2	96.2	97.8	94.7	97.0	98.3	95.9	97.7	98.6	96.8
Sri Lanka	87.2	92.0	82.2	88.7	92.9	84.6	90.2	93.7	86.9	91.6	94.5	88.9
Sudan	38.7	53.1	24.2	44.9	58.6	31.2	50.8	63.5	38.3	57.1	68.3	46.0
Suriname	90.0	93.1	86.9	91.8	94.3	89.3	93.0	95.2	91.0	94.2	95.9	92.6
Swaziland	66.0	68.5	64.0	71.6	73.7	69.8	76.0	77.6	74.7	79.8	80.9	78.7
Syria	59.4	77.6	40.8	64.9	81.9	47.5	69.9	85.4	54.1	74.4	88.3	60.4
Tajikistan	96.4	98.1	94.7	97.8	98.9	96.8	98.7	99.3	98.1	99.2	99.6	98.9
Tanzania	56.4	70.9	42.6	63.1	75.8	51.1	69.3	80.2	59.0	75.2	84.1	66.6
Thailand	90.2	94.0	86.5	93.4	95.6	91.2	94.2	96.4	92.0	95.6	97.2	94.0
Togo	38.4	54.4	23.1	44.4	60.5	28.9	50.7	66.5	35.4	57.1	72.2	42.6
Trinidad and Tobago	96.1	97.5	94.6	96.8	98.0	95.6	97.6	98.6	96.7	98.2	99.0	97.5
Tunisia	52.7	66.2	39.1	59.1	71.7	46.4	64.5	76.0	53.0	70.8	81.4	60.1
Turkey	76.4	87.6	64.3	79.3	89.8	68.5	82.0	91.7	72.2	85.2	93.6	76.7
Uganda	50.7	64.8	37.2	56.1	69.2	43.4	61.9	73.7	50.4	67.3	77.7	57.1
United Arab Emirates	69.1	70.0	66.7	71.4	71.5	71.0	73.8	73.2	75.1	76.5	75.2	79.5
Uruguay	95.4	94.8	95.8	96.6	96.1	97.0	97.3	96.9	97.7	97.8	97.4	98.2
Venezuela	87.5	88.8	86.2	90.1	90.9	89.2	91.5	92.1	90.9	93.0	93.3	92.7
Vietnam	86.7	92.8	81.2	89.0	93.8	84.5	91.1	94.8	87.8	93.3	95.7	91.0
Yemen	26.1	46.9	8.6	32.8	55.4	13.0	40.1	62.1	18.4	46.2	67.4	25.0
Zambia	63.5	74.9	53.1	68.2	78.5	58.9	73.2	82.0	65.1	78.0	85.2	71.2
Zimbabwe	83.4	88.6	78.3	86.8	91.3	82.5	89.8	93.5	86.1	92.7	95.5	89.9

Source: UNESCO *Statistical Yearbook 1999;* <http://unescostat.unesco.org/uisen/stats/stats0.htm>. Underlying data from United Nations Educational, Scientific and Cultural Organization (UNESCO).

B21. ILLITERACY

B21-1. Estimated Number of Illiterates Age 15 to 19 Years and Share of Age Group Population of the Total All Ages, Both Sexes, 1990 and 1995

	1990		1995	
	Number of illiterates, age 15-19	Number of illiterates, age 15-19 as percentage of total illiterates of all ages	Number of illiterates, age 15-19	Number of illiterates, age 15-19 as percentage of total illiterates of all ages
Afghanistan	959,321	15.5	1,000,932	12.3
Algeria	523,842	8.0	439,946	6.7
Argentina	58,948	6.0	61,699	6.6
Bahrain	1,186	2.0	952	1.7
Bangladesh	6,913,729	17.0	6,997,389	15.5
Benin	218,263	12.7	205,047	11.4
Bolivia	40,288	5.0	30,854	4.1
Brazil	1,447,201	7.8	1,295,491	7.1
Brunei	311	1.3	220	1.0
Bulgaria	4,609	2.9	3,601	2.9
Burkina Faso	674,675	16.0	703,715	15.3
Burundi	303,187	14.7	318,309	14.3
Cameroon	241,273	8.8	218,804	8.1
Cape Verde	4,196	6.3	3,612	5.6
Central African Republic	20,041	2.4	11,030	1.5
Chile	17,968	3.3	12,170	2.5
China	4,874,856	2.6	2,451,160	1.5
Colombia	131,212	6.1	114,427	5.6
Comoros	20,718	16.2	22,904	16.0
Congo, Dem.Rep. (Zaire)	106,443	2.3	67,986	1.6
Congo, Rep.	13,572	3.5	9,656	2.7
Costa Rica	5,718	4.9	5,745	5.0
Côte d'Ivoire	550,820	13.5	576,113	13.3
Cuba	4,988	1.1	2,300	0.6
Dominican Republic	89,971	9.9	78,945	8.7
Ecuador	37,320	4.9	31,064	4.3
Egypt	1,957,778	11.0	2,101,885	11.1
El Salvador	132,546	14.5	136,726	14.0
Equatorial Guinea	2,257	4.2	1,700	3.5
Estonia	218	5.7	218	8.5
Ethiopia	2,616,701	14.7	2,700,438	14.2
Fiji	945	1.9	703	1.6
Gabon	8,317	2.6	5,779	2.0
Ghana	274,161	8.0	225,597	6.7
Greece	2,906	0.7	2,246	0.8
Guatemala	N/A	N/A	N/A	N/A
Guyana	184	1.2	155	1.4
Haiti	296,490	13.0	286,342	12.1
Honduras	102,463	12.5	106,298	12.2
Hong Kong SAR , (China)	4,488	1.1	3,720	1.0
Hungary	2,348	3.2	2,051	3.0
India	31,559,230	11.3	29,407,110	10.1
Indonesia	659,530	2.7	408,541	1.9
Iran	755,310	6.2	682,614	5.7
Iraq	540,152	11.2	458,618	9.5
Israel	2,402	1.4	1,260	0.7
Italy	8,808	0.8	7,395	0.8
Jamaica	24,002	8.9	18,775	7.4
Jordan	9,136	2.2	4,694	1.1
Kenya	216,515	6.4	191,524	5.9
Kuwait	20,430	6.2	14,810	7.4

B21-1. Estimated Number of Illiterates Age 15 to 19 Years and Share of Age Group Population of the Total All Ages, Both Sexes, 1990 and 1995 *(continued)*

	1990		1995	
	Number of illiterates, age 15-19	Number of illiterates, age 15-19 as percentage of total illiterates of all ages	Number of illiterates, age 15-19	Number of illiterates, age 15-19 as percentage of total illiterates of all ages
Latvia	364	3.6	335	6.3
Liberia	129,756	13.8	136,989	13.5
Libya	20,880	2.8	12,829	1.8
Lithuania	543	1.6	521	3.3
Malawi	323,962	13.7	353,126	13.7
Malaysia	84,669	3.9	59,380	2.9
Maldives	980	10.9	1,050	11.3
Mali	527,872	14.3	507,961	13.0
Malta	384	1.3	303	1.2
Mauritania	115,553	16.0	130,750	16.2
Mauritius	6,862	4.7	6,105	4.4
Mexico	425,241	6.6	325,115	5.2
Mozambique	646,877	12.5	655,616	12.4
Myanmar (Burma)	520,652	10.7	472,926	9.6
Nepal	1,280,883	15.4	1,422,563	15.5
Nicaragua	116,688	16.9	147,865	18.0
Niger	652,765	18.3	745,622	18.3
Nigeria	2,088,388	7.9	1,721,675	6.6
Pakistan	6,473,883	14.4	6,603,041	13.6
Panama	10,320	6.2	8,260	5.1
Paraguay	16,668	7.0	15,160	6.5
Peru	90,748	4.9	75,737	4.4
Philippines	153,918	6.1	117,286	5.3
Poland	5,697	6.2	6,423	7.7
Portugal	1,654	0.2	1,551	0.2
Qatar	2,042	2.5	2,118	2.6
Romania	11,277	2.0	7,757	2.0
Russia	20,370	1.4	21,450	3.9
Rwanda	195,559	11.7	186,240	11.0
Senegal	434,837	15.3	465,900	15.1
Singapore	1,471	0.6	1,008	0.5
South Africa	489,706	10.6	489,341	10.3
South Korea, Rep.	8,928	1.0	7,885	1.1
Spain	8,323	0.7	6,268	0.7
Sri Lanka	76,407	5.8	67,696	5.5
Sudan	996,881	12.3	1,019,302	12.0
Swaziland	11,249	9.9	10,138	8.9
Syria	224,186	10.2	210,770	9.3
Tanzania	492,488	9.4	416,608	8.1
Thailand	110,079	3.5	78,535	3.0
Togo	115,058	10.9	109,729	10.1
Trinidad and Tobago	352	1.5	247	1.3
Tunisia	110,908	5.5	77,594	4.0
Turkey	337,099	4.3	218,723	3.0
Uganda	504,351	12.5	505,745	12.1
United Arab Emirates	7,567	2.8	6,535	2.4
Uruguay	2,869	3.8	2,352	3.6
Venezuela	67,779	5.2	56,803	4.6
Vietnam	123,049	3.2	104,779	3.6
Zambia	88,756	7.8	74,432	6.9
Zimbabwe	91,768	9.4	79,849	8.5

N/A Not Available

Source: UNESCO Statistical Yearbook 1999; <http://unescostat.unesco.org/uisen/stats/stats0.htm>. Underlying data from United Nations Educational, Scientific and Cultural Organization (UNESCO).

B21-2. Percentage of Women Ages 15 to 19 with No Education, by Country, various years

Country	Year of survey	Percent
Bolivia	1994	2.7
Botswana	1988	5.5
Brazil *	1991	6.1
Burkina	1993	73.2
Burundi	1987	73.3
Cameroon	1991	25.7
Colombia	1990	2.3
Dominican Republic	1991	3.0
Ecuador	1987	3.2
Egypt	1992	23.6
El Salvador	1985	9.1
Ghana	1993	19.0
Guatemala	1987	22.4
Indonesia	1991	3.0
Jordan	1990	3.0
Kenya	1993	4.3
Liberia	1986	36.7
Madagascar	1992	14.5
Malawi	1992	30.3
Mexico	1987	3.9
Morocco	1992	45.8
Namibia	1992	6.6
Niger	1992	80.5
Nigeria	1990	33.6
Pakistan	1990/1991	54.9
Peru	1991/1992	1.1
Philippines	1993	1.1
Rwanda	1992	20.9
Senegal	1992/1993	60.7
Sri Lanka	1987	15.8
Sudan	1989/1990	23.5
Tanzania	1991/1992	14.9
Thailand	1987	7.5
Togo	1988	37.6
Tunisia	1988	35.4
Turkey	1993	7.4
Uganda	1988/1989	20.7
Yemen	1991/1992	60.4
Zambia	1992	10.1
Zimbabwe	1988	2.5

* Data are only for some parts of the country.

Source: U.S. Bureau of the Census, International Data Base; <http://www.census.gov/ipc/prod/ipc95-1/ipc95_1j.pdf>. Underlying data from *Trends in Adolescent Fertility and Contraceptive Use in the Developing World*, by Thomas M. McDevitt with Arjun Adlakha, Timothy B. Fowler and Vera Harris-Bourne; IPC/95-1. Table 11.

C. Health and Nutrition

GENERAL OVERVIEW

The statistics in this section detail the features of health care systems available to children: government expenditure on health, access to sanitation and safe drinking water, and availability of hospitals and trained health personnel. We have defined health care broadly to include food aid because of the close connection between nutrition and health.

A large portion of this section focuses on immunization, which the World Health Organization views as a fundamental cornerstone of global health, a key component of economic development and an essential first step in enabling children to reach their physical and intellectual potential. During the last two decades the world community made tremendous gains in raising immunization rates. Close to 90 percent of the world's children are now routinely vaccinated against the key immunizable diseases of childhood. Vaccination saves the lives of 2.5 million children annually and remains the single most feasible and cost-effective way of ensuring good health. Yet 30 million children born each year in poor countries are still unprotected. The result is nearly 3 million children dying annually from vaccine-preventable illnesses.

EXPLANATION OF INDICATORS

C1-1. Central government expenditures for health care: This indicator presents the public financial resources allotted to a country's health care system as a percentage of the total government's expenditures. Expenditures comprise government budgets and external borrowings and grants, including donations from international agencies and nongovernmental organizations. The table says nothing about what part of a population reaps the benefit from expenditures, and so we cannot relate these figures specifically to children. It is presented as a general measure of government concern for health care. The money spent on health care relative to the rest of a country's economic activity is usually small in developing countries as compared to developed countries because poorer countries are often focused on concerns such as sanitation projects, highways, and mass transit, as well as building up military capacity.

C2-1. Access to safe water: Access to safe water is an important factor in maintaining basic health, especially of newborns and young children. Unfortunately, 1.1 billion people in the developing world have no safe water. In looking at this measure, one must remember that it is an indicator of access as well as water safety. According to the World Health Organization (WHO), access to safe water means that a household member need not spend a disproportionate amount of his or her day obtaining it. In many developing countries, however, the daily chore of collecting water is a huge burden on millions of lives, usually women and girls, who may spend up to four hours each day collecting water for domestic use. This in turn directly hampers these children's chances to attend school.

C3-1. Access to sanitation: Access to sanitation facilities is one of the most important aspects of maintaining basic health standards. It is a fundamental human right that safeguards health and human dignity, yet 2.9 billion people have no sanitary facilities. Adequate sanitation facilities protect children from the many health problems—including dysentery, cholera, and other serious infections—posed by poor disposal of human waste. The World Health Organization defines sanitation facilities as any means that effectively disposes of excreta in ways that will prevent human, animal, and insect contact with it. Included are a variety of methods and devices, such as pit latrines and flush toilets with sewage hookups.

C4-1. Hospital beds: The World Health Organization defines hospitals as medical institutions permanently staffed at any given time by at least one physician. Hospital beds are all beds available in public, private, general, and specialized hospitals and rehabilitation centers. C4 presents figures for the total population; there are no figures for children's access to hospitals. The measure is included because it is a reflection of the general level of a nation's health care. Lack of accessibility to hospitals and clinics is a major problem in developing countries, and especially in rural areas, which weighs heavily on children. Without adequate clinic and hospital facilities, curable diseases and conditions go untreated, and invariably result in death. Even some industrialized and developed countries have inadequate health care services for certain portions of their population due to lack of geographic accessibility or prohibitive medical costs.

C5-1–C5-3. Health Care Professionals: The next three tables present absolute numbers and rate per 1,000 population for health care professionals—physicians, dentists, and nurses/midwives. These indicators are for total population; data are not available for rate of health care workers to child population. The figures are included because they give a snapshot of the level of development of a country's health care system. The ratio of health care professionals to population measures one of the most advanced features of the health care system: the extent of personnel dedicated to patient care needs.

C6-1. Births attended by skilled personnel: This indicator is based on national reports of the proportion of births attended by skilled health personnel or skilled attendant: doctors (specialist or non-specialist) and persons with midwifery skills who can diagnose and manage obstetrical complications as well as normal deliveries. The presence of a skilled attendant is a measure of the quality of care available to the mother and newborn.

C7-1–C7-19. Vaccination and immunization: Vaccination protects children against some of the most dangerous diseases of childhood—diphtheria, hepatitis B, measles, pertussis (whooping cough), polio, tuberculosis, and tetanus—saving millions of children's lives annually. The tables in this section give a broad overview of the status of immunization as well as a detailed picture of vaccination by disease. C7-1 provides figures on the percent of routinely administered vaccines that are financed by the national government. C7-2 is a summary of the state of vaccination, while C7-3 looks at the percent of children immunized by age one, the age by which WHO recommends all children should have been vaccinated. The next five tables present detailed figures on the percent of the population immunized against specific diseases over time. Although not dealing with children, C7-9 is a significant indicator of newborn health; it reports percentage of pregnant women fully immunized against tetanus. Maternal immunization protects children against neonatal tetanus resulting from unsanitary birth practices, such as cutting the umbilical cord with an unclean blade.

C8-1–C8-3. Vitamin and mineral supplements: Simple supplements can prevent many diseases that cripple or kill children. The three tables in this cluster highlight coverage for two of the most important supplements: vitamin A and iodized salt. Vitamin A deficiency blinds over 350,000 children a year. Iodine deficiency delays physical and mental development, adversely effecting not only the health of an individual but the physical and economic future of whole communities.

C9-1. Oral Rehydration Treatment (ORT): Diarrhea causes dehydration and malnutrition that leads to the death of over three million children each year. It is usually caused by poor hygiene, lack of clean drinking water, and overcrowding. Although diarrhea can be deadly, scientists have developed a simple, inexpensive way of controlling its effects through the use of Oral Rehydration Salts or homemade rehydration fluids. ORT saves millions of children's lives each year.

C10-1–C10-2. Food aid: Food aid is important in developing nations where poverty is severe or where natural disasters and civil unrest have disrupted agriculture and normal food distribution. C10-1 and C10-2 furnish statistics on food aid to children for selected countries with food shortages. The figures are for cereal and non-cereal aid. Cereal food aid is defined as cereal grain and products such as wheat, coarse grains, flour, and the cereal component of blended foods. Non-cereal food aid includes products such as skimmed milk powder, vegetable oil, butter oil, meat, fish, pulses (legumes like lentils, beans, and peas), sugar, and dried fruit.

C11-1. Breast-fed babies: For the first few months of a baby's life, breast milk alone is the best possible foods. UNICEF estimates that if every baby were exclusively breast-fed from birth an estimated 1.5 million lives would be saved each year. And not just saved, but enhanced. Breast milk protects babies from diarrhea and acute respiratory infections—two leading causes of infant death. It also contains hundreds of antibodies and enzymes needed for good health. Children who are breast-fed have lower rates of childhood cancers, including leukemia and lymphoma. They are less susceptible to pneumonia, asthma, allergies, childhood diabetes, gastrointestinal illnesses, and infections that can damage their hearing. Breast-feeding also has an economic benefit; the purchase of breast milk substitutes becomes a liability to the economies of developing countries, as imported substitutes are bought with scarce foreign exchange, siphoning it away from vital priorities.

C1. CENTRAL GOVERNMENT EXPENDITURES FOR HEALTH CARE

C1-1. Percent of Central Government Expenditure Allocated to Health, 1992–1998

	Percent
Albania	6
Angola	6
Argentina	3
Australia	14
Austria	13
Bahamas	15
Bahrain	10
Bangladesh	5
Belarus	4
Belgium	2
Belize	8
Benin	6
Bhutan	10
Bolivia	3
Botswana	5
Brazil	6
Bulgaria	6
Burkina Faso	7
Burundi	3
Cameroon	4
Canada	5
Chad	8
Chile	12
China	0
Colombia	5
Congo, Dem. Rep. (Zaire)	1
Costa Rica	22
Côte d'Ivoire	4
Croatia	14
Cuba	23
Cyprus	6
Czech Republic	18
Denmark	1
Dominican Republic	11
Ecuador	11
Egypt	3
El Salvador	10
Estonia	16
Ethiopia	5
Fiji	9
Finland	3
France	16
Gambia, the	7
Georgia	4
Germany	17
Ghana	7
Greece	7
Grenada	10
Guatemala	11
Guinea	3
Guinea-Bissau	1
Honduras	10
Hungary	6
Iceland	23
India	2
Indonesia	3
Iran	6
Ireland	15
Israel	14
Italy	11

C1-1. Percent of Central Government Expenditure Allocated to Health, 1992–1998 *(continued)*

	Percent
Jamaica	7
Japan	2
Jordan	9
Kenya	6
South Korea, Rep.	1
Kuwait	8
Latvia	11
Lebanon	2
Lesotho	13
Liberia	5
Lithuania	14
Luxembourg	2
Madagascar	7
Malawi	7
Malaysia	6
Maldives	11
Mali	2
Malta	9
Mauritania	4
Mauritius	8
Mexico	3
Mongolia	4
Morocco	3
Mozambique	5
Myanmar	4
Namibia	10
Nepal	7
Netherlands, the	15
New Zealand	16
Nicaragua	13
Nigeria	1
Norway	4
Oman	7
Pakistan	1
Panama	21
Papua New Guinea	9
Paraguay	7
Peru	5
Philippines	3
Poland	10
Portugal	9
Romania	7
Russia	2
Rwanda	5
Saint Vincent and the Grena	11
Saudi Arabia	6
Seychelles	8
Sierra Leone	10
Singapore	7
Somalia	1
Spain	6
Sri Lanka	5
Sweden	2
Switzerland	16
Syria	4
Tanzania	6
Thailand	9
Togo	5
Tonga	7
Trinidad and Tobago	9
Tunisia	7
Turkey	2

C1-1. Percent of Central Government Expenditure Allocated to Health, 1992–1998 *(continued)*

	Percent
Uganda	2
United Arab Emirates	7
United Kingdom	14
United States	20
Uruguay	6
Venezuela	10
Yemen	4
Zambia	10
Zimbabwe	8

Source: The State of the World's Children, 2000: Table 6. Economic indicators; <http://www.unicef.org/sowc00/stat4.htm>. Underlying data from United Nations Children's Fund (UNICEF).

C2. ACCESS TO SAFE WATER

C2-1. Percent of Population with Access to Safe Water, Total, Urban and Rural, 1999

	Percent of population using improved drinking water sources		
	Total	Urban	Rural
Afghanistan	13	19	11
Algeria	94	98	88
Andorra	100	100	100
Angola	38	34	40
Antigua and Barbuda	91	95	88
Argentina	79	85	30
Armenia	84	N/A	N/A
Australia	100	100	100
Austria	100	100	100
Bahamas, the	96	98	86
Bangladesh	97	99	97
Barbados	100	100	100
Belarus	100	100	100
Belize	76	83	69
Benin	63	74	55
Bhutan	62	86	60
Bolivia	79	93	55
Botswana	N/A	100	N/A
Brazil	83	89	58
Bulgaria	100	100	100
Burkina Faso	N/A	84	N/A
Burundi	N/A	96	N/A
Cambodia	30	53	25
Cameroon	62	82	42
Canada	100	100	99
Cape Verde	74	64	89
Central African Republic	60	80	46
Chad	27	31	26
Chile	94	99	66
China	75	94	66
Colombia	91	98	73
Comoros	96	98	95
Congo, Dem. Rep. (Zaire)	45	89	26
Congo, Rep.	51	71	17
Cook Islands	100	100	100
Costa Rica	98	98	98
Côte d'Ivoire	77	90	65
Croatia	95	N/A	N/A

C2-1. Percent of Population with Access to Safe Water, Total, Urban and Rural, 1999 *(continued)*

| | Percent of population using improved drinking water sources | | |
	Total	Urban	Rural
Cuba	95	99	82
Cyprus	100	100	100
Denmark	100	100	100
Djibouti	100	100	100
Dominica	97	100	90
Dominican Republic	79	83	70
Ecuador	71	81	51
Egypt	95	96	94
El Salvador	74	88	61
Equatorial Guinea	43	45	42
Eritrea	46	63	42
Ethiopia	24	77	13
Fiji	47	43	51
Finland	100	100	100
Gabon	70	73	55
Gambia, the	62	80	53
Georgia	76	89	61
Ghana	64	87	49
Grenada	94	97	93
Guatemala	92	97	88
Guinea	48	72	36
Guinea-Bissau	49	29	55
Guyana	94	98	91
Haiti	46	49	45
Honduras	90	97	82
Hungary	99	100	98
India	88	92	86
Indonesia	76	91	65
Iran	95	99	89
Iraq	85	96	48
Jamaica	71	81	59
Jordan	96	100	84
Kazakhstan	91	98	82
Kenya	49	87	31
Kiribati	47	82	25
Kyrgyzstan	77	98	66
Laos	90	59	100
Lebanon	100	100	100
Lesotho	91	98	88
Libya	72	72	68
Macedonia, FYRO	99	99	99
Madagascar	47	85	31
Malawi	57	95	44
Malaysia	95	96	90
Maldives	100	100	100
Mali	65	74	61
Malta	100	100	100
Mauritania	37	34	40
Mauritius	100	100	100
Mexico	86	94	63
Moldova	100	100	100
Monaco	100	100	100
Mongolia	60	77	30
Morocco	82	100	58
Mozambique	60	86	43
Myanmar (Burma)	68	88	60
Namibia	77	100	67

C2-1. Percent of Population with Access to Safe Water, Total, Urban and Rural, 1999 *(continued)*

	Percent of population using improved drinking water sources		
	Total	**Urban**	**Rural**
Nepal	81	85	80
Netherlands, the	100	100	100
New Zealand	N/A	100	N/A
Nicaragua	79	95	59
Niger	59	70	56
Nigeria	57	81	39
Niue	100	100	100
North Korea, Dem. Rep.	100	100	100
Norway	100	100	100
Oman	39	41	30
Pakistan	88	96	84
Palau	79	100	20
Panama	87	88	86
Papua New Guinea	42	88	32
Paraguay	79	95	58
Peru	77	87	51
Philippines	87	92	80
Romania	58	91	16
Russia	99	100	96
Rwanda	41	60	40
Saint Kitts and Nevis	98	N/A	N/A
Saint Lucia	98	N/A	N/A
Saint Vincent and Grenadines	93	N/A	N/A
Samoa	99	95	100
Saudi Arabia	95	100	64
Senegal	78	92	65
Sierra Leone	28	23	31
Singapore	100	100	na
Slovakia	100	100	100
Slovenia	100	100	100
Solomon Islands	71	94	65
South Africa	86	92	80
South Korea, Rep.	92	97	71
Sri Lanka	83	91	80
Sudan	75	86	69
Suriname	95	94	96
Sweden	100	100	100
Switzerland	100	100	100
Syria	80	94	64
Tanzania	54	80	42
Thailand	80	89	77
Togo	54	85	38
Tonga	100	100	100
Trinidad and Tobago	86	N/A	N/A
Turkey	83	82	84
Turkmenistan	58	91	31
Tuvalu	100	100	100
Uganda	50	72	46
United Kingdom	100	100	100
United States	100	100	100
Uruguay	98	98	93
Uzbekistan	85	96	78
Vanuatu	88	63	94
Venezuela	84	88	58
Vietnam	56	81	50
Yemen	69	85	64
Zambia	64	88	48
Zimbabwe	85	100	77

N/A Not Available.

Source: The State of the World's Children, 2001: Table 3. Health; <http://www.unicef.org/sowc01/stat4.htm>. Underlying data from United Nations Children's Fund (UNICEF).

C3. ACCESS TO SANITATION

C3-1. Percent of Population with Access to Adequate Sanitation, Total, Urban and Rural, 1999

	Percent of population using adequate sanitation facilities		
	Total	Urban	Rural
Afghanistan	12	25	8
Algeria	73	90	47
Andorra	100	100	100
Angola	44	70	30
Antigua and Barbuda	96	98	94
Argentina	85	89	48
Armenia	67	N/A	N/A
Australia	100	100	100
Austria	100	100	100
Bahamas, the	93	93	94
Bangladesh	53	82	44
Barbados	100	100	100
Belize	42	59	21
Benin	23	46	6
Bhutan	69	65	70
Bolivia	66	82	38
Brazil	72	81	32
Bulgaria	100	100	100
Burkina Faso	29	88	16
Burundi	N/A	79	N/A
Cambodia	18	58	10
Cameroon	92	99	85
Canada	100	100	99
Cape Verde	71	95	32
Central African Republic	31	43	23
Chad	29	81	13
Chile	97	98	93
China	38	68	24
Colombia	85	97	51
Comoros	98	98	98
Congo, Dem. Rep. (Zaire)	20	53	6
Congo, Rep.	N/A	14	N/A
Cook Islands	100	100	100
Costa Rica	96	98	95
Croatia	100	N/A	N/A
Cuba	95	96	91
Cyprus	100	100	100
Djibouti	91	99	50
Dominican Republic.	71	75	64
Ecuador	59	70	37
Egypt	94	98	91
El Salvador	83	88	78
Equatorial Guinea	53	60	46
Eritrea	13	66	1
Estonia	N/A	93	N/A
Ethiopia	15	58	6
Fiji	43	75	12
Finland	100	100	100
Gabon	21	25	4
Gambia, the	37	41	35
Georgia	99	99	99
Ghana	63	62	64
Grenada	97	96	97
Guatemala	85	98	76

C3-1. Percent of Population with Access to Adequate Sanitation, Total, Urban and Rural, 1999 *(continued)*

	Percent of population using adequate sanitation facilities		
	Total	**Urban**	**Rural**
Guinea	58	94	41
Guinea-Bissau	47	88	34
Guyana	87	97	81
Haiti	28	50	16
Honduras	77	94	57
Hungary	99	100	98
India	31	73	14
Indonesia	66	87	52
Iran	81	86	74
Iraq	79	93	31
Jamaica	84	98	66
Jordan	99	100	98
Kazakhstan	99	100	98
Kenya	86	96	81
Kiribati	48	54	44
Kyrgyzstan	100	100	100
Laos	46	84	34
Lebanon	99	100	87
Lesotho	92	93	92
Libya	97	97	96
Macedonia, FYRO	93	99	83
Madagascar	42	70	30
Malawi	77	96	70
Malaysia	98	99	98
Maldives	56	100	41
Mali	69	93	58
Malta	100	100	100
Mauritania	33	44	19
Mauritius	99	100	99
Mexico	73	87	32
Moldova	N/A	100	N/A
Monaco	100	100	100
Mongolia	30	46	2
Morocco	75	100	42
Mozambique	43	69	26
Myanmar (Burma)	46	65	39
Namibia	41	96	17
Nepal	27	75	20
Netherlands, the	100	100	100
Nicaragua	84	96	68
Niger	20	79	5
Nigeria	63	85	45
Niue	100	100	100
North Korea, Dem. Rep.	99	99	100
Oman	92	98	61
Pakistan	61	94	42
Palau	100	100	100
Panama	94	99	87
Papua New Guinea	82	92	80
Paraguay	95	95	95
Peru	76	90	40
Philippines	83	92	71
Romania	53	86	10
Rwanda	8	12	8
Saint Kitts and Nevis	96	N/A	N/A
Saint Vincent and Grenadines	96	N/A	N/A

C3-1. Percent of Population with Access to Adequate Sanitation, Total, Urban and Rural, 1999 *(continued)*

	Percent of population using adequate sanitation facilities		
	Total	**Urban**	**Rural**
Samoa	99	95	100
Saudi Arabia	100	100	100
Senegal	70	94	48
Sierra Leone	28	23	31
Singapore	100	100	na
Slovakia	100	100	100
Solomon Islands	34	98	18
South Africa	86	99	73
South Korea, Rep.	63	76	4
Sri Lanka	83	91	80
Sudan	62	87	48
Suriname	83	100	34
Sweden	100	100	100
Switzerland	100	100	100
Syria	90	98	81
Tanzania	90	98	86
Thailand	96	97	96
Togo	34	69	17
Trinidad and Tobago	88	N/A	N/A
Turkey	91	98	70
Turkmenistan	100	100	100
Tuvalu	100	100	100
Uganda	75	96	72
United Kingdom	100	100	100
United States	100	100	100
Uruguay	95	96	89
Uzbekistan	100	100	100
Vanuatu	100	100	100
Venezuela	74	75	69
Vietnam	73	86	70
Yemen	45	87	31
Zambia	78	99	64
Zimbabwe	68	99	51

N/A Not Available

Source: The State of the World's Children, 2001: Table 3. Health; <http://www.unicef.org/sowc01/stat4.htm>. Underlying data from United Nations Children's Fund (UNICEF).

C4. HOSPITAL BEDS

C4-1. Population per Hospital Bed, Selected Countries, 1995–1996

	People per hospital bed
Brazil	334
Bosnia and Herzegovina	320
Albania	313
Spain	250
Portugal	244
United States	244
South Korea, Rep.	228
United Kingdom	213
Georgia	208
Denmark	204
Ireland	201
Canada	196
Macedonia, FYRO	193
Yugoslavia	188
Malta	184
Slovenia	174
Israel	167
Poland	161
Sweden	159
Italy	156
Czech Republic	150
Slovakia	134
Romania	132
Armenia	131
Estonia	124
Uzbekistan	120
Kyrgyzstan	113
France	113
Hungary	111
Austria	107
Finland	107
Germany	103
Azerbaijan	101
Latvia	97
Kazakhstan	97
Lithuania	95
Bulgaria	94
Netherlands, the	88
Russia	85
Ukraine	85
Moldova	82
Belarus	81
Norway	75

Source: World Health Organization, Statistics (WHOSIS); <http://www.who.int/whosis>. Underlying data from World Health Organization (WHO).

C5. HEALTH CARE PROFESSIONALS

C5-1. Physicians, Number and Rate per 100,000, 1990s

	Year of survey	Number	Rate per 100,000
Albania	1995	4,848	141
Algeria	1993	22,202	83
Antigua and Barbuda	1992	49	76
Argentina	1992	87,226	268
Armenia	1994	11,077	312
Austria	1993	25,701	327
Azerbaijan	1994	29,112	390
Bahamas	1992	361	141
Bahrain	1993	59	11
Bangladesh	1994	21,319	18
Barbados	1992	290	113
Belarus	1994	38,506	379
Belgium	1993	36,681	365
Belize	1994	97	47
Benin	1992	318	6
Bhutan	1994	115	20
Bolivia	1992	3,432	51
Brazil	1992	202,541	134
Bulgaria	1994	29,396	333
Burundi	1993	333	6
Cambodia	1993	5,642	58
Cameroon	1993	909	7
Canada	1992	61,418	221
Cape Verde	1991-1993	103	29
Central African Republic	1991-1993	174	6
Chad	1994	144	2
Chile	1992	14,447	108
China	1993	1,372,471	115
Colombia	1994	35,640	105
Comoros	1992	58	10
Congo, Rep.	1995	688	27
Cook Islands	1994	21	111
Costa Rica	1992	3,824	126
Croatia	1994	9,058	201
Cuba	1992	55,395	518
Cyprus	1993	1,677	231
Czech Republic	1994	30,185	293
Denmark	1992	14,617	283
Djibouti	1995	115	20
Dominica	1992	33	46
Dominican Republic	1992	5,587	77
Ecuador	1992	11,657	111
Egypt	1995	127,121	202
El Salvador	1992	4,806	91
Equatorial Guinea	1995	83	21
Eritrea	1993	64	2
Estonia	1994	4,810	312
Ethiopia	1994	2,214	4
Fiji	1994	295	38
Finland	1994	13,686	269
France	1993	160,982	280
Gabon	1994	248	19
Gambia	1991-1993	17	2
Georgia	1994	23,770	436
Germany	1993	258,023	319
Ghana	1994	747	4

C5-1. Physicians, Number and Rate per 100,000, 1990s *(continued)*

	Year of survey	Number	Rate per 100,000
Greece	1993	40,150	387
Grenada	1992	46	50
Guatemala	1992	8,520	90
Guinea	1993	920	15
Guinea-Bissau	1994	187	18
Guyana	1992	264	33
Haiti	1992	1,059	16
Honduras	1992	1,106	22
Hungary	1994	34,283	337
India	1992	424,524	48
Indonesia	1993	22,234	12
Iraq	1993	9,922	51
Ireland	1993	5,893	167
Israel	1993	24,100	459
Jamaica	1992	1,349	57
Japan	1992	219,704	177
Jordan	1994	8,213	158
Kazakhstan	1994	61,360	360
Kenya	1992	3,554	15
Kiribati	1993	10	13
Kuwait	1995	2,754	178
Kyrgyzstan	1994	14,451	310
Latvia	1994	7,821	303
Lebanon	1994	5,568	191
Lesotho	1993	93	5
Libya	1993	6,916	137
Lithuania	1994	14,804	399
Luxembourg	1993	841	213
Macedonia, FYRO	1993	4,644	219
Madagascar	1995	3,614	24
Malawi	1993	257	2
Malaysia	1993	8,279	43
Maldives	1993	45	19
Mali	1995	413	4
Malta	1993	901	250
Mauritania	1993	233	11
Mauritius	1992	916	85
Mexico	1992	92,390	107
Micronesia	1992	46	46
Monaco	1992	93	300
Mongolia	1992	6,053	268
Morocco	1994	9,006	34
Myanmar (Burma)	1995	13,214	28
Namibia	1992	330	23
Nepal	1995	1,162	5
New Zealand	1994	7,521	210
Nicaragua	1992	3,122	82
Niger	1992	225	3
Nigeria	1992	21,325	21
Niue	1994	2	200
Oman	1995	2,596	120
Pakistan	1994	71,055	52
Panama	1992	2,908	119
Papua New Guinea	1993	736	18
Paraguay	1992	2,977	67
Peru	1992	16,070	73
Philippines	1992	7,107	11
Portugal	1993	28,658	291

C5-1. Physicians, Number and Rate per 100,000, 1990s *(continued)*

	Year of survey	Number	Rate per 100,000
Qatar	1992	739	143
Republic of Moldova	1994	15,754	356
Romania	1994	40,453	176
Russia	1994	560,478	380
Saint Kitts and Nevis	1992	37	89
Saint Lucia	1992	47	35
Saint Vincent and the Grenadines	1992	49	46
Samoa	1992	60	38
Sao Tome and Principe	1992	40	32
Saudi Arabia	1994	28,969	166
Senegal	1992	520	7
Seychelles	1993	75	104
Singapore	1994	4,301	147
Slovakia	1992	17,192	325
Slovenia	1994	4,252	219
Somalia	1993	358	4
South Africa	1992	22,908	59
South Korea, Rep.	1992	55,229	127
Spain	1992	157,887	400
Sri Lanka	1994	4,114	23
Sudan	1994	2,736	10
Suriname	1992	162	40
Sweden	1993	26,026	299
Switzerland	1992	21,021	301
Syria	1995	15,980	109
Tajikistan	1994	12,479	210
Tanzania	1994	1,205	4
Thailand	1993	13,532	24
Togo	1994	225	6
Trinidad and Tobago	1992	1,126	90
Tunisia	1995	5,960	67
Turkey	1993	61,158	103
Turkmenistan	1994	14,165	353
Tuvalu	1993	8	89
Uganda	1991-1993	722	4
Ukraine	1994	220,939	429
United Arab Emirates	1994	3,126	168
United Kingdom	1993	94,955	164
United States	1992	612,314	245
Uruguay	1992	9,616	309
Uzbekistan	1994	74,874	335
Venezuela	1992	38,753	194
Yemen	1995	3,770	26
Zimbabwe	1995	1,632	14

Source: World Health Organization, Statistics (WHOSIS); <http://www.who.int/whosis>. Underlying data from World Health Organization (WHO).

C5-2. Dentists, Number and Rate per 100,000, 1990s

	Year of survey	Number	Rate per 100,000
Albania	1993	1,322	39
Antigua and Barbuda	1990-1995	11	17
Argentina	1990-1995	22,029	66
Armenia	1994	982	28
Austria	1992	2,973	38
Azerbaijan	1994	2,364	32
Bahamas	1990-1995	58	22
Bahrain	1993	64	12
Bangladesh	1992	448	0
Barbados	1990-1995	34	13
Belarus	1994	5,421	53
Belize	1994	17	8
Benin	1992	15	0
Bhutan	1994	7	0
Bolivia	1990-1995	414	6
Botswana	1992	14	1
Brazil	1990-1995	118,442	77
Brunei	1991-1993	27	10
Bulgaria	1994	5,797	66
Burkina Faso	1992	17	0
Burundi	1991-1993	12	0
Cambodia	1992	71	1
Cameroon	1992	17	0
Canada	1990-1995	15,098	53
Cape Verde	1992	3	1
Central African Republic	1991-1993	6	0
Chad	1994	2	0
Chile	1990-1995	5,984	44
Colombia	1994	21,418	62
Comoros	1992	4	1
Cook Islands	1994	7	37
Costa Rica	1990-1995	1,213	38
Croatia	1994	2,320	52
Cuba	1990-1995	8,952	83
Cyprus	1993	581	80
Czech Republic	1994	6,112	59
Djibouti	1995	12	2
Dominica	1990-1995	1	1
Dominican Republic	1990-1995	518	7
Ecuador	1990-1995	1,504	14
Egypt	1995	15,733	25
El Salvador	1990-1995	1,133	21
Equatorial Guinea	1993	3	1
Estonia	1994	843	55
Ethiopia	1992	16	0
Fiji	1994	36	5
Finland	1992	4,606	92
France	1992	38,376	67
Gabon	1994	4	0
Gambia	1994	3	0
Georgia	1994	80	1
Germany	1992	56,183	70
Ghana	1992	95	1
Greece	1992	10,425	101
Grenada	1990-1995	6	7
Guatemala	1990-1995	1,267	13
Guinea	1993	36	1
Guinea-Bissau	1992	2	0

C5-2. Dentists, Number and Rate per 100,000, 1990s *(continued)*

	Year of survey	Number	Rate per 100,000
Guyana	1990-1995	8	1
Haiti	1990-1995	135	2
Honduras	1990-1995	1,140	22
India	1992	10,751	1
Indonesia	1993	5,321	3
Iraq	1993	1,945	10
Ireland	1992	1,131	32
Israel	1993	6,886	131
Italy	1992	10,814	19
Jamaica	1990-1995	215	9
Jordan	1994	1,975	38
Kazakhstan	1994	2,222	13
Kenya	1992	664	3
Kuwait	1995	418	27
Kyrgyzstan	1994	1,261	27
Latvia	1994	982	38
Lebanon	1994	2,565	88
Libya	1993	606	12
Lithuania	1994	1,847	50
Macedonia, FYRO	1993	1,106	52
Madagascar	1991-1993	283	2
Malawi	1993	29	0
Malaysia	1992	1,501	8
Maldives	1992	4	2
Malta	1993	109	30
Mauritania	1993	20	1
Mauritius	1992	141	13
Mexico	1990-1995	5,291	6
Monaco	1992	40	129
Morocco	1994	1,324	5
Myanmar (Burma)	1992	970	2
Namibia	1992	51	4
New Zealand	1991-1993	1,287	37
Nicaragua	1990-1995	475	12
Niger	1992	15	0
Nigeria	1992	2,995	3
Oman	1995	151	7
Pakistan	1995	9,835	7
Panama	1990-1995	548	22
Paraguay	1990-1995	1,372	30
Peru	1990-1995	1,347	6
Philippines	1992	1,614	3
Poland	1993	18,309	48
Qatar	1992	109	21
Republic of Moldova	1994	1,958	44
Romania	1994	5,999	26
Russia	1994	65,000	44
Rwanda	1992	9	0
Saint Kitts and Nevis	1990-1995	8	18
Saint Lucia	1990-1995	8	6
Saint Vincent and the Grenadines	1990-1995	5	5
Sao Tome and Principe	1992	5	4
Saudi Arabia	1994	2,618	15
Senegal	1992	115	1
Seychelles	1993	13	18
Singapore	1992	806	29
Slovakia	1992	2,580	49
Slovenia	1994	1,030	53

C5-2. Dentists, Number and Rate per 100,000, 1990s *(continued)*

	Year of survey	Number	Rate per 100,000
Somalia	1994	9	0
South Africa	1992	3,768	10
South Korea, Rep.	1993	19,059	43
Sri Lanka	1992	381	2
Sudan	1994	274	1
Suriname	1990-1995	41	10
Swaziland	1992	3	0
Switzerland	1992	3,420	49
Syria	1995	8,210	56
Tajikistan	1994	960	16
Tanzania	1992	83	0
Trinidad and Tobago	1990-1995	139	11
Tunisia	1995	1,068	12
Turkey	1993	11,091	19
Turkmenistan	1994	810	20
Tuvalu	1991-1993	1	11
Uganda	1991-1993	21	0
Ukraine	1994	18,769	36
United Arab Emirates	1994	502	27
United Kingdom	1992	23,004	40
United States	1990-1995	160,770	63
Uruguay	1990-1995	3,474	111
Uzbekistan	1994	4,329	19
Venezuela	1990-1995	10,223	50
Yemen	1995	145	1
Zimbabwe	1993	138	1

Source: World Health Organization, Statistics (WHOSIS); <http://www.who.int/whosis>. Underlying data from World Health Organization (WHO).

C5-3. Nurses/Midwives, Number and Rate per 100,000, 1990s

	Year of survey	Number	Rate per 100,000
Albania	1995	14,559	423
Antigua and Barbuda	1993	151	233
Argentina	1993	18,241	54
Armenia	1994	29,491	831
Austria	1995	42,197	530
Azerbaijan	1994	80,737	1081
Bahamas	1993	691	258
Bahrain	1994	1,587	289
Bangladesh	1995	6,491	5
Barbados	1993	840	323
Belarus	1995	117,668	1160
Belize	1994	160	76
Benin	1992	1,622	33
Bhutan	1994	91	6
Bolivia	1993	1,766	25
Brazil	1993	64,159	41
Bulgaria	1994	57,493	652
Burundi	1992	986	17
Cambodia	1993	13,185	136
Canada	1993	276,067	958
Cape Verde	1992	205	57
Central African Republic	1992	1,374	45
Chad	1994	365	6
Chile	1993	5,805	42
China	1993	1,056,096	88

C5-3. Nurses/Midwives, Number and Rate per 100,000, 1990s *(continued)*

	Year of survey	Number	Rate per 100,000
Colombia	1994	16,927	49
Comoros	1992	191	33
Congo, Rep.	1992	1,158	49
Cook Islands	1994	102	537
Costa Rica	1993	3,107	95
Croatia	1994	21,149	470
Cuba	1993	81,780	752
Cyprus	1993	3,086	425
Czech Republic	1995	97,204	944
Dominica	1993	187	263
Dominican Republic	1993	1,509	20
Ecuador	1993	3,733	34
Egypt	1995	139,707	222
El Salvador	1993	2,096	38
Equatorial Guinea	1993	129	34
Estonia	1995	9,736	636
Ethiopia	1993	4,209	8
Fiji	1994	1,661	215
Finland	1995	111,535	2184
France	1992	224,679	392
Gabon	1994	722	56
Gambia	1992	250	25
Georgia	1994	47,011	863
Greece	1992	28,682	278
Grenada	1993	220	239
Guatemala	1993	3,009	30
Guinea	1993	202	3
Guinea-Bissau	1994	476	45
Guyana	1993	718	88
Haiti	1993	896	13
Honduras	1993	907	17
Indonesia	1993	128,066	67
Iraq	1993	12,451	64
Israel	1995	37,772	671
Jamaica	1993	1,664	69
Japan	1992	795,810	641
Jordan	1994	11,644	224
Kazakhstan	1995	149,482	874
Kenya	1992	5,879	23
Kiribati	1993	147	193
Kuwait	1995	7,240	468
Kyrgyzstan	1994	41,000	879
Latvia	1995	16,047	628
Lebanon	1994	3,556	122
Lesotho	1993	650	33
Libya	1993	18,476	366
Lithuania	1995	36,143	977
Macedonia, FYRO	1993	7,074	334
Madagascar	1992	7,398	55
Malawi	1993	638	6
Malaysia	1993	30,821	160
Maldives	1994	31	13
Mali	1992	918	9
Malta	1993	4,292	1189
Mauritania	1993	574	27
Mauritius	1992	2,598	241
Mexico	1993	36,011	40
Micronesia	1992	373	327

C5-3. Nurses/Midwives, Number and Rate per 100,000, 1990s *(continued)*

	Year of survey	Number	Rate per 100,000
Monaco	1992	460	1484
Mongolia	1992	10,278	452
Morocco	1994	24,899	94
Myanmar (Burma)	1995	20,223	43
Namibia	1992	1,153	81
Nepal	1995	1,189	5
New Zealand	1994	44,102	1249
Nicaragua	1993	2,304	56
Niger	1992	1,379	17
Nigeria	1992	144,952	142
Niue	1994	20	1000
Oman	1995	6,273	290
Pakistan	1994	43,726	32
Panama	1993	2,487	98
Papua New Guinea	1993	3,967	97
Paraguay	1993	470	10
Peru	1993	11,214	49
Philippines	1992	27,274	43
Portugal	1994	29,855	304
Qatar	1992	1,830	354
Republic of Moldova	1995	45,185	1020
Romania	1994	98,610	430
Russia	1994	971,465	659
Saint Kitts and Nevis	1993	248	590
Saint Lucia	1993	246	177
Saint Vincent and the Grenadines	1993	206	187
Samoa	1992	307	186
Saudi Arabia	1994	60,729	348
Senegal	1992	2,711	35
Seychelles	1993	300	417
Singapore	1994	11,735	416
Slovenia	1995	13,359	686
Solomon Islands	1992	484	141
Somalia	1993	269	3
South Africa	1992	67,843	175
South Korea, Rep.	1992	101,391	232
Sri Lanka	1992	19,791	112
Sudan	1994	19,153	70
Suriname	1993	940	227
Sweden	1994	91,580	1048
Syria	1995	31,081	212
Tajikistan	1994	43,795	738
Tanzania	1992	12,509	46
Thailand	1993	57,194	99
Togo	1994	1,259	31
Trinidad and Tobago	1993	2,147	168
Tunisia	1995	25,176	283
Turkey	1993	89,872	151
Turkmenistan	1994	47,901	1195
Tuvalu	1993	39	433
Uganda	1992	5,351	28
Ukraine	1994	622,997	1211
United Arab Emirates	1994	5,974	321
United States	1993	2,264,582	878
Uruguay	1993	1,921	61
Uzbekistan	1994	230,725	1032
Venezuela	1993	16,103	77
Yemen	1995	7,396	51
Zimbabwe	1993	17,654	164

Source: World Health Organization, Statistics (WHOSIS); <http://www.who.int/whosis>. Underlying data from World Health Organization (WHO).

C6. BIRTHS ATTENDED BY SKILLED PERSONNEL

C6-1. Percent of Births Attended by Trained Health Personnel,* 1990–1999

	% of births attended by trained health personnel
Afghanistan	8
Albania	99
Algeria	77
Antigua and Barbuda	100
Argentina	97
Armenia	96
Australia	100
Austria	100
Azerbaijan	99
Bahamas	100
Bahrain	98
Bangladesh	8
Barbados	100
Belarus	100
Belgium	100
Belize	77
Benin	60
Bhutan	15
Bolivia	59
Bosnia and Herzegovina	97
Botswana	78
Brazil	92
Brunei	98
Bulgaria	100
Burkina Faso	27
Burundi	24
Cambodia	31
Cameroon	58
Canada	100
Cape Verde	54
Central African Republic	46
Chad	15
Chile	100
China	89
Colombia	85
Comoros	52
Cook Islands	99
Costa Rica	98
Côte d'Ivoire	47
Cuba	99
Cyprus	100
Czech Republic	99
Denmark	100
Djibouti	79
Dominica	98
Dominican Republic	99
Ecuador	64
Egypt	56
El Salvador	87
Equatorial Guinea	5
Eritrea	21
Ethiopia	8
Finland	100
France	99
Gabon	80
Gambia	44
Germany	100
Ghana	39
Greece	99

C6-1. Percent of Births Attended by Trained Health Personnel,* 1990–1999 *(continued)*

	% of births attended by trained health personnel
Grenada	99
Guatemala	35
Guinea	31
Guinea-Bissau	25
Guyana	95
Haiti	21
Honduras	55
Hungary	99
Iceland	100
India	34
Indonesia	43
Iran	86
Iraq	54
Ireland	100
Israel	99
Italy	100
Jamaica	95
Japan	100
Jordan	97
Kazakhstan	100
Kenya	44
Kiribati	72
Kuwait	98
Kyrgyzstan	98
Laos	14
Latvia	100
Lebanon	89
Lesotho	50
Liberia	58
Libya	94
Luxembourg	100
Macedonia, FYRO	95
Madagascar	47
Malawi	55
Malaysia	99
Maldives	90
Mali	24
Malta	98
Mauritania	40
Mauritius	97
Mexico	68
Micronesia	90
Mongolia	100
Morocco	43
Mozambique	44
Myanmar (Burma)	56
Namibia	68
Nepal	9
Netherlands, the	100
New Zealand	95
Nicaragua	65
Niger	18
Nigeria	31
Niue	99
North Korea, Dem. Rep.	100
Norway	100
Oman	91
Pakistan	18
Palau	99
Panama	86
Papua New Guinea	53

C6-1. Percent of Births Attended by Trained Health Personnel,* 1990–1999 *(continued)*

	% of births attended by trained health personnel
Paraguay	61
Peru	56
Philippines	56
Poland	99
Portugal	98
Qatar	98
Romania	99
Russia	99
Rwanda	26
Saint Kitts and Nevis	100
Saint Lucia	100
Saint Vincent and Grenadines	96
Samoa	76
Sao Tome and Principe	86
Saudi Arabia	90
Senegal	47
Seychelles	99
Singapore	100
Slovenia	100
Solomon Islands	85
Somalia	2
South Africa	82
South Korea, Rep.	98
Spain	96
Sri Lanka	94
Sudan	69
Suriname	91
Swaziland	56
Sweden	100
Switzerland	99
Syria	67
Tajikistan	79
Tanzania	38
Thailand	71
Togo	51
Tonga	92
Trinidad and Tobago	98
Tunisia	81
Turkey	81
Turkmenistan	96
Tuvalu	100
Uganda	38
Ukraine	100
United Arab Emirates	99
United Kingdom	98
United States	99
Uruguay	96
Uzbekistan	98
Vanuatu	79
Viet Nam	77
Yemen	22
Yugoslavia	93
Zambia	47
Zimbabwe	69

*Doctors, nurses, midwives, medical assistants, or other primary health care workers trained to give the necessary supervision, care, and advice to women during pregnency labor, and after delivery, to conduct deliveries on their own, and to care for the newborn and the infant, irrespective of outcome (live birth or fetal death).

Source: The State of the World's Children, 2000: Table 7. Women; <http://www.unicef.org/sowc00/stat4.htm>. Underlying data from United Nations Children's Fund (UNICEF).

C7. VACCINATION AND IMMUNIZATION

C7-1. Percent of Routine Childhood Vaccines Financed by Government for the Extended Programme of Immunization (EPI),* Selected Countries, 1995–1998

	Percent financed
Algeria	100
Antigua and Barbuda	100
Argentina	100
Bahamas	100
Bahrain	100
Bangladesh	100
Barbados	100
Belize	100
Botswana	100
Brazil	100
Burkina Faso	100
Cape Verde	100
Chad	100
Chile	100
China	100
Colombia	100
Costa Rica	100
Croatia	100
Dominica	100
Ecuador	100
Egypt	100
El Salvador	100
Ghana	100
Grenada	100
Guatemala	100
Guyana	100
Honduras	100
Indonesia	100
Iran	100
Jamaica	100
Jordan	100
Kiribati	100
Kuwait	100
Malaysia	100
Mali	100
Marshall Islands	100
Mauritius	100
Mexico	100
Morocco	100
Namibia	100
Nicaragua	100
Nigeria	100
Oman	100
Pakistan	100
Panama	100
Papua New Guinea	100
Peru	100
Philippines	100
Qatar	100
Romania	100
Russia	100
Saint Kitts and Nevis	100
Saint Lucia	100
Saint Vincent and Grenadines	100

C7-1. Percent of Routine Childhood Vaccines Financed by Government for the Extended Programme of Immunization (EPI),* Selected Countries, 1995–1998 *(continued)*

	Percent financed
Samoa	100
Saudi Arabia	100
Senegal	100
South Africa	100
Sri Lanka	100
Suriname	100
Swaziland	100
Syria	100
Thailand	100
Trinidad and Tobago	100
Tunisia	100
Turkey	100
United Arab Emirates	100
Uruguay	100
Venezuela	100
Yugoslavia	100
Zimbabwe	100
India	98
Cuba	97
Dominican Republic	96
Côte d'Ivoire	95
Equatorial Guinea	95
Vanuatu	90
Kazakhstan	80
Niger	80
Togo	80
Belarus	78
Iraq	75
Lebanon	75
Paraguay	75
Vietnam	73
Tuvalu	70
Bolivia	65
Solomon Islands	60
Nepal	53
Cook Islands	50
Fiji	50
Tonga	50
Uganda	50
Seychelles	43
Uzbekistan	42
Mongolia	40
Yemen	38
Turkmenistan	36
Gambia	30
Maldives	30
Moldova	29
Cameroon	27
Guinea	25
Haiti	25
Lesotho	25
Niue	25
Benin	15
Ethiopia	15
Macedonia, FYRO	10
Madagascar	10
Sudan	10

C7-1. Percent of Routine Childhood Vaccines Financed by Government for the Extended Programme of Immunization (EPI),* Selected Countries, 1995–1998 *(continued)*

	Percent financed
Tanzania	10
Zambia	10
Armenia	7
Micronesia	5
Central African Republic	4
Kenya	3
Sierra Leone	3
Burundi	2
Libya	2
Malawi	2
Ukraine	1
Afghanistan	0
Albania	0
Angola	0
Azerbaijan	0
Bhutan	0
Bosnia and Herzegovina	0
Cambodia	0
Congo	0
Eritrea	0
Georgia	0
Guinea-Bissau	0
Laos	0
Liberia	0
Mauritania	0
Mozambique	0
Myanmar (Burma)	0
Rwanda	0
Somalia	0
Tajikistan	0

*The immunizations in this programme include those against TB, DPT, polio and measles, as well as protecting babies against neonatal tetanus by vaccination of pregnant women. Other vaccines (e.g., against hepatitis B or yellow fever) may be included in the Programme in some countries.

Source: The State of the World's Children, 2000 Table 3. Health; <http://www.unicef.org/sowc00/stat4.htm>. Underlying data from United Nations Children's Fund (UNICEF).

C7-2. Immunization Coverage, All Vaccines,* Selected Countries, 1980–1998

	1980	1985	1990	1995	1998
Afghanistan	48	57	77	N/A	147
Albania	N/A	282	94	374	432
Algeria	N/A	N/A	204	289	250
American Samoa	128	N/A	94	178	267
Angola	N/A	127	130	209	232
Anguilla	86	279	297	290	387
Antigua and Barbuda	36	169	287	N/A	200
Argentina	211	225	282	288	291
Armenia	N/A	N/A	270	273	285
Australia	17	68	158	173	172
Austria	N/A	130	150	150	N/A
Azerbaijan	N/A	N/A	259	N/A	292
Bahamas	35	163	172	176	180
Bahrain	208	139	223	337	454

C7-2. Immunization Coverage, All Vaccines,* Selected Countries, 1980–1998 *(continued)*

	1980	1985	1990	1995	1998
Bangladesh	2	7	315	375	328
Barbados	160	171	272	185	190
Belarus	N/A	N/A	277	284	294
Belgium	N/A	N/A	180	177	N/A
Belize	107	191	258	258	264
Benin	N/A	66	271	348	321
Bermuda	39	104	125	178	N/A
Bhutan	68	157	313	339	411
Bolivia	58	75	151	259	240
Bosnia and Herzegovina	N/A	N/A	N/A	N/A	265
Botswana	133	231	201	331	342
Brazil	211	209	249	271	343
British Virgin Islands	95	161	297	297	295
Brunei	162	330	291	N/A	446
Bulgaria	N/A	297	296	384	387
Burkina Faso	N/A	59	65	282	N/A
Burundi	N/A	18	314	223	162
Cambodia	N/A	N/A	125	286	234
Cameroon	N/A	N/A	134	166	196
Canada	N/A	N/A	N/A	96	171
Cape Verde	N/A	157	353	223	280
Cayman Islands	47	240	267	269	371
Chad	N/A	N/A	24	139	149
Chile	260	273	272	285	373
China	N/A	225	295	290	291
Colombia	91	190	270	289	363
Comoros	N/A	28	357	297	248
Congo, Dem. Rep. (Zaire)	121	214	156	105	73
Congo, Rep.	N/A	156	309	194	N/A
Cook Islands	68	289	355	371	403
Costa Rica	226	238	277	277	369
Cote d'Ivoire	N/A	N/A	56	212	307
Croatia	N/A	N/A	N/A	280	277
Cuba	246	271	286	294	296
Cyprus	64	N/A	N/A	247	N/A
Czech Republic	N/A	N/A	N/A	194	290
Denmark	N/A	N/A	181	185	N/A
Djibouti	N/A	125	345	234	95
Dominica	118	272	288	N/A	296
Dominican Republic	112	114	254	241	295
Ecuador	120	192	244	241	269
Egypt	234	246	324	430	448
El Salvador	169	175	253	286	297
Equatorial Guinea	N/A	59	N/A	287	N/A
Eritrea	N/A	N/A	N/A	121	217
Estonia	254	264	261	269	278
Ethiopia	7	33	173	182	205
Fiji	182	225	265	375	N/A
Finland	N/A	N/A	278	298	N/A
France	N/A	37	236	N/A	N/A
French Polynesia	N/A	250	239	286	N/A
Gabon	N/A	184	336	215	N/A
Gambia	N/A	375	444	377	474
Georgia	N/A	N/A	252	265	273
Germany	N/A	105	215	N/A	N/A
Ghana	35	N/A	192	215	231
Greece	90	173	172	227	N/A
Grenada	32	126	154	165	192

C7-2. Immunization Coverage, All Vaccines,* Selected Countries, 1980–1998 *(continued)*

	1980	1985	1990	1995	1998
Guam	N/A	155	113	275	364
Guatemala	102	74	231	242	260
Guinea	N/A	N/A	116	286	231
Guinea-Bissau	N/A	96	234	254	N/A
Guyana	110	215	237	257	282
Haiti	43	110	143	115	131
Honduras	102	176	297	280	377
Hong Kong SAR, China	260	191	345	353	352
Hungary	296	198	297	300	299.7629
Iceland	N/A	N/A	198	197	N/A
India	33	106	369	345	218
Indonesia	68	117	332	409	238
Iran	85	227	333	391	466
Iraq	131	N/A	324	413	289
Ireland	72	233	81	N/A	N/A
Israel	232	178	180	N/A	372.1966
Italy	N/A	12	201	243	246
Jamaica	72	173	254	277	257
Japan	69	158	241	190	N/A
Jordan	93	145	179	250	282
Kazakhstan	N/A	N/A	270	279	348
Kenya	N/A	255	184	300	274
Kiribati	76	83	392	226	420
Kuwait	127	188	47	320	394
Kyrgyzstan	N/A	N/A	296	289	290
Laos	N/A	20	94	226	226
Latvia	N/A	N/A	282	258	346.7108
Lebanon	N/A	83	121	179	187
Lesotho	N/A	N/A	243	205	N/A
Liberia	N/A	6	N/A	568	120
Libya	215	206	230	287	290
Lithuania	N/A	N/A	260	280	357
Luxembourg	N/A	N/A	170	N/A	N/A
Macao	N/A	119	294	395	428
Macedonia, FYRO	N/A	N/A	N/A	308	N/A
Madagascar	21	101	257	235	243
Malawi	176	205	344	363	364
Malaysia	190	257	340	180	442
Maldives	9	140	378	386	430
Mali	N/A	N/A	204	201	196
Malta	N/A	159	243	N/A	323
Marshall Islands	N/A	N/A	190	297	N/A
Mauritania	N/A	12	197	224	N/A
Mauritius	177	243	307	338	352
Mexico	174	147	244	280	291
Micronesia	N/A	N/A	178	303	292
Moldova	N/A	N/A	N/A	314	389
Monaco	N/A	N/A	300	189	N/A
Mongolia	160	170	260	354	372
Montserrat	59	237	297	297	300
Morocco	N/A	158	320	349	307
Mozambique	N/A	151	185	242	305
Myanmar (Burma)	12	68	260	332	342
Namibia	N/A	N/A	50	262	292
Nauru	N/A	154	167	191	N/A
Nepal	23	135	268	232	294
Netherlands Antilles	N/A	N/A	N/A	N/A	N/A
Netherlands, the	187	189	191	191	289

C7-2. Immunization Coverage, All Vaccines,* Selected Countries, 1980–1998 *(continued)*

	1980	1985	1990	1995	1998
New Caledonia	N/A	159	N/A	370	181
New Zealand	80	104	110	259	331
Nicaragua	69	226	253	276	305
Niger	N/A	N/A	111	179	193
Nigeria	N/A	43	239	151	104
Niue	238	93	N/A	316	300
North Korea, Dem. Rep.	129	209	394	388	180
Norway	N/A	180	171	N/A	N/A
Oman	130	305	389	450	488
Pakistan	9	103	292	224	310
Palau	N/A	N/A	100	300	288
Panama	176	248	282	269	306
Papua New Guinea	141	176	323	255	194
Paraguay	93	242	291	251	245
Peru	94	170	220	288	374
Philippines	133	201	316	311	295
Poland	281	281	288	N/A	N/A
Portugal	72	181	262	289	439
Qatar	91	209	258	364	463
Romania	N/A	180	274	287	296
Russia	N/A	N/A	241	282	292.3343
Rwanda	N/A	212	257	355	N/A
Saint Helena	N/A	N/A	400	400	N/A
Saint Kitts and Nevis	76	180	198	198	398
Saint Lucia	85	212	270	290	263
Saint Vincent The Grenadines	26	264	287	295	300
Samoa	101	290	344	482	498
Sao Tome & Principe	N/A	208	326	288	242
Saudi Arabia	91	79	336	441	440
Senegal	N/A	134	251	289	294
Seychelles	N/A	271	383	494	484
Sierra Leone	88	N/A	337	174	245
Singapore	215	249	342	369	386
Slovakia	N/A	N/A	296	295	291
Slovenia	N/A	N/A	N/A	N/A	281
Solomon Islands	108	111	296	353	260
Somalia	23	101	N/A	N/A	169
South Africa	N/A	217	214	269	82
South Korea, Rep.	93	216	239	293	317
Spain	N/A	152	191	N/A	N/A
Sri Lanka	159	197	318	350	353
Sudan	3	29	267	316	271
Suriname	24	158	146	160	172
Swaziland	N/A	187	347	384	378
Sweden	N/A	204	194	207	N/A
Switzerland	N/A	N/A	188	N/A	N/A
Syria	62	109	332	422	438
Tajikistan	N/A	N/A	273	259	288
Tanzania	143	257	302	281	230
Thailand	115	164	335	462	N/A
Togo	N/A	N/A	278	191	155
Tokelau	30	43	377	347	500
Tonga	119	284	437	460	482
Trinidad and Tobago	38	108	168	180	340
Tunisia	169	225	299	320	424
Turcs and Caicos Islands	116	229	278	297	299
Turkey	164	N/A	175	229	N/A
Turkmenistan	N/A	N/A	263	282	297

C7-2. Immunization Coverage, All Vaccines,* Selected Countries, 1980–1998 *(continued)*

	1980	1985	1990	1995	1998
Tuvalu	122	303	370	375	457
Uganda	N/A	72	282	328	184
Ukraine	N/A	N/A	261	289	378
United Arab Emirates	60	117	N/A	368	383
United Kingdom	N/A	N/A	179	N/A	184
United States	181	193	N/A	338	363
Uruguay	183	209	293	280	261
Uzbekistan	N/A	N/A	266	N/A	292
Vanuatu	N/A	155	283	285	433
Venezuela	217	115	206	242	363
Viet Nam	N/A	131	279	368	436
Wallis & Futuna Islands	60	183	N/A	291	471
West Bank and Gaza	N/A	N/A	N/A	392	396
Yemen	12	44	278	189	237
Yugoslavia	N/A	266	251	236	N/A
Zambia	N/A	N/A	235	350	N/A
Zimbabwe	N/A	286	271	274	266

*Includes BCG (Bacille Calmette Guerin), HepB3 (hepatitis type B vaccine), Hib3 (haemophilus influenza type B), MCV, Pol3 (polio vaccine), TT2plus (tetanus toxoid), YFV (yellow fever vaccine)
N/A Not Available

Source: Vaccine Preventable Diseases Monitoring System, *1999 Global Summary,* Division of Vaccines and Biologicals of the WHO; <http://www.who.int/vaccines-surveillance/Coverage_03May00.xls>. Underlying data from World Health Organization (WHO).

C7-3. Percent of 1-Year-Old Children Fully Immunized Against Tuberculosis, Diphtheria, Pertussis, Tetanus, Polio, and Measles, Selected Countries, 1995–1998

	Percent fully immunized			
	TB*	DPT**	Polio	Measles
Afghanistan	33	34	35	36
Albania	87	96	97	89
Algeria	95	80	80	75
Andorra	N/A	90	90	90
Angola	71	36	36	65
Antigua and Barbuda	N/A	100	100	100
Argentina	99	83	88	99
Armenia	95	82	96	94
Australia	N/A	86	86	86
Austria	N/A	90	95	90
Azerbaijan	96	97	98	98
Bahamas	N/A	89	88	93
Bahrain	72	98	98	100
Bangladesh	91	68	68	62
Barbados	N/A	93	93	92
Belarus	98	97	98	98
Belgium	N/A	62	72	64
Belize	93	87	87	84
Benin	92	81	81	82
Bhutan	94	86	85	71
Bolivia	85	42	33	51
Bosnia and Herzegovina	99	87	90	80
Botswana	66	82	73	80
Brazil	99	94	96	96
Brunei	96	97	98	100
Bulgaria	98	96	97	95
Burkina Faso	72	37	42	46

C7-3. Percent of 1-Year-Old Children Fully Immunized Against Tuberculosis, Diphtheria, Pertussis, Tetanus, Polio, and Measles, Selected Countries, 1995–1998 *(continued)*

	Percent fully immunized			
	TB*	DPT**	Polio	Measles
Burundi	58	50	51	44
Cambodia	76	64	64	63
Cameroon	72	46	42	44
Canada	N/A	97	N/A	96
Cape Verde	84	80	79	66
Central African Republic	53	46	47	39
Chad	43	24	24	30
Chile	96	93	93	93
China	96	98	98	97
Colombia	82	70	72	75
Comoros	84	75	75	67
Congo	29	23	21	18
Congo, Dem. Republic (Zaire)	13	10	10	10
Cook Islands	99	95	95	94
Costa Rica	87	85	85	86
Côte d'Ivoire	84	61	61	66
Croatia	93	93	93	91
Cuba	99	98	97	99
Cyprus	N/A	98	98	90
Czech Republic	99	98	97	95
Denmark	N/A	89	100	84
Djibouti	35	23	23	21
Dominica	99	99	98	98
Dominican Republic	86	74	73	95
Ecuador	98	85	83	88
Egypt	97	96	96	98
El Salvador	99	99	99	98
Equatorial Guinea	99	81	81	82
Eritrea	71	60	60	52
Estonia	100	94	94	89
Ethiopia	74	58	57	46
Fiji	95	86	88	75
Finland	99	99	98	98
France	83	96	97	97
Gabon	72	54	54	32
Gambia	99	96	95	91
Georgia	91	86	92	90
Germany	N/A	95	95	88
Ghana	86	68	68	62
Greece	70	85	95	90
Grenada	N/A	97	95	97
Guatemala	88	89	91	81
Guinea	69	56	56	58
Guinea-Bissau	82	63	60	51
Guyana	93	90	90	93
Haiti	28	22	20	22
Honduras	96	97	98	99
Hungary	100	100	100	100
Iceland	98	98	99	98
India	79	73	73	66
Indonesia	83	62	70	60
Iran	98	100	100	100
Iraq	76	86	86	79
Ireland	N/A	N/A	63	N/A
Israel	N/A	93	92	94
Italy	N/A	95	96	55

C7-3. Percent of 1-Year-Old Children Fully Immunized Against Tuberculosis, Diphtheria, Pertussis, Tetanus, Polio, and Measles, Selected Countries, 1995–1998 *(continued)*

	Percent fully immunized			
	TB*	DPT**	Polio	Measles
Jamaica	90	88	88	88
Japan	91	100	98	94
Jordan	N/A	91	91	86
Kazakhstan	99	100	100	100
Kenya	94	76	78	71
Kiribati	97	88	83	77
Kuwait	N/A	93	94	100
Kyrgyzstan	94	97	97	98
Laos	56	55	67	71
Latvia	100	94	94	97
Lebanon	N/A	96	96	91
Lesotho	46	50	48	43
Liberia	28	19	19	31
Libya	100	97	95	92
Liechtenstein	N/A	N/A	N/A	N/A
Lithuania	99	93	88	97
Luxembourg	58	94	98	91
Macedonia, FYRO	97	97	97	98
Madagascar	80	68	68	65
Malawi	100	96	93	90
Malaysia	100	95	94	86
Maldives	99	97	97	98
Mali	84	52	52	57
Malta	96	92	92	60
Marshall Islands	81	86	86	93
Mauritania	69	28	28	20
Mauritius	87	90	90	85
Mexico	93	94	95	89
Micronesia	52	80	79	82
Moldova	99	97	98	99
Monaco	90	99	99	98
Mongolia	95	94	94	93
Morocco	90	93	93	91
Mozambique	99	77	78	87
Myanmar (Burma)	91	87	88	85
Namibia	85	74	74	63
Nauru	78	50	36	100
Nepal	86	76	70	73
Netherlands, the	N/A	97	97	96
New Zealand	N/A	81	82	81
Nicaragua	96	69	73	71
Niger	46	22	21	27
Nigeria	27	21	22	26
Niue	100	100	100	100
North Korea, Dem. Rep.	64	37	77	34
Norway	N/A	92	92	93
Oman	96	100	100	98
Pakistan	66	59	59	55
Palau	N/A	74	74	66
Panama	99	98	99	96
Papua New Guinea	33	58	46	59
Paraguay	83	81	81	N/A
Peru	96	99	99	90
Philippines	91	79	81	71
Poland	94	95	95	91
Portugal	88	97	96	96

C7-3. Percent of 1-Year-Old Children Fully Immunized Against Tuberculosis, Diphtheria, Pertussis, Tetanus, Polio, and Measles, Selected Countries, 1995–1998 *(continued)*

	Percent fully immunized			
	TB*	DPT**	Polio	Measles
Qatar	100	94	94	90
Romania	100	97	97	97
Russia	95	97	99	98
Rwanda	79	77	77	66
Saint Kitts and Nevis	99	98	98	99
Saint Lucia	85	88	88	90
Saint Vincent/Grenadines	99	99	99	99
Samoa	100	100	100	100
San Marino	97	98	100	96
Sao Tome and Principe	80	73	72	59
Saudi Arabia	92	94	94	93
Senegal	80	65	65	65
Seychelles	100	99	99	93
Sierra Leone	79	56	56	68
Singapore	98	96	96	96
Slovakia	92	99	99	99
Slovenia	98	91	90	93
Solomon Islands	72	69	69	64
Somalia	57	24	24	47
South Africa	95	73	73	76
South Korea, Rep.	75	74	71	85
Spain	N/A	88	81	78
Sri Lanka	90	94	94	91
Sudan	81	72	69	63
Suriname	N/A	90	90	82
Swaziland	85	76	76	62
Sweden	12	99	99	96
Syria	75	97	97	97
Tajikistan	98	94	95	95
Tanzania	83	74	75	72
Thailand	98	94	94	91
Togo	73	37	41	32
Tonga	100	97	97	96
Trinidad and Tobago	N/A	91	91	90
Tunisia	91	96	96	94
Turkey	73	79	79	76
Turkmenistan	98	99	100	99
Tuvalu	100	94	94	96
Uganda	69	46	47	30
Ukraine	97	98	98	96
United Arab Emirates	98	94	94	95
United Kingdom	99	95	96	95
United States	N/A	94	84	89
Uruguay	99	92	92	92
Uzbekistan	97	99	99	96
Vanuatu	99	93	87	94
Venezuela	80	38	64	94
Vietnam	98	96	96	89
Yemen	77	68	68	66
Yugoslavia	87	94	95	94
Zambia	81	70	70	69
Zimbabwe	73	70	70	65

* TB - Tuberculosis
**DPT - Diphtheria, pertussis (whooping cough) and tetanus
N/A Not Available

Source: The State of the World's Children, 2000: Table 3. Health; <http://www.unicef.org/sowc00/stat4.htm>. Underlying data from United Nations Children's Fund (UNICEF).

C7-4. Reported Percent of Children Fully Vaccinated for Diphtheria Toxoid, Tetanus Toxoid, and Pertussis (DTP-3), 1985, 1990, 1997

	1985	1990	1997
Afghanistan	15	25	37
Albania	96	94	99
Algeria	N/A	58	79
American Samoa	60	44	85
Andorra	N/A	N/A	90
Angola	8	24	41
Anguilla	100	99	99
Antigua and Barbuda	100	99	99
Argentina	63	86	88
Armenia	N/A	N/A	88
Australia	N/A	95	86
Austria	90	90	90
Azerbaijan	N/A	84	96
Bahamas	86	87	86
Bahrain	64	95	98
Bangladesh	2	69	98
Barbados	83	91	96
Belarus	N/A	85	97
Belgium	N/A	N/A	62
Belize	59	91	86
Benin	17	78	78
Bermuda	52	62	91
Bhutan	52	84	87
Bolivia	33	41	82
Bosnia and Herzegovina	N/A	N/A	79
Botswana	68	56	76
Brazil	65	66	79
British Virgin Islands	81	100	99
Brunei	88	100	99
Bulgaria	99	99	94
Burkina Faso	N/A	N/A	70
Burundi	N/A	86	N/A
Cambodia	N/A	38	70
Cameroon	50	36	44
Cape Verde	39	88	78
Cayman Islands	91	95	95
Central African Republic	20	61	N/A
Chad	N/A	20	24
Chile	91	97	91
China	78	97	96
Colombia	60	87	81
Comoros	N/A	94	48
Congo	54	77	23
Congo, Dem. Rep. (Zaire)	37	36	18
Cook Islands	78	93	91
Costa Rica	75	95	91
Côte d'Ivoire	25	N/A	70
Croatia	N/A	N/A	92
Cuba	91	92	99
Cyprus	N/A	N/A	98
Czech Republic	N/A	N/A	98
Denmark	N/A	95	N/A
Djibouti	30	85	62
Dominica	91	69	99
Dominican Republic	18	69	80
Ecuador	41	75	76
Egypt	95	87	94

C7-4. Reported Percent of Children Fully Vaccinated for Diphtheria Toxoid, Tetanus Toxoid, and Pertussis (DTP-3), 1985, 1990, 1997 *(continued)*

	1985	1990	1997
El Salvador	54	80	97
Equatorial Guinea	3	N/A	81
Eritrea	N/A	N/A	60
Estonia	84	76	85
Ethiopia	6	49	63
Fiji	69	82	86
Finland	N/A	90	N/A
France	N/A	95	97
French Polynesia	76	81	0
Gabon	14	78	0
Gambia, the	77	92	96
Georgia	N/A	69	92
Germany	N/A	80	N/A
Ghana	N/A	50	60
Greece	54	54	85
Grenada	61	81	95
Guam	97	56	N/A
Guatemala	21	66	78
Guinea	N/A	20	53
Guinea-Bissau	18	61	63
Guyana	75	82	88
Haiti	23	41	N/A
Honduras	59	84	94
Hong Kong SAR, China	87	84	88
Hungary	99	99	100
Iceland	N/A	99	N/A
India	41	92	90
Indonesia	15	87	91
Iran	51	91	100
Iraq	N/A	83	92
Ireland	45	65	N/A
Israel	92	91	92
Italy	12	83	60
Jamaica	60	86	90
Japan	83	87	N/A
Jordan	53	92	93
Kazakhstan	N/A	80	96
Kenya	70	42	36
Kiribati	37	97	91
Kuwait	90	N/A	96
Kyrgyzstan	N/A	99	98
Laos	4	18	60
Latvia	N/A	85	75
Lebanon	60	82	92
Lesotho	N/A	N/A	57
Libya	51	62	96
Lithuania	N/A	76	90
Luxembourg	N/A	90	94
Macao	21	83	88
Macedonia, FYRO	N/A	N/A	97
Madagascar	23	71	N/A
Malawi	52	87	95
Malaysia	59	89	91
Maldives	28	94	97
Mali	N/A	42	52
Malta	37	63	N/A
Marshall Islands	N/A	92	78

C7-4. Reported Percent of Children Fully Vaccinated for Diphtheria Toxoid, Tetanus Toxoid, and Pertussis (DTP-3), 1985, 1990, 1997 *(continued)*

	1985	1990	1997
Mauritania	N/A	33	28
Mauritius	85	85	N/A
Mexico	40	66	83
Micronesia	N/A	85	75
Moldova	N/A	N/A	97
Monaco	N/A	100	N/A
Mongolia	83	69	92
Montserrat	99	100	99
Morocco	51	81	95
Mozambique	29	46	61
Myanmar (Burma)	16	69	90
Namibia	N/A	N/A	63
Nauru	67	74	50
Nepal	32	80	78
Netherlands, the	97	97	95
New Caledonia	76	N/A	93
New Zealand	72	90	86
Nicaragua	35	66	94
Niger	N/A	22	28
Nigeria	9	56	45
Niue	N/A	N/A	100
North Korea, Dem. Rep.	55	98	0
Norway	85	86	N/A
Oman	60	98	99
Pakistan	30	83	74
Palau	N/A	100	91
Panama	73	86	95
Papua New Guinea	43	67	45
Paraguay	54	79	82
Peru	48	72	98
Philippines	59	88	83
Poland	94	96	0
Portugal	72	89	0
Qatar	71	82	92
Romania	95	96	97
Russia	N/A	60	N/A
Rwanda	50	57	77
Saint Helena	N/A	100	N/A
Saint Kitts and Nevis	92	100	99
Saint Lucia	87	91	98
Saint Vincent	90	98	99
Samoa	89	90	99
Sao Tome and Principe	48	92	73
Saudi Arabia	81	92	92
Senegal	54	66	65
Seychelles	86	99	98
Sierra Leone	N/A	83	26
Singapore	78	85	93
Slovakia	N/A	99	98
Slovenia	N/A	N/A	91
Solomon Islands	38	77	72
Somalia	22	N/A	0
South Africa	75	74	0
South Korea, Rep.	76	74	80
Spain	79	93	N/A
Sri Lanka	70	86	97
Sudan	8	62	79

C7-4. Reported Percent of Children Fully Vaccinated for Diphtheria Toxoid, Tetanus Toxoid, and Pertussis (DTP-3), 1985, 1990, 1997 *(continued)*

	1985	1990	1997
Suriname	84	83	85
Swaziland	61	89	67
Sweden	99	99	N/A
Switzerland	N/A	90	N/A
Syria	26	90	95
Tajikistan	N/A	94	95
Tanzania	67	78	74
Thailand	47	85	N/A
Togo	N/A	77	33
Tokelau	46	99	100
Tonga	92	94	95
Trinidad and Tobago	75	89	90
Tunisia	70	91	96
Turkey	N/A	74	79
Turkmenistan	N/A	79	98
Turks and Caicos Islands	72	97	99
Tuvalu	52	90	77
Uganda	14	77	58
Ukraine	N/A	79	N/A
United Arab Emirates	58	N/A	92
United Kingdom	N/A	85	95
United States	96	N/A	0
Uruguay	63	97	88
Uzbekistan	N/A	79	96
Vanuatu	30	76	66
Venezuela	49	61	60
Vietnam	42	85	95
Wallis and Futuna Islands	94	N/A	95
Yemen	10	89	57
Yugoslavia	89	89	94
Zambia	N/A	71	70
Zimbabwe	72	78	78

N/A Not Available

Source: Vaccine Preventable Diseases Monitoring System, Division of Vaccines and Biologicals of the WHO; <http://www.who.int/gpv-surv>. Underlying data from World Health Organization (WHO).

C7-5. Reported Percent of Children Fully Vaccinated for Hepatitis B, 1990, 1995, 1997

	1990	1995	1997
Albania	N/A	88	97
American Samoa	N/A	47	N/A
Andorra	N/A	N/A	74
Anguilla	N/A	N/A	75
Bahrain	N/A	95	95
Belgium	N/A	N/A	2
Bhutan	N/A	N/A	84
Botswana	N/A	73	N/A
Brunei	96	N/A	98
Bulgaria	N/A	95	77
Cook Islands	71	86	97
Cyprus	N/A	68	88
Dominican Republic	N/A	N/A	53
Egypt	N/A	91	93
Fiji	N/A	82	98

C7-5. Reported Percent of Children Fully Vaccinated for Hepatitis B, 1990, 1995, 1997 *(continued)*

	1990	1995	1997
French Polynesia	N/A	N/A	0
Gabon	N/A	N/A	0
Gambia, the	93	N/A	93
Georgia	N/A	N/A	0
Greece	N/A	12	50
Guam	N/A	91	95
Honduras	N/A	N/A	75
Hong Kong SAR, China	82	98	87
Indonesia	N/A	N/A	62
Iran	N/A	54	93
Iraq	N/A	57	65
Israel	N/A	N/A	95
Italy	95	95	95
Jordan	N/A	35	85
Kiribati	73	36	97
Kuwait	N/A	100	98
Latvia	N/A	3	N/A
Luxembourg	N/A	N/A	49
Macao	63	85	88
Macedonia, FYRO	N/A	21	N/A
Malaysia	N/A	N/A	87
Maldives	N/A	N/A	56
Marshall Islands	N/A	47	70
Micronesia	N/A	82	79
Moldova	N/A	19	87
Mongolia	N/A	89	88
Nauru	N/A	57	86
New Caledonia	N/A	93	27
New Zealand	N/A	88	104
Niue	N/A	90	100
North Korea	N/A	N/A	0
Oman	N/A	100	100
Palau	N/A	100	90
Papua New Guinea	20	22	43
Philippines	N/A	N/A	31
Poland	N/A	N/A	0
Portugal	N/A	6	0
Qatar	N/A	90	90
Romania	N/A	N/A	99
Samoa	N/A	96	99
Saudi Arabia	66	95	91
Seychelles	N/A	99	N/A
Singapore	74	91	94
Solomon Islands	N/A	68	73
Somalia	N/A	N/A	0
South Africa	N/A	N/A	0
South Korea, Rep.	N/A	100	N/A
Syria	N/A	74	84
Thailand	N/A	92	N/A
Tokelau	14	50	N/A
Tonga	94	91	95
Tunisia	N/A	N/A	90
Tuvalu	N/A	49	88
United Arab Emirates	N/A	90	90
United States	N/A	N/A	0
Vanuatu	N/A	66	72
Vietnam	N/A	N/A	4
Wallis and Futuna Islands	N/A	96	82

N/A   Not Available

Source: Vaccine Preventable Diseases Monitoring System, Division of Vaccines and Biologicals of the WHO; <http://www.who.int/gpv-surv>. Underlying data from World Health Organization (WHO).

C7-6. Reported Percent of Children Fully Vaccinated for Measles, 1985, 1990, 1997

	1985	1990	1997
Afghanistan	14	20	48
Albania	96	N/A	95
Algeria	N/A	53	74
American Samoa	N/A	63	N/A
Andorra	N/A	N/A	90
Angola	83	38	78
Anguilla	81	99	92
Antigua and Barbuda	69	89	93
Argentina	67	93	92
Armenia	N/A	95	92
Australia	68	86	87
Austria	40	60	90
Azerbaijan	N/A	82	97
Bahamas	79	86	93
Bahrain	50	87	95
Bangladesh	1	82	97
Barbados	88	87	92
Belarus	N/A	96	98
Belgium	N/A	85	64
Belize	49	86	98
Benin	23	73	82
Bermuda	52	63	88
Bhutan	43	79	84
Bolivia	21	53	98
Bosnia and Herzegovina	N/A	N/A	85
Botswana	68	55	79
Brazil	67	78	99
British Virgin Islands	40	100	99
Brunei	98	N/A	98
Bulgaria	99	98	93
Burkina Faso	38	N/A	68
Burundi	N/A	75	N/A
Cambodia	N/A	34	68
Cameroon	N/A	36	43
Cape Verde	54	79	82
Cayman Islands	94	82	92
Central African Republic	23	67	N/A
Chad	N/A	N/A	30
Chile	92	81	92
China	88	98	96
Colombia	53	82	89
Comoros	18	87	49
Congo	67	77	18
Congo, Dem. Rep. (Zaire)	41	37	20
Cook Islands	76	67	86
Costa Rica	81	90	99
Cote d'Ivoire	N/A	N/A	68
Croatia	N/A	N/A	93
Cuba	85	94	99
Cyprus	N/A	N/A	90
Czech Republic	N/A	N/A	96
Denmark	N/A	84	84
Djibouti	27	85	59
Dominica	93	96	99
Dominican Republic	24	96	80
Ecuador	54	67	75
Egypt	74	87	92
El Salvador	71	98	97

C7-6. Reported Percent of Children Fully Vaccinated for Measles, 1985, 1990, 1997 *(continued)*

	1985	1990	1997
Equatorial Guinea	11	N/A	82
Eritrea	N/A	N/A	53
Estonia	82	82	88
Ethiopia	12	38	52
Fiji	57	72	75
Finland	N/A	97	N/A
France	37	71	83
French Polynesia	79	62	0
Gabon	58	76	0
Gambia, the	75	86	91
Georgia	N/A	81	95
Germany	25	50	N/A
Ghana	N/A	52	59
Greece	77	76	90
Grenada	49	85	92
Guam	97	57	94
Guatemala	23	68	74
Guinea	N/A	25	56
Guinea-Bissau	35	53	51
Guyana	40	77	82
Haiti	21	31	N/A
Honduras	53	90	89
Hong Kong SAR, China	N/A	80	82
Hungary	99	99	100
Iceland	N/A	99	N/A
India	1	87	81
Indonesia	15	86	92
Iran	62	85	96
Iraq	N/A	83	98
Ireland	63	N/A	N/A
Israel	85	91	94
Italy	12	43	75
Jamaica	64	69	88
Japan	73	66	N/A
Jordan	39	87	95
Kazakhstan	N/A	95	97
Kenya	63	41	32
Kiribati	4	75	82
Kuwait	91	N/A	95
Kyrgyzstan	N/A	99	98
Laos	6	32	67
Latvia	N/A	97	97
Lebanon	23	39	89
Lesotho	N/A	87	53
Libya	50	59	92
Lithuania	N/A	89	96
Luxembourg	N/A	80	91
Macao	3	57	85
Macedonia, FYRO	N/A	N/A	98
Madagascar	28	57	N/A
Malawi	49	81	87
Malaysia	20	70	83
Maldives	47	96	96
Mali	N/A	43	56
Malta	10	80	N/A
Marshall Islands	N/A	52	52
Mauritania	N/A	38	20
Mauritius	61	76	N/A

C7-6. Reported Percent of Children Fully Vaccinated for Measles, 1985, 1990, 1997 *(continued)*

	1985	1990	1997
Mexico	64	78	97
Micronesia	N/A	81	74
Moldova	N/A	N/A	99
Monaco	N/A	100	N/A
Mongolia	18	92	98
Montserrat	41	100	99
Morocco	45	79	92
Mozambique	39	59	70
Myanmar (Burma)	N/A	68	88
Namibia	N/A	N/A	57
Nauru	N/A	N/A	121
Nepal	34	68	85
Netherlands, the	92	94	96
New Caledonia	15	N/A	41
New Zealand	N/A	90	114
Nicaragua	49	82	94
Niger	N/A	25	42
Nigeria	9	48	69
Niue	52	N/A	100
North Korea, Dem. Rep.	93	98	0
Norway	90	87	N/A
Oman	65	98	98
Pakistan	23	76	74
Palau	N/A	N/A	83
Panama	83	99	92
Papua New Guinea	54	66	40
Paraguay	46	70	61
Peru	53	64	94
Philippines	49	85	83
Poland	92	95	0
Portugal	70	85	0
Qatar	62	79	87
Romania	88	92	97
Russia	N/A	81	N/A
Rwanda	52	55	66
Saint Helena	N/A	100	N/A
Saint Kitts and Nevis	91	100	97
Saint Lucia	68	83	95
Saint Vincent	91	96	99
Samoa	81	89	99
Sao Tome and Principe	35	71	60
Saudi Arabia	79	88	92
Senegal	40	57	65
Seychelles	90	86	100
Sierra Leone	N/A	75	28
Singapore	75	84	89
Slovakia	N/A	99	98
Slovenia	N/A	N/A	82
Solomon Islands	N/A	70	68
Somalia	34	N/A	0
South Africa	70	79	0
South Korea, Rep.	89	93	85
Spain	79	97	N/A
Sri Lanka	20	80	94
Sudan	6	57	92
Suriname	73	65	78
Swaziland	49	86	57
Sweden	92	95	N/A

C7-6. Reported Percent of Children Fully Vaccinated for Measles, 1985, 1990, 1997 *(continued)*

	1985	1990	1997
Switzerland	N/A	90	N/A
Syria	30	87	93
Tajikistan	N/A	91	95
Tanzania	66	79	69
Thailand	22	70	N/A
Togo	N/A	65	38
Tokelau	N/A	99	87
Tonga	81	86	97
Trinidad and Tobago	34	79	88
Tunisia	65	88	92
Turkey	N/A	67	76
Turkmenistan	N/A	80	100
Turks and Caicos Islands	57	81	99
Tuvalu	92	95	100
Uganda	17	74	60
Ukraine	N/A	89	N/A
United Arab Emirates	49	N/A	95
United Kingdom	N/A	89	95
United States	97	N/A	0
Uruguay	59	97	80
Uzbekistan	N/A	85	88
Vanuatu	26	66	59
Venezuela	56	61	68
Vietnam	19	85	96
Wallis and Futuna Islands	N/A	N/A	75
Yemen	11	74	51
Yugoslavia	91	89	91
Zambia	N/A	68	69
Zimbabwe	78	76	73

N/A Not Available

Source: Vaccine Preventable Diseases Monitoring System, Division of Vaccines and Biologicals of the WHO; <http://www.who.int/gpv-surv>. Underlying data from World Health Organization (WHO).

C7-7. Reported Percent of Children Fully Vaccinated for Polio (Oral Polio Vaccine OPV-3), 1985, 1990, 1997

	1985	1990	1997
Afghanistan	15	25	37
Albania	94	N/A	99
Algeria	N/A	81	79
American Samoa	N/A	31	87
Angola	N/A	23	38
Anguilla	100	99	99
Antigua and Barbuda	100	99	99
Argentina	69	90	91
Armenia	N/A	93	95
Australia	N/A	72	86
Austria	90	90	95
Azerbaijan	N/A	90	98
Bahamas	84	86	86
Bahrain	64	95	98
Bangladesh	2	69	98
Barbados	83	90	96
Belarus	N/A	90	98
Belgium	N/A	95	72

C7-7. Reported Percent of Children Fully Vaccinated for Polio (Oral Polio Vaccine OPV-3), 1985, 1990, 1997 *(continued)*

	1985	1990	1997
Belize	61	86	85
Benin	16	78	78
Bermuda	52	62	94
Bhutan	52	84	87
Bolivia	30	50	82
Bosnia and Herzegovina	N/A	N/A	80
Botswana	67	53	80
Brazil	86	92	89
British Virgin Island.	81	100	96
Brunei	88	100	99
Bulgaria	99	99	96
Burkina Faso	N/A	N/A	70
Burundi	N/A	86	N/A
Cambodia	N/A	39	70
Cameroon	N/A	34	47
Cape Verde	39	87	77
Cayman Islands	91	95	96
Central African Republic	20	57	N/A
Chad	N/A	16	24
Chile	89	97	91
China	87	98	97
Colombia	61	93	82
Comoros	N/A	94	48
Congo	N/A	94	21
Congo, Dem. Rep. (Zaire)	68	36	18
Cook Islands	91	83	91
Costa Rica	72	95	93
Côte d'Ivoire	N/A	56	70
Croatia	N/A	N/A	92
Cuba	88	94	97
Cyprus	N/A	N/A	98
Denmark	N/A	97	N/A
Djibouti	30	85	62
Dominica	89	90	99
Dominican Republic	39	90	81
Ecuador	39	77	77
Egypt	84	87	94
El Salvador	54	80	96
Equatorial Guinea	4	N/A	81
Estonia	85	86	86
Ethiopia	6	49	64
Fiji	68	87	88
Finland	N/A	90	N/A
France	N/A	85	97
French Polynesia	76	81	0
Gabon	44	78	0
Gambia	55	94	98
Georgia	N/A	87	98
Germany	80	85	N/A
Ghana	N/A	50	61
Greece	96	96	95
Grenada	77	69	95
Guam	58	56	94
Guatemala	21	74	78
Guinea	N/A	20	53
Guinea-Bissau	18	60	60
Guyana	77	78	88

C7-7. Reported Percent of Children Fully Vaccinated for Polio (Oral Polio Vaccine OPV-3), 1985, 1990, 1997 *(continued)*

	1985	1990	1997
Haiti	19	40	N/A
Honduras	58	87	93
Hong Kong SAR, China	92	84	N/A
Hungary	99	99	100
Iceland	N/A	99	N/A
India	35	82	91
Indonesia	13	92	90
Iran	63	90	100
Iraq	N/A	83	92
Ireland	90	81	N/A
Israel	93	89	93
Italy	N/A	63	98
Jamaica	58	87	90
Japan	N/A	90	N/A
Jordan	54	92	98
Kazakhstan	N/A	85	100
Kenya	70	44	36
Kiribati	15	97	93
Kuwait	91	N/A	100
Kyrgyzstan	N/A	99	99
Laos	4	26	69
Latvia	N/A	92	76
Lebanon	60	82	92
Lesotho	N/A	78	55
Libya	62	62	96
Lithuania	N/A	77	95
Luxembourg	N/A	90	98
Macao	17	82	88
Macedonia, FYRO	N/A	N/A	97
Madagascar	20	71	N/A
Malawi	48	90	94
Malaysia	87	90	90
Maldives	28	94	97
Mali	N/A	42	52
Malta	84	86	N/A
Marshall Islands	N/A	89	71
Mauritania	N/A	33	28
Mauritius	85	86	N/A
Mexico	67	96	83
Micronesia	N/A	85	75
Moldova	N/A	N/A	98
Monaco	N/A	100	N/A
Mongolia	100	87	92
Montserrat	99	100	99
Morocco	51	81	95
Mozambique	25	46	61
Myanmar (Burma)	3	69	90
Namibia	N/A	N/A	64
Nauru	73	74	36
Nepal	20	79	78
Netherlands, the	97	97	95
New Caledonia	76	N/A	N/A
New Zealand	84	N/A	117
Nicaragua	80	87	99
Niger	N/A	22	28
Nigeria	10	55	45
Niue	N/A	N/A	100

C7-7. Reported Percent of Children Fully Vaccinated for Polio (Oral Polio Vaccine OPV-3), 1985, 1990, 1997 *(continued)*

	1985	1990	1997
North Korea, Dem. Rep.	65	99	0
Norway	90	84	N/A
Oman	60	98	99
Pakistan	30	83	74
Palau	N/A	100	90
Panama	71	86	99
Papua New Guinea	34	67	35
Paraguay	97	76	82
Peru	47	73	97
Philippines	54	88	83
Poland	94	96	0
Portugal	29	89	0
Qatar	71	82	92
Romania	92	92	97
Russia	N/A	69	N/A
Rwanda	56	58	77
Saint Helena	N/A	100	N/A
Saint Kitts and Nevis	89	100	99
Saint Lucia	44	90	98
Saint Vincent	89	92	99
Samoa	92	88	99
Sao Tome and Principe	48	90	73
Saudi Arabia	N/A	92	92
Senegal	54	66	65
Seychelles	86	99	98
Sierra Leone	N/A	83	26
Singapore	81	85	94
Slovakia	N/A	99	98
Slovenia	N/A	N/A	92
Solomon Islands	36	75	70
Somalia	22	N/A	0
South Korea, Rep.	80	74	81
South Africa	77	76	0
Spain	73	94	N/A
Sri Lanka	65	86	98
Sudan	8	62	78
Suriname	85	81	81
Swaziland	59	89	67
Sweden	98	99	N/A
Switzerland	N/A	98	N/A
Syria	26	90	95
Tajikistan	N/A	98	92
Tanzania	64	73	73
Thailand	47	89	N/A
Togo	N/A	78	33
Tokelau	43	99	100
Tonga	81	93	95
Trinidad and Tobago	74	89	91
Tunisia	70	91	96
Turkey	N/A	74	79
Turkmenistan	N/A	92	99
Turks and Caicos Is.	72	98	99
Tuvalu	97	90	78
Uganda	13	77	59
Ukraine	N/A	81	N/A
United Arab Emirates	58	N/A	92
United Kingdom	N/A	90	96

C7-7. Reported Percent of Children Fully Vaccinated for Polio (Oral Polio Vaccine OPV-3), 1985, 1990, 1997 *(continued)*

	1985	1990	1997
United States	96	N/A	0
Uruguay	58	97	88
Uzbekistan	N/A	90	97
Vanuatu	27	78	62
Venezuela	59	71	76
Vietnam	62	85	95
Wallis and Futuna Islands	94	N/A	95
Yemen	10	89	57
Yugoslavia	90	86	94
Zambia	N/A	70	70
Zimbabwe	76	78	79

N/A Not Available

Source: Vaccine Preventable Diseases Monitoring System, Division of Vaccines and Biologicals of the WHO; <http://www.who.int/gpv-surv>. Underlying data from World Health Organization (WHO).

C7-8. Reported Percent of Children Fully Vaccinated for Tuberculosis, 1985, 1990, 1997

	1985	1990	1997
Afghanistan	17	30	55
Albania	92	94	94
Algeria	N/A	65	94
Angola	28	48	70
Anguilla	98	100	99
Antigua and Barbuda	N/A	99	N/A
Argentina	89	99	99
Armenia	N/A	82	72
Azerbaijan	N/A	87	94
Bangladesh	2	91	100
Barbados	N/A	95	N/A
Belarus	N/A	91	98
Belize	81	86	95
Benin	27	74	89
Bhutan	59	87	92
Bolivia	24	48	93
Bosnia and Herzegovina	N/A	N/A	97
Botswana	68	50	59
Brazil	56	79	99
British Virgin Islands	40	100	99
Brunei	95	95	99
Bulgaria	99	99	97
Burkina Faso	17	N/A	73
Burundi	N/A	97	N/A
Cambodia	N/A	52	82
Cameroon	N/A	52	53
Cape Verde	64	97	80
Cayman Islands	55	90	86
Central African Republic	34	93	N/A
Chad	N/A	N/A	45
Chile	92	94	98
China	50	99	96
Colombia	76	95	96
Comoros	N/A	99	55
Congo	89	86	29
Congo, Dem. Rep. (Zaire)	69	46	25

C7-8. Reported Percent of Children Fully Vaccinated for Tuberculosis, 1985, 1990, 1997 *(continued)*

	1985	1990	1997
Cook Islands	99	100	84
Costa Rica	85	92	N/A
Côte d'Ivoire	N/A	N/A	73
Croatia	N/A	N/A	98
Cuba	98	98	99
Czech Republic	N/A	N/A	97
Djibouti	58	95	67
Dominica	90	68	99
Dominican Republic	51	23	88
Ecuador	99	100	99
Egypt	84	89	98
El Salvador	50	75	93
Equatorial Guinea	28	N/A	99
Eritrea	N/A	N/A	67
Estonia	97	93	99
Ethiopia	11	70	90
Fiji	100	100	95
Finland	N/A	91	N/A
France	N/A	80	N/A
French Polynesia	95	96	0
Gabon	50	96	0
Gambia	92	98	99
Georgia	v	84	76
Ghana	N/A	71	72
Greece	N/A	N/A	70
Guatemala	30	62	94
Guinea	N/A	50	69
Guinea-Bissau	33	90	82
Guyana	98	82	94
Haiti	70	72	N/A
Honduras	65	71	99
Hong Kong SAR, China	99	99	100
Hungary	N/A	99	100
India	29	97	96
Indonesia	65	93	100
Iran	79	95	91
Iraq	N/A	95	97
Ireland	80	N/A	N/A
Jamaica	51	98	97
Japan	85	85	N/A
Kazakhstan	N/A	90	99
Kenya	82	54	42
Kiribati	62	93	103
Kuwait	3	N/A	N/A
Kyrgyzstan	N/A	98	97
Laos	8	26	58
Latvia	N/A	93	100
Lesotho	N/A	78	54
Libya	82	91	99
Lithuania	N/A	94	98
Luxembourg	N/A		58
Macao	99	92	94
Macedonia, FYRO	N/A	N/A	97
Madagascar	31	98	N/A
Malawi	87	97	100
Malaysia	100	98	100
Maldives	45	99	99
Mali	N/A	82	76

C7-8. Reported Percent of Children Fully Vaccinated for Tuberculosis, 1985, 1990, 1997 *(continued)*

	1985	1990	1997
Malta	65	77	N/A
Marshall Islands	N/A	49	94
Mauritania	N/A	79	69
Mauritius	79	87	N/A
Mexico	16	70	97
Micronesia	N/A	12	48
Moldova	N/A	N/A	99
Monaco	N/A	100	N/A
Mongolia	52	81	96
Montserrat	97	100	99
Morocco	62	96	94
Mozambique	47	59	84
Myanmar (Burma)	45	67	94
Namibia	N/A	N/A	64
Nauru	81	93	78
Nepal	67	98	96
New Caledonia	68	N/A	100
New Zealand	20	20	N/A
Nicaragua	97	84	99
Niger	N/A	53	44
Nigeria	17	80	53
Niue	41	N/A	100
North Korea, Dem. Rep.	51	99	0
Oman	93	96	96
Pakistan	41	93	90
Panama	94	97	99
Papua New Guinea	66	89	67
Paraguay	99	90	87
Peru	70	83	98
Philippines	76	96	83
Poland	95	97	0
Portugal	82	88	0
Qatar	76	97	99
Romania	N/A	90	100
Russia	N/A	91	N/A
Rwanda	83	57	79
Saint Helena	N/A	100	N/A
Saint Kitts and Nevis	N/A	N/A	99
Saint Lucia	100	97	99
Saint Vincent	84	100	98
Samoa	97	97	99
Sao Tome and Principe	75	100	70
Saudi Arabia	N/A	90	91
Senegal	32	91	80
Seychelles	95	98	100
Sierra Leone	N/A	98	38
Singapore	93	99	98
Slovakia	N/A	98	90
Slovenia	N/A	N/A	98
Solomon Islands	50	87	73
Somalia	31	N/A	0
South Africa	70	59	0
Sri Lanka	71	84	96
Sudan	12	73	90
Swaziland	79	96	60
Sweden	14	N/A	N/A
Syria	48	92	100
Tajikistan	N/A	84	99

C7-8. Reported Percent of Children Fully Vaccinated for Tuberculosis, 1985, 1990, 1997 *(continued)*

	1985	1990	1997
Tanzania	90	85	82
Thailand	60	100	N/A
Togo	N/A	100	53
Tokelau	N/A	66	100
Tonga	100	99	100
Tunisia	83	88	93
Turkey	N/A	16	73
Turkmenistan	N/A	91	97
Turks and Caicos Islands	100	100	99
Tuvalu	90	95	100
Uganda	37	100	84
Ukraine	N/A	91	N/A
United Arab Emirates	10	N/A	98
United Kingdom	N/A	N/A	99
Uruguay	92	99	99
Uzbekistan	N/A	91	97
Vanuatu	83	96	60
Venezuela	N/A	74	98
Vietnam	50	87	96
Wallis and Futuna Islands	89	N/A	80
Yemen	20	100	62
Yugoslavia	85	76	87
Zambia	N/A	97	81
Zimbabwe	89	74	82

N/A Not Available

Source: Vaccine Preventable Diseases Monitoring System, Division of Vaccines and Biologicals of the WHO; <http://www.who.int/gpv-surv>. Underlying data from World Health Organization (WHO).

C7-9. Percentage of Pregnant Women Fully Immunized against Tetanus, 1995–1998

Country	Percent fully immunized
Afghanistan	19
Albania	65
Algeria	52
Angola	24
Armenia	N/A
Bahrain	80
Bangladesh	86
Belize	65
Benin	66
Bhutan	80
Bolivia	27
Botswana	54
Brazil	30
Brunei Darussalam	52
Burkina Faso	54
Burundi	9
Cambodia	31
Cameroon	49
Cape Verde	51
Central African Rep.	37
Chad	27
China	13
Colombia	57
Comoros	22

C7-9. Percentage of Pregnant Women Fully Immunized against Tetanus, 1995–1998 *(continued)*

Country	Percent fully immunized
Congo	30
Congo, Dem. Rep.	N/A
Cook Islands	29
Costa Rica	N/A
Côte d'Ivoire	44
Croatia	N/A
Cuba	70
Djibouti	16
Dominican Rep.	77
Ecuador	3
Egypt	61
El Salvador	N/A
Equatorial Guinea	70
Eritrea	34
Ethiopia	30
France	83
Gabon	4
Gambia	96
Georgia	N/A
Germany	80
Ghana	45
Guatemala	38
Guinea	48
GuineaN/ABissau	46
Guyana	88
Haiti	38
Honduras	N/A
India	80
Indonesia	53
Iran	75
Iraq	45
Jamaica	52
Jordan	22
Kazakhstan	N/A
Kenya	51
Kiribati	74
Korea, Dem. People's Rep.	5
Kuwait	8
Kyrgyzstan	N/A
Lao People's Dem. Rep.	32
Lebanon	N/A
Lesotho	N/A
Liberia	14
Libya	N/A
Madagascar	30
Malawi	81
Malaysia	71
Maldives	91
Mali	62
Mauritania	63
Mauritius	78
Meico	70
Mongolia	N/A
Morocco	33
Mozambique	41
Myanmar	78
Namibia	70
Nepal	65

C7-9. Percentage of Pregnant Women Fully Immunized against Tetanus, 1995–1998 *(continued)*

Country	Percent fully immunized
Nicaragua	42
Niger	19
Nigeria	29
Niue	40
Oman	96
Pakistan	58
Panama	N/A
Papua New Guinea	11
Paraguay	32
Peru	57
Philippines	38
Qatar	N/A
Rwanda	43
Samoa	99
Sao Tome and Principe	31
Saudi Arabia	66
Senegal	34
Seychelles	100
Sierra Leone	42
Solomon Islands	55
Somalia	41
South Africa	26
Spain	99
Sri Lanka	78
Sudan	55
Swaziland	79
Syria	53
Tanzania	27
TFYR Macedonia	91
Thailand	88
Togo	41
Tonga	93
Tunisia	80
Turkey	32
Turkmenistan	N/A
Tuvalu	71
Uganda	38
United Arab Emirates	N/A
Uzbekistan	N/A
Vanuatu	78
Viet Nam	92
Yemen	26
Yugoslavia	N/A
Zambia	N/A
Zimbabwe	58

N/A Not Available

Source: The State of the World's Children, 2000: Table 3. Health; <http://www.unicef.org/sowc00/stat4.htm>. Underlying data from United Nations Children's Fund (UNICEF).

C8. VITAMIN AND MINERAL SUPPLEMENTS

C8-1. Vitamin A Supplementation Coverage Rate (6–59 Months), 1998

Country	Percent covered
Bangladesh	95
Benin	100
Bhutan	87
Bolivia	73
Brazil	20
Burkina Faso	97
Burundi	15
Cambodia	80
Chad	0
Congo, Dem. Rep. (Zaire)	46
Congo, Rep.	93
Djibouti	41
Dominican Republic	16
Ecuador	69
Eritrea	86
Ethiopia	83
Ghana	90
Guatemala	57
Guinea	97
Haiti	60
Honduras	58
India	25
Indonesia	66
Iran	35
Iraq	89
Kenya	10
Laos	39
Madagascar	100
Malawi	34
Mali	93
Marshall Islands	35
Mauritania	80
Mauritius	0
Mexico	93
Micronesia	50
Mongolia	87
Morocco	75
Myanmar (Burma)	91
Namibia	83
Nepal	90
Nicaragua	63
Niger	82
Oman	98
Pakistan	1
Philippines	80
Rwanda	75
Senegal	0
Somalia	90
Sudan	80
Tanzania	80
Thailand	4
Uganda	95
Vietnam	98
Yemen	100
Yugoslavia	25
Zambia	91

Source: The State of the World's Children, 2000: Table 2. Nutrition; <http://www.unicef.org/sowc00/stat4.htm>. Underlying data from United Nations Children's Fund (UNICEF).

C8-2. Percentage of Households Consuming Iodized Salt, 1992–1998

Country	Percent
Algeria	92
Angola	10
Argentina	90
Bangladesh	78
Belarus	37
Belize	90
Benin	79
Bhutan	82
Bolivia	90
Botswana	27
Brazil	95
Burkina Faso	23
Burundi	80
Cambodia	7
Cameroon	82
Cape Verde	99
Central African Republic	65
Chad	55
Chile	97
China	83
Colombia	92
Congo, Dem. Rep.	90
Costa Rica	89
Croatia	70
Cuba	45
Dominican Republic	13
Ecuador	97
Egypt	0
El Salvador	91
Equatorial Guinea	20
Eritrea	80
Ethiopia	0
Fiji	31
Gambia, the	0
Ghana	10
Guatemala	64
Guinea	37
Haiti	10
Honduras	85
India	70
Indonesia	62
Iran	94
Iraq	10
Jamaica	100
Jordan	95
Kazakhstan	53
Kenya	100
Kyrgyzstan	27
Laos	93
Lebanon	92
Lesotho	73
Libya	90
Macedonia, FYRO	100
Madagascar	73
Malawi	58
Mali	9
Mauritania	3
Mauritius	0

C8-2. Percentage of Households Consuming Iodized Salt, 1992–1998 *(continued)*

Country	Percent
Mexico	99
Mongolia	68
Mozambique	62
Myanmar (Burma)	65
Namibia	59
Nepal	93
Nicaragua	86
Niger	64
Nigeria	98
North Korea, Dem. Rep.	5
Oman	65
Pakistan	19
Panama	92
Paraguay	79
Peru	93
Philippines	15
Russia	30
Rwanda	95
Senegal	9
Sierra Leone	75
South Africa	40
Sri Lanka	47
Sudan	0
Swaziland	26
Syria	40
Tajikistan	20
Tanzania	74
Thailand	50
Togo	73
Tunisia	98
Turkey	18
Turkmenistan	0
Uganda	69
Ukraine	4
Uzbekistan	0
Venezuela	65
Vietnam	65
Yemen	39
Yugoslavia	70
Zambia	78
Zimbabwe	80

Source: The State of the World's Children, 2000: Table 2. Nutrition; United Nations Children's Fund (UNICEF); <http://www.unicef.org/sowc00/stat4.htm>. Underlying data from Salt iodization - Multiple Indicator Cluster Surveys (MICS) and United Nations Children's Fund (UNICEF).

C8-3. Iodized Salt by Regions, 1996

Region	Number of countries in region	Number of countries with IDD problem & salt info.	Population consuming iodized salt	
			Percentage	Total (millions)
Sub-Saharan Africa	39	30	56	270
Middle East and North Africa	16	10	64	124
Asia	22	14	56	1609
Americas	22	19	81	367
CEE-NIS	21	10	24	78
Developing world	120	83	57	2448

Note: IDD = Iodine Deficiency Disorders, CEE-NIS = Central and East European-Newly Independent States.

Source: WHO Fact Sheet No. 121, November 1996, IODINE DEFICIENCY DISORDERS: Table 1. Consumption of Iodized Salt, by region; <http://www.who.int/inf-fs/en/fact121.html>. Underlying data from World Health Organization (WHO).

C9. ORAL REHYDRATION TREATMENT (ORT)

C9. Oral Rehydration Treatment (ORT): Percentage of All Cases of Diarrhea in Children Under Five Years of Age Treated with Oral Rehydration Salts and/or Recommended Home Fluids, 1990–1998

	ORT use rate (%) 1990-1998*
Afghanistan	36
Albania	N/A
Algeria**	98
Andorra	N/A
Angola	N/A
Antigua and Barbuda	N/A
Argentina	N/A
Armenia	30
Australia	N/A
Austria	N/A
Azerbaijan	N/A
Bahamas	N/A
Bahrain	39
Bangladesh	61
Barbados	N/A
Belarus	N/A
Belgium	N/A
Belize	N/A
Benin	33
Bhutan	85
Bolivia	48
Bosnia and Herzegovina	N/A
Botswana	43
Brazil	54
Brunei Darussalam	N/A
Bulgaria	N/A
Burkina Faso	18
Burundi	38
Cambodia	48
Cameroon	34
Canada	N/A
Cape Verde	83
Central African Rep.	34
Chad	29
Chile	N/A

C9. Oral Rehydration Treatment (ORT): Percentage of All Cases of Diarrhea in Children Under Five Years of Age Treated with Oral Rehydration Salts and/or Recommended Home Fluids, 1990–1998 *(continued)*

	ORT use rate (%) 1990-1998*
China	85
Colombia	53
Comoros	32
Congo	41
Congo, Dem. Rep.**	90
Cook Islands	N/A
Costa Rica	31
Côte d'Ivoire	29
Croatia	5
Cuba	N/A
Cyprus	N/A
Czech Rep.	N/A
Denmark	N/A
Djibouti	N/A
Dominica	N/A
Dominican Rep.	39
Ecuador	64
Egypt	95
El Salvador	69
Equatorial Guinea	N/A
Eritrea	38
Estonia	N/A
Ethiopia**	95
Fiji	N/A
Finland	N/A
France	N/A
Gabon	39
Gambia**	99
Georgia	14
Germany	N/A
Ghana	36
Greece	N/A
Grenada	N/A
Guatemala	22
Guinea**	80
Guinea-Bissau	N/A
Guyana	N/A
Haiti	31
Holy See	N/A
Honduras	32
Hungary	N/A
Iceland	N/A
India**	67
Indonesia	70
Iran	48
Iraq**	54
Ireland	N/A
Israel	N/A
Italy	N/A
Jamaica	N/A
Japan	N/A
Jordan	29
Kazakhstan	31
Kenya	69
Kiribati	N/A
Korea, Dem. People's Rep.	N/A

C9. Oral Rehydration Treatment (ORT): Percentage of All Cases of Diarrhea in Children Under Five Years of Age Treated with Oral Rehydration Salts and/or Recommended Home Fluids, 1990–1998 *(continued)*

	ORT use rate (%) 1990-1998*
Korea, Rep. of	N/A
Kuwait	N/A
Kyrgyzstan**	98
Lao People's Dem. Rep.	32
Latvia	N/A
Lebanon	82
Lesotho**	84
Liberia**	94
Libya	49
Liechtenstein	N/A
Lithuania	N/A
Luxembourg	N/A
Madagascar	23
Malawi	70
Malaysia	N/A
Maldives	18
Mali	29
Malta	N/A
Marshall Islands	N/A
Mauritania	51
Mauritius	N/A
Mexico	80
Micronesia, Fed. States of	N/A
Moldova, Rep. of	N/A
Monaco	N/A
Mongolia	80
Morocco	29
Mozambique	49
Myanmar**	96
Namibia**	100
Nauru	N/A
Nepal	29
Netherlands, the	N/A
New Zealand	N/A
Nicaragua	58
Niger	21
Nigeria**	86
Niue	N/A
Norway	N/A
Oman	61
Pakistan**	97
Palau	N/A
Panama**	94
Papua New Guinea	N/A
Paraguay	33
Peru	55
Philippines	64
Poland	N/A
Portugal	N/A
Qatar	54
Romania	N/A
Russian Federation	N/A
Rwanda	47
Saint Kitts and Nevis	N/A
Saint Lucia	N/A
Saint Vincent/Grenadines	N/A

C9. Oral Rehydration Treatment (ORT): Percentage of All Cases of Diarrhea in Children Under Five Years of Age Treated with Oral Rehydration Salts and/or Recommended Home Fluids, 1990–1998 *(continued)*

	ORT use rate (%) 1990-1998*
Samoa	N/A
San Marino	N/A
Sao Tome and Principe**	74
Saudi Arabia	53
Senegal	39
Seychelles	N/A
Sierra Leone	N/A
Singapore	N/A
Slovakia	N/A
Slovenia	N/A
Solomon Islands	N/A
Somalia	N/A
South Africa	N/A
Spain	N/A
Sri Lanka	34
Sudan	31
Suriname	N/A
Swaziland**	99
Sweden	N/A
Switzerland	N/A
Syria	61
Tajikistan	N/A
Tanzania	50
TFYR Macedonia	N/A
Thailand	95
Togo	23
Tonga	N/A
Trinidad and Tobago	N/A
Tunisia	81
Turkey	27
Turkmenistan	98
Tuvalu	N/A
Uganda	49
Ukraine	N/A
United Arab Emirates	42
United Kingdom	N/A
United States	N/A
Uruguay	N/A
Uzbekistan	37
Vanuatu	N/A
Venezuela	N/A
Viet Nam	N/A
Yemen	35
Yugoslavia**	99
Zambia	57
Zimbabwe	60

* Data refer to the most recent year available during the period specified in the column heading.
** Indicates data that refer to years or periods other than those specified in the column heading, differ from the standard definition, or refer to only part of a country.
N/A Not Available

Source: The State of the World's Children, 2000: Table 2. Nutrition; United Nations Children's Fund (UNICEF); <http://www.unicef.org/sowc00/stat5.htm>. Underlying data from Demographic and Health Surveys, Multiple Indicator Cluster Surveys (MICS), World Health Organization (WHO) and United Nations Children's Fund (UNICEF).

C10. FOOD AID

C10-1. Total Cereal Food Aid (from All Donor Countries) per Child (Age 0–19 Years), Selected Recipient Countries, 1998

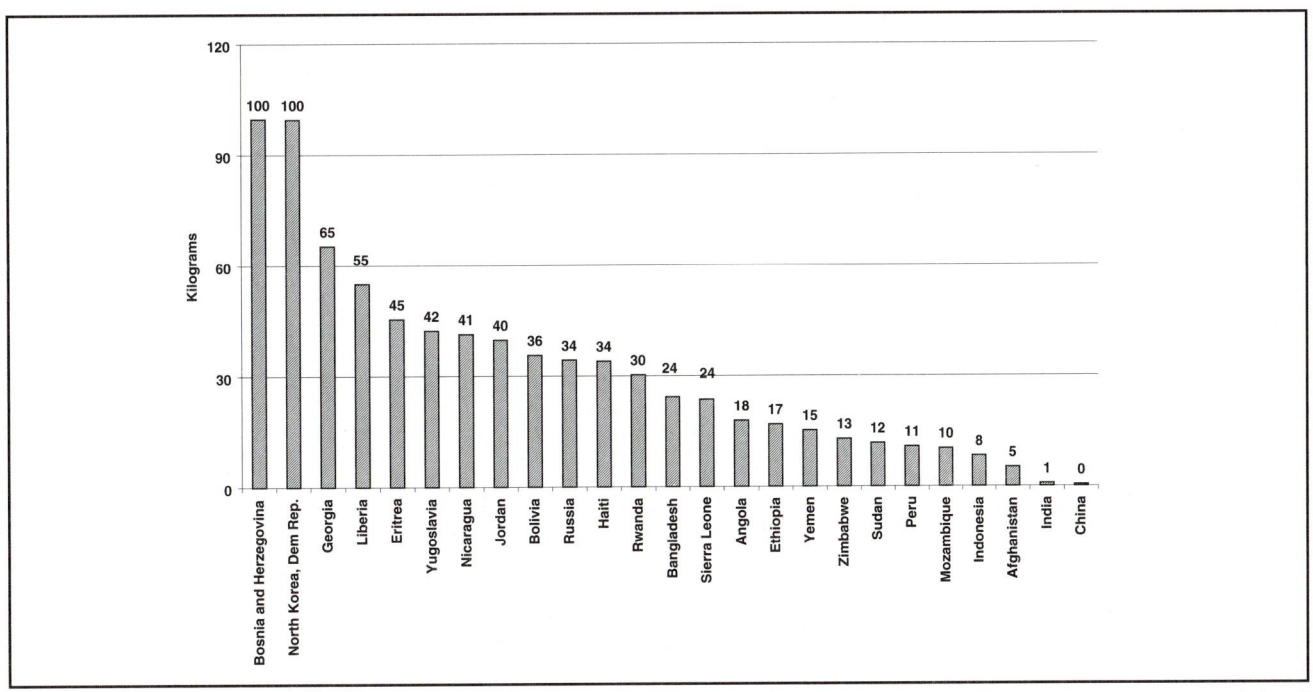

Source: Food and Agriculture Organization database (FAOSTAT) and U.S. Census International database; <http://apps.fao.org/cgi-bin/nph-db.pl> and <http://census.gov/>. Underlying data from Food and Agriculture Organization (FAO).

C10-2. Total Non-Cereal Food Aid (from All Donor Countries) per Child (Age 0–19 Years), Selected Recipient Countries, 1998

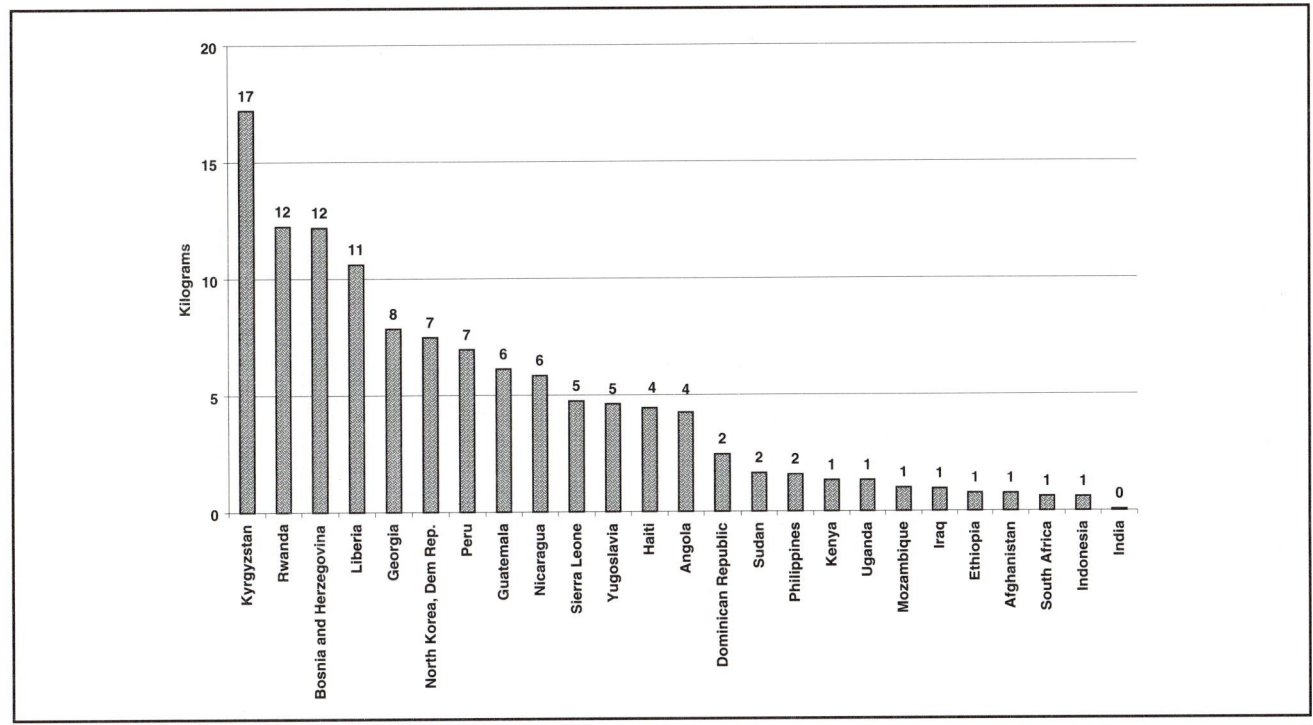

Source: Food and Agriculture Organization database (FAOSTAT) and U.S. Census International database; <http://apps.fao.org/cgi-bin/nph-db.pl> and <http://census.gov/>. Underlying data from Food and Agriculture Organization (FAO).

C11. BREAST-FED BABIES

C11-1. Percent of Children (0–3 Months, 6–9 Months, 20–26 Months) Who Are Exclusively Breast-fed, Selected Countries, 1990–1999

	Percent of Children Exclusively Breast-fed		
	0-3 months	6-9 months	20-26 months
Afghanistan	25	N/A	N/A
Algeria	48	29	21
Angola	12	70	49
Armenia	21	34	N/A
Azerbaijan	53	75	N/A
Bahrain	N/A	69	N/A
Bangladesh	52	69	90
Belize	24	49	N/A
Benin	15	97	65
Bolivia	61	80	32
Botswana	39	N/A	N/A
Brazil	42	30	17
Burkina Faso	5	56	N/A
Burundi	89	66	73
Cambodia	60	N/A	48
Cameroon	16	N/A	29
Cape Verde	18	N/A	N/A
Central African Republic	23	N/A	N/A
Chad	2	81	62
Chile	77	17	N/A
China	64	N/A	N/A
Colombia	16	61	17
Comoros	5	87	45
Congo, Dem. Rep. (Zaire)	32	40	64
Congo, Rep.	43	95	27
Costa Rica	35	47	12
Côte d'Ivoire	4	77	N/A
Croatia	24	N/A	N/A
Cuba	76	66	N/A
Dominican Republic	25	47	7
Ecuador	29	52	34
Egypt	53	37	N/A
El Salvador	16	76	68
Eritrea	66	45	60
Ethiopia	74	N/A	35
Gabon	32	N/A	N/A
Gambia	N/A	8	58
Ghana	37	N/A	66
Guatemala	50	56	43
Guinea	52	N/A	15
Haiti	3	83	25
Honduras	42	69	45
India	51	31	67
Indonesia	52	N/A	65
Iran	66	N/A	41
Iraq	N/A	N/A	25
Jordan	15	68	12
Kazakhstan	12	61	21
Kenya	17	94	54
Kyrgyzstan	31	N/A	79
Laos	36	N/A	31
Lesotho	54	47	52
Liberia	N/A	17	25

C11-1. Percent of Children (0–3 Months, 6–9 Months, 20–26 Months) Who Are Exclusively Breast-fed, Selected Countries, 1990–1999 *(continued)*

	Percent of Children Exclusively Breast-fed		
	0-3 months	6-9 months	20-26 months
Libya	N/A	N/A	39
Macedonia, FYRO	8	N/A	N/A
Madagascar	61	93	49
Malawi	11	78	68
Maldives	8	N/A	N/A
Mali	13	33	60
Mauritania	60	64	59
Mauritius	16	29	N/A
Mexico	38	36	21
Mongolia	93	84	74
Morocco	31	33	20
Mozambique	38	87	58
Myanmar (Burma)	N/A	78	75
Namibia	22	65	23
Nepal	83	63	88
Nicaragua	29	65	29
Niger	1	N/A	47
Nigeria	2	52	43
Oman	28	85	64
Pakistan	16	31	56
Panama	32	38	21
Papua New Guinea	75	74	66
Paraguay	7	59	15
Peru	63	83	43
Philippines	47	N/A	23
Rwanda	90	68	85
Senegal	16	69	50
Sierra Leone	N/A	94	41
Sri Lanka	24	60	66
Sudan	14	45	44
Swaziland	37	51	20
Syria	N/A	50	N/A
Tanzania	41	93	53
Thailand	4	71	27
Togo	15	N/A	77
Tunisia	12	N/A	16
Turkey	9	38	N/A
Turkmenistan	54	N/A	N/A
Uganda	70	64	40
United Arab Emirates	N/A	52	N/A
Uzbekistan	4	N/A	35
Yemen	25	79	41
Yugoslavia	6	35	13
Zambia	26	95	43
Zimbabwe	16	93	26

N/A Not Available

Source: The State of the World's Children, 2000: Table 2. Nutrition; United Nations Children's Fund (UNICEF); <http://www.unicef.org/sowc00/stat4.htm>. Underlying data from Demographic and Health Surveys, Multiple Indicator Cluster Surveys (MICS), World Health Organization (WHO), and United Nations Children's Fund (UNICEF).

D. Disease, Hunger and Malnutrition

GENERAL OVERVIEW

The impact of disease on the world's children is sobering. Every three seconds a young child dies, and in some countries one in five children does not reach his or her fifth birthday. This section gathers data on some of the major childhood killers, diseases such as diphtheria, malaria, measles, and tetanus. AIDS has had such a devastating impact on communities that we devote an entire chapter (Section E) to that epidemic. But infectious agents are not the only significant childhood killers. In developing countries, low birth weight and vitamin or mineral deficiencies kill millions and diminish the mental and physical capacities of still more. Surprisingly, traffic accidents account for thousands of deaths in the developing world, while injuries and cancer are leading causes of death in the industrial world.

Malnutrition, which affects more than one-third of the world's children, is a contributory factor in one-half of all child deaths. Hunger and under-nutrition also affect the children who survive, limiting their physical and mental development. In contrast, children in the industrial world are increasingly at risk for overweight and obesity, which can cause life-threatening conditions in the long term. According to the World Health Organization (WHO), obesity should be regarded as one of today's major principal neglected public health problems.

WHO records cases rather than deaths for specific diseases and does not break out figures for children. We have included these indicators because international health officials report that the diseases highlighted in this section kill mostly children and young adults. There are also no data dealing specifically with hunger among children. Nevertheless, we felt it imperative to present the general information available because hunger is a specter that haunts so many of the world's children.

EXPLANATION OF INDICATORS

D1-1–D1-14. Causes of death: This cluster of tables offers an overview of the major causes of death among the world's children. D1-1 summarizes causes worldwide; D1-2 and D1-3 look at cause of death by country income class. D1-4 then focuses on the developing world, where 97 percent of the under five deaths occur. The World Bank classifies countries into four categories based on per capita income (1998): High income ($9,361 or more), upper middle income ($3,031 to $9,360), lower middle income ($761 to $3,030), and low income ($760 or less). These figures, which change annually, are in 1998 dollars, which is the year of the table data. The final tables examine cause of death in 10 of the 40 nations for which the World Health Organization (WHO) collects country level information. These are a sample of nations by region and economic category. Unfortunately, WHO does not provide country-level data for African countries.

D2-1–D2-10. Preventable diseases: According to WHO estimates, close to three million children under five years of age die from vaccine preventable diseases annually, primarily in the developing world. Diphtheria, pertussis, measles, and tetanus are major killers, often in conjunction with malnutrition and other diseases such as pneumonia. Measles, for example, infects over 40 million children and kills about 900,000 under-fives each year; pertussis causes 200,000 to 300,000 fatalities. Each year about 200,000 infants die in the first month of life from neonatal tetanus, which occurs in newborns as a result of unsanitary birth practices, such as cutting the umbilical cord with an unclean blade. D2-1 gives an overview of deaths from preventable diseases; D2-2 to D2-7 present the number of reported deaths from specific preventable deaths by country over time. Three tables on polio complete this cluster. Polio was once a major killer and crippler of children. But as a result of a major campaign by international organizations, national governments, and private foundations, it was eradicated in much of the world by the end of the twentieth century. The World Health Organization reported fewer than 2,000 cases in 2000. D2-8 to D2-10 trace the history of this eradication, dramatically showing the progress that can be made when the international community mobilizes behind a health problem.

D3-1–D3-2. Malaria: These graphs present the number and percent of child deaths from malaria by World Health Organization region. As the charts indicate, malaria is most common in tropical and sub-tropical regions of the world, where it kills nearly 2.6 million people. Seventy-five per cent of these deaths are of children. Young children are especially vulnerable to malaria because they have not developed the partial immunity that results from surviving repeated infections. Child deaths due to malaria are particularly tragic since malaria can be treated with a variety of drugs. Its prevalence in the young population, especially in the developing countries, indicates inadequate and inaccessible health care services.

D4-1. Childhood cancer: Cancer is not a major cause of death among the world's children. Yet it is the chief cause of death due to disease in children under age 15 in the industrial world. This table presents statistics by gender for cancer deaths among selected developed nations.

D5-1. Deaths from preventable injuries: The World Health Organization includes fires, falls, car crashes, and drowning in its category of preventable injuries. According to UNICEF, these injuries cause more than 20,000 child (between 1 to 14 years) deaths each year in the world's industrialized countries and account for almost 40 percent of deaths in this age group. UNICEF studies associate the likelihood of a child being injured or killed with single parenthood, low maternal education, poor housing, large family size, parental drug or alcohol abuse, and poverty.

D6-1. Deaths from traffic accidents: Traffic accidents kill approximately 10,000 children each year in wealthy nations; in the rest of the world the figure is closer to 240,000 a year—the equivalent of two jumbo jets full of children crashing every day. The rate of child deaths in traffic accidents is today more than five times higher in Africa than in the European Union. It is more than three times higher in India than in the United States, even though Africa and India are still at the beginning of the growth curve in vehicle ownership. Although roads in the poor world carry fewer cars, they carry many more pedestrians and cyclists. Thus, there are higher chances of traffic casualties.

D7-1—D7-2. Vitamin and Mineral Deficiencies: Vitamin A deficiency (VAD) is a public health problem in more than 75 developing countries where over 200 million children are at risk from this largely preventable condition. VAD is associated with an increase in the severity of infections, particularly measles and diarrhoeal disease. At least 350,000 pre-school children become partially or totally blind every year from the condition, and about 60 percent of these children die within a few months of going blind. D7-1 ranks member nations of the World Health Organization on a scale of one to four in terms of progress toward eliminating VAD. A ranking of 1 designates countries moving toward elimination; 2 indicates nations that have acknowledged a problem but have not adequately tackled it; 3 denominates specific countries that have a problem but no plans for dealing with it. Nations with no problem or no data are ranked 4.

Iodine deficiency (D7-2) in early childhood can impair speech and hearing, motor development and physical growth. In both adults and children, chronic iodine deficiency causes goitre, a disorder characterized by swelling of the thyroid gland that can be seen as a growth in the neck. WHO estimated that the number of people with goitre was 750 million. Iodine deficiency has an enormous impact on communities and nations. The high costs associated with treating goitre, brain damage, and cretinism (a disease associated with physical deformity, dwarfism and mental retardation) are surpassed by the social and economic losses that result when generations are marked by diminished mental and physical capacities.

D8-1. Oral disease prevalence: The World Health Organization is just beginning to collect data on oral disease. To date the only general measure for children is DMFT (decayed, missing, or filled teeth) level per 12-year-old. The global average in 1999 was 2.2.

D9-1. Low birth weight or underweight: Low birth-weight is defined as less than 2,500 grams (about 5.5 pounds) at the time of birth. About 24 million low-birth-weight babies are born every year. Most of these are in developing countries, where one in five babies weighs less than the standard for a healthy-sized baby. Low birth weight is a major factor in the global total of more than 5 million yearly neonatal deaths. Low-birth-weight babies are much more likely to die in the first month of life than babies of normal weight, and those who survive are likely to be stunted for the rest of their lives. Children born underweight face increased risk of seizures, blindness and deafness, cerebral palsy, and mental retardation.

D10-1–D10-2. Childhood obesity: Child obesity is increasing worldwide at an alarming rate, although it is still relatively uncommon in the developing countries of Africa and Asia. The condition is linked to the sedentary lifestyle in technologically advanced countries where children spend considerable time with the computer and television. Increased consumption of junk food and unhealthy convenience meals exacerbate the problem. The consequences of obesity—which decreases productivity and increases the risk of heart disease, diabetes, hypertension, and early atherosclerosis—can be as serious as the consequences of underweight. Health professionals have very specific definitions of "overweight" and "obesity." Overweight is excess body weight compared to set standards. The excess weight may come from muscle, fat, bone, or water. Obesity refers specifically to having an abnormally high proportion of body fat. One of the more accurate ways of measuring overweight and obesity is the Body Mass Index (BMI). It is calculated by dividing a person's weight in kilograms by height in meters squared. D10-1 shows the cut-off points for BMI over which children are considered overweight and obese. D10-2 summarizes child obesity by continent.

D11-1–D11-5. Hunger: International organizations do not break out statistics for hunger among children. The United Nations estimates, however, that more than a third of the world's children are affected by food shortages. Because of the enormity of the problem, tables on hunger in the total population are presented in this cluster. D11-1 outlines the number and percent of the population undernourished over time. D11-2 presents the depth of hunger measured by the average dietary energy deficit of undernourished people—not of the population as a whole—expressed in kilocalories per person per day.

The higher the number, the deeper the hunger. Both tables include prevalence categories created by the U.N. Food and Agriculture Organization. The last three tables in the cluster show per capita consumption of total calories, protein, and cereals. The latter is important because cereals are the primary food source for majority of the world's population, especially the poor.

D12-1–D12-10. Malnutrition: Malnutrition, defined as the physiological condition resulting from inadequate food intake, contributes to more than half of all child deaths and to diminished capacities for those who survive. The following 10 tables and graphs present statistics on the impact of prolonged low levels of food intake, or undernutrition, on children. International organizations such as UNICEF and the World Health Organization look at three measures of undernutrition in assessing the nutritional status of children: stunting, wasting, and underweight. *Stunting* is low height for age. It usually reflects sustained periods of undernutrition. *Wasting* is low weight for height. It is generally caused by acute nutritional problems associated with a recent period of starvation or severe disease. *Underweight* is defined as low weight for age. It reflects both past and present episodes of undernutrition. The percentage underweight is a composite of stunting and wasting. Children who are underweight may be either short or thin. Underweight, stunting, and wasting are frequently part of a vicious cycle that includes poverty and disease. D12-1 to D12-4 provide a historical overview of undernutrition in the developing world; D12-5 to D12-10 offer a review of the 1990s. The data in these tables are obtained through surveys whose timing and frequency vary from country to country. Therefore, cross-country comparisons must be made cautiously.

D1. CAUSES OF DEATH

D1-1. Leading Causes of Death in the World, Ages 0 to 4 and 5 to 14, 1998

	Number
0-4 years	
Perinatal conditions	2,155,000
Acute lower respiratory infections	1,850,412
Diarrhoeal diseases	1,814,158
Measles	887,671
Malaria	793,368
Congenital abnormalities	404,849
HIV/AIDS	349,885
Pertussis	345,771
Tetanus	302,668
Protein-energy malnutrition	214,717
Drowning	125,301
Sexually Transmitted Diseases excluding HI	118,178
War injuries	103,323
Road traffic injuries	82,429
Meningitis	60,198
5-14 years	
Acute lower respiratory infections	213,429
Malaria	209,109
Road traffic injuries	161,956
Drowning	157,573
Diarrhoeal diseases	133,883
War injuries	57,285
Nephritis/nephrosis	44,640
Congenital abnormalities	43,056
Inflammatory cardiac disease	40,802
HIV/AIDS	39,042
Fires	38,968
Cerebrovascular disease	38,349
Tuberculosis	38,093
Interpersonal violence	34,938
Leukemia	34,503

Source: Injury: A Leading Cause of the Global Burden of Disease, Edited by Dr. E. Krug: Table 1. Violence and Injury Prevention, Department for Disability/ Injury Prevention and Rehabilitation, Social Change and Mental Health Cluster; <http://www.who.int/violence_injury_prevention/pages/ InjuryBofDtables.htm#World>. Underlying data from *World Health Report 1999* Database, World Health Organization (WHO).

D1-2. Leading Causes of Death, High-Income Countries,* Ages 0 to 4 and 5 to 14, 1998

Cause	Number
0-4 years	
Perinatal conditions	53,198
Congenital abnormalities	25,459
Acute lower respiratory infections	5,744
Measles	5,342
Diarrhoeal diseases	4,192
Pertussis	3,475
Road traffic injuries	2,328
Nutritional/endocrine isorders	1,853
Drowning	1,512
Interpersonal violence	1,311
Meningitis	1,144
Fires	1,048
Dementias	959
Inflammatory cardiac disease	851
Tetanus	741
5-14 years	
Road traffic injuries	5,313
Congenital abnormalities	1,491
Leukaemia	1,470
Drowning	1,159
Interpersonal violence	926
Acute lower respiratory infections	821
Nutritional/endocrine disorders	775
Self-inflicted injuries	702
Fires	666
Cerebrovascular disease	407
Inflammatory cardiac disease	396
Lymphoma	337
War injuries	301
Dementias	297
Falls	272

* Includes Andorra, Austria, Bahamas, Belgium, Canada, Cyprus, Denmark, Finland, France, Germany, Greece, Iceland, Ireland, Israel, Italy, Kuwait, Luxembourg, Monaco, Netherlands, the, Norway, Portugal, Qatar, San Marino, Spain, Sweden, Switzerland, United Arab Emirates, United Kingdom, and United States.

Source: Injury: A Leading Cause of the Global Burden of Disease, Edited by Dr. E. Krug: Table 7. Violence and Injury Prevention, Department for Disability/ Injury Prevention and Rehabilitation, Social Change and Mental Health Cluster; <http://www.who.int/violence_injury_prevention/pages/ InjuryBofDtables.htm#World>. Underlying data from *World Health Report 1999* Database, World Health Organization (WHO).

D1-3. Leading Causes of Death, Low- and Middle-Income Countries,* Ages 0 to 4 and 5 to 14, 1998

Cause	Number
0-4 years	
Perinatal conditions	2,101,802
Acute lower respiratory infections	1,844,668
Diarrheal diseases	1,809,966
Measles	882,329
Malaria	793,368
Congenital abnormalities	379,390
HIV/AIDS	349,712
Pertussis	342,296
Tetanus	301,927
Protein-energy malnutrition	214,112
Drowning	123,790
Sexually Transmitted Diseases excluding HIV	118,031
War injuries	102,859
Road traffic injuries	80,101
Meningitis	59,054
5-14 years	
Acute lower respiratory infections	212,608
Malaria	209,109
Road traffic injuries	156,643
Drowning	156,414
Diarrheal diseases	133,682
War injuries	56,984
Nephritis/nephrosis	44,510
Congenital abnormalities	41,565
Inflammatory cardiac disease	40,407
HIV/AIDS	38,876
Fires	38,302
Tuberculosis	38,076
Cerebrovascular disease	37,942
Interpersonal violence	34,012
Leukemia	33,033

*Includes Afghanistan, Albania, Algeria, Angola, Antigua and Barbuda, Argentina, Armenia, Azerbaijan, Bahrain, Bangladesh, Barbados, Belarus, Belize, Benin, Bhutan, Bolivia, Bosnia and Herzegovina, Botswana, Brazil, Bulgaria, Burkina Faso, Burundi, Cameroon, Cape Verde, Central African Republic, Chad, Chile, Colombia, Comoros, Congo, Rep., Costa Rica, Cote d'Ivoire, Croatia, Cuba, Czech Republic, Congo Dem. Rep. (Zaire), Djibouti, Dominica, Dominican Republic, Ecuador, Egypt, El Salvador, Equatorial Guinea, Eritrea, Estonia, Ethiopia, Gabon, Gambia, the, Georgia, Ghana, Grenada, Guatemala, Guinea, Guinea-Bissau, Guyana, Haiti, Honduras, Hungary, Indonesia, Iran , Iraq, Jamaica, Jordan, Kazakhstan, Kenya, Kyrgyzstan, Latvia, Lebanon, Lesotho, Liberia, Libya, Lithuania, Macedonia, FYRO, Madagascar, Malawi, Maldives, Mali, Malta, Mauritania, Mauritius, Mexico, Moldova, Morocco, Mozambique, Myanmar, Namibia, Nepal, Nicaragua, Niger, Nigeria, North Korea, Dem. Rep., Oman, Pakistan, Panama, Paraguay, Peru, Poland, Romania, Russia, Rwanda, Saint Kitts and Nevis, Saint Lucia, Saint Vincent and the Grenadines, Sao Tome and Principe, Saudi Arabia, Senegal, Seychelles, Sierra Leone, Slovakia, Slovenia, Somalia, South Africa, Sri Lanka, Sudan, Suriname, Swaziland, Syria, Tajikistan, Tanzania, Thailand, Togo, Trinidad and Tobago, Tunisia, Turkey, Turkmenistan, Uganda, Ukraine, Uruguay, Uzbekistan, Venezuela, Yemen, Yugoslavia, Zambia, and Zimbabwe.

Source: Injury: A Leading Cause of the Global Burden of Disease, Edited by Dr. E. Krug: Table 13. Violence and Injury Prevention, Department for Disability/ Injury Prevention and Rehabilitation, Social Change and Mental Health Cluster; <http://www.who.int/violence_injury_prevention/pages/ InjuryBofDtables.htm#World>. Underlying data from *World Health Report 1999* Database, World Health Organization (WHO).

D1-4. Causes of Death, Children under 5 Years of Age, in Developing Countries, mid-1990s

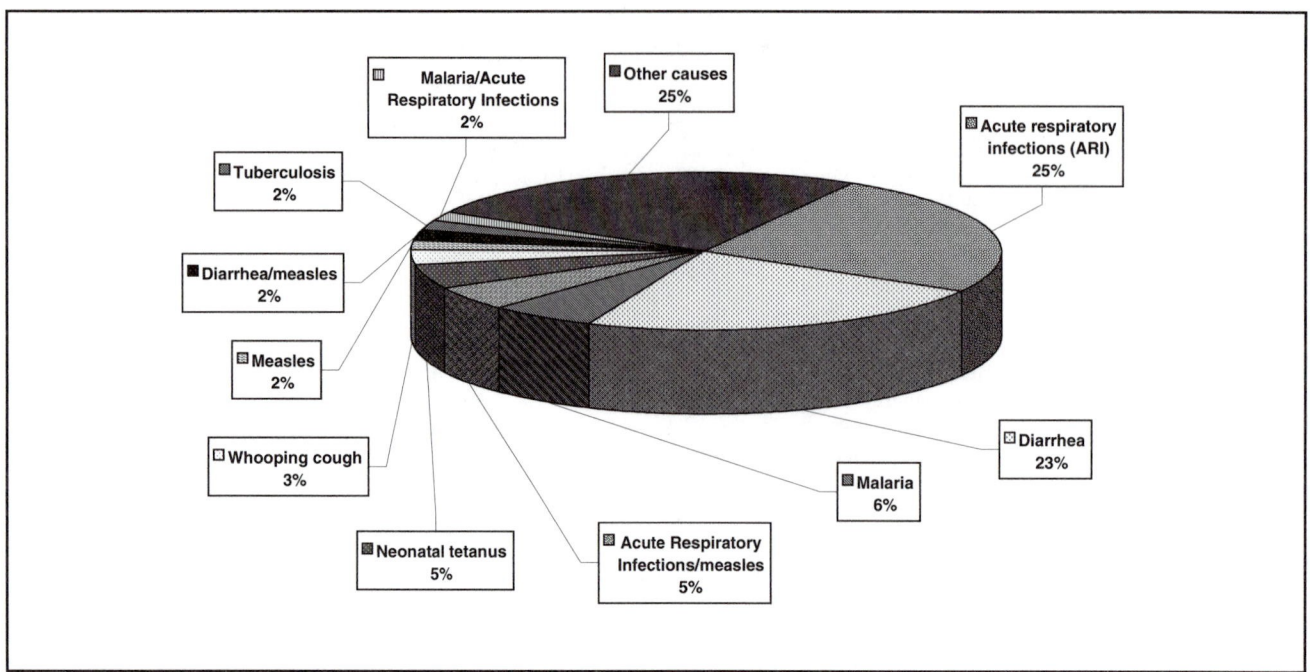

Source: The Progress of Nations 1996, United Nations Children's Fund (UNICEF); <http://www.unicef.org/pon96/leag1edu.htm>. Underlying data from World Health Organization (WHO).

D1-5. Infant Deaths: Numbers of Deaths and Death Rates, by Cause, Sex and Age, Argentina 1996

Causes of death	Number of infant deaths Less than 1 year			Rate per 100,000 infants Less than 1 year		
	Total	Male	Female	Total	Male	Female
All causes	14,099	8,070	6,029	2,087.4	2,330.6	1,831.6
Infectious and parasitic diseases	807	444	363	119.5	128.2	110.3
Intestinal infectious diseases	276	142	134	40.9	41.0	40.7
Whooping cough	13	8	5	1.9	2.3	1.5
Nutritional deficiencies	288	145	143	42.6	41.9	43.4
Diseases of the nervous system	268	162	106	39.7	46.8	32.2
Meningitis	160	102	58	23.7	29.5	17.6
Diseases of the respiratory system	1,279	758	521	189.4	218.9	158.3
Pneumonia	700	402	298	103.6	116.1	90.5
Influenza	3	3	N/R	0.4	0.9	N/R
Congenital anomalies	2,599	1,415	1,184	384.8	408.6	359.7
Spina bifida and hydrocephalus	291	157	134	43.1	45.3	40.7
Congenital anomalies of heart and circulatory system	1,046	597	449	154.9	172.4	136.4
Certain conditions originating in the perinatal period	6,746	3,926	2,820	998.8	1,133.8	856.7
Birth trauma	176	106	70	26.1	30.6	21.3
Hypoxia and birth asphyxia	2,802	1,725	1,077	414.8	498.2	327.2
Signs, symptoms and ill-defined conditions	674	385	289	99.8	111.2	87.8
Sudden infant death syndrome	N/A	N/A	N/A	N/A	N/A	N/A
Accidents	507	304	203	75.1	87.8	61.7

N/A Not Available
N/R None Reported

Source: 1997–1999 World Health Statistics Annual: Table 2. Infant Deaths: Numbers of Deaths and Death Rates, by Cause, Sex and Age; <http://www-nt.who.int/whosis/statistics/whsa/whsa_table2.cfm?path=statistics,whsa,whsa_table2&language=english>. Underlying data from World Health Organization (WHO).

D1-6. Leading Causes of Death, Ages 0 to 4 and 5 to 14, China 1998

Rank	Cause	Number
	0-4 years	
1	Perinatal conditions	186,196
2	Acute lower respiratory infections	171,681
3	Congenital abnormalities	56,563
4	Drowning	42,301
5	Diarrhoeal diseases	30,122
6	Protein-energy malnutrition	16,595
7	Pertussis	13,099
8	Interpersonal violence	11,461
9	Tetanus	9,218
10	Chronic obstructive pulmonary disease	8,879
11	Meningitis	8,128
12	Road traffic injuries	6,153
13	Tuberculosis	5,240
14	Poisoning	4,996
15	Leukaemia	4,807
	5-14 years	
1	Drowning	33,872
2	Road traffic injuries	14,618
3	Congenital abnormalities	9,179
4	Leukaemia	8,891
5	Acute lower respiratory infections	6,384
6	Self-inflicted injuries	5,253
7	Intestinal nematode infections	4,681
8	Poisoning	3,838
9	Interpersonal violence	2,813
10	Nephritis/nephrosis	2,792
11	Tuberculosis	2,207
12	Cerebrovascular disease	2,187
13	Vitamin A deficiency	2,006
14	Appendicitis	1,982
15	Diarrhoeal diseases	1,980

Source: *Injury: A Leading Cause of the Global Burden of Disease*, Edited by Dr. E. Krug: Table 39. Violence and Injury Prevention, Department for Disability/ Injury Prevention and Rehabilitation, Social Change and Mental Health Cluster; <http://www.who.int/violence_injury_prevention/pages/ InjuryBofDtables.htm#World>. Underlying data from *World Health Report 1999* Database, World Health Organization (WHO).

D1-7. Infant Deaths: Numbers of Deaths and Death Rates, by Cause, Sex and Age, Cuba 1996

	Number of infant deaths Less than 1 year			Rate per 100,000 infants Less than 1 year		
	Total	Male	Female	Total	Male	Female
All causes	1 109	645	464	790.6	901.6	675.1
Infectious and parasitic diseases	101	55	46	72.0	76.9	66.9
Intestinal infectious diseases	15	6	9	10.7	8.4	13.1
Whooping cough	N/A	N/A	N/A	N/A	N/A	N/A
Nutritional deficiencies	3	N/A	3	2.1	N/A	4.4
Diseases of the nervous system	58	34	24	41.3	47.5	34.9
Meningitis	39	25	14	27.8	34.9	20.4
Diseases of the respiratory system	67	42	25	47.8	58.7	36.4
Pneumonia	49	33	16	34.9	46.1	23.3
Influenza	N/A	N/A	N/A	N/A	N/A	N/A
Congenital anomalies	312	174	138	222.4	243.2	200.8
Spina bifida and hydrocephalus	12	5	7	8.6	7.0	10.2
Congenital anomalies of heart and circulatory system	169	96	73	120.5	134.2	106.2
Certain conditions originating in the perinatal period	442	280	162	315.1	391.4	235.7

D1-7. Infant Deaths: Numbers of Deaths and Death Rates, by Cause, Sex and Age, Cuba 1996 (continued)

	Number of infant deaths Less than 1 year			Rate per 100,000 infants Less than 1 year		
	Total	Male	Female	Total	Male	Female
Birth trauma	12	9	3	8.6	12.6	4.4
Hypoxia and birth asphyxia	302	192	110	215.3	268.4	160.0
Signs, symptoms and ill-defined conditions	6	3	3	4.3	4.2	4.4
Sudden infant death syndrome	4	2	2	2.9	2.8	2.9
Accidents	45	22	23	32.1	30.8	33.5
N/A Not Available						

Source: 1997–1999 World Health Statistics Annual: Table 2. Infant Deaths: Numbers of Deaths and Death Rates, by Cause, Sex and Age; <http://www-nt.who.int/whosis/statistics/whsa/whsa_table2.cfm?path=statistics,whsa,whsa_table2&language=english>. Underlying data from World Health Organization (WHO).

D1-8. Infant Deaths: Numbers of Deaths and Death Rates, by Cause, Sex and Age, Estonia 1998

	Number of infant deaths Less than 1 year			Rate per 100,000 infants Less than 1 year		
	Total	Male	Female	Total	Male	Female
All causes	114	63	51	929.2	994.2	859.7
Infectious and parasitic diseases	6	6	N/R	48.9	94.7	N/R
Intestinal infectious diseases	3	3	N/R	24.5	47.3	N/R
Whooping cough	N/R	N/R	N/R	N/R	N/R	N/R
Nutritional deficiencies	N/R	N/R	N/R	N/R	N/R	N/R
Diseases of the nervous system	N/R	N/R	N/R	N/R	N/R	N/R
Meningitis	N/R	N/R	N/R	N/R	N/R	N/R
Diseases of the respiratory system	12	7	5	97.8	110.5	84.3
Pneumonia	9	6	3	73.4	94.7	50.6
Influenza	N/R	N/R	N/R	N/R	N/R	N/R
Congenital anomalies	34	21	13	277.1	331.4	219.2
Spina bifida and hydrocephalus	3	3	N/R	24.5	47.3	N/R
Congenital anomalies of heart and circulatory system	16	7	9	130.4	110.5	151.7
Certain conditions originating in the perinatal period	45	20	25	366.8	315.6	421.4
Birth trauma	3	1	2	24.5	15.8	33.7
Hypoxia and birth asphyxia	21	7	14	171.2	110.5	236
Signs, symptoms and ill-defined conditions	4	3	1	32.6	47.3	16.9
Sudden infant death syndrome	4	3	1	32.6	47.3	16.9
Accidents	12	6	6	97.8	94.7	101.1
N/R None Reported						

Source: 1997–1999 World Health Statistics Annual: Table 2. Infant Deaths: Numbers of Deaths and Death Rates, by Cause, Sex and Age; <http://www-nt.who.int/whosis/statistics/whsa/whsa_table2.cfm?path=statistics,whsa,whsa_table2&language=english>. Underlying data from World Health Organization (WHO).

D1-9. Leading Causes of Death, Ages 0 to 4 and 5 to 14, India 1998

Rank	Cause	Number
	0-4 years	
1	Perinatal conditions	611,910
2	Acute lower respiratory infections	550,704
3	Diarrhoeal diseases	538,466
4	Measles	190,000
5	Congenital abnormalities	126,152
6	Tetanus	122,144
7	Pertussis	71,410
8	Protein-energy malnutrition	38,875
9	STDs excluding HIV	33,216
10	Road traffic injuries	21,976
11	Meningitis	17,927
12	Drowning	17,687
13	Fires	15,199
14	Tuberculosis	14,385
15	Interpersonal violence	13,648
	5-14 years	
1	Acute lower respiratory infections	71,971
2	Diarrhoeal diseases	44,256
3	Road traffic injuries	37,755
4	Drowning	31,595
5	Fires	16,117
6	Tetanus	15,726
7	Nephritis/nephrosis	15,398
8	Falls	11,478
9	Congenital abnormalities	11,315
10	Tropical diseases	10,849
11	Tuberculosis	9,181
12	Diabetes mellitus	8,122
13	Dengue fever	7,369
14	Self-inflicted injuries	6,576
15	Vitamin A deficiency	5,771

Source: Injury: A Leading Cause of the Global Burden of Disease, Edited by Dr. E. Krug: Violence and Injury Prevention, Department for Disability/Injury Prevention and Rehabilitation, Social Change and Mental Health Cluster; <http://www.who.int/violence_injury_prevention/pages/InjuryBofDtables.htm#World>. Underlying data from *World Health Report 1999* Database, World Health Organization (WHO).

D1-10. Infant Deaths: Numbers of Deaths and Death Rates, by Cause, Sex and Age, Israel 1996

	Number of infant deaths Less than 1 year			Rate per 100,000 infants Less than 1 year		
	Total	**Male**	**Female**	**Total**	**Male**	**Female**
All causes	767	414	353	632.1	663.2	599.3
Infectious and parasitic diseases	15	6	9	12.4	9.6	15.3
Intestinal infectious diseases	N/R	N/R	N/R	N/R	N/R	N/R
Whooping cough	N/R	N/R	N/R	N/R	N/R	N/R
Nutritional deficiencies	N/R	N/R	N/R	N/R	N/R	N/R
Diseases of the nervous system	15	8	7	12.4	12.8	11.9
Meningitis	1	N/R	1	0.8	N/R	1.7
Diseases of the respiratory system	24	11	13	19.8	17.6	22.1
Pneumonia	10	5	5	8.2	8	8.5
Influenza	N/R	N/R	N/R	N/R	N/R	N/R
Congenital anomalies	237	132	105	195.3	211.4	178.3
Spina bifida and hydrocephalus	16	5	11	13.2	8	18.7
Congenital anomalies of heart and circulatory system	86	51	35	70.9	81.7	59.4
Certain conditions originating in the perinatal period	350	194	156	288.5	310.8	264.8

D1-10. Infant Deaths: Numbers of Deaths and Death Rates, by Cause, Sex and Age, Israel 1996 (continued)

	Number of infant deaths Less than 1 year			Rate per 100,000 infants Less than 1 year		
	Total	Male	Female	Total	Male	Female
Birth trauma	8	5	3	6.6	8	5.1
Hypoxia and birth asphyxia	198	111	87	163.2	177.8	147.7
Signs, symptoms and ill-defined conditions	79	40	39	65.1	64.1	66.2
Sudden infant death syndrome	34	22	12	28	35.2	20.4
Accidents	16	11	5	13.2	17.6	8.5
N/R None Reported						

Source: 1997–1999 World Health Statistics Annual: Table 2. Infant Deaths: Numbers of Deaths and Death Rates, by Cause, Sex and Age; <http://www-nt.who.int/whosis/statistics/whsa/whsa_table2.cfm?path=statistics,whsa,whsa_table2&language=english>. Underlying data from World Health Organization (WHO).

D1-11. Infant Deaths: Numbers of Deaths and Death Rates, by Cause, Sex and Age, Japan 1997

	Number of infant deaths Less than 1 year			Rate per 100,000 infants Less than 1 year		
	Total	Male	Female	Total	Male	Female
All causes	4,403	2,414	1,989	369.5	395.2	342.5
Infectious and parasitic diseases	149	86	63	12.5	14.1	10.8
Intestinal infectious diseases	14	8	6	1.2	1.3	1.0
Whooping cough	2	2	N/R	0.2	0.3	N/R
Nutritional deficiencies	15	7	8	1.3	1.1	1.4
Diseases of the nervous system	84	51	33	7.0	8.3	5.7
Meningitis	20	9	11	1.7	1.5	1.9
Diseases of the respiratory system	191	114	77	16.0	18.7	13.3
Pneumonia	84	57	27	7.0	9.3	4.6
Influenza	3	2	1	0.3	0.3	0.2
Congenital anomalies	1,505	762	743	126.3	124.7	127.9
Spina bifida and hydrocephalus	21	11	10	1.8	1.8	1.7
Congenital anomalies of heart and circulatory system	726	370	356	60.9	60.6	61.3
Certain conditions originating in the perinatal period	1,250	695	555	104.9	113.8	95.6
Birth trauma	32	23	9	2.7	3.8	1.5
Hypoxia and birth asphyxia	577	322	255	48.4	52.7	43.9
Signs, symptoms and ill-defined conditions	537	318	219	45.1	52.1	37.7
Sudden infant death syndrome	496	290	206	41.6	47.5	35.5
Accidents	278	165	113	23.3	27.0	19.5
N/R None reported						

Source: 1997–1999 World Health Statistics Annual: Table 2. Infant Deaths: Numbers of Deaths and Death Rates, by Cause, Sex and Age; <http://www-nt.who.int/whosis/statistics/whsa/whsa_table2.cfm?path=statistics,whsa,whsa_table2&language=english>. Underlying data from, World Health Organization (WHO).

D1-12. Infant Deaths: Numbers of Deaths and Death Rates, by Cause, Sex and Age, Romania 1998

	Number of infant deaths Less than 1 year			Rate per 100,000 infants Less than 1 year		
	Total	Male	Female	Total	Male	Female
All causes	4 868	2 755	2 113	2051.4	2264.3	1827.5
Infectious and parasitic diseases	240	110	130	101.1	90.4	112.4
Intestinal infectious diseases	168	72	96	70.8	59.2	83.0
Whooping cough	N/A	N/A	N/A	N/A	N/A	N/A
Nutritional deficiencies	2	2	N/A	0.8	1.6	N/A
Diseases of the nervous system	114	66	48	48.0	54.2	41.5
Meningitis	35	20	15	14.7	16.4	13.0
Diseases of the respiratory system	1 574	883	691	663.3	725.7	597.6
Pneumonia	1 533	855	678	646.0	702.7	586.4
Influenza	N/A	N/A	N/A	N/A	N/A	N/A
Congenital anomalies	1 006	560	446	423.9	460.3	385.7
Spina bifida and hydrocephalus	141	72	69	59.4	59.2	59.7
Congenital anomalies of heart and circulatory system	400	235	165	168.6	193.1	142.7
Certain conditions originating in the perinatal period	1 529	940	589	644.3	772.6	509.4
Birth trauma	155	94	61	65.3	77.3	52.8
Hypoxia and birth asphyxia	647	405	242	272.7	332.9	209.3
Signs, symptoms and ill-defined conditions	8	4	4	3.4	3.3	3.5
Sudden infant death syndrome	N/A	N/A	N/A	N/A	N/A	N/A
Accidents	189	82	107	79.6	67.4	92.5

N/A Not Available

Source: 1997–1999 World Health Statistics Annual: Table 2. Infant Deaths: Numbers of Deaths and Death Rates, by Cause, Sex and Age; <http://www-nt.who.int/whosis/statistics/whsa/whsa_table2.cfm?path=statistics,whsa,whsa_table2&language=english>. Underlying data from, World Health Organization (WHO).

D1-13. Infant Deaths: Numbers of Deaths and Death Dates, by Cause, Sex and Age, United Kingdom 1997

	Number of infant deaths Less than 1 year			Rate per 100,000 infants Less than 1 year		
	Total	Male	Female	Total	Male	Female
All causes	4,253	2,391	1,862	586.0	642.7	526.3
Infectious and parasitic diseases	138	76	62	19.0	20.4	17.5
Intestinal infectious diseases	33	19	14	4.5	5.1	4.0
Whooping cough	3	2	1	0.4	0.5	0.3
Nutritional deficiencies	2	2	N/R	0.3	0.5	N/R
Diseases of the nervous system	131	68	63	18.0	18.3	17.8
Meningitis	30	13	17	4.1	3.5	4.8
Diseases of the respiratory system	189	98	91	26.0	26.3	25.7
Pneumonia	74	38	36	10.2	10.2	10.2
Influenza	3	1	2	0.4	0.3	0.6
Congenital anomalies	813	443	370	112.0	119.1	104.6
Spina bifida and hydrocephalus	26	18	8	3.6	4.8	2.3
Congenital anomalies of heart and circulatory system	315	174	141	43.4	46.8	39.9
Certain conditions originating in the perinatal period	2,189	1,223	966	301.6	328.8	273.0
Birth trauma	132	74	58	18.2	19.9	16.4
Hypoxia and birth asphyxia	624	359	265	86.0	96.5	74.9
Signs, symptoms and ill-defined conditions	481	300	181	66.3	80.6	51.2
Sudden infant death syndrome	423	266	157	58.3	71.5	44.4
Accidents	47	24	23	6.5	6.5	6.5

N/R None Reported

Source: 1997–1999 World Health Statistics Annual: Table 2. Infant Deaths: Numbers of Deaths and Death Rates, by Cause, Sex and Age; <http://www-nt.who.int/whosis/statistics/whsa/whsa_table2.cfm?path=statistics,whsa,whsa_table2&language=english>. Underlying data from, World Health Organization (WHO).

D1-14. Infant Deaths: Numbers of Deaths and Death Rates, by Cause, Sex and Age, United States of America 1997

	Number of infant deaths Less than 1 year			Rate per 100,000 infants Less than 1 year		
	Total	Male	Female	Total	Male	Female
All causes	28,045	15,788	12,257	722.6	795.1	646.7
Infectious and parasitic diseases	721	420	301	18.6	21.2	15.9
Intestinal infectious diseases	204	120	84	5.3	6.0	4.4
Whooping cough	6	3	3	0.2	0.2	0.2
Nutritional deficiencies	11	5	6	0.3	0.3	0.3
Diseases of the nervous system	424	218	206	10.9	11.0	10.9
Meningitis	97	40	57	2.5	2.0	3.0
Diseases of the respiratory system	813	501	312	20.9	25.2	16.5
Pneumonia	409	250	159	10.5	12.6	8.4
Influenza	12	7	5	0.3	0.4	0.3
Congenital anomalies	6,178	3,266	2,912	159.2	164.5	153.6
Spina bifida and hydrocephalus	194	87	107	5.0	4.4	5.6
Congenital anomalies of heart and circulatory system	2,092	1,149	943	53.9	57.9	49.8
Certain conditions originating in the perinatal period	12,935	7,308	5,627	333.3	368.1	296.9
Birth trauma	185	114	71	4.8	5.7	3.7
Hypoxia and birth asphyxia	3,487	2,031	1,456	89.9	102.3	76.8
Signs, symptoms and ill-defined conditions	3,773	2,268	1,505	97.2	114.2	79.4
Sudden infant death syndrome	2,991	1,812	1,179	77.1	91.3	62.2
Accidents	763	428	335	19.7	21.6	17.7

Source: 1997–1999 World Health Statistics Annual: Table 2. Infant Deaths: Numbers of Deaths and Death Rates, by Cause, Sex and Age; <http://www-nt.who.int/whosis/statistics/whsa/whsa_table2.cfm?path=statistics,whsa,whsa_table2&language=english>. Underlying data from World Health Organization (WHO).

D2. PREVENTABLE DISEASES

D2-1. Annual Deaths Due to Vaccine-Preventable Diseases, 2000

Disease	No. of preventable annual deaths
Hepatitis B *	900,000
Measles	888,000
Tetanus (including 215,000 neonatal deaths)	410,000
Haemophilus influenza type b	400,000
Pertussis	346,000
Yellow fever *	30,000
Diphtheria	5,000
Poliomyelitis (polio)	720
Total	2,979,720

* Most deaths do not occur in childhood.

Source: Bulletin of the World Health Organization, The International Journal of Public Health, Volume 78, Number 10, Bulletin 2000, 1172–1282. Special Theme— *Child Mortality; The Evolution of Child Health Programmes in Developing Countries: From Targeting Diseases to Targeting People,* By Mariam Claeson, & Ronald J. Waldman: Table 1. Annual deaths due to vaccine-preventable diseases; <http://www.who.int/bulletin/pdf/2000/issue10/bu0762.pdf>. Underlying data from World Health Organization (WHO).

D2-2. Number of Reported Cases of Diphtheria 1980, 1985, 1990, 1995, 1997

Country	1980	1985	1990	1995	1997
Afghanistan	1,939	3,179	368	N/A	N/A
Albania	3	3	18	5	1
Algeria	116	66	30	N/A	30
Angola	0	9	64	N/A	N/A
Argentina	86	45	4	4	0
Armenia	N/A	N/A	N/A	29	12
Australia	1	17	7	0	0
Austria	0	1	0	0	0
Azerbaijan	N/A	N/A	N/A	883	27
Bangladesh	1,559	204	711	282	96
Barbados	11	N/A	0	0	0
Belarus	N/A	N/A	N/A	322	96
Benin	127	16	N/A	N/A	N/A
Bolivia	30	31	4	5	3
Burkina Faso	725	51	0	0	N/A
Burundi	6	14	0	0	N/A
Cambodia	1,559	367	179	N/A	0
Canada	55	9	8	2	1
Chile	253	224	37	2	0
China	9,767	1,423	421	85	35
Colombia	263	32	16	6	1
Djibouti	411	1	0	0	N/A
Dominican Republic	187	100	27	13	25
Ecuador	16	44	3	154	19
Egypt	333	663	59	10	1
Estonia	N/A	N/A	N/A	19	3
Ethiopia	142	99	61	45	N/A
Georgia	N/A	N/A	N/A	419	286
Germany	19	4	6	4	1
Ghana	40	1	66	0	N/A
Guatemala	7	N/A	12	0	1
Guinea	0	0	37	N/A	0
Haiti	35	55	0	N/A	N/A
India	39,231	15,685	8,425	2,123	1,326
Indonesia	3,674	1,161	2,200	597	4,355
Iran	139	143	373	9	30
Iraq	1,122	1,348	10	133	290
Italy	30	5	0	1	0
Japan	66	9	5	N/A	N/A
Kazakhstan	N/A	N/A	N/A	1,105	160
Kenya	6,395	0	1	0	0
Kyrgyzstan	N/A	N/A	N/A	693	292
Laos	11	23	9	0	10
Laos	N/A	N/A	N/A	5,280	399
Latvia	N/A	N/A	N/A	369	42
Lesotho	13	26	37	N/A	N/A
Lithuania	N/A	N/A	N/A	43	2
Madagascar	227	1,963	252	179	N/A
Malawi	13	N/A	N/A	0	N/A
Malaysia	131	39	9	1	1
Mali	143	259	5	1	N/A
Mauritania	0	129	18	N/A	0
Moldova	N/A	N/A	N/A	418	46
Mongolia	0	0	1	128	69
Morocco	43	11	0	0	0
Mozambique	11	1	0	N/A	0
Myanmar (Burma)	830	268	181	28	5
Nepal	82	1,156	7	2,038	726

D2-2. Number of Reported Cases of Diphtheria 1980, 1985, 1990, 1995, 1997 *(continued)*

Country	1980	1985	1990	1995	1997
Niger	34	269	102	4	31
Nigeria	165	1,996	1,768	N/A	N/A
Pakistan	14,328	1,450	1,371	9	26
Paraguay	14	27	10	1	0
Peru	185	112	44	4	2
Philippines	1,910	1,669	921	173	138
Portugal	90	51	0	0	0
Russia	N/A	N/A	N/A	35,652	4,057
Rwanda	3	15	14	N/A	N/A
Saudi Arabia	99	65	1	1	1
Senegal	291	N/A	N/A	N/A	0
South Africa	57	46	34	N/A	3
South Korea, Rep.	51	2	0	N/A	0
Sri Lanka	37	10	0	0	3
Sudan	587	342	1,342	17	15
Sweden	4	10	0	0	0
Syria	366	400	80	61	59
Tajikistan	N/A	N/A	N/A	4,455	723
Thailand	1,918	762	58	19	38
Turkey	86	145	20	4	2
Turkmenistan	N/A	N/A	N/A	87	38
Uganda	181	N/A	95	N/A	N/A
Ukraine	20	12	0	0	0
United Kingdom	5	4	2	13	14
United States	3	3	4	0	5
Uzbekistan	N/A	N/A	N/A	638	34
Venezuela	31	4	0	0	0
Vietnam	1,730	2,361	509	167	152
Yemen	555	981	N/A	54	N/A
Zambia	12	35	4	N/A	0
Zimbabwe	8	4	0	0	0

N/A = Not available

Source: Number of reported cases, Department of Vaccines and Biologicals (V&B), formerly known as the Global Programme for Vaccines and Immunization; <http://www.who.int/gpv-surv/>. Underlying data from World Health Organization (WHO).

D2-3. Number of Reported Cases of Measles 1980, 1985, 1990, 1995, 1997

Country	1980	1985	1990	1995	1997
Afghanistan	32,455	14,457	1,609	N/A	N/A
Albania	N/A	0	428	0	2,387
Algeria	15,527	20,114	1,796	8,204	19,573
American Samoa	16	28	498	0	12
Angola	29,656	22,822	29,069	635	8,183
Antigua Barbuda	2,291	1	0	0	0
Argentina	16,102	9,240	2,022	655	125
Armenia	N/A	N/A	N/A	187	802
Australia	N/A	N/A	880	1,198	853
Bahamas	484	25	65	0	1
Bahrain	1,861	1,910	59	3	4
Bangladesh	11,077	11,699	1,705	4,995	10,329
Barbados	27	2	51	0	0
Belarus	N/A	N/A	N/A	1,516	135
Belize	607	7	61	4	0
Benin	18,635	13,210	N/A	10,469	9,521
Bhutan	1,642	819	173	148	169
Bolivia	4,181	217	984	76	8

D2-3. Number of Reported Cases of Measles 1980, 1985, 1990, 1995, 1997 *(continued)*

Country	1980	1985	1990	1995	1997
Botswana	4,091	1,684	1,218	478	5,032
Brazil	33,727	10,457	61,435	793	50,460
Bulgaria	10,763	972	150	172	23
Burkina Faso	13,713	17,461	9,804	5,669	1,438
Burundi	49,227	36,740	13,282	14,782	1,273
Cambodia	32,240	44,557	2,473	2,038	3,826
Cameroon	N/A	47,178	21,150	2,463	7,504
Canada	13,864	2,816	876	2,357	570
Cape Verde	1,279	3,048	0	10	8,584
Central African Republic	8,280	2,446	1,275	902	194
Chad	N/A	6,430	7,316	657	10,446
Chile	3,844	16,790	1,958	0	58
China	8,173	24,943	20,169	53,232	14,085
Colombia	9,222	5,572	17,520	410	43
Comoros	1,801	0	2,328	0	0
Congo, Dem. Rep. (Zaire)	32,596	19,508	4,564	5,443	5,766
Congo, Rep.	11,892	7,600	3,608	2,185	1,267
Cook Islands	363	50	36	7	194
Costa Rica	1,000	1	76	35	27
Cote d'Ivoire	7,633	8,892	17,799	30,039	9,665
Croatia	N/A	N/A	N/A	697	242
Cuba	3,924	3,874	17	1	0
Czech Republic	N/A	N/A	N/A	5	14
Denmark	28,249	13,187	180	20	61
Djibouti	N/A	108	104	8	N/A
Dominica	0	64	13	0	0
Dominican Republic	9,760	4,392	3,477	0	5
Ecuador	2,722	1,183	1,673	919	0
Egypt	839	5,554	887	1,833	4,606
El Salvador	2,315	1,413	1,124	0	0
Equatorial Guinea	N/A	464	32	44	0
Eritrea	N/A	N/A	N/A	185	777
Estonia	N/A	N/A	N/A	17	18
Ethiopia	10,690	1,008	1,836	562	1,113
Fiji	913	152	32	414	828
Finland	2,147	614	3	6	0
France	1,244	399	N/A	N/A	N/A
French Polynesia	379	1,927	30	7	518
Gabon	1,641	5,222	738	N/A	N/A
Gambia, the	284	1,628	N/A	130	1,500
Georgia	N/A	N/A	N/A	109	342
Germany	28,745	568	N/A	N/A	N/A
Ghana	17,148	64,517	32,246	40,276	37,261
Greece	13,464	1,484	245	112	126
Grenada	53	8	5	3	0
Guadeloupe	2	7	0	0	116
Guatemala	2,703	2,272	8,820	23	8
Guinea	8,552	2,969	12,756	1,085	10,170
Guinea-Bissau	1,332	1,328	259	528	498
Guyana	464	87	1	0	0
Haiti	507	2,111	1,414	N/A	0
Honduras	4,188	6,476	8,360	0	5
Hong Kong SAR, China	1,669	280	48	33	318
Hungary	1,198	20	N/A	19	24
Iceland	13	374	14	1	N/A
India	48,500	30,144	24,076	37,494	61,004
Indonesia	28,935	9,458	26,569	37,693	15,313
Iran	31,130	20,582	5,341	263	3,901

D2-3. Number of Reported Cases of Measles 1980, 1985, 1990, 1995, 1997 *(continued)*

Country	1980	1985	1990	1995	1997
Iraq	26,542	22,186	3,045	7,650	708
Ireland	1,106	9,903	556	231	173
Israel	215	3,005	212	25	10
Italy	27,452	9,504	5,223	37,054	28,096
Jamaica	36	67	3,651	15	0
Jordan	552	559	290	318	7,026
Kazakhstan	N/A	N/A	N/A	284	120
Kenya	28,473	45,956	11,536	3,322	3,339
Kiribati	170	2,015	30	4	25
Kuwait	1,382	2,061	71	12	26
Kyrgyzstan	N/A	N/A	N/A	17	998
Laos	13,219	2,810	3,259	N/A	N/A
Laos	1,380	1,492	2,168	3,174	671
Lebanon	N/A	N/A	N/A	3	134
Lesotho	7,935	7,362	2,195	304	0
Liberia	6,567	2,686	N/A	56	2,961
Libya	1,547	4,193	931	N/A	26
Lithuania	N/A	N/A	N/A	188	30
Luxembourg	63	62	16	1	1
Macao	73	265	19	3	3
Macedonia, FYRO	N/A	N/A	N/A	217	364
Madagascar	54,143	4,348	14,459	11,731	5,184
Malawi	31,614	61,045	N/A	4,218	10,845
Malaysia	8,727	5,163	563	654	627
Maldives	N/A	2,029	0	3,070	N/A
Mali	10,007	29,732	1,388	3,306	3,531
Malta	14	175	6	27	5
Marshall Islands	0	4	14	N/A	0
Mauritania	11,441	15,123	1,379	195	499
Mauritius	35	2	1	6	0
Mexico	29,730	23,410	3,246	244	28
Moldova	N/A	N/A	N/A	1,175	364
Mongolia	5,338	525	296	555	4
Morocco	21,383	4,216	1,577	2,380	2,512
Mozambique	30,070	16,507	18,082	4,166	15,324
Myanmar (Burma)	21,457	16,386	7,900	1,170	1,035
Namibia	N/A	N/A	N/A	1,723	5,359
Nauru	10	N/A	300	0	58
Nepal	561	952	182	4,810	11,669
Netherlands, the	178	24	16	184	21
New Caledonia	800	77	18	2	0
New Zealand	N/A	N/A	N/A	N/A	2,041
Nicaragua	3,784	956	19,150	5	0
Niger	36,811	64,689	20,463	2,450	32,649
Nigeria	31,034	30,696	50,146	12,393	21,385
Norway	1,322	1,312	95	18	N/A
Oman	10,630	4,161	1,262	68	12
Pakistan	28,573	26,686	21,785	1,720	1,848
Panama	2,096	4,295	1,891	19	0
Papua New Guinea	12,125	5,680	4,575	3,730	678
Paraguay	745	666	1,396	73	198
Peru	19,246	7,725	1,437	353	95
Philippines	26,765	62,959	42,938	3,913	9,218
Poland	24,882	35,680	56,471	759	261
Portugal	N/A	N/A	407	190	90
Puerto Rico	231	64	1,805	11	0
Qatar	392	1,410	314	0	439
Reunion	72	26	N/A	N/A	N/A

D2-3. Number of Reported Cases of Measles 1980, 1985, 1990, 1995, 1997 *(continued)*

Country	1980	1985	1990	1995	1997
Romania	10,476	5,007	4,691	2,188	23,579
Russia	N/A	N/A	N/A	6,630	2,893
Rwanda	14,866	16,760	8,970	28,874	787
Saint Kitts and Nevis	305	27	80	1	0
Saint Lucia	35	9	7	2	0
Saint Vincent	257	5	1	0	0
Samoa	376	1,095	0	0	0
San Marino	N/A	N/A	1	N/A	22
Sao Tome and Principe	519	62	10	23	0
Saudi Arabia	46,115	18,393	5,439	2,574	3,978
Senegal	29,144	N/A	5,004	N/A	6,594
Seychelles	3	10	13	0	3
Sierra Leone	3,625	3,351	830	344	361
Singapore	N/A	136	143	185	1,413
Slovakia	N/A	N/A	N/A	2	620
Slovenia	N/A	N/A	N/A	402	9
Solomon Islands	340	2	343	0	0
South Africa	19,193	17,884	10,624	8,845	1,337
South Korea, Rep.	5,097	1,283	3,415	71	2
Spain	14,250	15,127	21,650	8,845	0
Sri Lanka	5,032	8,798	4,004	408	195
Sudan	50,168	2,053	14,075	841	350
Suriname	254	110	27	0	0
Swaziland	N/A	3,253	1,465	171	609
Sweden	1,786	326	29	N/A	3
Switzerland	N/A	N/A	2,300	30	0
Syria	1,478	425	535	1,362	6,850
Tajikistan	N/A	N/A	N/A	160	3,882
Tanzania	63,100	46,032	14,920	3,160	7,287
Thailand	16,795	32,156	29,463	11,112	14,617
Togo	33,960	25,729	4,548	6,144	450
Tonga	2,336	412	65	0	1,081
Trinidad and Tobago	384	3,549	511	0	1
Tunisia	225	4,766	547	676	371
Turkey	8,618	14,695	11,372	13,463	22,795
Turkmenistan	N/A	N/A	N/A	393	377
Tuvalu	509	0	N/A	1	14
Uganda	13,415	N/A	2,637	42,659	12,562
Ukraine	2,796	2,400	1,187	671	243
United Kingdom	16,890	39,238	28,228	7,763	2,296
United States	13,506	2,822	27,786	309	138
Uruguay	141	160	110	5	2
Uzbekistan	N/A	N/A	N/A	295	264
Vanuatu	39	940	67	27	113
Venezuela	9,750	21,402	9,981	172	27
Vietnam	21,365	16,695	8,175	6,171	6,507
Wallis and Futuna Islands	342	N/A	N/A	13	0
Yemen	18,020	27,997	N/A	225	N/A
Yugoslavia	37,441	25,325	7,004	453	4,692
Zambia	33,123	51,000	6,748	8,533	7,140
Zimbabwe	23,650	22,290	13,728	8,529	12,971

N/A= Not available

Source: Number of reported cases, Department of Vaccines and Biologicals (V&B), formerly known as the Global Programme for Vaccines and Immunization; <http://www.who.int/gpv-surv/>. Underlying data from World Health Organization (WHO).

D2-4. Number of Reported Cases of Pertussis 1980, 1985, 1990, 1995, 1997

Country	1980	1985	1990	1995	1997
Afghanistan	15,748	8,531	411	N/A	N/A
Albania	137	172	329	141	78
Algeria	710	520	23	N/A	30
Angola	54,126	15,846	14,420	N/A	N/A
Argentina	27,208	4,654	1,974	844	638
Australia	124	587	862	4,099	10,242
Austria	186	301	234	91	114
Bahrain	106	7	0	0	0
Bangladesh	12,436	23,897	4,879	1,289	673
Belarus	N/A	N/A	N/A	227	455
Benin	2,694	2,646	N/A	1,055	N/A
Bhutan	464	213	3	5	0
Bolivia	2,596	964	155	36	138
Bosnia and Herzegovina	N/A	N/A	N/A	141	31
Botswana	110	28	22	15	19
Brunei	1	2	0	N/A	0
Bulgaria	154	40	26	77	44
Burkina Faso	3,888	5,078	713	419	N/A
Cambodia	20,798	25,023	1,690	N/A	1,665
Cameroon	N/A	11,126	5,498	4	0
Canada	2,872	2,376	6,266	9,799	3,688
Cape Verde	290	7	0	0	0
Central African Republic	4,340	2,443	46	6	11
Chad	N/A	1,496	N/A	N/A	5,498
Chile	2,795	633	63	424	825
China	23,824	16,226	20,015	5,482	8,678
Colombia	7,664	1,629	1,872	1,137	425
Congo, Dem. Rep. (Zaire)	15,335	1,590	N/A	N/A	N/A
Congo, Rep.	11,198	772	52	144	8
Costa Rica	960	133	75	21	30
Côte d'Ivoire	N/A	N/A	3,052	1,865	1,284
Croatia	N/A	N/A	N/A	252	567
Cuba	131	195	23	0	0
Cyprus	0	0	4	15	12
Czech Republic	N/A	N/A	N/A	19	114
Denmark	4,970	1,882	569	81	198
Djibouti	N/A	85	25	0	N/A
Dominican Republic	412	174	227	0	1
Ecuador	836	741	487	176	245
Egypt	49	18	1	1	0
El Salvador	1,005	464	212	4	2
Equatorial Guinea	N/A	4	67	N/A	0
Estonia	N/A	N/A	N/A	50	336
Ethiopia	23,429	5,148	922	626	N/A
Fiji	13	2	1	0	0
Finland	187	308	707	518	N/A
France	100	83	N/A	N/A	N/A
French Polynesia	7	6	13	2	69
Gabon	3,065	1,721	N/A	N/A	N/A
Gambia	157	56	N/A	N/A	0
Georgia	N/A	N/A	N/A	N/A	118
Germany	258	306	57	N/A	N/A
Ghana	13,216	8,704	2,651	1,147	N/A
Greece	3,083	1,020	752	204	105
Guam	0	0	0	2	13
Guatemala	1,513	1,507	138	34	567
Guinea	2,315	625	412	N/A	515
Guinea-Bissau	1,250	743	1,512	N/A	24

D2-4. Number of Reported Cases of Pertussis 1980, 1985, 1990, 1995, 1997 *(continued)*

Country	1980	1985	1990	1995	1997
Guyana	80	1	1	0	0
Haiti	812	1,373	913	N/A	N/A
Honduras	2,503	335	147	0	191
Hong Kong SAR, China	12	21	8	8	12
Hungary	22	21	12	3	0
Iceland	41	16	3	N/A	N/A
India	57,965	53,296	46,880	4,073	21,371
Indonesia	32,999	1,045	30,014	8,772	6,934
Iran	20,395	11,519	1,230	45	50
Iraq	16,687	2,768	122	483	578
Ireland	547	3,689	798	N/A	N/A
Israel	19	24	189	N/A	101
Italy	16,643	15,678	16,992	14,178	1,472
Jamaica	13	5	3	7	4
Japan	5,033	938	583	N/A	N/A
Jordan	437	35	4	4	4
Kazakhstan	N/A	N/A	N/A	504	268
Kenya	13,281	17,949	7,404	58	63
Kiribati	161	188	830	68	466
Kuwait	69	22	25	46	137
Kyrgyzstan	N/A	N/A	N/A	106	99
Laos	2,718	2,881	856	106	90
Latvia	N/A	N/A	0	58	152
Lebanon	N/A	N/A	N/A	4	14
Lesotho	2,020	186	34	N/A	N/A
Liberia	62	32	N/A	N/A	N/A
Libya	25	158	43	N/A	2
Lithuania	N/A	N/A	N/A	104	150
Luxembourg	46	17	3	1	0
Macedonia, FYRO	N/A	N/A	N/A	27	32
Madagascar	32,457	12,515	1,333	1,565	N/A
Malawi	29,769	25,712	N/A	0	N/A
Malaysia	97	150	24	8	3
Mali	2,811	4,165	430	162	N/A
Malta	2	140	106	59	12
Mauritania	7,576	5,958	383	N/A	N/A
Mauritius	0	0	12	N/A	N/A
Mexico	3,048	2,231	1,078	15	206
Moldova	N/A	N/A	N/A	123	327
Morocco	14,873	1,762	83	37	46
Mozambique	N/A	1,201	451	N/A	345
Myanmar (Burma)	26,878	10,238	7,882	871	120
Namibia	N/A	N/A	N/A	N/A	221
Nauru	0	N/A	166	0	0
Nepal	1,055	102	18	12,166	12,443
Netherlands, the	30	1,522	471	319	3,947
New Caledonia	48	5	1	N/A	5
New Zealand	0	N/A	91	10	284
Nicaragua	2,469	150	242	8	84
Niger	8,320	5,261	3,102	2,967	3,190
Nigeria	48,996	26,730	42,929	N/A	N/A
North Korea, Dem. Rep.	0	1,607	58	130	60
Norway	2,003	1,227	208	70	N/A
Oman	1,534	765	49	108	694
Pakistan	42,947	55,659	24,545	180	238
Panama	641	106	22	3	103
Papua New Guinea	2,693	1,757	2,084	2,814	2,871
Paraguay	652	363	115	13	27

D2-4. Number of Reported Cases of Pertussis 1980, 1985, 1990, 1995, 1997 *(continued)*

Country	1980	1985	1990	1995	1997
Peru	12,134	6,215	1,134	832	989
Philippines	19,844	19,628	4,135	22	24
Poland	232	304	292	550	N/A
Portugal	71	54	101	21	N/A
Puerto Rico	14	15	22	N/A	N/A
Qatar	219	129	18	0	3
Romania	11,441	1,810	817	510	263
Russia	N/A	N/A	N/A	20,626	27,275
Rwanda	16,189	1,573	177	N/A	N/A
Saudi Arabia	9,815	1,395	112	33	80
Senegal	22,792	N/A	1,041	N/A	0
Sierra Leone	1,619	1,637	N/A	N/A	0
South Korea, Rep.	1,554	479	174	3	13
Spain	N/A	60,564	10,075	3,741	N/A
Sri Lanka	542	536	271	64	229
Sudan	28,631	10,314	566	1,496	418
Swaziland	N/A	673	20	4	13
Sweden	5,221	10,839	10,697	N/A	N/A
Switzerland	N/A	N/A	N/A	17,000	N/A
Syria	430	286	39	961	925
Tajikistan	N/A	N/A	N/A	206	284
Tanzania	2,788	2,135	243	N/A	N/A
Thailand	4,820	2,533	486	117	110
Togo	3,901	2,440	431	60	14
Tunisia	4,106	482	68	1	0
Turkey	1,520	2,678	454	342	694
Turkmenistan	N/A	N/A	N/A	31	49
Uganda	2,122	N/A	913	N/A	N/A
Ukraine	228	49	96	29	16
United Kingdom	22,924	24,244	16,605	1,873	529
United States	1,730	3,589	4,570	4,315	5,461
Uruguay	192	399	161	69	12
Uzbekistan	N/A	N/A	N/A	263	197
Vanuatu	231	1,881	3	0	51
Venezuela	3,247	4,147	1,389	375	609
Vietnam	31,041	44,011	4,095	2,444	1,565
Yemen	15,332	17,506	N/A	184	N/A
Yugoslavia	6,710	3,744	2,169	424	218
Zambia	21,232	1,303	200	N/A	0
Zimbabwe	6,290	2,154	491	34	36

Source: Number of reported cases, Department of Vaccines and Biologicals (V&B), formerly known as the Global Programme for Vaccines and Immunization; <http://www.who.int/gpv-surv/>. Underlying data from World Health Organization (WHO).

D2-5. Number of Reported Cases of Neonatal Tetanus 1980, 1985, 1990, 1995, 1997

Country	1980	1985	1990	1995	1997
Afghanistan	16	N/A	3	N/A	N/A
Algeria	N/A	N/A	27	15	19
Angola	541	550	959	101	126
Argentina	N/A	19	8	3	4
Bangladesh	1,068	N/A	740	735	689
Benin	N/A	N/A	247	30	24
Bhutan	N/A	4	1	0	0
Bolivia	0	9	46	20	8
Botswana	N/A	2	2	0	0
Brazil	N/A	684	298	85	74
Burkina Faso	N/A	227	100	18	8
Burundi	N/A	127	25	12	1
Cambodia	N/A	N/A	N/A	8	34
Cameroon	N/A	537	382	57	171
Cape Verde	N/A	25	6	4	1
Chad	N/A	149	738	27	844
China	N/A	N/A	N/A	N/A	3,962
Colombia	N/A	252	165	35	24
Comoros	N/A	N/A	6	2	0
Congo, Dem. Rep. (Zaire)	N/A	208	120	83	107
Congo, Rep.	80	2	18	0	0
Côte d'Ivoire	N/A	N/A	364	311	241
Ecuador	28	91	88	51	25
Egypt	2,965	6,633	3,275	790	482
El Salvador	61	52	25	3	2
Ethiopia	N/A	151	39	N/A	27
Gabon	0	4	4	N/A	N/A
Gambia	N/A	27	44	6	0
Ghana	N/A	N/A	N/A	159	105
Guatemala	N/A	17	60	9	6
Guinea	N/A	80	53	120	280
Guinea-Bissau	N/A	108	45	5	5
Haiti	N/A	57	143	N/A	N/A
Honduras	N/A	20	39	3	1
India	N/A	N/A	9,313	1,783	3,011
Indonesia	954	662	1,577	807	546
Iran	N/A	N/A	26	13	14
Iraq	891	680	152	64	73
Jordan	23	8	9	2	2
Kenya	N/A	17	1,612	30	27
Kuwait	9	0	0	0	0
Laos	N/A	N/A	4	6	12
Laos	13	33	9	7	3
Liberia	207	N/A	N/A	24	84
Libya	N/A	15	1	N/A	0
Madagascar	N/A	N/A	208	7	45
Malawi	163	391	211	6	8
Malaysia	60	49	11	12	11
Mali	N/A	455	203	33	9
Mauritania	N/A	99	16	1	1
Mauritius	4	2	0	0	0
Mexico	N/A	N/A	145	67	41
Morocco	N/A	104	28	14	4
Mozambique	101	120	34	19	52
Myanmar (Burma)	124	96	27	31	20
Namibia	N/A	N/A	N/A	75	27
Nauru	N/A	N/A	4	0	0
Nepal	N/A	79	0	511	462

D2-5. Number of Reported Cases of Neonatal Tetanus 1980, 1985, 1990, 1995, 1997 *(continued)*

Country	1980	1985	1990	1995	1997
Nicaragua	157	30	15	4	1
Niger	N/A	115	39	61	33
Nigeria	N/A	N/A	1,060	388	656
Pakistan	1,085	576	1,067	1,580	2,053
Panama	19	12	5	1	1
Papua New Guinea	N/A	N/A	N/A	134	52
Paraguay	99	76	38	16	15
Peru	294	72	93	97	36
Philippines	1,506	1,244	291	288	338
Portugal	9	3	0	0	N/A
Saudi Arabia	N/A	N/A	13	25	26
Senegal	N/A	N/A	67	N/A	16
Sierra Leone	N/A	583	26	25	0
Solomon Islands	N/A	N/A	4	3	1
South Africa	166	136	58	9	9
Sri Lanka	339	76	5	7	8
Sudan	90	18	28	21	95
Swaziland	N/A	133	3	1	0
Syria	91	124	55	106	45
Tanzania	652	158	28	29	21
Thailand	664	564	212	38	25
Togo	217	118	42	13	14
Turkey	N/A	41	67	127	33
Uganda	N/A	N/A	129	307	158
Vanuatu	3	2	0	0	0
Venezuela	129	70	28	17	7
Vietnam	N/A	N/A	313	330	257
Yemen	7	61	N/A	12	N/A
Yugoslavia	17	6	0	N/A	3
Zambia	N/A	N/A	57	24	34
Zimbabwe	134	218	16	18	12

N/A = Not available

Source: Number of reported cases, Department of Vaccines and Biologicals (V&B), formerly known as the Global Programme for Vaccines and Immunization; <http://www.who.int/gpv-surv/>. Underlying data from World Health Organization (WHO).

D2-6. Estimated Number of Neonatal Tetanus Deaths, Selected Countries, 1999

	Estimate*
India	48,600
Nigeria	34,600
Pakistan	21,600
Ethiopia	13,400
Bangladesh	10,400
Congo, Dem. Rep. (Zaire)	10,000
Somalia	8,800
China	8,600
Afghanistan	4,200
Indonesia	4,100
Niger	3,600
Mozambique	3,000
Nepal	3,000
Angola	2,700
Chad	2,500
Mali	2,400
Senegal	2,300
Yemen	2,300
Sudan	2,200
Ghana	2,000
Burkina Faso	1,600
Cambodia	1,500
Cameroon	1,500
Côte d'Ivoire	1,100
Liberia	600
Mauritania	200
Guinea-Bissau	100
Total	196,900

* The numbers of deaths are estimated, as most neonatal deaths occur at home, before the baby reaches two weeks of age, and neither the birth nor the death is reported.

Source: The Progress of Nations, 2000 United Nations Children's Fund (UNICEF); <http://www.unicef.org/pon00/>. Underlying data from World Health Organization (WHO).

D2-7. Number of Reported Cases of Tetanus Toxoid 1980, 1985, 1990, 1995, 1997

Country	1980	1985	1990	1995	1997
Afghanistan	1,618	2,829	131	N/A	N/A
Albania	5	4	15	18	3
Algeria	86	343	38	N/A	1
Angola	1,185	893	1,826	N/A	0
Argentina	219	76	60	13	N/A
Australia	9	11	6	5	N/A
Bangladesh	2,855	363	2,511	3,114	5
Barbados	13	1	5	0	N/A
Belgium	4	1	2	3	27
Benin	499	636	N/A	184	8
Bhutan	3	34	0	0	N/A
Bolivia	153	57	80	28	0
Botswana	0	2	2	N/A	0
Brazil	3,098	2,623	1,498	779	0
Bulgaria	18	12	7	7	5
Burkina Faso	746	602	50	48	0
Burundi	256	256	65	35	1
Cambodia	2,089	1,169	219	430	5
Canada	3	9	2	4	N/A
Cape Verde	40	N/A	8	14	0

D2-7. Number of Reported Cases of Tetanus Toxoid 1980, 1985, 1990, 1995, 1997 *(continued)*

Country	1980	1985	1990	1995	1997
Central African Republic	217	124	34	87	0
Chad	8	217	1,603	N/A	0
Chile	31	26	22	11	N/A
Colombia	593	507	295	57	1
Comoros	N/A	N/A	N/A	N/A	1,627
Congo, Dem. Rep. (Zaire)	848	262	N/A	N/A	2
Congo, Rep.	167	250	27	0	N/A
Cook Islands	1	0	0	0	514
Costa Rica	17	6	3	6	0
Côte d'Ivoire	N/A	N/A	384	N/A	17
Croatia	N/A	N/A	N/A	17	N/A
Cuba	26	7	4	5	N/A
Dominican Republic	99	91	68	37	N/A
Ecuador	81	97	133	158	0
Egypt	6,644	9,286	4,952	1,097	N/A
El Salvador	98	82	56	3	0
Ethiopia	409	649	140	235	1
France	208	124	33	N/A	N/A
French Polynesia	8	4	2	0	0
Gabon	12	42	22	N/A	N/A
Gambia	567	889	N/A	N/A	0
Germany	21	18	18	N/A	N/A
Ghana	1,045	754	660	N/A	1
Greece	15	9	16	4	2
Grenada	3	2	0	1	0
Guam	0	0	1	2	1,425
Guatemala	60	101	85	8	0
Guinea	482	108	524	N/A	0
Guinea-Bissau	221	229	31	N/A	0
Guyana	20	7	0	0	0
Haiti	381	318	143	N/A	N/A
Honduras	31	47	78	7	0
Hong Kong SAR, China	15	31	4	23	23
Hungary	48	37	25	14	N/A
India	45,948	37,647	23,356	N/A	N/A
Indonesia	7,231	4,249	7,784	N/A	17
Iran	86	236	30	26	N/A
Iraq	1,045	1,398	N/A	99	N/A
Israel	2	3	0	N/A	99
Italy	176	160	123	136	12
Jamaica	10	0	6	9	N/A
Japan	50	43	47	N/A	N/A
Jordan	46	11	9	4	N/A
Kenya	831	884	1,692	N/A	165
Kiribati	0	10	3	4	0
Kuwait	15	1	2	1	1,886
Laos	1,015	88	27	7	N/A
Laos	461	424	N/A	N/A	16
Lebanon	N/A	0	N/A	15	3,129
Lesotho	1	0	27	N/A	N/A
Liberia	307	N/A	228	N/A	0
Libya	30	19	1	N/A	N/A
Macao	N/A	5	0	2	24
Madagascar	842	384	105	91	0
Malaysia	60	49	30	12	3
Maldives	2	0	N/A	N/A	51
Mali	294	452	365	71	7
Marshall Islands	0	0	0	N/A	2,119

D2-7. Number of Reported Cases of Tetanus Toxoid 1980, 1985, 1990, 1995, 1997 *(continued)*

Country	1980	1985	1990	1995	1997
Mauritania	12	135	24	N/A	0
Mexico	363	304	364	128	N/A
Moldova	N/A	N/A	N/A	3	7,323
Mongolia	0	1	1	6	44
Morocco	81	171	73	29	96
Mozambique	573	170	102	N/A	1
Myanmar (Burma)	2,423	1,759	769	N/A	53
Namibia	N/A	N/A	19	N/A	21
Nepal	116	246	35	N/A	1
Netherlands, the	8	3	2	3	9
New Caledonia	1	0	2	N/A	186
New Zealand	2	3	0	0	49
Nicaragua	382	137	46	8	N/A
Niger	346	115	220	220	N/A
Nigeria	3,095	2,679	2,703	N/A	515
North Korea, Dem. Rep.	537	804	N/A	3	N/A
Norway	3	1	1	2	3
Oman	48	64	3	8	0
Pakistan	2,738	8,143	4,080	1,687	2
Panama	31	11	7	2	N/A
Papua New Guinea	68	61	115	N/A	N/A
Paraguay	188	136	128	42	N/A
Peru	525	201	261	70	N/A
Philippines	3,080	3,474	2,286	1,443	3
Poland	89	86	65	43	1
Portugal	73	83	34	28	1
Puerto Rico	15	5	N/A	N/A	N/A
Qatar	7	5	0	0	77
Reunion	15	N/A	2	N/A	N/A
Romania	33	23	33	27	0
Russia	N/A	N/A	N/A	70	N/A
Rwanda	103	70	18	N/A	0
Sao Tome and Principe	12	20	N/A	N/A	3
Saudi Arabia	124	80	33	39	1
Senegal	1,378	N/A	109	N/A	N/A
Sierra Leone	871	631	103	N/A	0
Solomon Islands	14	0	46	0	1
Somalia	N/A	262	N/A	N/A	N/A
South Africa	288	251	117	N/A	111
South Korea, Rep.	1	5	0	N/A	N/A
Spain	500	74	54	38	39
Sri Lanka	1,243	481	183	66	0
Sudan	4,451	7,130	411	161	4
Suriname	11	0	27	0	N/A
Swaziland	N/A	230	1	N/A	N/A
Sweden	4	2	1	N/A	5
Switzerland	2	0	1	2	0
Syria	244	127	71	135	N/A
Tanzania	N/A	306	28	N/A	N/A
Thailand	1,818	1,455	813	349	5
Togo	436	273	107	N/A	0
Tonga	2	3	1	0	7
Trinidad and Tobago	28	2	10	1	N/A
Tunisia	121	43	12	8	N/A
Turkey	48	113	123	190	2
Uganda	48	N/A	288	13	0
Ukraine	N/A	N/A	N/A	72	2
Ukraine	14	8	3	7	340

D2-7. Number of Reported Cases of Tetanus Toxoid 1980, 1985, 1990, 1995, 1997 *(continued)*

Country	1980	1985	1990	1995	1997
United Kingdom	30	12	18	7	N/A
United States	95	83	64	34	N/A
Uruguay	15	10	3	2	N/A
Venezuela	476	197	127	56	0
Vietnam	1,948	1,658	628	464	0
Wallis and Futuna Islands	0	N/A	N/A	N/A	238
Yemen	405	247	N/A	N/A	N/A
Yugoslavia	99	74	57	23	88
Zambia	409	268	57	24	930

N/A = Not available

Source: Number of reported cases, Department of Vaccines and Biologicals (V&B), formerly known as the Global Programme for Vaccines and Immunization; <http://www.who.int/gpv-surv/>. Underlying data from World Health Organization (WHO).

D2-8. Progress in Polio Eradication, 1996–2000

	Total confirmed polio cases
Afghanistan	67
Angola	84
Bangladesh	75
Benin	1
Chad	16
Congo	25
Congo, Dem. Rep. (Zaire)	137
Egypt	3
Eritrea	1
Ethiopia	59
Gabon	1
Gambia, the	1
Ghana	23
India	208
Indonesia	30
Iraq	17
Myanmar (Burma)	17
Nepal	9
Niger	24
Nigeria	152
Pakistan	75
Sierra Leone	20
Somalia	39
Sudan	54
Thailand	7
Yemen	3

Source: The Department of Vaccines and Biologicals (V&B), formerly known as the Global Programme for Vaccines and Immunization; <http://www.polioeradication.org/afpextract.asp>. Global Polio Eradication Initiative Primary *Source:* World Health Organization (WHO).

D2-9. Number of Reported Cases of Polio 1980, 1985, 1990, 1995, 1997

Country	1980	1985	1990	1995	1997
Afghanistan	880	1,981	48	0	19
Algeria	116	66	2	4	0
American Samoa	0	0	0	0	0
Angola	32	14	94	152	15
Argentina	26	2	0	0	0
Armenia	N/A	N/A	N/A	3	0
Azerbaijan	N/A	N/A	N/A	5	0
Bahrain	6	0	0	0	0
Bangladesh	65	89	374	49	188
Belize	3	0	0	0	0
Benin	155	89	81	7	3
Bhutan	6	2	0	0	0
Bolivia	40	0	0	0	0
Botswana	1	3	0	0	3
Brazil	1,290	329	0	0	0
Burkina Faso	145	123	18	12	3
Burundi	43	25	10	10	0
Cambodia	591	931	63	130	8
Cameroon	255	134	38	8	21
Cape Verde	17	6	0	0	0
Chad	N/A	45	N/A	192	326
China	7,442	1,537	5,065	165	0
Colombia	129	5	4	0	0
Congo, Dem. Rep. (Zaire)	263	98	N/A	735	82
Côte d'Ivoire	47	18	28	117	6
Djibouti	N/A	N/A	7	0	0
Dominican Republic	147	2	0	0	0
Ecuador	11	0	1	0	0
Egypt	2,006	564	565	71	14
El Salvador	55	28	0	0	0
Eritrea	N/A	N/A	N/A	10	41
Ethiopia	234	92	81	199	19
France	10	1	0	1	0
Gabon	70	42	2	9	N/A
Gambia	1	2	1	0	1
Germany	7	0	1	0	0
Ghana	145	185	60	34	17
Guatemala	76	29	3	N/A	0
Guinea	32	21	155	54	2
Guinea-Bissau	3	22	2	0	1
Haiti	20	82	0	0	0
Honduras	3	4	0	0	0
Hong Kong SAR, China	2	1	0	0	0
India	18,975	22,584	10,408	3,263	2,262
Indonesia	182	88	465	12	506
Iran	80	53	15	101	13
Iraq	997	198	56	34	28
Ireland	1	0	0	0	0
Israel	11	2	0	0	0
Italy	1	0	0	0	0
Japan	4	0	0	0	N/A
Jordan	15	1	0	0	0
Kenya	455	368	1,528	12	14
Kuwait	32	2	0	0	0
Laos	1,166	523	18	8	0
Laos	138	87	3	1	5
Lebanon	N/A	3	2	0	0
Lesotho	36	29	0	0	0

D2-9. Number of Reported Cases of Polio 1980, 1985, 1990, 1995, 1997 *(continued)*

Country	1980	1985	1990	1995	1997
Liberia	98	2	N/A	0	0
Libya	30	2	5	0	0
Madagascar	68	21	39	0	10
Malawi	70	86	3	0	2
Malaysia	5	4	0	0	0
Maldives	1	0	0	0	0
Mali	234	271	63	26	2
Mauritania	159	141	7	5	5
Mexico	682	148	7	0	0
Morocco	52	15	0	0	0
Mozambique	65	26	1	0	4
Myanmar (Burma)	244	109	47	18	55
Namibia	N/A	N/A	0	15	2
Nepal	52	30	6	9	12
Nicaragua	21	0	0	N/A	0
Niger	311	146	32	40	56
Nigeria	816	959	1,873	439	383
North Korea, Dem. Rep.	0	0	0	7	0
Oman	37	33	0	0	0
Pakistan	2,980	2,159	777	508	961
Papua New Guinea	22	9	9	1	0
Paraguay	7	3	0	0	0
Peru	182	67	3	0	0
Philippines	432	557	85	40	0
Poland	3	0	0	0	0
Qatar	2	1	1	0	0
Romania	125	0	5	1	0
Russia	N/A	N/A	N/A	150	0
Rwanda	24	7	0	1	0
Sao Tome and Principe	4	0	0	0	0
Saudi Arabia	257	28	5	4	0
Sierra Leone	11	45	38	0	0
Somalia	N/A	6	N/A	N/A	1
South Africa	112	72	5	0	0
South Korea, Rep.	14	0	0	0	0
Spain	17	6	0	0	0
Sri Lanka	264	11	9	0	0
Sudan	4,151	171	4	22	33
Swaziland	192	13	0	0	0
Syria	312	25	13	4	0
Tanzania	91	340	3	N/A	10
Thailand	300	65	4	2	19
Togo	178	69	20	5	2
Tunisia	15	19	0	0	0
Turkey	182	88	21	32	6
Turkmenistan	N/A	N/A	N/A	8	0
Uganda	37	N/A	28	100	35
United Kingdom	3	2	0	0	0
Ukraine	48	7	0	0	0
United States	3	8	0	0	0
Vanuatu	2	0	0	0	0
Venezuela	11	8	0	0	0
Vietnam	1,741	1,600	723	137	1
Yemen	722	336	N/A	45	0
Yugoslavia	4	1	3	3	0
Zambia	276	128	79	6	5
Zimbabwe	32	69	0	1	3

N/A = Not available

Source: Number of reported cases, Department of Vaccines and Biologicals (V&B), formerly known as the Global Programme for Vaccines and Immunization, <http://www.who.int/gpv-surv/>. Underlying data from World Health Organization (WHO).

D2-10. Progress in Polio Eradication, 2000

World Health Region*	Year	Total confirmed polio cases
Africa		
	1996	1,949
	1997	1,087
	1998	993
	1999	2,860
	2000	544
Americas		
	1996	0
	1997	0
	1998	0
	1999	0
	2000	0
Eastern Mediterranean		
	1996	532
	1997	1,255
	1998	555
	1999	915
	2000	258
Europe		
	1996	193
	1997	7
	1998	26
	1999	0
	2000	0
South East Asia		
	1996	1,203
	1997	2,827
	1998	4,775
	1999	3,367
	2000	346
Western Pacific		
	1996	197
	1997	9
	1998	0
	1999	1
	2000	0
Global Totals		
	1996	4,074
	1997	5,185
	1998	6,349
	1999	7,143
	2000	1,148

*For breakdown of countries in WHO region, see Appendix 1.

Source: The Department of Vaccines and Biologicals (V&B), formerly known as the Global Programme for Vaccines and Immunization; Global Polio Eradication Initiative; <http://www.polioeradication.org/afpextract.asp>. Underlying data from World Health Organization (WHO).

D3. MALARIA

D3-1. Malaria Deaths in Children 0 to 14 Years, WHO Regions, 1998

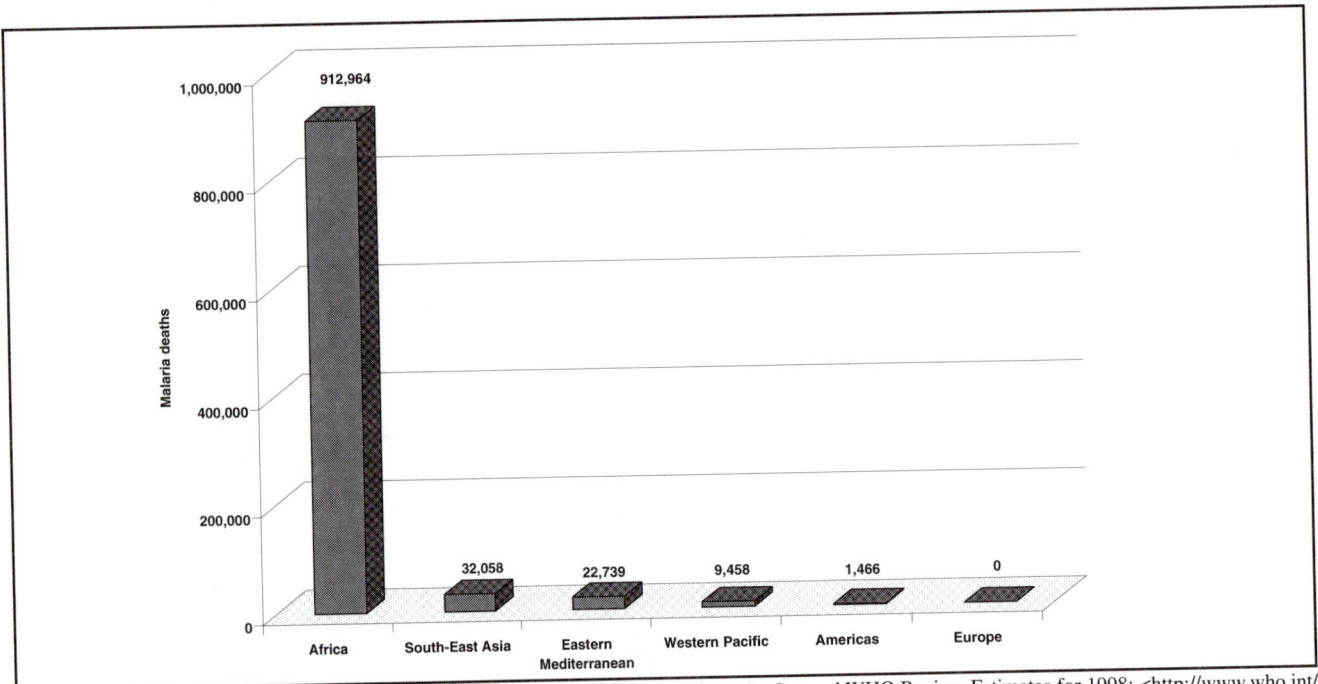

Source: World Health Report 1999, Annex: Table 8. Malaria: Magnitude of the Problem by Sex and WHO Region, Estimates for 1998; <http://www.who.int/whr/1999/en/pdf/mortality.pdf>. Underlying data from United Nation's Children's Fund (UNICEF).

D3-2. Percentage of Child Deaths (0–14 Years) to Total Malaria Deaths (All Age Groups), WHO Regions, 1998

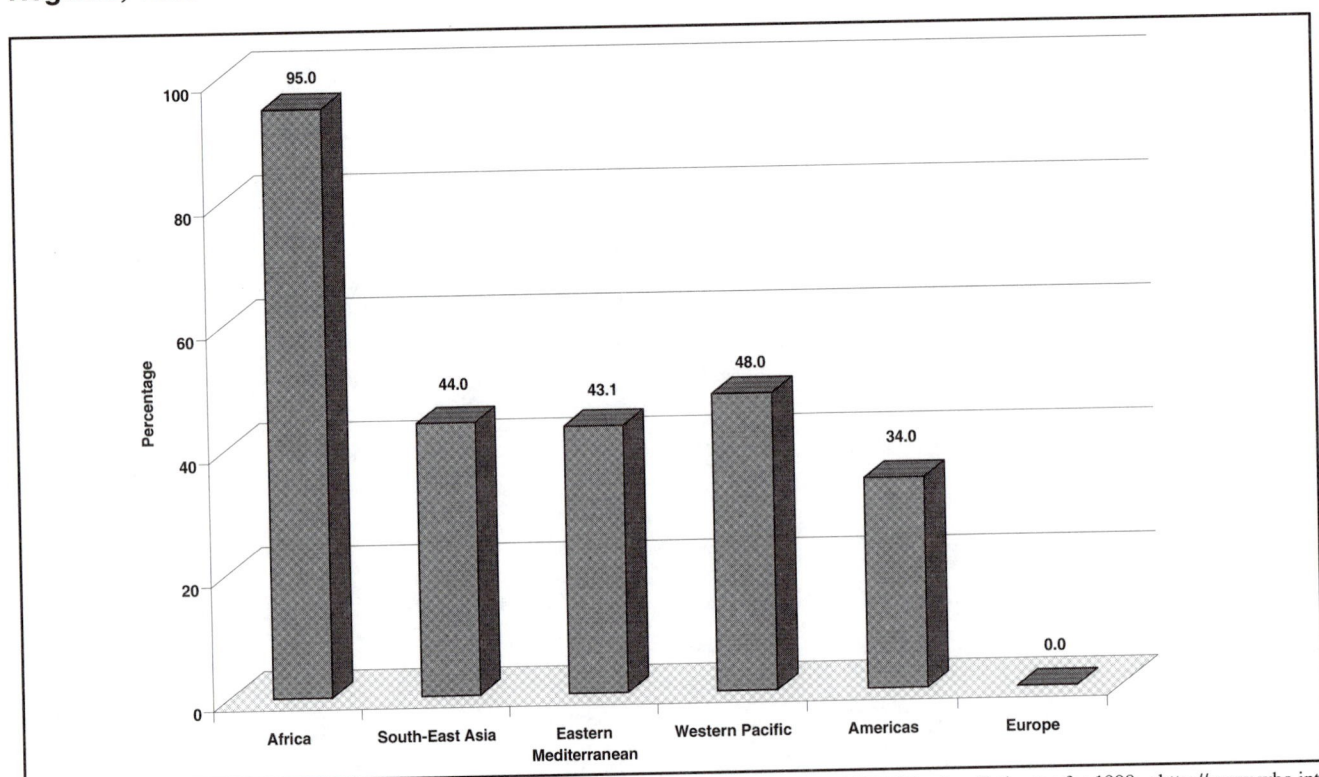

Source: World Health Report 1999, Annex: Table 8. Malaria: Magnitude of the Problem by Sex and WHO Region, Estimates for 1998; <http://www.who.int/whr/1999/en/pdf/mortality.pdf>. Underlying data from United Nation's Children's Fund (UNICEF).

D4. CHILDHOOD CANCER

D4-1. Adolescent (Age 10–15) Death Rate for Malignant Neoplasms, by Gender, per 100,000 Population, Selected Countries, 1998

	Male	Female
Austria	4.8	3.4
Belgium	5.6	4.0
Canada	10.4	8.5
Czech Republic	7.9	6.2
Denmark	5.9	4.7
England and Wales (UK)	5.4	4.3
Estonia	15.9	4.8
Finland	4.6	3.2
France	5.3	3.4
Germany	5.3	3.7
Greece	6.5	4.2
Hungary	8.9	4.7
Israel	5.4	5.4
Italy	7.3	4.3
Latvia	9.3	8.4
Lithuania	8.3	6.8
Northern Ireland (UK)	10.7	5.7
Norway	4.6	4.1
Poland	7.8	4.7
Russia	9.7	7.5
Scotland (UK)	4.6	3.3
Slovakia	8.5	5.0
Spain	6.6	4.5
Sweden	4.6	2.6

Source: Gender and Health in Adolescence, WHO Policy Series "Health Policy for Children and Adolescents," Issue 2. Health Policy for Children and Adolescents (HEPCA): Fig. 9. Age-Sex-Specific Death Rates for Malignant Neoplasms per 100,000 Population, 1998; <http://www.who.dk/HBSC/gender.pdf>. Underlying data from World Health Organization (WHO).

D5. DEATHS FROM PREVENTABLE INJURIES

D5-1. Rate of Child Injury Deaths, Annual Injury Deaths per 100,000 Children Aged 1 to 14, 1971–1975 and 1991–1995

	1971-1975	1991-1995
Australia	22.3	9.5
Austria	23.7	9.3
Belgium	20.0	9.2
Canada	27.8	9.7
Czech Republic	19.6	12.0
Denmark	19.6	12.0
Finland	24.7	8.2
France	19.4	9.1
Germany	28.4	8.3
Greece	13.5	7.6
Hungary	16.1	10.8
Ireland	17.2	8.3
Italy	16.3	6.1
Japan	22.4	8.4
Mexico	29.3	19.8
Netherlands, the	20.1	6.6
New Zealand	23.7	13.7
Norway	21.6	7.6

D5-1. Rate of Child Injury Deaths, Annual Injury Deaths per 100,000 Children Aged 1 to 14, 1971–1975 and 1991–1995 *(continued)*

	1971–1975	1991–1995
Poland	22.5	13.4
Portugal	31.1	17.8
Spain	13.7	8.1
Sweden	13.0	5.2
Switzerland	22.5	9.6
United Kingdom	14.3	6.1
United States	24.8	14.1

Source: A League Table of Child Deaths by Injury in Rich Nations, UNICEF, 2001; <http://www.unicef-icdc.org/publications/pdf/repcard2e.pdf>. Underlying data from Innocenti Report Card No.2, February 2001. UNICEF Innocenti Research Centre, Florence (UNICEF).

D6. DEATHS FROM TRAFFIC ACCIDENTS

D6-1. Deaths Due to Traffic Accidents Among Children Aged 0 to 14 per 100,000 Children in the Age Group, 1998

	Deaths per 100,000 children in age group
High income countries*	
West Pacific	4.7
Europe	4.7
Americas	4.8
East Mediterranean	8.0
Low and Middle Income countries*	
China	6.5
Europe	7.2
East Mediterranean	9.2
Americas	14.8
South-East Asia	17.8
West Pacific	18.2
India	18.5
Africa	23.2
* See Appendix for countries in these income groups.	

Source: A League Table Of Child Deaths By Injury In Rich Nations, UNICEF, 2001; <http://www.unicef-icdc.org/publications/pdf/repcard2e.pdf>. Underlying data from Innocenti Report Card No. 2, February 2001. UNICEF Innocenti Research Centre, Florence (UNICEF).

D7. VITAMIN AND MINERAL DEFICIENCIES

D7-1. Progress in Eliminating Vitamin A Deficiency, 1998

	Vitamin A ranking*
Afghanistan	2
Albania	4
Algeria	3
Angola	2
Argentina	4
Armenia	4
Australia	4
Austria	4
Azerbaijan	4
Bangladesh	1
Belarus	4
Belgium	4
Benin	1
Bhuton	1
Bolivia	2
Bosnia and Herzegovina	4
Botswana	3
Brazil	2
Bulgaria	4
Burkina Faso	1
Burundi	2
Cambodia	1
Cameroon	1
Canada	4
Central African Republic	2
Chad	2
Chile	4
China	2
Colombia	3
Congo	1
Congo Dem. Republic	2
Costa Rica	3
Côte d'Ivoire	2
Croatia	4
Cuba	4
Czech Republic	4
Denmark	4
Dominican Republic	2
Ecuador	2
Egypt	3
El Salvador	2
Eritrea	1
Estonia	4
Ethiopia	1
Finland	4
France	4
Gabon	3
Gambia	3
Georgia	4
Germany	4
Ghana	1
Greece	4
Guatemala	2
Guinea	1
Guinea-Bissau	2
Haiti	2

D7-1. Progress in Eliminating Vitamin A Deficiency, 1998 *(continued)*

	Vitamin A ranking*
Honduras	2
Hungary	4
India	2
Indonesia	3
Iran	2
Iraq	1
Ireland	4
Israel	4
Italy	4
Jamaica	4
Japan	4
Jordan	4
Kazakhstan	4
Kenya	2
Kuwait	4
Kyrgyzstan	4
Laos	1
Latvia	4
Lebanon	4
Lesotho	2
Liberia	1
Libya	4
Lithuania	4
Macedonia, FYRO	4
Madagascar	1
Malawi	1
Malaysia	4
Mali	1
Mauritania	1
Mauritius	3
Mexico	1
Moldova	4
Mongolia	1
Morocco	2
Mozambique	2
Myanmar	1
Namibia	1
Nepal	1
Netherlands, the	4
New Zealand	4
Nicaragua	2
Niger	1
Nigeria	2
North Korea, Dem. Rep.	4
Norway	4
Oman	1
Pakistan	2
Panama	4
Papua New Guinea	3
Paraguay	4
Peru	2
Philippines	1
Poland	4
Portugal	4
Romania	4
Russia	4
Rwanda	2
Saudi Arabia	4

D7-1. Progress in Eliminating Vitamin A Deficiency, 1998 *(continued)*

	Vitamin A ranking*
Senegal	3
Sierra Leone	2
Singapore	4
Slovakia	4
Slovenia	4
Somalia	1
South Africa	3
South Korea, Rep.	4
Spain	4
Sri Lanka	3
Sudan	1
Sweden	4
Switzerland	4
Syria	4
Tajikstan	3
Tanzania	1
Thailand	1
Togo	1
Trinidad and Tobago	4
Tunisia	4
Turkey	4
Turkmenistan	3
Uganda	1
Ukraine	4
United Arab Emirates	4
United Kingdom	4
United States	4
Uruguay	4
Uzbekistan	4
Venezuela	4
Vietnam	1
Yemen	1
Yugoslavia	4
Zambia	1
Zimbabwe	3

*What the rankings mean

1. Good coverage achieved. Vitamin A deficiency is a public health problem and/or high under-five mortality exists. Countries have achieved high vitamin A supplementation coverage and are working towards eliminating vitamin A deficiency as a public health problem.

2. Need to fulfil commitments. Vitamin A deficiency is a public health problem and/or high under-five mortality exists. Present coverage is inadequate.

3. Major push needed. Vitamin A deficiency is a problem and/or high under-five mortality exists. Present coverage is inadequate through routine systems, and there are no set plans to tackle this problem.

4. No problem or no data. Vitamin A deficiency is either not a public health problem or no data exist to show it is a problem. Furthermore, under-five mortality rate is low (less than 70 per 1,000). No large-scale action is being taken.

Source: The Progress of Nations, 1999; <http://www.unicef.org/pon99/>. United Nations Children's Fund (UNICEF).

D7-2. Percent of Age Group 6–11 Years with Visible Goitre, Selected Countries, 1985–1997

	% with visible goitre
Afghanistan	20
Albania	41
Algeria	9
Angola	7
Argentina	8
Armenia	40
Azerbaijan	20
Bangladesh	50
Belarus	22
Belgium	5
Belize	0
Benin	24
Bhutan	14
Bolivia	5
Botswana	8
Brazil	14
Bulgaria	20
Burkina Faso	16
Burundi	42
Cambodia	12
Cameroon	26
Cape Verde	26
Central African Republic	63
Chad	15
Chile	1
China	20
Colombia	7
Congo, Dem. Rep. (Zaire)	9
Congo, Rep.	8
Costa Rica	4
Côte d'Ivoire	6
Cuba	10
Denmark	5
Dominican Republic	5
Ecuador	10
Egypt	5
El Salvador	25
Ethiopia	31
France	5
Gabon	5
Georgia	64
Germany	10
Ghana	10
Greece	10
Guatemala	20
Guinea	55
Guinea-Bissau	19
Haiti	4
Honduras	9
India	9
Indonesia	28
Iran	30
Iraq	7
Italy	20
Kazakhstan	20
Kenya	7
Kyrgyzstan	20
Laos	25

D7-2. Percent of Age Group 6–11 Years with Visible Goitre, Selected Countries, 1985–1997

	% with visible goitre
Lebanon	15
Lesotho	43
Liberia	6
Libya	6
Macedonia, FYRO	19
Madagascar	15
Malawi	13
Malaysia	20
Maldives	24
Mali	29
Mauritius	0
Mexico	3
Mongolia	31
Morocco	20
Mozambique	20
Myanmar (Burma)	18
Namibia	35
Nepal	44
Netherlands, the	3
Nicaragua	4
Niger	9
Nigeria	20
Oman	10
Pakistan	32
Panama	13
Papua New Guinea	30
Paraguay	49
Peru	36
Philippines	7
Poland	10
Portugal	15
Romania	10
Rwanda	26
Senegal	12
Sierra Leone	7
Somalia	7
South Africa	2
Spain	10
Sri Lanka	14
Sudan	20
Syria	73
Tajikistan	20
Tanzania	37
Thailand	4
Togo	22
Tunisia	4
Turkey	36
Turkmenistan	20
Uganda	7
Ukraine	10
Uzbekistan	18
Venezuela	11
Vietnam	20
Yemen	32
Zambia	51
Zimbabwe	42

Source: The State of the World's Children, 1999; Table 2. Nutrition; <http://www.unicef.org/sowc99/>. Underlying data from United Nations Children's Fund (UNICEF).

D8. ORAL DISEASE PREVALENCE

D8-1. Mean Number of Decayed, Missing or Filled Teeth among 12-Year-Olds, various years

	Year	DMFT* in 12-Year-Olds
Afghanistan	1991	2.9
Albania	1994	2.2
Algeria	1987	2.3
Angola	1981	1.7
Anguilla	1991	2.5
Antigua and Baruda	1988-89	0.7
Argentina	1987	3.4
Armenia	1985-90	2.4
Australia	1996	0.9
Austria	1997	1.7
Bahamas, the	1981	1.6
Bahrein	1995	1.4
Bangladesh	1978-91	1.7
Barbados	1983	4.4
Belarus	1994	3.8
Belgium	1998	1.6
Belize	1989	6.0
Benin	1994	0.7
Bhutan	1985	1.4
Bolivia	1995	4.7
Botswana	1981	0.5
Brazil	1996	3.1
Brunei	1994	4.9
Bulgaria	1993	3.1
Burkina Faso	1993	1.7
Burundi	1987-88	1.0
Cambodia	1990	1.6
Cameroon	1988	1.5
Canada	1993	4.3
Cape Verde	1989	2.8
Cayman Islands	1995	1.7
Central African Republic	1986	4.1
Chile	1996	4.1
China	1995	1.0
Colombia	1984	4.8
Cook Islands	1995	1.3
Costa Rica	1996	4.8
Cote D'Ivoire	1993	2.6
Croatia	1991	2.6
Cuba	1998	1.4
Cyprus	1992	2.1
Czech Republic	1993	2.7
Denmark	2000	1.0
Djibouti	1990	0.9
Dominica	1989	2.5
Dominican Republic	1997	4.4
Ecuador	1996	3.0
Egypt	1991	1.2
El Salvador	1989	5.1
Estonia	1992	4.1
Ethiopia	1993	1.0
Fiji	1998	1.5
Finland	1994	1.2
France	1993	2.1
French Polynesia	1994	3.2
Gambia	1995	2.3

D8-1. Mean Number of Decayed, Missing or Filled Teeth among 12-Year-Olds, various years *(continued)*

	Year	DMFT* in 12-Year-Olds
Georgia	1985-90	2.4
Germany	1997	1.7
Ghana	1991	0.1
Gibraltar	1991	1.6
Greece	1993	1.6
Grenada	1991	5.5
Guatemala	1987-88	8.1 to 2.4
Guinea-Bissau	1986	0.5
Guyana	1995	1.3
Haiti	1994	2.2
Honduras	1997	3.7
Hong Kong, SAR (China)	1986	1.5
Hungary	1996	3.8
Iceland	1996	1.5
India	1993	1.4 to 3.8
Indonesia	1995	2.2
Iran	1995	2.0
Iraq	1990	1.1
Ireland	1992	1.9
Israel	1989	3.0
Italy	1996	2.1
Jamaica	1995	1.1
Japan	1999	2.4
Jordan	1995	3.3
Kazakstan	1985-90	2.1
Kenya	1986	0.9 to 1.8
Kiribati	1994	1.0
Kuwait	1993	2.6
Kyrgyzstan	1973	3.1
Laos	1991	1.9
Latvia	1998	4.2
Lebanon	1994	5.7
Lesotho	1991	0.4
Liberia	1977	0.4
Libya	1989	1.6
Liechtenstein	1988	3.4
Lithuania	1994	3.8
Luxembourg	1990	3.0
Macau	1994	2.0
Madagascar	1993	3.1
Malawi	1992-94	0.6 to 0.8
Malaysia	1997	1.9
Maldives	1984	2.1
Mali	1983	2.2
Malta	1986	1.6
Martinique	1988	6.3
Mauritania	1990	2.0
Mauritius	1993	4.9
Mexico	1991-92	2.5 to 5.1
Micronesia	1984	2.1
Moldova	1992	2.3
Mongolia	1990	2.6
Morocco	1999	2.5
Mozambique	1983	0.6 to 5.5
Myanmar (Burma)	1993	1.1
Namibia	1991	1.2
Nepal	1994	1.2

D8-1. Mean Number of Decayed, Missing or Filled Teeth among 12-Year-Olds, various years (continued)

	Year	DMFT* in 12-Year-Olds
Netherlands, the	1992-93	0.9
New Caledonia	1991	4.4
New Zealand	1993	1.5
Nicaragua	1997	2.8
Niger	1997	1.3
Nigeria	1990-91	0.7
Niue	1995	1.8
North Korea, Dem.Rep.	1991	3.0
Norway	1993	2.1
Oman	1993	1.5
Pakistan	1991	0.9
Panama	1997	3.6
Papua New Guinea	1995	1.7
Paraguay	1983	5.9
Peru	1990	7.0
Philippines	1998	4.6
Poland	1992	5.1
Portugal	1999	1.5
Reunion	1981	4.1
Romania	1995	3.4
Russia	1985-95	3.7
Rwanda	1993	0.3
Saint Kitts and Nevis	1979-83	5.5
Saint Lucia	1961	2.7
Saint Vincent and the Grenadines	1991	3.2
Samoa	1994	2.5
San Marino	1987	3.7
Saudi Arabia	1995	1.7
Senegal	1994	1.2
Serbia	1994	2.9 to 7.8
Sierra Leone	1986	1.3
Singapore	1995	1.0
Slovakia	1987	2.0 to 5.0
Slovenia	1998	1.8
Solomon Islands	1994	2.7
Somalia	1992	1.0
South Africa	1988-89	1.7
South Korea, Rep.	1995	3.1
Spain	1994	2.3
Sri Lanka	1994-95	1.4
Sudan	1990	1.4
Suriname	1992	2.7
Swaziland	1989	0.9
Sweden	1999	0.9
Switzerland	1992	1.2
Syria	1994	2.5
Tajikistan	1985-90	1.2
Tanzania	1994	0.3
Thailand	1994	1.6
Togo	1986	0.3
Tokelau	1999	4.9
Tonga	1998	3.1
Trinidad and Tobago	1989	4.9
Tunisia	1994	1.3
Turkey	1988	2.7
Turkmenistan	1985-90	2.6
Tuvalu	1994	2.0

D8-1. Mean Number of Decayed, Missing or Filled Teeth among 12-Year-Olds, various years (continued)

	Year	DMFT* in 12-Year-Olds
Uganda	1993	0.4
Ukraine	1992	4.4
United Arab Emirates	1995	1.6
United Kingdom	1996-97	1.1
United States	1991	1.4
Uruguay	1992	3.6
Uzbekistan	1996	1.4
Vanuatu	1994	1.2
Venezuela	1997	2.1
Vietnam	1990	1.8
Yemen	1987	3.1
Zaire	1987-91	0.4 to 1.1
Zambia	1982	2.3
Zimbabwe	1991	1.3

*DMFT = Mean number of decayed, missing or filled teeth

Source: WHO Oral Health Country/Area Profile Programme Department of Noncommunicable Diseases Surveillance/Oral Health WHO Collaborating Centre, Malmö University, Sweden; <http://www.whocollab.od.mah.se/countriesalphab.html> data extracted 2/28/2001. Underlying data from World Health Organization (WHO).

D9. LOW BIRTH WEIGHT OR UNDERWEIGHT

D9-1. Percent of Infants with Low Birth Weight,* 1990–1997

	Percent
Afghanistan	20
Albania	7
Algeria	9
Angola	19
Antigua and Barbuda	8
Argentina	7
Armenia	7
Australia	6
Austria	6
Azerbaijan	6
Bahrain	6
Bangladesh	50
Barbados	10
Belgium	6
Belize	4
Bolivia	5
Botswana	11
Brazil	8
Bulgaria	6
Burkina Faso	21
Cameroon	13
Canada	6
Cape Verde	9
Central African Republic	15
Chile	5
China	9
Colombia	9
Comoros	8
Congo	16

D9-1. Percent of Infants with Low Birth Weight,* 1990–1997 *(continued)*

	Percent
Congo, Dem. Rep. (Zaire)	15
Cook Islands	1
Costa Rica	7
Côte d'Ivoire	12
Cuba	7
Czech Republic	6
Denmark	6
Djibouti	11
Dominica	10
Dominican Republic	13
Ecuador	13
Egypt	10
El Salvador	11
Eritrea	13
Ethiopia	16
Fiji	12
Finland	4
France	5
Ghana	8
Greece	6
Grenada	9
Guatemala	15
Guinea	13
Guinea-Bissau	20
Guyana	15
Haiti	15
Honduras	9
Hungary	9
India	33
Indonesia	8
Iran	10
Iraq	15
Ireland	4
Israel	7
Italy	5
Jamaica	10
Japan	7
Jordan	10
Kazakhstan	9
Kenya	16
Kiribati	3
Kuwait	7
Kyrgyzstan	6
Laos	18
Lebanon	10
Lesotho	11
Libya	7
Madagascar	5
Malawi	20
Malaysia	8
Maldives	13
Mali	16
Marshall Islands	14
Mauritania	11
Mauritius	13
Mexico	7
Micronesia	9
Moldova	4
Mongolia	7
Morocco	9
Mozambique	20
Myanmar (Burma)	24
Namibia	16

D9-1. Percent of Infants with Low Birth Weight,* 1990–1997 *(continued)*

	Percent
New Zealand	6
Nicaragua	9
Niger	15
Nigeria	16
Norway	4
Oman	8
Pakistan	25
Palau	8
Panama	8
Papua New Guinea	23
Paraguay	5
Peru	11
Philippines	9
Portugal	5
Romania	7
Russia	6
Rwanda	17
Saint Kitts and Nevis	9
Saint Lucia	8
Saint Vincent and Grenadines	8
Samoa	6
Sao Tome and Principe	7
Saudi Arabia	7
Senegal	4
Seychelles	10
Sierra Leone	11
Singapore	7
Solomon Islands	20
Somalia	16
South Korea, Rep.	9
Spain	4
Sri Lanka	25
Sudan	15
Suriname	13
Swaziland	10
Sweden	5
Switzerland	5
Syria	7
Tanzania	14
Thailand	6
Togo	20
Tonga	2
Trinidad and Tobago	10
Tunisia	8
Turkey	8
Turkmenistan	5
Tuvalu	3
Uganda	13
United Arab Emirates	6
United Kingdom	7
United States	7
Uruguay	8
Vanuatu	7
Venezuela	9
Vietnam	17
Yemen	19
Zambia	13
Zimbabwe	10

*Low birth weight signifies a weight, measured immediately after birth, of less than 2,500 grams (5.5 pounds).

Source: The State of the World's Children, 2000; Table 2. Nutrition; <http://www.unicef.org/sowc00/stat4.htm Underlying data from United Nations Children's Fund (UNICEF).

D10. CHILDHOOD OBESITY

D10-1. Body Mass Index over which Children are Considered Overweight and Obese, by Age, 1999*

Age (years)	Overweight Body mass index		Obese Body mass index	
	Males	Females	Males	Females
2.0	18.4	18.0	20.1	20.1
2.5	18.1	17.8	19.8	19.5
3.0	17.9	17.6	19.6	19.4
3.5	17.7	17.4	19.4	19.2
4.0	17.6	17.3	19.3	19.1
4.5	17.5	17.2	19.3	19.1
5.0	17.4	17.1	19.3	19.2
5.5	17.5	17.2	19.5	19.3
6.0	17.6	17.3	19.8	19.7
6.5	17.7	17.5	20.2	20.1
7.0	17.9	17.8	20.6	20.5
7.5	18.2	18.0	21.1	21.0
8.0	18.4	18.3	21.6	21.6
8.5	18.8	18.7	22.2	22.2
9.0	19.1	19.1	22.8	22.8
9.5	19.5	19.5	23.4	23.5
10.0	19.8	19.9	24.0	24.1
10.5	20.2	20.3	24.6	24.8
11.0	20.6	20.7	25.1	25.4
11.5	20.9	21.2	25.6	26.1
12.0	21.2	21.7	26.0	26.7
12.5	21.6	22.1	26.4	27.2
13.0	21.9	22.6	26.8	27.8
13.5	22.3	23.0	27.2	28.2
14.0	22.6	23.3	27.6	28.6
14.5	23.0	23.7	28.0	28.9
15.0	23.3	23.9	28.3	29.1
15.5	23.6	24.2	28.6	29.3
16.0	23.9	24.4	28.9	29.4
16.5	24.2	24.5	29.1	29.6
17.0	24.5	24.7	29.4	29.7
17.5	24.7	24.8	29.7	29.8
18.0	25.0	25.0	30.0	30.0

* Obtained by averaging data from Brazil, Great Britain, Hong Kong, Netherlands, Singapore, and United States; based on six nationally representative datasets of body mass indices in childhood.
Note: BMI is calculated by dividing the individual's weight (in kilograms) by his or her height (in meters) squared: BMI = body weight (kg)/height2(m).

Source: The Childhood Obesity Working Group of the International Obesity Task Force, *Establishing A Standard Definition For Child Overweight And Obesity Worldwide: International Survey:* Table 2. by Tim J Cole, Mary C Bellizzi, Katherine M Flegal, William H Dietz. BMJ 2000;320:1240-1243 (6 May); <http://www.bmj.com/cgi/content/abridged/320/7244/1240> and <http://www.iotf.org/>. Underlying data from World Health Organization (WHO).

D10-2. Regional and Global Prevalence and Numbers of Overweight* Children under Five Years of Age, 1995

WHO Regions**	Percent overweight	Number overweight (million)
Africa	2.7	2.8
Americas	4.6	3.6
South-East Asia	0.6	1.0
Europe	N/A	N/A
Eastern Mediterranean	4.4	3.2
Western Pacific	3.7	5.2
World	3.6	21.9

N/A = Not available
* Percent more than +2 Standard Deviation above median height/weight.
** For breakdown of countries in WHO regions see appendix.

Source: Malnutrition—The Global Picture, WHO, Nutrition for Health and Development, January 2000; <http://www.who.int/nut/malnutrition_worldwide. htm#oao>. Underlying data from World Health Organization (WHO).

D11. HUNGER

D11-1. Prevalence of Undernourishment, Selected Developing Countries,* 1979–1981, 1990–1992, 1996–1998

	Prevalence Category (proportion of the population undernourished in 1996–98)	Number 1996–98 (millions)	Undernourished in total population		
			Percent 1979–81	Percent 1990–92	Percent 1996–98
Afghanistan	5	14.6	34	63	70
Angola	5	5	31	51	43
Bangladesh	5	46.8	42	35	38
Burundi	5	4.3	39	44	68
Central African Republic	5	1.4	22	46	41
Chad	5	2.7	69	58	38
Congo, Dem Rep, (Zaire)	5	29.3	38	37	61
Eritrea	5	2.2	N/A	N/A	65
Ethiopia	5	28.4	N/A	N/A	49
Haiti	5	4.8	48	64	62
Kenya	5	12.2	26	47	43
Liberia	5	1.1	22	49	46
Madagascar	5	5.8	18	33	40
Mongolia	5	1.1	16	34	45
Mozambique	5	10.7	54	67	58
Niger	5	4.5	34	42	46
North Korea, Dem. Rep.	5	13.2	19	19	57
Rwanda	5	2.3	24	37	39
Sierra Leone	5	1.9	40	45	43
Somalia	5	6.6	55	67	75
Tanzania	5	12.7	23	31	41
Yemen	5	5.7	39	37	35
Zambia	5	3.9	30	40	45
Zimbabwe	5	4.2	30	41	37
Armenia	4	0.7	N/A	N/A	21
Azerbaijan	4	2.4	N/A	N/A	32
Bolivia	4	1.8	26	25	23
Botswana	4	0.4	29	20	27
Burkina Faso	4	3.5	64	32	32
Cambodia	4	3.4	61	41	33
Cameroon	4	4.1	20	29	29

D11-1. Prevalence of Undernourishment, Selected Developing Countries,* 1979–1981, 1990–1992, 1996–1998 *(continued)*

	Prevalence Category (proportion of the population undernourished in 1996–98)	Undernourished in total population		
		Number 1996–98 (millions)	Percent 1979–81	Percent 1990–92	Percent 1996–98
Congo, Rep	4	0.9	29	34	32
Dominican Republic	4	2.2	25	29	28
Georgia	4	1.2	N/A	N/A	23
Guatemala	4	2.5	18	14	24
Guinea	4	2.1	30	37	29
Honduras	4	1.3	31	23	22
India	4	207.6	38	26	21
Laos	4	1.5	32	31	29
Lesotho	4	0.6	27	31	29
Malawi	4	3.2	26	47	32
Mali	4	3.4	60	24	32
Namibia	4	0.5	25	27	31
Nepal	4	6.2	47	21	28
Nicaragua	4	1.5	26	29	31
Pakistan	4	28.9	31	26	20
Papua New Guinea	4	1.3	31	26	29
Philippines	4	15.2	27	24	21
Senegal	4	2	20	21	23
Sri Lanka	4	4.5	22	28	25
Tajikistan	4	1.9	N/A	N/A	32
Thailand	4	12.2	25	31	21
Uganda	4	6	32	23	30
Vietnam	4	16.5	33	28	22
Algeria	3	1.4	9	5	5
Benin	3	0.8	37	21	14
Bosnia and Herzegovina	3	0.4	N/A	N/A	10
Brazil	3	15.9	15	13	10
Bulgaria	3	1.1	N/A	N/A	13
China	3	140.1	30	17	11
Colombia	3	5.2	22	17	13
Costa Rica	3	0.2	8	6	6
Côte d'Ivoire	3	1.9	8	15	14
Croatia	3	0.5	N/A	N/A	12
Cuba	3	2.1	4	4	19
Ecuador	3	0.5	11	8	5
El Salvador	3	0.6	17	12	11
Estonia	3	0.1	N/A	N/A	6
Gabon	3	0.1	13	11	8
Gambia, the	3	0.2	58	18	16
Ghana	3	1.9	62	29	10
Guyana	3	0.2	13	24	18
Indonesia	3	12..3	26	10	6
Iran	3	4.1	9	6	6
Iraq	3	3.5	4	9	17
Jamaica	3	0.2	9	12	10
Jordan	3	0.2	5	4	5
Kazakhstan	3	0.7	N/A	N/A	5
Kyrgyzstan	3	0.8	N/A	N/A	17
Macedonia, FYRO	3	0.1	N/A	N/A	7
Mauritania	3	0.3	35	15	13
Mauritius	3	0.1	10	6	6
Mexico	3	5.1	5	5	5
Moldova	3	0.5	N/A	N/A	11

D11-1. Prevalence of Undernourishment, Selected Developing Countries,* 1979–1981, 1990–1992, 1996–1998 *(continued)*

	Prevalence Category (proportion of the population undernourished in 1996–98)	Undernourished in total population		
		Number 1996–98 (millions)	Percent 1979–81	Percent 1990–92	Percent 1996–98
Morocco	3	1.4	10	5	5
Myanmar (Burma)	3	3.1	19	10	7
Nigeria	3	8.6	44	16	8
Panama	3	0.4	21	19	16
Paraguay	3	0.7	13	18	13
Peru	3	4.4	28	40	18
Russia	3	8.6	N/A	N/A	6
Sudan	3	5.1	24	30	18
Suriname	3	0	18	12	10
Swaziland	3	0.1	14	9	14
Togo	3	0.8	31	29	18
Trinidad and Tobago	3	0.2	6	12	13
Turkmenistan	3	0.4	N/A	N/A	10
Ukraine	3	2.6	N/A	N/A	5
Uzbekistan	3	2.6	N/A	N/A	11
Venezuela	3	3.7	4	11	16
Albania	2	0.1	9	14	3
Chile	2	0.6	7	8	4
Egypt	2	2.6	8	5	4
Kuwait	2	0.1	4	22	4
Latvia	2	0.1	N/A	N/A	4
Saudi Arabia	2	0.6	3	3	3
Slovakia	2	0.2	N/A	N/A	4
Slovenia	2	0.1	N/A	N/A	3
Uruguay	2	0.1	3	7	4
Yugoslavia	2	0.3	N/A	N/A	3
Argentina	1	0.4	N/A	N/A	N/A
Belarus	1	0.1	N/A	N/A	N/A
Czech Republic	1	0.1	N/A	N/A	N/A
Hong Kong, SAR (China)	1	0.1	N/A	N/A	N/A
Hungary	1	0.1	N/A	N/A	N/A
Lebanon	1	0.1	8	N/A	N/A
Libya	1	0	N/A	N/A	N/A
Lithuania	1	0.1	N/A	N/A	N/A
Malaysia	1	0.5	4	3	N/A
Poland	1	0.3	N/A	N/A	N/A
Romania	1	0.3	N/A	3	N/A
South Korea, Rep.	1	0.5	N/A	N/A	N/A
Syria	1	0.2	3	N/A	N/A
Tunisia	1	0.1	N/A	N/A	N/A
Turkey	1	1.2	3	N/A	N/A
United Arab Emirates	1	0	N/A	N/A	N/A

N/A = not available

*Table does not include countries with population of less than one million or having insufficient data.

Prevalence Category (proportion of the population undernourished in 1996–98):

1 = < 2.5% undernourished
2 = 2.5- 4% undernourished
3 = 5-19% undernourished
4 = 20- 34% undernourished
5 = =35% undernourished

Sources: Total population: UN World Population Prospects, 1998 Revision and *The State of Food Insecurity in the World, 2000;* <http://www.fao.org/docrep/x8200e/x8200e06.htm#P16_4884>. United Nations (UN) and the Food and Agriculture Organization (FAO).

D11-2. Food Availability and Depth of Hunger, Selected Developing Countries,* 1996–1998

		Food availability	Depth of hunger		
	Prevalence Cateogry (proportion undernourished in 1996–98	Dietary energy supply, DES (kcal/person/day)**	Dietary energy supply (DES) of the undernourished (kcal/person/day)**	Minimum energy requirement (kcal/person/day)**	Food deficit of the undernourished (kcal/person/day)**
Afghanistan	5	1,620	1,350	1,820	480
Angola	5	1,910	1,410	1,730	320
Bangladesh	5	2,060	1,460	1,790	340
Burundi	5	1,640	1,380	1,790	410
Central African Republic	5	2,000	1,490	1,800	310
Chad	5	2,070	1,490	1,820	330
Congo, Dem. Rep. (Zaire)	5	1,750	1,440	1,820	380
Eritrea	5	1,650	1,390	1,760	370
Ethiopia	5	1,840	1,410	1,750	340
Haiti	5	1,840	1,470	1,930	460
Kenya	5	1,970	1,530	1,820	290
Liberia	5	2,000	1,430	1,820	390
Madagascar	5	2,010	1,490	1,800	310
Mongolia	5	1,960	1,530	1,840	310
Mozambique	5	1,860	1,470	1,890	420
Niger	5	1,940	1,450	1,800	350
North Korea, Dem. Rep.	5	1,860	1,550	1,890	340
Rwanda	5	2,030	1,430	1,760	330
Sierra Leone	5	2,050	1,440	1,820	380
Somalia	5	1,550	1,330	1,820	490
Tanzania	5	2,000	1,500	1,800	300
Yemen	5	2,050	1,470	1,760	290
Zambia	5	1,960	1,470	1,810	340
Zimbabwe	5	2,140	1,510	1,850	340
Armenia	4	2,350	1,740	1,950	210
Azerbaijan	4	2,190	1,690	1,930	240
Bolivia	4	2,200	1,540	1,770	230
Botswana	4	2,210	1,600	1,840	240
Burkina Faso	4	2,160	1,520	1,810	290
Cambodia	4	2,060	1,490	1,760	270
Cameroon	4	2,190	1,590	1,850	260
Congo, Rep.	4	2,170	1,540	1,830	290
Dominican Republic	4	2,270	1,660	1,920	250
Georgia	4	2,320	1,730	1,940	210
Guatemala	4	2,180	1,510	1,750	250
Guinea	4	2,310	1,510	1,830	320
Honduras	4	2,340	1,490	1,760	270
India	4	2,470	1,520	1,810	290
Laos	4	2,120	1,430	1,710	280
Lesotho	4	2,230	1,580	1,860	280
Malawi	4	2,170	1,480	1,790	310
Mali	4	2,150	1,520	1,810	290
Namibia	4	2,130	1,570	1,830	260
Nepal	4	2,190	1,530	1,800	260
Nicaragua	4	2,190	1,500	1,800	300
Nigeria	4	2,760	1,620	1,830	210
Pakistan	4	2,430	1,490	1,760	270
Papua New Guinea	4	2,140	1,530	1,790	260
Philippines	4	2,390	1,520	1,790	270
Senegal	4	2,290	1,590	1,830	240
Sri Lanka	4	2,300	1,570	1,830	260
Tajikistan	4	2,160	1,630	1,880	250
Thailand	4	2,440	1,610	1,870	260
Uganda	4	2,140	1,500	1,780	280
Vietnam	4	2,410	1,520	1,800	280

D11-2. Food Availability and Depth of Hunger, Selected Developing Countries,* 1996–1998 *(continued)*

| | Prevalence Cateogry (proportion undernourished in 1996–98 | Food availability | Depth of hunger | | |
		Dietary energy supply, DES (kcal/person/day)**	Dietary energy supply (DES) of the undernourished (kcal/person/day)**	Minimum energy requirement (kcal/person/day)**	Food deficit of the undernourished (kcal/person/day)**
Algeria	3	2,980	1,640	1,830	190
Benin	3	2,540	1,570	1,790	220
Bosnia and Herzegovina	3	2,660	1,810	2,000	190
Brazil	3	2,960	1,650	1,900	250
Bulgaria	3	2,700	1,760	1,980	220
China	3	2,930	1,670	1,920	250
Colombia	3	2,580	1,590	1,810	220
Costa Rica	3	2,740	1,750	1,910	160
Côte d'Ivoire	3	2,610	1,610	1,840	230
Croatia	3	2,610	1,830	2,010	180
Cuba	3	2,420	1,740	1,960	210
Ecuador	3	2,710	1,650	1,810	160
El Salvador	3	2,540	1,590	1,790	200
Estonia	3	2,950	1,780	1,960	180
Gabon	3	2,540	1,680	1,840	160
Gambia	3	2,520	1,610	1,850	240
Ghana	3	2,670	1,620	1,830	210
Guyana	3	2,450	1,650	1,880	230
Indonesia	3	2,880	1,630	1,830	200
Iran	3	2,830	1,610	1,800	190
Iraq	3	2,340	1,560	1,770	210
Jamaica	3	2,660	1,720	1,920	200
Jordan	3	2,790	1,600	1,770	170
Kazakhstan	3	2,860	1,780	1,940	160
Kyrgyzstan	3	2,490	1,670	1,900	230
Macedonia, FYRO	3	2,780	1,800	1,970	170
Mauritania	3	2,630	1,600	1,840	240
Mauritius	3	2,940	1,720	1,900	180
Mexico	3	3,130	1,680	1,890	210
Moldova	3	2,690	1,740	1,950	210
Morocco	3	3,130	1,640	1,850	210
Myanmar (Burma)	3	2,830	1,630	1,830	200
Panama	3	2,450	1,590	1,820	230
Paraguay	3	2,570	1,610	1,830	220
Peru	3	2,390	1,570	1,810	240
Russia	3	2,840	1,800	1,970	170
Sudan	3	2,430	1,600	1,840	240
Suriname	3	2,640	1,720	1,910	190
Swaziland	3	2,490	1,630	1,840	210
Togo	3	2,460	1,560	1,820	260
Trinidad and Tobago	3	2,690	1,700	1,930	230
Turkmenistan	3	2,620	1,700	1,890	190
Ukraine	3	2,830	1,800	1,960	160
Uzbekistan	3	2,550	1,710	1,890	180
Venezuela	3	2,360	1,640	1,840	210
Albania	2	3,030	1,810	1,960	150
Chile	2	2,820	1,760	1,910	150
Egypt	2	3,280	1,700	1,900	190
Kuwait	2	3,050	1,710	1,890	180
Latvia	2	2,930	1,800	1,950	150
Saudi Arabia	2	2,850	1,710	1,860	150
Slovakia	2	2,960	1,870	2,020	160
Slovenia	2	2,970	1,850	1,990	150

D11-2. Food Availability and Depth of Hunger, Selected Developing Countries,* 1996–1998 *(continued)*

	Prevalence Cateogry (proportion undernourished in 1996–98)	Food availability	Depth of hunger		
		Dietary energy supply, DES (kcal/person/day)**	Dietary energy supply (DES) of the undernourished (kcal/person/day)**	Minimum energy requirement (kcal/person/day)**	Food deficit of the undernourished (kcal/person/day)**
Uruguay	2	2,810	1,760	1,910	150
Yugoslavia	2	3,040	1,840	1,990	150
Argentina	1	3,140	1,800	1,940	140
Belarus	1	3,160	1,820	1,960	130
Czech Republic	1	3,280	1,890	2,020	130
Hong Kong, SAR (China)	1	3,200	1,820	1,960	140
Hungary	1	3,350	1,860	2,000	140
Lebanon	1	3,270	1,730	1,890	160
Libya	1	3,250	1,730	1,860	130
Lithuania	1	3,110	1,810	1,950	140
Malaysia	1	2,890	1,690	1,830	140
Poland	1	3,330	1,860	1,990	130
Romania	1	3,280	1,870	2,010	130
South Korea, Rep.	1	3,120	1,790	1,920	130
Syria	1	3,350	1,660	1,820	160
Tunisia	1	3,260	1,730	1,860	130
Turkey	1	3,500	1,800	1,970	170
United Arab Emirates	1	3,370	1,850	1,990	140

*Table does not include countries with population of less than one million or having insufficient data.

**Kilocalorie (kcal) is a unit of measurement of energy. One kilocalorie equals 1,000 calories. In the International System of Units (ISU), the universal unit of energy is the joule (J). One kilocalorie = 4.184 kilojoules (kJ).

N/A = not available

Prevalence Category (proportion of the population undernourished in 1996–98):

1= < 2.5% undernourished

2 = 2.5 - 4% undernourished

3 = 5 - 19% undernourished

4 = 20 - 34% undernourished

5 = =35% undernourished

Sources: UN World Population Prospects, 1998 Revision and The State of Food Insecurity in the World, 2000; <http://www.fao.org/docrep/x8200e/x8200e06.htm#P16_4884>. United Nations (UN) and the Food and Agriculture Organization (FAO).

D11-3. Per Capita Calorie Consumption (Animal and Vegetable Products), in Grams, 1998

	Grams per capita
Afghanistan	1,774
Albania	2,976
Algeria	3,020
Angola	1,920
Antigua and Barbuda	2,451
Argentina	3,144
Armenia	2,356
Australia	3,191
Austria	3,531
Azerbaijan	2,191
Bahamas	2,545
Bangladesh	2,050
Barbados	2,978
Belarus	3,137
Belize	2,923
Benin	2,571
Bermuda	2,920
Bolivia	2,214

D11-3. Per Capita Calorie Consumption (Animal and Vegetable Products), in Grams, 1998 *(continued)*

	Grams per capita
Bosnia and Herzegovina	2,801
Botswana	2,160
Brazil	2,925
Brunei	2,851
Bulgaria	2,740
Burkina Faso	2,149
Burundi	1,578
Cambodia	2,078
Cameroon	2,209
Canada	3,167
Cape Verde	3,099
Central African Republic	2,056
Chad	2,171
Chile	2,844
China	2,974
Colombia	2,559
Comoros	1,857
Congo, Dem Rep. (Zaire)	1,701
Congo, Rep.	2,241
Costa Rica	2,780
Côte d'Ivoire	2,695
Croatia	2,854
Cuba	2,473
Cyprus	3,474
Czech Republic	3,292
Denmark	3,434
Djibouti	2,074
Dominica	2,997
Dominican Republic	2,278
Ecuador	2,724
Egypt	3,282
El Salvador	2,522
Eritrea	1,744
Estonia	3,058
Ethiopia	1,805
Fiji Islands	2,851
Finland	3,180
France	3,541
French Polynesia	2,924
Gabon	2,560
Gambia	2,559
Georgia	2,252
Germany	3,402
Ghana	2,586
Greece	3,630
Grenada	2,681
Guatemala	2,160
Guinea	2,315
Guinea-Bissau	2,410
Guyana	2,476
Haiti	1,876
Honduras	2,344
Hungary	3,407
Iceland	3,222
India	2,466
Indonesia	2,850
Iran	2,822

D11-3. Per Capita Calorie Consumption (Animal and Vegetable Products), in Grams, 1998 (continued)

	Grams per capita
Iraq	2,419
Ireland	3,622
Israel	3,466
Italy	3,608
Jamaica	2,711
Japan	2,874
Jordan	2,791
Kazakhstan	2,518
Kenya	1,968
Kiribati	2,976
Kuwait	3,060
Kyrgyzstan	2,535
Laos	2,175
Latvia	2,994
Lebanon	3,285
Lesotho	2,210
Liberia	1,979
Libya	3,267
Lithuania	3,104
Macedonia, FYRO	2,939
Madagascar	2,001
Malawi	2,226
Malaysia	2,901
Maldives	2,451
Mali	2,118
Malta	3,383
Mauritania	2,640
Mauritius	2,945
Mexico	3,144
Moldova Rep	2,763
Mongolia	2,010
Morocco	3,165
Mozambique	1,911
Myanmar (Burma)	2,833
Namibia	2,096
Nepal	2,170
Netherlands Antilles	2,659
Netherlands, the	3,282
New Caledonia	2,812
New Zealand	3,315
Nicaragua	2,208
Niger	1,966
Nigeria	2,882
North Korea, Dem. Rep.	1,900
Norway	3,425
Oceania	3,011
Pakistan	2,447
Panama	2,476
Papua New Guinea	2,168
Paraguay	2,577
Peru	2,420
Philippines	2,288
Poland	3,351
Portugal	3,691
Romania	3,263
Russia	2,835
Rwanda	2,036

D11-3. Per Capita Calorie Consumption (Animal and Vegetable Products), in Grams, 1998 (continued)

	Grams per capita
Sao Tome and Principe	2,200
Saudi Arabia	2,888
Senegal	2,277
Seychelles	2,462
Sierra Leone	2,045
Slovakia	2,953
Slovenia	2,950
Solomon Islands	2,130
Somalia	1,530
South Korea, Rep.	3,069
Spain	3,348
Sri Lanka	2,314
St Kitts and Nevis	2,766
St Lucia	2,842
St Vincent and the Grenadines	2,554
Sudan	2,444
Suriname	2,634
Swaziland	2,503
Sweden	3,113
Switzerland	3,222
Syria	3,378
Tajikistan	2,176
Tanzania	2,000
Thailand	2,463
Togo	2,513
Trinidad and Tobago	2,712
Tunisia	3,297
Turkey	3,554
Turkmenistan	2,684
Uganda	2,216
Ukraine	2,878
United Kingdom	3,256
United States	3,767
Untd Arab Emirtaes	3,372
Uruguay	2,866
Uzbekistan	2,564
Vanuatu	2,737
Venezuela	2,358
Vietnam	2,422
World	2,791
Yemen	2,087
Yugoslavia	2,963
Zambia	1,950
Zimbabwe	2,153

Source: Food and Agriculture Organization database (FAOSTAT); <http://apps.fao.org/lim500/nph-wrap.pl?FoodBalanceSheet&Domain=FoodBalanceSheet>. Underlying data from the Food and Agriculture Organization (FAO).

D11-4. Per Capita Protein Consumption (Animal and Vegetable Products), in Grams, 1998

	Grams per capita
Afghanistan	49.3
Albania	97.6
Algeria	82.2
Angola	40.9
Antigua and Barbuda	78.6
Argentina	99.1
Armenia	64.7
Australia	106.9
Austria	104.3
Azerbaijan	66.5
Bahamas, the	79.9
Bangladesh	44.4
Barbados	83.9
Belarus	88.7
Belize	64.3
Benin	60.7
Bermuda	91.2
Bolivia	56.5
Bosnia and Herzegovina	76.7
Botswana	68.7
Brazil	75.9
Brunei	81.5
Bulgaria	86.4
Burkina Faso	62.6
Burundi	48.2
Cambodia	48.1
Cameroon	50.9
Canada	99.4
Cape Verde	63.6
Central African Republic	43.9
Chad	64.2
Chile	78.5
China	81.8
Colombia	60.8
Comoros	42.3
Congo, Dem Rep. (Zaire)	27.5
Congo, Rep	46.1
Costa Rica	76.1
Côte d'Ivoire	52.9
Croatia	75.2
Cuba	51.6
Cyprus	111.6
Czech Republic	94.6
Denmark	104.9
Djibouti	44.2
Dominica	81.1
Dominican Republic	49.8
Ecuador	54.0
Egypt	89.7
El Salvador	62.6
Eritrea	55.7
Estonia	102.3
Ethiopia	52.7
Fiji Islands	69.5
Finland	103.8
France	114.5
French Polynesia	96.3
Gabon	72.5

D11-4. Per Capita Protein Consumption (Animal and Vegetable Products), in Grams, 1998 (continued)

	Grams per capita
Gambia	52.5
Georgia	64.6
Germany	97.9
Ghana	50.7
Greece	117.3
Grenada	66.3
Guatemala	56.4
Guinea	50.1
Guinea-Bissau	47.1
Guyana	71.9
Haiti	42.8
Honduras	58.1
Hungary	88.0
Iceland	111.7
India	58.9
Indonesia	62.8
Iran	73.9
Iraq	53.3
Ireland	112.1
Israel	111.4
Italy	110.7
Jamaica	66.6
Japan	94.1
Jordan	72.5
Kazakhstan	79.5
Kenya	51.2
Kiribati	71.9
Kuwait	95.4
Kyrgyzstan	84.6
Laos	53.7
Latvia	78.7
Lebanon	85.8
Lesotho	62.0
Liberia	35.7
Libya	81.2
Lithuania	93.8
Macedonia, FYRO	73.4
Madagascar	46.9
Malawi	55.4
Malaysia	72.9
Maldives	92.9
Mali	62.7
Malta	109.4
Mauritania	74.6
Mauritius	74.6
Mexico	86.1
Moldova	65.3
Mongolia	73.2
Morocco	83.2
Mozambique	37.4
Myanmar (Burma)	71.8
Namibia	56.4
Nepal	56.8
Netherlands Antilles	82.4
Netherlands, the	106.4
New Caledonia	83.2
New Zealand	102.9

D11-4. Per Capita Protein Consumption (Animal and Vegetable Products), in Grams, 1998 *(continued)*

	Grams per capita
Nicaragua	53.0
Niger	54.5
Nigeria	64.9
North Korea, Dem. Rep.	55.6
Norway	104.2
Pakistan	62.7
Panama	65.4
Papua New Guinea	45.2
Paraguay	72.3
Peru	61.9
Philippines	55.1
Poland	99.4
Portugal	116.2
Romania	101.7
Russia	88.3
Rwanda	47.3
Sao Tome and Principe	43.6
Saudi Arabia	76.6
Senegal	64.2
Seychelles	77.5
Sierra Leone	43.8
Slovakia	80.1
Slovenia	97.3
Solomon Islands	49.1
Somalia	48.3
South Africa	73.6
South Korea, Rep.	84.8
Spain	110.3
Sri Lanka	50.7
St Kitts and Nevis	75.8
St Lucia	84.6
St Vincent and the Grenadines	65.1
Sudan	77.7
Suriname	64.7
Swaziland	61.2
Sweden	100.6
Switzerland	88.9
Syria	88.0
Tajikistan	55.5
Tanzania	48.8
Thailand	57.2
Togo	61.4
Trinidad and Tobago	63.7
Tunisia	89.4
Turkey	99.8
Turkmenistan	75.3
Uganda	48.4
Ukraine	80.6
United Kingdom	96.1
United States	115.4
Untd Arab Emirates	105.5
Uruguay	86.8
Uzbekistan	71.8
Vanuatu	59.8
Venezuela	60.4
Vietnam	56.9
Yemen	57.0
Yugoslavia	90.2
Zambia	49.7
Zimbabwe	52.7

Source: Food and Agriculture Organization database (FAOSTAT); <http://apps.fao.org/lim500/nph-wrap.pl?FoodBalanceSheet&Domain=FoodBalanceSheet>. Underlying data from the Food and Agriculture Organization (FAO).

D11-5. Per Capita Supply of Total Cereals, in Kilograms, Selected Countries, 1994–1995

	Kilograms per capita
Algeria	234
Angola	61
Antigua and Barbuda	85
Argentina	127
Bangladesh	173
Barbados	108
Belize	102
Benin	101
Bolivia	121
Botswana	135
Brazil	105
Brunei	141
Burkina Faso	215
Burundi	37
Cambodia	170
Cameroon	106
Cape Verde	180
Central African Republic	48
Chad	125
Chile	137
China	184
Colombia	98
Comoros	86
Congo, Rep.	58
Congo, Dem. Rep. (Zaire)	35
Costa Rica	111
Côte d'Ivoire	114
Cuba	105
Cyprus	114
Djibouti	110
Dominica	106
Dominican Republic	91
Ecuador	93
Egypt	250
El Salvador	161
Fiji	145
Gabon	80
Gambia	134
Ghana	94
Grenada	95
Guatemala	148
Guinea	113
Guinea-Bissau	162
Guyana	145
Honduras	127
Hong Kong SAR, China	116
India	162
Indonesia	187
Iran	210
Iraq	140
Jamaica	98
Jordan	158
Kenya	129
Laos	180
Lebanon	137
Lesotho	185
Libya	193
Madagascar	113

D11-5. Per Capita Supply of Total Cereals, in Kilograms, Selected Countries, 1994–1995 *(continued)*

	Kilograms per capita
Malawi	158
Malaysia	127
Maldives	122
Mali	184
Mauritania	168
Mauritius	167
Mexico	178
Mongolia	121
Morocco	261
Mozambique	81
Myanmar	220
Namibia	126
Nepal	198
Nicaragua	129
Niger	221
Nigeria	126
North Korea, Dem. Rep.	159
Pakistan	154
Panama	128
Papua New Guinea	72
Paraguay	78
Peru	106
Philippines	139
Saint Kitts and Nevis	82
Saint Vincent and Grenadines	98
Saint Lucia	119
Saudi Arabia	168
Senegal	165
Seychelles	107
Sierra Leone	114
Solomon Islands	83
South Africa	184
South Korea, Rep.	165
Sri Lanka	148
Sudan	158
Suriname	150
Swaziland	153
Syria	234
Tanzania	107
Thailand	129
Togo	109
Trinidad and Tobago	112
Tunisia	205
Turkey	231
Uganda	58
United Arab Emirates	125
Uruguay	112
Vanuatu	55
Vietnam	178
Yemen	165
Zambia	159
Zimbabwe	154

Source: 1998 Human Development Report; United Nations Development Programme (UNDP): <http://www.undp.org/hdro/indicators.html>. Underlying data from the Food and Agriculture Organization (FAO).

D12. MALNUTRITION

D12-1. Global Estimates of the Prevalence and Number of Underweight, Stunted and Wasted Children under Five Years in Developing Countries, 1980–1992

	Underweight*		Stunted**		Wasted***	
	Percent	Number in 1,000s	Percent	Number in 1,000s	Percent	Number in 1,000s
Africa	27.4	31,600	38.6	44,600	7.2	8,300
Asia	42.0	154,100	47.1	172,800	10.8	39,600
Latin America	11.9	6,500	22.2	12,100	2.7	1,500
Oceania	29.1	300	41.9	400	5.6	100
All developing countries	35.8	192,500	42.7	223,900	9.2	49,500

Note: Figures are % Below -2 Standard Deviation of WHO reference value.
*Underweight is low weight for age.
**Stunted is low height for age.
***Wasted is low weight for height.

Source: The Worldwide Magnitude Of Protein-Energy Malnutrition: An Overview From The WHO Global Database On Child Growth, By M. de Onis, C. Monteiro, J. Akré, and G. Clugston: Table 3. <http://www.who.int/whosis/cgrowth/bulletin.htm>. Underlying data from World Health Organization (WHO).

D12-2. Regional Estimates of the Number of Underweight, Stunted and Wasted Children under Five Years in Developing Countries, Ranked by Descending Order, 1980–1992

	Underweight* (millions)	Stunted** (millions)	Wasted*** (millions)
Southern Asia	101.2	100.9	28.9
Eastern Asia	26.0	39.2	4.4
South-eastern Asia	21.8	24.9	4.4
Western Africa	12.2	17.5	3.5
Eastern Africa	11.5	14.1	2.2
Southern America	2.9	6.4	1.2
Central America	2.8	5.5	0.7
Northern Africa	2.4	4.8	0.7
Caribbean	0.6	0.9	0.1
Melanesia	0.2	0.3	0.0

Note: Figures are % Below -2 Standard Deviation of WHO reference value.
*Underweight is low weight for age.
**Stunted is low height for age.
***Wasted is low weight for height.

Source: The Worldwide Magnitude Of Protein-Energy Malnutrition: An Overview From The WHO Global Database On Child Growth, By M. de Onis, C. Monteiro, J. Akré, and G. Clugston: Table 5. <http://www.who.int/whosis/cgrowth/bulletin.htm>. Underlying data from World Health Organization (WHO).

D12-3. Regional Estimates of the Prevalence of Underweight, Stunted and Wasted Children under Five Years in Developing Countries, Ranked in Descending Order, 1980–1992

	Percent underweight*	Percent stunted**	Percent wasted***
Southern Asia	60.5	60.3	17.3
South-eastern Asia	37.8	47.0	9.5
Western Africa	32.8	43.2	7.6
Eastern Africa	31.0	42.2	6.0
Melanesia	29.5	37.9	5.8
Eastern Asia	21.3	32.1	5.5
Caribbean	19.4	29.8	4.6
Central America	17.7	25.9	3.6
Northern Africa	11.3	25.4	2.2
Southern America	8.4	18.1	1.9

Note: Figures are % Below -2 Standard Deviation of WHO reference value.
*Underweight is low weight for age.
**Stunted is low height for age.
***Wasted is low weight for height.

Source: The Worldwide Magnitude Of Protein-Energy Malnutrition: An Overview From The WHO Global Database On Child Growth, By M. de Onis, C. Monteiro, J. Akré, and G. Clugston: Table 4. <http://www.who.int/whosis/cgrowth/bulletin.htm>. Underlying data from World Health Organization (WHO).

D12-4. Prevalence of Underweight, Stunted and Wasted Children under Five Years in Developing Countries, Based on National Surveys, 1980–1992

	Survey date	Percent underweight*	Percent stunted**	Percent wasted***
Algeria	1992	9.2	18.1	5.5
Bangladesh	1989-90	65.8	64.6	15.5
Barbados	1981	5.3	7.4	3.8
Bhutan	1986-88	37.9	56.1	4.1
Bolivia	1989	13.3	38.3	1.6
Brazil	1989	7.0	15.4	2.0
Burundi	1987	38.3	48.1	5.6
Cameroon	1991	13.6	24.4	3.0
Cape Verde	1983	19.0	14.9	4.8
Chile	1986	2.5	9.6	0.5
China	1987	21.3	32.1	3.6
Colombia	1986-89	10.1	16.6	2.9
Congo, Rep.	1987	23.5	27.1	5.4
Costa Rica	1982	6.0	7.8	2.0
Côte d'Ivoire	1986	12.4	17.2	8.6
Cuba	1987	N/A	N/A	0.5
Djibouti	1989	22.9	22.2	10.7
Dominican Republic	1991	10.4	19.4	1.1
Ecuador	1986	16.5	34.0	1.7
Egypt	1990	10.4	30.0	3.5
El Salvador	1988	15.2	29.9	N/A
Ethiopia	1992	47.7	64.2	8.0
Ghana	1987-88	27.1	30.5	7.3
Guatemala	1987	33.5	57.9	1.4
Guyana	1981	22.1	20.7	8.5
Haiti	1990	33.9	40.6	4.2
Honduras	1987	20.6	33.9	1.9
India	1988-90	63.9	62.1	19.2
Indonesia	1987	39.9	N/A	N/A
Iraq	1991	11.9	21.8	3.4
Jamaica	1989	7.2	8.7	3.4

D12-4. Prevalence of Underweight, Stunted and Wasted Children under Five Years in Developing Countries, Based on National Surveys, 1980–1992 *(continued)*

	Survey date	Percent underweight*	Percent stunted**	Percent wasted***
Jordan	1990	6.4	19.3	2.8
Kenya	1987	14.3	32.2	4.5
Kiribati	1985	12.9	28.3	10.8
Kuwait	1983-84	6.4	11.3	2.7
Laos	1984	36.7	40.1	10.5
Lesotho	1981	15.6	26.1	4.5
Madagascar	1983-84	32.8	33.5	11.8
Malawi	1992	27.2	48.6	5.4
Maldives	1983	N/A	N/A	6.3
Mali	1987	31.0	24.4	11.0
Mauritania	1990-91	47.6	56.9	15.8
Mauritius	1985	23.9	21.5	16.2
Mexico	1988	16.3	27.0	5.5
Morocco	1987	15.7	25.5	3.7
Mongolia	1992	12.3	26.4	1.7
Myanmar (Burma)	1983-85	38.0	49.7	11.0
Namibia	1992	26.2	28.4	8.6
Nicaragua	1980-82	10.5	21.8	0.6
Niger	1992	36.2	32.3	15.8
Nigeria	1990	35.7	43.1	9.1
Oman	1991	24.3	20.7	7.3
Pakistan	1990-91	40.4	50.0	9.2
Panama	1980	15.7	22.0	6.4
Papua New Guinea	1982-83	29.9	43.2	5.5
Paraguay	1990	3.7	16.6	0.3
Peru	1991-92	10.8	36.5	1.4
Philippines	1987	32.9	38.6	4.5
Rwanda	1991-92	28.6	52.2	5.2
Sao Tome and Principe	1986	17.0	26.0	5.0
Senegal	1991-92	21.6	29.1	5.5
Seychelles	1987-88	5.7	5.1	2.0
Sierra Leone	1990	28.7	34.7	8.5
Sri Lanka	1987	38.1	27.5	12.9
Sudan	1987	N/A	N/A	12.5
Swaziland	1983-84	9.7	30.3	0.9
Tanzania	1991-92	28.8	42.6	6.0
Thailand	1987	25.8	22.4	5.7
Togo	1988	24.4	29.6	5.3
Trinidad and Tobago	1987	6.9	5.0	3.8
Tunisia	1988	10.4	18.2	3.1
Uganda	1988-89	23.3	44.5	1.9
Uruguay	1987	7.4	15.9	N/A
Vanuatu	1983	19.7	19.1	N/A
Venezuela	1981-82	10.2	6.4	1.3
Vietnam	1987-89	45.0	56.5	9.4
Yemen	1991-1992	30.0	44.1	12.7
Zambia	1992	25.1	39.6	5.1
Zimbabwe	1988	11.5	29.0	1.3

Note: Figures are % Below -2 Standard Deviation of WHO reference value.
*Underweight is low weight for age.
**Stunted is low height for age.
***Wasted is low weight for height.

Source: The Worldwide Magnitude Of Protein-Energy Malnutrition: An Overview From The WHO Global Database On Child Growth, By M. de Onis, C. Monteiro, J. Akré, and G. Clugston: Table 2. <http://www.who.int/whosis/cgrowth/bulletin.htm>. Underlying data from World Health Organization (WHO).

D12-5. Number of Children Suffering from Undernutrition, by Region, 1990s

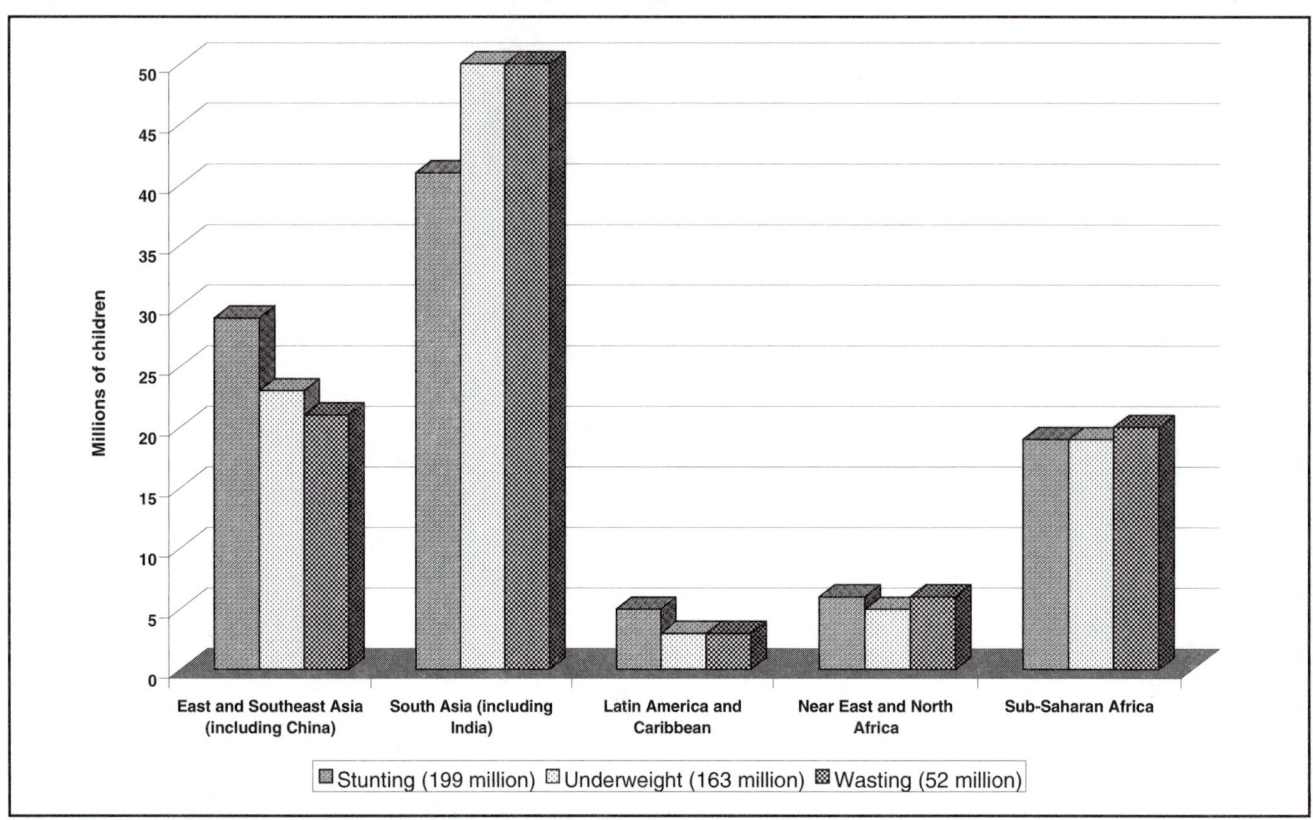

Source: The State Of Food Insecurity In The World: When People Must Live With Hunger And Fear Starvation, 1999; <http://www.fao.org/NEWS/1999/img/ SOFI99-E.PDF>. Underlying data from the Food and Agriculture Organization (FAO).

D12-6. Percent of Children under Five Suffering from Undernutrition, by Region, 1990s

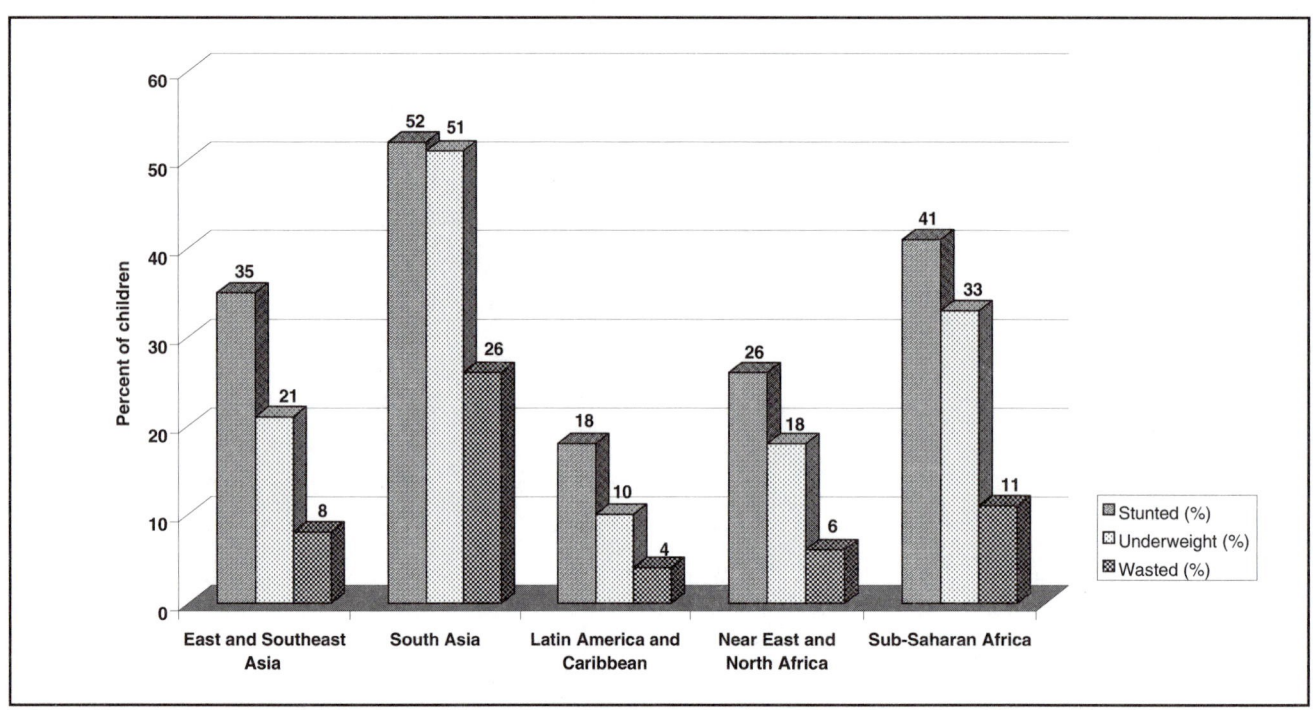

Source: The State Of Food Insecurity In The World: When People Must Live With Hunger And Fear Starvation, 1999; <http://www.fao.org/NEWS/1999/img/ SOFI99-E.PDF>. Underlying data from the Food and Agriculture Organization (FAO).

D12-7. Distribution of Countries According to Underweight Prevalence Among Preschool Children, 1990–1998

	Underweight* Prevalence				Countries with data available	Total number of countries in area
	Less than 10 percent	10 to 19 percent	20 to 29 percent	30 percent or more		
World	30	22	22	25	116	184
More developed regions	100	0	0	0	9	43
Less developed regions	24	24	24	27	107	141
Least developed countries	0	8	36	56	39	45
Africa	7	22	40	31	45	53
Asia and Oceania	21	26	13	39	38	57
Latin America and the Caribbean	63	25	13	0	24	31

*Underweight is low weight for age.

Source: *Charting the Progress of Populations*, United Nations Development Programme (UNDP), United Nations, 2000; Table IV.1. <http://www.undp.org/popin/wdtrends/chart/6.pdf>. Underlying data from the World Health Organization, *WHO Global Database on Child Growth and Malnutrition* (Geneva, 1997), and United Nations Children's Fund (UNICEF).

D12-8. Distribution of Population under Five Years of Age in the Less Developed Regions, by Underweight Prevalence, 1990–1998

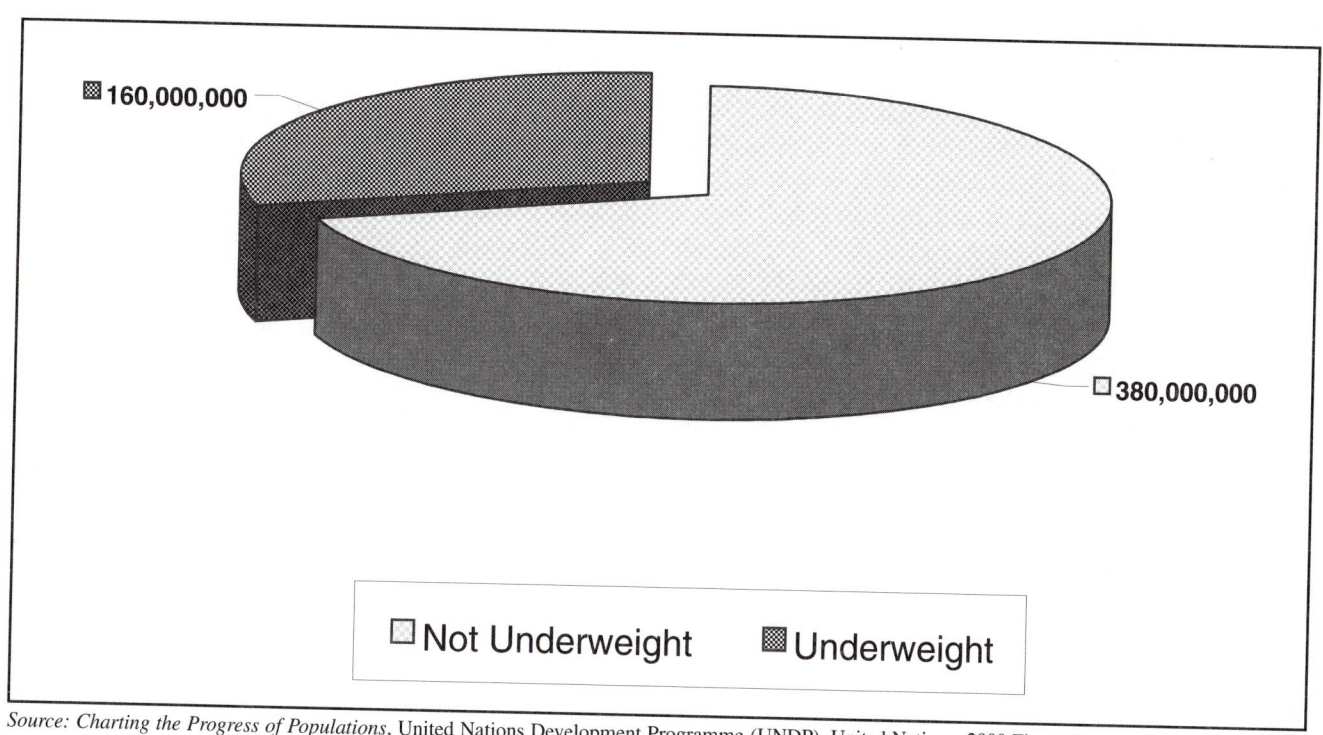

160,000,000

380,000,000

☐ Not Underweight   ▦ Underweight

Source: *Charting the Progress of Populations*, United Nations Development Programme (UNDP), United Nations, 2000 Figure IV.3; <http://www.undp.org/popin/wdtrends/chart/6.pdf>. Underlying data from the World Health Organization, *WHO Global Database on Child Growth and Malnutrition* (Geneva, 1997), and United Nations Children's Fund (UNICEF).

D12-9. Percent of Under-Fives Suffering from Moderate to Severe Underweight, Stunting, and Wasting, 1990–1998

	Percent Underweight*	Percent Wasting**	Percent Stunting***
Afghanistan	48	25	52
Algeria	13	9	18
Angola	42	6	53
Antigua and Barbuda	10	10	7
Azerbaijan	10	3	22
Bahrain	9	5	10
Bangladesh	56	18	55
Barbados	5	4	7
Belize	6	N/A	N/A
Benin	29	14	25
Bhutan	38	4	56
Bolivia	10	2	26
Botswana	17	11	29
Brazil	6	2	11
Burkina Faso	30	13	29
Burundi	37	9	43
Cambodia	52	13	56
Cameroon	22	6	29
Cape Verde	14	6	16
Central African Republic	27	7	34
Chad	39	14	40
Chile	1	0	2
China	16	N/A	34
Colombia	8	1	15
Comoros	26	8	34
Congo, Dem. Rep. (Zaire)	34	10	45
Congo, Rep.	17	4	21
Costa Rica	2	N/A	N/A
Côte d'Ivoire	24	8	24
Croatia	1	1	1
Cuba	9	3	N/A
Czech Republic	1	2	2
Djibouti	18	13	26
Dominica	5	2	6
Dominican Republic	6	1	11
Ecuador	17	2	34
Egypt	12	6	25
El Salvador	11	1	23
Eritrea	44	16	38
Ethiopia	48	8	64
Fiji	8	8	3
Gambia	26	N/A	30
Ghana	27	11	26
Guatemala	27	3	50
Guinea-Bissau	23	N/A	N/A
Guyana	12	12	10
Haiti	28	8	32
Honduras	18	2	40
Hungary	2	2	3
India	53	18	52
Indonesia	34	13	42
Iran	16	7	19
Iraq	23	10	31
Jamaica	10	4	6
Jordan	5	2	8
Kazakhstan	8	3	16
Kenya	22	6	33

D12-9. Percent of Under-Fives Suffering from Moderate to Severe Underweight, Stunting, and Wasting, 1990–1998 *(continued)*

	Percent Underweight*	Percent Wasting**	Percent Stunting***
Kiribati	13	11	28
Kuwait	6	3	12
Kyrgyzstan	11	3	25
Laos	40	11	47
Lebanon	3	3	12
Lesotho	16	5	44
Libya	5	3	15
Madagascar	40	7	48
Malawi	30	7	48
Malaysia	19	N/A	N/A
Maldives	43	17	27
Mali	40	23	30
Mauritania	23	7	44
Mauritius	16	15	10
Mexico	14	6	22
Mongolia	10	2	22
Morocco	9	2	23
Mozambique	26	8	36
Myanmar (Burma)	39	N/A	N/A
Namibia	26	9	28
Nepal	47	11	48
Nicaragua	12	2	25
Niger	50	21	41
Nigeria	36	9	43
North Korea, Dem. Rep.	60	19	60
Oman	23	13	23
Pakistan	38	N/A	N/A
Panama	7	1	9
Papua New Guinea	30	6	43
Paraguay	4	0	17
Peru	8	1	26
Philippines	28	6	30
Qatar	6	2	8
Romania	6	3	8
Russia	3	4	13
Rwanda	27	9	42
Sao Tome and Principe	16	5	26
Senegal	22	7	23
Seychelles	6	2	5
Sierra Leone	29	9	35
Solomon Islands	21	7	27
South Africa	9	3	23
Sri Lanka	34	14	18
Sudan	34	13	33
Swaziland	10	1	30
Syria	13	9	21
Tanzania	27	6	42
Thailand	19	6	16
Togo	25	12	22
Trinidad and Tobago	7	4	5
Tunisia	9	4	23
Turkey	10	N/A	N/A
Uganda	26	5	38
United Arab Emirates	14	15	17
United States	1	1	2
Uruguay	5	1	8
Uzbekistan	19	12	31

D12-9. Percent of Under-Fives Suffering from Moderate to Severe Underweight, Stunting, and Wasting, 1990–1998 *(continued)*

	Percent Underweight*	Percent Wasting**	Percent Stunting***
Vanuatu	20	N/A	19
Venezuela	5	3	13
Vietnam	41	14	44
Yemen	46	13	52
Yugoslavia	2	2	7
Zambia	24	4	42
Zimbabwe	15	6	32

*Underweight - Moderate and severe - below minus two standard deviations from median weight for age of reference population.
**Wasting - Moderate and severe - below minus two standard deviations from median weight for height of reference population.
***Stunting - Moderate and severe - below minus two standard deviations from median height for age of reference population.

Source: The State of the World's Children, 2000: Table 2. Nutrition; United Nations Children's Fund (UNICEF); <http://www.unicef.org/sowc00/stat4.htm>. Underlying data from Underweight, wasting and stunting - Demographic and Health Surveys (DHS), Multiple Indicator Cluster Surveys (MICS), World Health Organization (WHO) and UNICEF.

D12-10. Percentage of Children Under Five Who are Stunted*: Rural, Urban, and Rural/Urban Ratio, 1990–1998

	Rural	Urban	Rural/Urban ratio
Azerbaijan	29	17	1.7
Bolivia	38	19	2.0
Botswana	34	21	1.6
Brazil	19	8	2.4
Burkina Faso	31	19	1.6
Cameroon	30	17	1.8
China	39	9	4.3
Colombia	19	13	1.5
Congo, Dem. Rep. (Zaire)	52	28	1.9
Côte d'Ivoire	29	15	1.9
Dominican Republic	15	7	2.1
El Salvador	28	17	1.6
Ghana	30	16	1.9
Guatemala	57	35	1.6
Guinea	33	20	1.7
Haiti	35	24	1.5
Honduras	46	30	1.5
Iran	25	12	2.1
Kazakhstan	22	8	2.8
Malawi	50	34	1.5
Mali	33	22	1.5
Morocco	28	13	2.2
Nicaragua	33	16	2.1
Niger	42	27	1.6
Paraguay	22	10	2.2
Peru	40	16	2.5
Senegal	26	17	1.5
South Africa	27	16	1.7
Sri Lanka	19	11	1.7
Sudan	39	23	1.7
Tunisia	33	15	2.2
Turkey	27	16	1.7
Uganda	40	23	1.7
Viet Nam	47	15	3.1
Yemen	44	29	1.5
Zambia	49	33	1.5

*Stunted is low height for age.

Source: The Progress of Nations, 1999, United Nations Children's Fund (UNICEF); <http://www.unicef.org/pon99/>. Underlying data from Demographic and Health Surveys (DHS), Multiple Indicator Cluster Surveys (MICS), and other national surveys 1990-98.

E. Acquired Immunodeficiency Syndrome (AIDS)

GENERAL OVERVIEW

Acquired Immunodeficiency Syndrome (AIDS) is the late stage of infection caused by the Human Immunodeficiency Virus (HIV), which progressively damages the body's ability to protect itself from disease organisms. Although drug therapies that emerged in the mid-1990s have resulted in dramatic declines in AIDS deaths in the industrial world, the disease is a major killer in the developing world, particularly in sub-Saharan Africa. There, AIDS is endangering the future of nations and their children. It has slowed economic development, erased hard-won gains in heath care and education, and now threatens the social fabric.

The AIDS virus has infected more than 10 million young people around the world, making it the largest crisis facing the world's children today, according to the United Nations Children's Fund (UNICEF). Yet, the impact of AIDS on children extends far beyond infection and death. To date, the epidemic has left behind 13.2 million AIDS orphans, and at least 30 million children are thought to be living with parents who are HIV positive. In many African countries 20 to 25 percent of all households are fostering AIDS orphans. The long-term consequences of such shifts in socialization are incalculable. Even children whose families are not directly affected by the disease have been impacted by the crisis. Where AIDS is widespread, education is being impaired as the epidemic erodes the supply of teachers and dilutes the quality of education.

Because of the devastating effects AIDS has had, and will continue to have, on the world's children, we have separated AIDS statistics from the rest of the disease indicators. Topics covered in this section include AIDS prevalence, AIDS-related child deaths, adolescent behavior and knowledge of the disease, AIDS orphans, and the effect of the disease on education. All data on HIV/AIDS are subject to limitation. The quality of surveillance and reporting systems differ among nations, making intercountry comparisons difficult. The social stigma attached to the syndrome also makes people reluctant to report the disease. The number of reported cases, therefore, is much smaller then UN estimates, which attempt to compensate for underreporting.

EXPLANATION OF INDICATORS

E1-1. Beginning of the epidemic: Although a peripheral indicator, we have included this table to show the length of time a country has been faced with the AIDS epidemic. The epidemic developed at different rates in different parts of the world, and its impact on children, especially AIDS orphans, has become apparent only recently. The table includes only high-impact countries, primarily in sub-Saharan Africa. The dates in the table refer to the year when widespread transmission was first reported. They are not dates of first case, which may have occurred many years previously and are generally not known.

E2-1–E2-8. Children living with HIV/AIDS: This cluster of tables and graphs outline the magnitude of the HIV/AIDS epidemic among children. E2-1 and E2-2 summarize the global and regional picture, respectively; E2-3 offers a country breakdown. While the first tables combine figures for both HIV and AIDS, E2-4 focuses on full-blown cases of AIDS, the last step in the progression of the disease. E2-5 presents prevalence by nation. The age range (15–24) in this table goes beyond that of the handbook. Nevertheless, we have included the indicator because it is the only one that presents prevalence rates for youth. In a number of countries, the prevalence rate is higher among teenage girls than teenage boys. Experts see this as an indication that girls are more likely to have been infected by older men than by boys their own age. The last three indicators show how dramatically the disease is spreading in some countries and regions, particularly sub-Saharan Africa. The indicators in this cluster are not just a snapshot of the contemporary picture. They also are predictors of the future. Without massive international intervention, the majority of children living with HIV/AIDS will die.

E3-1–E3-7: AIDS deaths: AIDS has had a staggering impact on life expectancy and child survival rates in many parts of the world, particularly in sub-Saharan Africa. The UN estimates that in the most affected nations half of all 15-year-olds will eventually die of the disease. The youngest children are most at risk because children infected at birth rarely survive until their fifth birthday. In Botswana, for example, AIDS accounts for 64 percent of deaths of children under five, offsetting much of the country's impressive child health progress. In South Africa and Zimbabwe, AIDS is projected to account for a 100 percent increase in the number of deaths of children under five years. This is a dreadful toll, and the worst is yet to come as infection rates double and triple in many parts of the world. E3-1 and E3-2 offer a regional overview of the situation; E3-3 supplies a country breakdown. The remaining indicators in this cluster offer figures on deaths by age group with and without AIDS.

E4-1–E4-2. Teens and the AIDS Info Gap: UNAIDS reports a dangerous lack of knowledge among young people about how they can protect themselves from AIDS. Both boys and girls are in jeopardy—boys because of their sexual risk-taking and girls because in many countries they lack the social power to set the terms of relationships, given males' traditional dominance in sexual matters. According to UNAIDS, in many sub-Saharan counties, where AIDS rates are highest, a high percentage of boys and girls were unable to name a single method to avoid HIV infection. Even in countries with fairly low HIV/AIDS rates, there are exceedingly high percentages of young people unaware of protective measures. In Bangladesh, for example, 96 percent of girls and 88 percent of boys were unable to name any protection against HIV. The first table in this cluster presents figures on AIDS among teens; the second focuses on

HIV among pregnant girls. E4-3 and E4-4 look at condom use. The final three indicators survey teenage knowledge about the disease. We have included a table on a mother's knowledge that she can transmit AIDS to her child, even though the age range in the indicator extends far beyond the scope of this book, because her ignorance has a fatal impact on her child.

E5-1–E5-3. AIDS orphans:. AIDS orphans are defined as children who lose their mother to AIDS before reaching the age of 15. Some of these children have lost their father to AIDS as well. Neither words nor statistics can adequately capture the human tragedy of children grieving for dying or dead parents, stigmatized by society through association with HIV/AIDS, plunged into economic crisis and insecurity by their parents' death and struggling without services or support systems in impoverished communities. AIDS orphans are less likely to have their health care needs adequately met and are at greater risk of malnutrition, illness, abuse, and sexual exploitation than children orphaned by other causes. The first two tables in this cluster present cumulative numbers of AIDS orphans by region and country. The figures include children who are no longer alive, as well as those who are no longer under 15. E5-3 gives a clearer picture of the impact of the crisis, presenting the number of AIDS orphans per 10,000 children

E6-1. AIDS and education: For reasons that are not entirely clear, HIV is very high among teachers and school administrators, ultimately taking a high toll on education. An estimated 860,000 children in sub-Saharan Africa lost their teachers to AIDS in 1999. Schooling is disrupted not only when teachers die but also when teachers miss classes due to illness. In sub-Saharan Africa, HIV-positive teachers are leaving schools in remote areas that lack health care facilities and requesting postings in locations near hospitals. As teachers become ill and unable to work, some schools are closing. E6 shows numbers of primary school children who lost a teacher to AIDS in selected AIDS impact countries.

E1. BEGINNING OF THE EPIDEMIC

E1-1. High Impact HIV/AIDS Countries, with Years When Widespread Transmission of HIV/AIDS Began

	Year
Benin	1968
Botswana	1985
Brazil	1980
Burkina Faso	1974
Burundi	1976
Cambodia	1987
Cameroon	1968
Central African Republic	1972
Chad	1976
Congo, Dem. Rep. (Zaire)	1974
Congo, Rep.	1976
Côte d'Ivoire	1978
Eritrea	1983
Ethiopia	1980
Gabon	1974
Guinea-Bissau	1974
Haiti	1976
India	1986
Kenya	1974
Lesotho	1983
Liberia	1978
Malawi	1975
Mozambique	1985
Namibia	1985
Nigeria	1974
Rwanda	1970
Sierra Leone	1978
South Africa	1985
Tanzania	1976
Thailand	1985
Togo	1978
Uganda	1976
Zambia	1976
Zimbabwe	1976

Source: World Population Prospects, the 1998 Revision: Volume III. Analytical Report; Table III.1. United Nations Population Division. Underlying data from Joint United Nations Programme on HIV/AIDS (UNAIDS*),* Report on the Global HIV/AIDS Pandemic, June 1998, and World Health Organization (WHO).

E2. CHILDREN LIVING WITH HIV/AIDS

E2-1. Global Estimates of the HIV/AIDS Epidemic, Number of Children (<15 years) Affected, 1999 and 2000

	1999	2000
Children newly infected with HIV	620,000	600,000
Children living with HIV/AIDS	1,300,000	1,400,000
AIDS deaths of children	500,000	500,000
Total number of AIDS deaths of children since the beginning of the epidemic	3,800,000	4,300,000
Total number of AIDS orphans* since the beginning of the epidemic	13,200,000	N/A

N/A Not Available.
*Children who lost their mother or both parents to AIDS when they were under the age of 15.

Source: Report on the global HIV/AIDS epidemic—June 2000 and Report on the global HIV/AIDS epidemic—December 2000; <http://www.unaids.org/wac/2000/wad00/files/wad2000Master/index.htm> and <http://www.unaids.org/epidemic_update/report/Epi_report.pdf>. Underlying data from Joint United Nations Programme on HIV/AIDS (UNAIDS).

E2-2. Estimated Number of Children (<15 years) Living with HIV/AIDS, by Regions, 2000

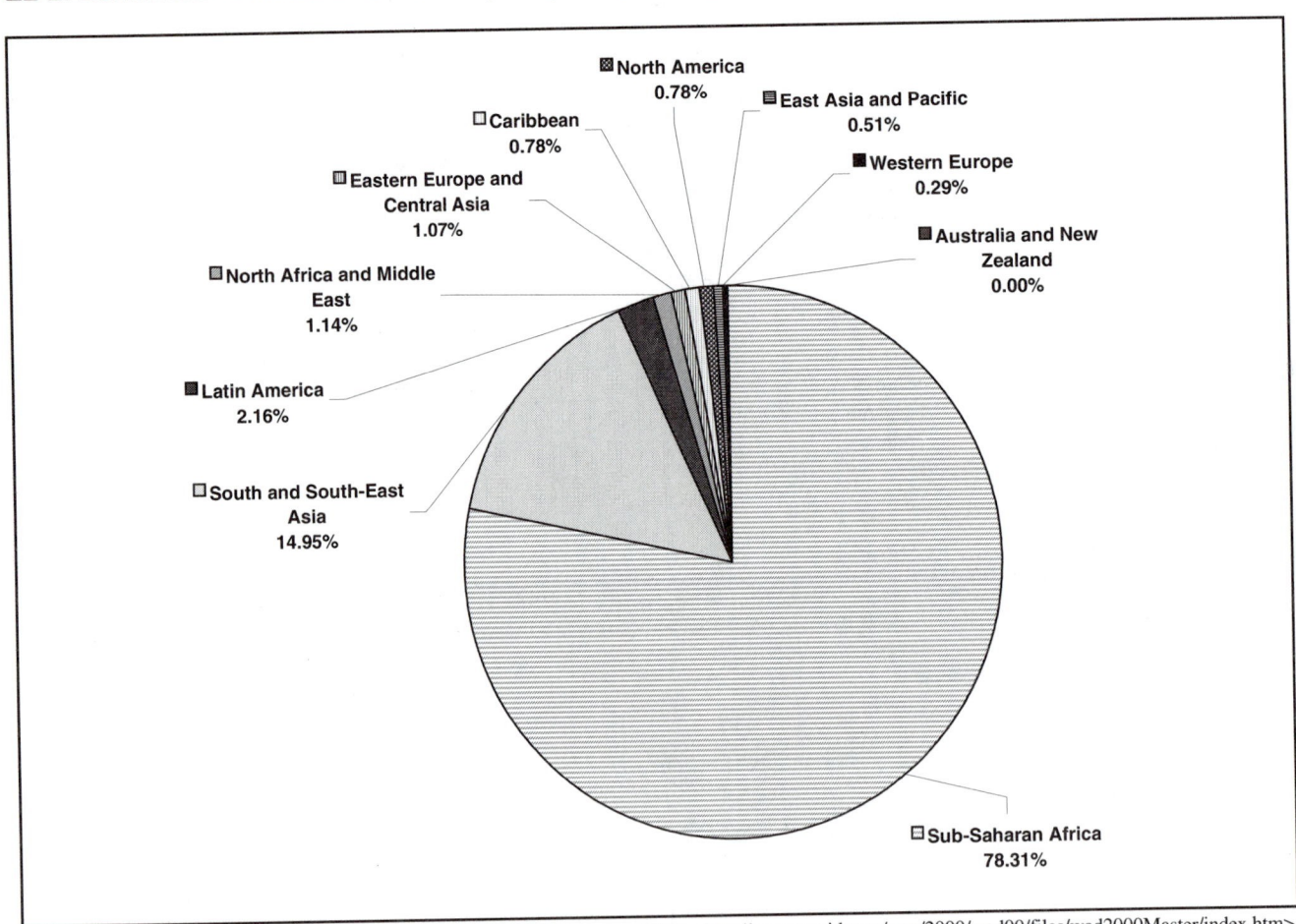

Source: Joint United Nations Programme on HIV/AIDS (UNAIDS), December 2000; <http://www.unaids.org/wac/2000/wad00/files/wad2000Master/index.htm>. Underlying data from World Health Organization (WHO).

E2-3. Estimated Number of Children (0–14) Living with HIV/AIDS as Percentage of Total Adults and Children, end 1999

	Estimated number of people living with HIV/AIDS	Estimated number of children living with HIV/AIDS	Estimated number of children living with HIV/AIDS as % of total a HIV/AIDS population
World Total	**34,300,000**	**1,300,000**	**3.8**
Sub-Saharan Africa	**24,500,000**	**1,000,000**	**4.1**
Angola	160,000	7,900	4.9
Benin	70,000	3,000	4.3
Botswana	290,000	10,000	3.4
Burkina Faso	350,000	20,000	5.7
Burundi	360,000	19,000	5.3
Cameroon	540,000	22,000	4.1
Central African Republic	240,000	8,900	3.7
Chad	92,000	4,000	4.3
Congo, Dem. Rep.	1,100,000	53,000	4.8
Congo, Rep.	86,000	4,000	4.7
Côte d'Ivoire	760,000	32,000	4.2
Djibouti	37,000	1,500	4.1
Equatorial Guinea	1,100	<100	9.0
Ethiopia	3,000,000	150,000	5.0
Gabon	23,000	780	3.4
Gambia, the	13,000	520	4.0
Ghana	340,000	14,000	4.1
Guinea	55,000	2,700	4.9
Guinea-Bissau	14,000	560	4.0
Kenya	2,100,000	78,000	3.7
Lesotho	240,000	8,200	3.4
Liberia	39,000	2,000	5.1
Madagascar	11,000	450	4.1
Malawi	800,000	40,000	5.0
Mali	100,000	5,000	5.0
Mauritania	6,600	260	3.9
Mozambique	1,200,000	52,000	4.3
Namibia	160,000	6,600	4.1
Niger	64,000	3,300	5.2
Nigeria	2,700,000	120,000	4.4
Rwanda	400,000	22,000	5.5
Senegal	79,000	3,300	4.2
Sierra Leone	68,000	3,300	4.9
South Africa	4,200,000	95,000	2.3
Swaziland	130,000	3,800	2.9
Tanzania	1,300,000	59,000	4.5
Togo	130,000	6,300	4.8
Uganda	820,000	53,000	6.5
Zambia	870,000	40,000	4.6
Zimbabwe	1,500,000	56,000	3.7
East Asia & Pacific	**530,000**	**5,200**	**1.0**
China	500,000	4,800	1.0
Hong Kong, SAR (China)	2,500	<100	4.0
Japan	10,000	<100	1.0
Papua New Guinea	5,400	220	4.1
South Korea, Rep.	3,800	<100	2.6
Australia & New Zealand	**15,000**	**190**	**1.3**
Australia	14,000	140	1.0
New Zealand	1,200	<100	8.3
South & South-East Asia	**5,600,000**	**200,000**	**3.6**
Bangladesh	13,000	130	1.0
Cambodia	220,000	5,400	2.5
India	3,700,000	160,000	4.3

E2-3. Estimated Number of Children (0–14) Living with HIV/AIDS as Percentage of Total Adults and Children, end 1999 *(continued)*

	Estimated number of people living with HIV/AIDS	Estimated number of children living with HIV/AIDS	Estimated number of children living with HIV/AIDS as % of total a HIV/AIDS population
Indonesia	52,000	680	1.3
Laos	1,400	<100	7.1
Malaysia	49,000	550	1.1
Myanmar (Burma)	530,000	14,000	2.6
Nepal	34,000	930	2.7
Pakistan	74,000	1,600	2.2
Philippines	28,000	1,300	4.6
Singapore	4,000	<100	2.5
Sri Lanka	7,500	200	2.7
Thailand	755,000	13,900	1.8
Vietnam	100,000	2,500	2.5
Eastern Europe & Central Asia	**420,000**	**15,000**	**3.6**
Armenia	<500	<100	20.0
Azerbaijan	<500	<100	20.0
Belarus	14,000	<100	7.1
Croatia	350	<100	28.6
Czech Republic	2,200	<100	4.5
Estonia	<500	<100	20.0
Georgia	<500	<100	20.0
Hungary	2,500	<100	4.0
Kazakstan	3,500	<100	2.9
Kyrgyzstan	<100	<100	100.0
Latvia	1,250	<100	8.0
Lithuania	<500	<100	20.0
Moldova	4,500	100	2.2
Romania	7,000	5,000	71.4
Russia	130,000	1,800	1.4
Slovakia	400	<100	25.0
Tajikistan	<100	<100	100.0
Turkmenistan	<100	<100	100.0
Ukraine	240,000	7,500	3.1
Uzbekistan	<100	<100	100.0
Western Europe	**520,000**	**4,100**	**0.8**
Austria	9,000	<100	1.1
Belgium	7,700	300	3.9
Denmark	4,300	<100	2.3
Finland	1,100	<100	9.1
France	130,000	1,000	0.8
Germany	37,000	500	1.4
Greece	8,000	<100	1.3
Iceland	200	<100	50.0
Ireland	2,200	170	7.7
Italy	95,000	700	0.7
Macedonia, FYRO	<100	<100	100.0
Netherlands, the	15,000	100	0.7
Norway	1,600	<100	6.2
Portugal	36,000	500	1.4
Slovenia	200	<100	50.0
Spain	120,000	<100	0.1
Sweden	3,000	<100	3.3
Switzerland	17,000	<100	0.6
United Kingdom	31,000	500	1.6
North Africa & Middle East	**220,000**	**8,000**	**3.6**
Cyprus	400	<100	25.0
Israel	2,400	<100	4.2

E2-3. Estimated Number of Children (0–14) Living with HIV/AIDS as Percentage of Total Adults and Children, end 1999 *(continued)*

	Estimated number of people living with HIV/AIDS	Estimated number of children living with HIV/AIDS	Estimated number of children living with HIV/AIDS as % of total a HIV/AIDS population
North America	**900,000**	**11,000**	**1.2**
Canada	49,000	500	1.0
United States of America	850,000	10,000	1.2
Caribbean	**360,000**	**9,600**	**2.7**
Bahamas, the	6,900	150	2.2
Barbados	1,800	<100	5.6
Cuba	1,950	<100	5.1
Dominican Republic	130,000	3,800	2.9
Haiti	210,000	5,200	2.5
Jamaica	9,900	230	2.3
Trinidad and Tobago	7,800	180	2.3
Latin America	**1,300,000**	**28,000**	**2.2**
Argentina	130,000	4,400	3.4
Belize	2,400	<100	4.2
Bolivia	4,200	<100	2.4
Brazil	540,000	9,900	1.8
Chile	15,000	260	1.7
Colombia	71,000	900	1.3
Costa Rica	12,000	290	2.4
Ecuador	19,000	330	1.7
El Salvador	20,000	560	2.8
Guatemala	73,000	1,600	2.2
Guyana	15,000	140	0.9
Honduras	63,000	4,400	7.0
Mexico	150,000	2,400	1.6
Nicaragua	4,900	<100	2.0
Panama	24,000	670	2.8
Paraguay	3,000	<100	3.3
Peru	48,000	640	1.3
Suriname	3,000	110	3.7
Uruguay	6,000	<100	1.7
Venezuela	62,000	580	0.9

Source: Report on the Global HIV/AIDS Epidemic—June 2000, <http://www.unaids.org/epidemic_update/report/Epi_report.pdf>. Underlying data from Joint United Nations Programme on HIV/AIDS (UNAIDS).

E2-4. AIDS Cases 0–14 Age Group as Percentage of Total Reported AIDS Cases, late 1990s

	Reporting period	Percent of total reported cases
Algeria	1997-1999	1
Argentina	1996-1998	8
Australia	1998-1999	1
Austria	1997-1999	1
Bahamas	1996-1998	4
Bahrain	1997-1999	3
Barbados	1996-1998	4
Belgium	1997-1999	5
Belize	1995-1996	5
Benin	1997	3
Bolivia	1995-1998	5
Botswana	1997-1998	10
Brazil	1996-1998	4
Brunei	1998-1999	0

E2-4. AIDS Cases 0–14 Age Group as Percentage of Total Reported AIDS Cases, late 1990s (continued)

	Reporting period	Percent of total reported cases
Bulgaria	1997-1999	0
Burkina Faso	1997	3
Burundi	1997-1998	7
Cameroon	1998	10
Canada	1996-1998	2
Cape Verde	1996-1998	8
Chad	1996-1998	8
Chile	1997-1999	1
China	1996-1997	1
Colombia	1997-1999	2
Congo, Rep.	1998	4
Costa Rica	1997-1999	1
Côte d'Ivoire	1997-1998	2
Croatia	1997-1999	3
Cuba	1997-1999	0
Cyprus	1997-1999	0
Czech Republic	1997-1999	0
Denmark	1997-1999	2
Djibouti	1997-1998	1
Dominica	1997-1999	8
Dominican Republic	1997-1999	6
Ecuador	1996-1998	3
Egypt	1997-1999	3
El Salvador	1997-1999	5
Eritrea	1997-1999	5
Ethiopia	1996-1998	5
Finland	1997-1999	2
France	1997-1998	2
Gambia	1996-1998	11
Georgia	1997-1999	0
Germany	1997-1999	0
Ghana	1996-1998	1
Greece	1997-1999	2
Grenada	1996-1997	19
Guatemala	1996-1998	4
Guinea	1996-1998	4
Guinea-Bissau	1996-1998	3
Guyana	1996-1998	2
Honduras	1996-1997	6
Hong Kong, SAR (China)	1998-1999	2
Hungary	1997-1999	1
Indonesia	1997-1998	3
Iran	1997-1998	2
Ireland	1997-1999	5
Israel	1997-1999	3
Italy	1997-1999	1
Jamaica	1997-1999	9
Japan	1996-1998	1
Jordan	1997-1999	4
Kazakhstan	1997-1999	0
Laos	1996-1997	2
Latvia	1997-1999	0
Lesotho	1998	17
Liberia	1998	0
Lithuania	1997-1999	0
Luxembourg	1997-1999	0
Malawi	1996-1997	12
Malaysia	1997-1999	1
Mali	1997-1999	4

E2-4. AIDS Cases 0–14 Age Group as Percentage of Total Reported AIDS Cases, late 1990s *(continued)*

	Reporting period	Percent of total reported cases
Mauritius	1996-1998	20
Mexico	1996-1998	3
Moldova	1997-1999	6
Morocco	1997-1998	3
Mozambique	1996-1998	14
Myanmar (Burma)	1996-1998	1
Netherlands, the	1998-1999	0
New Zealand	1998-1999	3
Nicaragua	1997-1999	0
Niger	1998	4
Norway	1997-1998	3
Oman	1997-1999	9
Pakistan	1997-1999	5
Panama	1997-1999	7
Papua New Guinea	1996-1998	9
Paraguay	1996-1998	5
Peru	1997-1999	3
Philippines	1998-1999	1
Poland	1997-1999	2
Portugal	1997-1999	0
Romania	1997-1999	80
Russia	1997-1999	14
Saint Kitts and Nevis	1996-1997	0
Saint Lucia	1996-1998	14
Saint Vincent and the Grenadines	1996-1998	11
San Marino	1997-1999	0
Sao Tome and Principe	1997-1999	0
Saudi Arabia	1997-1999	3
Seychelles	1996-1998	0
Sierra Leone	1996-1998	4
Singapore	1997-1999	2
Slovenia	1997-1999	0
South Korea, Rep.	1998-1999	0
Spain	1997-1999	1
Sri Lanka	1996-1998	3
Sudan	1997-1999	3
Swaziland	1997-1998	4
Sweden	1997-1999	2
Switzerland	1997-1999	1
Syria	1997-1999	6
Tanzania	1996-1998	6
Thailand	1997-1999	4
Togo	1997-1998	5
Trinidad and Tobago	1996-1997	7
Tunisia	1997-1999	4
Turkey	1997-1999	1
Ukraine	1997-1999	3
United Kingdom	1997-1999	4
United States	1996-1998	1
Uruguay	1996-1998	4
Venezuela	1996-1997	2
Vietnam	1996-1998	1
West Bank and Gaza Strip	1997-1999	8
Yemen	1998	6
Yugoslavia	1997-1999	1
Zimbabwe	1998	16

Source: Weekly Epidemiological Record, Number 48, 3 December 1999, pp. 410 and 411; <http://www.who.int/wer/pdf/1999/wer7448.pdf>. Underlying data from World Health Organization (WHO).

E2-5. HIV Prevalence Rate (%) in Young People (15–24), Total Male and Female, 1999

	Male		Female	
	Low Estimate	High Estimate	Low Estimate	High Estimate
Angola	2.58	2.86	1.08	1.43
Argentina	0.23	0.34	0.68	1.04
Australia	0.01	0.02	0.07	0.21
Austria	0.07	0.13	0.10	0.29
Bahamas, the	2.41	2.93	3.15	4.55
Bangladesh	0.00	0.01	0.00	0.02
Barbados	0.76	0.92	0.99	1.43
Belarus	0.14	0.23	0.29	0.51
Belgium	0.07	0.14	0.05	0.16
Belize	0.77	0.98	1.75	2.59
Benin	1.58	2.91	0.50	1.29
Bolivia	0.03	0.04	0.10	0.15
Botswana	32.55	36.07	13.68	18.00
Brazil	0.23	0.33	0.55	0.84
Burkina Faso	4.07	7.51	1.28	3.33
Burundi	9.86	13.34	3.80	7.59
Cambodia	2.31	4.70	0.94	3.77
Cameroon	6.61	8.94	2.54	5.09
Canada	0.05	0.09	0.15	0.44
Central African Republic	11.96	16.18	4.61	9.21
Chad	2.55	3.51	1.52	2.31
Chile	0.06	0.09	0.23	0.35
China	0.02	0.03	0.07	0.18
Colombia	0.08	0.12	0.35	0.53
Congo, Dem. Rep. (Zaire)	4.31	5.84	1.66	3.32
Congo, Rep.	5.49	7.43	2.12	4.23
Costa Rica	0.22	0.33	0.51	0.78
Cote d'Ivoire	6.68	12.33	2.10	5.47
Croatia	0.01	0.01	0.02	0.03
Cuba	0.02	0.03	0.05	0.07
Cyprus	0.06	0.08	0.08	0.12
Czech Republic	0.03	0.03	0.05	0.07
Denmark	0.05	0.10	0.08	0.24
Djibouti	11.70	16.13	6.99	10.61
Dominican Republic	2.44	3.11	2.08	3.08
Ecuador	0.06	0.09	0.29	0.45
El Salvador	0.24	0.31	0.55	0.81
Equatorial Guinea	0.46	0.63	0.18	0.36
Ethiopia	9.98	13.75	5.96	9.04
Finland	0.02	0.03	0.02	0.05
France	0.15	0.30	0.16	0.49
Gabon	4.01	5.42	1.54	3.09
Gambia, the	1.52	2.82	0.48	1.25
Germany	0.03	0.05	0.05	0.14
Ghana	2.40	4.44	0.76	1.97
Greece	0.04	0.07	0.06	0.18
Guatemala	0.81	1.03	0.93	1.38
Guinea	1.01	1.86	0.32	0.82
Guinea-Bissau	1.74	3.22	0.55	1.43
Guyana	2.03	2.58	3.12	4.62
Haiti	2.56	3.26	3.94	5.83
Honduras	1.46	1.86	1.13	1.68
Hong Kong, SAR (China)	0.04	0.05	0.05	0.14
Hungary	0.01	0.02	0.07	0.10
Iceland	0.04	0.08	0.05	0.15
India	0.40	0.82	0.14	0.58
Indonesia	0.02	0.04	0.01	0.04

E2-5. HIV Prevalence Rate (%) in Young People (15–24), Total Male and Female, 1999 *(continued)*

	Male		Female	
	Low Estimate	**High Estimate**	**Low Estimate**	**High Estimate**
Ireland	0.03	0.06	0.03	0.09
Israel	0.05	0.06	0.05	0.07
Italy	0.16	0.31	0.14	0.43
Jamaica	0.36	0.44	0.48	0.70
Japan	0.01	0.01	0.02	0.04
Kazakstan	N/A	N/A	0.05	0.09
Kenya	11.07	14.98	4.26	8.52
Laos	0.05	0.05	0.02	0.05
Latvia	0.05	0.08	0.13	0.22
Lesotho	23.94	28.85	8.04	16.07
Liberia	1.51	2.78	0.47	1.23
Madagascar	0.12	0.14	0.02	0.06
Malawi	14.48	16.04	6.08	8.00
Malaysia	0.08	0.10	0.32	0.82
Mali	1.74	2.40	1.04	1.58
Mauritania	0.50	0.69	0.30	0.45
Mauritius	0.04	0.05	0.02	0.06
Mexico	0.05	0.08	0.33	0.48
Moldova	0.08	0.14	0.20	0.35
Mozambique	13.36	16.11	4.49	8.97
Myanmar (Burma)	1.13	2.30	0.42	1.67
Namibia	18.78	20.82	7.89	10.38
Nepal	0.13	0.26	0.06	0.23
Netherlands, the	0.06	0.11	0.09	0.27
New Zealand	0.01	0.02	0.03	0.08
Nicaragua	0.05	0.08	0.17	0.26
Niger	1.26	1.73	0.75	1.14
Nigeria	4.35	5.89	1.68	3.35
Norway	0.02	0.04	0.03	0.09
Pakistan	0.03	0.06	0.02	0.10
Panama	1.20	1.52	1.33	1.97
Papua New Guinea	0.16	0.33	0.03	0.13
Paraguay	0.03	0.04	0.11	0.16
Peru	0.14	0.21	0.31	0.48
Philippines	0.04	0.08	0.01	0.05
Portugal	0.17	0.33	0.29	0.86
Romania	0.02	0.02	0.02	0.02
Russia	0.09	0.15	0.19	0.32
Rwanda	9.04	12.23	3.48	6.96
Senegal	1.12	2.07	0.39	1.02
Sierra Leone	2.05	3.79	0.65	1.68
Singapore	0.10	0.21	0.09	0.35
Slovakia	0.01	0.01	0.02	0.02
Slovenia	0.01	0.01	0.03	0.04
South Africa	22.51	27.13	7.56	15.11
South Korea, Rep.	0.00	0.01	0.01	0.03
Spain	0.15	0.30	0.24	0.71
Sri Lanka	0.03	0.07	0.02	0.07
Suriname	0.70	0.89	1.07	1.59
Swaziland	25.88	31.19	8.69	17.37
Sweden	0.03	0.05	0.03	0.09
Switzerland	0.22	0.43	0.18	0.55
Tanzania	6.85	9.27	2.64	5.28
Thailand	1.53	3.11	0.47	1.89
Togo	3.89	7.18	1.22	3.18
Trinidad and Tobago	0.53	0.64	0.69	1.00
Uganda	6.65	8.99	2.56	5.12

E2-5. HIV Prevalence Rate (%) in Young People (15–24), Total Male and Female, 1999 *(continued)*

	Male		Female	
	Low Estimate	**High Estimate**	**Low Estimate**	**High Estimate**
Ukraine	0.60	0.98	0.95	1.63
United Kingdom	0.03	0.06	0.05	0.14
United States of America	0.16	0.30	0.25	0.75
Uruguay	0.17	0.25	0.33	0.49
Venezuela	0.12	0.17	0.52	0.79
Vietnam	0.09	0.10	0.15	0.38
Zambia	16.86	18.68	7.08	9.32
Zimbabwe	23.25	25.76	9.77	12.85
N/A Not Available				

Source: Report on the Global HIV/AIDS Epidemic—June 2000; <http://www.unaids.org/epidemic_update/report/index.html> and <http://www.unaids.org/epidemic_update/report/Final_Table_Eng_Xcel.xls>. Underlying data from Joint United Nations Programme on HIV/AIDS (UNIADS).

E2-6. Estimated Number of Children (<15 Years) Newly Infected with HIV during 2000, by Region

	Number
Sub-Saharan Africa	520,000
South and South-East Asia	65,000
North Africa and Middle East	11,000
Latin America	7,300
Caribbean	4,200
East Asia and Pacific	2,600
North America	less than 500
Western Europe	less than 500
Eastern Europe and Central Asia	600
Australia and New Zealand	less than 100
Total	611,700

Source: Joint United Nations Programme on HIV/AIDS (UNAIDS), December 2000; <http://www.unaids.org/wac/2000/wad00/files/wad2000Master/index.htm>. Underlying data from World Health Organization (WHO).

E2-7. Regional Distribution of Children (<15 Years) Newly Infected with HIV during 2000

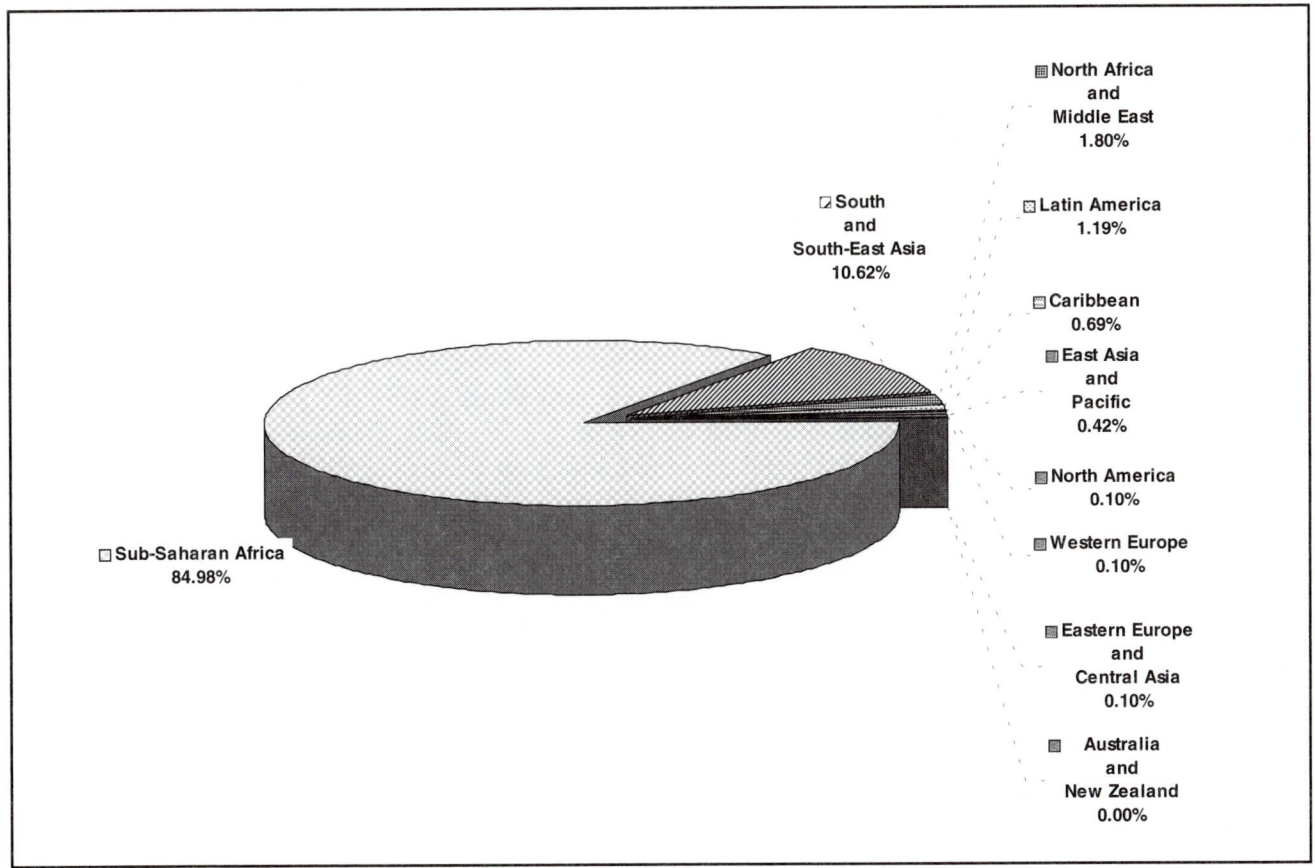

Source: Joint United Nations Programme on HIV/AIDS (UNAIDS), December 2000; <http://www.unaids.org/wac/2000/wad00/files/wad2000Master/index.htm>. Underlying data from World Health Organization (WHO).

E2-8. Increase in the Number of Children Living with HIV/AIDS, 1994 to 1997

Countries where the number of children living with HIV/AIDS has quadrupled	Number of children (age 0-14) infected
Namibia	5,000
China	1,400
Vietnam	1,100

Countries where the number of children living with HIV/AIDS has tripled	Number of children (age 0-14) infected
South Africa	80,000
India	48,000
Myanmar (Burma)	7,100
Cambodia	5,400
Swaziland	2,800
Dominican Republic	1,400
Malaysia	1,400

Countries where the number of children living with HIV/AIDS has doubled	Number of children (age 0-14) infected
Nigeria	99,000
Mozambique	54,000
Botswana	7,300
Angola	5,200
Lesotho	3,100
Benin	2,400
Pakistan	1,800
Djibouti	1,300

Note: The figures above are end-1997 estimates. In many countries, end-1999 estimates could be considerably higher.

Source: The Progress of Nations, 1999, data as at end-1997; http://www.unicef.org/pon99/ United Nations Children's Fund (UNICEF). Underlying data from Joint United Nations Programme on HIV/AIDS (UNAIDS) and World Health Organization (WHO).

E3. AIDS DEATHS

E3-1. Child Deaths (0–14 years) from AIDS, by Regions, end 1999

	Low Estimate	High Estimate
Sub-Saharan Africa	300,000	610,000
North Africa and Middle East	650	1,400
South and South East Asia	29000	54,000
East Asia and Pacific	650	1,200
Australia & New Zealand	less than 100	less than 100
Latin America	2600	4,600
North America	250	380
Caribbean	2000	3,800
Eastern Europe and Central Asia	N/A	N/A
Western Europe	N/A	N/A
World Total	335,150	675,380

N/A Not Available

Source: Report on the Global HIV/AIDS Epidemic—June 2000; <http://www.unaids.org/epidemic_update/report/Epi_report.pdf>. Underlying data from Joint United Nations Programme on HIV/AIDS (UNAIDS).

E3-2. Estimated Deaths in Children (<15 years) from HIV/AIDS during 2000

	Number	Percentage
Sub-Saharan Africa	440,000	88.9
South and South-East Asia	40,000	8.1
North Africa and Middle East	7,100	1.4
Caribbean	3,100	0.6
Latin America	3,000	0.6
East Asia and Pacific	1,000	0.2
Eastern Europe and Central Asia	less than 500	0.1
Australia and New Zealand	less than 100	0.0
North America	less than 100	0.0
Western Europe	less than 100	0.0
Total*	495,000	100.0

*Total does not add to 100 because of rounding.

Source: Report on the Global HIV/AIDS Epidemic—December 2000; <http://www.unaids.org/wac/2000/wad00/files/wad2000Master/index.htm>. Underlying data from Joint United Nations Programme on HIV/AIDS (UNAIDS) and World Health Organization (WHO).

E3-3. AIDS Deaths in Children (0–14), 1999

Country	Low Estimate	High Estimate
World Total	**330,000**	**670,000**
Sub-Saharan Africa	**300,000**	**610,000**
Angola	2,400	4,400
Benin	1,000	1,600
Botswana	3,700	5,100
Burkina Faso	6,000	12,000
Burundi	3,000	18,000
Cameroon	7,000	16,000
Central African Republic	3,000	5,500
Chad	1,100	2,300
Congo, Dem. Rep. (Zaire)	10,000	25,000
Congo, Rep.	870	2,600
Côte d'Ivoire	10,000	15,000
Djibouti	430	920
Equatorial Guinea	<100	<100
Ethiopia	35,000	91,000
Gabon	220	460
Gambia, the	140	300
Ghana	2,600	7,700
Guinea	830	1,500
Guinea-Bissau	150	330
Kenya	27,000	41,000
Lesotho	2,300	4,900
Liberia	540	1,200
Madagascar	150	240
Malawi	12,000	22,000
Mali	1,400	3,000
Mauritania	<100	160
Mozambique	11,000	32,000
Namibia	2,300	3,500
Niger	920	2,000
Nigeria	41,000	64,000
Rwanda	3,900	18,000
Senegal	1,100	1,700
Sierra Leone	910	2,000
South Africa	36,000	74,000
Swaziland	1,300	2,000
Tanzania	20,000	30,000

E3-3. AIDS Deaths in Children (0–14), 1999 *(continued)*

Country	Low Estimate	High Estimate
Togo	2,100	3,300
Uganda	18,000	32,000
Zambia	14,000	24,000
Zimbabwe	19,000	38,000
East Asia & Pacific	**650**	**1,200**
China	580	1000
Fiji	N/A	<100
Hong Kong, SAR (China)	<100	<100
Japan	<100	<100
Papua New Guinea	<100	130
South Korea, Rep.	<100	<100
Australia & New Zealand	**<100**	**<100**
Australia	<100	<100
New Zealand	<100	<100
South & South-East Asia	**29,000**	**54,000**
Bangladesh	<100	<100
Cambodia	1900	2,900
India	16000	33,000
Indonesia	240	360
Laos	<100	<100
Malaysia	<100	110
Myanmar (Burma)	4800	7,400
Nepal	260	550
Pakistan	450	970
Philippines	150	230
Singapore	<100	<100
Sri Lanka	<100	<100
Thailand	4700	7,300
Vietnam	300	460
North Africa & Middle East	**650**	**1,400**
Cyprus	<100	<100
Israel	<100	<100
North America	**250**	**380**
Canada	<100	<100
United States of America	250	380
Carribean	**2,000**	**3,800**
Bahamas, the	<100	<100
Barbados	<100	<100
Cuba	<100	<100
Dominican Republic	470	710
Haiti	1400	3,000
Jamaica	<100	<100
Trinidad and Tobago	<100	<100
Latin America	**2,600**	**4,600**
Argentina	<100	120
Belize	<100	<100
Bolivia	<100	<100
Brazil	800	1,200
Chile	<100	<100
Colombia	<100	160
Costa Rica	<100	<100
Ecuador	<100	<100
El Salvador	<100	<100
Guatemala	460	970
Guyana	<100	<100
Honduras	450	680
Mexico	210	380
Nicaragua	<100	<100

E3-3. AIDS Deaths in Children (0–14), 1999 *(continued)*

Country	Low Estimate	High Estimate
Panama	<100	120
Paraguay	<100	<100
Peru	200	360
Suriname	<100	<100
Uruguay	<100	<100
Venezuela	<100	120
World Total	**330,000**	**670,000**

N/A Not Available

Source: Report on the Global HIV/AIDS Epidemic—June 2000; <http://www.unaids.org/epidemic_update/report/index.html> and <http://www.unaids.org/epidemic_update/report/Final_Table_Eng_Xcel.xls> Underlying data from Joint United Nations Programme on HIV/AIDS (UNIADS).

E3-4. Cumulative Projected Number of Deaths with and without AIDS, by Age Group, Selected Countries, 1985–2005

Country	Cumulative projected number of deaths in 1,000s		
	0-4 years	5-14 years	0-65+ years
24 African countries*			
With AIDS	30,763	10,237	77,827
Without AIDS	28,363	9,696	67,150
Additional deaths	2,400	542	10,677
Percentage difference	8.5	5.6	15.9
5 African countries**			
With AIDS	7,490	2,226	18,232
Without AIDS	6,402	2,012	13,652
Additional deaths	1,088	214	4,580
Percentage difference	17.0	10.6	33.5
India			
With AIDS	48,795	13,260	176,948
Without AIDS	48,503	13,178	174,284
Additional deaths	293	82	2,664
Percentage difference	0.6	0.6	1.5
Thailand			
With AIDS	899	287	7,540
Without AIDS	848	270	6,808
Additional deaths	51	17	731
Percentage difference	6.0	6.3	10.7
Brazil			
With AIDS	3,347	642	23,089
Without AIDS	3,301	626	22,455
Additional deaths	46	16	634
Percentage difference	1.4	2.6	2.8
Haiti			
With AIDS	544	128	1,823
Without AIDS	503	119	1,633
Additional deaths	41	9	190
Percentage difference	8.2	7.6	11.6

*24 African countries where the demographic impact of AIDS is high, are: Benin, Botswana, Burkina Faso, Burundi, Cameron, Central African Republic, Chad, Congo, Republic, Dote d'Ivoire, Congo, Democratic Rep., Eritrea, Guinea-Bissau, Kenya, Lesotho, Malawi, Mozambique, Namibia, Rwanda, Sierra Leone, Togo, Uganda, Tanzania, Zambia, and Zimbabwe.
**5 countries, Botswana, Malawi, Uganda, Zambia, and Zimbabwe, with the highest HIV seroprevalence level in 1994.

Source: World Population Prospects, the 1996 Revision, 1998: Table 32. Underlying data from United Nations, Department of Economic and Social Affairs, Population Division.

E3-5. Infant Mortality Rate (under 1 Year of Age), Life Expectancy, and Child Mortality (under Age 5) with and without AIDS, Selected Countries, 1998

	Infant Mortality Rates (deaths per 1,000 live births)		Life expectancy		Child mortality (deaths per 1,000 live births)	
	With AIDS	Without AIDS	With AIDS	Without AIDS	With AIDS	Without AIDS
Botswana	59.3	36.4	40.1	61.5	121.1	57.4
Brazil	37.0	33.5	64.4	71.4	47.3	37.5
Burkina Faso	109.2	101.1	46.1	55.4	179.1	156.5
Burundi	101.2	92.1	45.6	55.4	157.1	131.0
Cambodia	106.8	104.2	48.0	50.7	179.7	171.9
Cameroon	76.9	70.7	51.4	58.6	128.1	109.6
Central African Republic	105.7	97.7	46.8	56.3	162.6	140.2
Côte d'Ivoire	95.9	86.7	46.2	56.5	149.2	122.7
Dem. Rep. Congo (Zaire)	101.6	97.1	49.3	54.4	152.7	139.3
Ethiopia	125.7	115.4	40.9	50.9	197.6	169.2
Guyana	48.7	45.4	62.3	65.7	71.4	61.3
Haiti	99.0	95.6	51.4	55.5	155.7	145.9
Honduras	41.9	38.6	65.0	69.2	61.2	50.4
Kenya	59.4	44.7	47.6	65.6	107.0	64.9
Lesotho	78.3	71.2	54.0	62.0	120.2	98.3
Malawi	133.8	117.9	36.6	51.1	231.6	190.3
Myanmar (Burma)	78.4	76.3	54.5	57.1	113.1	106.4
Namibia	66.8	44.0	41.5	65.3	125.5	62.1
Nigeria	70.7	65.9	53.6	57.8	139.0	124.4
Rep. Congo	102.7	94.0	47.1	57.2	166.3	142.5
Rwanda	113.3	101.3	41.9	53.9	181.9	148.5
South Africa	52.0	43.3	55.7	65.4	95.5	69.7
Swaziland	103.4	83.8	38.5	58.1	168.1	114.4
Tanzania	96.9	89.2	46.4	55.2	160.1	137.8
Thailand	30.8	29.7	69.0	71.3	40.8	36.2
Uganda	92.9	81.3	42.6	54.1	164.5	132.9
Zambia	92.6	72.0	37.1	56.2	181.2	125.7
Zimbabwe	61.8	35.9	39.2	64.9	123.4	50.5

Note: infant mortality, life expectancy, and child mortality is for both sexes combined.

Source: World Population Profile: 1998, with a Special Chapter Focusing on HIV/AIDS in the Developing World, Population Composition and Distribution; <http://wwwcensusgov/ipc/prod/wp98/wp98pdf>. Underlying data from U.S. Department of Commerce, Economics and Statistics Administration, Bureau of the Census, International Data Base and unpublished tables.

E3-6. Projected Infant Mortality Rate (under 1 Year of Age), Life Expectancy, and Child Mortality (under Age 5) with and without AIDS, Selected Countries, 2010

	Infant Mortality Rates (deaths per 1,000 live births)		Life expectancy		Child mortality (deaths per 1,000 live births)	
	With AIDS	Without AIDS	With AIDS	Without AIDS	With AIDS	Without AIDS
Botswana	55.2	26.3	37.8	66.3	119.5	38.3
Brazil	22.3	18.4	67.7	75.5	31.4	20.6
Burkina Faso	86.6	73.7	45.6	60.7	144.7	108.7
Burundi	79.6	66.3	45.3	60.8	128.6	90.9
Cambodia	81.7	78.1	52.8	56.7	133.9	123.9
Cameroon	63.8	52.9	49.8	63.2	108.3	78.0
Central African Republic	79.8	71.6	50.9	61.9	122.7	99.1
Côte d'Ivoire	74.8	61.8	46.7	61.8	120.9	84.2
Dem. Rep. Congo (Zaire)	77.0	70.4	51.9	59.8	116.2	97.3
Ethiopia	112.4	95.4	38.6	54.7	183.4	136.7
Guyana	50.1	36.9	51.1	67.9	86.6	48.7
Haiti	83.4	80.1	54.4	58.8	129.1	119.0
Honduras	32.1	23.5	59.7	73.4	55.2	29.3
Kenya	53.9	32.9	43.7	69.2	105.2	45.4
Lesotho	71.1	52.8	44.7	65.9	121.9	70.7
Malawi	113.1	88.4	34.8	56.8	202.6	136.0
Myanmar (Burma)	55.7	52.4	58.8	62.8	80.3	70.1
Namibia	57.2	28.3	38.9	70.1	118.8	37.5
Nigeria	57.4	41.4	46.3	64.9	112.7	68.2
Rep. Congo	77.5	67.3	49.0	62.4	125.9	97.1
Rwanda	97.1	74.7	37.6	59.2	166.4	105.5
South Africa	50.7	32.3	48.0	68.2	99.5	48.5
Swaziland	85.3	58.6	37.1	63.2	152.2	77.5
Tanzania	77.8	65.2	46.1	60.7	131.3	95.8
Thailand	18.7	17.8	72.9	75.1	25.0	21.2
Uganda	68.6	58.5	47.6	59.5	120.6	92.2
Zambia	81.7	58.4	37.8	60.1	160.7	96.9
Zimbabwe	53.7	24.0	38.8	69.5	115.6	31.8

Note: Infant mortality, life expectancy, and child mortality are for both sexes combined.

Source: World Population Profile: 1998, with a Special Chapter Focusing on HIV/AIDS in the Developing World, Population Composition and Distribution. <http://wwwcensusgov/ipc/prod/wp98/wp98pdf>. Underlying data from U.S. Department of Commerce, Economics and Statistics Administration, Bureau of the Census, International Data Base and unpublished tables.

E3-7. Under-5 Mortality with and without AIDS (Number of Under-5-year Deaths per 1,000 Live Births) Selected Countries, 1995–2000 and 2010–2015

	Deaths per 1,000 live births, 1995–2000		Deaths per 1,000 live births, 2010–2015	
	With AIDS	**Without AIDS**	**With AIDS**	**Without AIDS**
Benin	133	129	97	89
Botswana	107	53	86	27
Brazil	48	46	34	34
Burkina Faso	171	156	120	112
Burundi	179	160	132	119
Cambodia	134	131	89	82
Cameroon	114	105	81	59
Central African Republic	157	136	112	95
Chad	174	168	128	124
Congo, Dem. Rep. (Zaire)	139	130	89	83
Congo, Rep.	132	116	88	78
Cote d'Ivoire	136	117	90	77
Eritrea	146	139	93	88
Ethiopia	184	165	122	111
Gabon	135	127	102	85
Guinea-Bissau	203	199	167	149
Haiti	105	100	79	73
India	89	89	59	56
Kenya	104	81	87	44
Lesotho	130	121	90	77
Liberia	174	133	73	66
Malawi	220	190	156	136
Mozambique	183	160	165	116
Namibia	122	93	125	53
Nigeria	147	141	111	104
Rwanda	202	176	143	121
Sierra Leone	263	257	190	186
South Africa	87	62	98	39
Tanzania	130	110	97	84
Thailand	35	33	21	18
Togo	129	114	87	76
Uganda	173	146	118	102
Zambia	147	111	95	74
Zimbabwe	117	74	84	40

Source: World Population Prospects, the 1998 Revision Volume III. Analytical Report; Table III.13. United Nations Population Division. Underlying data from Joint United Nations Programme on HIV/AIDS (UNAIDS), Report on the Global HIV/AIDS Pandemic, June 1998, and World Health Organization (WHO).

E4. TEENS AND THE AIDS INFO GAP

E4-1. Number of Teens (Age 15–19) Living with HIV/AIDS, 1999

	Number
Western Europe	
Spain	5,400
Portugal	3,300
France	2,600
Italy	2,200
Germany	1,000
United Kingdom	600
Belgium	400
Greece	400
Switzerland	300
Netherlands, the	100
Subtotal	16,300
Eastern Europe	
Ukraine	18,000
Russia	2,300
Poland	1,100
Subtotal	21,400
Total 13 European countries	37,700
North America	
United States	17,000

Sources: UNICEF, *Progress of the Nations, 1999,* Data as at end-1997; <http://www.unicef.org/pon99/> />. United Nations Children's Fund (UNICEF). Underlying data from Hamers and Downs at the European Centre for the Epidemiological Monitoring of AIDS (CESES), 1999; the United States Center for Disease Control and Prevention.

E4-2. HIV Rates among Pregnant Girls (Age 15–19) Attending Ante-Natal Clinics in Major Urban Areas, Selected Countries, 1995–1998

	Percentage HIV positive
Botswana	31
Zimbabwe	26
Swaziland	23
South Africa*	21
Mozambique	19
Rwanda	19
Malawi	17
Zambia	17
Burundi	16
Ethiopia	16
Côte d'Ivoire	14
Kenya	13
Namibia*	11
Uganda	10
Gabon	7
Tanzania	7
Burkina Faso*	6
Cameroon	5
Cambodia*	3
Ghana	3
Congo, Dem. Rep.	2
Haiti	2
Thailand	2
Brazil*	1
Guinea	1
Myanmar	1

* Also includes girls outside major urban areas.

Source: Progress of the Nations, 1999; <http://www.unicef.org/pon99/>. Underlying data from U.S. Bureau of the Census, National AIDS programs, Joint United Nations Programme on HIV/AIDS (UNAIDS)/ World Health Organization (WHO).

E4-3. Percentage of Young Adults (15–19 Years) Who Ever Used a Condom for Sexual Intercourse, various years

Country	Year	Age group	Male	Female
Angola	1997	14-19	19.0	9.1
Brazil	1996	15-19	N/A	17.3
Burkina Faso	1993	15-19	N/A	5.3
Cameroon	1991	15-19	N/A	8.7
Canada (Quebec only)	1991	15-19	85.0	85.0
Eritrea	1995	15-19	N/A	0.2
Ghana	1988	15-19	N/A	1.6
Haiti	1995	15-19	N/A	3.9
Kenya	1989	15-19	N/A	1.5
Kenya	1993	15-19	N/A	3.2
Madagascar	1992	15-19	N/A	1.0
Malawi	1992	15-19	N/A	1.0
Mali	1996	15-19	N/A	3.6
Nigeria	1990	15-19	N/A	1.6
Rwanda	1992	15-19	N/A	0.2
Senegal	1993	15-19	N/A	1.2
South Africa	1998	15-19	N/A	28.4
Tanzania	1992	15-19	N/A	1.8
Tanzania	1996	15-19	10.0	3.5
Uganda	1989	15-19	N/A	0.6
Uganda	1995	15-19	N/A	4.9
Zimbabwe	1988	15-19	N/A	4.6
Zimbabwe	1994	15-19	N/A	6.4

Source: Global HIV/AIDS & STD Surveillance, UNAIDS/WHO Epidemiological Fact Sheet, 2000 update, and Demographic and Health Survey; <http://www.who.int/emc-hiv/fact_sheets/africa.html>. Underlying data from World Health Organization (WHO).

E4-4. Reported Condom Use in Risk Sex (Age Group Less than 19 Years), Selected Countries, various years

Country	Year	Geographic coverage area	Age group	Male*	Female*	All*
Angola	1997	All	14-19	38.1	36.3	N/A
Canada	1992	only Province of British Columbia	15-19	57-71	45-69	N/A
Djibouti	1995	All	15-19	N/A	N/A	56.5
Mozambique	1997	All	15-19	20.0	18.0	21.0
Tanzania	1996	All	15-19	25.4	18.7	15.9
Uganda	1995	Rural	15-19	20.0	0.0	17.0
Uganda	1995	Urban	15-19	70.0	22.0	39.0

*Proportion of people reporting the use of a condom during the most recent intercourse of risk.

Source: Global HIV/AIDS & STD Surveillance, UNAIDS/WHO Epidemiological Fact Sheet, 2000 update, and Demographic and Health Survey; <http://www.who.int/emc-hiv/fact_sheets/africa.html>. Underlying data from World Health Organization (WHO).

E4-5. Percentage of Children (Aged 15–19) Who Do Not Know Any Way to Protect Themselves against HIV/AIDS, by Gender, 1994–1999

	Male	**Female**
Bangladesh	88	96
Mozambique	62	74
Chad	45	66
Niger	43	66
Thailand	35	51
Comoros	20	42
Mali	28	40
Bolivia	26	33
Peru	22	32
Cameroon	18	31
Nicaragua	15	27
Kenya	17	26
Zambia	10	23
Côte d'Ivoire	8	22
Zimbabwe	8	17
Uganda	11	16
Brazil	9	11

Source: Progress of the Nations, 2000, United Nations Children's Fund (UNICEF); <http://www.unicef.org/pon00/>. Underlying data from Demographic and Health Surveys (DHS), 1994–1999.

E4-6. Percentage of Girls (15–19 Years Old) Who Do Not Know That a Person with AIDS May Look Healthy, 1994–1999

	Percent
Chad	83
Niger	81
Nepal	80
Lesotho	73
Madagascar	68
Bangladesh	67
Cambodia	66
Mozambique	66
Benin	62
Mali	62
Guatemala	57
Papua New Guinea	56
Mongolia	54
South Africa	51
Vietnam	50
Cape Verde	47
Central African Republic	47
Cameroon	45
Eritrea	45
Côte d'Ivoire	41
Tanzania	40
Romania	39
Turkey	39
Togo	37
Comoros	35
Kenya	33
Peru	32
Malawi	31
Zimbabwe	31
Haiti	28
Zambia	26
Uganda	23
Brazil	22
Dominican Republic	14

Source: The Progress of Nations 2000; <http://www.unicef.org/pon00/>, United Nations Children's Fund (UNICEF). Underlying data from DHS and other nationwide surveys, 1994-1999.

E4-7. Percentage of Women (Aged 15–49) Who Know That the AIDS Virus Can Be Transmitted from a Mother to Her Child, 1994–1999

	Percent
Dominican Republic	96
Zimbabwe	92
Zambia	88
Kenya	85
Uganda	85
South Africa	84
Peru	79
Haiti	74
Tanzania	73
Central African Republic	70
Côte d'Ivoire	66
Cameroon	65
Benin	62
Madagascar	58
Mali	41
Chad	36
Niger	26

Source: The Progress of Nations 2000; <http://www.unicef.org/pon00/>, United Nations Children's Fund (UNICEF). Underlying data from DHS and other nationwide surveys, 1994-1999.

E5. AIDS ORPHANS

E5-1. Cumulative Number of Children Estimated to Have Been Orphaned by AIDS* at Age 14 or Younger, end 1999

	Number	Percentage
Sub-Saharan Africa	12,100,000	91.6
South and South-East Asia	850,000	6.4
Latin America	110,000	0.8
Caribbean	85,000	0.6
North America	70,000	0.5
North Africa and Middle East	15,000	0.1
Western Europe	9,000	0.1
East Asia and Pacific	5,600	0.0
Eastern Europe and Central Asia	500	0.0
Australia and New Zealand	less than 500	0.0
Total**	13,200,000	100.0

*HIV negative children who have lost their mother or both parents to AIDS before the age of 15 years.
**total does not add to 100 because of rounding.

Source: Joint United Nations Programme on HIV/AIDS (UNAIDS) and World Health Organization (WHO), December 2000; <http://www.unaids.org/wac/2000/wad00/files/wad2000Master/index.htm>.

E5-2. AIDS Orphans (Cumulative), 1999

	Cumulative orphans*
World Total	**13,200,000**
Sub-Saharan Africa	**12,100,000**
Angola	98,000
Benin	22,000
Botswana	66,000
Burkina Faso	320,000
Burundi	230,000
Cameroon	270,000
Central African Republic	99,000
Chad	68,000
Congo, Dem. Rep. (Zaire)	680,000
Congo, Rep.	53,000
Côte d'Ivoire	420,000
Djibouti	7,200
Equatorial Guinea	860
Ethiopia	1,200,000
Gabon	8,600
Gambia, the	9,600
Ghana	170,000
Guinea	30,000
Guinea-Bissau	6,100
Kenya	730,000
Lesotho	35,000
Liberia	31,000
Madagascar	2,600
Malawi	390,000
Mali	45,000
Mozambique	310,000
Namibia	67,000
Niger	31,000
Nigeria	1,400,000
Rwanda	270,000
Senegal	42,000
Sierra Leone	56,000
South Africa	420,000
Swaziland	12,000
Tanzania	1,100,000
Togo	95,000
Uganda	1,700,000
Zambia	650,000
Zimbabwe	900,000
East Asia & Pacific	**5,600**
China	4,500
Papua New Guinea	1,100
South Korea, Rep.	<100
Australia & New Zealand	**<500**
South & South-East Asia	**850,000**
Bangladesh	610
Cambodia	13,000
Indonesia	2,000
Laos	280
Malaysia	680
Myanmar (Burma)	43,000
Nepal	2,500
Pakistan	7,900
Philippines	1,500
Singapore	120
Sri Lanka	600

E5-2. AIDS Orphans (Cumulative), 1999 *(continued)*

	Cumulative orphans*
Thailand	75,000
Vietnam	3,200
Eastern Europe & Central Asia	**500**
Western Europe	**9,000**
North Africa & Middle East	**15,000**
North America	**70,000**
Canada	1,000
United States of America	70,000
Caribbean	**85,000**
Bahamas, the	970
Barbados	190
Cuba	190
Dominican Republic	7,900
Haiti	74,000
Jamaica	1,200
Trinidad and Tobago	930
Latin America	**110,000**
Argentina	8,900
Belize	420
Bolivia	260
Brazil	41,000
Chile	770
Colombia	2,800
Costa Rica	1,300
Ecuador	1,500
El Salvador	2,600
Guatemala	5,200
Guyana	1,100
Honduras	19,000
Mexico	14,000
Nicaragua	520
Panama	2,100
Paraguay	400
Peru	8,900
Suriname	480
Uruguay	330
Venezuela	1,100
World Total	**13,200,000**

* Cumulative total includes children who may no longer be alive, and also who are no longer under 14.

Source: Report on the Global HIV/AIDS Epidemic—June 2000; <http://www.unaids.org/epidemic_update/report/index.html> and <http://www. unaids.org/ epidemic_update/report/Final_Table_Eng_Xcel.xls>. Underlying data from Joint United Nations Programme on HIV/AIDS (UNIADS).

E5-3. Number of Children (0 to 15 years) per 10,000 Who Have Lost Their Mother or Both Parents to AIDS, Selected Countries,* 1997

	Number per 10,000
Uganda	1,100
Zambia	890
Zimbabwe	700
Malawi	580
Togo	400
Botswana	390
Burundi	380
Côte d'Ivoire	380
Congo, Rep.	360
Tanzania	360
Rwanda	350
Central African Republic	340
Burkina Faso	290
Kenya	280
Ethiopia	250
Mozambique	180
Sierra Leone	170
Liberia	150
Congo, Dem. Rep. (Zaire)	140
Chad	130
Gambia, the	120
Ghana	110
Namibia	110
South Africa	110
Cameroon	100
Haiti	100
Lesotho	100
Gabon	90
Senegal	90
Nigeria	60
Mali	50
Guinea	40
Angola	30
Benin	30
Niger	30
Thailand	30
Cambodia	20
Guinea-Bissau	20
Honduras	20
Jamaica	20
Trinidad and Tobago	20
Dominican Republic	10
Mauritania	10
United States	10
Panama	9
El Salvador	8
Myanmar (Burma)	8
Costa Rica	6
Guatemala	6
Papua New Guinea	6
Uruguay	4
India	3
Argentina	2
Ecuador	2
Madagascar	2
Malaysia	2
Mexico	2

E5-3. Number of Children (0 to 15 years) per 10,000 Who Have Lost Their Mother or Both Parents to AIDS, Selected Countries,* 1997 *(continued)*

	Number per 10,000
Chile	1
Colombia	1
Laos	1
Nepal	1
New Zealand	1
Nicaragua	1
Pakistan	1
Paraguay	1
Peru	1
Sri Lanka	1
Venezuela	1
Vietnam	1
Afghanistan	Less than 1
Armenia	Less than 1
Australia	Less than 1
Azerbaijan	Less than 1
Bangladesh	Less than 1
Bhutan	Less than 1
Bolivia	Less than 1
Canada	Less than 1
China	Less than 1
Cuba	Less than 1
Egypt	Less than 1
Georgia	Less than 1
Indonesia	Less than 1
Iran	Less than 1
Iraq	Less than 1
Israel	Less than 1
Japan	Less than 1
Jordan	Less than 1
Kazakhstan	Less than 1
Kuwait	Less than 1
Kyrgyzstan	Less than 1
Lebanon	Less than 1
Libya	Less than 1
Mongolia	Less than 1
North Korea, Dem. Rep.	Less than 1
Oman	Less than 1
Philippines	Less than 1
Saudi Arabia	Less than 1
Singapore	Less than 1
South Korea, Rep.	Less than 1
Syria	Less than 1
Tajikstan	Less than 1
Tunisia	Less than 1
Turkey	Less than 1
Turkmenistan	Less than 1
Uzbekistan	Less than 1
Yemen	Less than 1

* Comparable data on the number of children orphaned by AIDS are not available for many of the developed countries or those in transition, so these countries have been excluded from this table.

Note: These estimations do not include those children who have lost only their father.

Source: The Progress of Nations, 1999, data as at end-1997; <http://www.unicef.org/pon99/>. Underlying data from United Nations Children's Fund (UNICEF), Joint United Nations Programme on HIV/AIDS (UNIADS), and World Health Organization (WHO).

E6. AIDS AND EDUCATION

E6-1. Primary School Children Who Lost a Teacher to AIDS, Selected Countries, 1999

South Africa	100,000
Kenya	95,000
Zimbabwe	86,000
Nigeria	85,000
Uganda	81,000
Zambia	56,000
Malawi	52,000
Ethiopia	51,000
Tanzania	49,000
Congo, Dem. Rep. (Zaire)	27,000

Source: The Progress of Nations, 2000; <http://www.unicef.org/pon00/>. Underlying data from United Nations Children's Fund (UNICEF) and Joint United Nations Programme on HIV/AIDS (UNAIDS).

F. Economics

GENERAL OVERVIEW

The tables and graphs in this section sketch the economic world of today's children. The first clusters offer general data that provide context for the later indictors' focus, which is specifically on children. Figures for the GDP and GNP are benchmarks of a country's health. Indebtedness and financial assistance are important because they affect a nation's ability to deliver basic social services to its children.

Sadly, a major portion of this chapter must deal with poverty. In the $30 trillion global economy of the twenty-first century, half of humanity is desperately impoverished. Although there are not specific measures of child poverty, the World Bank estimates that more than half a billion children—representing a staggering 40 percent of all children in developing countries—are still struggling to survive on less than 1 dollar a day. One of the most dramatic economic manifestations of poverty is child labor. Firm figures on child labor are hard to come by because most children work in informal, family-owned businesses beyond the reach of official statistics. The International Labour Organization, however, estimates that 120 million children aged 5 to 14 work full time to support their parents and siblings, and a further 130 million work part-time. Seventy-five percent of these child laborers work six or more days a week. About 80 percent of children's work is unpaid because they work in family-based agriculture.

Yet, poverty cannot be reduced to dollars and cents. Poverty causes lifelong damage to children's minds and bodies. It is the main cause of millions of preventable child deaths each year, and it also causes tens of millions of children to go hungry or miss school. Children growing up in poverty are likely to have children who grow up in poverty, perpetuating the cycle. It is, therefore, important to use the indicators in this section in conjunction with those of health, disease, and education in other sections to derive a full portrait of poverty.

EXPLANATION OF INDICATORS

F1-1–F1-3. Gross domestic product and gross national product per capita: Although the tables and charts in this cluster present figures for the population as a whole, they are important in understanding the general economic world in which children live. The first indicator presents the per capita gross domestic product (GDP). F1-2 and F1-3 show gross national product (GNP) by region and nation. The GDP is the total output of goods and services for final use produced by an economy. The GNP is the sum of value added by all resident producers plus net receipts of income from nonresident sources. GDP per capita and GNP per capita are the total GDP or GNP of a country divided by its population. These indicators help relate a country's economic output to the size of its population. F1-2 also includes information by economic class. The World Bank classifies countries into four income categories based on the most recent (1999) GNP per capita figures (per month): high income ($9,266 or more); upper middle income ($2,996 to $9,265); lower middle income ($756 to $2,995); and low income ($755 or less). What the latest GNP figures do not indicate is that the average GNP of the world's poorest countries slipped from $240 per person in 1990 to $232 in 1996. This contrasts with an average GNP surge from $20,900 to $27,000 per person in the wealthiest countries during the same period.

F2-1–F2-4. Indebtedness: The following four indicators present a picture of countries' debt. Debt takes a heavy toll on children's rights and development. When a country's debt becomes disproportionately large compared to its GNP, or when debt service takes a large proportion of the national budget, debt slows growth, inhibits foreign investment, creates instability, and soaks up money that could be spent on health, education, and other vital services. According to the World Bank, many African countries spend more than twice as much on financing debt as on basic social services such as health care, nutrition, safe water, adequate sanitation, and education.

F2-1, debt per capita, shows trends in official external debt per capita from 1970 to 1996 for developing countries. F2-2 shows external debt as percentage of GNP, and F2-3 shows central government expenditure on debt services, which are indicators of the burden of debt.

In 2000, 41 developing nations fell into a special category the International Monetary Fund (IMF) and the World Bank labeled Heavily Indebted Poor Countries (HIPC). All of these countries, presented in F2-4, have unsustainable debt. Changing debt liability to investment in children is key to ending poverty in these HIPC countries.

F3-1–F3-2. Official Development Assistance (ODA): Foreign aid is often essential for developing countries to finance economic and human development. Yet despite economic growth in donor nations during the 1990s, ODA has fallen to record lows. According to the Organisation for Economic Co-operation and Development, the proportion of GNP that its member nations devote to international assistance stands at less than one-half percent, far shorter than the UN target of 0.7 percent. With tightening development assistance, people—mostly children—suffer the consequences. F3-1, official development assistance and ODA inflow as a percent of recipient GNP, is an indication of a developing nation's dependence on aid. F3-2, aid as a proportion of donor country's gross national product (GNP), is a measure of donor nations' ability and willingness to provide aid to needy countries.

F4-1–F4-2. Spending for basic social services: One of the most critical aspects of government expenditures, especially in developing countries, is the budget allocation to basic social services. These essentials comprise basic health care, including reproductive health, basic education, nutrition programs, sanitation, and safe water supply. The World Bank and International Monetary Fund recommend that developing countries allocate at least 20 percent of their budgets for the basic social services for its population, including children. Yet many nations fail to meet this target. As a consequence, millions of children are deprived of services and destined to live and die in poverty. F4-1 shows the percent of central government expenditures on basic social services. F4-2 provides figures on the amount of official development assistance spent in this area.

F5-1–F5-2. Human Poverty Index (HPI): The United Nations Development Programme (UNDP) introduced the HPI to bring together different dimensions of deprivation. In lieu of extensive specific data for children, the HPI (calculated for the total population) gives an overview of poverty among nations. Because the dimensions of poverty differ in the industrial and developing worlds, the UNDP established two poverty indexes.

HPI-1 (F5-1), for the developing world, measures deprivation in the basic dimensions of human development. The variables used are the percentage of people born today expected to die before age 40; the percentage of adults who are illiterate; the percentage of people without access to health services and safe water; and the percentage of underweight children.

HPI-2 (F5-2), for industrialized countries, measures the percentage of people born today expected to die before age 60; the percentage of people whose ability to read and write is not adequate to be functional; the proportion of people who are income poor; and, the proportion of the long-term (12 months or more) unemployed.

As with all composite indicators, in which several measures are combined, it is important to recognize that the final index may hide differences in the component variables—thus areas or countries with markedly different profiles of poverty may end up with a similar index value.

F6-1–F6-3. International Poverty Line (IPL): The World Bank has established two international poverty lines to permit meaningful comparison among nations with different economies and standards of living: $1.08 a day and $2.15 a day at 1993 international prices (equivalent to $1 and $2 in 1985 prices) adjusted to account for differences in purchasing power across countries. The $1 per person per day poverty line is also known as the extreme poverty line. The share and number of people living on less than $2 per day is a more relevant threshold for middle income economies such as those of East Asia and Latin America. These IPL measures are for consumption, not income; they show both the extent and depth of poverty. F6-1 presents percentage of population living on less than $1 and $2 a day. F6-2 and F6-3 show the regional distribution of poverty over time.

F7-1–F7-2. Child poverty in the industrial world: Not all children living in poverty are found in developing nations. One child out of six—or 47 million children—in the industrialized nations of the Organisation for Economic Co-operation and Development are poor. In many of these nations there is a vast income gap between "have" and "have not" children. F7-1 presents the percent of children living in relative poverty, defined as living in a household where income is less than half of the national median. The data in F7-2 contrast the after-tax household incomes of rich and poor families of four. In this table poor means poorer than 90 percent but richer than 10 percent of the poorest households in the country; rich means richer than 90 percent but poorer than 10 percent of the richest households.

F8-1–F8-2. Poverty and household composition: The shape of the household is an important factor in a child's economic well being. Children living in large households and children living with one parent, usually the mother, are at greater risk of poverty than those in small household or in two-parent families. F8-1 presents statistics on household size and poverty for 21 developing countries. Comparisons between countries in this table are not valid because the figures in the table are based on each nation's definition of poverty. There are very few data on the impact of single-parent homes on children and the data that are available (F8-2) are almost 10 years old. Nevertheless, those data are included here because single-parent families are increasing in the industrialized world.

F9-1. Minimum work age: This table presents the official or legal minimum working age in selected countries. The minimum age for basic work ranges from 12 to 16 years; the minimum age for hazardous work (work likely to jeopardize health, safety or morals) from 12 to 21 years. In reality many developing countries rarely observe these laws. Poor parents often push children out to work at very early ages to help support the family. In many developing Asian countries, children as young as four are pledged by their parents to factory owners in exchange for meager loans (sometimes less than $15). This debt is handed down through the generations; frequently children are placed in bonded labor because their grandparents never repaid their debts.

F10-1. Children's work places: Table F10 lists the economic areas that employ child labor in a selected group of countries. What it fails to show is that child labor almost always involves long hours under unhealthy conditions. Sometimes the work is backbreaking; often it is dangerous. In Tanzania children harvesting coffee and tea work for 60 hours each week under harsh conditions. Many Peruvian children toil in hot and acid-smelling brick-making factories. In Brazil children working on tobacco plantations suffer frequent snakebites; and in Mexico and the southwestern United States child laborers are often exposed to pesticides.

F11-1–F11-2. Size of child labor force: The child labor force includes children in paid employment as well as those self-employed, such as unpaid family workers. The International Labor Organization estimates that about 80 percent of children's work falls in the later category. The tables in this cluster present the labor force by country as percent of the total child population in two age cohorts, 1 to 14, and 15 to 19, engaged in the production of goods and services. The child labor force has been decreasing slowly over the past few decades, and as these indicators show, the International Labor Organization projects the numbers will decrease further.

F12-1–F12-2. Distribution of child labor: Child labor is not distributed evenly, even within the developing word. Instead, United Nations studies have shown that there is a close correlation between depth of poverty and child participation in the labor force. Participation is extremely high (30 to 60 percent) in areas with per capita income of $500 or less, but it declines quite rapidly, to 10 to 30 percent, in areas with incomes between $500 and $1,000. Table F12-1 gives the regional distribution of economically active children, while F12-2 presents figures for selected countries with high percentages of child labor.

F13-1. Youth unemployment: A country's youth unemployment rate is the number of youth seeking employment as a percentage of the total number of working and work-seeking youth. In every country, the youth unemployment rate is higher than the total unemployment rate. Teenage unemployment results in social and economic trauma at a personal, community, and national level. For young people, work is more than earning an income: It is a critical phase in the transition from dependent childhood to independent adulthood and a source of emotional and social well being. Many studies suggest that there is an association between unemployment and a decline in the psychological health of the teenage population. F13 presents teen unemployment in the context of total unemployment for nine industrial nations between 1994 and 1998. The statistics are not comparable among nations because of differences in the age-range definition of "teenage."

F1. GROSS DOMESTIC AND NATIONAL PRODUCT PER CAPITA

F1-1. Gross Domestic Product (GDP) per Capita, 1998

	$ U.S.
Albania	910
Algeria	1,580
Angola	620
Antigua and Barbuda	9,230
Argentina	8,250
Armenia	500
Australia	19,290
Austria	26,230
Azerbaijan	500
Bahamas, the	13,180
Bahrain	8,320
Bangladesh	340
Barbados	8,540
Belarus	2,200
Belgium	24,320
Belize	2,850
Benin	390
Bermuda	36,000
Bhutan	520
Bolivia	1,080
Botswana	3,120
Brazil	4,690
Brunei	15,410
Bulgaria	1,480
Burkina Faso	240
Burundi	140
Cambodia	250
Cameroon	610
Canada	19,160
Cape Verde	1,190
Central African Republic	300
Chad	230
Chile	5,310
China	770
Colombia	2,520
Comoros	370
Congo, Dem. Rep. (Zaire)	140
Congo, Rep.	700
Costa Rica	2,970
Côte d'Ivoire	760
Croatia	4,830
Cyprus	11,940
Czech Republic	5,480
Denmark	32,990
Djibouti	800
Dominica	3,420
Dominican Republic	1,920
Ecuador	1,510
Egypt	1,350
El Salvador	1,960
Equatorial Guinea	1,060
Eritrea	170
Estonia	3,590
Ethiopia	110
Fiji	2,000
Finland	23,970
France	24,250
French Polynesia	16,590
Gabon	4,680
Gambia, the	340
Georgia	940

F1-1. Gross Domestic Product (GDP) per Capita, 1998 *(continued)*

	$ U.S.
Germany	26,010
Ghana	410
Greece	11,480
Greenland	22,410
Grenada	3,570
Guatemala	1,750
Guinea	510
Guinea-Bissau	180
Guyana	850
Haiti	510
Honduras	870
Hong Kong, SAR (China)	24,890
Hungary	4,730
Iceland	28,810
India	440
Indonesia	460
Iran	1,830
Ireland	22,120
Israel	16,860
Italy	20,350
Jamaica	2,490
Japan	29,930
Jordan	1,620
Kazakhstan	1,410
Kenya	400
Kiribati	520
Kuwait	13,490
Kyrgyzstan	360
Laos	250
Latvia	2,610
Lebanon	4,090
Lesotho	390
Lithuania	2,900
Luxembourg	40,760
Macau	14,780
Macedonia, FYRO	1,240
Madagascar	260
Malawi	160
Malaysia	3,270
Maldives	1,400
Mali	250
Malta	9,210
Marshall Islands	1,620
Mauritania	390
Mauritius	3,620
Mexico	4,110
Micronesia	1,870
Moldova	380
Mongolia	400
Morocco	1,280
Mozambique	230
Namibia	1,860
Nepal	210
Netherlands, the	24,320
New Zealand	13,940
Nicaragua	420
Niger	200
Nigeria	340
Norway	32,920
Oman	6,500
Pakistan	480
Palau	6,990

F1-1. Gross Domestic Product (GDP) per Capita, 1998 *(continued)*

	$ U.S.
Panama	3,310
Papua New Guinea	810
Paraguay	1,650
Peru	2,530
Philippines	870
Poland	4,100
Portugal	10,700
Puerto Rico	12,440
Qatar	12,830
Romania	1,700
Russia	1,880
Rwanda	250
Samoa	1,040
Sao Tome and Principe	290
Saudi Arabia	6,210
Senegal	520
Seychelles	6,800
Sierra Leone	130
Singapore	26,670
Slovakia	3,780
Slovenia	9,850
Solomon Islands	720
South Africa	3,220
South Korea, Rep.	6,910
Spain	14,050
Sri Lanka	840
St. Kitts and Nevis	7,120
St. Lucia	4,010
St. Vincent and the Grenadines	2,790
Sudan	370
Suriname	820
Swaziland	1,230
Sweden	25,590
Switzerland	37,100
Syria	1,140
Tajikistan	350
Tanzania	250
Thailand	1,820
Togo	340
Tonga	1,750
Trinidad and Tobago	4,970
Tunisia	2,140
Turkey	3,130
Turkmenistan	500
Uganda	320
Ukraine	870
United Arab Emirates	17,340
United Kingdom	22,980
United States	30,450
Uruguay	6,260
Uzbekistan	850
Vanuatu	1,320
Venezuela	4,090
Vietnam	360
Yemen	260
Zambia	350
Zimbabwe	540

Source: World Bank; <http://www.worldbank.org/>, and Organization for Economic Co-operation and Development (OECD).

F1-2. Gross National Product (GNP) per Capita by Regions and Income Class, 1999

	$ U.S.
Luxembourg	42,930
Liechtenstein	A
Switzerland	38,380
Bermuda	A
Norway	33,470
Denmark	32,050
Japan	32,030
United States	31,910
San Marino	A
Iceland	29,540
Cayman Islands	A
Sweden	26,750
Germany	25,620
Austria	25,430
Monaco	A
Netherlands	25,140
Finland	24,730
Belgium	24,650
Hong Kong, China	24,570
Brunei*	24,620
France**	24,170
Singapore	24,150
United Kingdom	23,590
Ireland	21,470
Australia	20,950
Italy	20,170
Canada	20,140
United Arab Emirates*	17,870
French Polynesia	16,930
Israel	16,310
New Caledonia	15,160
Spain	14,800
New Zealand	13,990
Greece	12,110
Cyprus	11,950
Portugal	11,030
Slovenia	10,000
Malta	9,210
Antigua and Barbuda	8,990
Barbados	8,600
Korea, Rep.	8,490
Bahrain*	7,640
Argentina	7,550
Saudi Arabia*	6,900
Seychelles	6,500
St. Kitts and Nevis	6,330
Uruguay	6,220
Czech Republic	5,020
Trinidad and Tobago	4,750
Hungary	4,640
Chile	4,630
Croatia	4,530
Mexico	4,440
Brazil	4,350
Poland	4,070
St. Lucia	3,820
Slovakia	3,770
Lebanon	3,700

F1-2. Gross National Product (GNP) per Capita by Regions and Income Class, 1999 *(continued)*

	$ U.S.
Venezuela	3,680
Costa Rica	3,570
Mauritius	3,540
Grenada	3,440
Estonia	3,400
Malaysia	3,390
Gabon	3,300
Dominica	3,260
Botswana	3,240
South Africa	3,170
Panama	3,080
Turkey	2,900
Belize	2,730
Lithuania	2,640
St. Vincent and the Grenadines	2,640
Belarus	2,620
Jamaica	2,430
Latvia	2,430
Fiji	2,310
Russia	2,250
Colombia	2,170
Peru	2,130
Tunisia	2,090
Thailand	2,010
Dominican Republic	1,920
El Salvador	1,920
Namibia	1,890
Micronesia	1,830
Iran, Islamic Rep.	1,810
West Bank and Gaza	1,780
Tonga	1,730
Guatemala	1,680
Macedonia, FYRO	1,660
Suriname*	1,660
Jordan	1,630
Paraguay	1,560
Algeria	1,550
Romania	1,470
Bulgaria	1,410
Egypt	1,380
Ecuador	1,360
Swaziland	1,350
Cape Verde	1,330
Kazakhstan	1,250
Bosnia and Herzegovina	1,210
Maldives	1,200
Morocco	1,190
Vanuatu	1,180
Equatorial Guinea	1,170
Samoa	1,070
Philippines	1,050
Bolivia	990
Syria	970
Albania	930
Kiribati	910
Ukraine	840
Sri Lanka	820
Papua New Guinea	810

F1-2. Gross National Product (GNP) per Capita by Regions and Income Class, 1999 *(continued)*

	$ U.S.
Djibouti	790
China	780
Guyana	760
Honduras	760
Solomon Islands	750
Uzbekistan	720
Côte d'Ivoire	670
Turkmenistan	670
Georgia	620
Cameroon	600
Indonesia	600
Congo, Rep.	550
Lesotho	550
Zimbabwe	530
Bhutan	510
Senegal	500
Armenia	490
Guinea	490
Pakistan	470
Azerbaijan	460
Haiti	460
India	440
Moldova	410
Nicaragua	410
Ghana	400
Mauritania	390
Mongolia	390
Benin	380
Bangladesh	370
Vietnam	370
Kenya	360
Yemen	360
Comoros	350
Gambia, the	330
Sudan	330
Zambia	330
Uganda	320
Togo	310
Kyrgyzistan	300
Central African Republic	290
Laos	290
Tajikistan	280
Angola	270
São Tomé and Principe	270
Cambodia	260
Nigeria	260
Tanzania	260
Madagascar	250
Rwanda	250
Burkina Faso	240
Mali	240
Mozambique	220
Nepal	220
Chad	210
Eritrea	200
Niger	190
Malawi	180
Guinea-Bissau	160

F1-2. Gross National Product (GNP) per Capita by Regions and Income Class, 1999 *(continued)*

	$ U.S.
Sierra Leone	130
Burundi	120
Congo, Dem. Rep. (Zaire)*	100
Ethiopia	100

A 1999 data not available; ranking is approximate.
* Figures are the most recent estimate from 1997 or 1998.
** Data include French overseas departments.

Source: World Development Indicators 2001; <http://www.worldbank.org/data/databytopic/GNPPC.pdf >. Underlying data from World Bank.

F1-3. Gross National Product (GNP) per Capita, 1999

	$ U.S.
Low income	420
Middle income	1,980
Lower middle	1,200
Upper middle	4,870
Low & middle income	1,240
East Asia & Pacific	1,010
Europe & Central Asia	2,160
Latin America and Carribbean	3,800
Middle East & North Africa	2,060
South Asia	440
Sub-Saharan Africa	490
High income	26,440
European Monetary Union	22,250
World	5,020

Note: World Bank classifies countries into four categories—High income ($9,266 or more), Upper middle income ($2,996 to $9,265), Lower middle income ($756 to $2995), and Low income ($755 or less).

Source: World Development Indicators 2001; <http://www.worldbank.org/data/databytopic/GNPPC.pdf >. Underlying data from World Bank.

F2. INDEBTEDNESS

F2-1. External Debt per Capita, Developing Countries, 1970 to 1996

	1970 ($US)	1980 ($US)	1990 ($US)	1991 ($US)	1992 ($US)	1993 ($US)	1994 ($US)	1995 ($US)	1996 ($US)
Algeria	67	103	764	107	102	95	1,011	105	111
Argentina	242	96	832	188	204	208	1,901	222	262
Bangladesh	N/A	5	36	12	12	13	110	12	13
Brazil	60	58	474	78	83	91	752	93	107
Chile	318	109	921	144	141	150	1,285	175	189
China	N/A	0	4	5	6	7	51	8	11
Colombia	104	26	210	51	50	54	482	60	76
Côte d'Ivoire	N/A	90	627	139	145	144	1,327	123	131
Czech Republic	N/A	37	368	62	73	89	777	104	195
Egypt	54	45	341	57	53	51	533	52	48
Hungary	N/A	91	943	206	213	235	2,196	274	263
India	15	3	24	10	10	11	93	11	9
Indonesia	28	14	112	37	45	45	397	53	62
Iran	N/A	11	79	15	26	38	179	35	31
Malaysia	46	48	378	86	109	139	890	149	194
Mexico	132	84	677	121	127	146	1,245	150	162
Morocco	62	47	374	94	83	79	791	79	76
Nigeria	17	14	103	37	32	32	342	33	29
Pakistan	49	12	87	18	21	20	189	22	23
Peru	243	54	427	89	88	100	861	108	114
Philippines	57	34	268	46	48	52	455	55	54
Poland	N/A	25	233	129	126	117	1,386	110	106
Russia	0	3	30	40	53	75	458	82	85
South Africa	N/A	N/A	N/A	N/A	2	17	N/A	46	56
Sudan	N/A	27	195	54	55	55	513	55	52
Syria	N/A	40	282	130	140	142	1,297	136	133
Thailand	27	18	151	50	74	92	654	113	153
Turkey	77	42	341	86	97	116	842	108	126

Source: Handbook of International Economic Statistics, Central Intelligence Agency, Directorate of Intelligence, Table 13; <http://www.cia.gov/cia/di/products/hies/hiestabs.xls>. Underlying data from U.S. Bureau of the Census, International Data Base.

F2-2. Total External Debt as a Percentage of Gross National Product (GNP), late 1990s

	Percent
Afghanistan	N/A
Albania	28
Algeria	69
Angola	232
Argentina	39
Armenia	38
Australia	9
Austria	12
Azerbaijan	12
Bangladesh	35
Belarus	5
Belgium	0
Benin	77
Bhutan	27
Bolivia	68
Bosnia and Herzegovina	41
Botswana	11
Brazil	24
Bulgaria	101
Burkina Faso	54

F2-2. Total External Debt as a Percentage of Gross National Product (GNP), late 1990s *(continued)*

	Percent
Burundi	113
Cambodia	70
Cameroon	109
Canada	10
Central African Republic	88
Chad	65
Chile	42
China	17
Colombia	35
Congo, Dem. Rep. (Zaire)	232
Congo. Rep.	278
Costa Rica	38
Côte d'Ivoire	165
Croatia	35
Cuba	N/A
Czech Republic	42
Denmark	26
Dominican Republic.	29
Ecuador	87
Egypt	39
El Salvador	29
Eritrea	9
Estonia	14
Ethiopia	159
Finland	36
France	N/A
Gabon	96
Gambia, the	108
Georgia	28
Germany	19
Ghana	89
Greece	25
Guatemala	23
Guinea	95
Guinea-Bissau	366
Haiti	38
Honduras	103
Hungary	55
India	27
Indonesia	65
Iran	10
Iraq	N/A
Ireland	N/A
Israel	25
Italy	5
Jamaica	98
Japan	0
Jordan	117
Kazakhstan	19
Kenya	65
Kuwait	28
Kyrgyzstan	43
Laos	132
Latvia	9
Lebanon	33
Lesotho	52
Liberia	189
Libya	N/A

F2-2. Total External Debt as a Percentage of Gross National Product (GNP), late 1990s *(continued)*

	Percent
Lithuania	16
Macedonia, FYRO	71
Madagascar	119
Malawi	89
Malaysia	51
Mali	119
Mauritania	235
Mauritius	57
Mexico	38
Moldova	52
Mongolia	73
Morocco	59
Mozambique	249
Myanmar (Burma)	N/A
Namibia	2
Nepal	49
Netherlands, the	13
New Zealand	34
Nicaragua	306
Niger	86
Nigeria	85
North Korea, Dem. Rep.	N/A
Oman	34
Pakistan	47
Panama	75
Papua New Guinea	56
Paraguay	21
Peru	50
Philippines	53
Poland	29
Portugal	N/A
Romania	33
Russia	26
Rwanda	60
Saudi Arabia	15
Senegal	83
Sierra Leone	141
Singapore	0
Slovakia	52
Slovenia	12
Somalia	307
South Africa	20
South Korea, Rep.	33
Spain	12
Sri Lanka	51
Sudan	182
Sweden	37
Switzerland	0
Syria	126
Tajikistan	45
Tanzania	1
Thailand	63
Togo	93
Trinidad and Tobago	39
Tunisia	63
Turkey	47
Turkmenistan	63
Uganda	56

F2-2. Total External Debt as a Percentage of Gross National Product (GNP), late 1990s (continued)

	Percent
Ukraine	18
United Arab Emirates	28
United Kingdom	6
United States	16
Uruguay	33
Uzbekistan	11
Venezuela	42
Vietnam	89
Yemen	77
Yugoslavia	N/A
Zambia	185
Zimbabwe	58

Source: The Progress of Nations, 1999, United Nations Children's Fund (UNICEF); <http://www.unicef.org/pon99/>. Underlying data from *Global Development Finance 1999* and *World Bank Atlas 1999,* World Bank; and IMF, *Government Finance Statistics Yearbook, 1998.*

F2-3. Central Government Expenditure on Debt Services, Selected Countries, various years

	Year(s)	% of central government expenditures on debt services
Belize	1996	6
Benin	1997	11
Bolivia	1997	10
Brazil	1995	20
Burkina Faso	1997	10
Cameroon	1996-97	36
Chile	1996	3
Colombia	1997	8
Costa Rica	1996	13
Côte d'Ivoire	1994-96	35
Dominican Republic	1997	10
El Salvador	1996	27
Honduras	1992	21
Jamaica	1996	31
Kenya	1995	40
Malawi	1997	40
Namibia	1996-97	3
Nepal	1997	15
Nicaragua	1996	14
Niger	1995	33
Philippines	1992	31
South Africa	1996-97	8
Sri Lanka	1996	22
Tanzania	1994-95	46
Thailand	1997	1
Uganda	1994-95	9
Zambia	1997	40

Sources: The Progress of Nations, 1999, United Nations Children's Fund (UNICEF); <http://www.unicef.org/pon99/>. Underlying data from *Country Experiences in Assessing the Adequacy, Equity and Efficiency of Public Spending on Basic Social Services,* October 1998, and unpublished documents, United Nations Development Programme (UNDP).

F2-4. Heavily Indebted Poor Countries Initiative (HIPC) Countries, December 2000

Angola*
Bolivia
Burkina Faso
Burundi*
Cameroon
Central African Republic*
Chad
Congo, Dem. Rep. (Zaire)*
Congo, Rep.*
Côte d'Ivoire
Equatorial Guinea
Ethiopia**
Ghana
Guinea
Guinea-Bissau*
Guyana
Honduras
Kenya
Laos
Liberia*
Madagascar
Mali
Mauritania
Mozambique
Myanmar (Burma)*
Nicaragua
Niger
Rwanda*
Sao Tome and Principe
Sierra Leone*
Somalia*
Sudan
Tanzania
Togo
Uganda
Vietnam
Yemen
Zambia

*Countries affected by some kind of conflicts.
**Cessation of hostilities signed on June 18, 2000. A peace agreement was signed with Eritrea on December 13, 2000.

Source: The Progress of Nations, 1999, United Nations Children's Fund (UNICEF) <http://www.unicef.org/pon99/debtdat2.htm> and *Poverty Trends and Voices of the Poor,* World Bank, December 2000 <http://www.worldbank.org/hipc/Grouping_Final.xls>.

F3. OFFICIAL DEVELOPMENT ASSISTANCE (ODA)

F3-1. Official Development Assistance (ODA) Inflow and ODA Inflow as a Percentage of Recipient GNP, 1997

	Million $US	% of recipient GNP
Afghanistan	279	5
Albania	155	7
Algeria	248	1
Angola	436	14
Antigua and Barbuda	4	1
Argentina	222	0
Armenia	168	8
Azerbaijan	182	5
Bahamas, the	4	0
Bahrain	84	2
Bangladesh	1,009	2
Barbados	3	0
Belize	14	2
Benin	225	10
Bhutan	70	8
Bolivia	717	9
Bosnia and Herzegovina	863	N/A
Botswana	125	2
Brazil	487	0
Brunei	4	0
Burkina Faso	370	13
Burundi	119	13
Cambodia	372	12
Cameroon	501	6
Cape Verde	110	25
Central African Republic	92	8
Chad	225	13
Chile	136	0
China	2,040	0
Colombia	274	0
Comoros	28	11
Congo	268	14
Congo, Dem. Rep. (Zaire)	168	3
Cook Islands	10	16
Costa Rica	0	0
Côte d'Ivoire	444	4
Croatia	44	0
Cuba	67	1
Cyprus	30	0
Djibouti	87	N/A
Dominica	14	6
Dominican Republic	76	1
Ecuador	172	1
Egypt	1,947	2
El Salvador	294	3
Equatorial Guinea	24	5
Eritrea	123	15
Ethiopia	637	10
Fiji	44	2
Gabon	40	1
Gambia, the	40	10
Georgia	246	6
Ghana	493	7
Grenada	8	3

F3-1. Official Development Assistance (ODA) Inflow and ODA Inflow as a Percentage of Recipient GNP, 1997 *(continued)*

	Million $US	% of recipient GNP
Guatemala	302	2
Guinea	382	9
Guinea-Bissau	125	47
Guyana	272	40
Haiti	332	11
Honduras	308	7
India	1,678	0
Indonesia	832	0
Iran	196	0
Iraq	281	N/A
Israel	2,217	2
Jamaica	71	2
Jordan	462	5
Kazakhstan	131	1
Kenya	457	5
Kiribati	16	22
Kuwait	6	0
Kyrgyzstan	240	11
Laos	341	17
Lebanon	239	2
Lesotho	93	7
Liberia	95	7
Libya	9	0
Macedonia, FYRO	149	7
Madagascar	838	22
Malawi	350	16
Malaysia	-241	0
Maldives	26	8
Mali	455	16
Malta	22	1
Marshall Islands	63	65
Mauritania	250	22
Mauritius	42	1
Mexico	108	0
Micronesia	96	44
Moldova	63	3
Mongolia	248	25
Morocco	462	1
Mozambique	963	36
Myanmar (Burma)	45	0
Namibia	166	5
Nauru	3	N/A
Nepal	414	8
Nicaragua	421	21
Niger	341	17
Nigeria	202	1
Niue	5	N/A
North Korea, Dem. Rep.	202	1
Oman	20	0
Pakistan	597	1
Palau	39	N/A
Panama	124	1
Papua New Guinea	349	8
Paraguay	116	1
Peru	488	1
Philippines	689	1
Qatar	3	0

F3-1. Official Development Assistance (ODA) Inflow and ODA Inflow as a Percentage of Recipient GNP, 1997 *(continued)*

	Million $US	% of recipient GNP
Rwanda	592	43
Saint Kitts and Nevis	7	3
Saint Lucia	24	5
Saint Vincent and Grenadines	6	2
Samoa	28	14
Sao Tome and Principe	33	81
Saudi Arabia	15	0
Senegal	427	9
Seychelles	15	3
Sierra Leone	130	18
Singapore	16	0
Slovenia	97	0
Solomon Islands	42	12
Somalia	104	10
South Africa	497	0
South Korea, Rep.	-160	0
Sri Lanka	345	2
Sudan	187	2
Suriname	77	14
Swaziland	27	2
Syria	199	1
Tajikistan	101	5
Tanzania	963	14
Thailand	626	0
Togo	124	8
Tonga	28	16
Trinidad and Tobago	33	1
Tunisia	194	1
Turkey	-1	0
Turkmenistan	11	0
Tuvalu	10	N/A
Uganda	840	12
United Arab Emirates	8	0
Uruguay	57	0
Uzbekistan	130	1
Vanuatu	27	11
Venezuela	28	0
Vietnam	997	4
Yemen	366	8
Yugoslavia	97	N/A
Zambia	618	19
Zimbabwe	327	4

Source: The State of the World's Children, 2000: Table 6. Economic indicators; <http://www.unicef.org/sowc00/stat4.htm>. Underlying data from United Nations Children's Fund (UNICEF).

F3-2. Official Development Assistance as Percent of Donor Nations' GNP, Total Aid, Aid Per Person and Change in Aid Per Person, Selected Countries, 1990–1998

	ODA as % of donor nations' GNP, 1990	ODA as % of donor nations' GNP, 1998	Total aid, 1998 (billion US $)	Aid per person, 1998 (US $)	Change per person, 1990–1998 (US $)
Australia	0.34	0.27	1.0	52	0
Austria	0.25	0.22	0.5	56	-1
Belgium	0.46	0.35	0.9	87	-13
Canada	0.44	0.29	1.7	55	-22
Denmark	0.94	0.99	1.7	323	83
Finland	0.65	0.32	0.4	77	-64
France	0.6	0.4	5.7	98	-36
Germany	0.42	0.26	5.6	68	-22
Ireland	0.16	0.3	0.2	54	37
Italy	0.31	0.2	2.3	40	-19
Japan	0.31	0.28	10.6	84	0
Luxembourg	0.21	0.65	0.1	265	194
Netherlands, the	0.92	0.8	3.0	194	11
New Zealand	0.23	0.27	0.1	34	5
Norway	1.17	0.91	1.3	299	29
Portugal	0.25	0.24	0.3	26	7
Spain	0.2	0.24	1.4	35	11
Sweden	0.91	0.72	1.6	177	-36
Switzerland	0.32	0.32	0.9	123	1
United Kingdom	0.27	0.27	3.9	66	11
United States	0.21	0.1	8.8	32	-22
Average/Total	0.33	0.24	51.9	63	-12

Note: Amounts in 1998 dollars.

Source: The Progress of Nations, 2000, United Nations Children's Fund (UNICEF); <http://www.unicef.org/pon00/>. Underlying data from *Development Co-operation* "1995 and 1999 reports" Organisation for Economic Co-operation and Development (OECD); and *World Population Prospects, 1998 revision,* Population Division, United Nations (UN).

F4. SPENDING FOR BASIC SOCIAL SERVICES

F4-1. Percent of Central Government Expenditure on Basic Social Services and Debt Service, Selected Countries, various years

	Year(s)	% of central government expenditure on basic social services	% of central government expenditure on debt services
Belize	1996	20	6
Benin	1997	10	11
Bolivia	1997	17	10
Brazil	1995	9	20
Burkina Faso	1997	20	10
Cameroon	1996-97	4	36
Chile	1996	11	3
Colombia	1997	17	8
Costa Rica	1996	13	13
Côte d'Ivoire	1994-96	11	35
Dominican Republic	1997	9	10
El Salvador	1996	13	27
Honduras	1992	13	21
Jamaica	1996	10	31
Kenya	1995	13	40
Malawi	1997	8	40
Namibia	1996-97	19	3
Nepal	1997	14	15

F4-1. Percent of Central Government Expenditure on Basic Social Services and Debt Service, Selected Countries, various years *(continued)*

	Year(s)	% of central government expenditure on basic social services	% of central government expenditure on debt services
Nicaragua	1996	9	14
Niger	1995	20	33
Philippines	1992	8	31
South Africa	1996-97	14	8
Sri Lanka	1996	13	22
Tanzania	1994-95	15	46
Thailand	1997	15	1
Uganda	1994-95	21	9
Zambia	1997	7	40

Sources: *The Progress of Nations, 1999*, United Nations Children's Fund (UNICEF); <http://www.unicef.org/pon99/>. Underlying data from *Country Experiences in Assessing the Adequacy, Equity and Efficiency of Public Spending on Basic Social Services*, October 1998, and unpublished documents, United Nations Development Programme (UNDP).

F4-2. Percent of Total Aid Spent on Basic Social Services, various years

	Year	%
Benin	1996	18
Bolivia	1996	8
Burkina Faso	1996	18
Cameroon	1996	8
Côte d'Ivoire	1994	9
Kenya	1995	20
Mali	1996	23
Namibia	1996	30
Nicaragua	1996	15
Niger	1995	18
Peru	1996	5
Sri Lanka	1996	5
Tanzania	1996	10
Uganda	1996	16
Viet Nam	1996	5
Zambia	1996	13

Sources: *The Progress of Nations, 1999*, United Nations Children's Fund (UNICEF), <http://www.unicef.org/pon99/>. Underlying data from *Country Experiences in Assessing the Adequacy, Equity and Efficiency of Public Spending on Basic Social Services*, October 1998, and unpublished documents, United Nations Development Programme (UNDP).

F5. HUMAN POVERTY INDEX (HPI)

F5-1. Human Poverty Index (HPI-1) for Developing Countries, 1998

Rank		Value
1	Uruguay	3.9
2	Costa Rica	4.0
3	Cuba	4.6
4	Chile	4.7
5	Trinidad and Tobago	5.1
6	Fiji	8.4
7	Jordan	8.8
8	Panama	8.9
9	Bahrain	9.6
10	Guyana	10.0
11	Colombia	10.4
12	Mexico	10.4
13	Lebanon	10.8
14	Mauritius	11.6
15	Venezuela	12.4
16	Jamaica	13.4
17	Qatar	13.7
18	Malaysia	14.0
19	Libya	15.3
20	Dominican Republic	15.4
21	Brazil	15.6
22	Philippines	16.1
23	Paraguay	16.4
24	Turkey	16.4
25	Peru	16.5
26	Ecuador	16.8
27	Bolivia	17.4
28	United Arab Emirates	17.9
29	Thailand	18.7
30	China	19.0
31	Iran	19.2
32	Syria	19.3
33	South Africa	20.2
34	El Salvador	20.2
35	Sri Lanka	20.3
36	Tunisia	21.9
37	Cape Verde	22.0
38	Oman	22.7
39	Honduras	23.3
40	Lesotho	23.3
41	Nicaragua	24.2
42	Algeria	24.8
43	Maldives	25.4
44	Namibia	26.6
45	Swaziland	27.4
46	Indonesia	27.7
47	Vietnam	28.2
48	Botswana	28.3
49	Guatemala	29.2
50	Tanzania	29.2
51	Kenya	29.5
52	Zimbabwe	30.0
53	Myanmar	31.4
54	Congo, Rep.	31.9
55	Egypt	32.3
56	Iraq	32.9

F5-1. Human Poverty Index (HPI-1) for Developing Countries, 1998 *(continued)*

Rank		Value
57	Comoros	33.0
58	India	34.6
59	Ghana	35.4
60	Sudan	35.5
61	Rwanda	37.5
62	Nigeria	37.6
63	Togo	37.8
64	Zambia	37.9
65	Morocco	38.4
66	Cameroon	38.5
67	Uganda	39.7
68	Pakistan	40.1
69	Malawi	41.9
70	Bangladesh	43.6
71	Haiti	45.2
72	Côte d 'Ivoire	45.8
73	Senegal	47.9
74	Benin	48.8
75	Gambia, the	49.0
76	Yemen	49.4
77	Mauritania	49.7
78	Guinea-Bissau	50.2
79	Mozambique	50.7
80	Nepal	51.3
81	Mali	51.4
82	Central African Republic	53.0
83	Ethiopia	55.3
84	Burkina Faso	58.4
85	Niger	64.7

Source: Human Development Report 2000; <http://www.undp.org/hdr2000/english/presskit/hpi-1.pdf>. Underlying data from United Nations Development Programme (UNDP).

F5-2. Human Poverty Index (HPI-2) for Developed Countries, 1998

Rank		Value
1	Uruguay	3.9
1	Norway	7.3
2	Sweden	7.6
3	Netherlands, the	8.2
4	Finland	8.6
5	Denmark	9.3
6	Germany	10.4
7	Luxembourg	10.5
8	France	11.1
9	Japan	11.2
10	Spain	11.6
11	Canada	11.8
12	Italy	11.9
13	Australia	12.2
14	Belgium	12.4
15	New Zealand	12.8
16	United Kingdom	14.6
17	Ireland	15.0
18	United States	15.8

Source: Human Development Report 2000; <http://www.undp.org/hdr2000/english/presskit/hpi-1.pdf>. Underlying data from United Nations Development Programme (UNDP).

F6. INTERNATIONAL POVERTY LINE (IPL)

F6-1. International Poverty Line: People Surviving on $1 and $2 per Day, various years

	Survey year	Population below $1 per day (%)	Population below $2 per day (%)
Albania	1995	less than 2	15.1
Bangladesh	1996	29.1	77.8
Belarus	1998	less than 2	less than 2
Bolivia	1990	11.3	38.6
Botswana	1985-86	33.3	61.4
Brazil	1997	5.1	17.4
Bulgaria	1995	less than 2	7.8
Burkina Faso	1994	61.2	85.8
Central African Republic	1993	6.6	84.0
Chile	1994	4.2	20.3
China	1998	18.5	53.7
China	1996	11.0	28.7
Costa Rica	1996	9.6	26.3
Côte d'Ivoire	1995	12.3	49.4
Czech Republic	1993	less than 2	less than 2
Dominican Republic	1996	3.2	16.0
Ecuador	1995	20.2	52.3
Egypt	1995	3.1	52.7
El Salvador	1996	25.3	51.9
Estonia	1995	4.9	17.7
Ethiopia	1995	31.3	76.4
Gambia, the	1992	53.7	84.0
Guatemala	1989	39.8	64.3
Honduras	1996	40.5	68.8
Hungary	1993	less than 2	4.0
India	1997	44.2	86.2
Indonesia	1999	15.2	66.1
Jamaica	1996	3.2	25.2
Jordan	1997	less than 2	7.4
Kazakhstan	1996	1.5	15.3
Kenya	1994	26.5	62.3
Latvia	1998	less than 2	8.3
Lesotho	1993	43.1	65.7
Lithuania	1996	less than 2	7.8
Madagascar	1993	60.2	88.8
Mali	1994	72.8	90.6
Mauritania	1995	3.8	22.1
Mexico	1995	17.9	42.5
Moldova	1992	7.3	31.9
Mongolia	1995	13.9	50.0
Morocco	1990-91	less than 2	7.5
Mozambique	1996	37.9	78.4
Namibia	1993	34.9	55.8
Nepal	1995	37.7	82.5
Nicaragua	1993	3.0	18.1
Niger	1995	61.4	85.3
Nigeria	1997	70.2	90.8
Pakistan	1996	31.0	84.7
Panama	1997	10.3	25.1
Paraguay	1995	19.4	38.5
Peru	1996	15.5	41.4
Poland	1993	5.4	10.5
Portugal	1994	less than 2	less than 2
Romania	1994	2.8	27.5
Russia	1998	7.1	25.1

F6-1. International Poverty Line: People Surviving on $1 and $2 per Day, various years (*continued*)

	Survey year	Population below $1 per day (%)	Population below $2 per day (%)
Rwanda	1983-85	35.7	84.6
Senegal	1995	26.3	67.8
Sierra	1989	57.0	74.5
Singapore	1992	less than 2	less than 2
Slovak Republic	1993	less than 2	less than 2
Slovenia	1993	11.5	35.8
South Korea, Rep.	1993	less than 2	less than 2
Spain	1995	6.6	45.4
Tanzania	1993	19.9	59.7
Thailand	1998	less than 2	28.2
Trinidad and Tobago	1992	12.4	39.0
Tunisia	1990	less than 2	11.6
Turkey	1994	2.4	18.0
Turkmenistan	1993	20.9	59.0
Uganda	1992	36.7	77.2
Ukraine	1996	less than 2	23.7
Uruguay	1989	less than 2	6.6
Uzbekistan	1993	3.3	26.5
Venezuela	1996	14.7	36.4
Yemen	1998	5.1	35.5
Zambia	1996	72.6	91.7
Zimbabwe	1990-91	36.0	64.2

Source: World Development Indicators, 2000: Table 2.7; <http://www.worldbank.org/data/wdi2000/pdfs/tab2_7.pdf>. Underlying data from World Bank.

F6-2. Population Living on Less Than $2 Per Day and Headcount Index* in Developing and Transitional Economies, Selected Years, 1987–1998

Regions	Population covered by at least one survey (percent)	1990 Number	1990 Percent	1993 Number	1993 Percent	1996 Number	1996 Percent	1998 (est.) Number	1998 (est.) Percent
East Asia and the Pacific (with China)*	90.8	1084.4	66.1	1035.8	60.5	863.9	48.6	892.2	49.1
East Asia and the Pacific (excluding China)	71.1	284.9	57.3	271.6	51.6	236.3	42.8	260.1	45.0
Eastern Europe and Central Asia	81.7	43.8	9.6	79.4	17.2	92.7	19.9	92.9	19.9
Latin America and the Caribbean	88.0	167.2	38.1	162.2	35.1	179.8	37.0	182.9	36.4
Middle East and North Africa	52.5	58.7	24.8	61.7	24.1	60.6	22.2	62.4	21.9
South Asia	97.9	976.0	86.8	1017.8	85.4	1069.5	85.0	1095.9	84.0
Sub-Saharan Africa	72.9	388.2	76.4	427.8	77.8	457.7	76.9	474.8	75.6
World Total	**88.1**	**2718.4**	**61.7**	**2784.8**	**60.1**	**2724.1**	**56.1**	**2801.0**	**56.0**
World Total (excluding China)**	84.2	1918.8	58.8	2020.5	58.6	2096.5	57.7	2168.9	57.6

*The headcount index is the percentage of the population below the poverty line.

**Because of the enormous number of people in China, counts are given with and without inclusion of China.

Note: The numbers are estimated from those countries in each region for which at least one survey was available during the period 1985–98. These surveys can include: Household Living Standards Survey (LSMS); Household Income and Expenditures Surveys; Family Budget Surveys; and Household Consumption Surveys.

Source: World Development Report (WDR) on Poverty and Development 2000/01: Table 2; <http://www.worldbank.org/poverty/data/trends/income.htm>. Underlying data from World Bank.

F6-3. Population Living on Less Than $1 per Day and Headcount Index* in Developing and Transitional Economies, Selected Years, 1987–1998

Regions	Population covered by at least one survey (percent)	Number of people living on less than $1 a day (millions) 1990	Headcount index* (percent) 1990	Number of people living on less than $1 a day (millions) 1993	Headcount index* (percent) 1993	Number of people living on $1 a day (millions) 1996	Headcount index* (percent) 1996	Number of people living on less than $1 a day (millions) 1998 (est.)	Headcount index* (percent) 1998 (est.)
East Asia and the Pacific (with China)**	90.8	452.4	27.6	431.9	25.2	265.1	14.9	278.3	15.3
East Asia and the Pacific (excluding China)**	71.1	92.0	18.5	83.5	15.9	55.1	10.0	65.1	11.3
Eastern Europe and Central Asia	81.7	7.1	1.6	18.3	4.0	23.8	5.1	24.0	5.1
Latin America and the Caribbean	88.0	73.8	16.8	70.8	15.3	76.0	15.6	78.2	15.6
Middle East and North Africa	52.5	5.7	2.4	5.0	1.9	5.0	1.8	5.5	1.9
South Asia	97.9	495.1	44.0	505.1	42.4	531.7	42.3	522.0	40.0
Sub-Saharan Africa	72.9	242.3	47.7	273.3	49.7	289.0	48.5	290.9	46.3
World Total	88.1	1276.4	29.0	1304.3	28.1	1190.6	24.5	1198.9	24.0
World Total (excluding China)**	84.2	915.9	28.1	955.9	27.7	980.5	27.0	985.7	26.2

*The headcount index is the percentage of the population below the poverty line.

**Because of the enormous number of people in China, counts are given with and without inclusion of China.

Notes: The numbers are estimated from those countries in each region for which at least one survey was available during the period 1985–98. These surveys can include: Household Living Standards Survey (LSMS); Household Income and Expenditures Surveys; Family Budget Surveys; and Household Consumption Surveys.

Source: World Development Report (WDR) on Poverty and Development 2000/01: Table 1; <http://www.worldbank.org/poverty/data/trends/income.htm>. Underlying data from World Bank.

F7. CHILD POVERTY IN THE INDUSTRIAL WORLD

F7-1. Children Living in Relative* Poverty in OECD Countries, late 1990s

	Percent
Mexico	26.2
United States	22.4
Italy	20.5
United Kingdom	19.8
Turkey	19.7
Ireland	16.8
Canada	15.5
Poland	15.4
Australia	12.6
Greece	12.3
Spain	12.3
Japan	12.2
Germany	10.7
Hungary	10.3
France	7.9
Netherlands, the	7.7
Czech Republic	5.9
Denmark	5.1
Luxembourg	4.5
Belgium	4.4
Finland	4.3
Norway	3.9
Sweden	2.6

* Relative poverty is defined here as living in a household where income is less than half of the national median.

Source: The Progress of Nations, 2000, United Nations Children's Fund (UNICEF); <http://www.unicef.org/pon00/>. Underlying data from, *A league table of child poverty in rich nations,* Innocenti Report Card No.1, UNICEF Innocenti Research Centre, UNICEF.

F7-2. Gap Between Rich and Poor Children, Selected Countries, early 1990s

	Annual household income (in US $)**—Poor child	Annual household income (in US$)—Rich child
Australia	11,510	19,860
Austria	14,320	39,910
Belgium	16,680	47,260
Canada	13,660	56,170
Denmark	17,270	46,330
Finland	17,300	41,990
France	13,000	44,840
Germany, West*	15,260	51,870
Ireland	6,690	27,190
Israel	7,870	33,390
Italy	12,550	44,280
Luxembourg	15,400	50,070
Netherlands, the	14,580	42,260
Norway	16,580	43,830
Sweden	18,830	46,150
Switzerland	18,830	59,500
United Kingdom	11,580	43,930
United States	10,920	65,540

* Before unification of Germany.
**All figures are in 1991 dollars, with other currencies converted using adjustments for national differences in purchasing power.

Source: The Progress of Nations 1996, United Nations Children's Fund (UNICEF); Chart adapted from The New York Times 14 August 1995, citing Luxembourg Income Study data; <http://www.unicef.org/pon96/ingap.htm>. Underlying data from United Nations Children's Fund (UNICEF).

F8. POVERTY AND HOUSEHOLD COMPOSITION

F8-1. Number of Children in Poor and Non-Poor Households, Selected Countries, 1998

Country	Household/family characteristic	Number of children in poor households	Number of children in non-poor households	Number of children in all households
Argentina	Number of children under 15	3.0	0.4	1.3
Bolivia	Number of children under 15	3.4	1.3	2.3
Brazil	Number of children under 15	3.6	0.8	1.8
Chile	Number of children under 15	2.5	0.9	1.5
Costa Rica	Number of children under 15	3.3	1.0	2.0
Ecuador	Number of children under 15	3.4	1.4	2.9
El Salvador	Number of children under 15	3.7	1.1	2.4
Guyana	Number of children under 17	2.6	1.4	1.8
Honduras	Number of children under 15	4.2	1.7	3.1
Indonesia	Number of children under 9	1.7	N/A	1.2
Mexico	Number of children under 15	4.0	1.1	2.3
Nepal	Number of children under 14	3.5	2.5	N/A
Nicaragua	Number of children under 15	4.9	1.8	3.3
Panama	Number of children under 15	3.2	0.8	1.9
Paraguay	Number of children under 15	4.3	1.3	2.8
Peru	Number of children under 15	3.7	1.1	2.4
Uruguay	Number of children under 15	2.8	0.5	1.2
Malawi	Household size	5.4	4.2	5.0
Mali	Household size	11.5	9.2	10.4
Philippines	Household size	6.0	5.0	N/A
Tanzania	Household size	7.2	5.0	6.0

N/A   Not Available
Note: The poor and the non-poor households have been defined at the national level.

Source: Poverty Reduction Begins with Children UNICEF; <http://www.unicef.org/pubsgen/poverty/povred.pdf> and <http://www.unicef.org/pubsgen/poverty/>. Underlying data from Inter-American Development Bank (1998) and various poverty assessments reports by the World Bank.

F8-2. Percent of Children Living Below the Poverty Line,* Two-Parent Family and Solo Mother Family, 1990–1992

	Children in two-parent family (percent)	Children in solo mother family (percent)
Sweden	2.2	5.2
Denmark	2.5	7.3
Finland	1.9	7.5
Belgium	3.2	10
Italy	9.5	13.9
Norway	1.9	18.4
Netherlands, the	3.1	39.5
Canada	7.4	50.2
Australia	7.7	56.2
United States	11.1	59.5

*The poverty line is defined as 50% of national median income after taxes and transfers.

Source: The Progress of Nations 1996, United Nations Children's Fund (UNICEF); <http://www.unicef.org/pon96/ingap.htm>. Underlying data from Luxembourg Income Study, Working Paper No. 127.

F9. MINIMUM WORK AGE

F9-1. Minimum Ages for Work, 1990s

	Ratification of ILO Convention No. 138, Date and Year	Minimum Age—Basic Work	Minimum Age—Hazardous Work	Comments
Bangladesh	**	12 to 15	12 to 18	Basic and hazardous ages apply only to certain occupations.
Brazil	**	14	18 to 21	Basic age exempts apprentices.
Egypt	**	14	15 to 17	Children 12-14 can participate in seasonal agricultural work.
Guatemala	4/1/90	14	16	Children 12-13 can work with Ministry of Labor approval.
India	**	14	14 to 18	Basic and hazardous ages apply only to certain occupations.
Kenya	4/1/79	16	16 to 18	Basic age applies only to industrial undertakings.
Mexico	**	14	16 to 18	
Nepal	5/1/97	14	16	Basic age applies only to certain enterprises.
Nicaragua	11/1/81	14	18	
Pakistan	**	14	14 to 21	Basic and hazardous ages apply only to certain occupations.
Peru	**	12 to 16	18	Basic age varies by sector.
Philippines	6/1/98	15	18	
South Africa	**	15	18	
Tanzania	*	12 to 15	18	Basic age is 12; 15 for industry.
Thailand	**	15	18	
Turkey	*	15	18	

* Country ratified Convention No. 138. However, the official instrument of ratification has not been registered with the ILO.
** Country has not ratified ILO convention Number 138.

Source: By the Sweat & Toil of Children (Volume V), Efforts to Eliminate Child Labor; <http://www.dol.gov/dol/ilab/public/media/reports/iclp/sweat5/chap3.htm#Table III-1>. Underlying data from U.S. Department of Labor.

F10. CHILDREN'S WORK PLACES

F10-1. Sample of Children's Work Places, 1990s

Country	Agriculture and Fishing	Manufacturing, Mining and Quarrying	Services
Bangladesh	Shrimp and other seafood; tobacco	*Bidis* (cigarettes); garments	Bakeries and confectioneries; carpentry; commercial sex workers; communications; domestic servants; hotels; porters; restaurants; small retail shops; street vendors; transport workers
Brazil	Animal husbandry; cocoa; coffee; cotton; dairy farms; fishing; fruits and vegetables (e.g. apples; bananas; beans; Brazil nuts; cassava; corn; garlic; grapes; guava; oranges and other citrus fruits; peanuts; pineapple; potatoes; rice; tomatoes; watermelon); poultry; rubber; sisal; sugar cane; tea; tobacco; tree resin	Ceramics; charcoal; crates; electronics; footwear; furniture; garments; handicrafts; leather tanning; metallurgy; plastics; rock salt; sawmills/wood-pulp; stone quarrying; textiles; tin-ore and gold mining	Auto repair; bakeries; car washers; commercial sex workers; construction; domestic servants; drug trafficking; garbage pickers; messengers/delivery boys; newspaper delivery; parking garage guards; retail shops; shoeshines; small businesses; street vendors; wood delivery
Egypt	Cotton; jasmine	Bricks; carpets; footwear; handicrafts; leather tanning; plastics; textiles	Auto repair; domestic servants; garbage collection; scavengers; shop assistants; small workshops; street vendors
Guatemala	Beans; broccoli; cardamom; coffee; cotton; flowers; macadamia nuts; melons; raspberries; snow peas; sugar cane; tea	Bricks; fireworks; lime extracting; stone quarrying	Car washers; commercial sex workers; construction; domestic servants; scavengers; shoeshines; stonemasons; street vendors
India	Animal husbandry; *cinchona* (quinine); cardamom; cashew nuts; coffee; fishing; forestry; rubber; small scale agriculture; tea; tobacco	Aluminum; base metals; *bidis* (cigarettes); brassware; bricks; cardboard boxes; carpets; fireworks; footwear; garments and textiles; gemstones; glass; jewelry; leather tanning; locks; matches; mining; packaging and manufacturing workshops; seafood processing; silk; slates; soccer balls and other sporting goods; stainless steel silverware; stone breaking; stone quarrying; synthetic jewels; tiles	Auto repair; bakeries; bus/taxi conductors; cement recyclers; commercial sex workers; construction; domestic servants; flower shops; hotels; rag pickers; railway porters; restaurants; rickshaw pullers; shoeshines; street barbers; street vendors; tea shops
Kenya	Animal husbandry; coffee; corn; dairy products; fishing; pineapples; rice; sisal; sugar cane; tea; wheat	Mining; salt harvesting; soapstone carving; stone quarrying	Bus/taxi conductors; commercial sex workers; domestic servants; scavengers; street vendors; tourism
Mexico	Coffee; fruits and vegetables (e.g. broccoli; cucumbers; eggplant; grapes; onions; peppers snow-peas; strawberries; tomatoes); tobacco	Apparel; bricks; fireworks; footwear; traditional handicrafts	Auto repair shops; bars; cafes; car washers; cashiers; commercial sex workers; construction; domestic servants; drug trafficking; grocery packers; hawkers; public markets; shoeshines; small workshops; street performers; street vendors; trash collectors; windshield wipers
Nepal	Animal husbandry; small-scale agriculture; tea	Baskets; bricks; carpets; garments; iron smithing; mining; pottery; stone quarrying; stone breaking; wood products	Bakeries; bus/taxi conductors; commercial sex workers; construction; domestic servants; hotels; porters; restaurants; sewing; tea shops; transportation; weaving
Nicaragua	Animal husbandry; bananas; beans; coffee; corn; cotton; fishing; forestry; rice; sugar; tobacco	Rock breaking	Cargo loaders; car washers; cemetery assistants; commercial sex workers; domestic servants; scavengers; shoeshines; small shops; stevedores; street vendors; vehicle guards
Pakistan	Fishing; small-scale agriculture; tobacco	Bricks; carpets; footwear; furniture; garments; handicrafts; leather tanning; paper and packaging; power looms; soccer balls and other sporting goods; stone/brick crushing; surgical instruments	Auto and engineering workshops; commercial sex workers; construction; domestic servants; scavengers; shop assistants; tailoring
Peru	Asparagus; coca; coffee; cotton; fruit; rice; shrimp	Bricks; fireworks; gold mining; *moralla* (dehydrated potatoes) processing; pumice stone; stone quarrying	Bus/taxi conductors; car washers; commercial sex workers; domestic servants; leaflet distributors; market workers; messengers; street entertainers; street vendors; scavengers; vehicle guards
Philippines	Fishing; forestry/ logging; fruits and vegetables (e.g. corn); palm plantations; poultry farms; rattan; rice; seaweed; sugar cane	Charcoal production; coconut processing; cooking oil; fireworks; fish packing/processing; food products; garments and embroidery; gold mining; handicrafts; mat-weaving/sewing; metal working; print shops; sardine factory; stone quarrying; wood and rattan/buri/bamboo furniture; wood products	Bars; car guards; car washers; catering; commercial sex workers; construction; cooks; dancers; domestic servants; entertainers; gas stations; grocery/bakeshops; janitors; newspapers sales; porters; receptionists; restaurants; stevedores; street vendors; wholesale/retail trade
South Africa	Corn; fruits and vegetables; sugar cane; tobacco	Bricks; textiles	Car parkers; car washers; coal carriers; catering; commercial sex workers; corner cafes; domestic servants; retail shops; taxi fare collectors
Tanzania	Animal husbandry; cloves; coffee; corn; green algae (seaweed); fishing; pyrethrum; rubber; sisal; sugar cane; tea; tobacco; wheat	Cotton ginning; fish processing; gemstones; mining; sawmills; stone crushing; stone quarrying	Auto repair; bars; cafes; carpentry; car washers; commercial sex workers; domestic servants; markets; restaurants; scavengers; shoeshines; small shops; street vendors; tourism
Thailand	Fishing; garlic; lychee; onions; rubber; shrimp and other seafood; sugar cane	Artificial flowers; candy wrapping; dolls; embroidery; fishing net production; footwear; garments; gems; glass; leather; paper cups; plastic products; rattan and wood furniture; shrimp and seafood processing; silver jewelry	Bakeries; car washers; commercial sex workers construction; delivery boys/porters; domestic servants; gas stations; *karaoke*; mechanical repair shops; restaurants; retail shops; street vendors
Turkey	Animal husbandry; corn; cotton; fruits and vegetables (e.g. apricots, figs, lemons, nuts, oranges, raisins); tea; tobacco; wheat	Auto parts manufacturing; bricks; carpets; cement; footwear/leather; garments; metal industry; textiles	Auto repair; commercial sex workers; domestic servants; hotels; scavengers; shoeshines; street vendors; tourism; windshield washers

Source: By the Sweat & Toil of Children (Volume V), Efforts to Eliminate Child Labor, 1998; <http://www.dol.gov/dol/ilab/public/media/reports/iclp/sweat5/appendixc.htm>. Underlying data from U.S. Department of Labor.

F11. SIZE OF CHILD LABOR FORCE

F11-1. Children Age 10–14 in Labor Force as Percentage of Total Children in the Age Group, 1970, 1980, 1990, 2000, 2010

	1970	1980	1990	2000	2010
Afghanistan	29.18	27.92	26.32	24.18	22.07
Albania	4.84	3.59	1.91	0.31	0.00
Algeria	11.44	7.06	3.26	0.00	0.00
Angola	31.37	29.74	28.10	26.08	24.33
Argentina	8.89	7.77	6.65	2.40	0.00
Armenia	0.00	0.00	0.00	0.00	0.00
Australia	1.23	0.00	0.00	0.00	0.00
Austria	3.62	0.00	0.00	0.00	0.00
Azerbaijan	0.00	0.00	0.00	0.00	0.00
Bahamas, the	2.64	0.00	0.00	0.00	0.00
Bahrain	3.50	0.00	0.00	0.00	0.00
Bangladesh	40.83	34.79	32.46	27.74	23.73
Barbados	2.09	0.00	0.00	0.00	0.00
Belarus	0.00	0.00	0.00	0.00	0.00
Belgium	0.63	0.00	0.00	0.00	0.00
Belize	5.06	1.00	2.88	1.87	1.21
Benin	34.44	30.28	28.56	26.47	24.53
Bhutan	65.81	62.51	59.18	51.05	42.96
Bolivia	21.08	18.94	17.36	11.35	5.30
Bosnia and Herzegovina	4.33	0.66	0.04	0.00	0.00
Botswana	32.29	25.88	19.44	14.39	9.99
Brazil	20.33	19.02	17.80	14.43	10.95
Brunei	7.51	0.00	0.00	0.00	0.00
Bulgaria	0.65	0.44	0.00	0.00	0.00
Burkina Faso	75.14	70.89	58.70	43.46	28.20
Burundi	50.79	49.99	49.42	48.50	47.60
Cambodia	27.48	26.56	25.59	23.74	21.97
Cameroon	38.87	33.92	27.53	22.96	18.38
Canada	1.62	0.00	0.00	0.00	0.00
Cape Verde	17.34	16.04	14.71	13.55	12.27
Central African Republic	45.05	39.41	33.77	28.57	23.38
Chad	41.88	41.61	39.98	36.64	33.29
Chile	2.95	0.32	0.00	0.00	0.00
China	39.03	30.48	15.24	7.86	0.00
Colombia	14.43	11.79	7.21	6.02	5.10
Comoros	45.84	44.70	40.94	37.56	34.18
Congo, Dem. Rep. (Zaire)	36.50	33.23	30.53	28.60	26.91
Congo, Rep.	28.29	27.47	26.64	25.41	24.21
Costa Rica	10.84	9.73	6.82	4.13	2.59
Côte d'Ivoire	34.60	28.44	22.26	18.65	15.63
Croatia	1.85	0.07	0.00	0.00	0.00
Cuba	1.48	0.00	0.00	0.00	0.00
Cyprus	6.10	3.81	0.00	0.00	0.00
Czech Republic	1.91	0.00	0.00	0.00	0.00
Denmark	0.81	0.00	0.00	0.00	0.00
Dominican Republic	31.57	24.77	19.01	13.22	7.32
Ecuador	15.80	9.49	6.54	4.31	2.09
Egypt	23.57	18.33	13.21	9.25	4.50
El Salvador	17.80	17.11	16.58	13.71	10.84
Equatorial Guinea	42.72	40.42	35.81	32.00	28.28
Eritrea	46.13	43.79	40.82	38.42	36.01
Estonia	0.00	0.00	0.00	0.00	0.00
Ethiopia	48.51	46.32	43.47	41.10	38.79
Fiji	8.38	5.27	0.00	0.00	0.00
Finland	0.55	0.00	0.00	0.00	0.00
France	2.59	0.00	0.00	0.00	0.00
Gabon	35.57	29.08	22.66	14.07	5.48
Gambia, the	45.89	44.39	40.15	33.83	27.95
Georgia	0.00	0.00	0.00	0.00	0.00

F11-1. Children Age 10–14 in Labor Force as Percentage of Total Children in the Age Group, 1970, 1980, 1990, 2000, 2010 (continued)

	1970	1980	1990	2000	2010
Germany	1.11	0.00	0.00	0.00	0.00
Ghana	16.29	16.22	14.55	12.00	9.44
Greece	10.00	4.59	0.00	0.00	0.00
Guatemala	24.23	18.99	18.26	14.18	10.08
Guinea	43.31	41.15	36.98	31.09	25.20
Guinea-Bissau	45.19	43.36	40.38	36.73	33.07
Guyana	2.90	1.98	0.00	0.00	0.00
Haiti	41.50	32.86	27.82	22.78	18.08
Honduras	18.92	14.20	9.89	7.14	4.36
Hong Kong, SAR (China)	6.48	5.97	0.00	0.00	0.00
Hungary	1.60	0.44	0.35	0.00	0.00
Iceland	1.44	0.00	0.00	0.00	0.00
India	25.46	21.44	16.68	12.07	7.46
Indonesia	18.52	13.49	11.30	7.82	4.33
Iran	19.54	13.58	6.83	2.58	0.00
Iraq	16.49	11.21	3.65	2.23	0.00
Ireland	2.25	1.22	0.00	0.00	0.00
Israel	1.26	0.00	0.00	0.00	0.00
Italy	4.12	1.55	0.43	0.33	0.27
Jamaica	0.55	0.45	0.21	0.00	0.00
Japan	1.92	0.00	0.00	0.00	0.00
Jordan	6.11	3.88	1.39	0.00	0.00
Kazakhstan	0.00	0.00	0.00	0.00	0.00
Kenya	44.96	45.05	43.37	39.17	34.96
Kuwait	4.68	0.00	0.00	0.00	0.00
Kyrgyzstan	0.00	0.00	0.00	0.00	0.00
Laos	33.01	31.03	29.05	25.36	21.67
Latvia	0.00	0.00	0.00	0.00	0.00
Lebanon	6.23	4.78	0.00	0.00	0.00
Lesotho	30.92	27.71	23.52	20.73	17.97
Liberia	31.08	25.72	21.84	15.39	8.93
Libya	12.79	8.67	0.49	0.00	0.00
Lithuania	0.00	0.00	0.00	0.00	0.00
Luxembourg	1.02	0.00	0.00	0.00	0.00
Macau	7.71	7.22	0.00	0.00	0.00
Macedonia, FYRO	4.31	0.83	0.05	0.02	0.02
Madagascar	41.73	40.19	37.59	34.07	30.98
Malawi	50.70	45.22	38.87	31.49	24.09
Malaysia	8.38	7.97	3.99	2.33	0.00
Maldives	30.10	23.14	7.67	3.81	0.00
Mali	62.49	61.19	57.93	51.13	44.35
Malta	2.15	1.38	1.13	0.00	0.00
Mauritania	33.32	29.58	25.84	22.10	18.35
Mauritius	5.75	4.84	3.98	2.00	0.00
Mexico	10.28	9.46	8.59	4.88	1.16
Moldova	5.14	3.28	0.00	0.00	0.00
Mongolia	4.23	3.53	2.45	1.35	0.00
Morocco	21.55	20.93	10.56	0.64	0.00
Mozambique	40.67	39.49	35.19	32.41	29.61
Myanmar (Burma)	29.72	27.91	26.07	22.94	19.79
Namibia	40.15	33.57	25.99	17.37	8.72
Nepal	63.10	55.56	48.26	42.07	35.79
Netherlands, the	1.72	0.00	0.00	0.00	0.00
New Zealand	0.05	0.00	0.00	0.00	0.00
Nicaragua	22.86	19.30	15.99	12.00	7.96
Niger	48.80	47.79	46.77	43.57	40.35
Nigeria	30.80	29.22	27.60	23.91	20.22
North Korea, Dem. Rep.	5.58	2.79	0.00	0.00	0.00
Norway	0.05	0.00	0.00	0.00	0.00
Oman	9.49	5.55	1.00	0.00	0.00
Pakistan	25.17	22.88	20.11	15.39	10.63
Panama	8.01	5.85	4.53	2.50	0.00

F11-1. Children Age 10–14 in Labor Force as Percentage of Total Children in the Age Group, 1970, 1980, 1990, 2000, 2010 *(continued)*

	1970	1980	1990	2000	2010
Papua New Guinea	39.02	27.62	21.53	17.18	13.21
Paraguay	16.98	14.56	9.91	5.84	1.77
Peru	5.01	4.45	3.16	1.80	1.06
Philippines	17.65	14.10	10.64	5.44	0.00
Poland	0.57	0.00	0.00	0.00	0.00
Portugal	13.35	7.89	2.37	1.19	0.00
Qatar	4.42	0.00	0.00	0.00	0.00
Romania	0.70	0.41	0.33	0.00	0.00
Russia	0.00	0.00	0.00	0.00	0.00
Rwanda	43.28	42.52	42.09	41.35	40.63
Saudi Arabia	9.25	4.53	0.00	0.00	0.00
Senegal	46.92	42.92	35.41	27.30	19.19
Sierra Leone	21.74	19.42	17.08	13.90	11.31
Singapore	3.44	1.71	0.00	0.00	0.00
Slovakia	1.91	0.00	0.00	0.00	0.00
Slovenia	4.33	0.01	0.00	0.00	0.00
Solomon Islands	41.74	39.56	33.56	24.23	14.88
Somalia	39.88	37.66	34.50	31.30	28.19
South Africa	2.71	0.86	0.00	0.00	0.00
South Korea, Rep.	9.37	0.36	0.00	0.00	0.00
Spain	5.29	0.00	0.00	0.00	0.00
Sri Lanka	5.63	0.00	2.86	2.00	0.00
Sudan	34.06	33.32	31.36	27.41	23.49
Suriname	0.71	0.55	0.49	0.42	0.38
Swaziland	19.13	17.20	15.27	12.25	9.06
Sweden	0.50	0.00	0.00	0.00	0.00
Switzerland	0.20	0.00	0.00	0.00	0.00
Syria	16.15	13.89	9.21	2.35	0.00
Tajikistan	0.00	0.00	0.00	0.00	0.00
Tanzania	45.57	42.84	42.06	36.90	31.73
Thailand	30.20	25.21	20.23	12.21	4.95
Togo	40.42	36.12	30.38	26.82	23.68
Trinidad and Tobago	1.30	0.55	0.00	0.00	0.00
Tunisia	12.19	5375.00	0.00	0.00	0.00
Turkey	28.25	20.52	16.02	7.78	2.29
Turkmenistan	0.00	0.00	0.00	0.00	0.00
Uganda	50.38	48.85	46.83	43.78	40.74
Ukraine	0.00	0.00	0.00	0.00	0.00
United Arab Emirates	6.68	0.00	0.00	0.00	0.00
United Kingdom	0.02	0.00	0.00	0.00	0.00
United States	1.76	0.00	0.00	0.00	0.00
Uruguay	6.60	4.17	3.15	1.00	0.00
Uzbekistan	0.00	0.00	0.00	0.00	0.00
Venezuela	6.06	4.09	1.90	0.00	0.00
Vietnam	26.27	21.78	13.01	5.21	0.00
Yemen	27.80	26.45	21.57	18.74	15.98
Yugoslavia	5.13	0.37	0.02	0.00	0.00
Zambia	21.11	18.99	16.92	15.61	14.49
Zimbabwe	41.06	36.73	31.83	27.04	22.47

Source: STAT Working papers, Economically active population 1950–2010, Six volumes, 1997. Underlying data from International Labour Office of the International Labour Organization (ILO), Bureau of Statistics.

F11-2. Children Age 15–19 in Labor Force as Percentage of Total Children in the Age Group, 1970, 1980, 1990, 2000, 2010

	1970	1980	1990	2000	2010
Afghanistan	56.59	54.64	52.16	48.54	45.04
Albania	51.91	43.99	40.57	37.86	35.33
Algeria	34.08	28.85	24.03	21.74	20.00
Angola	79.17	77.43	75.68	74.12	72.62
Argentina	47.12	44.03	41.16	38.12	35.13
Armenia	29.51	31.47	26.57	24.16	22.15
Australia	66.38	63.36	59.72	53.05	46.38
Austria	62.79	58.05	49.51	41.71	33.86
Azerbaijan	31.47	35.23	28.88	26.35	24.25
Bahamas, the	50.53	41.11	37.26	31.42	25.48
Bahrain	24.17	19.55	16.93	14.60	12.60
Bangladesh	66.72	64.52	61.86	59.33	56.61
Barbados	51.75	49.72	39.46	35.86	32.38
Belarus	36.61	33.20	25.08	23.20	21.57
Belgium	34.01	23.68	10.84	10.11	9.50
Belize	50.21	47.25	39.99	38.24	36.06
Benin	78.57	59.94	56.60	50.81	45.83
Bhutan	79.53	75.67	71.79	66.81	61.89
Bolivia	48.18	44.17	42.87	41.12	39.65
Bosnia and Herzegovina	46.83	23.07	20.36	18.86	15.75
Botswana	60.95	52.50	44.04	39.80	36.31
Brazil	53.42	54.85	56.72	55.80	54.50
Brunei	28.99	26.70	19.01	16.93	14.91
Bulgaria	31.66	29.72	23.79	17.31	12.92
Burkina Faso	85.06	82.27	77.33	71.31	65.61
Burundi	86.45	85.07	84.07	82.47	80.93
Cambodia	63.67	63.06	61.59	60.51	59.45
Cameroon	60.41	53.96	50.74	47.43	44.14
Canada	41.89	55.16	57.06	49.04	41.01
Cape Verde	55.84	56.26	58.19	54.18	49.77
Central African Republic	78.23	69.13	60.00	56.21	52.68
Chad	65.67	64.83	63.98	62.45	60.93
Chile	32.07	28.25	25.78	23.28	21.26
China	77.92	76.58	67.03	58.63	20.21
Colombia	36.85	34.18	37.03	35.81	34.70
Comoros	59.66	58.29	56.97	55.59	54.20
Congo, Dem. Rep. (Zaire)	64.55	60.74	57.68	54.44	51.56
Congo, Rep.	46.32	47.39	47.86	46.39	44.93
Costa Rica	45.68	43.70	42.85	39.09	35.30
Côte d'Ivoire	58.32	54.42	50.53	47.86	45.39
Croatia	38.64	22.22	20.27	18.79	17.54
Cuba	40.62	32.73	26.50	24.03	22.05
Cyprus	47.86	46.68	46.23	43.47	40.57
Czech Republic	40.12	29.03	33.46	29.31	26.08
Denmark	62.19	61.16	68.32	57.99	47.66
Dominican Republic	43.30	39.82	37.42	34.61	32.16
Ecuador	44.23	38.80	38.07	34.78	31.81
Egypt	42.24	35.95	32.32	29.51	27.83
El Salvador	48.89	46.77	45.23	42.23	38.72
Equatorial Guinea	60.53	58.94	56.35	54.45	52.59
Eritrea	70.10	67.92	66.25	63.87	61.53
Estonia	39.11	30.57	29.22	24.76	20.39
Ethiopia	62.19	60.08	58.43	56.75	55.04
Fiji	38.42	36.50	40.24	36.20	32.14
Finland	45.76	39.68	35.73	30.45	25.69
France	40.59	21.80	10.58	9.45	8.53
Gabon	63.08	60.03	55.71	52.21	48.87
Gambia, the	71.87	69.87	66.07	62.62	59.15
Georgia	32.02	34.10	28.26	25.66	23.52
Germany	64.86	54.31	42.39	34.23	26.04
Ghana	55.78	54.01	50.91	46.35	41.79
Greece	40.91	33.31	22.93	20.38	18.43

F11-2. Children Age 15–19 in Labor Force as Percentage of Total Children in the Age Group, 1970, 1980, 1990, 2000, 2010 *(continued)*

	1970	1980	1990	2000	2010
Guatemala	51.58	49.06	49.09	45.84	42.26
Guinea	77.15	73.64	67.36	63.20	59.03
Guinea-Bissau	62.35	61.11	59.83	58.57	57.31
Guyana	46.53	44.45	41.55	39.36	37.00
Haiti	65.62	50.53	42.15	40.22	38.46
Honduras	50.89	47.13	44.01	42.92	42.10
Hong Kong, SAR (China)	53.28	42.40	31.87	25.43	17.94
Hungary	58.64	53.61	47.47	42.33	37.23
Iceland	60.04	59.90	50.27	43.67	37.07
India	64.11	51.95	47.61	44.39	41.21
Indonesia	47.24	44.43	41.99	38.58	35.54
Iran	40.14	34.88	32.64	30.50	28.99
Iraq	30.79	25.00	17.84	15.57	13.73
Ireland	51.77	43.45	25.76	22.88	20.63
Israel	35.74	27.63	23.24	19.84	17.04
Italy	50.22	37.89	29.55	25.91	23.09
Jamaica	54.52	45.94	36.11	30.51	25.80
Japan	35.76	18.82	18.79	15.81	13.65
Jordan	31.99	24.21	19.53	17.35	15.85
Kazakhstan	37.45	35.14	29.79	26.57	23.84
Kenya	73.76	73.31	71.43	67.55	63.67
Kuwait	25.62	20.76	11.84	10.32	9.06
Kyrgyzstan	33.22	34.03	26.61	23.87	21.65
Laos	79.41	78.19	76.89	73.26	69.60
Latvia	37.65	32.24	30.74	25.56	20.42
Lebanon	28.67	27.44	28.65	27.90	27.32
Lesotho	52.34	48.61	45.31	42.35	39.36
Liberia	53.95	51.35	45.84	41.53	37.61
Libya	34.74	29.52	23.30	20.94	19.03
Lithuania	30.97	24.25	23.40	20.64	18.51
Luxembourg	53.93	46.34	29.04	25.46	22.67
Macau	48.59	57.26	38.08	34.01	30.65
Macedonia, FYRO	41.11	24.80	19.89	18.09	16.59
Madagascar	67.02	64.94	61.44	58.88	56.31
Malawi	68.37	65.65	62.69	59.52	56.51
Malaysia	42.82	40.65	36.76	33.39	29.97
Maldives	65.73	64.47	56.39	52.58	49.34
Mali	76.77	75.56	72.64	68.06	63.47
Malta	46.39	45.62	37.65	34.01	29.91
Mauritania	67.59	64.06	60.23	56.95	53.65
Mauritius	41.33	39.15	38.38	36.26	34.46
Mexico	42.80	42.50	43.92	41.97	39.99
Moldova	47.97	38.81	28.55	25.12	22.43
Mongolia	71.66	66.20	58.72	51.99	45.45
Morocco	47.51	46.68	44.14	38.17	32.13
Mozambique	71.41	70.50	66.75	64.57	62.38
Myanmar	70.87	68.32	65.83	61.30	56.82
Namibia	58.96	61.06	43.16	39.11	35.77
Nepal	76.38	67.52	62.88	56.45	49.70
Netherlands, the	48.76	40.36	42.91	37.78	33.01
New Zealand	58.67	56.42	54.02	49.75	46.49
Nicaragua	45.00	44.00	45.32	42.79	40.16
Niger	77.05	75.91	74.78	72.74	70.70
Nigeria	56.66	53.80	51.06	47.32	43.61
North Korea, Dem. Rep.	53.10	42.89	30.85	24.49	19.45
Norway	40.82	38.28	34.90	30.40	26.50
Oman	32.21	25.57	18.31	15.52	13.46
Pakistan	48.02	45.87	43.10	40.65	39.07
Panama	46.41	33.43	33.71	31.30	29.18
Papua New Guinea	69.22	64.86	59.98	56.12	52.48
Paraguay	55.00	53.16	45.68	42.34	39.50
Peru	32.28	28.19	25.06	21.49	18.26

F11-2. Children Age 15–19 in Labor Force as Percentage of Total Children in the Age Group, 1970, 1980, 1990, 2000, 2010 *(continued)*

	1970	1980	1990	2000	2010
Philippines	42.33	39.11	35.91	33.33	31.20
Poland	43.19	38.80	29.00	26.50	24.43
Portugal	61.50	65.67	45.75	40.39	34.83
Qatar	34.83	22.03	14.15	11.45	10.29
Romania	53.82	35.06	35.62	30.73	27.02
Russia	40.43	34.90	27.40	24.09	21.30
Rwanda	87.07	85.59	84.72	83.28	81.89
Saudi Arabia	38.00	29.31	23.45	15.54	9.78
Senegal	65.52	63.28	61.04	58.11	55.15
Sierra Leone	48.17	46.17	44.14	41.54	39.22
Singapore	48.49	47.99	28.47	21.43	14.41
Slovakia	36.80	30.92	34.05	30.18	27.10
Slovenia	46.85	30.95	23.48	21.86	20.48
Solomon Islands	81.80	80.52	77.23	69.61	61.96
Somalia	66.09	62.98	61.08	58.50	55.99
South Africa	53.36	47.64	41.25	36.76	32.75
South Korea, Rep.	43.61	34.13	16.13	13.69	11.26
Spain	49.96	39.48	30.13	26.25	23.34
Sri Lanka	37.63	32.10	29.14	26.80	24.75
Sudan	46.86	44.63	41.96	40.20	38.67
Suriname	27.30	22.63	22.29	21.24	20.20
Swaziland	49.16	44.37	39.57	37.71	36.18
Sweden	47.33	44.11	39.33	33.53	29.22
Switzerland	61.21	54.41	52.78	45.23	37.83
Syria	41.38	37.93	33.48	31.02	28.99
Tajikistan	38.43	39.52	29.97	26.67	23.70
Tanzania	78.75	74.32	73.07	69.83	66.65
Thailand	75.96	72.03	68.13	62.28	56.44
Togo	58.71	57.48	54.53	52.94	51.34
Trinidad and Tobago	38.00	37.95	29.99	27.56	25.07
Tunisia	42.55	47.42	39.13	36.49	33.95
Turkey	63.41	59.90	57.48	52.68	48.10
Turkmenistan	42.10	40.23	34.90	30.60	26.31
Uganda	80.79	78.66	77.44	73.78	70.12
Ukraine	43.59	35.76	26.78	23.42	20.81
United Arab Emirates	45.62	27.89	15.05	11.43	8.90
United Kingdom	65.63	56.63	59.76	48.69	37.62
United States	40.81	46.31	43.40	38.86	34.31
Uruguay	46.86	41.37	42.24	36.67	31.16
Uzbekistan	39.84	37.98	30.58	27.23	24.37
Venezuela	37.78	35.94	33.26	30.96	29.01
Vietnam	75.95	76.45	70.30	52.21	34.08
Yemen	42.42	41.21	38.74	36.82	35.22
Yugoslavia	35.48	28.09	22.19	21.14	20.19
Zambia	68.71	67.13	65.81	64.01	62.13
Zimbabwe	54.59	52.08	49.57	48.34	47.17

Source: STAT Working papers, Economically active population 1950–2010, Six volumes, 1997. Underlying data from International Labour Office of the International Labour Organization (ILO), Bureau of Statistics.

F12. DISTRIBUTION OF CHILD LABOR

F12-1. Distribution and Labor Force Participation Rates of Children (10–14 Years), by Region, mid-1990s

Region	Working children (1,000s)	Percent of world's total working children	Percent of children in total labor force
Eastern Asia	22,448	31.60	32.9
Southern Asia	20,143	28.40	24.2
Eastern Africa	7,965	11.20	23.9
Western Africa	5,785	8.20	21.6
South-Eastern Asia	5,587	7.90	20.0
South America	3,485	4.90	14.0
Middle Africa	1,848	2.60	12.8
Western Asia	1,109	1.60	11.1
Central America	1,022	1.40	10.3
Northern Africa	982	1.40	6.8
Caribbean	216	0.30	6.7
Melanesia	147	0.20	5.8
Southern Africa	100	0.10	4.8
Southern Europe	84	0.10	4.6
Eastern Europe	4	0.00	0.8
Polynesia	1	0.00	0.1
Northern Europe	1	0.00	0.0
Australia and New Zealand	0	0.00	0.0
Western Europe	0	0.00	0.0
Micronesia	0	0.00	0.0
North America	0	0.00	0.0
Asia	49,287	69.50	15.3
Africa	16,680	23.50	22.0
Americas	4,723	6.70	7.9
Oceania	148	0.20	6.9
Europe	89	0.10	0.3
World	70,927	100.00	13.7

Source: Child Labor: Issues and Directions for the World Bank, Annex, World Bank; <http://wbln0018.worldbank.org/HDNet/HDdocs.nsf/ f879b8f845ed3915852566500051f549/1bc81c2e1b5234fc852566b1000c47f7?OpenDocument>. Underlying data from the World Bank.

F12-2. Total Number and Percent of Child Laborers in the Child Population, Selected Countries, various years

Country	Age Range	Number of Children in Age Range (in millions)	Estimated Number of Child Workers in Age Range (in thousands)	Percentage of Children in Age Range Working
Bangladesh	5 to 14	34.5	6,584	19.1
Brazil	5 to 14	33.9	4,349	12.8
Egypt	6 to 14	10.9	1,309	12.0
Guatemala	7 to 14	3.7	152	4.1
India	5 to 14	210.0	11,285	5.4
Kenya	10 to 14	3.8	1,558	41.3
Mexico	12 to 14	6.6	1,137	17.3
Nepal	5 to 14	6.2	2,596	41.7
Nicaragua	10 to 14	0.6	60	9.9
Pakistan	5 to 14	40.0	3,313	8.0
Peru	6 to 14	4.8	196	4.1
Philippines	5 to 14	17.5	1,863	10.6
South Africa	10 to 14	4.6	200	4.3
Tanzania	10 to 14	3.9	1,523	39.5
Thailand	6 to 14	5.6	1,495	12.6
Turkey	6 to 14	11.9	1,495	12.6

Note: While total population estimates are for 1996, child labor data are from various years.

Source: By the Sweat & Toil of Children (Volume V), Efforts to Eliminate Child Labor, 1998; <http://www.dol.gov/dol/ilab/public/media/reports/iclp/sweat5/ chap2.htm#Table II-1>. Underlying data from U.S. Department of Labor.

F13. YOUTH UNEMPLOYMENT

F13-1. Civilian Teenage Unemployment Rates in Percent by Age, Selected Countries, 1994–1998

Age Group	Canada	Australia	Japan	France	Germany	Italy	Sweden	United Kingdom	United States
1994									
All working ages	10.4	9.7	2.9	12.8	8.5	11.3	9.6	9.6	6.1
Under 25 years	16.5	17.3	5.5	29.1	8.5	32.4	23	16.2	12.5
Teenagers (*)	18.9	23	7.7	36.9	6	37	25	18.6	17.6
20-24 years	15	13.8	5	27.9	9.4	30.8	22.4	14.9	9.7
1995									
All working ages	9.5	8.5	3.2	12	8.2	12	9.1	8.6	5.6
Under 25 years	15.6	15.4	6.2	27.4	8.4	33.8	19.9	15.3	12.1
Teenagers (*)	18.5	20.6	8.4	30.9	7	37.2	21.1	17.3	17.3
20-24 years	13.7	12	5.7	26.8	9	32.6	19.5	14.2	9.1
1996									
All working ages	9.7	8.6	3.4	12.6	8.9	12.1	9.9	8.2	5.4
Under 25 years	16.1	15.7	6.7	27.8	9.4	33.9	21.4	14.7	12
Teenagers (*)	20.1	20.8	9.3	32.1	7.7	36.8	22.8	17.8	16.7
20-24 years	13.6	12.3	6.2	27.1	10.1	33.3	21	13	9.3
1997									
All working ages	9.2	8.6	3.4	12.8	9.9	12.3	10.1	7.1	4.9
Under 25 years	16.7	16.3	6.7	29.3	10.5	33.7	21.4	13.5	11.3
Teenagers (*)	21.8	20.6	9.3	33.7	8.7	36.5	24.5	N/A	16
20-24 years	13.6	13.4	6.2	28.5	11.3	32.8	20.4	N/A	8.5
1998									
All working ages	8.3	8	4.1	12.2	9.4	12.3	8.4	6.1	4.5
Under 25 years	15.2	15.2	7.8	26.5	9.7	33.6	17.2	12.3	10.4
Teenagers (*)	20	20	10.9	N/A	8.3	37	21.2	N/A	14.6
20-24 years	12.3	11.9	7.2	N/A	10.4	32.5	15.9	N/A	7.9

N/A Not Available.

(*) 16-to-19-year-olds in the United States, France, Sweden and the United Kingdom; 15-to-19-year-olds in Canada, Australia, Japan, and Italy.

Source: Comparative Civilian Labor Force Statistics Ten Countries 1959–1998, Table 9; <ftp://ftp.bls.gov/pub/special.requests/ForeignLabor/flslforc.txt>. Underlying data from U.S. Department of Labor, Bureau of Labor Statistics, Office of Productivity and Technology.

G. Family, Social Environment and Behavior

GENERAL OVERVIEW

This section outlines some of the most basic dimensions of a child's world. It opens with two composite indicators, the Human Development Index and the Child Risk Measure, which international agencies use to obtain a broad view of a society's achievement in key areas of a child's life and to assess overall risks for children. The next clusters deal with the family and child care alternatives. These are followed by sets of indicators on sexual behavior and marriage. The final groupings deal with behavior, primarily food habits, and leisure activities.

Despite the importance of many of the topics in this section, the data available are extremely limited. This is particularly true of indictors outlining behaviors. For example, the international community is increasingly concerned about adolescent sexual behavior in light of the AIDs epidemic, yet data on sexual activity exists for only a few industrialized nations. We know little about children's daily lives, even in developed nations, and nothing about daily life in the developing world. In part, the lack of statistics on behavior reflects the international community's traditional focus on collecting information needed to ensure child survival. Nevertheless, it is also a reflection of the fact that, until recently, the community did not regard childrens' behavior as significant. The WHO Regional Office for Europe has compiled some of the most comprehensive data available. We have relied on this study for a large portion of the behavioral material in this section. It is important to remember, however, that researchers cannot generalize from this data, even about other sections of the developed world.

EXPLANATION OF INDICATORS

G1-1. Human Development Index (HDI): The HDI, developed by the United Nations Development Programme, measures the average achievements in a country in three basic dimensions—health, education, and living standard. A composite index, it contains three variables—life expectancy at birth, educational attainment, and Gross Domestic Product GDP per capita. Its value ranges from 0 to 1. The HDI value for a country shows the distance that it has already covered towards the maximum possible value of 1.

G2-1. The Child Risk Measure (CRM): UNICEF created the CRM in 1999 to quantify the risks children face in different societies until age 18. It is a composite of five factors: under-five mortality rate, percent of children moderately or severely underweight, percent of primary school age children not attending school, HIV/AIDS prevalence rate for 15- to 49-year-olds, and armed conflict prevalence. A higher rating represents higher risk. UNICEF included statistics on AIDS and armed conflict in the measure so that the CRM would reflect both present and future risk.

G3-1–G3-2. Households: Although household statistics deal only indirectly with children, they are indicators of the social environment in which children live. G3-1 presents the average number of persons living in a household; G3-2 offers statistics on type of household for nine industrial countries. A household is defined as all the people who are current residents of a housing unit, such as a house, an apartment, a mobile home, or a group of rooms. Households are classified as "married-couple, with or without children," "single parent," "one person," or "other." The last category includes two or more families living together or any other group of related or unrelated people who share living arrangements.

G4-1. Average family size: A family consists of a householder and one or more other people living in the same household who are related to the householder by birth, marriage, or adoption.

G5-1. Children living away from parents: In many developing countries, large numbers of adolescents, especially those from rural areas, do not live with their biological parents. Instead, they live with relatives or family friends in nearby cities because parents think the children will have better access to education and work. Unfortunately, this arrangement can led to abuse or mistreatment. UN studies have indicated that children living away from their parents work longer hours, have lower school enrollment ratio, and have higher rates of morbidity and mortality than siblings who remain at home. In sub-Saharan Africa, girls are very likely to end up as household servants,

G6-1. Foster care and foster children: Foster care is defined as giving or receiving a home and parental care, and upbringing, usually on a short-term basis, of children who are unrelated by blood or adoption. Foster care is provided for children whose natural parents are dead, absent, or unfit or unable to look after them. As in the previous section, data collected by UNICEF is limited to the former Soviet bloc. Foster children frequently face the same problems as those in institutions.

G7-1–G7-2. Institutional and state care: With the fall of Communism in the late 1980s, the West became aware of the plight of Eastern Bloc children in poorly staffed and maintained state facilities. These children live in large-scale institutions, such as infant homes, orphanages, homes for the disabled, and hospitals. Children under institutional or state care carry risks of high death rates, disabilities, emotional harm, and the withering of family ties. They also lack access to a full range of educational opportunities and have limited opportunities for play and recreation. G7-1 surveys the rate of infants age 0–3 per 1,000 children in state care; G7-2 presents data on children 0–17 in institutions for the disabled. Information on the reasons for entry of children into public care is not available, nor are the data on whether entry is with parents' approval or whether it has been legally enforced. Similarly, many countries provide no data on exits from public care.

G8-1–G8-2. Adoption: G8-1 presents the absolute number of adoptions for the nations of the former Soviet Bloc over a nine-year period beginning shortly after the fall of Communism. G8-2 gives the adoption rate for the same nations over the same period. Adoption is to raise a child of some other biological parents as if it were your own, in accordance with formal legal procedures. Adoption offers the best prospects for a secure upbringing for young children who have no chance of remaining with or returning to their own parents. Higher numbers of adoptions can be interpreted as the results of increasing numbers of orphans, which in turn are the result of a higher adult mortality due to conflicts, wars, and poverty.

G9-1–G9-2. Children of divorce: Divorce has long-term economic and emotional consequences for children. Yet international statistics on the number of children affected by divorce is extremely limited. Data in this cluster are confined to countries in the former Soviet Bloc. G9-1 gives the total number of children involved in divorce; G9-2 shows the rate per 100,000 population aged 0 to 17 years.

G10-1. Working mothers: This table traces the growth in the percentage of working mothers with small children for selected industrial countries. Throughout the world, women bear most of the responsibility for raising children. As many mothers move into the labor force, reliable child care has become a crucial issue in many countries.

G11-1–G11-2. Sexual activity: Given the fact that unintended pregnancy and sexually transmitted diseases have a serious long-term impact on health and the quality of life, understanding adolescent sexual behavior is a priority. Nevertheless, international data on this topic are sparse. G11-1 supplies data, for nine geographic areas, on the percentage of 15-year-olds who are sexually active. G11-2 presents, for six locations, the mean age of sexual initiation by gender.

G12-1. Contraception: This table breaks down contraceptive use among 15 to 19 year old married women by method in selected developing countries. Modern methods include condoms, injectables, intrauterine device (IUD)'s, pills, vaginal methods (spermicides, diaphragms, or caps), and voluntary sterilization of a woman or her partner; traditional methods of contraception include periodic abstinence, rhythm, withdrawal, douche, and folk methods. According to the U.S. Census International Programs Center, contraceptive prevalence is relatively low among married adolescent females because these young women are often under social pressures to have children.

G13-1. Teenage abortions: Abortion, in legal terms, is any interruption of pregnancy before 28 weeks of gestation. Induced abortions are subject to governmental regulation in most countries. This regulation varies from complete prohibition in some countries to services provided by governmental health agencies in others. The figures on teenage abortions are extremely limited. This table focuses exclusively on former Eastern Bloc countries. The figures include only legal, regulated abortions; there are no statistics for illegal procedures.

G14-1–G14-6. Married adolescents: This cluster of tables gives an overview of adolescent marriage (G14-1 and G14-2) with an emphasis on the marriage of young girls (G14-3–G14-6). The data in these tables include diverse types of socially accepted unions, in various societies—monogamous marriage, forms of cohabitation, and polygamy. The figures are conservative; the United Nations believes that the early marriage is under-reported globally. Experts use age of marriage is an indicator of the status of young women. A young girl often does not have a say in whether and whom she will marry, and she is frequently subordinate to her older partner in fundamental family decisions, such as when to have children and how many to have. Early marriage is closely linked to early, repeated and unplanned childbearing, which has long-term health and economic consequences for both the young mother and the child.

G15-1–G15-5. Tobacco and alcohol: G15-1 to G15-4 present data on teenage tobacco and alcohol use in 28 developed nations. There are no comparable data for the rest of the world. G15-1 and G15-2 provide the percent of teenagers smoking and number of cigarettes smoked by age and gender. G15-3 shows how smoking patterns for 15-year-olds have changed over time. G15-4 offers figures on alcohol consumption by age and gender. Most countries have some regulations to protect children and adolescents against smoking and alcohol consumption. Owing to the cultural meaning of drinking and smoking, and depending on the balance of power between the national interest in health promotion and the influence of industries affecting health, preventive strategies differ. One of the most common is setting legal ages for buying alcohol and tobacco. G15-5 presents this information for the 28 nations for which consumption information is available.

G16-1–G16-4. Food habits: This cluster offers statistics on eating patterns for teenagers from 28 developed nations. The first three tables cover consumption of "junk food": potato chips and fried potatoes; candy and chocolate; and soft drinks. Experts are increasingly concerned about the amount of junk food children eat because of the long-term risks of obesity, high blood pressure and other health problems. But these indexes are not only an indicator of future health problems. Daily consumption of junk food also reflects money spent on luxuries rather on food necessities and is an indicator of the economic affluence of a society. To contrast unhealthy and healthy eating habits, the cluster of tables ends with data on fruit consumption (G16-4). Intake of fruits is important in promoting health benefits in childhood because it may help reduce the risk of cancer, cardiovascular diseases and adult-onset diabetes mellitus.

G17-1. Dental care: Considering the amount of chocolate, sweets, and soft drinks students consume daily, brushing teeth more than once a day is very important. Students in Sweden, Denmark, and Switzerland are most likely to brush their teeth more than once a day, with overall levels over 80 percent. In contrast, less than half of students brush their teeth more than once a day in Lithuania, Belgium, and Greece. In all countries and for all age groups, girls brush more frequently than boys, a difference that increases with age. For both genders, brushing more than once a day increases with age in most countries.

G18-1–G18-2. Leisure activities: Playing computer games and watching TV are popular recreation activities for children in developed countries. G18-1 shows the proportions of students playing computer games for four or more hours a week by age and gender. The indicator shows large gender differences, with boys far more likely than girls to play these games. G18-2 presents data on student television viewing habits. The indicator focuses on television watching for long periods daily, a practice that many educators, psychologists and health officials deem injurious to adolescents.

G19-1. Exercise: This indicator measures how many times a week students took part in vigorous activity outside school hours. Vigorous physical activity is defined as the equivalent of at least slow jogging. It is considered vital for the long-term health of children. Across most countries surveyed, the gender difference is pronounced. Regular exercise is more common among boys than among girls and declines with age, especially for girls.

G1. HUMAN DEVELOPMENT INDEX (HDI)

G1-1. Human Development Index, 2000

Rank	Country	Value
	High human development*	
1	Canada	0.935
2	Norway	0.934
3	United States	0.929
4	Australia	0.929
5	Iceland	0.927
6	Sweden	0.926
7	Belgium	0.925
8	Netherlands	0.925
9	Japan	0.924
10	United Kingdom	0.918
11	Finland	0.917
12	France	0.917
13	Switzerland	0.915
14	Germany	0.911
15	Denmark	0.911
16	Austria	0.908
17	Luxembourg	0.908
18	Ireland	0.907
19	Italy	0.903
20	New Zealand	0.903
21	Spain	0.899
22	Cyprus	0.886
23	Israel	0.883
24	Singapore	0.881
25	Greece	0.875
26	Hong Kong, SAR (China)	0.872
27	Malta	0.865
28	Portugal	0.864
29	Slovenia	0.861
30	Barbados	0.858
31	South Korea,Rep.	0.854
32	Brunei	0.848
33	Bahamas, the	0.844
34	Czech Republic	0.843
35	Argentina	0.837
36	Kuwait	0.836
37	Antigua and Barbuda	0.833
38	Chile	0.826
39	Uruguay	0.825
40	Slovakia	0.825
41	Bahrain	0.820
42	Qatar	0.819
43	Hungary	0.817
44	Poland	0.814
45	United Arab Emirates	0.810
46	Estonia	0.801
	Medium human development**	
47	Saint Kitts and Nevis	0.798
48	Costa Rica	0.797
49	Croatia	0.795
50	Trinidad and Tobago	0.793
51	Dominica	0.793
52	Lithuania	0.789
53	Seychelles	0.786
54	Grenada	0.785

G1-1. Human Development Index, 2000 *(continued)*

Rank	Country	Value
55	Mexico	0.784
56	Cuba	0.783
57	Belarus	0.781
58	Belize	0.777
59	Panama	0.776
60	Bulgaria	0.772
61	Malaysia	0.772
62	Russia	0.771
63	Latvia	0.771
64	Romania	0.770
65	Venezuela	0.770
66	Fiji	0.769
67	Suriname	0.766
68	Colombia	0.764
69	Macedonia, FYRO	0.763
70	Georgia	0.762
71	Mauritius	0.761
72	Libya	0.760
73	Kazakhstan	0.754
74	Brazil	0.747
75	Saudi Arabia	0.747
76	Thailand	0.745
77	Philippines	0.744
78	Ukraine	0.744
79	Saint Vincent and the Grenadines	0.738
80	Peru	0.737
81	Paraguay	0.736
82	Lebanon	0.735
83	Jamaica	0.735
84	Sri Lanka	0.733
85	Turkey	0.732
86	Oman	0.730
87	Dominican Republic	0.729
88	Saint Lucia	0.728
89	Maldives	0.725
90	Azerbaijan	0.722
91	Ecuador	0.722
92	Jordan	0.721
93	Armenia	0.721
94	Albania	0.713
95	Samoa	0.711
96	Guyana	0.709
97	Iran	0.709
98	Kyrgyzstan	0.706
99	China	0.706
100	Turkmenistan	0.704
101	Tunisia	0.703
102	Moldova	0.700
103	South Africa	0.697
104	El Salvador	0.696
105	Cape Verde	0.688
106	Uzbekistan	0.686
107	Algeria	0.683
108	Vietnam	0.671
109	Indonesia	0.670
110	Tajikistan	0.663
111	Syria	0.660
112	Swaziland	0.655

G1-1. Human Development Index, 2000 *(continued)*

Rank	Country	Value
113	Honduras	0.653
114	Bolivia	0.643
115	Namibia	0.632
116	Nicaragua	0.631
117	Mongolia	0.628
118	Vanuatu	0.623
119	Egypt	0.623
120	Guatemala	0.619
121	Solomon Islands	0.614
122	Botswana	0.593
123	Gabon	0.592
124	Morocco	0.589
125	Myanmar	0.585
126	Iraq	0.583
127	Lesotho	0.569
128	India	0.563
129	Ghana	0.556
130	Zimbabwe	0.555
131	Equatorial Guinea	0.555
132	São Tomé and Principe	0.547
133	Papua New Guinea	0.542
134	Cameroon	0.528
135	Pakistan	0.522
136	Cambodia	0.512
137	Comoros	0.510
138	Kenya	0.508
139	Congo, Rep.	0.507
	Low human development***	
140	Laos	0.484
141	Madagascar	0.483
142	Bhutan	0.483
143	Sudan	0.477
144	Nepal	0.474
145	Togo	0.471
146	Bangladesh	0.461
147	Mauritania	0.451
148	Yemen	0.448
149	Djibouti	0.447
150	Haiti	0.440
151	Nigeria	0.439
152	Congo, Dem. Rep. (Zaire)	0.430
153	Zambia	0.420
154	Côte d'Ivoire	0.420
155	Senegal	0.416
156	Tanzania	0.415
157	Benin	0.411
158	Uganda	0.409
159	Eritrea	0.408
160	Angola	0.405
161	Gambia	0.396
162	Guinea	0.394
163	Malawi	0.385
164	Rwanda	0.382
165	Mali	0.380
166	Central African Republic	0.371
167	Chad	0.367
168	Mozambique	0.341
169	Guinea-Bissau	0.331

G1-1. Human Development Index, 2000 *(continued)*

Rank	Country	Value
170	Burundi	0.321
171	Ethiopia	0.309
172	Burkina Faso	0.303
173	Niger	0.293
174	Sierra Leone	0.252

*HDI of .8 and above
**HDI of .500-.799
***HDI less than .500

Source: United Nations (UN) Development Programme, *Human Development Report 2000;* <http://www.undp.org/hdr2000/english/presskit/hdi.pdf> and <http://www.undp.org/hdr2000/english/book/back1.pdf>.

G2. THE CHILD RISK MEASURE (CRM)

G2-1. The Child Risk Measure, 1999

	Risk measure level
Afghanistan	94
Albania	17
Algeria	26
Angola	96
Argentina	5
Armenia	N/A
Australia	Less than 5
Austria	Less than 5
Azerbaijan	24
Bangladesh	47
Belarus	11
Belgium	Less than 5
Benin	45
Bhutan	46
Bolivia	21
Bosnia/Herzegovina	N/A
Botswana	42
Brazil	8
Bulgaria	7
Burkina Faso	60
Burundi	74
Cambodia	60
Cameroon	47
Canada	Less than 5
Central African Rep.	62
Chad	67
Chile	8
China	13
Colombia	16
Congo	51
Congo, Dem. Rep.	76
Costa Rica	Less than 5
Côte d'Ivoire	51
Croatia	10
Cuba	6
Czech Rep.	8
Denmark	Less than 5
Dominican Rep.	16
Ecuador	13

G2-1. The Child Risk Measure, 1999 *(continued)*

	Risk measure level
Egypt	21
El Salvador	22
Eritrea	74
Estonia	10
Ethiopia	85
Finland	Less than 5
France	Less than 5
Gabon	32
Gambia	35
Georgia	27
Germany	Less than 5
Ghana	36
Greece	6
Guatemala	33
Guinea	69
Guinea-Bissau	80
Haiti	47
Honduras	18
Hungary	Less than 5
India	45
Indonesia	34
Iran	17
Iraq	39
Ireland	Less than 5
Israel	No data
Italy	Less than 5
Jamaica	8
Japan	Less than 5
Jordan	11
Kazakhstan	12
Kenya	46
Korea, Dem.	50
Korea, Rep.	5
Kuwait	24
Kyrgyzstan	13
Lao PDR	42
Latvia	8
Lebanon	18
Lesotho	46
Liberia	74
Libya	6
Lithuania	N/A
Macedonia, FYRO	11
Madagascar	49
Malawi	55
Malaysia	14
Mali	64
Mauritania	45
Mauritius	11
Mexico	11
Moldova, Rep.	N/A
Mongolia	25
Morocco	21
Mozambique	63
Myanmar	44
Namibia	42
Nepal	44
Netherlands	Less than 5
New Zealand	Less than 5

G2-1. The Child Risk Measure, 1999 *(continued)*

	Risk measure level
Nicaragua	22
Niger	80
Nigeria	59
Norway	Less than 5
Oman	17
Pakistan	49
Panama	9
Papua New Guinea	55
Paraguay	8
Peru	19
Philippines	31
Poland	Less than 5
Portugal	Less than 5
Romania	6
Russian Fed.	11
Rwanda	70
Saudi Arabia	24
Senegal	38
Sierra Leone	95
Singapore	Less than 5
Slovakia	N/A
Slovenia	Less than 5
Somalia	92
South Africa	25
Spain	Less than 5
Sri Lanka	39
Sudan	59
Sweden	Less than 5
Switzerland	Less than 5
Syria	13
Tajikistan	N/A
Tanzania	53
Thailand	22
Togo	46
Trinidad/Tobago	10
Tunisia	8
Turkey	15
Turkmenistan	21
U. Arab Emirates	16
Uganda	57
Ukraine	N/A
United Kingdom	Less than 5
United States	Less than 5
Uruguay	6
Uzbekistan	23
Venezuela	16
Viet Nam	31
Yemen	49
Yugoslavia	29
Zambia	58
Zimbabwe	48

N/A   Not Available

Source: The Progress of Nations, 1999; <http://www.unicef.org/pon99/>. Underlying data from United Nations Children's Fund (UNICEF).

G3. HOUSEHOLDS

G3-1. Average Household Size, 1990

	In persons
Afghanistan	5.9
Algeria	7.0
American Samoa	7.0
Antigua and Barbuda	3.2
Argentina	3.9
Armenia	4.4
Australia	3.0
Austria	3.0
Azerbaijan	4.5
Bahamas, the	4.3
Bahrain	6.6
Bangladesh	5.3
Barbados	3.6
Belarus	3.0
Belgium	3.0
Belize	5.3
Benin	5.4
Bolivia	4.6
Botswana	4.8
Brazil	4.2
Brunei	5.8
Bulgaria	3.0
Burkina Faso	6.2
Burundi	4.6
Cameroon	5.2
Canada	3.0
Cape Verde	5.2
Central African Republic	4.7
Chile	4.5
China	4.0
Colombia	5.2
Comoros	5.3
Congo, Dem. Rep. (Zaire)	5.0
Congo, Rep.	5.3
Cook Islands	4.9
Costa Rica	4.3
Côte d'Ivoire	6.0
Croatia	3.0
Cuba	4.0
Czech Republic	3.0
Denmark	2.0
Djibouti	6.6
Dominica	3.6
Dominican Republic	4.5
Ecuador	4.8
Egypt	4.9
El Salvador	5.0
Estonia	3.0
Ethiopia	4.5
Fiji	5.7
Finland	3.0
France	3.0
French Guiana	3.3
French Polynesia	4.7
Gambia, the	8.4
Georgia	3.7

G3-1. Average Household Size, 1990 *(continued)*

	In persons
Germany	2.0
Ghana	4.8
Greece	3.0
Grenada	4.2
Guadeloupe	3.8
Guam	4.0
Guatemala	5.2
Guinea	6.5
Guinea-Bissau	7.9
Guyana	5.1
Haiti	4.5
Honduras	5.4
Hong Kong SAR, China	3.4
Hungary	3.0
India	5.5
Indonesia	4.5
Iran	5.1
Iraq	7.3
Ireland	3.0
Israel	3.5
Italy	3.0
Jamaica	4.2
Japan	3.0
Jordan	6.9
Kazakhstan	3.6
Kenya	5.2
Kiribati	6.4
Kuwait	6.5
Kyrgyzstan	4.3
Latvia	3.0
Lesotho	5.1
Liberia	5.0
Libya	6.4
Liechtenstein	3.0
Lithuania	3.0
Luxembourg	3.0
Madagascar	4.5
Malawi	3.0
Malaysia	4.9
Maldives	6.8
Mali	5.0
Malta	3.0
Marshall Islands	7.0
Martinique	3.8
Mauritania	5.5
Mauritius	4.4
Mexico	5.0
Micronesia	7.5
Moldova	3.0
Monaco	2.0
Morocco	6.0
Mozambique	4.3
Myanmar (Burma)	5.2
Namibia	6.0
Nepal	5.6
Netherlands	3.0
Netherlands-Antilles	4.1
New Caledonia	4.0

G3-1. Average Household Size, 1990 *(continued)*

	In persons
New Zealand	3.0
Niger	6.4
Nigeria	4.7
Northern Mariana Islands	4.6
Norway	3.0
Pakistan	6.5
Palau	5.0
Panama	4.4
Papua New Guinea	4.5
Paraguay	4.7
Peru	5.9
Philippines	5.6
Poland	3.0
Portugal	3.0
Puerto Rico	3.7
Qatar	5.6
Reunion	3.8
Russia	3.0
Rwanda	4.7
Samoa	6.7
San Marino	3.0
Sao Tome and Principe	3.8
Saudi Arabia	7.4
Seychelles	4.5
Sierra Leone	5.7
Singapore	4.2
Slovenia	3.0
Solomon Islands	6.5
Somalia	5.3
South Korea, Rep.	3.7
Spain	4.0
Sri Lanka	5.2
St. Kitts & Nevis	3.4
St. Lucia	4.6
St. Vincent and the Grenadines	3.9
Sudan	6.3
Sweden	3.0
Switzerland	3.0
Syria	6.0
Tajikistan	5.7
Tanzania	5.2
Thailand	4.4
Togo	5.1
Tonga	6.2
Trinidad and Tobago	4.5
Tunisia	5.4
Turkey	5.2
Turkmenistan	5.2
Uganda	5.4
Ukraine	2.8
United Arab Emirates	4.8
United Kingdom	2.5
United States	2.6
Uruguay	3.4
Uzbekistan	5.2
Vanuatu	5.0
Venezuela	4.8

G3-1. Average Household Size, 1990 *(continued)*

	In persons
Vietnam	4.8
Virgin Islands	3.3
Yemen	5.8
Zambia	5.6
Zimbabwe	5.2

Source: World's Women 1995: Table 2. Household families and childbearing. Underlying data from United Nations (UN).

G3-2. Distribution of Households by Type, Selected Countries, various years

Country	Year	Total	Married couple-total	Married couple-with children	Married couple-without children	Single parent	One person	Other
Canada:								
	1961	100	78	51	27	4	9	9
	1971	100	74	47	28	5	13	8
	1981	100	67	36	31	5	20	8
	1991	100	63	30	33	6	23	9
Denmark:								
	1976	100	45	24	21	5	(NA)	(NA)
	1983	100	44	23	21	5	(NA)	(NA)
	1990	100	40	19	21	5	(NA)	(NA)
	1992	100	39	18	21	4	50	7
	1993	100	39	18	21	4	50	7
France:								
	1968	100	70	44	27	4	20	5
	1975	100	69	42	27	4	22	5
	1982	100	67	40	27	4	25	4
	1990	100	65	39	26	7	26	2
	1992	100	64	37	27	7	27	2
	1993	100	64	37	27	7	27	2
Germany:								
	1961	100	67	44	22	11	21	2
	1970	100	65	42	23	6	27	3
	1980	100	61	37	24	7	30	3
	1990	100	54	31	23	6	35	4
	1992	100	55	31	24	7	34	4
	1993	100	54	31	24	7	34	4
Japan:								
	1960	100	65	49	16	3	17	14
	1970	100	64	45	20	2	20	13
	1980	100	68	43	26	2	20	10
	1990	100	65	33	32	2	23	10
Netherlands, the:								
	1961	100	78	55	22	6	12	5
	1971	100	74	52	22	5	17	4
	1981	100	67	44	23	6	21	6
	1985	100	60	39	22	7	28	5
	1990	100	64	36	28	5	30	1
	1992	100	63	34	29	5	31	1
	1993	100	63	33	30	5	31	1
Sweden:								
	1960	100	66	36	31	4	20	10
	1970	100	64	30	34	3	25	7
	1980	100	58	25	33	3	33	6
	1985	100	55	22	33	3	36	6
	1990	100	52	20	32	3	40	5

G3-2. Distribution of Households by Type, Selected Countries, various years *(continued)*

Country	Year	Total	Married couple- total	Married couple- with children	Married couple- without children	Single parent	One person	Other
United Kingdom:								
	1961	100	74	38	36	2	12	12
	1971	100	70	34	35	3	18	9
	1981	100	64	31	34	5	22	9
	1990	100	61	25	36	6	26	7
	1992	100	60	24	36	6	27	7
	1993	100	60	25	35	7	27	6
United States:								
	1960	100	74	44	30	4	13	8
	1970	100	71	40	30	5	17	7
	1980	100	61	31	30	8	23	9
	1990	100	56	26	30	8	25	11
	1992	100	55	26	29	9	25	11
	1993	100	55	26	29	9	25	11

Source: Statistical Abstract of the United States 1995: Table 1365. Percent Distribution of Households, by Type and Country; <http://www.census.gov/prod/2/gen/96statab/app5.pdf>. Underlying data from U.S. Bureau of Labor Statistics, Monthly Labor Review, March 1990; and unpublished data.

G4. AVERAGE FAMILY SIZE

G4-1. Average Size of Family, Selected Countries, 1997–1998

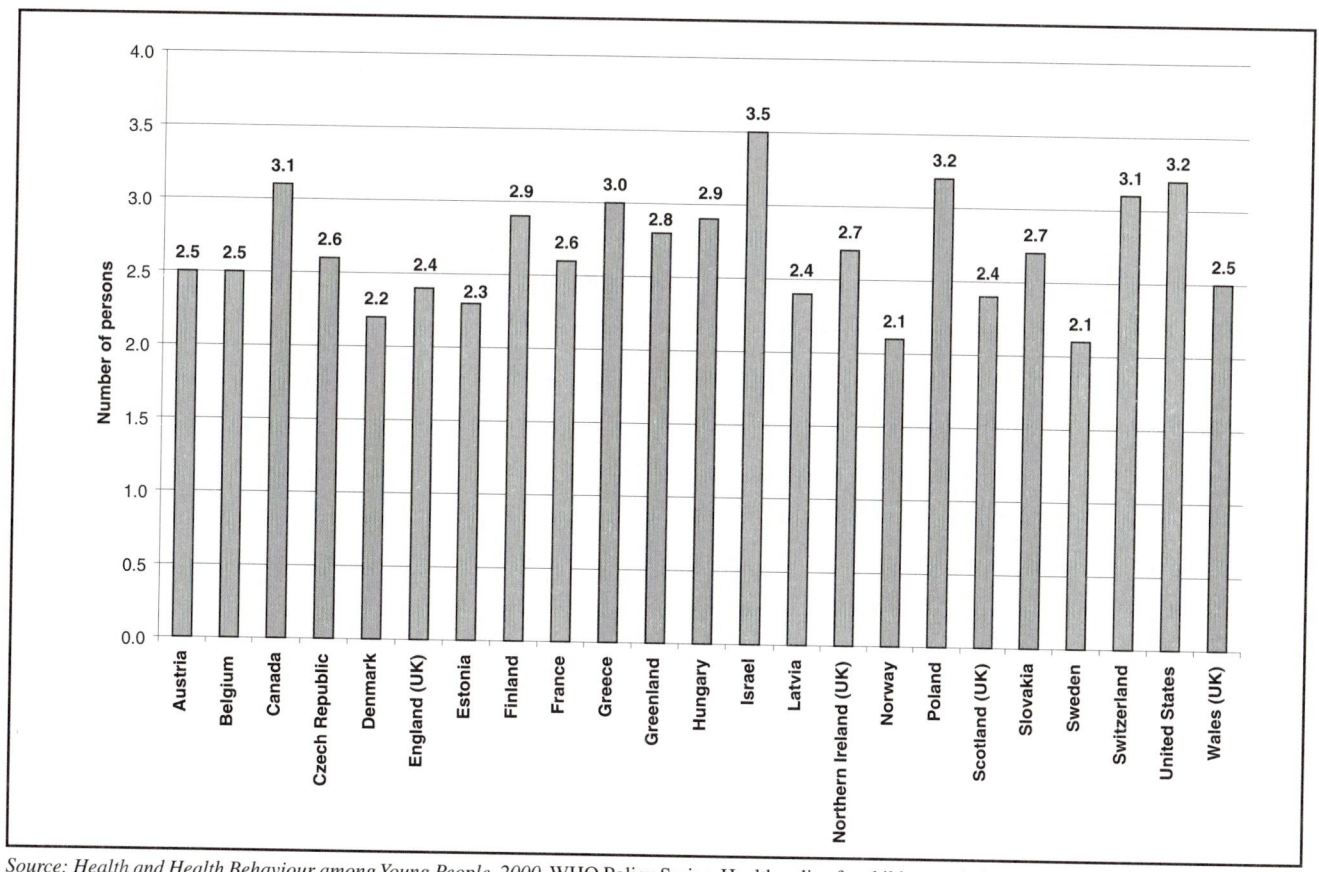

Source: Health and Health Behaviour among Young People, 2000, WHO Policy Series: Health policy for children and adolescents, Issue 1, International Report 2/1/2000; <http://www.eurochild.gla.ac.uk/documents/monee/welcome.htm>. Underlying data from The Health Behaviour in School-Aged Children (HBSC) study by the WHO Regional Office for Europe.

G5. CHILDREN LIVING AWAY FROM PARENTS

G5-1. Percent of Adolescent Children Aged 12 to 14 Living with Neither Parent, Selected Countries, 1992–1996

	Girls	Boys
Benin	33	19
Brazil	12	9
Burkina Faso	21	16
Cameroon	26	24
Central African Republic	28	25
Colombia	14	13
Comoros	28	23
Côte d'Ivoire	36	25
Dominican Republic	27	18
Ghana	30	20
Guatemala	9	8
Haiti	36	26
Indonesia	9	7
Kazakhstan	10	5
Kenya	19	15
Madagascar	22	21
Mali	18	11
Morocco	8	9
Namibia	42	36
Niger	26	16
Nigeria	22	16
Pakistan	4	4
Paraguay	17	12
Philippines	11	9
Senegal	21	20
Tanzania	23	22
Turkey	3	3
Uganda	31	27
Uzbekistan	2	2
Zambia	28	25
Zimbabwe	27	24

Source: The World's Women 2000, United Nations (UN); Chapter 2, chart 2.22.

G6. FOSTER CARE AND FOSTER CHILDREN

G6-1. Rate of Children in Foster Care (Children in Foster Care per 100,000 Aged 0–17 Years), Selected Countries, 1990–1998

	1990	1991	1992	1993	1994	1995	1996	1997	1998
Albania	N/A	N/A	N/A	N/A	N/A	N/A	N/A	N/A	N/A
Armenia	N/A	N/A	N/A	N/A	N/A	N/A	N/A	N/A	N/A
Azerbaijan	241.2	254.3	265.6	271.9	277.8	269.6	273.2	281.1	286.1
Belarus	377.6	370.5	373.8	380.4	222.3	264.6	317.8	376.6	453.8
Bosnia-Herzegovina	N/A	N/A	N/A	N/A	N/A	N/A	N/A	N/A	N/A
Bulgaria	N/A	N/A	N/A	N/A	N/A	N/A	N/A	N/A	N/A
Croatia	N/A	N/A	N/A	N/A	N/A	N/A	N/A	N/A	N/A
Czech Republic	279.3	286	285.3	293.1	302.7	318.3	341.1	349.3	361.5
Estonia	N/A	N/A	457.2	623.1	568.8	580.3	678.7	686.2	1,075.20
Georgia	N/A	N/A	N/A	N/A	N/A	N/A	30	59.7	58.3
Hungary	341.8	332.7	337.5	343.2	346.3	345.5	349.5	361.7	641.3
Kazakhstan	N/A	N/A	N/A	N/A	N/A	N/A	N/A	N/A	N/A
Kyrgyzstan	N/A	N/A	234.7	278.5	330.3	291.3	306.2	321.3	302.6
Latvia	N/A	N/A	N/A	502.4	724.3	885	971.4	1,124.10	1,346.30
Lithuania	459.6	492.1	523.3	545.6	543.5	607.7	654.3	707.8	763.8
Macedonia	N/A	107.9	231.3	203.8	212.5	209.1	245.3	237.6	233.2
Moldova	N/A	347.4	283.3	277.7	278.8	287.2	299.1	339.4	384.2
Poland	1,270.20	1,219.10	1,184.30	1,196.00	1,232.80	1,303.90	1,385.30	1,468.50	1,538.30
Romania	N/A	N/A	119.5	134.9	139.4	181	195.1	N/A	N/A
Russia	424.9	451	480.1	514.6	585	666.1	748.6	809.1	858.7
Slovakia	143.9	147.8	149.7	155	155.4	155.1	160.4	156	170.8
Slovenia	523.7	524.6	539	521	711.6	710.5	788.5	814.1	793.8
Tajikistan	N/A	N/A	N/A	N/A	N/A	N/A	N/A	N/A	N/A
Turkmenistan	N/A	N/A	N/A	N/A	N/A	N/A	N/A	N/A	N/A
Ukraine	289.4	304.3	313.6	326.5	339.3	374.6	409.8	447.8	488.1
Uzbekistan	N/A	N/A	170.3	168.7	171.8	173	181.1	190.4	204.5
Yugoslavia	621.2	621	716.6	688.5	605.3	314.8	301.7	319.3	N/A

N/A Not Available

Source: TransMONEE 2000 database; <http://www.eurochild.gla.ac.uk/documents/monee/welcome.htm>, UNICEF Innocenti Research Centre, Florence. Underlying data from United Nations Children's Fund (UNICEF).

G7. INSTITUTIONAL AND STATE CARE

G7-1. Rate of Infants in State Institutions (Infants per 100,000 Children Aged 0–3 Years), Selected Countries, 1990–1998

	1990	1991	1992	1993	1994	1995	1996	1997	1998
Albania	N/A	N/A	N/A	N/A	56.9	75.2	77.7	84.4	66.4
Armenia	11.6	10.8	13.2	12.5	13.9	15.3	17.9	N/A	N/A
Azerbaijan	34	32.4	25.9	26.4	26.7	24.4	24.2	27.3	27
Belarus	164.7	162.6	168.6	184.2	205.9	223.6	241.6	287	325.6
Bosnia-Herzegovina	N/A	N/A	N/A	N/A	N/A	N/A	N/A	N/A	N/A
Bulgaria	861.8	863.7	923.4	1,009.9	1,084.2	1,089.0	1,205.8	1,263.1	1,299.6
Croatia	N/A	N/A	61.4	N/A	57.1	N/A	70.7	N/A	N/A
Czech Republic	509	492	460.5	455.8	466.7	498.7	517.7	533.2	571.7
Estonia	148.9	154.5	168.4	181.2	185.8	213.1	244.4	261.4	N/A
Georgia	70.7	57.6	36.1	41.5	33.8	39.7	64.9	56.4	79.9
Hungary	390.1	376.6	390.5	396.7	385	382.5	384.2	374	378.9
Kazakhstan	119.2	121.3	112.4	133.1	148.6	172.6	202	217.1	267.3
Kyrgyzstan	N/A	47.2	47.5	42.4	50.7	48.8	52.3	50.6	51.7
Latvia	497.4	461.1	488.5	575.4	661	737.1	803.4	877.2	996.5
Lithuania	202.7	216.2	218.5	245.4	215.7	254.4	296.4	312.6	324.1
Macedonia	N/A	51.3	140.8	64.3	81	85.6	63.6	194.3	199.8
Moldova	175	182	172.2	182.1	198.1	195.8	217.7	248.3	285.8
Poland	190.9	196.9	193.5	193.2	N/A	N/A	N/A	N/A	N/A
Romania	597.1	604.5	653.8	750.3	1,074.00	887.7	938.9	944.3	836.4
Russia	203.5	209.2	226.2	250.7	278.8	306	346.1	334.1	365
Slovakia	170.7	170.5	206.2	215.3	238.3	240.2	272.6	N/A	N/A
Slovenia	28.7	27.6	25.8	40.1	34.3	23.9	N/A	N/A	N/A
Tajikistan	58.2	56.8	55.8	37.4	30.9	27.4	23.7	22.2	19.2
Turkmenistan	61.3	53.9	48.1	47.8	42	45	30.9	35.4	42.1
Ukraine	151.3	150.4	150.9	160.9	177.5	200.1	223	236.8	274
Uzbekistan	35.3	33	33.5	31.9	31.6	29.3	29.9	30.1	30.2
Yugoslavia	48.2	N/A	43.8	N/A	52.6	N/A	73	N/A	N/A

N/A Not Available

Source: TransMONEE 2000 database; <http://www.eurochild.gla.ac.uk/documents/monee/welcome.htm> UNICEF Innocenti Research Centre, Florence. Underlying data from United Nations Children's Fund (UNICEF).

G7-2. Rate of Children in Institutions* for the Disabled (Children in Institutions per 100,000 Aged 0–17 Years), Selected Countries, 1990–1997

	1989	1990	1991	1992	1993	1994	1995	1996	1997
Armenia	11.7	14.7	14.4	14.7	16.5	22.1	26.4	30.0	N/A
Azerbaijan	128.7	121.0	105.4	90.1	86.5	77.5	65.5	75.5	82.9
Belarus	596.4	589.9	499.9	498.0	453.1	449.7	467.5	452.2	458.2
Bosnia and Herzegovina	N/A	140.0	N/A	N/A	N/A	N/A	N/A	125.3	N/A
Bulgaria	N/A	108.4	105.7	98.1	115.1	129.5	121.5	125.2	121.0
Croatia	N/A	N/A	N/A	248.6	N/A	276.6	N/A	298.4	N/A
Czech Republic	394.0	413.8	412.8	429.5	443.3	462.4	496.4	519.2	544.4
Estonia	143.2	152.8	136.9	125.0	110.0	107.1	105.9	124.1	132.1
Yugoslavia	N/A	142.7	N/A	137.3	N/A	144.7	N/A	156.0	N/A
Macedonia, FYRO	N/A	N/A	156.2	175.0	143.1	150.5	146.5	146.4	148.3
Georgia	136.4	119.9	108.6	95.3	129.2	91.5	76.3	102.8	109.5
Hungary	34.8	34.2	31.2	31.4	30.5	31.4	31.7	31.4	30.7
Latvia	N/A	N/A	N/A	N/A	75.4	70.1	72.4	72.7	76.5
Lithuania	N/A	251.0	217.2	209.4	191.3	177.7	185.5	192.2	188.6
Moldova	744.4	681.8	621.0	426.6	354.8	360.5	345.9	361.2	387.0
Poland	315.3	287.4	298.3	308.5	314.8	305.0	307.9	308.7	313.8

G7-2. Rate of Children in Institutions* for the Disabled (Children in Institutions per 100,000 Aged 0–17 Years), Selected Countries, 1990–1997 *(continued)*

	1989	1990	1991	1992	1993	1994	1995	1996	1997
Romania	N/A	105.0	124.0	128.6	131.9	127.4	134.4	130.4	131.3
Russia	659.6	636.7	589.2	550.6	528.2	533.5	530.2	544.7	558.9
Slovakia	258.1	261.2	266.5	271.2	283.8	287.0	295.6	297.3	299.3
Slovenia	353.6	357.1	376.9	412.6	332.6	279.3	308.2	313.1	270.1
Ukraine	81.9	78.7	73.0	69.1	66.8	67.1	67.8	67.3	67.7

N/A Not Available

* Definitions of types of institutions may vary by country; includes both physically and mentally disabled.

Source: TransMONEE 2000 database; <http://www.eurochild.gla.ac.uk/documents/monee/welcome.htm>; UNICEF Innocenti Research Centre, Florence. Underlying data from United Nations Children's Fund (UNICEF).

G8. ADOPTION

G8-1. Absolute Number of Adoptions, Selected Countries, 1990–1998

Country	1990	1991	1992	1993	1994	1995	1996	1997	1998
Albania	N/A	N/A	N/A	N/A	69	86	117	62	N/A
Armenia	312	216	184	168	447	521	207	N/A	N/A
Azerbaijan	608	526	462	375	521	396	455	411	458
Belarus	N/A	N/A	N/A	247	329	261	250	197	209
Bosnia-Herzegovina	N/A	N/A	N/A	N/A	N/A	N/A	N/A	N/A	N/A
Bulgaria	2,550	2,319	2,191	1,994	2,098	2,100	2,081	2,130	2,058
Croatia	232	107	118	220	309	175	180	157	N/A
Czech Republic	499	530	475	463	543	628	575	634	499
Estonia	N/A	N/A	262	318	284	270	269	227	193
Georgia	N/A	N/A	N/A	N/A	N/A	N/A	106	435	166
Hungary	958	1,016	923	892	914	940	1,030	911	850
Kazakhstan	N/A	N/A	N/A	N/A	N/A	N/A	N/A	N/A	N/A
Kyrgyzstan	N/A	N/A	8,379	9,998	10,375	8,772	9,431	8,905	8,777
Latvia	584	641	615	469	422	387	384	404	373
Lithuania	N/A	N/A	332	115	308	220	418	421	362
Macedonia	280	255	208	198	187	175	207	196	172
Moldova	N/A	N/A	N/A	N/A	296	338	323	311	313
Poland	3,629	3,360	3,021	2,810	2,600	2,495	2,529	2,441	2,425
Romania	N/A	N/A	N/A	N/A	N/A	2,595	2,320	1,007	N/A
Russia	12,828	12,964	13,942	15,264	16,310	13,523	12,050	14,270	13,178
Slovakia	395	399	369	449	415	514	522	451	476
Slovenia	132	141	117	103	132	74	79	57	61
Tajikistan	N/A	N/A	N/A	N/A	N/A	N/A	N/A	N/A	N/A
Turkmenistan	N/A	N/A	N/A	N/A	N/A	N/A	N/A	N/A	N/A
Ukraine	5,821	6,548	6,461	6,765	7,765	7,567	4,801	5,441	5,479
Uzbekistan	N/A	N/A	6,870	6,285	5,284	5,580	5,672	5,610	5,689
Yugoslavia	N/A	N/A	N/A	N/A	N/A	N/A	N/A	N/A	N/A

N/A Not Available

Source: TransMONEE 2000 database; <http://www.eurochild.gla.ac.uk/documents/monee/welcome.htm> UNICEF Innocenti Research Centre, Florence. Underlying data from United Nations Children's Fund (UNICEF).

G8-2. Gross Adoption Rate (Rates per 100,000 Children Aged 0–3 Years), Selected Countries, 1990–1998

Country	1990	1991	1992	1993	1994	1995	1996	1997	1998
Albania	N/A	N/A	N/A	N/A	22.6	28.6	39.9	21.6	N/A
Armenia	102.5	71.2	61.1	57.8	166.5	217.2	96.5	N/A	N/A
Azerbaijan	85.8	72.5	62.7	51.3	72.9	58.3	69.2	61.9	68.3
Belarus	N/A	N/A	N/A	45.7	65.3	55.7	57.4	48.5	54.4
Bosnia-Herzegovina	N/A	N/A	N/A	N/A	N/A	N/A	N/A	N/A	N/A
Bulgaria	577.9	551.3	557	542.5	603.2	639.1	668.1	725	744.4
Croatia	N/A	47.2	54.9	106	150.8	88	92.3	80	N/A
Czech Republic	96.7	103.6	93.7	92.7	111.8	137.1	134.8	160	133.6
Estonia	N/A	N/A	309.9	418	417	436.6	471.1	422.3	373.1
Georgia	N/A	N/A	N/A	N/A	N/A	N/A	45.3	197.8	78.9
Hungary	195.3	206.9	188	183.1	190.5	201	227.6	208.7	202.6
Kazakhstan	N/A	N/A	N/A	N/A	N/A	N/A	N/A	N/A	N/A
Kyrgyzstan	N/A	N/A	1,686.2	2,057.7	2,210.1	1,921.4	2,125.7	2,078.1	2,091.9
Latvia	362.2	415.7	426.8	356.5	354.4	360.6	400.2	466.3	466.4
Lithuania	N/A	N/A	147.7	53.5	152.1	116.9	240.1	258.1	231.9
Macedonia	N/A	204.4	166.4	159.3	153	140.1	164.6	156.7	137.5
Moldova	N/A	N/A	N/A	N/A	109.2	131.9	134.7	148.2	171
Poland	157.4	150.3	139.2	133.8	127.7	128	136.6	137.8	143.4
Romania	N/A	N/A	N/A	N/A	N/A	264.3	243.4	107.9	N/A
Russia	141.1	152.5	178.6	215.6	252.4	225.5	213.9	263.4	249.8
Slovakia	122.4	126.7	119.3	148.1	140.6	182.9	196.6	179.3	198.1
Slovenia	135.1	149.8	131.2	121.6	161.8	93.2	101.3	74.4	81.4
Tajikistan	N/A	N/A	N/A	N/A	N/A	N/A	N/A	N/A	N/A
Turkmenistan	N/A	N/A	N/A	N/A	N/A	N/A	N/A	N/A	N/A
Ukraine	201.1	235.6	243.3	269	327.9	341.3	231.3	278.9	297.3
Uzbekistan	N/A	N/A	257.9	233.6	196.8	210.8	218.4	221.4	231.9
Yugoslavia	N/A	N/A	N/A	N/A	N/A	N/A	N/A	N/A	N/A

N/A Not Available

Source: TransMONEE 2000 database; <http://www.eurochild.gla.ac.uk/documents/monee/welcome.htm>, UNICEF Innocenti Research Centre, Florence. Underlying data from United Nations Children's Fund (UNICEF).

G9. CHILDREN OF DIVORCE

G9-1. Absolute Number of Children Aged 0–17 Involved in Divorce (in thousands), Selected Countries, 1990–1998

	1990	1991	1992	1993	1994	1995	1996	1997	1998
Albania	2.5	2.1	N/A	2.1	1.2	1.4	1.2	0.9	N/A
Armenia	3.6	3.2	2.7	2.8	3	2.2	2.3	2.2	1.5
Azerbaijan	9.9	8	6.5	4.8	4	2.5	2.2	3.6	3.7
Belarus	31.6	35.9	38.8	45	42.9	40.5	42.3	45.5	44.7
Bosnia-Herzegovina	N/A	N/A	N/A	N/A	N/A	N/A	N/A	N/A	N/A
Bulgaria	12.7	12	10.3	7.8	7	9.3	8.6	8.1	9
Croatia	6.7	6.3	4.6	5.9	5.8	5.5	4.7	5	4.9
Czech Republic	35.2	32	31.1	32.5	33.1	32.8	34.7	33.3	32.2
Estonia	5.3	5.4	6.2	5.1	4.8	7	5.6	5.1	4.3
Georgia	4.4	4.5	1.9	N/A	1.6	1.5	1	0.9	1.8
Hungary	26.1	25.4	22.9	22.9	23.3	24.9	21	24.9	25.3
Kazakhstan	40.5	45.8	47.4	43.6	39.2	37.1	39.3	36.4	37.6
Kyrgyzstan	7	8.3	7.1	6.5	5.1	5.8	6.6	6.8	6.7
Latvia	9.6	10	13.7	9.2	8.1	7.7	5.6	5.8	5.6
Lithuania	12	15.2	13.8	13.3	11.5	11	12.1	12.2	12.4
Macedonia	N/A	N/A	N/A	N/A	N/A	N/A	N/A	N/A	N/A
Moldova	11.6	12.9	14.3	13.5	12.2	13	N/A	N/A	9.4
Poland	45.1	35.8	33.5	28.4	32.8	40.6	42.2	44.6	45.8
Romania	27.7	30.5	23.6	21.6	32.8	27.2	26.8	26.9	30.3
Russia	466.1	522.2	569.1	593.8	613.4	588.1	463.5	454.5	389.7
Slovakia	13.5	10.3	9.7	9.7	10.3	6.8	7	N/A	6.8
Slovenia	2	1.9	2	2	2	1.5	2	1.9	2
Tajikistan	7	7.8	6	4.9	3.8	4.1	N/A	N/A	N/A
Turkmenistan	4.8	6.2	6	5.8	6.2	6.5	7.3	6.1	5.7
Ukraine	158.5	170.7	186.7	184.7	N/A	N/A	N/A	N/A	N/A
Uzbekistan	26.3	29	27.6	21.7	19.1	16.8	18	19.4	9.4
Yugoslavia	6.3	4.9	4.1	4.2	4.5	5	4.7	4.6	4.8

N/A Not Available

Source: TransMONEE 2000 database; <http://www.eurochild.gla.ac.uk/documents/monee/welcome.htm>, UNICEF Innocenti Research Centre, Florence. Underlying data from United Nations Children's Fund (UNICEF).

G9-2. Rate of Children Involved in Divorce (Children Involved in Divorce during the Year per 100,000 Population Aged 0–17 Years), Selected Countries, 1990–1998

	1990	1991	1992	1993	1994	1995	1996	1997	1998
Albania	2	1.7	N/A	1.6	1	1	0.9	0.7	N/A
Armenia	2.9	2.5	2.1	2.2	2.3	1.7	1.8	1.8	1.3
Azerbaijan	3.6	2.8	2.3	1.6	1.4	0.9	0.7	1.2	1.2
Belarus	11.3	12.9	13.9	16.2	15.6	15	16	17.6	17.7
Bosnia-Herzegovina	N/A	N/A	N/A	N/A	N/A	N/A	N/A	N/A	N/A
Bulgaria	5.9	5.7	5	3.9	3.6	5	4.7	4.6	5.3
Croatia	N/A	5.5	4.2	5.5	5.4	5.2	4.6	5	4.9
Czech Republic	12.8	11.8	11.7	12.6	13.2	13.5	14.8	14.7	14.7
Estonia	12.8	13.1	15.5	13.3	12.8	19.1	15.6	14.6	12.6
Georgia	2.8	2.9	1.2	N/A	1	1	0.7	0.7	1.3
Hungary	10	9.9	9.1	9.3	9.8	10.7	9.3	11.3	11.7
Kazakhstan	6.7	7.6	7.9	7.3	6.7	6.5	7.1	6.8	7.2
Kyrgyzstan	3.7	4.3	3.6	3.3	2.6	3	3.4	3.4	3.3
Latvia	14.1	14.7	20.6	14.3	12.8	12.4	9.3	9.9	9.8
Lithuania	12	15.2	13.8	13.4	11.7	11.4	12.7	13	13.5
Macedonia	N/A	N/A	N/A	N/A	N/A	N/A	N/A	N/A	N/A
Moldova	8.1	9	10	9.6	8.7	9.4	8.9	N/A	8.4
Poland	4	3.2	3	2.6	3	3.8	4	4.3	4.6
Romania	4.2	4.7	3.7	3.5	5.5	4.7	4.7	4.9	5.7
Russia	11.6	13.1	14.3	15.2	15.9	15.5	12.5	12.5	11
Slovakia	8.4	6.5	6.1	6.2	6.8	4.5	4.8	N/A	4.9
Slovenia	4	3.9	4.1	4.2	4.3	3.3	4.5	4.5	4.9
Tajikistan	2.7	2.9	2.2	1.7	1.3	1.4	N/A	N/A	N/A
Turkmenistan	2.8	3.5	3.3	3.2	3.2	3.1	3.4	2.9	2.7
Ukraine	11.9	12.9	14.2	14.1	N/A	N/A	N/A	N/A	N/A
Uzbekistan	2.7	2.9	2.7	2.1	1.8	1.6	1.7	1.8	0.9
Yugoslavia	2.2	1.7	1.4	1.5	1.6	1.8	1.7	1.7	1.8

N/A Not Available

Source: TransMONEE 2000 database; <http://www.eurochild.gla.ac.uk/documents/monee/welcome.htm>, UNICEF Innocenti Research Centre, Florence. Underlying data from United Nations Children's Fund (UNICEF).

G10. WORKING MOTHERS

G10-1. Working Mothers with Children Under Three Years of Age, Selected Countries, 1983, 1992, 1997

	1983 percent	1992 percent	1997 percent
Belgium	50	62	69
Canada	42	54	62
Denmark	N/A	43	45
France	48	52	51
Greece	27	42	45
Ireland	18	37	48
Italy	38	42	42
Luxembourg	34	37	46
Netherlands, the	18	42	59
Portugal	N/A	69	69
Spain	N/A	31	39
United Kingdom	21	45	55
United States	42	49	58

Source: The World's Women 2000, United Nations (UN); Chapter 2, chart 2.18.

G11. SEXUAL ACTIVITY

G11-1. Percent of 15-Year-Olds Who Are Sexually Active, Selected Countries, 1997–1998

	Boys	Girls
Finland	23	30
France	30	20
Hungary	47	34
Israel*	44	11
Latvia	36	19
Northern Ireland (UK)	30	26
Poland	30	13
Scotland (UK)	33	37
United States	38	38

* Refers to 15-year-old Jewish secular population only.

Source: Health and Health Behaviour among Young People, 2000, WHO Policy Series: Health policy for children and adolescents, Issue 1, International Report 2/1/2000; <http://www.ruhbc.ed.ac.uk/hbsc/download/hbsc.pdf> and <http://www.who.dk/document/e67880.pdf> Underlying data from The Health Behaviour in School-Aged Children (HBSC) study by the WHO Regional Office for Europe.

G11-2. Mean Age of Sexual Initiation, Selected Countries, 1997–1998

	Boys	Girls
France	14.7	14.3
Israel	15.5	14.6
Latvia	15.0	14.9
Northern Ireland (UK)	14.7	14.0
Scotland (UK)	14.4	14.3
United States	14.2	13.8

Source: Health and Health Behaviour among Young People, 2000, WHO Policy Series: Health policy for children and adolescents, Issue 1, International Report 2/1/2000, Table 10.1; <http://www.ruhbc.ed.ac.uk/hbsc/download/hbsc.pdf> and <http://www.who.dk/document/e67880.pdf>. Underlying data from The Health Behaviour in School-Aged Children (HBSC) study by the WHO Regional Office for Europe.

G12. CONTRACEPTION

G12-1. Percentage of Currently Married Women Ages 15 to 19 Using Contraception by Method and Country, Selected Countries, various years

	Year of survey	No method	All methods	Modern methods-all	Traditional
Bangladesh	1993/94	75.3	24.7	19.7	5.1
Belize	1991	73.8	26.2	24.4	1.7
Bolivia	1994	69.8	30.2	9.4	20.8
Botswana	1988	82.8	17.2	14.6	2.7
Brazil *	1991	58.7	41.3	38.3	3.0
Burkina Faso	1993	94.1	5.9	2.3	3.7
Burundi	1987	95.7	4.3	0.6	3.7
Cameroon	1991	81.6	18.4	1.4	16.9
Colombia	1990	63.1	36.9	31.9	5.0
Costa Rica	1993	47.0	53.0	44.0	9.0
Dominican Republic	1991	82.6	17.4	13.2	4.0
Ecuador	1989	75.0	25.0	18.0	7.0
Egypt	1992	86.7	13.3	12.7	0.6
El Salvador	1993	77.7	22.3	18.9	3.4
Ghana	1993	87.0	13.0	8.1	5.0
Guatemala	1987	94.6	5.4	2.5	2.8
India	1992/93	92.9	7.1	4.0	3.1
Indonesia	1991	70.0	30.0	29.1	0.9
Jamaica	1993	41.2	58.8	54.4	4.4
Jordan	1990	87.7	12.3	3.9	8.4
Kenya	1993	89.7	10.3	6.2	4.1
Liberia	1986	97.9	2.1	2.0	0.1
Madagascar	1992	93.6	6.4	0.6	5.9
Malawi	1992	92.7	7.3	3.4	3.9
Mali	1987	91.4	8.6	1.4	7.2
Mauritius	1991	53.7	46.3	28.3	17.9
Mexico	1987	70.3	29.7	24.4	5.3
Morocco	1992	76.7	23.3	22.2	1.2
Namibia	1992	79.5	20.5	16.5	3.9
Nicaragua	1992/93	76.8	23.2	20.7	2.5
Niger	1992	97.8	2.2	0.8	1.3
Nigeria	1990	98.7	1.3	0.6	0.7
Pakistan	1990/91	97.4	2.6	1.8	0.7
Panama	1984	77.4	22.6	19.7	2.9
Paraguay	1990	64.6	35.4	26.2	9.2
Peru	1991/92	70.9	29.1	11.0	18.2
Philippines	1993	82.8	17.2	9.7	7.6
Rwanda	1992	89.2	10.8	7.1	3.7
Senegal	1992/93	98.0	2.0	0.4	1.6
Sri Lanka	1987	79.7	20.3	10.8	9.5
Sudan *	1989/90	96.2	3.8	2.2	1.6
Tanzania	1994	85.0	15.0	8.3	6.7
Thailand	1987	57.0	43.0	40.4	2.6
Togo	1988	83.3	16.7	2.0	14.6
Trinidad and Togago	1987	57.6	42.4	30.2	12.2
Tunisia	1988	88.9	11.1	9.6	1.6
Turkey	1993	75.9	24.1	9.3	14.8
Uganda	1988/89	98.3	1.7	1.2	0.5
Yemen	1991/92	94.9	5.1	1.3	3.8
Zambia	1992	91.3	8.7	3.5	5.2
Zimbabwe	1988	70.0	30.0	28.4	1.7

* Data are only for some parts of the country.

Source: Trends in Adolescent Fertility and Contraceptive Use in the Developing World, by Thomas M. McDevitt with Arjun Adlakha, Timothy B. Fowler and Vera Harris-Bourne, IPC/95-1, Table 15, 1995; < http://www.census.gov/ipc/prod/ipc95-1/ipc95_1j.pdf>. Underlying data from U.S. Bureau of the Census.

G13. TEENAGE ABORTIONS

G13-1. Number of Abortions Registered during the Year to Women under 20 Years Old, Selected Countries, 1995–1998

	Number of Abortions in 1,000s			
	1995	**1996**	**1997**	**1998**
Albania	0.9	0.3	N/A	N/A
Armenia	N/A	N/A	0.9	0.8
Azerbaijan	1.0	0.6	0.6	1.0
Belarus	13.1	13.8	14.0	14.1
Bulgaria	11.1	11.4	10.6	9.1
Czech Republic	6.5	6.1	5.3	5.2
Estonia	2.2	2.4	2.3	2.3
Georgia	4.0	1.7	1.3	1.0
Hungary	14.7	13.2	12.2	10.8
Kazakhstan	24.2	21.7	13.3	10.9
Kyrgyzstan	5.9	3.9	3.7	2.5
Latvia	2.6	2.6	2.5	2.0
Lithuania	1.7	1.8	1.5	1.5
Moldova	4.4	4.4	3.7	2.9
Romania	39.6	36.7	26.7	21.4
Russia	304.1	273.7	258.1	242.3
Slovakia	3.4	3.0	2.7	2.6
Slovenia	0.8	0.8	0.7	0.9
Tajikistan	2.9	2.6	1.8	1.9
Uzbekistan	9.1	7.8	6.2	4.9
Yugoslavia	3.0	2.5	N/A	N/A

Source: TransMONEE 2000 database; <http://www.eurochild.gla.ac.uk/Documents/monee/queries/t02.htm>, UNICEF Innocenti Research Centre, Florence. Underlying data from United Nations Children's Fund (UNICEF).

G14. MARRIED ADOLESCENTS

G14-1. Percent of 15- to 19-Year-Olds Who Are Currently Married or Cohabiting, 1986–1996

	Males	**Females**
Bangladesh	7	48
Bolivia	3	15
Botswana	1	6
Brazil	2	14
Burkina Faso	3	44
Burundi	4	6
Cameroon	3	41
Central African Republic	6	39
China	1	3
Colombia	6	14
Côte d'Ivoire	3	26
Dominican Republic	6	18
Ecuador	4	17
Egypt	3	14
El Salvador	4	24
France	1	4
Germany	0	2
Ghana	2	20
Guatemala	8	24
India	6	38
Indonesia	2	17

G14-1. Percent of 15- to 19-Year-Olds Who Are Currently Married or Cohabiting, 1986–1996 *(continued)*

	Males	Females
Japan	0	2
Kenya	3	15
Liberia	3	32
Madagascar	9	21
Malawi	6	36
Mali	1	72
Mexico	7	18
Morocco	2	12
Namibia	-	7
Niger	14	57
Nigeria	-	37
Pakistan	4	24
Paraguay	1	14
Peru	3	10
Philippines	4	7
Poland	1	8
Rwanda	3	8
Senegal	1	29
Sri Lanka	1	7
Sudan	3	15
Tanzania	3	26
Thailand	4	16
Togo	2	27
Trinidad and Tobago	1	20
Tunisia	0	4
Turkey	5	13
Uganda	8	47
United Kingdom	3	11
United States	1	8
Yemen	13	24
Zambia	2	27
Zimbabwe	2	19

Source: Progress of Nations 1998; <http://www.unicef.org/pon98/>, United Nations Children Fund (UNICEF). Underlying data from The Alan Guttmacher Institute, *Into a New World, Young Women's Sexual and Reproductive Lives,* New York, 1998.

G14-2. Percentage of 15- to 19-Year-Olds Married, Selected Countries, 2000

	Boys	Girls
Sub-Saharan Africa		
Congo, Dem. Rep. (Zaire)	5	74
Congo, Rep.	12	56
Mali	5	50
Niger	4	70
Uganda	11	50
Asia		
Afghanistan	9	54
Bangladesh	5	51
Nepal	14	42
Middle East		
Iraq	15	28
Syria	4	25
Yemen	5	24
Latin America and Caribbean		
Honduras	7	30
Cuba	7	29
Guatemala	8	24

Source: "Early Marriage Child Spouses," *Unicef Innocenti Digest,* No.7 March 2001, page 5; <http://www.unicef.org/hpphotocaption/7mar01-earlymarriage.htm>,UNICEF Innocenti Research Centre, Florence, Italy. Underlying data from UN Population Division, Department of Economic and Social Affairs, World Marriage Patterns 2000.

G14-3. Percent of Women Aged 15–19 Married, 1985–1996

	Percent
Niger	72.5
Bangladesh	65.4
Sierra Leone	57.5
United Arab Emirates	55.0
Afghanistan	53.3
Gambia, the	52.7
Benin	51.4
Mozambique	47.7
Nepal	45.7
India	43.5
Mali	42.9
Ethiopia	41.7
Côte d'Ivoire	41.3
Senegal	40.9
Central African Republic	40.8
Malawi	38.6
Uganda	37.3
Cameroon	37.3
Tanzania	35.7
Madagascar	34.3
Burkina Faso	33.0
Congo, Dem. Rep. (Zaire)	31.0
Maldives	30.9
Pakistan	29.1
Cuba	26.9
Sudan	26.0
Equatorial Guinea	25.7
Iran	25.5
Syria	24.6
Yemen	23.2
Marshall Islands	22.5
Guatemala	22.5
Zambia	21.9
Panama	21.3
Egypt	20.2
Sao Tome and Principe	19.9
Zimbabwe	19.2
Papua New Guinea	18.8
Venezuela	18.4
Solomon Islands	18.3
Iraq	18.2
Kenya	18.2
Ecuador	17.4
Lesotho	17.3
Georgia	16.5
Brazil	16.5
Paraguay	16.5
Colombia	16.3
Bulgaria	16.1
Myanmar (Burma)	16.0
Kiribati	15.7
Congo	15.7
El Salvador	15.6
Costa Rica	15.4
Turkey	15.1
Armenia	15.1
Mexico	15.1
Rwanda	15.0

G14-3. Percent of Women Aged 15–19 Married, 1985–1996 *(continued)*

	Percent
Comoros	14.9
Ukraine	14.7
Mauritania	14.3
Thailand	14.2
Peru	14.2
Qatar	14.1
Indonesia	13.5
Uzbekistan	13.3
Bolivia	13.1
Fiji	12.8
Kuwait	12.6
Puerto Rico	12.3
Argentina	12.3
Morocco	12.1
Chile	11.6
Guyana	11.6
Vanuatu	11.3
Mauritius	11.3
Tajikistan	11.3
Vietnam	11.2
Uruguay	11.2
Moldova	11.1
Yugoslavia	10.6
Russia	10.5
Kyrgyzstan	10.4
Sri Lanka	9.7
Micronesia	9.3
Philippines	9.3
Algeria	9.3
Jordan	9.3
Romania	9.0
Azerbaijan	8.9
Kazakhstan	8.9
Belize	8.9
Swaziland	8.8
Trinidad and Tobago	8.7
Latvia	8.2
Haiti	8.0
Belarus	7.9
Brunei	7.8
Cyprus	7.5
Djibouti	7.4
Malaysia	7.4
Estonia	7.2
Slovakia	6.9
Burundi	6.6
Cape Verde	6.6
Bahrain	6.5
Namibia	6.4
Lithuania	6.3
Turkmenistan	6.2
Virgin Islands, US	5.9
Tonga	5.9
Seychelles	5.6
Guam	5.6
Portugal	5.6
Greece	5.5
Croatia	5.1
Botswana	5.1
Israel	4.9

G14-3. Percent of Women Aged 15–19 Married, 1985–1996 *(continued)*

	Percent
Denmark	4.9
American Samoa	4.7
China	4.6
Italy	4.6
Poland	4.4
South Africa	4.3
Czech Republic	4.2
Northern Mariana Islands	4.1
Hungary	4.0
United States	3.9
Samoa	3.7
Bahamas	3.6
Palau	3.4
French Polynesia	3.3
Tunisia	3.0
Malta	3.0
Austria	2.7
Canada	2.6
Belgium	2.4
Luxembourg	2.4
Macau	2.3
Spain	2.3
Slovenia	2.1
Reunion	2.0
Cook Islands	1.9
New Caledonia	1.7
Netherlands Antilles	1.6
Hong Kong, SAR (China)	1.6
Germany	1.5
Australia	1.5
Australia	1.5
Switzerland	1.4
Singapore	1.3
New Zealand	1.1
New Zealand	1.1
Guadeloupe	1.1
United Kingdom	1.0
San Marino	0.9
Liechtenstein	0.8
Netherlands	0.8
France	0.8
St. Vincent and the Grenadines	0.8
St. Lucia	0.7
Finland	0.6
Japan	0.6
Japan	0.6
Barbados	0.6
Sweden	0.5
South Korea, Rep.	0.5
Norway	0.5
Martinique	0.5
Jamaica	0.5
St. Kitts and Nevis	0.5
Grenada	0.5
Dominica	0.4
Ireland	0.3
Iceland	0.2

Source: World's Women, 1995; <http://www.un.org/Depts/unsd/gender/>. Underlying data from United Nations (UN).

G14-4. Percentage of Women Aged 25–29 Married before Age 18, Selected Countries, late 1990s

	Percent
Latin America	
Guatemala	39
Dominican Republic	38
Paraguay	24
South Central and Southeast Asia	
Bangladesh	81
Nepal	68
Pakistan	37
Indonesia	34
Sub-Saharan Africa	
Niger	77
Mali	70
Burkina Faso	62
Mozambique	57
Malawi	55
Cote d'Ivoire	44
Cameroon	43
Benin	40
Middle East and North Africa	
Yemen	64
Egypt	30

Source: "Early Marriage Child Spouses," *Unicef Innocenti Digest*, No.7 March 2001, page 5; <http://www.unicef.org/hpphotocaption/7mar01-earlymarriage.htm>,UNICEF Innocenti Research Centre, Florence, Italy. Underlying data from Population Council.

G14-5. Countries with the Lowest Women's Mean Age (Below 19 Years) at Marriage, 1985–1996

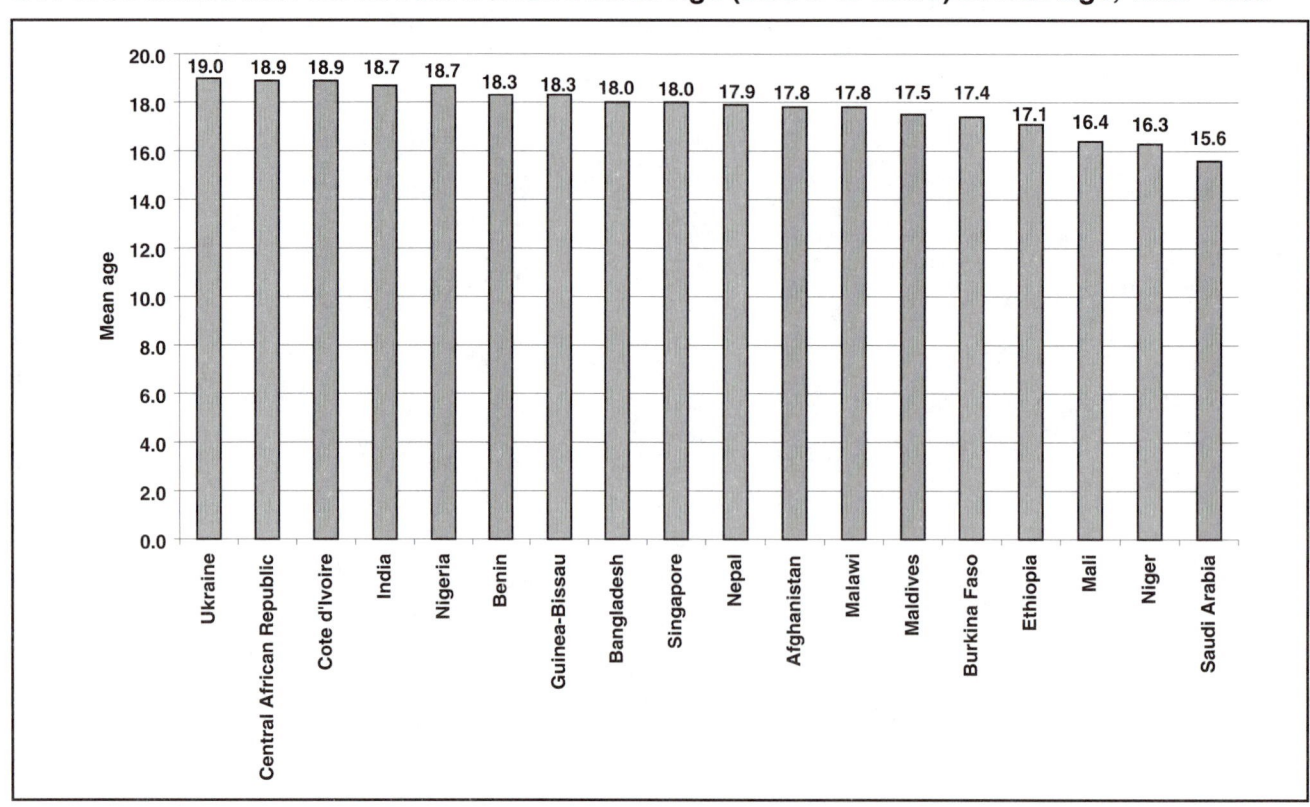

Source: World's Women, 1995; <http://www.un.org/Depts/unsd/gender/>. Underlying data from United Nations (UN).

G14-6. Marriage and Level of Education of Young Women, Selected Countries, various years

Country (year of data)	Percent of 15–19-year-old women married	Average age at 1st marriage of women	% of women with 7+ years school-married before age 20	% of women with 7+ years school-married at age 20 or older
Sub-Saharan Africa				
Botswana (1988)	6	25	55	71
Cameroon (1991)	44	19	27	77
Mali (1987)	75	16	6	19
Niger (1992)	59	18	1	17
Uganda (1988/89)	41	19	20	43
Latin America				
Guatemala (1987)	26	21	9	34
Mexico (1987)	20	22	32	72
Middle East				
Egypt (1992)	14	22	25	60
Yemen (1991/92)	25	21	6	21
Asia				
China (1987/88)	5	22	28	60
Indonesia (1991)	20	22	18	58
Pakistan (1990/91)	25	21	8	25

Source: "Early Marriage: Child Spouses," *Unicef Innocenti Digest,* No.7 March 2001, page 6; <http://www.unicef.org/hppphotocaption/7mar01-earlymarriage.htm>,UNICEF Innocenti Research Centre, Florence, Italy. Underlying data from Sexual Relationships and Marriage Worldwide, Alan Guttmacher Institute 1995.

G15. TOBACCO AND ALCOHOL

G15-1. Percent of Students Who Report Smoking Daily, 11-Year-Olds, 13-Year-Olds, 15-Year-Olds, Males and Females, Selected Countries, 1997–1998

	11-Year-Olds		**13-Year-Olds**		**15-Year-Olds**	
	percent male	percent female	percent male	percent female	percent male	percent female
Austria	0.3	0.1	5	3	20	26
Belgium (Flemish)	1.0	0.0	6	4	21	20
Canada	1.0	1.0	8	8	17	21
Czech Republic	1.0	0.2	6	3	16	11
Denmark	0.4	0.1	3	4	15	21
England (UK)	1.0	1.0	7	8	21	24
Estonia	0.0	1.0	4	1	17	8
Finland	0.2	0.4	7	8	19	20
France	1.0	0.5	5	6	20	25
Germany	1.0	0.1	9	9	22	25
Greece	0.1	0.5	3	2	13	14
Greenland	2.0	2.0	19	29	45	56
Hungary	1.0	0.0	6	3	29	20
Ireland	1.0	0.4	8	6	19	16
Israel	4.0	2.0	6	3	17	7
Latvia	2.0	0.1	8	3	27	12
Lithuania	1.0	0.3	6	1	15	6
Northern Ireland (UK)	1.0	1.0	7	10	16	24
Norway	1.0	0.1	5	4	18	21
Poland	1.0	0.4	3	2	22	14
Portugal	1.0	1.0	3	2	13	10
Russian Federation	0.4	0.0	7	3	20	14
Scotland (UK)	1.0	2.0	5	8	19	24
Slovakia	1.0	0.3	4	2	20	10
Sweden	0.0	0.3	2	2	10	16
Switzerland	0.5	0.0	3	4	17	17
United States	2.0	1.0	5	3	13	12
Wales (UK)	1.0	1.0	6	12	18	23

Source: Health and Health Behaviour among Young People, 2000; Figure 9.2, WHO Policy Series: Health policy for children and adolescent, Issue 1, International Report 2/1/2000, Table 10.1; <http://www.ruhbc.ed.ac.uk/hbsc/download/hbsc.pdf>. Underlying data from The Health Behaviour in School-Aged Children (HBSC) study by the WHO Regional Office for Europe.

G15-2. Median Number of Cigarettes Smoked Weekly, 11-Year-Olds, 13-Year-Olds, 15-Year-Olds, Males and Females, Selected Countries, 1997–1998

	11-Year-Olds		13-Year-Olds		15-Year-Olds	
	males	females	males	females	males	males
Austria	1	1	5	3	3	20
Belgium	1	1	7	4	21	20
Canada	2	2	10	7	20	25
Czech Republic	2	2	5	3	14	10
Denmark	2	1	8	5	30	28
England (UK)	2	1	10	5	30	20
Estonia	1	4.5	5	1	20	10
Finland	2	2.5	10	9	26	20
France	4.5	2.5	4.5	3	7	10
Germany	3	5	10	9	29.5	20
Greece	7	4.5	7	6	35	30
Greenland	7	3.5	11.5	15	30	30
Hungary	1	1	3	3	24	12
Ireland	1	2	10	5	25	20
Israel	5	3.5	5	4	20	10
Latvia	2	1	7	3	20	10
Lithuania	2	1	5	3	12	4
Northern Ireland (UK)	3	3	10	10	30	30
Norway	1	2.5	5	5	25	20
Poland	1	2.5	3	2	20	10
Portugal	2	2.5	5	3	20	20
Russia	1	1	9	4.5	20	10
Scotland (UK)	2	2	5	8	30	30
Slovakia	2	2	5	3	30	15
Sweden	1	2	4	4	10	20
Switzerland	1	1	4	4	20	20
United States	1.5	3	4	3	20	10
Wales (UK)	4.5	2	11.5	12	30	30

Source: Health and Health Behaviour among Young People, 2000, Table 9.2, WHO Policy Series: Health policy for children and adolescents, Issue 1, International Report 2/1/2000, Table 10.1; <http://www.ruhbc.ed.ac.uk/hbsc/download/hbsc.pdf>. Underlying data from The Health Behaviour in School-Aged Children (HBSC) study by the WHO Regional Office for Europe.

G15-3. Percent of 15-Year-Olds Who Report Smoking Daily, Selected Countries, 1994 and 1998

	Boys		Girls	
	1994	1998	1994	1998
Austria	21	20	21	26
Belgium	19	21	14	20
Canada	16	17	21	21
Czech Republic	11	16	6	
Denmark	10	15	17	21
Estonia	16	17	3	8
Finland	25	19	19	20
France	18	20	18	25
Germany	16	22	19	25
Hungary	19	29	13	20
Israel	6	17	5	7
Latvia	22	27	8	12
Lithuania	9	15	2	6
Norway	16	18	15	21
Poland	17	22	8	14
Russia	13	20	5	14
Slovakia	13	20	3	10
Sweden	10	10	13	16
United Kingdom	N/A	N/A	N/A	N/A
Northern Ireland (UK)	20	16	20	24
Scotland (UK)	17	19	21	24
United States	10	13	10	12

N/A Not available

Source: The Progress of Nations, 2000; <http://www.unicef.org/pon00/> and <http://www.ruhbc.ed.ac.uk/hbsc/download/hbsc.pdf>. Underlying data from United Nations Children's Fund (UNICEF) and WHO Regional Office for Europe.

G15-4. Percent of Students Who Report Drinking Beer, Wine or Spirits at Least Weekly, 11-Year-Olds, 13-Year-Olds, 15-Year-Olds, Males and Females, Selected Countries, 1997–1998

	11-Year-Olds		13-Year-Olds		15-Year-Olds	
	males	females	males	females	males	females
Austria	3	1	8	4	39	23
Belgium	7	2	11	6	38	22
Canada	3	2	10	6	22	17
Czech Republic	15	8	16	9	32	19
Denmark	4	2	11	9	46	38
England (UK)	14	9	22	16	47	36
Estonia	6	2	7	3	21	10
Finland	2	0.3	5	4	11	8
France	6	3	12	5	31	15
Germany	2	0.3	10	5	29	22
Greece	20	8	27	16	52	31
Greenland	1	0	3	6	13	10
Hungary	3	1	8	4	29	11
Ireland	7	1	8	6	27	12
Israel	18	6	20	9	26	10
Latvia	2	0.4	9	4	28	12
Lithuania	5	2	10	4	16	9
Northern Ireland (UK)	5	1	14	6	33	20
Norway	1	0.2	4	3	16	12
Poland	3	1	7	3	20	8
Portugal	4	1	9	3	29	9
Russia	6	3	11	9	28	24
Scotland (UK)	8	4	17	11	37	33
Slovakia	11	6	14	9	32	16
Sweden	3	1	6	4	17	11
Switzerland	4	0.5	5	3	19	9
United States	8	7	10	11	23	15
Wales (UK)	12	5	24	16	53	36

Source: Health and Health Behaviour among Young People, 2000, Figure 9.5, WHO Policy Series: Health policy for children and adolescents, Issue 1, International Report 2/1/2000, Table 10.1; <http://www.ruhbc.ed.ac.uk/hbsc/download/hbsc.pdf> and <http://www.who.dk/document/e67880.pdf>. Underlying data from The Health Behaviour in School-Aged Children (HBSC) study by the WHO Regional Office for Europe.

G15-5. Legal Age for Buying Cigarettes and Legal Age for Buying Alcoholic Beverages, Selected Countries, 1997–1998

	Legal age for buying cigarettes (years)	Legal age for buying alcoholic beverages (years)
Austria	16	16
Belgium	NR	16
Canada	18-19	18-19
Czech Republic	16	18
Denmark	NR	15
England	16	18
Estonia	N/A	N/A
Finland	18	18
France	NR	16
Germany	16	16
Greece	NR	NR
Greenland	15	18
Hungary	18	16
Ireland	16	18
Israel	NR	18
Latvia	18	18
Lithuania	18	21
Northern Ireland	16	18
Norway	18	18
Poland	18	18
Portugal	NR	16

G15-5. Legal Age for Buying Cigarettes and Legal Age for Buying Alcoholic Beverages, Selected Countries, 1997–1998 *(continued)*

	Legal age for buying cigarettes (years)	Legal age for buying alcoholic beverages (years)
Russia	18	18
Scotland	16	18
Slovakia	18	18
Sweden	18	18-20
Switzerland	NR	16
United States	18-21	21
Wales	16	18

NR Not Restricted
N/A Not Available

Source: Health and Health Behaviour among Young People, 2000; Table 11.2, WHO Policy Series: Health policy for children and adolescents, Issue 1, International Report 2/1/2000, Table 10.1; <http://www.ruhbc.ed.ac.uk/hbsc/download/hbsc.pdf> and <http://www.who.dk/document/e67880.pdf> Underlying data from The Health Behaviour in School-Aged Children (HBSC) study by the WHO Regional Office for Europe.

G16. FOOD HABITS

G16-1. Percent of Students Who Report Eating Potato Crisps Every Day, 11-Year-Olds, 13-Year-Olds, 15-Year-Olds, Males and Females, Selected Countries, 1997–1998

	11-Year-Olds		13-Year-Olds		15-Year-Olds	
	male	female	male	female	male	female
Austria	18	12	14	9	12	6
Belgium	13	12	14	8	12	8
Canada	21	16	21	13	16	11
Czech Republic	16	15	16	11	10	6
Denmark	8	5	6	3	5	2
England (UK)	61	60	63	62	60	50
Estonia	26	22	21	10	11	5
France	25	20	21	15	22	15
Germany	21	14	16	11	10	7
Greece	34	24	27	23	18	15
Greenland	20	12	7	11	11	12
Hungary	22	18	18	15	12	12
Ireland	54	54	60	58	56	50
Israel	33	33	30	28	34	27
Latvia	35	28	29	19	25	19
Lithuania	23	18	16	13	13	9
Northern Ireland (UK)	77	82	78	82	71	75
Norway	12	5	12	5	10	5
Poland	41	36	37	27	25	19
Portugal	32	21	31	22	21	17
Russia	35	33	36	34	39	27
Scotland (UK)	73	73	66	65	63	61
Slovakia	33	28	23	17	21	12
Sweden	8	4	6	3	6	4
Switzerland	12	7	13	9	12	7
United States	36	33	33	34	31	26
Wales (UK)	47	49	44	48	45	37

Source: Health and Health Behaviour among Young People, 2000; Figure 8.2, WHO Policy Series: Health policy for children and adolescents, Issue 1, International Report 2/1/2000, Table 10.1; <http://www.ruhbc.ed.ac.uk/hbsc/download/hbsc.pdf> and <http://www.who.dk/document/e67880.pdf>. Underlying data from The Health Behaviour in School-Aged Children (HBSC) study by the WHO Regional Office for Europe.

G16-2. Percent of Students Who Report Eating Sweets or Chocolate Every Day, 11-Year-Olds, 13-Year-Olds, 15-Year-Olds, Males and Females, Selected Countries, 1997–1998

	11-Year-Olds		13-Year-Olds		15-Year-Olds	
	male	female	male	female	male	female
Austria	32	32	39	39	43	42
Belgium	31	33	31	29	33	24
Canada	27	23	28	24	25	22
Czech Republic	49	49	44	47	45	38
Denmark	25	19	27	27	31	27
England (UK)	56	55	67	59	62	54
Estonia	65	64	63	62	64	60
Finland	19	12	23	22	24	14
France	45	42	42	45	47	40
Germany	49	48	48	47	45	41
Greece	34	30	43	44	43	47
Greenland	42	40	43	44	38	42
Hungary	61	60	64	63	57	64
Ireland	71	72	80	77	80	75
Israel	57	63	55	57	59	54
Latvia	49	46	51	47	43	47
Lithuania	43	49	48	46	42	38
Northern Ireland (UK)	73	75	79	81	78	81
Norway	19	13	28	20	30	27
Poland	50	51	51	48	44	44
Portugal	50	54	64	60	60	55
Russia	50	53	52	63	51	58
Scotland (UK)	74	71	79	74	78	71
Slovakia	61	64	62	62	49	58
Sweden	19	14	27	27	31	28
Switzerland	39	37	44	40	44	40
United States	49	51	51	54	53	51
Wales (UK)	46	43	48	50	50	41

Source: Health and Health Behaviour among Young People, 2000; Figure 8.4, WHO Policy Series: Health policy for children and adolescents, Issue 1, International Report 2/1/2000, Table 10.1; <http://www.ruhbc.ed.ac.uk/hbsc/download/hbsc.pdf> and <http://www.who.dk/document/e67880.pdf>. Underlying data from The Health Behaviour in School-Aged Children (HBSC) study by the WHO Regional Office for Europe.

G16-3. Percent of Students Who Report Drinking Soft Drinks Every Day, 11-Year-Olds, 13-Year-Olds, 15-Year-Olds, Males and Females, Selected Countries, 1997–1998

	11-Year-Olds		13-Year-Olds		15-Year-Olds	
	percent male	percent female	percent male	percent female	percent male	percent female
Austria	33	26	43	33	39	26
Belgium	40	39	50	46	55	39
Canada	43	34	55	44	60	46
Czech Republic	48	44	49	46	52	36
Denmark	21	14	29	20	40	22
England (UK)	59	55	67	56	67	53
Estonia	39	34	44	25	41	25
Finland	19	9	19	9	22	6
France	41	32	42	30	42	27
Germany	48	42	54	42	54	37
Greece	49	33	60	43	61	41
Greenland	46	35	53	44	64	55
Hungary	46	37	53	45	58	45
Ireland	64	56	71	59	75	51
Israel	72	68	76	65	78	64
Latvia	41	30	39	26	37	23
Lithuania	35	31	36	26	30	19
Northern Ireland (UK)	69	70	79	75	78	71
Norway	21	14	26	18	37	24
Poland	46	34	47	36	48	38

G16-3. Percent of Students Who Report Drinking Soft Drinks Every Day, 11-Year-Olds, 13-Year-Olds, 15-Year-Olds, Males and Females, Selected Countries, 1997–1998 *(continued)*

	11-Year-Olds		13-Year-Olds		15-Year-Olds	
	percent male	percent female	percent male	percent female	percent male	percent female
Portugal	49	40	56	47	58	42
Russia	37	32	38	29	36	30
Scotland (UK)	65	60	76	60	77	57
Slovakia	52	49	50	49	55	44
Sweden	22	14	28	15	32	19
Switzerland	44	37	52	42	56	45
United States	64	60	68	68	72	66
Wales (UK)	60	56	59	56	59	44

Source: Health and Health Behaviour among Young People, 2000; Figure 8.5, WHO Policy Series: Health policy for children and adolescents, Issue 1, International Report 2/1/2000, Table 10.1, <http://www.ruhbc.ed.ac.uk/hbsc/download/hbsc.pdf> and <http://www.who.dk/document/e67880.pdf>. Underlying data from The Health Behaviour in School-Aged Children (HBSC) study by the WHO Regional Office for Europe.

G16-4. Percent of Students Who Report Eating Fruit Every Day, 11-Year-Olds, 13-Year-Olds, 15-Year-Olds, Males and Females, Selected Countries, 1997–1998

	11-Year-Olds		13-Year-Olds		15-Year-Olds	
	male	female	male	female	male	female
Austria	69	78	63	77	55	69
Belgium	46	54	46	48	39	53
Canada	69	76	64	69	61	65
Czech Republic	82	89	81	85	77	82
Denmark	59	70	59	66	48	59
England (UK)	63	70	58	63	52	57
Estonia	67	62	70	69	56	65
Finland	58	62	50	58	43	56
France	58	55	57	53	53	59
Germany	71	76	64	69	51	63
Greece	87	85	81	83	75	76
Greenland	31	41	31	38	29	36
Hungary	81	84	80	82	76	79
Ireland	75	82	70	77	66	75
Israel	71	75	74	78	73	78
Latvia	65	64	68	56	59	59
Lithuania	66	67	62	62	57	58
Northern Ireland (UK)	73	85	70	76	63	71
Norway	59	63	46	54	35	50
Poland	85	87	82	85	78	79
Portugal	92	94	92	93	91	95
Russia	65	72	65	69	66	67
Scotland (UK)	69	75	61	70	54	60
Slovakia	77	80	76	81	70	78
Sweden	70	79	67	75	58	69
Switzerland	58	60	52	60	44	59
United States	61	67	60	61	53	58
Wales (UK)	55	62	50	58	39	55

Source: Health and Health Behaviour among Young People, 2000; Figure 8.1, WHO Policy Series: Health policy for children and adolescents, Issue 1, International Report 2/1/2000, Table 10.1; <http://www.ruhbc.ed.ac.uk/hbsc/download/hbsc.pdf> and <http://www.who.dk/document/e67880.pdf>. Underlying data from The Health Behaviour in School-Aged Children (HBSC) study by the WHO Regional Office for Europe.

G17. DENTAL CARE

G17-1. Percent of Students Who Report Brushing Their Teeth More Than Once a Day, 11-Year-Olds, 13-Year-Olds, 15-Year-Olds, Males and Females, Selected Countries, 1997–1998

	11-Year-Olds		13-Year-Olds		15-Year-Olds	
	male	female	male	female	male	female
Austria	58	73	55	74	61	79
Belgium	33	44	35	55	42	62
Canada	55	67	56	74	59	80
Czech Republic	60	73	54	73	56	77
Denmark	80	85	79	88	78	88
England (UK)	62	76	60	82	64	84
Estonia	46	65	47	69	48	69
Finland	28	42	28	50	31	61
France	54	69	60	76	53	79
Germany	69	82	66	79	66	82
Greece	42	53	36	53	35	64
Greenland	53	70	44	71	52	69
Hungary	49	64	47	68	55	78
Ireland	47	61	44	67	46	74
Israel	57	69	54	73	54	71
Latvia	47	63	39	56	42	65
Lithuania	36	47	27	47	33	53
Northern Ireland (UK)	55	75	50	76	56	84
Norway	65	72	62	74	64	82
Poland	52	70	55	74	52	79
Portugal	54	73	51	76	56	78
Russia	56	72	57	70	53	74
Scotland (UK)	57	66	56	73	56	78
Slovakia	47	66	47	69	47	74
Sweden	82	88	81	90	82	92
Switzerland	78	84	77	84	73	89
United States	65	75	66	81	63	82
Wales (UK)	56	71	56	76	60	82

Source: Health and Health Behaviour among Young People, 2000; Figure 8.7, WHO Policy Series: Health policy for children and adolescents, Issue 1, International Report 2/1/2000, Table 10.1; <http://www.ruhbc.ed.ac.uk/hbsc/download/hbsc.pdf> and <http://www.who.dk/document/e67880.pdf>. Underlying data from The Health Behaviour in School-Aged Children (HBSC) study by the WHO Regional Office for Europe.

G18. LEISURE ACTIVITIES

G18-1. Percent of Students Who Report Playing Computer Games Four Hours or More a Week, 11-Year-Olds, 13-Year-Olds, 15-Year-Olds, Males and Females, Selected Countries, 1997–1998

	11-Year-Olds		13-Year-Olds		15-Year-Olds	
	male	female	male	female	male	female
Austria	23	5	35	8	42	7
Belgium	23	6	23	7	28	6
Canada	39	13	41	11	37	5
Czech Republic	24	7	26	5	31	3
Denmark	41	6	42	7	40	4
England (UK)	27	6	36	7	31	3
Estonia	18	6	23	4	24	5
Finland	45	9	50	9	45	4
France	27	7	29	8	26	7
Germany	25	6	41	8	46	7
Greece	21	6	29	6	36	4
Greenland	16	7	21	6	19	5
Hungary	15	3	20	3	16	2
Ireland	31	7	35	10	28	6
Latvia	20	6	22	5	19	3

G18-1. Percent of Students Who Report Playing Computer Games Four Hours or More a Week, 11-Year-Olds, 13-Year-Olds, 15-Year-Olds, Males and Females, Selected Countries, 1997–1998 *(continued)*

	11-Year-Olds		13-Year-Olds		15-Year-Olds	
	male	female	male	female	male	female
Lithuania	21	9	24	6	24	4
Northern Ireland (UK)	42	16	46	14	37	9
Norway	29	7	41	8	46	5
Poland	25	5	27	5	25	4
Portugal	15	3	24	5	27	4
Russia	23	9	28	6	28	4
Scotland (UK)	45	9	45	8	36	4
Slovakia	29	13	31	9	26	5
Sweden	28	6	39	7	34	3
Switzerland	26	11	31	11	33	8
United States	28	16	27	12	22	8
Wales (UK)	40	12	44	9	40	6

Source: Health and Health Behaviour among Young People, 2000; Figure 7.4, WHO Policy Series: Health policy for children and adolescents, Issue 1, International Report 2/1/2000, Table 10.1; <http://www.ruhbc.ed.ac.uk/hbsc/download/hbsc.pdf> and <http://www.who.dk/document/e67880.pdf>. Underlying data from The Health Behaviour in School-Aged Children (HBSC) study by the WHO Regional Office for Europe.

G18-2. Percent of Students Who Report Watching Television Four Hours or More a Day, 11-Year-Olds, 13-Year-Olds, 15-Year-Olds, Males and Females, Selected Countries, 1997–1998

	11-Year-Olds		13-Year-Olds		15-Year-Olds	
	male	female	male	female	male	female
Austria	17	9	25	20	22	20
Belgium	22	18	23	19	20	18
Canada	31	23	29	24	24	18
Czech Republic	30	28	34	26	34	24
Denmark	21	14	25	23	22	19
England (UK)	24	20	31	31	29	28
Estonia	34	30	39	39	39	31
Finland	25	25	28	25	21	15
France	15	12	16	15	17	14
Germany	20	15	22	22	25	19
Greece	28	25	28	24	29	21
Greenland	37	33	35	33	38	26
Hungary	35	26	33	29	26	20
Ireland	28	21	28	20	19	16
Israel	47	47	45	45	40	32
Latvia	41	30	47	33	36	23
Lithuania	45	41	56	48	46	41
Northern Ireland (UK)	27	25	34	32	28	23
Norway	19	13	26	21	28	22
Poland	45	29	40	31	38	24
Portugal	28	26	32	28	26	25
Russia	31	31	43	39	36	33
Scotland (UK)	30	27	30	28	27	26
Slovakia	53	45	52	48	46	32
Sweden	19	18	28	23	25	19
Switzerland	11	9	13	12	18	16
United States	36	34	33	28	27	18
Wales (UK)	31	32	38	44	38	38

Source: Health and Health Behaviour among Young People, 2000; Figure 7.3, WHO Policy Series: Health policy for children and adolescents, Issue 1, International Report 2/1/2000, Table 10.1, <http://www.ruhbc.ed.ac.uk/hbsc/download/hbsc.pdf> and <http://www.who.dk/document/e67880.pdf>. Underlying data from The Health Behaviour in School-Aged Children (HBSC) study by the WHO Regional Office for Europe.

G19. EXERCISE

G19-1. Percent of Students Who Report Exercising Twice a Week or More, Selected Countries, 1997–1998

	11-Year-Olds		13-Year-Olds		15-Year-Olds	
	male	female	male	female	male	female
Austria	89	83	92	79	87	65
Belgium	79	59	78	53	72	50
Canada	70	57	73	55	75	54
Czech Republic	83	77	82	75	80	66
Denmark	78	65	80	63	69	56
England (UK)	78	73	82	63	79	50
Estonia	89	82	88	82	84	62
Finland	86	74	83	66	79	64
France	80	54	80	53	72	46
Germany	83	74	86	74	83	66
Greece	88	75	87	64	80	45
Greenland	58	46	64	46	60	37
Hungary	74	63	72	57	67	45
Ireland	87	82	87	78	81	59
Israel	84	61	80	57	76	48
Latvia	73	54	71	43	71	43
Lithuania	72	55	74	41	77	42
Northern Ireland (UK)	93	89	90	83	90	63
Norway	76	69	80	70	71	65
Poland	74	64	78	60	71	49
Portugal	87	71	87	62	80	54
Russian	77	69	78	51	77	50
Scotland (UK)	89	82	90	75	85	61
Sweden	77	59	77	62	71	55
Switzerland	86	61	83	65	81	57
United States	74	65	75	62	74	54
Wales (UK)	87	82	89	71	82	56

Source: Health and Health Behaviour among Young People, 2000; Figure 7.1, WHO Policy Series: Health policy for children and adolescents, Issue 1, International Report 2/1/2000, Table 10.1; <http://www.ruhbc.ed.ac.uk/hbsc/download/hbsc.pdf> and <http://www.who.dk/document/e67880.pdf>. Underlying data from The Health Behaviour in School-Aged Children (HBSC) study by the WHO Regional Office for Europe.

H. Crime, Violence and War

GENERAL OVERVIEW

The tables and charts in this section provide data on children as both perpetrators and victims of crime and violence. The first clusters (H1–H4) give an overview of criminal behavior and children in the criminal justice system. With the exception of statistics on drug use, there are few international indicators on juvenile crime. The most detailed figures come from a study of former Yugoslavian and Soviet nations conducted by the Centre for Europe's Children. Virtually no data are available for the developing world, where the majority of the world's children live. All comparisons among nations must be made with caution because of the wide variation in national juvenile justice systems and methods of reporting juvenile crimes.

The next group of clusters (H5–H8) present data on children as victims of violence. We have defined "violence" broadly to include not only homicide but also sexual exploitation and female genital mutilation. Data on children as victims is very limited, and the figures presented underestimate the extent of the problem. We were not able to include one of the most important aspects of violence against children, child abuse, because no international statistics are available on the subject.

The final clusters in this section (H9–H11) deal with children and war. Armed conflicts around the globe continue to disrupt and shorten the lives of millions of children. The UN High Commissioner for Refugees estimates that in the late 1990s there were 20 million children displaced within national borders as a consequence of armed conflicts and internal fighting. Sadly, children are often active participants in wars. According to UNICEF, 300,000 children under 18 are serving as regular soldiers, guerrilla fighters, porters, spies, sexual slaves, and even suicide commandos in conflicts around the world. For children the impact of war lasts long after hostilities have ceased because of the systematic use of landmines in conflicts. Although the UN does not break

out statistics for children, it reports that landmine victims are overwhelmingly women and children. UNICEF estimates that landmines kill or injure as many as 500 children each month around the world.

EXPLANATION OF INDICATORS

H1-1–H1-5. Illegal drug use: Substance abuse has many serious health and social consequences for adolescents. Health problems range from eating disorders to imbalance in brain chemistry, damage to pulmonary functions, strokes, and death from heart attacks. Possession and use of illegal drugs can lead to a variety of legal penalties and permanent criminal record for the young offender. The five tables in this cluster present data on the percentage of youth who have tried drugs—cannabis, ecstasy, cocaine, heroin, and inhalants—at least once in their lives. Because age range and date of survey differ from country to country, the statistics are not comparable among nations.

H2-1. Age of criminal responsibility: The Convention on the Rights of the Child calls for nations to establish a minimum age "below which children shall be presumed not to have the capacity to infringe the penal law." The Convention, however, does not set a specific age for criminal responsibility, and it varies greatly among nations. International standards, such as the Beijing Rules for juvenile justice, recommend that the age of criminal responsibility be based on emotional, mental, and intellectual maturity and that it not be fixed too low. The Committee on the Rights of the Child, which monitors countries' implementation of the Convention, has recommended that the age be guided by the best interests of the child.

H3-1–H3-4. Juvenile crimes: Juvenile crimes refer to all offenses committed by children under the age of 18. They are largely crimes against property, but the statistics in H3-1 to H3-3 include violent crimes (homicide, forcible rape, robbery, aggravated assault, and extortion) as well as involvement in organized crime. Tables H3-1 and H3-2 present absolute numbers of crimes committed by juveniles and juvenile crime rate, respectively. H3-3 breaks out absolute numbers of homicides. (The Centre for Europe's Children, which compiled the data, does not provide figures on juvenile homicide rate.) H3-4 lists the percentage of juveniles involved in specific crimes for 11 nations. The data for this table are based on police statistics, not judicial statistics. Because the legal definitions of punishable offences vary from country to country, the numbers should not be compared among countries and must be interpreted with caution.

H4-1–H4-4. Juvenile prisoners: The tables in this cluster present figures on juvenile sentencing (H4-1 and H4-2) and juvenile prisoners (H4-3 and H4-4). Despite international concerns about juvenile justice systems, available international statistics on juveniles in justice systems are limited and, in the case of juvenile prisoners, old. Statistics cannot be compared among countries because of differences in legal systems.

H5-1. Homicide, suicide and firearm-related deaths: In 1996 the World Health Assembly declared violence a leading worldwide public health problem. Yet there are few international statistical studies of adolescent violence. H5 compares the rate of homicide, suicide, and firearm-related deaths between the United States and 25 other industrial nations taken as a whole. The rates and ratios must be used with caution. The integration of non-U.S. figures masks differences among nations. Although the U.S. Centers for Disease Control, who compiled the table, reports that rates in all other countries were lower than that in the United States, they varied substantially from one nation to another. Reporting systems also varied. Only one-half of the countries distinguish between death by firearms and other explosives. Therefore, firearm deaths may have been overstated slightly for countries, including the United States, that do not make the distinction.

H6-1. Commercial sexual exploitation: Commercial sexual exploitation of children includes all forms of prostitution, pornography, and trafficking or "selling" of children for sexual purposes. The UN has declared it a form of violence against the child. In 1996 the First World Congress Against Sexual Exploitation of Children agreed to implement an Agenda for Action to eradicate the problem. The agenda called for each participating nation to develop a National Plan of Action to coordinate and identify the measures needed to end the practice in its country. H6 indicates progress toward that goal.

Some nations do not have formal action plans; instead they have general plans for protecting children's rights.

H7-1. Violence against girls: The United Nations views violence against women as a major health and human rights issue. According to the World Health Organization (WHO), at least one in five of the world's female population has been physically or sexually abused some time in their life. WHO does not break out figures by age, and comparative statistics on violence against girls are very rare. H7 presents the percentage of sex crime victims under age 15 for seven selected countries or cities. The sex crimes include attempted and completed rape as well as sexual assaults such as molestation. The table also offers figures on the percentage of victims who knew their attacker. Although rape and sexual assault may be perpetrated by strangers, a high percentage of rapists are acquaintances, "friends," relatives, and those in positions of trust or power.

H8-1–H8-2. Female genital mutilation (FGM): One of the worst kinds of violence against girls is the cultural, social, and religious practice of female genital mutilation (sometimes called female circumcision). According to the Department of Women's Health Systems and Community Health of the World Health Organization, approximately 2 million girls go through genital mutilation every year. The number of girls and women who have been subjected to female genital mutilation is estimated at over 130 million worldwide. FGM is practiced by Muslims, Christians, animists and nonbelievers in a range of communities, most commonly in Africa. Apart from the immediate fear and pain, the consequences can include prolonged bleeding, infection, infertility, and death. The psychological complications may be submerged deep in the girl child's subconscious and may trigger behavioral disturbances later. The tables in this cluster present legal status of FGM in Africa and estimates of the numbers and percentages of women who suffer female genital mutilation (FMG).

H9-1–H9-4. Refugee children: Refugees are persons who have fled or been expelled from their country or region of origin for the safety of another region or country. Natural catastrophe, war or military occupation, or fear of religious, racial, or political persecution can cause their flight. Once displaced from their own land, they face tremendous economic hardships and social stigmatization. Children loose continuity in education as well as the sense of secure family atmosphere. H9-1 and H9-2 present numbers of child refugees by country of origin and country of asylum respectively. H9-3 and H9-4 focus on the most vulnerable part of the refugee population, children under five.

I10-1–I10-5. Children in the military: The UN defines a child soldier as any person below 18 years of age who is recruited for military purposes into an armed force or group, or who participates in lethal violence in a political (non-criminal) context. At the turn of the twenty-first century there were hundreds of thousands of children serving in the military, either in governmental forces or in armed insurgent groups. Many entered as a result of coercion, abduction, severe economic need, or deception. Boys are not the only child soldiers. UNICEF estimates that one-third of the children fighting in Ethiopia, Uganda, and El Salvador were girls. Aside from the obvious danger of injury and death, these children are at high risk for drug addiction, malnutrition, sexually transmitted diseases, and unwanted pregnancies. Child soldiers are also left with complex mental problems as a result of witnessing and participating in wartime atrocities. The Convention on the Rights of the Child cites 15 as the minimum permissible age for military service, but many nations and nongovernmental groups use children far below that age. H10-1 presents the minimum legal age for recruitment into the armed forces; H10-2 lists the lowest age at which children can volunteer. The last three tables detail the groups using child soldiers, countries in which children have participated in armed conflicts, and girls recruited in armed forces.

H11-1–H11-2. Landmines: Landmines maim and kill thousands of children annually, most long after hostilities have ended. In more than 60 countries around the world children face danger every day, walking through mine fields to find food or firewood or to go to school. Their natural curiosity and love of play increases their risk. The victims are often from the poorest segment of society. In addition to killing and maiming, these "inexpensive tools of terror" also damage the child's physical and social world and can be devastating to the child's future development. Despite an international campaign to ban landmines, the UN estimates that approximately 2.5 million new mines are laid each year. H11-1 presents the number of landmines by nation for 1994 and 1997. H11-2 contrasts mines cleared and mines remaining for selected countries in 1997.

H1. ILLEGAL DRUG USE

H1-1. Percentage of Youth Who Have Tried Cannabis* At Least Once in Their Life, 1990–1997

	Date of data	Age range	Percent
Australia	1996	12 to 17	36.4
Austria	1994	13 to 18	8.7
Bahamas, the	1990	16 to 29	16.6
Belgium	1996	15 to 16	18.9
Bolivia	1996	12 to 24	3.6
Brazil	1997	10 to 19	7.6
Bulgaria	1995	14 to 18	15.0
Canada	1994	15 to 24	33.6
Chile	1996	12 to 25	22.7
Colombia	1996	12 to 24	4.6
Costa Rica	1992	18 to 19	3.1
Croatia	1995	15 to 16	9.0
Cyprus	1995	15 to 16	5.0
Czech Republic	1995	15 to 16	21.5
Denmark	1995	16 to 19	28.0
Dominican Republic	1992	12 to 24	1.8
Estonia	1995	15 to 16	7.5
Finland	1995	15 to 16	5.2
France	1993	15 to 16	11.6
Germany	1995	18 to 24	21.2
Hong Kong SAR, China	1992	12 to 16	0.7
Hungary	1995	15 to 16	4.8
Iceland	1995	15 to 16	10.0
Ireland	1995	15 to 16	37.0
Italy	1995	15 to 16	18.5
Jamaica	1990	13 to 19	17.0
Kenya	1993	12 to 18	12.0
Lithuania	1995	15 to 16	1.5
Luxembourg	1995	15 to 16	6.0
Malta	1995	15 to 16	8.5
Mexico	1993	12 to 25	2.8
Namibia	1991	12 to 18	7.0
Netherlands, the	1996	12 to 19	20.9
Norway	1996	15 to 20	12.3
Panama	1991	12 to 24	2.2
Peru	1995	12 to 19	1.7
Poland	1995	15 to 18	12.2
Portugal	1995	13 to 20	8.5
Slovakia	1996	15 to 29	15.7
Slovenia	1995	15 to 16	13.0
Spain	1996	14 to 18	26.0
Suriname	1995	12 to 18	5.0
Swaziland	1997	15 to 24	9.9
Sweden	1997	15 to 16	6.8
Switzerland	1990	15 to 24	25.0
Ukraine	1995	15 to 16	14.5
United Kingdom	1995	11 to 16	37.0
United States	1996	13 to 17	35.9
Zimbabwe	1994	12 to 18	6.0

* Derived from hemp, as marijuana or hashish.
Note: These data are not directly comparable among countries.

Source: Global Illicit Drug Trends 1999, ODCCP Studies on Drug and Crime—Statistics, United Nations Office for Drug Control and Crime Prevention (ODCCP), New York 1999, UN Publication Sales No. E.99.XI.16, Table 144; <http://www.undcp.org/pdf/report_1999-06-01_1.pdf>. Underlying data from United Nations (UN).

H1-2. Percentage of Youth Who Have Tried Cocaine at Least Once in Their Life, 1990–1997

	Date of data	Age range	Percent
Australia	1996	12 to 17	3.6
Austria	1994	15 to 16	2.0
Bahamas, the	1990	16 to 29	6.4
Belgium	1994	12 to 24	1.0
Bolivia	1996	12 to 24	2.3
Brazil	1997	10 to 19	2.0
Canada	1994	15 to 24	3.7
Chile	1996	12 to 25	3.4
Colombia	1996	12 to 24	0.8
Costa Rica	1992	18 to 19	1.0
Czech Republic	1995	12 to 18	0.5
Denmark	1995	15 to 16	0.4
Dominican Republic	1992	12 to 24	1.4
Finland	1995	15 to 16	0.2
France	1993	15 to 16	1.1
Germany	1995	18 to 24	3.0
Greece	1993	15 to 16	0.7
Hungary	1995	15 to 16	0.8
Ireland	1995	15 to 16	2.0
Italy	1995	18 to 25	0.3
Kenya	1993	12 to 18	4.5
Luxembourg	1992	15 to 16	0.9
Malta	1991	11 to 17	1.6
Netherlands, the	1996	12 to 19	2.9
New Zealand	1990	15 to 24	2.1
Norway	1996	15 to 20	0.5
Panama	1991	12 to 24	1.8
Peru	1995	12 to 19	0.3
Poland	1995	15 to 18	0.8
Portugal	1995	13 to 20	0.8
Slovakia	1996	15 to 29	1.5
Spain	1996	14 to 18	3.2
Swaziland	1997	15 to 24	1.4
Sweden	1997	15 to 16	0.5
United Kingdom	1995	15 to 16	3.0
United States	1996	13 to 17	6.0

Note: These data are not directly comparable among countries.

Source: Global Illicit Drug Trends 1999, ODCCP Studies on Drug and Crime—Statistics, United Nations Office for Drug Control and Crime Prevention (ODCCP), New York 1999, UN Publication Sales No. E.99.XI.16, Table 146; <http://www.undcp.org/pdf/report_1999-06-01_1.pdf>. Underlying data from United Nations (UN).

H1-3. Percentage of Youth who Have Tried "Ecstasy"* at Least Once in Their Life, 1990–1997

	Date of data	Age range	Percent
Australia	1996	12 to 17	3.6
Austria	1996	12 to 20	3.2
Belgium	1996	15 to 16	6.0
Croatia	1995	15 to 16	2.5
Cyprus	1995	15 to 16	1.5
Denmark	1995	15 to 16	0.5
Finland	1995	15 to 16	0.2
Germany	1995	18 to 24	5.1
Hungary	1995	15 to 16	0.8
Iceland	1995	15 to 16	1.5
Ireland	1995	15 to 16	9.0
Italy	1995	15 to 16	4.0
Luxembourg	1992	15 to 16	0.9
Malta	1995	15 to 16	1.5
Netherlands, the	1996	12 to 19	5.6
New Zealand	1990	15 to 24	1.4
Norway	1996	15 to 20	1.7
Poland	1995	15 to 16	0.5
Portugal	1995	15 to 16	0.5
Slovakia	1995	15 to 18	0.3
Slovenia	1995	15 to 16	1.5
Spain	1996	14 to 18	5.1
Suriname	1995	12 to 18	0.4
Swaziland	1997	15 to 24	0.3
Sweden	1997	15 to 16	0.8
United Kingdom	1996	15 to 16	8.3
United States	1995	19 to 22	3.1

* Originally, the term "ecstasy" was used as street name for the psychoactive substance MDMA (3,4-methylenedioxy-methamphetamine).
Note: These data are not directly comparable among countries.

Source: Global Illicit Drug Trends 1999, ODCCP Studies on Drug and Crime—Statistics, United Nations Office for Drug Control and Crime Prevention (ODCCP), New York 1999, UN Publication Sales No. E.99.XI.16, Table 145; <http://www.undcp.org/pdf/report_1999-06-01_1.pdf>. Underlying data from United Nations (UN).

H1-4. Percentage of Youth Who Have Tried Heroin at Least Once in Their Life, 1990–1997

	Date of data	Age range	Percent
Australia	1996	12 to 17	3.6
Australia	1995	14 to 24	1.4
Belgium	1996	15 to 16	1.1
Chile	1995	12 to 18	0.5
Colombia	1992	12 to 24	0.1
Croatia	1995	15 to 15	0.9
Czech Republic	1995	12 to 18	0.6
Denmark	1995	15 to 16	2.0
Finland	1995	15 to 16	0.1
France	1993	15 to 16	0.8
Germany	1995	18 to 24	1.0
Greece	1995	15 to 16	2.0
Hong Kong SAR, China	1992	12 to 16	0.4
Hungary	1995	15 to 16	0.5
Ireland	1995	15 to 16	2.0
Italy	1995	15 to 16	2.0
Netherlands, the	1996	12 to 19	1.1
New Zealand	1990	15 to 24	0.3
Norway	1996	15 to 20	0.6
Poland	1995	15 to 18	0.7
Portugal	1995	13 to 20	1.3
Slovakia	1995	15 to 29	1.9
Spain	1996	14 to 18	0.6

H1-4. Percentage of Youth Who Have Tried Heroin at Least Once in Their Life, 1990–1997 *(continued)*

	Date of data	Age range	Percent
Swaziland	1997	15 to 24	0.7
Sweden	1997	15 to 16	0.5
United Kingdom	1995	15 to 16	2.0
United States	1995	13 to 22	1.2
Note: These data are not directly			

Source: Global Illicit Drug Trends 1999, ODCCP Studies on Drug and Crime—Statistics, United Nations Office for Drug Control and Crime Prevention (ODCCP), New York 1999, UN Publication Sales No. E.99.XI.16, Table 147; <http://www.undcp.org/pdf/report_1999-06-01_1.pdf>. Underlying data from United Nations (UN).

H1-5. Percentage of Youth Who Have Tried Inhalants at Least Once in Their Life, 1990–1997

	Date of data	Age range	Percent
Australia	1996	12 to 17	7.7
Belgium	1996	15 to 16	3.6
Bolivia	1996	12 to 24	11.8
Brazil	1997	10 to 19	16.0
Canada	1994	15 to 24	1.4
Chile	1995	12 to 18	3.4
Colombia	1996	12 to 24	5.9
Croatia	1995	15 to 16	13.8
Cyprus	1995	15 to 16	2.0
Czech Republic	1995	15 to 16	7.5
Denmark	1995	15 to 16	7.0
Dominican Republic	1992	12 to 24	3.6
Estonia	1995	15 to 16	7.5
Finland	1995	15 to 16	4.4
France	1993	15 to 16	5.5
Germany	1995	18 to 24	1.7
Greece	1993	15 to 16	6.3
Hong Kong SAR, China	1992	12 to 16	0.4
Hungary	1995	15 to 16	5.3
Iceland	1995	15 to 16	8.7
Italy	1995	15 to 16	7.5
Kenya	1993	12 to 18	19.0
Lithuania	1995	15 to 16	17.0
Luxembourg	1995	15 to 16	2.6
Malta	1995	15 to 16	19.0
Mexico	1993	12 to 25	0.6
Netherlands, the	1990	10 to 17	3.0
New Zealand	1990	15 to 24	1.8
Norway	1996	15 to 20	6.2
Panama	1991	12 to 24	3.2
Peru	1995	12 to 19	3.0
Poland	1995	15 to 18	9.9
Portugal	1995	15 to 20	3.3
Slovakia	1996	15 to 29	6.1
Spain	1996	14 to 18	3.3
Swaziland	1997	15 to 24	12.0
Sweden	1997	15 to 16	9.6
Ukraine	1995	15 to 16	5.5
United Kingdom	1995	15 to 16	25.5
United States	1996	13 to 17	20.0
Zimbabwe	1994	12 to 18	13.5
Note: These data are not directly comparable among countries.			

Source: Global Illicit Drug Trends 1999, ODCCP Studies on Drug and Crime—Statistics, United Nations Office for Drug Control and Crime Prevention (ODCCP), New York 1999, UN Publication Sales No. E.99.XI.16, Table 148; <http://www.undcp.org/pdf/report_1999-06-01_1.pdf>. Underlying data from United Nations (UN).

H2. AGE OF CRIMINAL RESPONSIBILITY

H2-1. Minimum Age at Which Children Are Subject to Penal Law in Countries with 10 Million or More Children Under 18 Years Old

	Age
Mexico	*6-12
Bangladesh	7
India	7
Myanmar (Burma)	7
Nigeria	7
Pakistan	7
South Africa	7
Sudan	7
Tanzania	7
Thailand	7
United States	**7
Indonesia	8
Kenya	8
Scotland, (UK)	8
Ethiopia	9
Iran	***9
Philippines	9
Nepal	10
England, (UK)	10
Wales, (UK)	10
Ukraine	10
Turkey	11
South Korea, Rep.	12
Morocco	12
Uganda	12
Algeria	13
France	13
Poland	13
Uzbekistan	13
China	14
Germany	14
Italy	14
Japan	14
Russia	14
Vietnam	14
Egypt	15
Argentina	16
Brazil	****18
Colombia	****18
Peru	****18

*Most states 11 or 12 years; age 11 for federal crimes.
**Age determined by state, minimum age is 7 in most states under common law.
***Age 9 for girls, 15 for boys.
****Official age of criminal responsibility. From age 12 children's actions are subject to juvenile legal proceedings.

Source: CRC Country Reports (1992-1996), *Juvenile Justice and Juvenile Delinquency in Central and Eastern Europe*, 1995; United Nations, *Implementation of UN Mandates on Juvenile Justice in ESCAP*, 1994; Geert Cappelaere, Children's Rights Centre, University of Gent, Belgium; <http://www.unicef.org/pon97/stat3a.htm>. Underlying data *from The Progress of Nations 1997,* United Nations Children's Fund (UNICEF).

H3. JUVENILE CRIMES

H3-1. Crimes by or with the Participation of Juveniles, in Thousands, Selected Countries, 1990–1998

	1990	1991	1992	1993	1994	1995	1996	1997	1998
Albania	N/A	N/A	N/A	N/A	N/A	N/A	N/A	1.8	N/A
Armenia	0.3	0.4	N/A	N/A	N/A	0.4	0.5	0.6	0.5
Azerbaijan	0.5	0.6	1.1	0.9	0.9	0.9	0.8	0.8	0.7
Belarus	7.5	7.6	8.4	9.5	10.0	10.7	9.9	10.0	9.9
Bosnia-Herzegovina	N/A	N/A	N/A	N/A	0.3	0.5	N/A	N/A	N/A
Bulgaria	6.9	11.7	15.1	15.1	15.3	15.3	14.5	18.0	18.9
Croatia	2.7	2.1	2.5	3.3	3.0	2.2	2.3	2.1	1.9
Czech Republic	N/A	13.7	17.1	18.9	21.7	21.1	22.7	19.1	16.7
Estonia	N/A	N/A	1.0	1.6	1.8	2.4	2.3	2.2	2.3
Georgia	0.8	0.9	0.8	0.6	0.5	0.7	0.7	0.6	0.7
Hungary	12.3	13.5	15.5	15.0	14.5	14.3	13.5	14.0	12.9
Kazakhstan	10.8	12.4	13.0	12.8	11.2	9.7	8.8	7.4	7.2
Kyrgyzstan	1.3	1.6	1.7	1.2	1.2	1.2	1.4	1.5	1.3
Latvia	2.4	2.3	3.3	2.5	2.2	2.6	3.0	3.6	4.0
Lithuania	2.5	2.7	3.6	4.3	4.4	4.6	5.3	5.3	5.0
Macedonia, FYR	3.6	3.7	5.2	5.0	5.4	4.9	N/A	5.9	N/A
Moldova	3.1	3.0	2.2	2.0	2.2	2.1	2.0	2.3	2.5
Poland	60.5	62.8	66.2	72.2	75.8	82.6	70.1	73.0	78.8
Romania	9.2	17.4	15.0	22.2	24.3	26.5	28.8	33.2	43.8
Russia	164.7	173.8	200.6	223.7	221.6	209.8	202.9	182.8	189.3
Slovakia	5.6	7.0	7.6	9.3	8.8	8.9	7.9	7.4	6.8
Slovenia	4.3	4.7	6.8	5.6	5.6	4.5	4.2	4.6	6.1
Tajikistan	1.2	1.5	1.3	1.1	1.1	1.0	0.9	0.6	0.5
Turkmenistan	1.2	1.2	1.1	0.9	0.8	N/A	N/A	N/A	0.6
Ukraine	28.8	28.8	34.9	37.9	40.7	41.6	41.8	40.1	39.1
Uzbekistan	5.6	5.7	6.1	5.3	4.4	3.6	3.2	3.2	3.0
Yugoslavia	5.4	4.9	5.8	7.4	5.8	5.3	5.4	6.0	4.9

N/A Not Available

Source: Centre for Europe's Children, TransMONEE 2000 on-line database; <http://www.eurochild.gla.ac.uk/Documents/monee/queries/t07.htm>. Underlying data from Innocenti Research Centre, Florence, United Nations Children's Fund (UNICEF).

H3-2. Crime Rate per 100,000 Juveniles Age 14–17, Selected Countries, 1990–1998

	1990	1991	1992	1993	1994	1995	1996	1997	1998
Albania	N/A	N/A	N/A	N/A	N/A	N/A	N/A	661.6	N/A
Armenia	105.6	151.1	N/A	N/A	N/A	148.7	162.4	207.2	179.9
Azerbaijan	97.2	105.5	197.3	172.3	162.0	161.3	131.9	129.8	116.2
Belarus	1,275.9	1,305.1	1,431.1	1,590.7	1,666.4	1,755.5	1,597.7	1,571.6	1,511.1
Bosnia-Herzegovina	201.4	N/A	N/A	N/A	141.6	237.4	N/A	N/A	N/A
Bulgaria	1,309.3	2,208.7	2,907.1	2,980.8	3,083.6	3,173.2	3,081.0	3,917.6	4,202.0
Croatia	N/A	797.2	965.1	1,263.5	1,130.0	833.9	884.4	821.2	747.3
Czech Republic	N/A	2,467.8	3,098.9	3,508.9	4,119.2	4,174.6	4,771.9	4,299.8	3,959.1
Estonia	N/A	N/A	1,489.9	2,438.4	1,707.0	2,290.7	2,171.0	2,043.6	2,084.3
Georgia	225.0	264.7	250.3	177.4	154.5	203.8	198.2	180.4	199.5
Hungary	1,787.5	1,898.7	2,175.4	2,193.4	2,231.2	2,328.4	2,327.0	2,538.4	2,462.7
Kazakhstan	905.0	1,030.8	1,074.7	1,060.6	936.8	828.8	757.8	643.0	625.9
Kyrgyzstan	375.7	442.0	479.2	345.3	330.1	318.5	383.4	385.2	312.0
Latvia	1,714.1	1,685.0	2,410.3	1,890.8	1,629.8	1,940.6	2,230.2	2,599.7	2,782.5
Lithuania	1,178.3	1,278.2	1,691.3	2,057.8	2,121.1	2,169.4	2,538.5	2,488.7	2,307.8
Macedonia, FYR	N/A	2,849.2	3,959.0	3,783.7	4,113.6	3,716.0	N/A	4,443.4	N/A
Moldova	1,036.4	1,022.9	746.4	671.5	745.6	701.8	650.6	807.0	916.3
Poland	2,449.5	2,489.8	2,583.1	2,783.4	2,902.5	3,129.0	2,618.6	2,700.1	2,902.6
Romania	604.1	1,101.6	934.3	1,402.9	1,553.1	1,733.7	1,955.1	2,366.2	3,288.1
Russia	1,986.9	2,070.6	2,359.0	2,599.1	2,550.5	2,387.5	2,274.5	1,994.4	2,006.4

H3-2. Crime Rate per 100,000 Juveniles Age 14–17, Selected Countries, 1990–1998 *(continued)*

	1990	1991	1992	1993	1994	1995	1996	1997	1998
Slovakia	2,076.3	2,502.4	2,673.4	3,260.8	3,061.6	3,124.5	2,801.1	2,684.9	2,540.6
Slovenia	3,629.2	3,943.5	5,633.3	4,592.1	4,623.5	3,705.0	3,527.9	3,970.6	5,393.3
Tajikistan	277.9	337.8	291.5	238.9	236.2	193.5	178.2	111.5	91.3
Turkmenistan	382.6	392.1	350.4	268.7	216.9	N/A	N/A	N/A	136.2
Ukraine	973.7	977.1	1,189.0	1,293.4	1,391.2	1,428.1	1,431.6	1,352.6	1,295.6
Uzbekistan	324.1	327.4	345.7	291.2	238.6	187.9	164.4	156.7	142.8
Yugoslavia	816.7	755.1	894.4	1,147.7	895.3	826.6	847.7	936.8	775.9

N/A Not Available

Source: Centre for Europe's Children, TransMONEE 2000 on-line database; <http://www.eurochild.gla.ac.uk/Documents/monee/queries/t07.htm>. Underlying data from Innocenti Research Centre, Florence, United Nations Children's Fund (UNICEF).

H3-3. Homicides Committed by or with Participation of Juveniles (Absolute Numbers), Selected Countries, 1990–1998

	1990	1991	1992	1993	1994	1995	1996	1997	1998
Albania	N/A	N/A	N/A	N/A	N/A	N/A	N/A	N/A	N/A
Armenia	N/A	5	N/A	N/A	N/A	4	3	N/A	N/A
Azerbaijan	7	14	18	19	24	20	22	27	17
Belarus	27	21	22	36	32	29	59	57	70
Bosnia-Herzegovina	33	N/A	2	2	11	17	N/A	N/A	N/A
Bulgaria	N/A	23	27	38	30	46	29	38	24
Croatia	9	16	14	9	6	4	9	6	5
Czech Republic	14	15	17	14	21	15	9	8	16
Estonia	N/A	N/A	N/A	11	15	8	11	14	13
Georgia	14	15	12	5	7	N/A	N/A	8	3
Hungary	N/A	N/A	N/A	N/A	N/A	N/A	N/A	N/A	N/A
Kazakhstan	86	95	62	113	93	144	110	146	145
Kyrgyzstan	N/A	N/A	N/A	N/A	N/A	N/A	N/A	N/A	N/A
Latvia	4	10	9	6	24	9	12	12	10
Lithuania	2	7	11	14	22	30	28	27	23
Macedonia, FYR	4	6	9	6	5	4	N/A	3	N/A
Moldova	17	11	16	9	11	11	11	7	15
Poland	17	19	21	22	33	26	36	36	29
Romania	36	45	44	41	35	31	32	36	30
Russia	472	504	603	1,009	1,311	1,215	1,143	1,068	1,024
Slovakia	6	6	8	8	8	7	9	8	9
Slovenia	3	1	3	2	4	3	6	2	8
Tajikistan	4	7	5	7	10	10	9	4	6
Turkmenistan	18	11	13	12	11	8	4	13	14
Ukraine	124	134	143	159	178	191	232	232	251
Uzbekistan	N/A	N/A	N/A	N/A	N/A	N/A	N/A	N/A	N/A
Yugoslavia	17	29	38	41	34	41	37	28	40

N/A Not Available

Source: Centre for Europe's Children, TransMONEE 2000 on-line database; <http://www.eurochild.gla.ac.uk/Documents/monee/queries/t07.htm>. Underlying data from Innocenti Research Centre, Florence, United Nations Children's Fund (UNICEF).

H3-4. Percent of Juveniles Responsible for Total Offenses, 1997

	Argentina (age range not available)	Canada (12-17 years)	France (13-18 years)	Germany (14-17 years)	India (7-16 years)	Japan (14-19 years)	the Netherlands (12-17 years)	New Zealand (0-16 years)	Russia (14-17 years)	Swaziland (12-18 years)	United Kingdom (10-17 years)
Murder	13.83	10.58	7.40	6.42	0.50	5.80	6.00	2.88	5.70	5.78	6.00
Sex offences (including rape)	16.43	15.58	14.10	7.37	0.50	22.80	20.00	12.81	16.80	11.96	18.00
Rape	22.47	N/A	17.20	8.05	0.90	27.70	17.00	10.61	16.00	22.02	12.00
Serious assault	12.14	11.87	14.60	20.07	0.40	39.80	18.00	7.63	5.70	14.79	27.00
Theft (all kinds)	29.30	24.22	32.10	20.36	1.60	55.70	23.00	41.61	18.60	22.66	32.00
Aggravated theft	26.80	39.59	35.40	23.83	1.40	35.80	25.00	40.97	N/A	30.29	46.00
Robbery and violent theft	26.42	37.85	38.50	32.27	0.20	53.10	27.00	39.02	21.80	25.18	47.00
Breaking and entering	3.85	40.00	34.10	20.16	2.50	32.30	24.00	41.14	N/A	17.10	44.00
Theft of motor cars	23.71	37.48	32.40	27.58	N/A	40.00	N/A	42.52	N/A	4.84	44.00
Other thefts	17.62	17.87	30.90	20.00	1.70	58.60	21.00	41.75	18.10	0.93	31.00
Fraud	3.84	6.93	3.60	5.84	0.20	6.30	7.00	7.87	1.20	2.85	10.00
Counterfeit currency offences	13.28	13.37	11.30	9.40	0.10	3.10	6.00	14.71	6.00	10.00	N/A
Drug offences	16.17	12.46	16.10	14.09	0.00	8.10	4.00	9.03	9.50	10.56	12.00
Total number of offences contain	17.37	22.20	19.40	12.87	0.20	42.20	17.00	22.89	11.80	17.67	24.00

N/A   Not available separately

Source: International Crime Statistics, 1997, International Criminal Police Organization (ICPO-INTERPOL).

H4. JUVENILE PRISONERS

H4-1. Juvenile Sentencing Rate (Sentences per 100,000 Population Aged 14 to 17 Years), Selected Countries, 1990–1998

	1990	1991	1992	1993	1994	1995	1996	1997	1998
Albania	N/A	N/A	N/A	N/A	N/A	N/A	N/A	N/A	N/A
Armenia	54.8	82.0	128.6	150.8	143.1	109.6	130.7	150.7	97.1
Azerbaijan	55.0	56.8	100.6	125.2	112.3	107.2	76.8	77.6	58.6
Belarus	743.3	761.2	800.6	998.2	1010.2	1060.2	1018.7	898.6	941.7
Bosnia-Herzegovina	N/A	N/A	N/A	N/A	N/A	N/A	N/A	N/A	N/A
Bulgaria	188.6	204.4	193.4	101.8	136.4	136.2	251.8	363.7	577.8
Croatia	N/A	501.8	476.9	734.8	724.3	591.5	506.8	420.4	363.4
Czech Republic	418.3	631.0	755.3	963.5	1146.8	1242.2	1325.6	1446.4	1089.7
Estonia	N/A	N/A	1471.4	1502.3	1104.5	1318.1	1457.0	1551.6	1382.8
Georgia	N/A	146.4	99.6	N/A	N/A	N/A	145.7	104.9	103.4
Hungary	751.5	871.4	969.6	966.2	1161.4	1417.3	1334.8	1354.6	1538.2
Kazakhstan	575.7	633.4	753.3	814.4	677.7	620.6	490.7	490.3	410.1
Kyrgyzstan	247.0	232.4	274.0	320.3	228.4	330.8	281.8	300.1	277.2
Latvia	780.9	702.1	839.2	908.2	858.1	796.1	912.7	1199.0	1160.6
Lithuania	538.4	580.9	736.9	1019.6	1113.4	958.1	1040.9	922.8	983.5
Macedonia, FYRO	N/A	1035.4	1097.4	1398.5	1172.3	894.6	876.3	560.1	700.2
Moldova	538.6	569.6	516.8	505.7	579.2	601.5	535.7	514.0	575.2
Poland	412.8	477.5	475.9	497.6	599.1	483.3	747.4	717.2	N/A
Romania	129.6	239.8	286.0	438.2	584.1	639.7	703.6	842.2	839.7
Russia	956.3	1013.3	1070.0	1219.3	1282.3	1325.6	1356.3	1315.5	1398.4
Slovakia	522.0	871.4	346.8	953.1	1082.4	1427.2	1058.6	1332.6	1122.8
Slovenia	841.5	901.1	927.8	905.4	848.1	413.1	419.3	531.3	565.5
Tajikistan	125.4	149.0	125.1	140.1	151.8	110.6	N/A	N/A	N/A
Turkmenistan	216.6	216.0	226.9	N/A	N/A	N/A	N/A	N/A	N/A
Ukraine	427.7	387.1	396.5	497.5	578.3	574.2	652.0	620.2	602.3
Uzbekistan	160.1	199.8	217.4	N/A	N/A	N/A	N/A	N/A	N/A
Yugoslavia	458.1	391.2	460.1	569.5	574.1	506.9	420.5	413.0	472.4

N/A Not Available

Source: Centre for Europe's Children, TransMONEE 2000 on-line database; <http://www.eurochild.gla.ac.uk/Documents/monee/queries/t07.htm>. Underlying data from Innocenti Research Centre, Florence, United Nations Children's Fund (UNICEF).

H4-2. Juveniles Sentenced for Criminal Activity, Absolute Numbers in Thousands, Selected Countries, 1990–1998

	1990	1991	1992	1993	1994	1995	1996	1997	1998
Albania	N/A	N/A	N/A	N/A	N/A	N/A	N/A	N/A	N/A
Armenia	0.1	0.2	0.3	0.4	0.4	0.3	0.4	0.4	0.3
Azerbaijan	0.3	0.3	0.5	0.7	0.6	0.6	0.4	0.5	0.3
Belarus	4.4	4.5	4.7	5.9	6.1	6.5	6.3	5.7	6.2
Bosnia-Herzegovina	N/A	N/A	N/A	N/A	N/A	N/A	N/A	N/A	N/A
Bulgaria	1.0	1.1	1.0	0.5	0.7	0.7	1.2	1.7	2.6
Croatia	1.6	1.3	1.2	1.9	1.9	1.5	1.3	1.1	0.9
Czech Republic	2.3	3.5	4.2	5.2	6.0	6.3	6.3	6.4	4.6
Estonia	N/A	N/A	1.0	1.0	1.2	1.4	1.6	1.7	1.5
Georgia	N/A	0.5	0.3	N/A	N/A	N/A	0.5	0.4	0.4
Hungary	5.2	6.2	6.9	6.6	7.5	8.7	7.8	7.4	8.0
Kazakhstan	6.9	7.6	9.1	9.8	8.1	7.3	5.7	5.7	4.7
Kyrgyzstan	0.9	0.8	1.0	1.2	0.8	1.2	1.1	1.2	1.1
Latvia	1.1	1.0	1.1	1.2	1.1	1.1	1.2	1.7	1.7
Lithuania	1.1	1.2	1.5	2.1	2.3	2.0	2.2	2.0	2.1
Macedonia, FYRO	1.2	1.4	1.5	1.9	1.5	1.2	1.2	0.7	0.9
Moldova	1.6	1.7	1.5	1.5	1.7	1.8	1.6	1.5	1.6
Poland	10.2	12.1	12.2	12.9	15.7	12.8	20.0	19.4	N/A
Romania	2.0	3.8	4.6	6.9	9.1	9.8	10.4	11.8	11.2

H4-2. Juveniles Sentenced for Criminal Activity, Absolute Numbers in Thousands, Selected Countries, 1990–1998 *(continued)*

	1990	1991	1992	1993	1994	1995	1996	1997	1998
Russia	79.3	85.0	91.0	104.9	111.4	116.5	121.0	120.6	131.9
Slovakia	1.4	2.4	1.0	2.7	3.1	4.1	3.0	3.7	3.0
Slovenia	1.0	1.1	1.1	1.1	1.0	0.5	0.5	0.6	0.6
Tajikistan	0.6	0.7	0.6	0.7	0.7	0.5	N/A	N/A	N/A
Turkmenistan	0.7	0.7	0.7	N/A	N/A	N/A	N/A	N/A	N/A
Ukraine	12.7	11.4	11.6	14.6	16.9	16.7	19.0	18.4	18.2
Uzbekistan	2.8	3.5	3.9	N/A	N/A	N/A	N/A	N/A	N/A
Yugoslavia	3.0	2.6	3.0	3.7	3.7	3.3	2.7	2.6	3.0

N/A Not Available

Source: Centre for Europe's Children, TransMONEE 2000 on-line database; <http://www.eurochild.gla.ac.uk/Documents/monee/queries/t07.htm>. Underlying data from Innocenti Research Centre, Florence, United Nations Children's Fund (UNICEF).

H4-3. Young Adult Prisoners, 1987 and 1990

	Young adult (as % of total prisoners) 1987	Young adult (as % of total prisoners) 1990
Austria	1	3
Finland	N/A	7
France	13	11
Greece	6	N/A
Hungary	N/A	6
Iceland	9	5
Ireland	28	N/A
Italy	2	1
Luxembourg	7	6
Netherlands, the	18	28
Norway	8	6
Portugal	10	8
Spain	10	6
Sweden	4	5
Switzerland	2	N/A
United Kingdom	25	21

N/A Not Available

Source: "Social Stress and Social Change," *Human Development Report 1997*, p. 213; <http://www.undp.org/hdro/indicators.html>. United Nations Development Programme (UNDP).

H4-4. Juvenile Prisoners, Selected Countries, 1994

	Juvenile prisoners (as % of total prisoners) 1994
Armenia	1.5
Belarus	6.6
Belgium	3.6
Brunei	8.0
Bulgaria	3.0
Croatia	0.9
Cyprus	12.2
Czech Republic	7.5
Denmark	1.3
El Salvador	18.6
Estonia	7.7
Georgia	0.9
Greece	5.9
Hong Kong, SAR (China)	17.4
Indonesia	31.4
Israel	0.8
Italy	1.4
Jamaica	6.6
Kyrgyzstan	1.8
Lesotho	20.6
Macedonia, FYRO	1.8
Madagascar	2.4
Malaysia	0.7
Malta	1.3
Mauritius	1.6
Moldova	2.3
Portugal	6.9
Qatar	4.5
Samoa	12.4
Singapore	1.2
Slovenia	2.2
South Korea, Rep.	23.4
Sudan	0.8
Swaziland	11.6
Sweden	0.2
Turkey	1.7
Uganda	1.0
Ukraine	5.9
Zambia	0.1

Source: Human Development Report 1999; <http://www.undp.org/hdro/>. United Nations Development Programme (UNDP).

H5. HOMICIDE, SUICIDE AND FIREARM-RELATED DEATHS

H5-1. Rates* of Homicide, Suicide, and Firearm-Related Deaths** Among Children Under Age 15, United States and 25 Other Industrialized Countries,*** 1990–1995

Age group (years)	Total homicide	Total suicide	Firearm-related deaths				
			Homicide	Suicide	Unintentional	Intention undermined	Total
0–4							
U.S.	4.1	0	0.43	0	0.15	0.01	0.59
Non-U.S.	0.95	0	0.05	0	0.01	0.01	0.07
Ratio U.S.:Non-U.S.	4.3:1	8.6:1	15.0:1	1.0:1	8.4:1		
5–14							
U.S.	1.75	0.84	1.22	0.49	0.46	0.06	2.23
Non-U.S.	0.3	0.4	0.07	0.05	0.05	0.01	0.18
Ratio U.S.:Non-U.S.	5.8:1	2.1:1	17.4:1	9.8:1	9.2:1	6.0:1	12.4:1
0–14							
U.S.	2.57	0.55	0.94	0.32	0.36	0.04	1.66
Non-U.S.	0.51	0.27	0.06	0.03	0.04	0.01	0.14
Ratio U.S.:Non-U.S.	5.0:1	2.0:1	15.7:1	10.7:1	9.0:1	4.0:1	11.9:1

*Per 100,000 children in each age group and for 1 year during 1990–1995.

**Homicides, suicides, homicides by firearm, suicides by firearm, unintentional deaths caused by firearm, and firearm-related deaths for which intention was undetermined.

***Australia, Austria, Belgium, Canada, Denmark, England and Wales, Finland, France, Germany, Hong Kong, Ireland, Israel, Italy, Japan, Kuwait, Netherlands, New Zealand, Northern Ireland, Norway, Scotland, Singapore, Sweden, Spain, Switzerland, and Taiwan. In this analysis, Hong Kong, Northern Ireland, and Taiwan are considered as countries.

Source: Rates of Homicide, Suicide, and Firearm-Related Death Among Children—26 Industrialized Countries, Morbidity and Mortality Weekly Report (MMWR), February 7, 1997 / Vol. 46 / No. 5, pp 101–105, Table 1; <http://www.cdc.gov/ftp://ftp.cdc.gov/pub/Publications/mmwr/wk/mm4605.pdf>. Underlying data from Centers for Disease Control and Prevention (CDC).

H6. COMMERCIAL SEXUAL EXPLOITATION

H6-1. Countries Taking Action Against the Sexual Exploitation of Children, 1999

	Countries that adopted the Stockholm Agenda for Action	Countries with a National Plan of Action and countries that are developing a National Plan in 1999	Countries with a general plan to protect children
Afghanistan	yes		
Albania	yes		
Algeria	yes		
Andorra	yes		
Angola	yes		
Antigua and Barbuda	yes		
Australia	yes	*	
Azerbaijan	yes		
Bahamas		*	
Bangladesh	yes		
Barbados	yes		
Belarus	yes		
Belgium	yes		
Belize	yes		
Bhutan	yes		
Bolivia	yes		
Bosnia and Herzegovina	yes		
Brazil	yes		
Brunei	yes		
Bulgaria	yes	*	
Burkina Faso	yes		

H6-1. Countries Taking Action Against the Sexual Exploitation of Children, 1999 *(continued)*

	Countries that adopted the Stockholm Agenda for Action	Countries with a National Plan of Action and countries that are developing a National Plan in 1999	Countries with a general plan to protect children
Cameroon	yes		
Canada	yes		
Cape Verde	yes		
Central African Republic	yes	*	
Chad	yes		
Colombia	yes		
Comoros	yes	*	
Congo, Rep.	yes		
Cook Islands	yes		
Costa Rica	yes		
Croatia	yes		
Cuba	yes		
Cyprus	yes		
Czech Republic	yes		
Denmark	yes	+	
Dominican Republic		*	
Egypt		*	
Equatorial Guinea		*	
Eritrea		*	
Ghana	yes		
Greece	yes		
Grenada	yes		
Guatemala	yes		
Guinea Bissau	yes		
Guyana	yes		
Haiti	yes		
Honduras	yes		
Hungary	yes		
Iceland	yes	*	
India	yes		
Indonesia	yes		
Iran	yes		
Iraq	yes	*	
Ireland	yes	*	
Israel	yes		
Italy	yes		
Ivory Coast	yes		
Jamaica	yes		
Japan	yes	*	
Jordan	yes		
Kazakhstan	yes		
Kenya	yes		
Kuwait	yes		
Kyrgyzstan	yes		
Laos	yes		
Latvia	yes		
Lebanon		+	
Lesotho		*	
Liberia	yes		
Liechtenstein	yes		
Lithuania	yes		
Macedonia	yes		
Madagascar	yes		
Malawi	yes		
Malaysia	yes	*	
Maldives	yes	*	
Mali	yes		
Malta	yes		
Marshall Islands	yes		

H6-1. Countries Taking Action Against the Sexual Exploitation of Children, 1999 *(continued)*

	Countries that adopted the Stockholm Agenda for Action	Countries with a National Plan of Action and countries that are developing a National Plan in 1999	Countries with a general plan to protect children
Mauritania	yes		
Mauritius	yes		
Mexico	yes		
Monaco	*		
Myanmar (Burma)	yes		
North Korea, Dem. Rep.	yes		
Norway	yes	*	
Oman	yes	+	
Pakistan	yes		
Palau	yes	+	
Panama	yes		
Papua New Guinea	yes	*	
Paraguay	yes		
Peru	yes		
Philippines	yes		
Poland	yes		yes
Portugal	yes		yes
Qatar	yes		yes
Saint Lucia	yes		
Saint Vincent and the Grenadines	yes		
Samoa	yes	+	
San Marino	yes	*	
Sao Tome and Principe	yes		yes
Saudi Arabia	yes	?	
Senegal	yes	+	
Seychelles		*	
Sierra Leone	yes		
Singapore	yes		
Slovakia	yes		
Slovenia	yes		
Solomon Islands	yes	*	yes
Somalia	yes	+	
South Africa	yes	+	
South Korea, Rep.	yes	*	
Spain	yes	+	
Sri Lanka		*	
Sudan		+	
Suriname	yes		
Swaziland	yes		
Sweden	yes		
Switzerland	yes		
Syria	yes		
Taiwan	yes	+	
Tanzania		+	
Thailand	yes		
Togo	yes		
Tonga	yes		
Trinidad and Tobago	yes		
Tunisia	yes	*	
Turkmenistan	yes		
Tuvalu	yes		
Ukraine	yes		
United Arab Emirates	yes		
Vatican City	yes		
Venezuela	yes		

* Countries with a National Plan of Action in 1999.
+ Countries developing a National Plan of Action in 1999.

Source: A Step Forward 1998–99, The third report on the implementation of the Agenda for Action adopted at the World Congress against Commercial Sexual Exploitation of Children, Stockholm, Sweden, 28 August 1996; <http://www.ecpat.net/a4a99/appen5.htm>. Underlying data from End Child Prostitution Child Pornography and Trafficking (ECPAT) International.

H7. VIOLENCE AGAINST GIRLS

H7-1. Sex Crimes Against Girls, Selected Countries/Cities, early 1990s

Country (city)	Percent of all sexual assault victims		Percent of attackers known to child victim
	Aged 15 or less	Aged 10 or less	
Peru (Lima)	N/A	18	60
Malaysia	58	18	68
Mexico (City)	36	23	67
Guatemala (City)	40	N/A	61
Papua New Guinea	47	13	N/A
Chile (Santiago)	58	32	72
United States	62	29	78
N/A = Not available			

Source: Violence against women: a priority health issue; Violence and Injury Prevention; <http://www.who.int/violence_injury_prevention/vaw/infopack.htm#The%20girl%20child>. Underlying data from L. Heise. "Violence Against Women: The Hidden Health Burden." *World Health Statistics Quarterly*, 1993, Volume 46, Number 1, Pages 78–85, World Health Organization (WHO).

H8. FEMALE GENITAL MUTILATION (FGM)

H8-1. Legal Status and Estimates of the Numbers and Percentages of Women Who Suffer Female Genital Mutilation (FGM) in Africa, mid-1990s

	Estimated % of women who have suffered FGM	Estimated number of women (millions) who have suffered FGM, 1994	Government has published policy opposing FGM	FGM prohibited under specific FGM law	FGM prohibited under medical code of practice
Benin	50	1.3	Yes	No	No
Burkina Faso[1]	70	3.5	Yes	No	No
Cameroon	20	1.3	Yes	No	No
Central African Republic[2]	50	0.8	Yes	No	No
Chad	60	1.9	Yes	No	No
Cote d'Ivoire	60	4.1	No	No	No
Djibouti[3]	98	0.3	Yes	No	No
Egypt	80	24.2	Yes	No	Yes
Eritrea	90****	1.6	Yes	No	No
Ethiopia	90	23.9	Yes	No	No
Gambia	89	0.5	Yes	No	No
Ghana[4]	30	2.6	Yes	Yes	***
Guinea[5]	50	1.6	Yes	No	No
Guinea-Bissau	50	0.3	No	No	No
Kenya	50	6.8	Yes	No	No
Liberia	60	0.9	Yes	No	No
Mali	80	4.3	Yes	No	No
Mauritania	25	0.3	No	No	No
Niger	20	0.9	No	No	No
Nigeria	60	32.8	Yes	No	No
Senegal	20	0.8	Yes	No	No
Sierra Leone	90	2.0	Yes	No	No
Somalia	98	4.5	Yes**	No	No
Sudan	89	9.7	Yes	*	No
Tanzania	10	1.5	No	No	No
Togo	50	1.0	Yes	No	No
Uganda	5	0.5	No	No	No
Zaire	5	1.1	No	No	No

* Past government policy opposed FGM, but the policy of current ruling groups is unknown.

** FGM is not covered by a medical code, but this may be unnecessary since the practice is illegal.

*** FGM is not covered by a medical code, but this may be unnecessary since the practice is illegal.

**** This estimate predates Eritrea's independence and assumes that FGM prevalence is equivalent to Ethiopia's.

[1] Law outlawing FGM passed in October 1996

[2] Law outlawing FGM enacted since 1966

[3] Penal code outlawing FGM enacted in 1994

[4] Law prohibiting FGM enacted in 1994

[5] Article 256 of Penal Code prohibits FGM

Source: The Progress of Nations 1996, United Nations Children's Fund (UNICEF) and Department of Women's Health Health Systems and Community Health World Health Organization (WHO) 1999, *Female Genital Mutilation Programmes to Date: What Works and What Doesn't, A Review*; Annex 4; <http://www.unicef.org/pon96/contents.htm> and <http://www.who.int/frh-whd/PDFfiles/Programmes%20to%20Date.pdf>. Underlying data from Nahid Toubia, January 1996 update from her study, *Female Genital Mutilation: A Call for Global Action, Women, Ink.*, New York, revised edition, 1995; Office of Asylum Affairs, Bureau of Democracy, Human Rights and Labor, U.S. Department of State, 1997; and country assessment reports.

H8-2. Prevalence Rates for Female Genital Mutilation (FGM), January 2001

	Year of data	Prevalence (%) of all women*
Benin	1996	50
Burkina Faso	1999	72
Cameroon	1998	20
Central African Republic	1994	43
Chad	1996-1997	60
Congo, Dem. Rep. (Zaire)	unknown	5
Côte d'Ivoire	1994	43
Djibouti	unknown	98
Egypt	1995	97
Eritrea	1995	95
Ethiopia	1984-1990	85
Gambia, the	1985	80
Ghana	1998	30
Guinea	1999	99
Guinea-Bissau	1990	50
Kenya	1998	38
Liberia	1986	60
Mali	1996	94
Mauritania	1987	25
Niger	1998	5
Nigeria	various years	40-50
Senegal	1999	20
Sierra Leone	1987	90
Somalia	1982-1993	98-100
Sudan	1990	89
Tanzania	1996	18
Togo	1996	12
Uganda	1995-1996	5
Yemen	1997	23

* Based on representative sample surveys.

Source: Women's Health, *Female Genital Mutilation*, January 2001; <http://www.who.int/frh-whd/FGM/prevalence_rates_for_fgm.htm>. Underlying data from World Health Organization (WHO).

H9. REFUGEE CHILDREN

H9-1. Refugee Children Age 0–17, Male, Female, and Total, by Country of Origin, 1998

	Country/territory of asylum	Male	Female	Total
Afghanistan	Belarus	150	140	290
	Bulgaria	N/A	30	30
	India	3,760	3,610	7,370
	Kazakhstan	180	180	360
	Pakistan	293,300	327,100	620,400
	Saudi Arabia	30	30	60
	Slovakia	10	10	20
	Tajikistan	80	70	150
	Turkmenistan	350	540	890
	Ukraine	80	60	140
Algeria	Tunisia	30	10	40
Angola	Brazil	140	130	270
	Congo, Rep.	10	N/A	10
	Ukraine	50	40	90
	Zambia	29,600	30,700	60,300
Azerbaijan	Armenia	12,030	12,410	24,440
Bhutan	Nepal	23,090	22,910	46,000

H9-1. Refugee Children Age 0–17, Male, Female, and Total, by Country of Origin, 1998 *(continued)*

	Country/territory of asylum	Male	Female	Total
Bosnia and Herzegovina	Croatia	3,000	2,800	5,800
	Macedonia, FYRO	80	90	170
	Turkey	100	100	200
Burundi	Cameroon	50	100	150
	Kenya	70	90	160
	Rwanda	360	300	660
	Swaziland	20	10	30
	Tanzania	80,110	78,260	158,370
Cambodia	Thailand	100	80	180
Chad	Burkina Faso	40	10	50
	Cameroon	1,500	1,020	2,520
	Congo, Rep.	60	50	110
	Niger	50	50	100
Colombia	Ecuador	30	10	40
Congo, Rep.	Cameroon	20	20	40
	Côte d'Ivoire	30	30	60
	Gabon	30	30	60
	Ukraine	30	30	60
Cuba	Argentina	N/A	N/A	N/A
Congo, Dem. Rep. (Zaire)	Angola	2,670	2,680	5,350
	Benin	10	30	40
	Brazil	20	10	30
	Burundi	30	40	70
	Cameroon	40	60	100
	Congo, Rep.	60	60	120
	Kenya	70	60	130
	Malawi	40	40	80
	Rwanda	10,460	9,260	19,720
	Sudan	110	170	280
	Swaziland	20	20	40
	Uganda	1,620	1,750	3,370
	Tanzania	16,020	17,400	33,420
El Salvador	Belize	140	140	280
	Belize	630	630	1,260
	Guatemala	30	30	60
	Mexico	100	60	160
Eritrea	Sudan	45,200	44,010	89,210
Ethiopia	Djibouti	180	220	400
	Kenya	1,060	1,510	2,570
	Somalia	80	60	140
	Sudan	3,220	2,900	6,120
	Yemen	50	40	90
Ghana	Togo	3,130	4,090	7,220
Guatemala	Belize	280	280	560
	Mexico	7,520	7,590	15,110
Guinea-Bissau	Gambia, the	20	30	50
	Guinea	620	660	1,280
	Senegal	110	120	230
Indonesia	Papua New Guinea	1,170	930	2,100
Iran	India	20	20	40
	Iraq	5,100	4,400	9,500
	Pakistan	90	80	170
	Turkey	80	80	160
Iraq	Jordan	140	120	260
	Kuwait	130	80	210
	Lebanon	450	410	860
	Pakistan	210	180	390
	Saudi Arabia	1,020	1,020	2,040

H9-1. Refugee Children Age 0–17, Male, Female, and Total, by Country of Origin, 1998 *(continued)*

	Country/territory of asylum	Male	Female	Total
	Syria	870	830	1,700
	Turkey	190	160	350
	Ukraine	20	40	60
Laos	Thailand	60	50	110
Liberia	Brazil	N/A	10	10
	Cameroon	40	20	60
	Côte d'Ivoire	31,820	32,960	64,780
	Ghana	2,810	2,900	5,710
	Guinea	32,800	40,600	73,400
	Guinea-Bissau	N/A	10	10
	Mali	20	40	60
Mali	Niger	470	700	1,170
Mauritania	Senegal	14,040	13,280	27,320
Myanmar (Burma)	Bangladesh	6,400	6,400	12,800
	India	80	80	160
	Thailand	230	230	460
Nicaragua	Belize	40	40	80
	Guatemala	60	80	140
Nigeria	Benin	120	100	220
Palestinians	Kuwait	120	120	240
	Libya	130	140	270
Peru	Argentina	30	20	50
	Bolivia	20	20	40
	Chile	30	30	60
Russia	Kazakhstan	120	120	240
Rwanda	Angola	50	50	100
	Benin	50	50	100
	Burkina Faso	50	10	60
	Cameroon	320	240	560
	Congo, Rep.	1,050	950	2,000
	Côte d'Ivoire	60	40	100
	Kenya	1,710	640	2,350
	Malawi	30	30	60
	Togo	40	40	80
	Uganda	2,430	2,270	4,700
	Tanzania	1,400	1,210	2,610
	Zimbabwe	20	20	40
Senegal	Gambia	80	170	250
	Guinea-Bissau	1,530	1,400	2,930
Sierra Leone	Côte d'Ivoire	410	420	830
	Gambia	240	340	580
	Ghana	120	120	240
	Guinea	92,630	100,900	193,530
	Guinea-Bissau	40	N/A	40
	Liberia	8,950	8,720	17,670
	Mali	70	50	120
Somalia	Djibouti	5,450	5,680	11,130
	Egypt	560	500	1,060
	Eritrea	680	640	1,320
	Ethiopia	54,730	52,880	107,610
	India	40	30	70
	Kenya	36,490	38,800	75,290
	Lebanon	10	10	20
	Libya	160	240	400
	Malawi	40	50	90
	Pakistan	240	180	420
	Russia	30	20	50
	Syria.	100	90	190
	Uganda	400	330	730

H9-1. Refugee Children Age 0–17, Male, Female, and Total, by Country of Origin, 1998 *(continued)*

	Country/territory of asylum	Male	Female	Total
	Tanzania	1,200	1,010	2,210
	Yemen	9,030	8,880	17,910
Sri Lanka	Thailand	10	10	20
Sudan	Central African Rep.	12,500	10,100	22,600
	Chad	3,630	700	4,330
	Egypt	340	340	680
	Eritrea	20	20	40
	Ethiopia	15,730	14,460	30,190
	Kenya	12,090	9,370	21,460
	Lebanon	60	50	110
	Syria	20	20	40
	Uganda	50,310	47,010	97,320
	Zimbabwe	20	20	40
Tajikistan	Kazakhstan	170	170	340
	Turkmenistan	250	400	650
Togo	Benin	270	260	530
	Ghana	150	150	300
Turkey	Iraq	3,370	3,350	6,720
Uganda	Kenya	1,030	900	1,930
Vietnam	China	51,150	45,200	96,350
	Hong Kong, SAR (China	90	120	210
Yemen	Egypt	130	150	280
	Syria	110	100	210
Yugoslavia	Albania	3,580	2,810	6,390
	Bosnia and Herzegovina	250	380	630
	Croatia	60	50	110
	Macedonia, FYRO	130	120	250

Source: Refugees and Others of Concern to UNHCR—1998 Statistical Overview Table III.5. UNHCR Assisted Refugees by Origin, Gender and Age, end–1998; <http://www.unhcr.ch/statist/98oview/intro.htm>. Underlying data from United Nations High Commission for Refugees (UNHCR).

H9-2. Refugee Children Age 0–17, Male, Female, and Total, by Country of Asylum, 1998

	Male	Female	Total
Albania	3,610	2,770	6,380
Angola	2,690	2,810	5,500
Argentina	60	50	110
Armenia	12,000	12,400	24,400
Bangladesh	6,500	6,400	12,900
Belarus	160	160	320
Belize	1,110	1,110	2,220
Benin	500	470	970
Bolivia	20	20	40
Bosnia and Herzegovina	250	390	640
Brazil	220	200	420
Bulgaria	0	50	50
Burkina Faso	130	60	190
Burundi	30	50	80
Cameroon	2,040	1,570	3,610
Central African Republic	13,000	10,500	23,500
Chad	3,600	700	4,300
Chile	40	40	80
China	51,000	45,300	96,300
Colombia	30	10	40
Congo, Rep.	1,220	1,070	2,290
Côte d'Ivoire	32,300	33,600	65,900
Croatia	3,090	2,770	5,860

H9-2. Refugee Children Age 0–17, Male, Female, and Total, by Country of Asylum, 1998 *(continued)*

	Male	Female	Total
Djibouti	5,590	5,870	11,460
Ecuador	50	30	80
Egypt	1,100	1,040	2,140
Eritrea	700	660	1,360
Ethiopia	70,600	67,400	138,000
Gabon	60	70	130
Gambia, the	360	580	940
Ghana	3,060	3,160	6,220
Guatemala	90	110	200
Guinea	126,200	142,200	268,400
Guinea-Bissau	1,600	1,450	3,050
Hong Kong SAR (China)	90	120	210
India	3,890	3,740	7,630
Iraq	8,400	7,800	16,200
Jordan	170	130	300
Kazakhstan	470	470	940
Kenya	52,700	51,500	104,200
Kuwait	250	200	450
Lebanon	560	520	1,080
Liberia	8,900	8,800	17,700
Libya	310	400	710
Macedonia, FYRO	210	210	420
Malawi	110	130	240
Malaysia	20	0	20
Mali	120	120	240
Mexico	7,700	7,600	15,300
Nepal	23,100	22,700	45,800
Niger	520	780	1,300
Pakistan	293,900	327,600	621,500
Papua New Guinea	1,170	930	2,100
Philippines	20	20	40
Romania	50	60	110
Russia	30	30	60
Rwanda	10,900	9,700	20,600
Saudi Arabia	1,060	1,060	2,120
Senegal	14,200	13,300	27,500
Slovakia	20	20	40
Somalia	80	60	140
South Africa	500	310	810
Sudan	48,600	47,200	95,800
Swaziland	90	90	180
Syria	1,150	1,060	2,210
Tajikistan	80	70	150
Tanzania	98,800	97,800	196,600
Thailand	410	380	790
Togo	3,200	4,100	7,300
Tunisia	40	30	70
Turkey	480	480	960
Turkmenistan	600	940	1,540
Uganda	54,900	51,400	106,300
Ukraine	260	270	530
Venezuela	20	20	40
Yemen	9,100	9,000	18,100
Zambia	42,100	42,700	84,800
Zimbabwe	80	70	150

Source: Refugees and Others of Concern to UNHCR—1998 Statistical Overview: Table III.1. UNHCR Assisted Refugees by Gender and Age, 1998; <http://www.unhcr.ch/statist/98oview/intro.htm>. Underlying data from United Nations High Commission for Refugees (UNHCR).

H9-3. Refugee Children Less Than Five Years of Age as Percentage of Total Refugee Population, by Country of Origin, end 1998

	Country/territory of asylum	% of total refugee population
Afghanistan	Belarus	5.6
	Bulgaria	0.0
	India	4.2
	Kazakhstan	67.9
	Pakistan	15.4
	Saudi Arabia	6.3
	Slovakia	6.7
	Tajikistan	4.8
	Turkmenistan	26.3
	Ukraine	10.7
Algeria	Tunisia	8.3
Angola	Brazil	12.6
	Congo, Rep.	0.0
	Ukraine	20.0
	Zambia	15.8
Azerbaijan	Armenia	2.5
Bhutan	Nepal	13.3
Bosnia and Herzegovina	Croatia	2.0
	Macedonia, FYRO	8.0
	Turkey	4.8
Burundi	Cameroon	8.3
	Kenya	10.7
	Rwanda	10.4
	Swaziland	10.0
	Tanzania	17.6
Cambodia	Thailand	9.5
Chad	Burkina Faso	10.0
	Cameroon	14.4
	Congo, Rep.	0.0
	Niger	11.8
Colombia	Ecuador	8.3
Congo, Rep.	Cameroon	10.0
	Côte d'Ivoire	20.0
	Gabon	15.4
	Ukraine	15.4
Cuba	Argentina	0.0
Congo, Dem. Rep. (Zaire)	Angola	13.4
	Benin	0.0
	Brazil	8.3
	Burundi	16.7
	Cameroon	7.7
	Congo, Rep.	3.3
	Kenya	10.5
	Malawi	15.4
	Rwanda	23.6
	Sudan	69.7
	Swaziland	20.0
	Uganda	28.1
	Tanzania	20.1
El Salvador	Belize	13.6
	Belize	13.4
	Guatemala	10.0
	Mexico	2.3
Eritrea	Sudan	21.6
Ethiopia	Djibouti	10.8
	Kenya	8.4
	Somalia	14.7

H9-3. Refugee Children Less Than Five Years of Age as Percentage of Total Refugee Population, by Country of Origin, end 1998 *(continued)*

	Country/territory of asylum	% of total refugee population
	Sudan	15.7
	Yemen	3.2
Ghana	Togo	26.3
Guatemala	Belize	13.6
	Mexico	17.8
Guinea-Bissau	Gambia, the	16.7
	Guinea	10.7
	Senegal	5.2
Indonesia	Papua New Guinea	21.4
Iran	India	0.0
	Iraq	15.9
	Pakistan	6.4
	Turkey	1.9
Iraq	Jordan	9.0
	Kuwait	6.1
	Lebanon	10.2
	Pakistan	10.6
	Saudi Arabia	12.0
	Syria	8.8
	Turkey	12.0
	Ukraine	15.4
Laos	Thailand	9.5
Liberia	Brazil	4.8
	Cameroon	0.0
	Côte d'Ivoire	15.7
	Ghana	6.1
	Guinea	18.0
	Guinea-Bissau	0.0
	Mali	10.0
Mali	Niger	4.5
Mauritania	Senegal	5.3
Myanmar (Burma)	Bangladesh	21.2
	India	8.5
	Thailand	7.1
Nicaragua	Belize	16.7
	Guatemala	3.4
Nigeria	Benin	12.7
Palestinians	Kuwait	6.0
	Libya	17.7
Peru	Argentina	7.1
	Bolivia	3.0
	Chile	5.0
Russia	Kazakhstan	68.6
Rwanda	Angola	12.5
	Benin	10.3
	Burkina Faso	6.7
	Cameroon	6.0
	Congo, Rep.	19.4
	Côte d'Ivoire	13.0
	Kenya	11.5
	Malawi	18.2
	Togo	23.8
	Uganda	21.9
	Tanzania	20.8
	Zimbabwe	7.7
Senegal	Gambia	12.3
	Guinea-Bissau	13.7

H9-3. Refugee Children Less Than Five Years of Age as Percentage of Total Refugee Population, by Country of Origin, end 1998 *(continued)*

	Country/territory of asylum	% of total refugee population
Sierra Leone	Côte d'Ivoire	15.9
	Gambia	6.5
	Ghana	6.6
	Guinea	16.2
	Guinea-Bissau	10.3
	Liberia	14.7
	Mali	11.4
Somalia	Djibouti	6.0
	Egypt	1.9
	Eritrea	23.1
	Ethiopia	13.3
	India	5.3
	Kenya	12.1
	Lebanon	6.3
	Libya	16.0
	Malawi	13.3
	Pakistan	7.6
	Russia	13.3
	Syria	3.6
	Uganda	13.1
	Tanzania	18.2
	Yemen	9.6
Sri Lanka	Thailand	0.0
Sudan	Central African Rep.	18.2
	Chad	19.8
	Egypt	8.9
	Eritrea	13.3
	Ethiopia	20.8
	Kenya	12.5
	Lebanon	11.9
	Syria	20.0
	Uganda	21.6
	Zimbabwe	18.2
Tajikistan	Kazakhstan	73.9
	Turkmenistan	30.0
Togo	Benin	9.0
	Ghana	9.5
Turkey	Iraq	16.7
Uganda	Kenya	6.4
Vietnam	China	6.7
	Hong Kong SAR, China	4.9
Western Sahara	Cuba	0.0
Yemen	Egypt	6.1
	Syria	4.3
Yugoslavia	Albania	6.0
	Bosnia and Herzegovina	14.7
	Croatia	5.4
	Macedonia, FYRO	12.0

Source: Refugees and Others of Concern to UNHCR—1998 Statistical Overview: Table III.5. UNHCR Assisted Refugees by Origin, Gender and Age, end–1998; <http://www.unhcr.ch/statist/98oview/intro.htm>. Underlying data from United Nations High Commission for Refugees (UNHCR).

H9-4. Refugee Children Less Than Five Years of Age as Percentage of Total Refugee Population, by Country of Asylum, end 1998

	% of total refugee population*
Albania	5.9
Angola	13.2
Argentina	4.3
Armenia	2.5
Bangladesh	21.0
Belarus	5.3
Belize	12.9
Benin	9.4
Bolivia	2.8
Bosnia and Herzegovina	14.9
Brazil	9.4
Bulgaria	0.0
Burkina Faso	5.3
Burundi	20.0
Cameroon	11.2
Central African Republic	18.4
Chad	19.7
Chile	7.1
China	6.7
Colombia	0.0
Congo, Rep.	16.3
Côte d'Ivoire	15.7
Croatia	1.9
Djibouti	6.3
Ecuador	3.8
Egypt	4.2
Eritrea	22.4
Ethiopia	15.1
Gabon	8.5
Gambia, the	8.9
Ghana	6.4
Guatemala	4.9
Guinea	16.7
Guinea-Bissau	12.6
Hong Kong SAR, China	4.8
India	4.3
Iraq	15.9
Jordan	9.0
Kazakhstan	70.7
Kenya	11.8
Kuwait	5.9
Lebanon	9.8
Liberia	14.6
Libya	15.5
Macedonia, FYRO	10.0
Malawi	16.3
Malaysia	10.0
Mali	13.0
Mexico	17.5
Nepal	13.3
Niger	4.9
Pakistan	15.4
Papua New Guinea	21.4
Philippines	14.3
Romania	8.8
Russia	10.5
Rwanda	23.2

H9-4. Refugee Children Less Than Five Years of Age as Percentage of Total Refugee Population, by Country of Asylum, end 1998 *(continued)*

	% of total refugee population*
Saudi Arabia	12.2
Senegal	5.3
Slovakia	3.7
Somalia	14.7
South Africa	0.0
Sudan	21.3
Swaziland	10.0
Syria	7.7
Tajikistan	4.8
Tanzania	18.1
Thailand	7.1
Togo	26.3
Tunisia	7.1
Turkey	7.1
Turkmenistan	27.7
Uganda	21.7
Ukraine	15.3
Venezuela	0.0
Yemen	9.5
Zambia	15.5
Zimbabwe	8.5

*Refugee populations of 100 and above only.

Source: Refugees and Others of Concern to UNHCR—1998 Statistical Overview; Table III.1. UNHCR Assisted Refugees by Gender and Age, 1998; <http://www.unhcr.ch/statist/98oview/intro.htm>. Underlying data from United Nations High Commission for Refugees (UNHCR).

H10. CHILDREN IN THE MILITARY

H10-1. Countries Recruiting Under-18 Children into the Armed Forces, July 1999

	Minimum age for official recruitment*	Minimum age for participation**
Angola	17 (conscripts)	
Australia	17 (volunteers)	18
Austria	17 (volunteers)	
Bangladesh	16 (volunteers)	
Belgium (1)	16 (volunteers)	
Bhutan	16 (volunteers)	
Bosnia and Herzegovina	16 (volunteers)	
Brazil	17 (volunteers)	
Burundi	16 (volunteers)	
Canada	16 (volunteers)	18
Chile	16 (volunteers)	
Croatia (3)	17 (volunteers)	18
Cuba	16 (conscripts)	
Cyprus	17 (volunteeers)	
El Salvador	16 (volunteers)	
Estonia	17 (volunteers)	
Finland (2)	17 (conscripts)	18
France	17 (volunteers)	
Germany	17 (volunteers)	18
Germany	16 (border guards)	
Honduras	17 (volunteers)	
India	16 (volunteers)	18
Indonesia	17 (volunteers)	
Iran	16 (volunteers)	
Iraq	15 (volunteers)	

H10-1. Countries Recruiting Under-18 Children into the Armed Forces, July 1999 *(continued)*

	Minimum age for official recruitment*	Minimum age for participation**
Ireland	16 (volunteers)	
Israel	17 (volunteers)	
Italy	17 (volunteers)	
Japan	15 (military schools)	18
Jordan	17 (volunteers)	
Laos	15 (conscripts)	
Libya	17 (volunteers)	
Luxembourg	17 (volunteers)	
Macedonia, FYRO	17 (volunteers)	
Mauritania	16 (volunteers)	
Mexico	16 (volunteers)	
Namibia	16 (conscripts)	
Netherlands, the	17 (volunteers)	18
New Zealand	17 (volunteers)	18
Nicaragua	17 (volunteers)	
Norway (2) (3)	17 (volunteers)	18
Norway (2) (3)	16 (home guards)	
Pakistan	16 (volunteers)	
Peru	16 (volunteers)	
Poland	17 (volunteers)	
Qatar	17 (volunteers)	
Rwanda	16 (volunteers)	
Slovakia	16 (volunteers)	
Slovenia	17 (volunteers)	
South Korea, Rep.	17 (volunteers)	
Sudan	16 (volunteers)	
Switzerland	16 (volunteers)	
Uganda	13 (volunteers - exceptionally)	
United Kingdom	16 (volunteers)	17
United States	17 (volunteers)	
Yugoslavia	17 (volunteers)	

Note: Conscription: Conscription is the legal obligation of citizens falling into a specified category to perform a stated period of compulsory military service. Conscription shows the duration of service in monts and whether conscription is selective; volunteers: The minimum age for voluntary recruitment. If a country has several different recruitment ages, the lowest is given.

* Recruitment includes conscripting, enlisting or otherwise accepting a person into armed forces.

**The age for participation is only given where it is different from the age for recruitment.

(1) Planning to raise to 18.

(2) Being raised to 18.

(3) In armed conflict, these countries retain the possibility to conscript from 16 years, or, in the case of Greece, 17 years.

Source: Children: The Invisible Soldiers, statements to the UN Working Group on the draft Optional Protocol, reports to the Committee on the Rights of the Child, research carried out by the Coalition; <http://www.child-soldiers.org/countryposition.htm>. Data extracted 24/10/1999, United Nations (UN).

H10-2. Lowest Age at Which Children Can Volunteer in the Armed Forces (Governmental or Non-governmental), 1996–1997

	Lowest age (in years), 1996-1997
Uganda	5
Sierra Leone	6
Congo, Dem. Rep. (Zaire)	7
Myanmar (Burma)	7
Rwanda	7
Sudan	7
Turkey	7
Angola	8
Burundi	8
Cambodia	8
Colombia	8
Sri Lanka	8
Iran	9
Peru	9
Afghanistan	10
Albania	10
Iraq	10
Liberia	10
Philippines	10
Bhutan	11
India	11
Somalia	11
Chad	12
Ethiopia	12
Israel	12
Lebanon	12
Mexico	12
Paraguay	12
Comoros	13
Papua New Guinea	13
Yugoslavia	13
Congo, Rep.	14
Libya	14
Azerbaijan	14 or 17
Algeria	15
Laos	15
Taiwan	15
United Kingdom	15
Australia	16
Bangladesh	16
Canada	16
Chile	16
Croatia	16
El Salvador	16
Greece	16
Mauritania	16
Netherlands, the	16
New Zealand	16
Pakistan	16
Tajikistan	16
Namibia	16 *
Austria	17
Finland	17
Germany	17
Guinea-Bissau	17
Indonesia	17
Ireland	17

H10-2. Lowest Age at Which Children Can Volunteer in the Armed Forces (Governmental or Non-governmental), 1996–1997 *(continued)*

	Lowest age (in years), 1996-1997
Luxembourg	17
Morocco	17
Nicaragua	17
Norway	17
Poland	17
Russia	17
United States	17

* Known but not confirmed.

Note: All information about child soldiers relates to children below 18 years of age, if not otherwise specified.

Source: Rädda Barnen—Swedish Save the Children database, ChildWar; military recruitment of children worldwide; <http://www.rb.se:8082/www/childwar.nsf/HTML/Forsta?openDocument>.

H10-3. Military Recruitment of Children Less than 18 Years (Armed Force, Number, Type of Force), 1996–1997

	Armed force (forces listed by names)	Number of children (less than 18 years) in troops	Type of forces**
Afghanistan	Northern Alliance	More than 60,000	(Former Gov.)
	Talebaan	25,000	(Governmental)
Albania	Armed Forces	54,000	Governmental
	Paramilitary	13,500	Governmental
	Rebels	*	Non-governmental
Algeria	AIS	2,000 *	Non-governmental
	Armed Forces	122,000	Governmental
	FIDA	*	Non-governmental
	GIA	Less than 3000	Non-governmental
	LIDD	*	Non-governmental
	Paramilitary	181,200	Governmental
Angola	FAA	112,500	Governmental
	FDC	N/A	Non-governmental
	FLEC-FAC	1,500-2,000	Non-governmental
	FLEC-Renovada	1,500-2,000	Non-governmental
	Reaction Police	15,000	Governmental
	UNITA	25,000-30,000	Non-governmental
Antigua and Barbuda	Armed Forces	150	Governmental
Argentina	Armed Forces	70,500	Governmental
Armenia	Armed Forces	53,400	Governmental
	Paramilitary	1,000	Governmental
Australia	Armed Forces	55,200	Governmental
Austria	Armed Forces	40,500	Governmental
Azerbaijan	Armed Forces	69,900	Governmental
	Karabakh forces	20,000-25,000	Karabakh "goverment"
	Militia	More than 15,000	Governmental
	Popular Front	20,000	Governmental
Bahamas, the	Defence Force	860	Governmental
Bahrain	Armed Forces	11,000	Governmental
Bangladesh	Ansars	20,000	Governmental
	Armed Forces	137,000	Governmental
	Armed Police	5,000	Governmental
	Bangladesh Rifles	30,000	Governmental
	Shanti Bahini	5,000	Non-governmental
Barbados	Armed Forces	610	Governmental
Belarus	Armed Forces	80,900	Governmental
Belgium	Armed Forces	41,750	Governmental
Belize	Armed Forces	1,050	Governmental

H10-3. Military Recruitment of Children Less than 18 Years (Armed Force, Number, Type of Force), 1996–1997 *(continued)*

	Armed force (forces listed by names)	Number of children (less than 18 years) in troops	Type of forces**
Benin	Armed Forces	4,800	Governmental
Bhutan	Armed Forces	11,000	Governmental
	Militias	More than 2,200	Governmental
	Royal Bhutan Police	8,000	Governmental
	Royal Body Guard	2,000	Governmental
Bolivia	Armed Forces	32,500	Governmental
Bosnia and Herzegovina	Armed Forces	40,000	Governmental
Botswana	Armed Forces	9,000	Governmental
Brazil	Armed Forces	291,000	Governmental
Brunei	Armed Forces	5,000	Governmental
Bulgaria	Armed Forces	80,760	Governmental
Burkina Faso	Armed Forces	10,000	Governmental
Burundi	Armed Forces	45,000	Governmental
	Hutu rebels	More than 5,000	Non-governmental
Cambodia	Armed Forces	149,000	Governmental
	Village militias	35,000	Governmental
Cameroon	Armed Forces	22,100	Governmental
Canada	Armed Forces	60,600	Governmental
	Paramilitary	9,350	Governmental
Cape Verde	Armed Forces	1,100	Governmental
Chad	Armed Forces	30,350	Governmental
	FARF	*	Non-governmental
	FNR	600	Non-governmental
	FNT	1,000	Non-governmental
	Gendarmerie	4,500	Governmental
	MDD	600	Non-governmental
Chile	Armed Forces	93,000	Governmental
	Carabineros	29,500	Governmental
	FPMR	800	Non-governmental
	MIR	Less than 500	Non-governmental
China	Armed Forces	2,480,000	Governmental
	Armed Police	1,100,000	Governmental
Colombia	Armed forces	144,000	Governmental
	AUC	4,000-6,000	(Governmental)
	ELN	5,000	Non-governmental
	EPL	500	Non-governmental
	FARC	10,000-15,000	Non-governmental
	National Police	87,000	Governmental
Comoros	Anjouan separatists	*	Non-governmental
	Armed Forces	900	Governmental
Congo, Rep.	Armed forces	10,000	Governmental
	Cocoye	*	Non-governmental
	Ninjas	4,000	Non-governmental
	Paramilitary	2,000	Governmental
Congo, Dem. Rep. (Zaire)	Armed Forces	55,000-75,000	Governmental
	Mai-Mai	2,500-15,000	(Governmental)
	MLC	5,000-10,000	Non-governmental
	National Police	*	Governmental
	RCD	40,000-60,000	Non-governmental
Costa Rica	Armed Forces	8,400	Governmental
Cote d' Ivoire	Armed Forces	13,900	Governmental
Croatia	Armed Forces	61,000	Governmental
	Police	40,000	Governmental
Cuba	Armed Forces	65,000	Governmental
	Border Guards	6,500	Governmental
	Civil Defence Force	50,000	Governmental

H10-3. Military Recruitment of Children Less than 18 Years (Armed Force, Number, Type of Force), 1996–1997 *(continued)*

	Armed force (forces listed by names)	Number of children (less than 18 years) in troops	Type of forces**
	State Security	20,000	Governmental
	Youth Labour Army	65,000	Governmental
Cyprus	Armed Forces	10,000	Governmental
	Turkish Forces	4,500	Non-governmental
Czech Republic	Armed Forces	58,200	Governmental
Denmark	Armed Forces	24,300	Governmental
Djibouti	Armed Forces	9,600	Governmental
	FRUD	*	Non-governmental
Dominican Republic	Armed Forces	24,500	Governmental
Ecuador	Armed Forces	57,100	Governmental
Egypt	Al-Gama'a al-Islamiya	*	Non-governmental
	Al-Jihad	*	Non-governmental
	Armed Forces	450,000	Governmental
	Central Security Force	150,000	Governmental
	Guard Forces	82,000	Governmental
El Salvador	Armed Forces	24,600	Governmental
	National Civilian Police	12,000	Governmental
Equatorial Guinea	Armed Forces	1,320	Governmental
Eritrea	Afars	*	Non-governmental
	Armed Forces	180,000-200,000	Governmental
	EIJ	4,000 *	Non-governmental
	ELF-AI	3,000	Non-governmental
	ELF-NC	*	Non-governmental
Estonia	Armed Forces	4,800	Governmental
	Border Guard	2,800	Governmental
Ethiopia	Al-Ittihad	Non-governmental	
	ARDUF	*	Non-governmental
	Armed Forces	325,500	Governmental
	OLF	More than 100	Non-governmental
	ONLF	*	Non-governmental
Fiji	Armed Forces	3,500	Governmental
Finland	Armed Forces	31,700	Governmental
	Frontier Guard	3,400	Governmental
France	Armed Forces	317,300	Governmental
Gabon	Armed Forces	4,700	Governmental
Gambia, the	Armed Forces	800	Governmental
Georgia	Abkhazia forces	5,000	Abkh. "government"
	Armed Forces	26,000	Governmental
	South Ossetia	2,000	Non-governmental
Germany	Armed Forces	332,800	Governmental
	Border Guard	24,500	Governmental
	Coast Guard	550	Governmental
Ghana	Armed Forces	7,000	Governmental
Greece	Armed Forces	165,670	Governmental
	Coast Guard	4,000	Governmental
	Gendarmerie	26,500	Governmental
Guatemala	Armed Forces	31,400	Governmental
	National Police	7,000	Governmental
Guinea	Armed Forces	9,700	Governmental
Guinea-Bissau	Armed Forces	9,250	Governmental
	Rebels/junta	7,000	Non-governmental
Guyana	Armed Forces	1,600	Governmental
Haiti	National Police Force	5,300	Governmental
Honduras	Armed Forces	8,300	Governmental
	Security Forces	6,000	Governmental
Hungary	Armed Forces	43,440	Governmental

H10-3. Military Recruitment of Children Less than 18 Years (Armed Force, Number, Type of Force), 1996–1997 *(continued)*

	Armed force (forces listed by names)	Number of children (less than 18 years) in troops	Type of forces**
India	Armed Forces	1,173,000	Governmental
	Assam insurgent	*	Non-governmental
	Kashmir insurgent	3,000	Non-governmental
	Manipur insurgent	12,000-15,000	Non-governmental
	Nagaland insurgent	3,000	Non-governmental
	Paramilitary	1,090,000	Governmental
	Tripura insurgent	14,000-16,000	Non-governmental
Indonesia	Armed Forces	298,000	Governmental
	Fretilin	170 *	Non-governmental
	GAM	50	Non-governmental
	Militias/East Timor	Less than 10,000	(Governmental)
	OPM	150	Non-governmental
	Paramilitary	1,706,000	Governmental
Iran	Armed Forces	545,600	Governmental
	Basij	200,000	Governmental
	KDP-Iran	1,200-1,800	Non-governmental
	Komala	200	Non-governmental
	Law Enforcement	40,000	Governmental
	NLA	15,000-30,000	Non-governmental
Iraq	Armed Forces	429,000	Governmental
	Border Guards	20,000	Governmental
	KDP	15,000	Non-governmental
	PUK	10,000	Non-governmental
	Saddam's Youth	10,000-15,000	Governmental
	SAIRI	4,000	Non-governmental
	Security Troops	15,000	Governmental
	SPK	500	Non-governmental
Ireland	Armed Forces	11,500	Governmental
Israel	Armed Forces	173,500	Governmental
	Hamas	300	Non-governmental
	Hizbollah	*	Non-governmental
	Islamic Jihad	350	Non-governmental
	Palest. Auto. Areas	35,000	Pal. security
	Paramilitary	6,050	Governmental
	PFLP-GC	600	Non-governmental
	PLA	4,500	Non-governmental
	PNLA/PLO	8,000	Non-governmental
Italy	Armed Forces	265,500	Governmental
Jamaica	Defence Force	2,830	Governmental
Japan	Armed Forces	236,300	Governmental
Jordan	Armed Forces	104,000	Governmental
Kazakhstan	Armed Forces	65,800	Governmental
Kenya	Armed Forces	24,200	Governmental
	Police	5,000	Governmental
Korea, North	Armed Forces	1,082,000	Governmental
Korea, South	Armed Forces	672,000	Governmental
Kuwait	Armed Forces	15,300	Governmental
Kyrgyzstan	Armed Forces	9,200	Governmental
	Islamic rebels	400-100,0	Non-governmental
Laos	Armed Forces	29,100	Governmental
	Self Defence Forces	More than 100,000	Governmental
	ULNLF	2,000	Non-governmental
Latvia	Armed Forces	5,730	Governmental
Lebanon	Amal	*	Non-governmental
	Armed Forces	67,900	Governmental
	Hezbollah	300-5,000	Non-governmental

H10-3. Military Recruitment of Children Less than 18 Years (Armed Force, Number, Type of Force), 1996–1997 *(continued)*

	Armed force (forces listed by names)	Number of children (less than 18 years) in troops	Type of forces**
	Internal Security Force	13,000	Governmental
	PNLA/PLO	3,000	Non-governmental
	SLA	2,500	Non-governmental
Lesotho	Armed Forces	2,000	Governmental
Liberia	Armed Forces	*	Governmental
Libya	Armed Forces	65,000	Governmental
Lithuania	Armed Forces	12,130	Governmental
Luxembourg	Armed Forces	768	Governmental
	Gendarmerie	612	Governmental
Macedonia	Armed Forces	16,000	Governmental
Madagascar	Armed Forces	21,000	Governmental
Malawi	Armed Forces	5,000	Governmental
Malaysia	Armed Forces	105,000	Governmental
Mali	Armed Forces	7,350	Governmental
Malta	Armed Forces	1,900	Governmental
Mauritania	Armed Forces	15,650	Governmental
	Gendarmerie	5,000	Governmental
	National Guard	2,000	Governmental
Mauritius	Paramilitary	1,500	Governmental
Mexico	Armed Forces	178,770	Governmental
	Defence Militia	14,000	Governmental
	EPR	*	Non-governmental
	ERPI	*	Non-governmental
	EZLN	More than 3,000	Non-governmental
	Paramilitaries	*	(Governmental)
Moldova	Armed Forces	10,650	Governmental
Mongolia	Armed Forces	9,100	Governmental
Morocco	Armed Forces	196,300	Governmental
	Polisario	3,000-6,000	Non-governmental
Mozambique	MDAF	5,100-6,100	Governmental
Myanmar (Burma)	ABSDF	2,000	Non-governmental
	Armed Forces	354,000	Governmental
	KA	More than 1,000	Non-governmental
	KNLA	4,000	Non-governmental
	People's Militia	35,000	Governmental
	Peoples Police Force	50,000	Governmental
	SSA	*	Non-governmental
	UWSA	12,000	Former opposition party
Namibia	Armed Forces	9,000	Governmental
	Caprivi rebels	*	Non-governmental
Nepal	Armed Forces	46,000	Governmental
	Police Force	40,000	Governmental
Netherlands, the	Armed Forces	56,380	Governmental
	Constabulary	3,600	Governmental
New Zealand	Armed Forces	9,530	Governmental
Nicaragua	Armed Forces	16,000	Governmental
Niger	Armed Forces	5,300	Governmental
Nigeria	Armed Forces	94,000	Governmental
	Security Police	2,000	Governmental
Norway	Armed Forces	31,000	Governmental
Oman	Armed Forces	43,500	Governmental
Pakistan	Armed Forces	587,000	Governmental
	MQM	*	Non-governmental
	Paramilitary	247,000	Governmental
Panama	Paramilitary	11,800	Governmental
Papua New Guinea	Armed Forces	4,300	Governmental

H10-3. Military Recruitment of Children Less than 18 Years (Armed Force, Number, Type of Force), 1996–1997 *(continued)*

	Armed force (forces listed by names)	Number of children (less than 18 years) in troops	Type of forces**
	BRA	1,000	Non-governmental
Paraguay	Armed Forces	20,200	Governmental
	National Police	14,800	Governmental
Peru	Armed Forces	115,000	Governmental
	MRTA	600	Non-governmental
Paramilitary	78,000-100,000	Governmental	
	Sendero Lum.	1,500-2,000	Non-governmental
Philippines	Abu Sayyaf	500	Non-governmental
	Armed Forces	110,000	Governmental
	CAFGU	60,000	Governmental
	Coast Guard	3,500	Governmental
	MILF	8,000-35000 *	Non-governmental
	MIRG	900	Non-governmental
	MNLF	5,000	Non-governmental
	National Police	40,500	Governmental
	NPA	8,000	Non-governmental
Poland	Armed Forces	240,650	Governmental
	Border Guards	13,500	Governmental
	Police	7,000	Governmental
Portugal	Armed Forces	49,700	Governmental
Qatar	Armed Forces	11,800	Governmental
Romania	Armed Forces	207,000	Governmental
Russia	Armed Forces	1,004,100	Governmental
	Chechnya forces	*	Chechnya "government"
	Daghestan rebels	More than 1,200	Non-governmental
	Paramilitary	478,000	Governmental
Rwanda	Armed Forces	37,000-47,000	Governmental
	Hutu opposition	7,000	Non-governmental
Sao Tome	Armed Forces	900	Governmental
Saudi Arabia	Armed Forces	105,500	Governmental
Senegal	Armed Forces	11,000	Governmental
	CMDF	2,000-,3000	Non-governmental
	Gendarmerie	5,800	Governmental
Seychelles	Armed Forces	450	Governmental
Sierra Leone	AFRC	3,000-5,000	Non-governmental
	Armed Forces	3,000	Governmental
	Civil Defence Forces	30,000?	Governmental
	RUF	8,000-10,000	Non-governmental
Singapore	Armed Forces	73,000	Governmental
Slovakia	Armed Forces	44,880	Governmental
Slovenia	Armed Forces	9,550	Governmental
Somalia	Ali Mahdi faction	10,000	Gov(?)
	SNF	2,000-3,000	Non-governmental
	SNM	5,000-6,000	Somaliland "government
	SPM	2,000-3,000	Non-governmental
	SSDF	3,000	Non-governmental
	USC/Aideed	*	Non-governmental
South Africa	Police Service	69,950	Governmental
	SANDF	69,950	Governmental
Spain	Armed Forces	186,500	Governmental
	ETA	*	Non-governmental
Sri Lanka	Armed Forces	110,000-120,000	Governmental
	Home Guard	15,200	Governmental
	LTTE	6,000-10,000	Non-governmental
	National Guard	15,000	Governmental
	Police Force	70,100	Governmental

H10-3. Military Recruitment of Children Less than 18 Years (Armed Force, Number, Type of Force), 1996–1997 *(continued)*

	Armed force (forces listed by names)	Number of children (less than 18 years) in troops	Type of forces**
Sudan	Armed Forces	94,700	Governmental
	Beja Congress	500	Non-governmental
	New Sudan Brigade	2,000	Non-governmental
	PDF	15,000-40,000	Governmental
	SAF	500	Non-governmental
	SPLA	20,000-30,000	Non-governmental
	SSIM	Former opposition party	
Suriname	Armed Forces	1,800	Governmental
Swaziland	Armed Forces	2,700	Governmental
Sweden	Armed Forces	53,100	Governmental
Switzerland	Armed Forces	3,470	Governmental
Syria	Armed Forces	316,000	Governmental
Taiwan	Armed Forces	376,000	Governmental
	Customs Service	650	Governmental
	Maritime Police	1,000	Governmental
	Security Groups	25,000	Governmental
Tajikistan	Armed Forces	7,000-,9000	Governmental
	Border Guards	1,200	Governmental
	UTO	5,000a	Non-governmental
Tanzania	TPDF	34,000	Governmental
Thailand	Armed Forces	306,000	Governmental
Togo	Armed Forces	6,950	Governmental
Tonga	Armed Forces	300	Governmental
Trinidad and Tobago	Armed Forces	2,700	Governmental
Tunisia	Armed Forces	35,000	Governmental
Turkey	Armed Forces	639,000	Governmental
	Coast Guard	2,200	Governmental
	Gendarmerie	200,000	Governmental
	PKK	10,000-12,000	Non-governmental
Turkmenistan	Armed Forces	17,000-19,000	Governmental
Uganda	ADF	More than 1,000	Non-governmental
	LRA	12,000	Non-governmental
	Paramilitary	600	Governmental
	UNRF II	More than 1,000	Non-governmental
	UPDF	30,000-40,000	Governmental
	WNBF	2,000	Non-governmental
Ukraine	Armed Forces	311,400	Governmental
United Arab Emirates	Armed Forces	64,500	Governmental
United Kingdom	Armed Forces	212,400	Governmental
United States	Armed Forces	1,401,600	Governmental
	CAP	53,000	Governmental
Uruguay	Armed Forces	25,600	Governmental
Uzbekistan	Armed Forces	74,000	Governmental
Vanuatu	Armed Forces	300	Governmental
Venezuela	Armed Forces	79,000	Governmental
Vietnam	Armed Forces	484,000	Governmental
Yemen	Armed Forces	66,300	Governmental
Yugoslavia	Armed Forces	108,700	Governmental
	KLA	17,000	Non-governmental
	Serb militias	*	(Governmental)
Zambia	Armed Forces	21,600	Governmental
Zimbabwe	Armed Forces	39,000	Governmental

* Known but not confirmed.

**Type of force: Governmental forces are regular national armed forces—army, navy and air force—as well as paramilitary forces. Non-governmental forces are allother armed forces or groups.

Note: All information about child soldiers relates to children below 18 years of age, if not otherwise specified.

Source: Rädda Barnen—Swedish Save the Children database, ChildWar; military recruitment of children worldwide; <http://www.rb.se:8082/www/childwar.nsf/HTML/Forsta?openDocument>.

H10-4. Countries in Which There Is Evidence of Children Under 15 Being Used in Ongoing or Recently-ended Armed Conflicts, June 1999

	Children participating
Afghanistan	Yes
Algeria	Yes
Angola	Yes
Azerbaijan (Nagorno-Karabakh)	Not reported but there is some evidence
Bangladesh	Not reported but there is some evidence
Burundi	Yes
Cambodia	Yes
Colombia	Yes
Cong. Dem. Rep. (Zaire)	Yes
Congo, Rep.	Yes
India (Andhra Pradesh, Kashmir)	Yes
Indonesia (East Timor)	Yes
Iran	Yes
Iraq	Yes
Israel (Occupied Territories)	Yes
Lebanon	Yes
Liberia	Yes
Mexico	Yes
Myanmar	Yes
Pakistan	Not reported but there is some evidence
Papua New Guinea (Bougainville)	Not reported but there is some evidence
Peru	Yes
Philippines	Yes
Russia (Chechnya)	Yes
Rwanda	Not reported but there is some evidence
Sierra Leone	Yes
Somalia	Yes
Sri Lanka	Yes
Sudan	Yes
Tajikistan	Not reported but there is some evidence
Turkey	Yes
Uganda	Not reported but there is some evidence
Yugoslavia (Kosovo)	Not reported but there is some evidence

Source: Rädda Barnen—Swedish Save the Children database, ChildWar; military recruitment of children worldwide and Child Soldiers Organization; <http://www.rb.se:8082/www/childwar.nsf/HTML/Forsta?openDocument> and <http://www.child-soldiers.org/countries_in_which_there_is_evid.htm>.

H10-5. Girls Recruited in the Armed Forces, July 1999

	Type of armed forces *	Girls recruited in the armed forces?
Afghanistan	Governmental	No
	Former Government	No **
Albania	Non-governmental	No **
Algeria	Non-governmental	No **
Angola	Non-governmental	Yes
Australia	Governmental	Yes
Bhutan	Governmental	No
Burundi	Non-governmental	Yes
Cambodia	Governmental	No
Colombia	Governmental	Yes
	Non-governmental	Yes
Congo, Dem. Rep. (Zaire)	Non-governmental	Yes
Ethiopia	Governmental	No
Guatemala	Governmental	No

H10-5. Girls Recruited in the Armed Forces, July 1999 *(continued)*

	Type of armed forces *	Girls recruited in the armed forces?
India	Non-governmental	Yes
Iraq	Governmental	Yes
Lebanon	Non-governmental	Yes
Myanmar (Burma)	Governmental	Yes
	Non-governmental	Yes **
Paraguay	Governmental	No
Peru	Non-governmental	Yes
	Governmental	Yes
Philippines	Non-governmental	Yes **
Rwanda	Non-governmental	Yes **
Sierra Leone	Non-governmental	Yes
Sri Lanka	Non-governmental	Yes
Sudan	Governmental	Yes **
	Non-governmental	Yes **
Tajikistan	Governmental	No **
Turkey	Non-governmental	Yes
Uganda	Non-governmental	Yes
United Kingdom	Governmental	Yes

* Selected forces.
** Known but not confirmed.
Note: 1) All information about child soldiers relates to children below 18 years of age, if not otherwise specified. 2) Type of force: Governmental forces are regular national armed forces—army, navy and air force—as well as paramilitary forces. Non-governmental forces are all other armed forces or groups.

Source: Rädda Barnen—Swedish Save the Children database, ChildWar; military recruitment of children worldwide; <http://www.rb.se:8082/www/childwar.nsf/HTML/Forsta?openDocument>.

H11. LANDMINES

H11-1. Total Estimated Number of Landmines, 1994 and 1997

	1994	1997
Afghanistan	10,000,000	10,000,000
Angola	9,000,000 to 20,000,000	15,000,000
Austria	Affected	Unknown
Azerbaijan	Affected	100,000
Bosnia and Herzegovina	Affected	3,000,000
Burundi	Affected	Unknown
Cambodia	7,000,000 to 9,000,000	6,000,000
Chad	Affected	70,000
China	Affected	10,000,000
Colombia	Affected	1,500
Costa Rica	1,000 to 2,000	Unknown
Croatia	1,000,000	3,000,000
Cyprus	Affected	17,000
Denmark	N/A	9,900
Ecuador	N/A	60,000
Egypt	Affected	23,000,000
El Salvador	Affected	10,000
Eritrea	1,000,000 to 2,000,000	1,000,000
Ethiopia	500,000	500,000
Falkland Islands	25,000 to 30,000	25,000
Georgia	Affected	150,000
Germany	Affected	Unknown
Guatemala	Affected	1,500
Honduras	Affected	35,000
Iran	N/A	16,000,000

H11-1. Total Estimated Number of Landmines, 1994 and 1997 *(continued)*

	1994	1997
Iraq (Kurd area)	Affected	10,000,000
Israel	Affected	N/A
Jordan	Affected	206,193
Latvia	Affected	17,000
Lebanon	20,000	8,795
Liberia	1,000	18,250
Libya	Affected	Unknown
Mauritania	Affected	Unknown
Mexico	Affected	N/A
Moldova	Affected	N/A
Mongolia	Affected	N/A
Morocco	Affected	N/A
Mozambique	Less than 1,000,000	3,000,000
Myanmar (Burma)	Affected	Unknown
Namibia	Affected	50,000
Nicaragua	132,000	108,297
Panama	N/A	N/A
Russia (Chechnya)	N/A	Unknown
Rwanda	50,000	250,000
Senegal	N/A	Unknown
Sierra Leone	Affected	N/A
Somalia	Affected	1,000,000
South Africa	N/A	N/A
South Korea, Rep.	Affected	206,193
Sri Lanka	Affected	Unknown
Sudan	Affected	1,000,000
Syria	Affected	Unknown
Tadjikistan	Affected	Unknown
Thailand	Affected	Unknown
Tunisia	Affected	Unknown
Turkey	Affected	Unknown
Uganda	Affected	Unknown
Ukraine	N/A	1,000,000
Vietnam	N/A	3,500,000
Yemen	20,000	100,000
Yugoslavia	N/A	500,000
Zaire	N/A	Unknown
Zambia	N/A	N/A
Zimbabwe	Affected	Unknown

Affected = Affected regions/countries (degree varies).
Unknown = Quantity of landmines unknown.
N/A = Not available.

Sources: UN Landmine Database (Demining Program and country reports); U.S. Army National Ground Intelligence Center estimates; and U.S. Department of State. Report released by the U.S. Department of State, Bureau of Political-Military Affairs, Office of Humanitarian Demining Programs, Washington, DC, September 1998 Table A-1. Mine-Affected Countries; <http://www.state.gov/www/global/arms/rpt_9809_demine_nxa.html>. Underlying data from United Nations (UN).

H11-2. Estimated Existing and Cleared Landmines, 1997

	Mines remaining	Mines cleared
Afghanistan	10,000,000	363,000
Angola	15,000,000	80,000
Bosnia/Herzegovina	6,000,000	N/A
Cambodia	10,000,000	62,000
China	10,000,000	280,000
Croatia	3,000,000	250,000
Egypt	23,000,000	11,000,000
Iran	16,000,000	200,000
Iraq	10,000,000	21,000
Mozambique	3,000,000	17,000
Viet Nam	3,500,000	59,000
Other countries	6,214,000	3,228,000

Source: Progress of Nations, 1997; <http://www.unicef.org/pon97/>. Underlying data from Department of Humanitarian Affairs, United Nations (UN).

Appendixes

1. World Health Organization Regional and Economic Groupings

Africa Region (46 Member States)	Region of the Americas (35 Member States)	Eastern Mediterranean Region (22 Member States)	European Region (51 Member States)	South-East Asia Region (10 Member States)	Western Pacific Region (27 Member States)
Low and middle income	**Low and middle income**	**Low and middle income**	**Low and middle income**	**Low and middle income**	**Low and middle income**
Algeria	Antigua and Barbuda	Afghanistan	Albania	Bangladesh	Cambodia
Angola	Argentina	Bahrain	Armenia	Bhutan	China
Benin	Barbados	Djibouti	Azerbaijan	India	Cook Islands
Botswana	Belize	Egypt	Belarus	Indonesia	Fiji
Burkina Faso	Bolivia	Iran	Bosnia and Herzegovina	Maldives	Kiribati
Burundi	Brazil	Iraq	Bulgaria	Myanmar (Burma)	Laos
Cameroon	Chile	Jordan	Croatia	Nepal	Malaysia
Cape Verde	Colombia	Lebanon	Czech Republic	North Korea, Dem. Rep.	Marshall Islands
Central African Republic	Costa Rica	Libya	Estonia	Sri Lanka	Micronesia
Chad	Cuba	Morocco	Georgia	Thailand	Mongolia
Comoros	Dominica	Oman	Hungary		Nauru
Congo, Dem. Rep (Zaire)	Dominican Republic	Pakistan	Kazakhstan		Niue
Congo, Rep.	Ecuador	Saudi Arabia	Kyrgyzstan		Palau
Cote d'Ivoire	El Salvador	Somalia	Latvia		Papua New Guinea
Equatorial Guinea	Grenada	Sudan	Lithuania		Philippines
Eritrea	Guatemala	Syria	Macedonia, FYRO		Samoa
Ethiopia	Guyana	Tunisia	Malta		Solomon Islands
Gabon	Haiti	Yemen	Moldova		Tonga
Gambia	Honduras	**High income**	Poland		Tuvalu
Ghana	Jamaica	Cyprus	Romania		Vanuatu
Guinea	Mexico	Kuwait	Russia		Viet Nam
Guinea-Bissau	Nicaragua	Qatar	Slovakia		**High income**
Kenya	Panama	United Arab Emirates	Slovenia		Australia
Lesotho	Paraguay	Uzbekistan	Tajikistan		Brunei
Liberia	Peru		Turkey		Japan
Madagascar	Saint Kitts and Nevis		Turkmenistan		New Zealand
Malawi	Saint Lucia		Ukraine		Singapore
Mali	Saint Vincent and the Grenadines		Yugoslavia		South Korea, Rep.
Mauritania	Suriname		**High income**		
Mauritius	Trinidad and Tobago		Andorra		
Mozambique	Uruguay		Austria		
Namibia	Venezuela		Belgium		
Niger	**High income**		Denmark		
Nigeria	Bahamas, the		Finland		
Rwanda	Canada		France		
Sao Tome and Principe	United States of America		Germany		
Senegal			Greece		
Seychelles			Iceland		
Sierra Leone			Ireland		
South Africa			Israel		
Swaziland			Italy		
Tanzania			Luxembourg		
Togo			Monaco		
Uganda			Netherlands		
Zambia			Norway		
Zimbabwe			Portugal		
			San Marino		
			Spain		
			Sweden		
			Switzerland		
			United Kingdom		

1. World Health Organization Regional and Economic Groupings *(continued)*

UNICEF Development Regions*

MORE DEVELOPED REGIONS

Northern America: Canada and the United States.

Asia and Oceania: Australia, Israel, Japan and New Zealand.

Europe: Austria, Belgium, Denmark, Finland, France, Germany, Greece, Iceland, Ireland, Italy, Luxembourg, Monaco, Netherlands, Norway, Portugal, San Marino, Spain, Sweden, Switzerland and the United Kingdom.

COUNTRIES IN TRANSITION

Albania, Armenia, Azerbaijan, Belarus, Bosnia and Herzegovina, Bulgaria, Croatia, Czech Republic, Estonia, Georgia, Hungary, Kazakhstan, Kyrgyzstan, Latvia, Lithuania, Poland, Republic of Moldova, Romania, Russian Federation, Slovakia, Slovenia, Tajikistan, The Former Yugoslav Republic of Macedonia, Turkmenistan, Ukraine, Uzbekistan and Yugoslavia.

LESS DEVELOPED REGIONS

Sub-Saharan Africa: Angola, Benin, Botswana, Burkina Faso, Burundi, Cameroon, Cape Verde, Central African Republic, Chad, Comoros, Congo, Côte d'Ivoire, Democratic Republic of the Congo, Djibouti, Equatorial Guinea, Eritrea, Ethiopia, Gabon, Gambia, Ghana, Guinea, Guinea-Bissau, Kenya, Lesotho, Liberia, Madagascar, Malawi, Mali, Mauritania, Mauritius, Mozambique, Namibia, Niger, Nigeria, Rwanda, Sao Tome and Principe, Senegal, Seychelles, Sierra Leone, Somalia, South Africa, Sudan, Swaziland, Togo, Uganda, United Republic of Tanzania, Zambia and Zimbabwe.

Arab States: Algeria, Bahrain, Djibouti, Egypt, Iraq, Jordan, Kuwait, Lebanon, Libyan Arab Jamahiriya, Mauritania, Morocco, Oman, Palestinian Autonomous Territories, Qatar, Saudi Arabia, Somalia, Sudan, Syrian Arab Republic, Tunisia, United Arab Emirates and Yemen.

Latin America and the Caribbean: Antigua and Barbuda, Argentina, Bahamas, Barbados, Belize, Bolivia, Brazil, British Virgin Islands, Chile, Colombia, Costa Rica, Cuba, Dominica, Dominican Republic, Ecuador, El Salvador, Grenada, Guatemala, Guyana, Haiti, Honduras, Jamaica, Mexico, Netherlands Antilles, Nicaragua, Panama, Paraguay, Peru, Saint Kitts and Nevis, Saint Lucia, Saint Vincent and the Grenadines, Suriname, Trinidad and Tobago, Uruguay and Venezuela.

Eastern Asia and Oceania: Brunei Darussalam, Cambodia, China, Cook Islands, Democratic People's Republic of Korea, Fiji, Hong Kong Special Administrative Region of China, Indonesia, Kiribati, Lao People's Democratic Republic, Macau, Malaysia, Mongolia, Myanmar, Papua New Guinea, Philippines, Republic of Korea, Samoa, Singapore, Solomon Islands, Thailand, Tonga, Tuvalu, Vanuatu and Viet Nam.

Southern Asia: Afghanistan, Bangladesh, Bhutan, India, Islamic Republic of Iran, Maldives, Nepal, Pakistan and Sri Lanka.

LEAST DEVELOPED COUNTRIES

Afghanistan, Angola, Bangladesh, Benin, Bhutan, Burkina Faso, Burundi, Cambodia, Cape Verde, Central African Republic, Chad, Comoros, Democratic Republic of the Congo, Djibouti, Equatorial Guinea, Eritrea, Ethiopia, Gambia, Guinea, Guinea-Bissau, Haiti, Kiribati, Lao People's Democratic Republic, Lesotho, Liberia, Madagascar, Malawi, Maldives, Mali, Mauritania, Mozambique, Myanmar, Nepal, Niger, Rwanda, Samoa, Sao Tome and Principe, Sierra Leone, Solomon Islands, Somalia, Sudan, Togo, Tuvalu, Uganda, United Republic of Tanzania, Vanuatu, Yemen and Zambia.

*This classification is based on the sum of development indicators such as literacy, school enrollment, gross domestic product etc.

Heavily Indebted Poor Countries

Angola	Congo, Rep.	Kenya	Nicaragua	Togo
Benin	Côte d'Ivoire	Laos	Niger	Uganda
Bolivia	Ethiopia	Liberia	Rwanda	Vietnam
Burkina Faso	Gambia, the	Madagascar	Sierra Leone	Yemen
Burundi	Ghana	Malawi	São Tomé and Príncipe	Zambia
Cameroon	Guinea	Mali	Senegal	
Central African Republic	Guinea-Bissau	Mauritania	Somalia	
Chad	Guyana	Mozambique	Sudan	
Congo, Dem Rep. (Zaire)	Honduras	Myanmar (Burma)	Tanzania	

2. Declaration of the Rights of the Child

2. Declaration of the Rights of the Child
Proclaimed by United nation's General Assembly
Resolution 1386 (XIV) of November 20th, 1959

Whereas the peoples of the United Nations have, in the Charter, reaffirmed their faith in fundamental human rights and in the dignity and worth of the human person, and have determined to promote social progress and better standards of life in larger freedom,

Whereas the United Nations has, in the Universal Declaration of Human Rights, proclaimed that everyone is entitled to all the rights and freedoms set forth therein, without distinction of any kind, such as race, color, sex, language, religion, political or other opinion, national or social origin, property, birth or other status,

Whereas the child, by reason of his physical and mental immaturity, needs special safeguards and care, including appropriate legal protection, before as well as after birth,

Whereas the need for such special safeguards has been stated in the Geneva Declaration of the Rights of the Child of 1924, and recognized in the Universal Declaration of Human Rights and in the statutes of specialized agencies and international organizations concerned with the welfare of children,

Whereas mankind owes to the child the best it has to give, *Now therefore, The General Assembly Proclaims* this Declaration of the Rights of the Child to the end that he may have a happy childhood and enjoy for his own good and for the good of society the rights and freedoms herein set forth, and calls upon parents, upon men and women as individuals, and upon voluntary organizations, local authorities and national Governments to recognize these rights and strive for their observance by legislative and other measures progressively taken in accordance with the following principles:

Principle 1

The child shall enjoy all the rights set forth in this Declaration. Every child, without any exception whatsoever, shall be entitled to these rights, without distinction or discrimination on account of race, color, sex, language, religion, political or other opinion, national or social origin, property, birth or other status, whether of himself or of his family.

Principle 2

The child shall enjoy special protection, and shall be given opportunities and facilities, by law and by other means, to enable him to develop physically, mentally, morally, spiritually and socially in a healthy and normal manner and in conditions of freedom and dignity. In the enactment of laws for this purpose, the best interests of the child shall be the paramount consideration.

Principle 3

The child shall be entitled from his birth to a name and a nationality.

Principle 4

The child shall enjoy the benefits of social security. He shall be entitled to grow and develop in health; to this end, special care and protection shall be provided both to him and to his mother, including adequate pre-natal and post-natal care. The child shall have the right to adequate nutrition, housing, recreation and medical services.

Principle 5

The child who is physically, mentally or socially handicapped shall be given the special treatment, education and care required by his particular condition.

Principle 6

The child, for the full and harmonious development of his personality, needs love and understanding. He shall, wherever possible, grow up in the care and under the responsibility of his parents, and, in any case, in an atmosphere of affection and of moral and material security; a child of tender years shall not, save in exceptional circumstances, be separated from his mother. Society and the public authorities shall have the duty to extend particular care to children without a family and to those without adequate means of support. Payment of State and other assistance towards the maintenance of children of large families is desirable.

Principle 7

The child is entitled to receive education, which shall be free and compulsory, at least in the elementary stages. He shall be given an education which will promote his general culture and enable him, on a basis of equal opportunity, to develop his abilities, his individual judgement, and his sense of moral and social responsibility, and to become a useful member of society.

The best interests of the child shall be the guiding principle of those responsible for his education and guidance; that responsibility lies in the first place with his parents.

The child shall have full opportunity for play and recreation, which should be directed to the same purposes as education; society and the public authorities shall endeavor to promote the enjoyment of this right.

Principle 8

The child shall in all circumstances be among the first to receive protection and relief.

2. Declaration of the Rights of the Child *(continued)*

> *Principle 9*
>
> The child shall be protected against all forms of neglect, cruelty and exploitation. He shall not be the subject of traffic, in any form.
>
> The child shall not be admitted to employment before an appropriate minimum age; he shall in no case be caused or permitted to engage in any occupation or employment which would prejudice his health or education, or interfere with his physical, mental or moral development.
>
> *Principle 10*
>
> The child shall be protected from practices which may foster racial, religious and any other form of discrimination. He shall be brought up in a spirit of understanding, tolerance, friendship among peoples, peace and universal brotherhood, and in full consciousness that his energy and talents should be devoted to the service of his fellow men.

3. Convention on the Rights of the Child (CRC)

> ### 3. Convention on the Rights of the Child (CRC)
> **Adopted and opened for signature, ratification and accession by United Nation's General Assembly Resolution 44/25 of November 20th, 1989**
> ***Entry into force* September 2nd, 1990, in accordance with article 49**
>
> *Preamble*
>
> The States Parties to the present Convention, Considering that, in accordance with the principles proclaimed in the Charter of the United Nations, recognition of the inherent dignity and of the equal and inalienable rights of all members of the human family is the foundation of freedom, justice and peace in the world,
>
> Bearing in mind that the peoples of the United Nations have, in the Charter, reaffirmed their faith in fundamental human rights and in the dignity and worth of the human person, and have determined to promote social progress and better standards of life in larger freedom,
>
> Recognizing that the United Nations has, in the Universal Declaration of Human Rights and in the International Covenants on Human Rights, proclaimed and agreed that everyone is entitled to all the rights and freedoms set forth therein, without distinction of any kind, such as race, colour, sex, language, religion, political or other opinion, national or social origin, property, birth or other status,
>
> Recalling that, in the Universal Declaration of Human Rights, the United Nations has proclaimed that childhood is entitled to special care and assistance,
>
> Convinced that the family, as the fundamental group of society and the natural environment for the growth and well-being of all its members and particularly children, should be afforded the necessary protection and assistance so that it can fully assume its responsibilities within the community,
>
> Recognizing that the child, for the full and harmonious development of his or her personality, should grow up in a family environment, in an atmosphere of happiness, love and understanding,
>
> Considering that the child should be fully prepared to live an individual life in society, and brought up in the spirit of the ideals proclaimed in the Charter of the United Nations, and in particular in the spirit of peace, dignity, tolerance, freedom, equality and solidarity,
>
> Bearing in mind that the need to extend particular care to the child has been stated in the Geneva Declaration of the Rights of the Child of 1924 and in the Declaration of the Rights of the Child adopted by the General Assembly on 20 November 1959 and recognized in the Universal Declaration of Human Rights, in the International Covenant on Civil and Political Rights (in particular in articles 23 and 24), in the International Covenant on Economic, Social and Cultural Rights (in particular in article 10) and in the statutes and relevant instruments of specialized agencies and international organizations concerned with the welfare of children,
>
> Bearing in mind that, as indicated in the Declaration of the Rights of the Child, "the child, by reason of his physical and mental immaturity, needs special safeguards and care, including appropriate legal protection, before as well as after birth",
>
> Recalling the provisions of the Declaration on Social and Legal Principles relating to the Protection and Welfare of Children, with Special Reference to Foster Placement and Adoption Nationally and Internationally; the United Nations Standard Minimum Rules for the Administration of Juvenile Justice (The Beijing Rules) ; and the Declaration on the Protection of Women and Children in Emergency and Armed Conflict,
>
> Recognizing that, in all countries in the world, there are children living in exceptionally difficult conditions, and that such children need special consideration,
>
> Taking due account of the importance of the traditions and cultural values of each people for the protection and harmonious development of the child,

3. Convention on the Rights of the Child (CRC) *(continued)*

Recognizing the importance of international co-operation for improving the living conditions of children in every country, in particular in the developing countries,

Have agreed as follows:

PART I

Article 1

For the purposes of the present Convention, a child means every human being below the age of eighteen years unless under the law applicable to the child, majority is attained earlier.

Article 2

1. States Parties shall respect and ensure the rights set forth in the present Convention to each child within their jurisdiction without discrimination of any kind, irrespective of the child's or his or her parent's or legal guardian's race, color, sex, language, religion, political or other opinion, national, ethnic or social origin, property, disability, birth or other status.

2. States Parties shall take all appropriate measures to ensure that the child is protected against all forms of discrimination or punishment on the basis of the status, activities, expressed opinions, or beliefs of the child's parents, legal guardians, or family members.

Article 3

1. In all actions concerning children, whether undertaken by public or private social welfare institutions, courts of law, administrative authorities or legislative bodies, the best interests of the child shall be a primary consideration.

2. States Parties undertake to ensure the child such protection and care as is necessary for his or her well-being, taking into account the rights and duties of his or her parents, legal guardians, or other individuals legally responsible for him or her, and, to this end, shall take all appropriate legislative and administrative measures.

3. States Parties shall ensure that the institutions, services and facilities responsible for the care or protection of children shall conform with the standards established by competent authorities, particularly in the areas of safety, health, in the number and suitability of their staff, as well as competent supervision.

Article 4

States Parties shall undertake all appropriate legislative, administrative, and other measures for the implementation of the rights recognized in the present Convention. With regard to economic, social and cultural rights, States Parties shall undertake such measures to the maximum extent of their available resources and, where needed, within the framework of international co-operation.

Article 5

States Parties shall respect the responsibilities, rights and duties of parents or, where applicable, the members of the extended family or community as provided for by local custom, legal guardians or other persons legally responsible for the child, to provide, in a manner consistent with the evolving capacities of the child, appropriate direction and guidance in the exercise by the child of the rights recognized in the present Convention.

Article 6

1. States Parties recognize that every child has the inherent right to life.

2. States Parties shall ensure to the maximum extent possible the survival and development of the child.

Article 7

1. The child shall be registered immediately after birth and shall have the right from birth to a name, the right to acquire a nationality and. as far as possible, the right to know and be cared for by his or her parents.

2. States Parties shall ensure the implementation of these rights in accordance with their national law and their obligations under the relevant international instruments in this field, in particular where the child would otherwise be stateless.

Article 8

1. States Parties undertake to respect the right of the child to preserve his or her identity, including nationality, name and family relations as recognized by law without unlawful interference.

2. Where a child is illegally deprived of some or all of the elements of his or her identity, States Parties shall provide appropriate assistance and protection, with a view to re-establishing speedily his or her identity.

Article 9

1. States Parties shall ensure that a child shall not be separated from his or her parents against their will, except when competent authorities subject to judicial review determine, in accordance with applicable law and procedures, that such separation is necessary for the best interests of the child. Such determination may be necessary in a particular case such as one involving abuse or neglect of the child by the parents, or one where the parents are living separately and a decision must be made as to the child's place of residence.

2. In any proceedings pursuant to paragraph 1 of the present article, all interested parties shall be given an opportunity to participate in the proceedings and make their views known.

3. Convention on the Rights of the Child (CRC) *(continued)*

3. States Parties shall respect the right of the child who is separated from one or both parents to maintain personal relations and direct contact with both parents on a regular basis, except if it is contrary to the child's best interests. 4. Where such separation results from any action initiated by a State Party, such as the detention, imprisonment, exile, deportation or death (including death arising from any cause while the person is in the custody of the State) of one or both parents or of the child, that State Party shall, upon request, provide the parents, the child or, if appropriate, another member of the family with the essential information concerning the whereabouts of the absent member(s) of the family unless the provision of the information would be detrimental to the well-being of the child. States Parties shall further ensure that the submission of such a request shall of itself entail no adverse consequences for the person(s) concerned.

Article 10

1. In accordance with the obligation of States Parties under article 9, paragraph 1, applications by a child or his or her parents to enter or leave a State Party for the purpose of family reunification shall be dealt with by States Parties in a positive, humane and expeditious manner. States Parties shall further ensure that the submission of such a request shall entail no adverse consequences for the applicants and for the members of their family.

2. A child whose parents reside in different States shall have the right to maintain on a regular basis, save in exceptional circumstances personal relations and direct contacts with both parents. Towards that end and in accordance with the obligation of States Parties under article 9, paragraph 1, States Parties shall respect the right of the child and his or her parents to leave any country, including their own, and to enter their own country. The right to leave any country shall be subject only to such restrictions as are prescribed by law and which are necessary to protect the national security, public order (ordre public), public health or morals or the rights and freedoms of others and are consistent with the other rights recognized in the present Convention.

Article 11

1. States Parties shall take measures to combat the illicit transfer and non-return of children abroad.

2. To this end, States Parties shall promote the conclusion of bilateral or multilateral agreements or accession to existing agreements.

Article 12

1. States Parties shall assure to the child who is capable of forming his or her own views the right to express those views freely in all matters affecting the child, the views of the child being given due weight in accordance with the age and maturity of the child.

2. For this purpose, the child shall in particular be provided the opportunity to be heard in any judicial and administrative proceedings affecting the child, either directly, or through a representative or an appropriate body, in a manner consistent with the procedural rules of national law.

Article 13

1. The child shall have the right to freedom of expression; this right shall include freedom to seek, receive and impart information and ideas of all kinds, regardless of frontiers, either orally, in writing or in print, in the form of art, or through any other media of the child's choice.

2. The exercise of this right may be subject to certain restrictions, but these shall only be such as are provided by law and are necessary:

(a) For respect of the rights or reputations of others; or

(b) For the protection of national security or of public order (ordre public), or of public health or morals.

Article 14

1. States Parties shall respect the right of the child to freedom of thought, conscience and religion.

2. States Parties shall respect the rights and duties of the parents and, when applicable, legal guardians, to provide direction to the child in the exercise of his or her right in a manner consistent with the evolving capacities of the child.

3. Freedom to manifest one's religion or beliefs may be subject only to such limitations as are prescribed by law and are necessary to protect public safety, order, health or morals, or the fundamental rights and freedoms of others.

Article 15

1. States Parties recognize the rights of the child to freedom of association and to freedom of peaceful assembly.

2. No restrictions may be placed on the exercise of these rights other than those imposed in conformity with the law and which are necessary in a democratic society in the interests of national security or public safety, public order (ordre public), the protection of public health or morals or the protection of the rights and freedoms of others.

Article 16

1. No child shall be subjected to arbitrary or unlawful interference with his or her privacy, family, home or correspondence, nor to unlawful attacks on his or her honor and reputation.

2. The child has the right to the protection of the law against such interference or attacks.

3. Convention on the Rights of the Child (CRC) *(continued)*

Article 17

States Parties recognize the important function performed by the mass media and shall ensure that the child has access to information and material from a diversity of national and international sources, especially those aimed at the promotion of his or her social, spiritual and moral well-being and physical and mental health. To this end, States Parties shall:

(a) Encourage the mass media to disseminate information and material of social and cultural benefit to the child and in accordance with the spirit of article 29;

(b) Encourage international co-operation in the production, exchange and dissemination of such information and material from a diversity of cultural, national and international sources;

(c) Encourage the production and dissemination of children's books;

(d) Encourage the mass media to have particular regard to the linguistic needs of the child who belongs to a minority group or who is indigenous;

(e) Encourage the development of appropriate guidelines for the protection of the child from information and material injurious to his or her well-being, bearing in mind the provisions of articles 13 and 18.

Article 18

1. States Parties shall use their best efforts to ensure recognition of the principle that both parents have common responsibilities for the upbringing and development of the child. Parents or, as the case may be, legal guardians, have the primary responsibility for the upbringing and development of the child. The best interests of the child will be their basic concern.

2. For the purpose of guaranteeing and promoting the rights set forth in the present Convention, States Parties shall render appropriate assistance to parents and legal guardians in the performance of their child-rearing responsibilities and shall ensure the development of institutions, facilities and services for the care of children.

3. States Parties shall take all appropriate measures to ensure that children of working parents have the right to benefit from child-care services and facilities for which they are eligible.

Article 19

1. States Parties shall take all appropriate legislative, administrative, social and educational measures to protect the child from all forms of physical or mental violence, injury or abuse, neglect or negligent treatment, maltreatment or exploitation, including sexual abuse, while in the care of parent(s), legal guardian(s) or any other person who has the care of the child.

2. Such protective measures should, as appropriate, include effective procedures for the establishment of social programmes to provide necessary support for the child and for those who have the care of the child, as well as for other forms of prevention and for identification, reporting, referral, investigation, treatment and follow-up of instances of child maltreatment described heretofore, and, as appropriate, for judicial involvement.

Article 20

1. A child temporarily or permanently deprived of his or her family environment, or in whose own best interests cannot be allowed to remain in that environment, shall be entitled to special protection and assistance provided by the State.

2. States Parties shall in accordance with their national laws ensure alternative care for such a child.

3. Such care could include, inter alia, foster placement, kafalah of Islamic law, adoption or if necessary placement in suitable institutions for the care of children. When considering solutions, due regard shall be paid to the desirability of continuity in a child's upbringing and to the child's ethnic, religious, cultural and linguistic background.

Article 21

States Parties that recognize and/or permit the system of adoption shall ensure that the best interests of the child shall be the paramount consideration and they shall:

(a) Ensure that the adoption of a child is authorized only by competent authorities who determine, in accordance with applicable law and procedures and on the basis of all pertinent and reliable information, that the adoption is permissible in view of the child's status concerning parents, relatives and legal guardians and that, if required, the persons concerned have given their informed consent to the adoption on the basis of such counseling as may be necessary;

(b) Recognize that inter-country adoption may be considered as an alternative means of child's care, if the child cannot be placed in a foster or an adoptive family or cannot in any suitable manner be cared for in the child's country of origin; (c) Ensure that the child concerned by inter-country adoption enjoys safeguards and standards equivalent to those existing in the case of national adoption;

(d) Take all appropriate measures to ensure that, in inter-country adoption, the placement does not result in improper financial gain for those involved in it;

(e) Promote, where appropriate, the objectives of the present article by concluding bilateral or multilateral arrangements or agreements, and endeavor, within this framework, to ensure that the placement of the child in another country is carried out by competent authorities or organs.

3. Convention on the Rights of the Child (CRC) *(continued)*

Article 22

1. States Parties shall take appropriate measures to ensure that a child who is seeking refugee status or who is considered a refugee in accordance with applicable international or domestic law and procedures shall, whether unaccompanied or accompanied by his or her parents or by any other person, receive appropriate protection and humanitarian assistance in the enjoyment of applicable rights set forth in the present Convention and in other international human rights or humanitarian instruments to which the said States are Parties.

2. For this purpose, States Parties shall provide, as they consider appropriate, co-operation in any efforts by the United Nations and other competent intergovernmental organizations or non-governmental organizations co-operating with the United Nations to protect and assist such a child and to trace the parents or other members of the family of any refugee child in order to obtain information necessary for reunification with his or her family. In cases where no parents or other members of the family can be found, the child shall be accorded the same protection as any other child permanently or temporarily deprived of his or her family environment for any reason, as set forth in the present Convention.

Article 23

1. States Parties recognize that a mentally or physically disabled child should enjoy a full and decent life, in conditions, which ensure dignity, promote self-reliance and facilitate the child's active participation in the community.

2. States Parties recognize the right of the disabled child to special care and shall encourage and ensure the extension, subject to available resources, to the eligible child and those responsible for his or her care, of assistance for which application is made and which is appropriate to the child's condition and to the circumstances of the parents or others caring for the child.

3. Recognizing the special needs of a disabled child, assistance extended in accordance with paragraph 2 of the present article shall be provided free of charge, whenever possible, taking into account the financial resources of the parents or others caring for the child, and shall be designed to ensure that the disabled child has effective access to and receives education, training, health care services, rehabilitation services, preparation for employment and recreation opportunities in a manner conducive to the child's achieving the fullest possible social integration and individual development, including his or her cultural and spiritual development

4. States Parties shall promote, in the spirit of international cooperation, the exchange of appropriate information in the field of preventive health care and of medical, psychological and functional treatment of disabled children, including dissemination of and access to information concerning methods of rehabilitation, education and vocational services, with the aim of enabling States Parties to improve their capabilities and skills and to widen their experience in these areas. In this regard, particular account shall be taken of the needs of developing countries.

Article 24

1. States Parties recognize the right of the child to the enjoyment of the highest attainable standard of health and to facilities for the treatment of illness and rehabilitation of health. States Parties shall strive to ensure that no child is deprived of his or her right of access to such health care services.

2. States Parties shall pursue full implementation of this right and, in particular, shall take appropriate measures:

(a) To diminish infant and child mortality;

(b) To ensure the provision of necessary medical assistance and health care to all children with emphasis on the development of primary health care;

(c) To combat disease and malnutrition, including within the framework of primary health care, through, inter alia, the application of readily available technology and through the provision of adequate nutritious foods and clean drinking-water, taking into consideration the dangers and risks of environmental pollution;

(d) To ensure appropriate pre-natal and post-natal health care for mothers;

(e) To ensure that all segments of society, in particular parents and children, are informed, have access to education and are supported in the use of basic knowledge of child health and nutrition, the advantages of breastfeeding, hygiene and environmental sanitation and the prevention of accidents;

(f) To develop preventive health care, guidance for parents and family planning education and services.

3. States Parties shall take all effective and appropriate measures with a view to abolishing traditional practices prejudicial to the health of children.

4. States Parties undertake to promote and encourage international co-operation with a view to achieving progressively the full realization of the right recognized in the present article. In this regard, particular account shall be taken of the needs of developing countries.

Article 25

States Parties recognize the right of a child who has been placed by the competent authorities for the purposes of care, protection or treatment of his or her physical or mental health, to a periodic review of the treatment provided to the child and all other circumstances relevant to his or her placement.

3. Convention on the Rights of the Child (CRC) *(continued)*

Article 26

1. States Parties shall recognize for every child the right to benefit from social security, including social insurance, and shall take the necessary measures to achieve the full realization of this right in accordance with their national law.

2. The benefits should, where appropriate, be granted, taking into account the resources and the circumstances of the child and persons having responsibility for the maintenance of the child, as well as any other consideration relevant to an application for benefits made by or on behalf of the child.

Article 27

1. States Parties recognize the right of every child to a standard of living adequate for the child's physical, mental, spiritual, moral and social development.

2. The parent(s) or others responsible for the child have the primary responsibility to secure, within their abilities and financial capacities, the conditions of living necessary for the child's development.

3. States Parties, in accordance with national conditions and within their means, shall take appropriate measures to assist parents and others responsible for the child to implement this right and shall in case of need provide material assistance and support programs, particularly with regard to nutrition, clothing and housing.

4. States Parties shall take all appropriate measures to secure the recovery of maintenance for the child from the parents or other persons having financial responsibility for the child, both within the State Party and from abroad. In particular, where the person having financial responsibility for the child lives in a State different from that of the child, States Parties shall promote the accession to international agreements or the conclusion of such agreements, as well as the making of other appropriate arrangements.

Article 28

1. States Parties recognize the right of the child to education, and with a view to achieving this right progressively and on the basis of equal opportunity, they shall, in particular:

(a) Make primary education compulsory and available free to all;

(b) Encourage the development of different forms of secondary education, including general and vocational education, make them available and accessible to every child, and take appropriate measures such as the introduction of free education and offering financial assistance in case of need;

(c) Make higher education accessible to all on the basis of capacity by every appropriate means;

(d) Make educational and vocational information and guidance available and accessible to all children;

(e) Take measures to encourage regular attendance at schools and the reduction of drop-out rates.

2. States Parties shall take all appropriate measures to ensure that school discipline is administered in a manner consistent with the child's human dignity and in conformity with the present Convention.

3. States Parties shall promote and encourage international cooperation in matters relating to education, in particular with a view to contributing to the elimination of ignorance and illiteracy throughout the world and facilitating access to scientific and technical knowledge and modern teaching methods. In this regard, particular account shall be taken of the needs of developing countries.

Article 29

1. States Parties agree that the education of the child shall be directed to:

(a) The development of the child's personality, talents and mental and physical abilities to their fullest potential;

(b) The development of respect for human rights and fundamental freedoms, and for the principles enshrined in the Charter of the United Nations;

(c) The development of respect for the child's parents, his or her own cultural identity, language and values, for the national values of the country in which the child is living, the country from which he or she may originate, and for civilizations different from his or her own;

(d) The preparation of the child for responsible life in a free society, in the spirit of understanding, peace, tolerance, equality of sexes, and friendship among all peoples, ethnic, national and religious groups and persons of indigenous origin;

(e) The development of respect for the natural environment.

2. No part of the present article or article 28 shall be construed so as to interfere with the liberty of individuals and bodies to establish and direct educational institutions, subject always to the observance of the principle set forth in paragraph 1 of the present article and to the requirements that the education given in such institutions shall conform to such minimum standards as may be laid down by the State.

Article 30

In those States in which ethnic, religious or linguistic minorities or persons of indigenous origin exist, a child belonging to such a minority or who is indigenous shall not be denied the right, in community with other members of his or her group, to enjoy his or her own culture, to profess and practice his or her own religion, or to use his or her own language.

3. Convention on the Rights of the Child (CRC) *(continued)*

Article 31

1. States Parties recognize the right of the child to rest and leisure, to engage in play and recreational activities appropriate to the age of the child and to participate freely in cultural life and the arts.

2. States Parties shall respect and promote the right of the child to participate fully in cultural and artistic life and shall encourage the provision of appropriate and equal opportunities for cultural, artistic, recreational and leisure activity.

Article 32

1. States Parties recognize the right of the child to be protected from economic exploitation and from performing any work that is likely to be hazardous or to interfere with the child's education, or to be harmful to the child's health or physical, mental, spiritual, moral or social development.

2. States Parties shall take legislative, administrative, social and educational measures to ensure the implementation of the present article. To this end, and having regard to the relevant provisions of other international instruments, States Parties shall in particular:

(a) Provide for a minimum age or minimum ages for admission to employment;

(b) Provide for appropriate regulation of the hours and conditions of employment;

(c) Provide for appropriate penalties or other sanctions to ensure the effective enforcement of the present article.

Article 33

States Parties shall take all appropriate measures, including legislative, administrative, social and educational measures, to protect children from the illicit use of narcotic drugs and psychotropic substances as defined in the relevant international treaties, and to prevent the use of children in the illicit production and trafficking of such substances.

Article 34

States Parties undertake to protect the child from all forms of sexual exploitation and sexual abuse. For these purposes, States Parties shall in particular take all appropriate national, bilateral and multilateral measures to prevent:

(a) The inducement or coercion of a child to engage in any unlawful sexual activity;

(b) The exploitative use of children in prostitution or other unlawful sexual practices;

(c) The exploitative use of children in pornographic performances and materials.

Article 35

States Parties shall take all appropriate national, bilateral and multilateral measures to prevent the abduction of, the sale of or traffic in children for any purpose or in any form.

Article 36

States Parties shall protect the child against all other forms of exploitation prejudicial to any aspects of the child's welfare.

Article 37

States Parties shall ensure that:

(a) No child shall be subjected to torture or other cruel, inhuman or degrading treatment or punishment. Neither capital punishment nor life imprisonment without possibility of release shall be imposed for offences committed by persons below eighteen years of age;

(b) No child shall be deprived of his or her liberty unlawfully or arbitrarily. The arrest, detention or imprisonment of a child shall be in conformity with the law and shall be used only as a measure of last resort and for the shortest appropriate period of time;

(c) Every child deprived of liberty shall be treated with humanity and respect for the inherent dignity of the human person, and in a manner which takes into account the needs of persons of his or her age. In particular, every child deprived of liberty shall be separated from adults unless it is considered in the child's best interest not to do so and shall have the right to maintain contact with his or her family through correspondence and visits, save in exceptional circumstances;

(d) Every child deprived of his or her liberty shall have the right to prompt access to legal and other appropriate assistance, as well as the right to challenge the legality of the deprivation of his or her liberty before a court or other competent, independent and impartial authority, and to a prompt decision on any such action.

Article 38

1. States Parties undertake to respect and to ensure respect for rules of international humanitarian law applicable to them in armed conflicts, which are relevant to the child.

2. States Parties shall take all feasible measures to ensure that persons who have not attained the age of fifteen years do not take a direct part in hostilities.

3. States Parties shall refrain from recruiting any person who has not attained the age of fifteen years into their armed forces. In recruiting among those persons who have attained the age of fifteen years but who have not attained the age of eighteen years, States Parties shall endeavor to give priority to those who are oldest.

3. Convention on the Rights of the Child (CRC) *(continued)*

4. In accordance with their obligations under international humanitarian law to protect the civilian population in armed conflicts, States Parties shall take all feasible measures to ensure protection and care of children who are affected by an armed conflict.

Article 39

States Parties shall take all appropriate measures to promote physical and psychological recovery and social reintegration of a child victim of: any form of neglect, exploitation, or abuse; torture or any other form of cruel, inhuman or degrading treatment or punishment; or armed conflicts. Such recovery and reintegration shall take place in an environment, which fosters the health, self-respect and dignity of the child.

Article 40

1. States Parties recognize the right of every child alleged as, accused of, or recognized as having infringed the penal law to be treated in a manner consistent with the promotion of the child's sense of dignity and worth, which reinforces the child's respect for the human rights and fundamental freedoms of others and which takes into account the child's age and the desirability of promoting the child's reintegration and the child's assuming a constructive role in society.

2. To this end, and having regard to the relevant provisions of international instruments, States Parties shall, in particular, ensure that:

(a) No child shall be alleged as, be accused of, or recognized as having infringed the penal law by reason of acts or omissions that were not prohibited by national or international law at the time they were committed;

(b) Every child alleged as or accused of having infringed the penal law has at least the following guarantees:

(i) To be presumed innocent until proven guilty according to law;

(ii) To be informed promptly and directly of the charges against him or her, and, if appropriate, through his or her parents or legal guardians, and to have legal or other appropriate assistance in the preparation and presentation of his or her defense;

(iii) To have the matter determined without delay by a competent, independent and impartial authority or judicial body in a fair hearing according to law, in the presence of legal or other appropriate assistance and, unless it is considered not to be in the best interest of the child, in particular, taking into account his or her age or situation, his or her parents or legal guardians;

(iv) Not to be compelled to give testimony or to confess guilt; to examine or have examined adverse witnesses and to obtain the participation and examination of witnesses on his or her behalf under conditions of equality;

(v) If considered to have infringed the penal law, to have this decision and any measures imposed in consequence thereof reviewed by a higher competent, independent and impartial authority or judicial body according to law;

(vi) To have the free assistance of an interpreter if the child cannot understand or speak the language used;

(vii) To have his or her privacy fully respected at all stages of the proceedings. 3. States Parties shall seek to promote the establishment of laws, procedures, authorities and institutions specifically applicable to children alleged as, accused of, or recognized as having infringed the penal law, and, in particular:

(a) The establishment of a minimum age below which children shall be presumed not to have the capacity to infringe the penal law;

(b) Whenever appropriate and desirable, measures for dealing with such children without resorting to judicial proceedings, providing that human rights and legal safeguards are fully respected.

4. A variety of dispositions, such as care, guidance and supervision orders; counseling; probation; foster care; education and vocational training programs and other alternatives to institutional care shall be available to ensure that children are dealt with in a manner appropriate to their well-being and proportionate both to their circumstances and the offence.

Article 41

Nothing in the present Convention shall affect any provisions which are more conducive to the realization of the rights of the child and which may be contained in:

(a) The law of a State party; or

(b) International law in force for that State.

PART II

Article 42

States Parties undertake to make the principles and provisions of the Convention widely known, by appropriate and active means, to adults and children alike.

Article 43

1. For the purpose of examining the progress made by States Parties in achieving the realization of the obligations undertaken in the present Convention, there shall be established a Committee on the Rights of the Child, which shall carry out the functions hereinafter, provided.

3. Convention on the Rights of the Child (CRC) *(continued)*

2. The Committee shall consist of ten experts of high moral standing and recognized competence in the field covered by this Convention. The members of the Committee shall be elected by States Parties from among their nationals and shall serve in their personal capacity, consideration being given to equitable geographical distribution, as well as to the principal legal systems.

3. The members of the Committee shall be elected by secret ballot from a list of persons nominated by States Parties. Each State Party may nominate one person from among its own nationals.

4. The initial election to the Committee shall be held no later than six months after the date of the entry into force of the present Convention and thereafter every second year. At least four months before the date of each election, the Secretary-General of the United Nations shall address a letter to States Parties inviting them to submit their nominations within two months. The Secretary-General shall subsequently prepare a list in alphabetical order of all persons thus nominated, indicating States Parties which have nominated them, and shall submit it to the States Parties to the present Convention.

5. The elections shall be held at meetings of States Parties convened by the Secretary-General at United Nations Headquarters. At those meetings, for which two thirds of States Parties shall constitute a quorum, the persons elected to the Committee shall be those who obtain the largest number of votes and an absolute majority of the votes of the representatives of States Parties present and voting.

6. The members of the Committee shall be elected for a term of four years. They shall be eligible for re-election if re-nominated. The term of five of the members elected at the first election shall expire at the end of two years; immediately after the first election, the names of these five members shall be chosen by lot by the Chairman of the meeting.

7. If a member of the Committee dies or resigns or declares that for any other cause he or she can no longer perform the duties of the Committee, the State Party which nominated the member shall appoint another expert from among its nationals to serve for the remainder of the term, subject to the approval of the Committee.

8. The Committee shall establish its own rules of procedure.

9. The Committee shall elect its officers for a period of two years.

10. The meetings of the Committee shall normally be held at United Nations Headquarters or at any other convenient place as determined by the Committee. The Committee shall normally meet annually. The duration of the meetings of the Committee shall be determined, and reviewed, if necessary, by a meeting of the States Parties to the present Convention, subject to the approval of the General Assembly.

11. The Secretary-General of the United Nations shall provide the necessary staff and facilities for the effective performance of the functions of the Committee under the present Convention.

12. With the approval of the General Assembly, the members of the Committee established under the present Convention shall receive emoluments from United Nations resources on such terms and conditions as the Assembly may decide.

Article 44

1. States Parties undertake to submit to the Committee, through the Secretary-General of the United Nations, reports on the measures they have adopted which give effect to the rights recognized herein and on the progress made on the enjoyment of those rights:

(a) Within two years of the entry into force of the Convention for the State Party concerned;

(b) Thereafter every five years.

2. Reports made under the present article shall indicate factors and difficulties, if any, affecting the degree of fulfillment of the obligations under the present Convention. Reports shall also contain sufficient information to provide the Committee with a comprehensive understanding of the implementation of the Convention in the country concerned.

3. A State Party which has submitted a comprehensive initial report to the Committee need not, in its subsequent reports submitted in accordance with paragraph 1 (b) of the present article, repeat basic information previously provided.

4. The Committee may request from States Parties further information relevant to the implementation of the Convention.

5. The Committee shall submit to the General Assembly, through the Economic and Social Council, every two years, reports on its activities.

6. States Parties shall make their reports widely available to the public in their own countries.

Article 45

In order to foster the effective implementation of the Convention and to encourage international co-operation in the field covered by the Convention:

(a) The specialized agencies, the United Nations Children's Fund, and other United Nations organs shall be entitled to be represented at the consideration of the implementation of such provisions of the present Convention as fall within the scope of their mandate. The Committee may invite the specialized agencies, the United Nations Children's Fund and other competent bodies as it may consider appropriate to provide expert advice on the implementation of the Convention in areas falling within the scope of their respective mandates. The Committee may invite the specialized agencies, the United Nations Children's Fund, and other United Nations organs to submit reports on the implementation of the Convention in areas falling within the scope of their activities;

3. Convention on the Rights of the Child (CRC) *(continued)*

(b) The Committee shall transmit, as it may consider appropriate, to the specialized agencies, the United Nations Children's Fund and other competent bodies, any reports from States Parties that contain a request, or indicate a need, for technical advice or assistance, along with the Committee's observations and suggestions, if any, on these requests or indications;

(c) The Committee may recommend to the General Assembly to request the Secretary-General to undertake on its behalf studies on specific issues relating to the rights of the child;

(d) The Committee may make suggestions and general recommendations based on information received pursuant to articles 44 and 45 of the present Convention. Such suggestions and general recommendations shall be transmitted to any State Party concerned and reported to the General Assembly, together with comments, if any, from States Parties.

PART III

Article 46

The present Convention shall be open for signature by all States.

Article 47

The present Convention is subject to ratification. Instruments of ratification shall be deposited with the Secretary-General of the United Nations.

Article 48

The present Convention shall remain open for accession by any State. The instruments of accession shall be deposited with the Secretary-General of the United Nations.

Article 49

1. The present Convention shall enter into force on the thirtieth day following the date of deposit with the Secretary-General of the United Nations of the twentieth instrument of ratification or accession.

2. For each State ratifying or acceding to the Convention after the deposit of the twentieth instrument of ratification or accession, the Convention shall enter into force on the thirtieth day after the deposit by such State of its instrument of ratification or accession.

Article 50

1. Any State Party may propose an amendment and file it with the Secretary-General of the United Nations. The Secretary-General shall thereupon communicate the proposed amendment to States Parties, with a request that they indicate whether they favor a conference of States Parties for the purpose of considering and voting upon the proposals. In the event that, within four months from the date of such communication, at least one third of the States Parties favor such a conference, the Secretary-General shall convene the conference under the auspices of the United Nations. Any amendment adopted by a majority of States Parties present and voting at the conference shall be submitted to the General Assembly for approval.

2. An amendment adopted in accordance with paragraph 1 of the present article shall enter into force when it has been approved by the General Assembly of the United Nations and accepted by a two-thirds majority of States Parties.

3. When an amendment enters into force, it shall be binding on those States Parties which have accepted it, other States Parties still being bound by the provisions of the present Convention and any earlier amendments which they have accepted.

Article 51

1. The Secretary-General of the United Nations shall receive and circulate to all States the text of reservations made by States at the time of ratification or accession.

2. A reservation incompatible with the object and purpose of the present Convention shall not be permitted.

3. Reservations may be withdrawn at any time by notification to that effect addressed to the Secretary-General of the United Nations, who shall then inform all States. Such notification shall take effect on the date on which it is received by the Secretary-General

Article 52

A State Party may denounce the present Convention by written notification to the Secretary-General of the United Nations. Denunciation becomes effective one year after the date of receipt of the notification by the Secretary-General.

Article 53

The Secretary-General of the United Nations is designated as the depositary of the present Convention.

Article 54

The original of the present Convention, of which the Arabic, Chinese, English, French, Russian and Spanish texts are equally authentic, shall be deposited with the Secretary-General of the United Nations.

IN WITNESS THEREOF the undersigned plenipotentiaries, being duly authorized thereto by their respective governments, have signed the present Convention.

4. Signatories to the Convention on the Rights of the Child (CRC)

COUNTRIES RATIFIED	Signature Date	Entry into Force Date
Afghanistan	27/09/90	27/04/94
Albania	26/01/90	28/03/92
Algeria	26/01/90	16/05/93
Andorra	2/10/95	1/2/96
Angola	14/02/90	4/1/91
Antigua and Barbuda	12/3/91	4/11/93
Argentina	29/06/90	3/1/91
Armenia	N/A	22/07/93
Australia	22/08/90	16/01/91
Austria	26/01/90	5/9/92
Azerbaijan	N/A	12/9/92
Bahamas	30/10/90	22/03/91
Bahrain	N/A	14/03/92
Bangladesh	26/01/90	2/9/90
Barbados	19/04/90	8/11/90
Belarus	26/01/90	31/10/90
Belgium	26/01/90	15/01/92
Belize	2/3/90	2/9/90
Benin	25/04/90	2/9/90
Bhutan	4/6/90	2/9/90
Bolivia	8/3/90	25/07/90
Bosnia and Herzegovina	N/A	6/3/92
Botswana	N/A	13/04/95
Brazil	26/01/90	24/10/90
Brunei	N/A	26/01/96
Bulgaria	31/05/90	3/7/91
Burkina Faso	26/01/90	30/09/90
Burundi	8/5/90	18/11/90
Cambodia	22/09/92	14/11/92
Cameroon	25/09/90	10/2/93
Canada	28/05/90	12/1/92
Cape Verde	N/A	4/7/92
Central African Republic	30/07/90	23/05/92
Chad	30/09/90	1/11/90
Chile	26/01/90	12/9/90
China	29/08/90	1/4/92
Colombia	26/01/90	27/02/91
Comoros	30/09/90	21/07/93
Congo, Dem. Rep. (Zaire)	20/03/90	27/10/90
Congo, Rep.	N/A	13/11/93
Cook Islands	N/A	6/7/97
Costa Rica	26/01/90	20/09/90
Côte d'Ivoire	26/01/90	6/3/91
Croatia	N/A	8/10/91
Cuba	26/01/90	20/09/91
Cyprus	5/10/90	9/3/91
Czech Republic	N/A	1/1/93
Denmark	26/01/90	18/08/91
Djibouti	30/09/90	5/1/91
Dominica	26/01/90	12/4/91
Dominican Republic	8/8/90	11/7/91
Ecuador	26/01/90	2/9/90
Egypt	5/2/90	2/9/90
Egypt	5/2/90	2/9/90
El Salvador	26/01/90	2/9/90
Equatorial Guinea	N/A	15/07/92
Eritrea	20/12/93	2/9/94
Estonia	N/A	20/11/91
Ethiopia	N/A	13/06/91
Fiji	2/7/93	12/9/93

4. Signatories to the Convention on the Rights of the Child (CRC) *(continued)*

COUNTRIES RATIFIED	Signature Date	Entry into Force Date
Finland	26/01/90	20/07/91
France	26/01/90	6/9/90
Gabon	26/01/90	11/3/94
Gambia, the	5/2/90	7/9/90
Georgia	N/A	2/7/94
Germany	26/01/90	5/4/92
Ghana	29/01/90	2/9/90
Greece	26/01/90	10/6/93
Grenada	21/02/90	5/12/90
Guatemala	26/01/90	2/9/90
Guinea	N/A	2/9/90
Guinea-Bissau	26/01/90	19/09/90
Guyana	30/09/90	13/02/91
Haiti	20/01/90	8/7/95
Holy See (Vatican City)	20/04/90	2/9/90
Honduras	31/05/90	9/9/90
Hungary	14/03/90	6/11/91
Iceland	26/01/90	27/11/92
India	N/A	11/1/93
Indonesia	26/01/90	5/10/90
Iran	5/9/91	12/8/94
Iraq	N/A	15/07/94
Ireland	30/09/90	28/10/92
Ireland	30/09/90	28/10/92
Israel	3/7/90	2/11/91
Italy	26/01/90	5/10/91
Jamaica	26/01/90	13/06/91
Japan	21/09/90	22/05/94
Jordan	29/08/90	23/06/91
Kazakhstan	16/02/94	11/9/94
Kenya	26/01/90	2/9/90
Kiribati	N/A	10/1/96
Kuwait	7/6/90	20/11/91
Kyrgyzstan	N/A	6/11/94
Laos	N/A	7/6/91
Latvia	N/A	14/05/92
Lebanon	26/01/90	13/06/91
Lesotho	21/08/90	9/4/92
Liberia	26/04/90	4/7/93
Libya	N/A	15/05/93
Liechtenstein	30/09/90	21/01/96
Lithuania	N/A	1/3/92
Luxembourg	21/03/90	6/4/94
Macedonia, FYRO	17/09/91	
Madagascar	19/04/90	18/04/91
Malawi	N/A	1/2/91
Malaysia	N/A	19/03/95
Maldives	21/08/90	13/03/91
Mali	26/01/90	20/10/90
Malta	26/01/90	30/10/90
Marshall Islands	14/04/93	3/11/93
Mauritania	26/01/90	15/06/91
Mauritius	N/A	2/9/90
Mexico	26/01/90	21/10/90
Mexico	26/01/90	21/10/90
Micronesia	N/A	4/6/93
Moldova	N/A	25/02/93
Monaco	N/A	21/07/93
Mongolia	26/01/90	2/9/90
Morocco	26/01/90	21/07/93

4. Signatories to the Convention on the Rights of the Child (CRC) *(continued)*

COUNTRIES RATIFIED	Signature Date	Entry into Force Date
Mozambique	30/09/90	26/05/94
Myanmar (Burma)	N/A	14/08/91
Namibia	26/09/90	30/10/90
Nauru	N/A	26/08/94
Nepal	26/01/90	14/10/90
Netherlands, the	26/01/90	7/3/95
New Zealand	1/10/90	6/5/93
Nicaragua	6/2/90	4/11/90
Niger	26/01/90	30/10/90
Nigeria	26/01/90	19/05/91
Niue	N/A	19/01/96
North Korea, Dem. Rep.	23/08/90	21/10/90
Norway	26/01/90	7/2/91
Oman	N/A	8/1/97
Pakistan	20/09/90	12/12/90
Palau	N/A	3/9/95
Panama	26/01/90	11/1/91
Papua New Guinea	30/09/90	31/03/93
Paraguay	4/4/90	25/10/90
Peru	26/01/90	4/10/90
Philippines	26/01/90	20/09/90
Poland	26/01/90	7/7/91
Portugal	26/01/90	21/10/90
Qatar	8/12/92	3/5/95
Romania	26/01/90	28/10/90
Russia	26/01/90	15/09/90
Rwanda	26/01/90	23/02/91
Saint Kitts and Nevis	26/01/90	2/9/90
Saint Lucia	N/A	16/07/93
Saint Vincent and the Grenadines	20/09/93	25/11/93
Samoa	30/09/90	29/12/94
San Marino	N/A	25/12/91
Sao Tome and Principe	N/A	13/06/91
Saudi Arabia	N/A	25/02/96
Senegal	26/01/90	2/9/90
Seychelles	N/A	7/10/90
Sierra Leone	13/02/90	2/9/90
Singapore	N/A	4/11/95
Slovakia	v	1/1/93
Slovenia	N/A	25/06/91
Solomon Islands	N/A	9/5/95
South Africa	29/01/93	16/07/95
South Korea, Rep.	25/09/90	20/12/91
Spain	26/01/90	5/1/91
Sri Lanka	26/01/90	11/8/91
Sudan	24/07/90	2/9/90
Suriname	26/01/90	31/03/93
Swaziland	22/08/90	6/10/95
Sweden	26/01/90	2/9/90
Switzerland	1/5/91	26/03/97
Syria	18/09/90	14/08/93
Tajikistan	N/A	25/11/93
Tanzania	1/6/90	10/7/91
Thailand	N/A	26/04/92
Togo	26/01/90	2/9/90
Tonga	N/A	6/12/95
Trinidad and Tobago	30/09/90	4/1/92
Tunisia	26/02/90	29/02/92
Turkey	14/09/90	4/5/95
Turkmenistan	N/A	19/10/93

4. Signatories to the Convention on the Rights of the Child (CRC) *(continued)*

COUNTRIES RATIFIED	Signature Date	Entry into Force Date
Tuvalu	N/A	22/10/95
Uganda	17/08/90	16/09/90
Ukraine	21/02/91	27/09/91
United Arab Emirates	N/A	2/2/97
United Kingdom	19/04/90	15/01/92
Uruguay	26/01/90	20/12/90
Uzbekistan	N/A	29/07/94
Vanuatu	30/09/90	6/8/93
Venezuela	26/01/90	13/10/90
Vietnam	26/01/90	2/9/90
Yemen	13/02/90	31/05/91
Yugoslavia	26/01/90	2/2/91
Zambia	30/09/90	5/1/92
Zimbabwe	8/3/90	11/10/90

COUNTRIES SIGNED BUT NOT RATIFIED

Somalia*	N/A	
United States**	16/02/95	

N/A   Not Available

*Ratification of the Convention on the Rights of the Child is not possible at this time. Somalia does not currently have an internationally recognized government.   Because of this, Somalia cannot sign or ratify any legal international treaties.

**The United States has signed, but not ratified. Although the USA does have an internationally recognized government, it has not ratified the convention as of December 2000.

Source: United Nations (UN). <http://untreaty.un.org/English/sample/EnglishInternetBible/partI/chapterIV/treaty15.asp and http://www.unhchr.ch/tbs/doc.nsf>

5. UNICEF's Response to HIV/AIDS Epidemic

In response to HIV/AIDS epidemic's impact on the world population, United Nations Children's Fund (UNICEF) has set the following program priorities at the beginning of the 21st century:

1.To ensure that all young people know the facts about HIV and how to prevent it. This includes programs for injecting-drug users, on the control of sexually transmitted infections (STIs) and youth life skills, and on lifestyle promotion.

2.To support efforts to expand access to services to prevent parent-to-child transmission of HIV, which includes clearer guidance on the use of anti-retroviral therapy and infant feeding in the context of prevention of mother-to-child transmission (PMTCT) projects, access to voluntary counseling and testing, and the reduction of stigma and discrimination for women living with HIV.

3.To provide care and support by strengthening programming for orphans and vulnerable children infected/affected by AIDS and by expanding life skills training for young people. In this context, UNICEF is positioning schools as the hub in every community in the struggle against AIDS. It is working with ministries of education to dedicate time and attention to the introduction of life skills into the curricula and learning of young children. It is also negotiating with the private sector for low-cost supply of essential HIV/AIDS-related drugs;

4.To protect young people and women from HIV in situations of conflict and emergency.

UNICEF has integrated the above-mentioned priorities in all its programming at the country level and globally, and is stepping up its response in the key areas of prevention of mother-to-child transmission and care and support for children infected/affected by HIV.

Source: UNAIDS, UN, UNICEF, WHO, Special session of the General Assembly on HIV/AIDS, Report of the Secretary-General report, 16 February 2001, <http://www.unaids.org/whatsnew/others/un_special/SGreport1.doc>

6. International Labour Organization C138 Minimum Age Convention, 1973

PREAMBLE

The General Conference of the International Labour Organisation,

Having been convened at Geneva by the Governing Body of the International Labour Office, and having met in its Fifty-eighth Session on 6 June 1973, and

Having decided upon the adoption of certain proposals with regard to minimum age for admission to employment, which is the fourth item on the agenda of the session, and

Noting the terms of the Minimum Age (Industry) Convention, 1919, the Minimum Age (Sea) Convention, 1920, the Minimum Age (Agriculture) Convention, 1921, the Minimum Age (Trimmers and Stokers) Convention, 1921, the Minimum Age (Non-Industrial Employment) Convention, 1932 the Minimum Age (Sea) Convention (Revised), 1936, the Minimum Age (Industry) Convention (Revised), 1937, the Minimum Age (Non-Industrial Employment) Convention (Revised), 1937, the Minimum Age (Fishermen) Convention, 1959, and the Minimum Age (Underground Work) Convention, 1965, and

Considering that the time has come to establish a general instrument on the subject, which would gradually replace the existing ones applicable to limited economic sectors, with a view to achieving the total abolition of child labour, and Having determined that these proposals shall take the form of an international Convention, adopts the twenty-sixth day of June of the year one thousand nine hundred and seventy-three, the following convention, which may be cited as the Minimum Age Convention, 1973:

Article 1

Each Member for which this Convention is in force undertakes to pursue a national policy designed to ensure the effective abolition of child labour and to raise progressively the minimum age for admission to employment or work to a level consistent with the fullest physical and mental development of young persons.

Article 2

1. Each Member which ratifies this Convention shall specify, in a declaration appended to its ratification, a minimum age for admission to employment or work within its territory and on means of transport registered in its territory; subject to Articles 4 to 8 of this Convention, no one under that age shall be admitted to employment or work in any occupation.

2. Each Member which has ratified this Convention may subsequently notify the Director- General of the International Labour office, by further declarations, that it specifies a minimum age higher than that previously specified.

3. The minimum age specified in pursuance of paragraph 1 of this Article shall not be less than the age of completion of compulsory schooling and, in any case, shall not be less than 15 years.

4. Notwithstanding the provisions of paragraph 3 of this Article, a Member whose economy and educational facilities are insufficiently developed may, after consultation with the organisations of employers and workers concerned, where such exist, initially specify a minimum age of 14 years.

5. Each Member which has specified a minimum age of 14 years in pursuance of the provisions of the preceding paragraph shall include in its reports on the application of this Convention submitted under article 22 of the constitution of the International Labour Organisation a statement—
   (a) that its reason for doing so subsists; or
   (b) that it renounces its right to avail itself of the provisions in question as from a stated date.

Article 3

1. The minimum age for admission to any type of employment or work which by its nature or the circumstances in which it is carried out, is likely to jeopardise the health, safety or morals of young persons shall not be less than 18 years.

2. The types of employment or work to which paragraph 1 of this Article applies shall be determined by national laws or regulations or by the competent authority, after consultation with the organisations of employers and workers concerned, where such exist.

3. Notwithstanding the provisions of paragraph 1 of this Article national laws or regulations or the competent authority may, after consultation with the organisations of employers and workers concerned, where such exist, authorise employment or work as from the age of 16 years on condition that the health, safety and morals of the young persons concerned are fully protected and that the young persons have received adequate specific instruction or vocational training in the relevant branch of activity.

Article 4

1. In so far as necessary, the competent authority, after consultation with the organisations of employers and workers concerned, where such exist, may exclude from the application of this Convention limited categories of employment or work in respect of which special and substantial problems of application arise.

2. Each Member which ratifies this Convention shall list in its first report on the application of the Convention submitted under article 22 of the Constitution of the International Labour Organisation any categories which may have been excluded in pursuance of

6. International Labour Organization C138 Minimum Age Convention, 1973 *(continued)*

paragraph 1 of this Article, giving the reasons for such exclusion, and shall state in subsequent reports the position of its law and practice in respect of the categories excluded and the extent to which effect has been given or is proposed to be given to the Convention in respect of such categories.

3. Employment or work covered by Article 3 of this Convention shall not be excluded from the application of the Convention in pursuance of this Article.

Article 5

1. A Member whose economy and administrative facilities are insufficiently developed may, after consultation with the organisations of employers and workers concerned, where such exist initially limit the scope of application of this Convention.

2. Each Member which avails itself of the provisions of paragraph 1 of this Article shall specify, in a declaration appended to its ratification, the branches of economic activity or types of undertakings to which it will apply the provisions of the Convention.

3. The provisions of the Convention shall be applicable as a minimum to the following: mining and quarrying; manufacturing; construction; electricity, gas and water; sanitary services; transport, storage and communication; and plantations and other agricultural undertakings mainly producing for commercial purposes, but excluding family and small-scale holdings producing for local consumption and not regularly employing hired workers.

4. Any Member which has limited the scope of application of this Convention in pursuance of this Article—
   (a) shall indicate in its reports under article 22 of the Constitution of the International Labour Organisation the general position as regards the employment or work of young persons and children in the branches of activity which are excluded from the scope of application of this Convention and any progress which may have been made towards wider application of the provisions of the Convention;
   (b) may at any time formally extend the scope of application by a declaration addressed to the Director-General of the International Labour Office.

Article 6

This Convention does not apply to work done by children and young persons in schools for general, vocational or technical education or in other training institutions, or to work done by persons at least 14 years of age in undertakings, where such work is carried out in accordance with conditions prescribed by the competent authority after consultation with the organisations of employers and workers concerned, where such exist, and is an integral part of-(a) a course of education or training for which a school or training institution is primarily responsible; (b) a programme of training mainly or entirely in an undertaking which programme has been approved by the competent authority; or (c) a programme of guidance or orientation designed to facilitate the choice of an occupation or of a line of training.

Article 7

1. National laws or regulations may permit the employment or work of persons 13 to 15 years of age on light work which is—
   (a) not likely to be harmful to their health or development; and
   (b) not such as to prejudice their attendance at school, their participation in vocational orientation or training programmes approved by the competent authority or their capacity to benefit from the instruction received.

2. National laws or regulations may also permit the employment or work of persons who are at least 15 years of age but have not yet completed their compulsory schooling on work which meets the requirements set forth in sub-paragraphs (a) and (b) of paragraph 1 of this Article.

3. The competent authority shall determine the activities in which employment or work may be permitted under paragraphs 1 and 2 of this Article and shall prescribe the number of hours during which and the conditions in which such employment or work may be undertaken.

4. Notwithstanding the provisions of paragraphs 1 and 2 of this Article, a Member which has availed itself of the provisions of paragraph 4 of Article 2 may, for as long as it continues to do so substitute the ages 12 and 14 for the ages 13 and 15 in paragraph 1 and the age 14 for the age 15 in paragraph 2 of this Article.

Article 8

1. After consultation with the organisations of employers and workers concerned, where such exist, the competent authority may, by permits granted in individual cases, allow exceptions to the prohibition of employment or work provided for in Article 2 of this Convention, for such purposes as participation in artistic performances.

2. Permits so granted shall limit the number of hours during which and pre-scribe the conditions in which employment or work is allowed.

Article 9

1. All necessary measures, including the provision of appropriate penalties, shall be taken by the competent authority to ensure the effective enforcement of the provisions of this Convention.

6. International Labour Organization C138 Minimum Age Convention, 1973 *(continued)*

2. National laws or regulations or the competent authority shall define the persons responsible for compliance with the provisions giving effect to the Convention.

3. National laws or regulations or the competent authority shall prescribe the registers or other documents which shall be kept and made available by the employer; such registers or documents shall contain the names and ages or dates of birth, duly certified wherever possible, of persons whom he employs or who work for him and who are less than 18 years of age.

Article 10

1. This Convention revises, on the terms set forth in this Article the Minimum Age (Industry) Convention, 1919, the Minimum Age (Sea) Convention, 1920, the Minimum Age (Agriculture) Convention, 1921 the Minimum Age (Trimmers and Stokers) Convention, 1921, the Minimum Age (Non-Industrial Employment) Convention, 1932, the Minimum Age (Sea) Convention (Revised), 1936, the Minimum Age (Industry) Convention (Revised), 1937, the Minimum Age (Non-Industrial Employment) Convention (Revised), 1937, the Minimum Age (Fishermen) Convention, 1959, and the Minimum Age (Underground Work) Convention, 1965. The coming into force of this Convention shall not close the Minimum Age (Sea) Convention (Revised), 1936, the Minimum Age (Industry) Convention (Revised), 1937, the Minimum Age (Non-Industrial Employment) Convention (Revised), 1937, the Minimum Age (Fishermen) Convention, 1959, or the Minimum Age (Underground Work) Convention, 1965, to further ratification.

2. The coming into force of this Convention shall not close the Minimum Age (Sea) Convention (Revised), 1936, the Minimum Age (Industry) Convention (Revised), 1937, the Minimum Age (Non-Industrial Employment) Convention (Revised), 1937, the Minimum Age (Fishermen) Convention, 1959, or the Minimum Age (Under-ground Work) Convention, 1965, to further ratification.

3. The Minimum Age (Industry) Convention, 1919, the Minimum Age (Sea) Convention, 1920, the Minimum Age (Agriculture) Convention 1921, and the Minimum Age (Trimmers and Stokers) Convention, 1921 shall be closed to further ratification when all the parties thereto have consented to such closing by ratification of this Convention or by a declaration communicated to the Director-General of the International Labour Office.

4. When the obligations of this Convention are accepted—
(a) by a Member which is a party to the Minimum Age (Industry) Convention (Revised), 1937, and a minimum age of not less than 15 years is specified in pursuance of Article 2 of this Convention this shall ipso jure involve the immediate denunciation of that convention,
(b) in respect of non-industrial employment as defined in the Minimum Age (Non-Industrial Employment) Convention, 1932, by a Member which is a party to that Convention, this shall ipso jure involve the immediate denunciation of that Convention,
(c) in respect of non-industrial employment as defined in the Minimum Age (Non-Industrial Employment) Convention (Revised), 1937 by a Member which is a party to that Convention, and a minimum age of not less than 15 years is specified in pursuance of Article 2 of this Convention, this shall ipso jure involve the immediate denunciation of that Convention,
(d) in respect of maritime employment, by a Member which is a party to the Minimum Age (Sea) Convention (Revised), 1936, and a minimum age of not less than 15 years is specified in pursuance of Article 2 of this Convention or the Member specifies that Article 3 of this convention applies to maritime employment, this shall ipso jure involve the immediate denunciation of that Convention,
(e) in respect of employment in maritime fishing, by a Member which is a party to the Minimum Age (Fishermen) Convention, 1959, and a minimum age of not less than 15 years is specified in pursuance of Article 2 of this Convention or the Member specifies that Article 3 of this Convention applies to employment in maritime fishing, this shall ipso jure involve the immediate denunciation of that convention,
(f) by a Member which is a party to the Minimum Age (underground Work) Convention, 1965, and a minimum age of not less than the age specified in pursuance of that Convention is specified in pursuance of Article 2 of this Convention or the Member specifies that such an age applies to employment underground in mines in virtue of Article 3 of this Convention, this shall ipso jure involve the immediate denunciation of that Convention, if and when this Convention shall have come into force.

5. Acceptance of the obligations of this Convention—
(a) shall involve the denunciation of the Minimum Age (Industry) Convention, 1919, in accordance with Article 12 thereof,
(b) in respect of agriculture shall involve the denunciation of the Minimum Age (Agriculture) Convention, 1921, in accordance with Article 9 thereof,
(c) in respect of maritime employment shall involve the denunciation of the Minimum Age (Sea) Convention, 1920, in accordance with Article 10 thereof, and of the Minimum Age (Trimmers and Stokers) Convention, 1921, in accordance with Article 12 thereof, if and when this Convention shall have come into force.

FINAL PROVISIONS

Article 11

The formal ratifications of this Convention shall be communicated to the Director-General of the International Labour office for registration.

6. International Labour Organization C138 Minimum Age Convention, 1973 *(continued)*

Article 12

1. This Convention shall be binding only upon those Members of the International Labour Organisation whose ratifications have been registered with the Director-General.

2. It shall come into force twelve months after the date on which the ratifications of two Members have been registered with the Director-General.

3. Thereafter, this Convention shall come into force for any Member twelve months after the date on which its ratifications has been registered.

Article 13

1. A Member which has ratified this Convention may denounce it after the expiration of ten years from the date on which the Convention first comes into force, by an Act communicated to the Director-General of the International Labour Office for registration. Such denunciation should not take effect until one year after the date on which it is registered.

2. Each Member which has ratified this Convention and which does not, within the year following the expiration of the period of ten years mentioned in the preceding paragraph, exercise the right of denunciation provided for in this Article, will be bound for another period' of ten years and, thereafter, may denounce this Convention at the expiration of each period of ten years under the terms provided for in this Article.

Article 14

1. The Director-General of the International Labour office shall notify all Members of the International Labour Organisation of the registration of all ratifications and denunciations communicated to him by the Members of the Organisation.

2. When notifying the Members of the Organisation of the registration of the second ratification communicated to him, the Director-General shall draw the attention of the Members of the Organisation to the date upon which the Convention will come into force.

Article 15

The Director-General of the International Labour Office shall communicate to the Secretary-General of the United Nations for registration in accordance with Article 102 of the Charter of the United Nations full particulars of all ratifications and acts of denunciation registered by him in accordance with the provisions of the preceding Articles.

Article 16

At such times as may consider necessary the Governing Body of the International Labour office shall present to the General Conference a report on the working of this Convention and shall examine the desirability of placing on the agenda of the Conference the question of its revision in whole or in part.

Article 17

1. Should the Conference adopt a new Convention revising this Convention in whole or in part, then, unless the new Convention otherwise provides:
   a) the ratification by a Member of the new revising convention shall ipso jure involve the immediate denunciation of this Convention notwithstanding the provisions of Article 13 above, if and when the new revising Convention shall have come into force;
   b) as from the date when the new revising Convention comes into force this Convention shall cease to be open to ratification by the Members.

2. This Convention shall in any case remain in force in its actual form and content for those Members which have ratified it but have not ratified the revising Convention.

Article 18

The English and French versions of the text of this Convention are equally authoritative.

7. C182 Worst Forms of Child Labour Convention, 1999*

Convention concerning the Prohibition and Immediate Action for the Elimination of the Worst Forms of Child Labour (Note/ This Convention has not yet come into force/ 19/11/2000)
Convention/C182
Place/Geneva
Session of the Conference/87
Date of adoption/17/06/1999

The General Conference of the International Labour Organization,

Having been convened at Geneva by the Governing Body of the International Labour Office, and having met in its 87th Session on 1 June 1999, and

Considering the need to adopt new instruments for the prohibition and elimination of the worst forms of child labour, as the main priority for national and international action, including international cooperation and assistance, to complement the Convention and the Recommendation concerning Minimum Age for Admission to Employment, 1973, which remain fundamental instruments on child labour, and

Considering that the effective elimination of the worst forms of child labour requires immediate and comprehensive action, taking into account the importance of free basic education and the need to remove the children concerned from all such work and to provide for their rehabilitation and social integration while addressing the needs of their families, and

Recalling the resolution concerning the elimination of child labour adopted by the International Labour Conference at its 83rd Session in 1996, and

Recognizing that child labour is to a great extent caused by poverty and that the long-term solution lies in sustained economic growth leading to social progress, in particular poverty alleviation and universal education, and

Recalling the Convention on the Rights of the Child adopted by the United Nations General Assembly on 20 November 1989, and

Recalling the ILO Declaration on Fundamental Principles and Rights at Work and its Follow-up, adopted by the International Labour Conference at its 86th Session in 1998, and

Recalling that some of the worst forms of child labour are covered by other international instruments, in particular the Forced Labour Convention, 1930, and the United Nations Supplementary Convention on the Abolition of Slavery, the Slave Trade, and Institutions and Practices Similar to Slavery, 1956, and

Having decided upon the adoption of certain proposals with regard to child labour, which is the fourth item on the agenda of the session, and

Having determined that these proposals shall take the form of an international Convention;

adopts this seventeenth day of June of the year one thousand nine hundred and ninety-nine the following Convention, which may be cited as the Worst Forms of Child Labour Convention, 1999.

Article 1

Each Member which ratifies this Convention shall take immediate and effective measures to secure the prohibition and elimination of the worst forms of child labour as a matter of urgency.

Article 2

For the purposes of this Convention, the term child shall apply to all persons under the age of 18.

Article 3

For the purposes of this Convention, the term the worst forms of child labour comprises

(a) all forms of slavery or practices similar to slavery, such as the sale and trafficking of children, debt bondage and serfdom and forced or compulsory labour, including forced or compulsory recruitment of children for use in armed conflict;
(b) the use, procuring or offering of a child for prostitution, for the production of pornography or for pornographic performances;
(c) the use, procuring or offering of a child for illicit activities, in particular for the production and trafficking of drugs as defined in the relevant international treaties;
(d) work which, by its nature or the circumstances in which it is carried out, is likely to harm the health, safety or morals of children.

Article 4

1. The types of work referred to under Article 3(d) shall be determined by national laws or regulations or by the competent authority, after consultation with the organizations of employers and workers concerned, taking into consideration relevant international standards, in particular Paragraphs 3 and 4 of the Worst Forms of Child Labour Recommendation, 1999.

7. C182 Worst Forms of Child Labour Convention, 1999* *(continued)*

2. The competent authority, after consultation with the organizations of employers and workers concerned, shall identify where the types of work so determined exist.

3. The list of the types of work determined under paragraph 1 of this Article shall be periodically examined and revised as necessary, in consultation with the organizations of employers and workers concerned.

Article 5

Each Member shall, after consultation with employers' and workers' organizations, establish or designate appropriate mechanisms to monitor the implementation of the provisions giving effect to this Convention.

Article 6

1. Each Member shall design and implement programmes of action to eliminate as a priority the worst forms of child labour.

2. Such programmes of action shall be designed and implemented in consultation with relevant government institutions and employers' and workers' organizations, taking into consideration the views of other concerned groups as appropriate.

Article 7

1. Each Member shall take all necessary measures to ensure the effective implementation and enforcement of the provisions giving effect to this Convention including the provision and application of penal sanctions or, as appropriate, other sanctions.

2. Each Member shall, taking into account the importance of education in eliminating child labour, take effective and time-bound measures to/
    (a) prevent the engagement of children in the worst forms of child labour;
    (b) provide the necessary and appropriate direct assistance for the removal of children from the worst forms of child labour and for their rehabilitation and social integration;
    (c) ensure access to free basic education, and, wherever possible and appropriate, vocational training, for all children removed from the worst forms of child labour;
    (d) identify and reach out to children at special risk; and
    (e) take account of the special situation of girls.

3. Each Member shall designate the competent authority responsible for the implementation of the provisions giving effect to this Convention.

Article 8

Members shall take appropriate steps to assist one another in giving effect to the provisions of this Convention through enhanced international cooperation and/or assistance including support for social and economic development, poverty eradication programmes and universal education.

Article 9

The formal ratifications of this Convention shall be communicated to the Director-General of the International Labour Office for registration.

Article 10

1. This Convention shall be binding only upon those Members of the International Labour Organization whose ratifications have been registered with the Director-General of the International Labour Office.

2. It shall come into force 12 months after the date on which the ratifications of two Members have been registered with the Director-General.

3. Thereafter, this Convention shall come into force for any Member 12 months after the date on which its ratification has been registered.

Article 11

1. A Member which has ratified this Convention may denounce it after the expiration of ten years from the date on which the Convention first comes into force, by an act communicated to the Director-General of the International Labour Office for registration. Such denunciation shall not take effect until one year after the date on which it is registered.

2. Each Member which has ratified this Convention and which does not, within the year following the expiration of the period of ten years mentioned in the preceding paragraph, exercise the right of denunciation provided for in this Article, will be bound for another period of ten years and, thereafter, may denounce this Convention at the expiration of each period of ten years under the terms provided for in this Article.

7. C182 Worst Forms of Child Labour Convention, 1999* *(continued)*

Article 12

1. The Director-General of the International Labour Office shall notify all Members of the International Labour Organization of the registration of all ratifications and acts of denunciation communicated by the Members of the Organization.

2. When notifying the Members of the Organization of the registration of the second ratification, the Director-General shall draw the attention of the Members of the Organization to the date upon which the Convention shall come into force.

Article 13

The Director-General of the International Labour Office shall communicate to the Secretary-General of the United Nations, for registration in accordance with article 102 of the Charter of the United Nations, full particulars of all ratifications and acts of denunciation registered by the Director-General in accordance with the provisions of the preceding Articles.

Article 14

At such times as it may consider necessary, the Governing Body of the International Labour Office shall present to the General Conference a report on the working of this Convention and shall examine the desirability of placing on the agenda of the Conference the question of its revision in whole or in part.

Article 15

1. Should the Conference adopt a new Convention revising this Convention in whole or in part, then, unless the new Convention otherwise provides —

  (a) the ratification by a Member of the new revising Convention shall ipso jure involve the immediate denunciation of this Convention, notwithstanding the provisions of Article 11 above, if and when the new revising Convention shall have come into force;
  (b) as from the date when the new revising Convention comes into force, this Convention shall cease to be open to ratification by the Members.

2. This Convention shall in any case remain in force in its actual form and content for those Members which have ratified it but have not ratified the revising Convention.

Article 16

The English and French versions of the text of this Convention are equally authoritative.

The foregoing is the authentic text of the Convention unanimously adopted by the General Conference of the International Labour Organization during its Eighty-seventh Session which was held at Geneva and declared closed on 17 June 1999.

IN FAITH WHEREOF we have appended our signatures this day of June 1999.

The President of the Conference, The Director-General of the International Labour Office

* On June 17th, 1999, when it was placed before the ILO delegates for a final recorded vote, the new Convention won the unanimous support with 415 delegates representing governments, employers, and workers voting in favor of the Convention, 0 voting against it, and 0 abstaining. It was the very first time in the history of the ILO that a new Convention had won unanimous support. By November 2000, Convention No. C182 was ratified by 49 countries: Barbados, Belarus, Belize, Botswana, Brazil, Bulgaria, Canada, Central African Republic, Chad, Chile, Denmark, Dominican Republic, Ecuador, El Salvador, Finland, Ghana, Hungary, Iceland, Indonesia, Ireland, Italy, Jordan, Kuwait, Libya, Malawi, Malaysia, Mali, Mauritius, Mexico, Namibia, Nicaragua, Niger, Panama, Papua New Guinea, Portugal, Qatar, Rwanda, Saint Kitts and Nevis, San Marino, Senegal, Seychelles, Slovakia, South Africa, Switzerland, Togo, Tunisia, United Kingdom, United States, Yemen.

8. Declaration on Social and Legal Principles Relating to the Protection and Welfare of Children, with Special Reference to Foster Placement and Adoption Nationally and Internationally

Adopted by United Nation's General Assembly
Resolution 41/85 of December 3rd, 1986

The General Assembly,

Recalling the Universal Declaration of Human Rights, the International Covenant on Economic, Social and Cultural Rights, the International Covenant on Civil and Political Rights, the International Convention on the Elimination of All Forms of Racial Discrimination and the Convention on the Elimination of All Forms of Discrimination against Women,

Recalling also the Declaration of the Rights of the Child, which it proclaimed by its resolution 1386 (XIV) of 20 November 1959,

Reaffirming principle 6 of that Declaration, which states that the child shall, wherever possible, grow up in the care and under the responsibility of his parents and, in any case, in an atmosphere of affection and of moral and material security,

Concerned at the large number of children who are abandoned or become orphans owing to violence, internal disturbance, armed conflicts, natural disasters, economic crises or social problems,

Bearing in mind that in all foster placement and adoption procedures the best interests of the child should be the paramount consideration,

Recognizing that under the principal legal systems of the world, various valuable alternative institutions exist, such as the kafalah of Islamic Law, which provide substitute care to children who cannot be cared for by their own parents,

Recognizing further that only where a particular institution is recognized and regulated by the domestic law of a State would the provisions of this Declaration relating to that institution be relevant and that such provisions would in no way affect the existing alternative institutions in other legal systems,

Conscious of the need to proclaim universal principles to be taken into account in cases where procedures are instituted relating to foster placement or adoption of a child, either nationally or internationally,

Bearing in mind, however, that the principles set forth hereunder do not impose on States such legal institutions as foster placement or adoption,

Proclaims the following principles:

A. GENERAL FAMILY AND CHILD WELFARE

Article 1

Every State should give a high priority to family and child welfare.

Article 2

Child welfare depends upon good family welfare.

Article 3

The first priority for a child is to be cared for by his or her own parents.

Article 4

When care by the child's own parents is unavailable or inappropriate, care by relatives of the child's parents, by another substitute— foster or adoptive— family or, if necessary, by an appropriate institution should be considered.

Article 5

In all matters relating to the placement of a child outside the care of the child's own parents, the best interests of the child, particularly his or her need for affection and right to security and continuing care, should be the paramount consideration.

Article 6

Persons responsible for foster placement or adoption procedures should have professional or other appropriate training.

Article 7

Governments should determine the adequacy of their national child welfare services and consider appropriate actions.

Article 8

The child should at all times have a name, a nationality and a legal representative. The child should not, as a result of foster placement, adoption or any alternative regime, be deprived or his or her name, nationality or legal representative unless the child thereby acquires a new name, nationality or legal representative.

8. Declaration on Social and Legal Principles Relating to the Protection and Welfare of Children, with Special Reference to Foster Placement and Adoption Nationally and Internationally *(continued)*

Article 9

The need of a foster or an adopted child to know about his or her background should be recognized by persons responsible for the child's care unless this is contrary to the child's best interests.

B. FOSTER PLACEMENT

Article 10

Foster placement of children should be regulated by law.

Article 11

Foster family care, though temporary in nature, may continue, if necessary, until adulthood but should not preclude either prior return to the child's own parents or adoption.

Article 12

In all matters of foster family care, the prospective foster parents and, as appropriate, the child and his or her own parents should be properly involved. A competent authority or agency should be responsible for supervision to ensure the welfare of the child.

C. ADOPTION

Article 13

The primary aim of adoption is to provide the child who cannot be cared for by his or her own parents with a permanent family.

Article 14

In considering possible adoption placements, persons responsible for them should select the most appropriate environment for the child.

Article 15

Sufficient time and adequate counseling should be given to the child's own parents, the prospective adoptive parents and, as appropriate, the child in order to reach a decision on the child's future as early as possible.

Article 16

The relationship between the child to be adopted and the prospective adoptive parents should be observed by child welfare agencies or services prior to the adoption. Legislation should ensure that the child is recognized in law as a member of the adoptive family and enjoys all the rights pertinent thereto.

Article 17

If a child cannot be placed in a foster or an adoptive family or cannot in any suitable manner be cared for in the country of origin, inter-country adoption may be considered as an alternative means of providing the child with a family.

Article 18

Governments should establish policy, legislation and effective supervision for the protection of children involved in inter-country adoption. Inter-country adoption should, wherever possible, only be undertaken when such measures have been established in the States concerned.

Article 19

Policies should be established and laws enacted, where necessary, for the prohibition of abduction and of any other act for illicit placement of children.

Article 20

In inter-country adoption, placements should, as a rule, be made through competent authorities or agencies with application of safeguards and standards equivalent to those existing in respect of national adoption. In no case should the placement result in improper financial gain for those involved in it.

Article 21

In inter-country adoption through persons acting as agents for prospective adoptive parents, special precautions should be taken in order to protect the child's legal and social interests.

Article 22

No inter-country adoption should be considered before it has been established that the child is legally free for adoption and that any pertinent documents necessary to complete the adoption, such as the consent of competent authorities, will become available. It must also be established that the child will be able to migrate and to join the prospective adoptive parents and may obtain their nationality.

8. Declaration on Social and Legal Principles Relating to the Protection and Welfare of Children, with Special Reference to Foster Placement and Adoption Nationally and Internationally *(continued)*

Article 23

In inter-country adoption, as a rule, the legal validity of the adoption should be assured in each of the countries involved.

Article 24

Where the nationality of the child differs from that of the prospective adoptive parents, all due weight shall be given to both the law of the State of which the child is a national and the law of the State of which the prospective adoptive parents are nationals. In this connection due regard shall be given to the child's cultural and religious background and interests.

9. Draft Optional Protocol to the Convention on the Rights of the Child on Involvement of Children in Armed Conflict

21 January 2000

Article 1

State Parties shall take all feasible measures to ensure that members of their armed forces who have not attained the age of 18 years do not take a direct part in hostilities.

Article 2

State Parties shall ensure that persons who have not attained the age of 18 years are not compulsorily recruited into their armed forces.

Article 3

States Parties shall raise the minimum age in years for the voluntary recruitment of persons into their national armed forces from that set out in Article 38(3) the Convention on the Rights of the Child, taking account of the principles contained in that article and recognize that under the Convention persons under 18 are entitled to special protection.

Each State Party shall deposit a binding declaration upon ratification of or accession to this Protocol which sets forth the minimum age at which it will permit voluntary recruitment into its national armed forces and a description of the safeguards that it has adopted to ensure that such recruitment is not forced or coerced.

States Parties which permit voluntary recruitment into their national armed forces under the age of 18 shall maintain safeguards to ensure, as a minimum, that:

- such recruitment is genuinely voluntary;
- such recruitment is done with the informed consent of the person's parents or legal guardians;
- such persons are fully informed of the duties involved in such military service, and
- such persons provide reliable proof of age prior to acceptance into national military service.

Each State Party may strenghten its declaration at any time by notification to that effect addressed to the Secretary-General of the United Nations who shall inform all States Par-ties. Such notification shall take effect on the date which it is received by the Secretary-General.

The requirement to raise the age in paragraph 1 does not apply to schools operated by or under the control of the armed forces of the States Parties, in keeping with Articles 28 and 29 of the Convention on the Rights of the Child.

Article 4

1. Armed groups, distinct from the armed forces of a State, should not, under any circumstances, recruit or use in hostilities persons under the age of 18 years.

2. State Parties shall take all feasible measures to prevent such recruitment and use, including the adoption of legal measures necessary to prohibit and criminalize such practices.

3. The application of the present article under this Protocol shall not affect the legal status of any party to an armed conflict.

Article 5

Nothing in the present Protocol shall be construed to preclude provisions in the law of a State Party or in international instruments and international humanitarian law which are more conducive to the realisation of the rights of the child.

9. Draft Optional Protocol to the Convention on the Rights of the Child on Involvement of Children in Armed Conflict *(continued)*

Article 6

1. Each State Party shall take all necessary legal, administrative and other measures to ensure the effective implementation and enforcement of the provisions of this Protocol within its jurisdiction.

2. States Parties undertake to make the principles and provisions of the present Protocol widely known and promoted by appropriate means, to adults and children alike.

3. States Parties shall take all feasible measures to ensure that persons within their jurisdiction recruited or used in hostilities contrary to this Protocol are demobilized or otherwise released from service. States Parties shall, when necessary, accord to these persons all appropriate assistance for their physical and psychological recovery, and their social reintegration.

Article 7

1. States Parties shall cooperate in the implementation of the present protocol, including in the prevention of any activity contrary to the protocol and in the rehabilitation and social reintegration of persons who are victims of acts contrary to this protocol, including through technical cooperation and financial assistance. Such assistance and cooperation will be undertaken in consultation among concerned States parties and other relevant international organisations.

2. States Parties, in a position to do so, shall provide such assistance through existing multilateral, bilateral, or other programmes, or inter aria, through a voluntary fund established in accordance with the General Assembly rules.

Article 8

1. Each State Party shall submit, within two years following the entry into force of the Protocol for that State Party, a report to the Committee on the Rights of the Child providing comprehensive information on the measures it has taken to implement the provisions of the Protocol, including the measures taken to implement the provisions on participation and recruitment.

2. Following the submission of the comprehensive report, each State Party shall include in the reports they submit to the Committee on the Rights of the Child in accordance with article 44 of the Convention, any further information with respect to the implementation of the Protocol. Other State Parties to the Protocol shall submit a report every five years.

3. The Committee on the Rights of the Child may request from State Parties further information relevant to the implementation of this Protocol.

Article 9

1. The present Protocol is open for signature by any State which is a party to the Convention or has signed it.

2. The present Protocol is subject to ratification or open to accession by any State. Instruments of ratification or accession shall be deposited with the Secretary-General of the United Nations.

3. The Secretary-General of the United Nations in his capacity as depositary of the Convention and the Protocol shall inform all States Parties to the Convention and all States which have signed the Convention of each instrument of declaration pursuant to article 3, ratification or accession to the Protocol.

Article 10

1. The present Protocol shall enter into force three months after the deposit of the tenth instrument of ratification or accession.

2. For each State ratifying the present Protocol or acceding to it after its entry into force the present Protocol shall enter into force one month after the date of the deposit of its own instrument of ratification or accession.

Article 11

1. Any State Party may denounce the present Protocol at any time by written notification to the Secretary-General of the United Nations, who shall thereafter inform the other States Parties to the Convention and all States which have signed the Convention. Denunciation shall take effect one year after the date of receipt of the notification by the Secretary-General of the United Nations. If, however on the expiry of that year the denouncing State Party is engaged in armed conflict, the denunciation shall not take effect before the end of the armed conflict.

2. Such a denunciation shall not have the effect of releasing the State Party from its obligations under the present Protocol in regard to any act which occurs prior to the date at which the denunciation becomes effective. Nor shall such a denunciation prejudice in any way the continued consideration of any matter which is already under consideration by the Committee prior to the date at which the denunciation becomes effective.

Article 12

1. Any State Party may propose an amendment and file it with the Secretary-General of the United Nations. The Secretary-General shall thereupon communicate the proposed amendment to States Parties, with a request that they indicate whether they favour a

9. Draft Optional Protocol to the Convention on the Rights of the Child on Involvement of Children in Armed Conflict *(continued)*

conference of States Parties for the purpose of considering and voting upon the proposals. In the event that, within four months from the date of such communication, at least one third of the States Parties favour such a conference, the Secretary-General shall convene the conference under the auspices of the United Nations. Any amendment adopted by a majority of States Parties present and voting at the conference shall be submitted to the General Assembly for approval.

2. An amendment adopted in accordance with paragraph I of the present article shall enter into force when it has been approved by the General Assembly of the United Nations and accepted by a two-thirds majority of States Parties.

When an amendment enters into force, it shall be binding on those States Parties which have accepted it, other States Parties still being bound by the provisions of the present Protocol and any earlier amendments which they have accepted.

Article 13

1. The present Protocol, of which the Arabic, Chinese, English, French, Russian and Spanish texts are equally authentic, shall be deposited in the archives of the United Nations.

2. The Secretary-General of the United Nations shall transmit certified copies of the present Protocol to all States Parties to the Convention and all States which have signed the Convention.

* * * * * * * * * *

CHAIRMANS' TEXT

PPI: Encouraged by the overwhelming support for the Convention on the Rights of the Child, demonstrating the widespread commitment that exists to strive for the promotion and protection of the rights of the child.

PP2: Reaffirming that the rights of children require special protection and call for continuous improvement of the situation of children without distinction, as well as for their development and education in conditions of peace and security.

PP3: Disturbed by the harmful and widespread impact of armed conflict on children and the long-term consequences this has for durable peace, security and development.

PP4: Condemning the targeting of children in situations of armed conflict and direct attacks on objects protected under international law, including places generally having a significant presence of children, such as schools and hospitals.

PP5: Noting the adoption of the Statute of the International Criminal Court, in particular the inclusion of conscripting or enlisting children under the age of fifteen years or using them to participate actively in hostilities as a war crime in both international and non international armed conflicts.

PP6: Considering therefore that to strengthen further the implementation of rights recognized in the Convention on the Rights of the Child, there is a need to increase the protection of children from involvement in armed conflict.

PP7: Noting that article 1 of the Convention on the Rights of the Child specifies that, for the purposes of that Convention, a child means every human being below the age of 18 years unless under the law applicable to the child, majority is attained earlier.

PP8: Convinced that an Optional Protocol to the Convention, raising the age of possible recruitment of persons into armed forces and their participation in hostilities, will contribute effectively to the implementation of the principle that the best interests of the child are to be a primary consideration in all actions concerning children.

PP9: Noting that the twenty-sixth international Conference of the Red Cross and Red Crescent in December 1995 recommended inter alia that parties to conflict take -every feasible step to ensure that children under the age of 18 years do not take part in hostilities.

PP10: Welcoming also the unanimous adoption in June 1999, of the ILO Convention 182 on the Prohibition and Immediate Action for the Elimination of the Worst Forms of Child Labour, which prohibits inter alia forced or compulsory recruitment of children for use in armed conflict.

PP11: Condemning with gravest concern the recruitment, training and use within and across national borders of children in hostilities by armed groups distinct from the armed forces of a State, and recognizing the responsibility of those who recruit,train and use children in this regard.

PP12: Recalling the obligation of each party to an armed conflict to abide by the provisions of international humanitarian law.

PP13: Stressing that this Protocol is without prejudice to the purposes and principles contained in the Charter of the United Nations, including article 51 and relevant norms of humanitarian law.

PP14: Bearing in mind that conditions of peace and security based on full respect of the purposes and principles contained in the Charter of the United Nations and observance of applicable human rights instruments are indispensable for the full protection of children, in particular during armed conflicts and foreign occupation.

9. Draft Optional Protocol to the Convention on the Rights of the Child on Involvement of Children in Armed Conflict *(continued)*

PP15: Recognizing the special needs of those children who are particularly vulnerable to recruitment or use in hostilities contrary to this Protocol due to their economic or social status or gender.

PP16: Mindful also of the necessity to take into consideration the economic, social and political root causes of the involvement of children in armed conflicts.

PP17: Convinced of the need to strengthen international cooperation in implementation of this protocol, as well as physical and psychosocial rehabilitation and social reintegration of children who are victims of armed conflict.

PP18: Encouraging the participation of the community and, in particular, children and child victims in the dissemination of information and education programmes concerning the implementation of the Protocol.

10. Optional Protocols to the Convention on the Rights of the Child on the Involvement of Children in Armed Conflict and on the Sale of Children, Child Prostitution and Child Pornography

ANNEX I

Optional Protocol to the Convention on the Rights of the Child on the involvement of children in armed conflict

The States Parties to the present Protocol,

Encouraged by the overwhelming support for the Convention on the Rights of the Child,1 demonstrating the widespread commitment that exists to strive for the promotion and protection of the rights of the child,

Reaffirming that the rights of children require special protection, and calling for continuous improvement of the situation of children without distinction, as well as for their development and education in conditions of peace and security,

Disturbed by the harmful and widespread impact of armed conflict on children and the long-term consequences it has for durable peace, security and development,

Condemning the targeting of children in situations of armed conflict and direct attacks on objects protected under international law, including places that generally have a significant presence of children, such as schools and hospitals,

Noting the adoption of the Rome Statute of the International Criminal Court, in particular, the inclusion therein as a war crime, of conscripting or enlisting children under the age of 15 years or using them to participate actively in hostilities in both international and non-international armed conflicts,

Considering therefore that to strengthen further the implementation of rights recognized in the Convention on the Rights of the Child there is a need to increase the protection of children from involvement in armed conflict,

Noting that article 1 of the Convention on the Rights of the Child specifies that, for the purposes of that Convention, a child means every human being below the age of 18 years unless, under the law applicable to the child, majority is attained earlier,

Convinced that an optional protocol to the Convention that raises the age of possible recruitment of persons into armed forces and their participation in hostilities will contribute effectively to the implementation of the principle that the best interests of the child are to be a primary consideration in all actions concerning children,

Noting that the twenty-sixth International Conference of the Red Cross and Red Crescent in December 1995 recommended, inter alia, that parties to conflict take every feasible step to ensure that children below the age of 18 years do not take part in hostilities,

Welcoming the unanimous adoption, in June 1999, of International Labour Organization Convention No. 182 on the Prohibition and Immediate Action for the Elimination of the Worst Forms of Child Labour, which prohibits, inter alia, forced or compulsory recruitment of children for use in armed conflict,

Condemning with the gravest concern the recruitment, training and use within and across national borders of children in hostilities by armed groups distinct from the armed forces of a State, and recognizing the responsibility of those who recruit, train and use children in this regard,

Recalling the obligation of each party to an armed conflict to abide by the provisions of international humanitarian law,

Stressing that the present Protocol is without prejudice to the purposes and principles contained in the Charter of the United Nations, including Article 51, and relevant norms of humanitarian law,

10. Optional Protocols to the Convention on the Rights of the Child on the Involvement of Children in Armed Conflict and on the Sale of Children, Child Prostitution and Child Pornography *(continued)*

Bearing in mind that conditions of peace and security based on full respect of the purposes and principles contained in the Charter and observance of applicable human rights instruments are indispensable for the full protection of children, in particular during armed conflicts and foreign occupation,

Recognizing the special needs of those children who are particularly vulnerable to recruitment or use in hostilities contrary to the present Protocol owing to their economic or social status or gender,

Mindful of the necessity of taking into consideration the economic, social and political root causes of the involvement of children in armed conflicts,

Convinced of the need to strengthen international cooperation in the implementation of the present Protocol, as well as the physical and psychosocial rehabilitation and social reintegration of children who are victims of armed conflict,

Encouraging the participation of the community and, in particular, children and child victims in the dissemination of informational and educational programmes concerning the implementation of the Protocol,

Have agreed as follows:

Article 1

States Parties shall take all feasible measures to ensure that members of their armed forces who have not attained the age of 18 years do not take a direct part in hostilities.

Article 2

States Parties shall ensure that persons who have not attained the age of 18 years are not compulsorily recruited into their armed forces.

Article 3

1. States Parties shall raise the minimum age for the voluntary recruitment of persons into their national armed forces from that set out in article 38, paragraph 3, of the Convention on the Rights of the Child,1 taking account of the principles contained in that article and recognizing that under the Convention persons under the age of 18 years are entitled to special protection.

2. Each State Party shall deposit a binding declaration upon ratification of or accession to the present Protocol that sets forth the minimum age at which it will permit voluntary recruitment into its national armed forces and a description of the safeguards it has adopted to ensure that such recruitment is not forced or coerced.

3. States Parties that permit voluntary recruitment into their national armed forces under the age of 18 years shall maintain safeguards to ensure, as a minimum, that:

(a) Such recruitment is genuinely voluntary;

(b) Such recruitment is carried out with the informed consent of the person's parents or legal guardians;

(c) Such persons are fully informed of the duties involved in such military service;

(d) Such persons provide reliable proof of age prior to acceptance into national military service.

4. Each State Party may strengthen its declaration at any time by notification to that effect addressed to the Secretary-General of the United Nations, who shall inform all States Parties. Such notification shall take effect on the date on which it is received by the Secretary-General.

5. The requirement to raise the age in paragraph 1 of the present article does not apply to schools operated by or under the control of the armed forces of the States Parties, in keeping with articles 28 and 29 of the Convention on the Rights of the Child.

Article 4

1. Armed groups that are distinct from the armed forces of a State should not, under any circumstances, recruit or use in hostilities persons under the age of 18 years.

2. States Parties shall take all feasible measures to prevent such recruitment and use, including the adoption of legal measures necessary to prohibit and criminalize such practices.

3. The application of the present article shall not affect the legal status of any party to an armed conflict.

Article 5

Nothing in the present Protocol shall be construed as precluding provisions in the law of a State Party or in international instruments and international humanitarian law that are more conducive to the realization of the rights of the child.

10. Optional Protocols to the Convention on the Rights of the Child on the Involvement of Children in Armed Conflict and on the Sale of Children, Child Prostitution and Child Pornography *(continued)*

Article 6

1. Each State Party shall take all necessary legal, administrative and other measures to ensure the effective implementation and enforcement of the provisions of the present Protocol within its jurisdiction.

2. States Parties undertake to make the principles and provisions of the present Protocol widely known and promoted by appropriate means, to adults and children alike.

3. States Parties shall take all feasible measures to ensure that persons within their jurisdiction recruited or used in hostilities contrary to the present Protocol are demobilized or otherwise released from service. States Parties shall, when necessary, accord to such persons all appropriate assistance for their physical and psychological recovery and their social reintegration.

Article 7

1. States Parties shall cooperate in the implementation of the present Protocol, including in the prevention of any activity contrary thereto and in the rehabilitation and social reintegration of persons who are victims of acts contrary thereto, including through technical cooperation and financial assistance. Such assistance and cooperation will be undertaken in consultation with the States Parties concerned and the relevant international organizations.

2. States Parties in a position to do so shall provide such assistance through existing multilateral, bilateral or other programmes or, inter alia, through a voluntary fund established in accordance with the rules of the General Assembly.

Article 8

1. Each State Party shall, within two years following the entry into force of the present Protocol for that State Party, submit a report to the Committee on the Rights of the Child providing comprehensive information on the measures it has taken to implement the provisions of the Protocol, including the measures taken to implement the provisions on participation and recruitment.

2. Following the submission of the comprehensive report, each State Party shall include in the reports it submits to the Committee on the Rights of the Child, in accordance with article 44 of the Convention, any further information with respect to the implementation of the Protocol. Other States Parties to the Protocol shall submit a report every five years.

3. The Committee on the Rights of the Child may request from States Parties further information relevant to the implementation of the present Protocol.

Article 9

1. The present Protocol is open for signature by any State that is a party to the Convention or has signed it.

2. The present Protocol is subject to ratification and is open to accession by any State. Instruments of ratification or accession shall be deposited with the Secretary-General of the United Nations.

3. The Secretary-General, in his capacity as depositary of the Convention and the Protocol, shall inform all States Parties to the Convention and all States that have signed the Convention of each instrument of declaration pursuant to article 3.

Article 10

1. The present Protocol shall enter into force three months after the deposit of the tenth instrument of ratification or accession.

2. For each State ratifying the present Protocol or acceding to it after its entry into force, the Protocol shall enter into force one month after the date of the deposit of its own instrument of ratification or accession.

Article 11

1. Any State Party may denounce the present Protocol at any time by written notification to the Secretary-General of the United Nations, who shall thereafter inform the other States Parties to the Convention and all States that have signed the Convention. The denunciation shall take effect one year after the date of receipt of the notification by the Secretary-General. If, however, on the expiry of that year the denouncing State Party is engaged in armed conflict, the denunciation shall not take effect before the end of the armed conflict.

2. Such a denunciation shall not have the effect of releasing the State Party from its obligations under the present Protocol in regard to any act that occurs prior to the date on which the denunciation becomes effective. Nor shall such a denunciation prejudice in any way the continued consideration of any matter that is already under consideration by the Committee on the Rights of the Child prior to the date on which the denunciation becomes effective.

10. Optional Protocols to the Convention on the Rights of the Child on the Involvement of Children in Armed Conflict and on the Sale of Children, Child Prostitution and Child Pornography *(continued)*

Article 12

1. Any State Party may propose an amendment and file it with the Secretary-General of the United Nations. The Secretary-General shall thereupon communicate the proposed amendment to States Parties with a request that they indicate whether they favour a

conference of States Parties for the purpose of considering and voting upon the proposals. In the event that, within four months from the date of such communication, at least one third of the States Parties favour such a conference, the Secretary-General shall convene the conference under the auspices of the United Nations. Any amendment adopted by a majority of States Parties present and voting at the conference shall be submitted to the General Assembly of the United Nations for approval.

2. An amendment adopted in accordance with paragraph 1 of the present article shall enter into force when it has been approved by the General Assembly and accepted by a two-thirds majority of States Parties.

3. When an amendment enters into force, it shall be binding on those States Parties that have accepted it, other States Parties still being bound by the provisions of the present Protocol and any earlier amendments they have accepted.

Article 13

1. The present Protocol, of which the Arabic, Chinese, English, French, Russian and Spanish texts are equally authentic, shall be deposited in the archives of the United Nations.

2. The Secretary-General of the United Nations shall transmit certified copies of the present Protocol to all States Parties to the Convention and all States that have signed the Convention.

ANNEX II

Optional Protocol to the Convention on the Rights of the Child on the sale of children, child prostitution and child pornography

The States Parties to the present Protocol,

Considering that, in order further to achieve the purposes of the Convention on the Rights of the Child1 and the implementation of its provisions, especially articles 1, 11, 21, 32, 33, 34, 35 and 36, it would be appropriate to extend the measures that States Parties should undertake in order to guarantee the protection of the child from the sale of children, child prostitution and child pornography,

Considering also that the Convention on the Rights of the Child recognizes the right of the child to be protected from economic exploitation and from performing any work that is likely to be hazardous or to interfere with the child's education, or to be harmful to the child's health or physical, mental, spiritual, moral or social development,

Gravely concerned at the significant and increasing international traffic in children for the purpose of the sale of children, child prostitution and child pornography,

Deeply concerned at the widespread and continuing practice of sex tourism, to which children are especially vulnerable, as it directly promotes the sale of children, child prostitution and child pornography,

Recognizing that a number of particularly vulnerable groups, including girl children, are at greater risk of sexual exploitation and that girl children are disproportionately represented among the sexually exploited,

Concerned about the growing availability of child pornography on the Internet and other evolving technologies, and recalling the International Conference on Combating Child Pornography on the Internet, held in Vienna in 1999, in particular its conclusion calling for the worldwide criminalization of the production, distribution, exportation, transmission, importation, intentional possession and advertising of child pornography, and stressing the importance of closer cooperation and partnership between Governments and the Internet industry,

Believing that the elimination of the sale of children, child prostitution and child pornography will be facilitated by adopting a holistic approach, addressing the contributing factors, including underdevelopment, poverty, economic disparities, inequitable socio-economic structure, dysfunctioning families, lack of education, urban-rural migration, gender discrimination, irresponsible adult sexual behaviour, harmful traditional practices, armed conflicts and trafficking in children,

Believing also that efforts to raise public awareness are needed to reduce consumer demand for the sale of children, child prostitution and child pornography, and believing further in the importance of strengthening global partnership among all actors and of improving law enforcement at the national level,

Noting the provisions of international legal instruments relevant to the protection of children, including the Hague Convention on Protection of Children and Cooperation in Respect of Intercountry Adoption, the Hague Convention on the Civil Aspects of International Child Abduction, the Hague Convention on Jurisdiction, Applicable Law, Recognition, Enforcement and Cooperation in Respect of Parental Responsibility and Measures for the Protection of Children, and International Labour Organization Convention No. 182 on the Prohibition and Immediate Action for the Elimination of the Worst Forms of Child Labour,

10. Optional Protocols to the Convention on the Rights of the Child on the Involvement of Children in Armed Conflict and on the Sale of Children, Child Prostitution and Child Pornography *(continued)*

Encouraged by the overwhelming support for the Convention on the Rights of the Child, demonstrating the widespread commitment that exists for the promotion and protection of the rights of the child,

Recognizing the importance of the implementation of the provisions of the Programme of Action for the Prevention of the Sale of Children, Child Prostitution and Child Pornography and the Declaration and Agenda for Action adopted at the World Congress against Commercial Sexual Exploitation of Children, held in Stockholm from 27 to 31 August 1996, and the other relevant decisions and recommendations of pertinent international bodies,

Taking due account of the importance of the traditions and cultural values of each people for the protection and harmonious development of the child,

Have agreed as follows:

Article 1

States Parties shall prohibit the sale of children, child prostitution and child pornography as provided for by the present Protocol.

Article 2

For the purposes of the present Protocol:

(a) Sale of children means any act or transaction whereby a child is transferred by any person or group of persons to another for remuneration or any other consideration;

(b) Child prostitution means the use of a child in sexual activities for remuneration or any other form of consideration;

(c) Child pornography means any representation, by whatever means, of a child engaged in real or simulated explicit sexual activities or any representation of the sexual parts of a child for primarily sexual purposes.

Article 3

1. Each State Party shall ensure that, as a minimum, the following acts and activities are fully covered under its criminal or penal law, whether such offences are committed domestically or transnationally or on an individual or organized basis:

(a) In the context of sale of children as defined in article 2:

(i) Offering, delivering or accepting, by whatever means, a child for the purpose of:

a. Sexual exploitation of the child;

b. Transfer of organs of the child for profit;

c. Engagement of the child in forced labour;

(ii) Improperly inducing consent, as an intermediary, for the adoption of a child in violation of applicable international legal instruments on adoption;

(b) Offering, obtaining, procuring or providing a child for child prostitution, as defined in article 2;

(c) Producing, distributing, disseminating, importing, exporting, offering, selling or possessing for the above purposes child pornography as defined in article 2.

2. Subject to the provisions of the national law of a State Party, the same shall apply to an attempt to commit any of the said acts and to complicity or participation in any of the said acts.

3. Each State Party shall make such offences punishable by appropriate penalties that take into account their grave nature.

4. Subject to the provisions of its national law, each State Party shall take measures, where appropriate, to establish the liability of legal persons for offences established in paragraph 1 of the present article. Subject to the legal principles of the State Party, such liability of legal persons may be criminal, civil or administrative.

5. States Parties shall take all appropriate legal and administrative measures to ensure that all persons involved in the adoption of a child act in conformity with applicable international legal instruments.

Article 4

1. Each State Party shall take such measures as may be necessary to establish its jurisdiction over the offences referred to in article 3, paragraph 1, when the offences are commited in its territory or on board a ship or aircraft registered in that State.

10. Optional Protocols to the Convention on the Rights of the Child on the Involvement of Children in Armed Conflict and on the Sale of Children, Child Prostitution and Child Pornography *(continued)*

2. Each State Party may take such measures as may be necessary to establish its jurisdiction over the offences referred to in article 3, paragraph 1, in the following cases:
(a) When the alleged offender is a national of that State or a person who has his habitual residence in its territory;

(b) When the victim is a national of that State.

3. Each State Party shall also take such measures as may be necessary to establish its jurisdiction over the aforementioned offences when the alleged offender is present in its territory and it does not extradite him or her to another State Party on the ground that the offence has been committed by one of its nationals.

4. The present Protocol does not exclude any criminal jurisdiction exercised in accordance with internal law.

Article 5

1. The offences referred to in article 3, paragraph 1, shall be deemed to be included as extraditable offences in any extradition treaty existing between States Parties and shall be included as extraditable offences in every extradition treaty subsequently concluded between them, in accordance with the conditions set forth in such treaties.

2. If a State Party that makes extradition conditional on the existence of a treaty receives a request for extradition from another State Party with which it has no extradition treaty, it may consider the present Protocol to be a legal basis for extradition in respect of such offences. Extradition shall be subject to the conditions provided by the law of the requested State.

3. States Parties that do not make extradition conditional on the existence of a treaty shall recognize such offences as extraditable offences between themselves subject to the conditions provided by the law of the requested State.

4. Such offences shall be treated, for the purpose of extradition between States Parties, as if they had been committed not only in the place in which they occurred but also in the territories of the States required to establish their jurisdiction in accordance with article 4.

5. If an extradition request is made with respect to an offence described in article 3, paragraph 1, and the requested State Party does not or will not extradite on the basis of the nationality of the offender, that State shall take suitable measures to submit the case to its competent authorities for the purpose of prosecution.

Article 6

1. States Parties shall afford one another the greatest measure of assistance in connection with investigations or criminal or extradition proceedings brought in respect of the offences set forth in article 3, paragraph 1, including assistance in obtaining evidence at their disposal necessary for the proceedings.

2. States Parties shall carry out their obligations under paragraph 1 of the present article in conformity with any treaties or other arrangements on mutual legal assistance that may exist between them. In the absence of such treaties or arrangements, States Parties shall afford one another assistance in accordance with their domestic law.

Article 7

States Parties shall, subject to the provisions of their national law:
(a) Take measures to provide for the seizure and confiscation, as appropriate, of:

(i) Goods, such as materials, assets and other instrumentalities used to commit or facilitate offences under the present protocol;

(ii) Proceeds derived from such offences;

(b) Execute requests from another State Party for seizure or confiscation of goods or proceeds referred to in subparagraph (a) (i) and (ii);

(c) Take measures aimed at closing, on a temporary or definitive basis, premises used to commit such offences.

Article 8

1. States Parties shall adopt appropriate measures to protect the rights and interests of child victims of the practices prohibited under the present Protocol at all stages of the criminal justice process, in particular by:

(a) Recognizing the vulnerability of child victims and adapting procedures to recognize their special needs, including their special needs as witnesses;

(b) Informing child victims of their rights, their role and the scope, timing and progress of the proceedings and of the disposition of their cases;

10. Optional Protocols to the Convention on the Rights of the Child on the Involvement of Children in Armed Conflict and on the Sale of Children, Child Prostitution and Child Pornography *(continued)*

(c) Allowing the views, needs and concerns of child victims to be presented and considered in proceedings where their personal interests are affected, in a manner consistent with the procedural rules of national law;

(d) Providing appropriate support services to child victims throughout the legal process;

(e) Protecting, as appropriate, the privacy and identity of child victims and taking measures in accordance with national law to avoid the inappropriate dissemination of information that could lead to the identification of child victims;

(f) Providing, in appropriate cases, for the safety of child victims, as well as that of their families and witnesses on their behalf, from intimidation and retaliation;

(g) Avoiding unnecessary delay in the disposition of cases and the execution of orders or decrees granting compensation to child victims.

2. States Parties shall ensure that uncertainty as to the actual age of the victim shall not prevent the initiation of criminal investigations, including investigations aimed at establishing the age of the victim.

3. States Parties shall ensure that, in the treatment by the criminal justice system of children who are victims of the offences described in the present Protocol, the best interest of the child shall be a primary consideration.

4. States Parties shall take measures to ensure appropriate training, in particular legal and psychological training, for the persons who work with victims of the offences prohibited under the present Protocol.

5. States Parties shall, in appropriate cases, adopt measures in order to protect the safety and integrity of those persons and/or organizations involved in the prevention and/or protection and rehabilitation of victims of such offences.

6. Nothing in the present article shall be construed to be prejudicial to or inconsistent with the rights of the accused to a fair and impartial trial.

Article 9

1. States Parties shall adopt or strengthen, implement and disseminate laws, administrative measures, social policies and programmes to prevent the offences referred to in the present Protocol. Particular attention shall be given to protect children who are especially vulnerable to such practices.

2. States Parties shall promote awareness in the public at large, including children, through information by all appropriate means, education and training, about the preventive measures and harmful effects of the offences referred to in the present Protocol. In fulfilling their obligations under this article, States Parties shall encourage the participation of the community and, in particular, children and child victims, in such information and education and training programmes, including at the international level.

3. States Parties shall take all feasible measures with the aim of ensuring all appropriate assistance to victims of such offences, including their full social reintegration and their full physical and psychological recovery.

4. States Parties shall ensure that all child victims of the offences described in the present Protocol have access to adequate procedures to seek, without discrimination, compensation for damages from those legally responsible.

5. States Parties shall take appropriate measures aimed at effectively prohibiting the production and dissemination of material advertising the offences described in the present Protocol.

Article 10

1. States Parties shall take all necessary steps to strengthen international cooperation by multilateral, regional and bilateral arrangements for the prevention, detection, investigation, prosecution and punishment of those responsible for acts involving the sale of children, child prostitution, child pornography and child sex tourism. States Parties shall also promote international cooperation and coordination between their authorities, national and international non-governmental organizations and international organizations.

2. States Parties shall promote international cooperation to assist child victims in their physical and psychological recovery, social reintegration and repatriation.

3. States Parties shall promote the strengthening of international cooperation in order to address the root causes, such as poverty and underdevelopment, contributing to the vulnerability of children to the sale of children, child prostitution, child pornography and child sex tourism.

4. States Parties in a position to do so shall provide financial, technical or other assistance through existing multilateral, regional, bilateral or other programmes.

10. Optional Protocols to the Convention on the Rights of the Child on the Involvement of Children in Armed Conflict and on the Sale of Children, Child Prostitution and Child Pornography *(continued)*

Article 11

Nothing in the present Protocol shall affect any provisions that are more conducive to the realization of the rights of the child and that may be contained in:

(a) The law of a State Party;

(b) International law in force for that State.

Article 12

1. Each State Party shall, within two years following the entry into force of the present Protocol for that State Party, submit a report to the Committee on the Rights of the Child providing comprehensive information on the measures it has taken to implement the provisions of the Protocol.

2. Following the submission of the comprehensive report, each State Party shall include in the reports they submit to the Committee on the Rights of the Child, in accordance with article 44 of the Convention, any further information with respect to the implementation of the present Protocol. Other States Parties to the Protocol shall submit a report every five years.

3. The Committee on the Rights of the Child may request from States Parties further information relevant to the implementation of the present Protocol.

Article 13

1. The present Protocol is open for signature by any State that is a party to the Convention or has signed it.

2. The present Protocol is subject to ratification and is open to accession by any State that is a party to the Convention or has signed it. Instruments of ratification or accession shall be deposited with the Secretary-General of the United Nations.

Article 14

1. The present Protocol shall enter into force three months after the deposit of the tenth instrument of ratification or accession.

2. For each State ratifying the present Protocol or acceding to it after its entry into force, the Protocol shall enter into force one month after the date of the deposit of its own instrument of ratification or accession.

Article 15

1. Any State Party may denounce the present Protocol at any time by written notification to the Secretary-General of the United Nations, who shall thereafter inform the other States Parties to the Convention and all States that have signed the Convention. The denunciation shall take effect one year after the date of receipt of the notification by the Secretary-General.

2. Such a denunciation shall not have the effect of releasing the State Party from its obligations under the present Protocol in regard to any offence that occurs prior to the date on which the denunciation becomes effective. Nor shall such a denunciation prejudice in any way the continued consideration of any matter that is already under consideration by the Committee on the Rights of the Child prior to the date on which the denunciation becomes effective.

Article 16

1. Any State Party may propose an amendment and file it with the Secretary-General of the United Nations. The Secretary-General shall thereupon communicate the proposed amendment to States Parties with a request that they indicate whether they favour a conference of States Parties for the purpose of considering and voting upon the proposals. In the event that, within four months from the date of such communication, at least one third of the States Parties favour such a conference, the Secretary-General shall convene the conference under the auspices of the United Nations. Any amendment adopted by a majority of States Parties present and voting at the conference shall be submitted to the General Assembly of the United Nations for approval.

2. An amendment adopted in accordance with paragraph 1 of the present article shall enter into force when it has been approved by the General Assembly and accepted by a two-thirds majority of States Parties.

3. When an amendment enters into force, it shall be binding on those States Parties that have accepted it, other States Parties still being bound by the provisions of the present Protocol and any earlier amendments they have accepted.

Article 17

1. The present Protocol, of which the Arabic, Chinese, English, French, Russian and Spanish texts are equally authentic, shall be deposited in the archives of the United Nations.

2. The Secretary-General of the United Nations shall transmit certified copies of the present Protocol to all States Parties to the Convention and all States that have signed the Convention.

Acronyms

AIDS	Acquired Immunodeficiency Syndrome	**LE**	Life Expectancy
ASER	Age-Specific Enrollment Ratio	**NAIR**	Net Apparent Intake Rate
CRC	Convention on the Rights of the Child	**OAD**	Official Development Assistance
CRM	Child Risk Measure	**OECD**	Organisation for Economic Co-operation and Development
DALE	Disability-Adjusted Life Expectancy		
DES	Dietary Energy Supply	**ORT**	Oral Re-hydration Therapy
DMFT	Decayed, Missing or Filled Teeth	**SLE**	School Life Expectancy
DPT3	Three doses of vaccine against diphtheria, pertussis (whooping cough) and tetanus	**U5MR**	Under-Five Mortality Rate
		UN	United Nations
FAO	Food and Agriculture Organization	**UNAIDS**	Joint United Nations Programme on HIV/AIDS; it is a partnership of United Nations Children's Fund, United Nations Development Programme, United Nations Population Fund, United Nations Educational, Scientific and Cultural Organization, World Health Organization, and World Bank.
FGM	Female Genital Mutilation		
GDP	Gross Domestic Product		
GER	Gross Enrollment Ratio		
GNP	Gross National Product		
HDI	Human Development Index		
HIPC	Highly Indebted Poor Countries		
HIV	Human Immunodeficiency Virus		
HLE	Healthy Life Expectancy		
HPI	Human Poverty Index	**UNDP**	United Nations Development Programme
ILO	International Labor Organization	**UNESCO**	United Nations Educational, Scientific and Cultural Organization
IMF	International Monetary Fund		
IMR	Infant Mortality Rate	**UNFPA**	United Nations Population Fund
INTERPOL	International Criminal Police Organization	**UNHCR**	United Nations High Commissioner for Refugees
IPL	International Poverty Line	**UNICEF**	United Nations Children's Fund
		UNPD	United Nations Population Division
		VAD	Vitamin A Deficiency
		WHO	World Health Organization

Glossary

Adolescents individuals who are between puberty and the completion of physical growth. The World Health Organization (WHO) considers adolescence the period between 10 and 19 years.

Adoption acceptance of a child as one's own by legal process.

Age dependency ratio, youth the ratio of dependents—people under age 15—to the working-age population—those age 15–64.

Age-specific enrollment ratio (ASER) the percentage of the population of a specified age enrolled in schools, irrespective of the level of education. The indicator shows the extent of the participation of a specified age cohort in educational activities.

AIDS orphans children who lose their mother to AIDS before reaching the age of 15 years.

Body mass index (BMI) is a ratio of weight for height often used to estimate body fat. It is obtained by dividing the weight (in kilograms) by the square of the height (in meters).

Caries decay or progressive decay of a tooth, or less commonly, decay of a bone

Child the Convention on the Rights of the Child defines as children all human beings under the age of 18, unless the relevant national laws recognize an earlier age of majority (article 1). The Convention emphasizes that States substituting an earlier age for specific purposes must do so in the context of the Convention's guiding principles – of non-discrimination (article 2), best interests of the child (article 3), maximum survival and development (article 6) and participation of children (article 12). States are free to employ ages over 18 as the upper benchmark for defining the child.

Child labor children employed for pay or profit. According to the US Department of Labor, any work that prevents a child from going to school or that restricts a child from accessing quality schooling.

Child risk measure (CRM) a composite indicator based on five factors: under-five mortality rate, percent of children moderately or severely underweight, percent of primary school age children not attending school, HIV/AIDS prevalence rate for 15- to 49-year-olds, and armed conflict prevalence.

Child soldier any person below 18 years of age who is recruited for military purposes into an armed force/group or who participates in lethal violence in a political (non-criminal) context.

Child trafficking recruitment, transportation, transfer, harboring or receipt of persons by the threat or use of kidnapping, force, fraud, deception o coercion, or by the giving or receiving of unlawful payments or benefits to achieve the consent of a person having control over another person, for the purpose of sexual exploitation or forced labor.

Conscription the legal obligation of citizens falling into a specified category to perform a stated period of compulsory military service.

Convention a list of issues that are agreed upon by different countries under an international organization, affecting the lives of people around the world.

Convention on the Rights of the Child (CRC) an international human rights treaty that protects children around the world and gives them the rights to:

1. Freedom from violence, abuse, hazardous employment, exploitation, abduction or sale.
2. Freedom from hunger and protection from diseases.
3. Free compulsory primary education.
4. Adequate health care.
5. Equal treatment regardless of gender, race or cultural background.
6. The right to express opinions and freedom of thought in matters affecting them.
7. Safe exposure/access to leisure, play, culture and art.

Debt services the sum of interest payments and repayments of principal on external public and publicly guaranteed long-term debts.

Dietary energy deficit the difference between the average daily dietary energy intake of an undernourished population and its average minimum energy requirement.

Dietary energy requirement the amount of dietary energy required by an individual to maintain body functions, health and normal activity.

Dietary energy supply (DES) food available for human consumption, expressed in kilocalories per person per day (kcal/person/day). At the country level, it is calculated as the food remaining for human use after deduction of all non-food consumption (exports, animal feed, industrial use, seed and wastage).

Disability-adjusted life expectancy (DALE) the expected number of years to be lived in what might be termed the equivalent of "full health." To calculate DALE, years of ill-health are weighted according to severity and subtracted from the expected overall life expectancy.

DMFT level the mean number of decayed, missing or filled teeth. It describes the amount—the prevalence—of dental caries in an individual. DMFT is obtained by calculating the number of Decayed (D), Missing (M), and Filled (F), or teeth (T).

DPT3, three doses of vaccine against diphtheria, pertussis (whooping cough), and tetanus.

Economically active population persons who furnish the supply of labor for the production of economic goods and services (employed and unemployed, including those seeking work for the first time), during a specified time reference period. Persons serving in the armed forces are also included.

Family a group of two people or more (one of whom is the householder) related by birth, marriage, or adoption and residing together; all such people (including related subfamily members) are considered as members of one family.

Female genital mutilation procedures involving partial or total removal of the external female genitalia or other injury to the female genital organs whether for cultural, religious or other non-therapeutic reasons.

Female infanticide the abortion of a fetus because it is female or the killing of an infant by a relative because it is female.

Fertility rate the number of children that would be born to a woman if she were to live to the end of her child-bearing years and bear children in accordance with prevailing age-specific fertility rates. It assumes there is no female mortality at child-bearing ages of the mother.

Goitre an enlargement of the thyroid gland visible as a swelling of the front of the neck.

Gross domestic product (GDP) the total output of goods and services for final use produced by an economy.

Gross enrollment ratio (GER) the number of children enrolled in schools at a level (primary or secondary), regardless of age, divided by the population of the age group which officially corresponds to the same level.

Gross national product (GNP) the sum of value added by all resident producers plus net receipts of income from nonresident sources.

Hazardous work for children includes

- work which exposed children to physical, emotional or sexual abuse;
- work underground, underwater, or at dangerous heights;
- work with dangerous machinery, equipment and tools, or which involved the manual transport of heavy loads;
- work in an unhealthy environment which might, for example, involve exposure to hazardous substances, agents or processes, or to extreme temperatures, noise levels, or vibrations;
- and work under particularly difficult conditions such as for long hours, during the night, or without the possibility of returning home each day.

Heavily Indebted Poor Countries (HIPC) a category created by the International Monetary Fund and the World Bank that includes countries having unsustainable debt

Household all the people who occupy a housing unit. A house, an apartment or other group of rooms, or a single room, is regarded as a housing unit when it is occupied or intended for occupancy as separate living quarters; that is, when the occupants do not live and eat with any other persons in the structure and there is direct access from the outside or through a common hall.

Human Development Index (HDI) a composite indicator measuring the average achievements in a country in three basic dimensions of human development: average of the life expectancy; educational attainment; and adjusted GDP per capita.

Human Poverty Index (HPI) a measure designed to capture the many dimensions of poverty beyond mere of lack of income. A composite indicator, the HPI looks at three types of deprivation: deprivation in longevity, deprivation in knowledge and deprivations in standard of living. The HPI is constructed separately for developing (HPI-1) and industrialized (HPI-2) countries.

HPI-1 (developing countries): deprivations in longevity are measured by the percentage of newborns not expected to survive to age 40. Deprivations in knowledge are measured by the percentage of adults who are illiterate. Deprivations in a decent standard of living are measured by three variables: the percentage of people without access to safe water, the percentage of people without access to health services, and the percentage of moderately and severely underweight children below the age of five.

HPI-2 (industrialized countries): deprivations in longevity are measured by the percentage of newborns not expected to survive to age 60. Deprivations in knowledge are measured by the percentage of people who are functionally illiterate. Deprivations in a decent standard of living are measured by the percentage of people living below the income poverty line, set at 50% of the median disposable household income. Social exclusion is measured by the rate of long-term (12 months or more) unemployment of the labor force.

Illiteracy rate the percentage of people who cannot, with understanding, read and write a short, simple statement about their everyday life. A person who can only write figures, his or her name or a memorized ritual phrase is not considered literate

Immunization rate the rate of vaccination coverage of children under one year of age. A child is considered adequately immunized against measles after receiving one dose of vaccine. A child is considered adequately immunized against DPT (diphtheria, pertussis or whooping cough, and tetanus) after receiving two or three doses of vaccine, depending on the immunization scheme.

Indicator a variable with characteristics of quality, quantity and time used to measure, directly or indirectly, changes in a situation and to appreciate the progress made in addressing it.

Infant mortality rate (IMR) the probability of an infant dying between birth and exactly one year of age times 1,000.

International Poverty Line (IPL) A monetary disignator established by the World Bank to permit meaningful comparisons of poverty among nations with different economies and standards of living. There are actually two poverty lines: $1.08 a day and $2.15 a day at 1993 international prices (equivalent to $1 and $2 in

1985 prices) adjusted to account for differences in purchasing power across countries.

Kilocalorie (kcal) a unit of measurement of energy. One kilocalorie equals 1 000 calories. In the International System of Units (ISU), the universal unit of energy is the joule (J). One kilocalorie = 4.184 kilojoules (kJ).

Landmines, anti-personnel devices designed to explode when a person walks on, or, in some cases, near them. They are often laid to protect military installations from enemy approach and may delay and inconvenience enemy forces. Anti-personnel landmines have been utilized to terrorize and demoralize civilian populations and to sabotage their livelihood by mining to block access to water supplies, firewood, grazing and agricultural lands, and traveling paths.

Life expectancy (LE) the number of years a newborn infant would live if prevailing patterns of mortality at the time of its birth were to stay the same throughout its life.

Low birth weight newborns weighing less than 2,500 grams, with the measurement taken within the first hours of life, before significant postnatal weight loss has occurred.

Malnutrition an abnormal physiological condition resulting from inadequacy or imbalance in food intake or from poor absorption of food consumed or imbalances in energy, protein and/or other nutrients.

Maternal mortality rate the number of maternal deaths divided by the number of live births for a given year, It is expressed per 100,000 live births. Maternal deaths are defined as those caused by deliveries and complications of pregnancy, child-birth and the puerperium.

Mothers' Index a composite indicator that measures the overall status of mothers by looking important data on both the woman and the child. For women, indicators used to calculate the Index are: lifetime risk of maternal death; modern contraceptive use; percent of births attended by trained personnel; percent of pregnant women with anemia; adult female literacy rate; and participation as national government officeholders. For children, the measures are: infant mortality rate; access to safe water; primary school enrollment; and nutritional status.

Net Apparent Intake Rate (NAIR) the number of new entrants (of official admission age) into the first grade of primary education. It is expressed as a percentage of the population of the same age.

Obesity having an abnormally high proportion of body fat. For adults it is defined as having a Body Mass Index greater than 30.

Oral Re-hydration Therapy (ORT) the treatment of diarrhea in children under five years of age with oral re-hydration salts and/or recommended home fluids.

Overweight excess body weight compared to set standards. The excess weight may come from muscle, fat, bone, or water. For adults overweight is defined as a Body Mass Index of between 25 and 30.

Pertussis whooping cough.

Population growth rate the average annual percent change in the population resulting from a surplus (or deficit) of births over deaths and the balance of migrants entering and leaving a country.

Population projections data on population and vital rates derived for future years based on statistics from population censuses, vital registration systems, or sample surveys pertaining to the recent past, and on assumptions about future trends.

Poverty, absolute poverty so extreme that if all income were used to buy only food, it could still not ensure even a minimum level of nutrition. It is usually defined as per capita income equivalent to less than one dollar per day at 1985 international prices, adjusted for purchasing power parity.

Prevalence the number of cases in a given population at a specified point in time.

Ratify when the government of a country formally accepts and uses the international convention in that country. Once a convention is ratified, it becomes legally binding on an international level.

Refugees persons who, owing to well-founded fear of being persecuted for reasons of race, religion, nationality, membership of particular social group or political opinion, are outside the country of their nationality and are unable to, or owing to such fear, are unwilling to avail themselves of the protection of that country; or who, not having a nationality and being outside the country of their former habitual residence, are unable or, owing to such fear, are unwilling to return to it.

Safe water includes treated surface water and untreated but uncontaminated water, such as from springs, sanitary wells, and protected boreholes. In urban areas the source may be a public fountain or standpipe located not more than 200 meters away. In rural areas the definition implies that members of the household do not have to spend a disproportionate part of the day fetching wa-ter. An adequate amount of water is that needed to satisfy metabolic, hygienic, and domestic requirements, usually about 20 liters of safe water a person per day.

Sanitation adequate excreta disposal facilities that can effectively prevent human, animal, and insect contact with excreta. Suitable facilities range from simple but protected pit latrines to flush toilets with sewerage. To be effective, all facilities must be correctly constructed and properly maintained.

School life expectancy (SLE) the total number of years of schooling that a child of a certain age can expect to receive in the future, assuming that the probability of his or her being enrolled in school at any particular age is equal to the current enrollment ratio for that age.

Sex ratio at birth the number of male live births per one female live birth.

State party a country that has ratified an international treaty.

Stunting low height-for-age, reflecting a sustained past episode or episodes of under-nutrition.

Under-five mortality rate (U5MR) the probability that a newborn baby will die before reaching age five, if subject to current age-specific mortality rates. It is expressed as deaths per 1,000 live births.

Undernourishment chronic food insecurity, in which food intake is insufficient to meet basic energy requirements on a continuing basis.

Under-nutrition the result of prolonged low level of food intake and/or poor absorption of food consumed. Manifestations include wasting, stunting or underweight, reduced cognitive ability, poor health status and low productivity.

Underweight low weight-for-age, reflecting a current condition resulting from either inadequate food intake, past episodes of under-nutrition or poor health conditions.

Vital statistics registration statistics of demographic events, such as births, deaths, marriages, and divorces.

Wasting low weight-for-height, generally the result of weight loss associated with a recent period of starvation or severe disease.

Youth the United Nations defines youth as people belonging to the age group 15–24 years.

Index

About the Author

DR. CHANDRIKA KAUL holds a Ph.D. in economic geography from Jiwaji University, India. Dr. Kaul has worked with economic development organizations specializing in international trade development and, for the last 21 years, has been a geography and statistics editor for numerous reference publishers. She is the editor of two other Oryx Press Statistical Handbooks: *Statistical Handbook on Poverty in the Developing World* and *Statistical Handbook on Consumption and Wealth in the United States.*